Lecture Notes in Computer Science 1698

Edited by G. Goos, J. Hartmanis and J. van Leeuwen

T0241026

Springer

Berlin
Heidelberg
New York
Barcelona
Hong Kong
London
Milan
Paris
Singapore
Tokyo

Massimo Felici Karama Kanoun
Alberto Pasquini (Eds.)

Computer Safety, Reliability and Security

18th International Conference, SAFECOMP'99
Toulouse, France, September 27-29, 1999
Proceedings

 Springer

Series Editors

Gerhard Goos, Karlsruhe University, Germany
Juris Hartmanis, Cornell University, NY, USA
Jan van Leeuwen, Utrecht University, The Netherlands

Volume Editors

Massimo Felici
ENEA (sp 088)
Via Anguillarese, 301, I-00060 Roma, Italy
E-mail: felici@casaccia.enea.it

Karama Kanoun
LAAS-CNRS
7, Avenue du Colonel Roche, F-31077 Toulouse Cedex 4, France
E-mail: kanoun@laas.fr

Alberto Pasquini
ENEA (sp 088)
Via Anguillarese, 301, I-00060 Roma, Italy
E-mail: pasquini@casaccia.enea.it

Cataloging-in-Publication data applied for

Die Deutsche Bibliothek - CIP-Einheitsaufnahme

Computer safety, reliability and security : 18th international
conference ; proceedings / SAFECOMP '99, Toulouse, France,
September 27 - 29, 1999. Massimo Felici ... (ed.). - Berlin ;
Heidelberg ; New York ; Barcelona ; Hong Kong ; London ; Milan ;
Paris ; Singapore ; Tokyo : Springer, 1999
   (Lecture notes in computer science ; Vol. 1698)
   ISBN 3-540-66488-2

CR Subject Classification (1998): D.1-4, E.4, C.3, F.3, K.6.5

ISSN 0302-9743
ISBN 3-540-66488-2 Springer-Verlag Berlin Heidelberg New York

© Springer-Verlag Berlin Heidelberg 1999
Printed in Germany

Typesetting: Camera-ready by author
SPIN: 10705000   06/3142 – 5 4 3 2 1 0   Printed on acid-free paper

Preface

The European Commission emphasizes, in its Fifth Research Framework, the "...emerging generic dependability requirements in the information society, stemming both from the ubiquity and volume of embedded and networked systems and services as well as from the global and complex nature of large-scale information and communication infrastructures, from citizens, administrations and business in terms of technologies, tools, systems, applications and services". The series of Conference on Computer Safety, Reliability, and Security (Safecomp) contributes to satisfy these requirements by reviewing the state of the art, experiences, and new trends in the relevant scientific and industrial areas. Safecomp is intended to be a platform for technology transfer among academia, industry, and research institutions, providing the opportunity for exchange of ideas, opinions, and visions among experts.

This year Safecomp celebrates the 20th anniversary, its first Conference having been organized in Stuttgart by EWICS (European Workshop on Industrial Computer Systems) in 1979, and we hope these Proceedings will contribute to the celebration by supporting Safecomp aims. The Proceedings include the 25 papers that have been presented orally at the Conference and the full version of the 14 papers that have been presented as posters, all of which were selected from 76 submissions. Papers almost uniformly take up Safecomp topics, dealing with the issues of Safety Assessment and Human Factors, Verification and Validation, Design for Safety, Formal Methods, and Security.

As General and Program Chair of Safecomp '99, respectively, we would like to thank all authors who submitted their work, the presenters, the members of the international program committee and the local organising committee, the external reviewers, the session chairmen, the sponsors and co-sponsors, and all those who contributed to the Conference with their efforts and support.

We hope this book will prove to be useful reading, and help you in your research activity and in the design, assessment, and use of industrial computer systems.

Karama Kanoun   Alberto Pasquini
General Chair   IPC Chair

International Program Committee

S.	Anderson	UK	
O.	Andersen	DK	
A.	Bertolino	I	
H.	Bezecny	D	
P.	Bishop	UK	
R.	Bloomfield	UK	
S.	Bologna	I	
F.	Cara	F	
Y.	Crouzet	F	
F.	Dafelmair	D	
W.	Ehrenberger	D	
G.	Dahll	N	
P.	Daniel	UK	
R.	Genser	A	
J.	Gorski	PL	
D.	Inverso	USA	
J.	Järvi	FIN	
M.	Kaâniche	F	
K.	Kanoun	F	(General Chair)
F.	Koornneef	NL	
V.	Maggioli	USA	
C.	Mazet	F	
C.	Mazuet	F	
M.	Van der Meulen	NL	
A.	Pasquini	I	(IPC Chair)
G.	Rabe	D	(EWICS Chair)
J.	Rainer	A	
F.	Redmill	UK	
F.	Saglietti	D	
E.	Schoitsch	A	
I.	Smith	UK	
T.	Skramstad	NO	
J.	Trienekens	NL	
U.	Voges	D	
S.	Wittmann	D	
A. J.	Zalewski	USA	

Organizing Committee

Alain Costes, F
Yves Crouzet, F
Massimo Felici, I

Mohamed Kaâniche, F
Karama Kanoun, F
Marie-Thérèse Ippolito, F

External Reviewers

Gerard Duin, NL
Robert Garnier, F
Stefania Gnesi, I
Frank Koob, D
Raffaela Mirandola, I
Helmut Schwigon, D
Petra Scrivani, I

Peter van Sprundel, NL
Mark Sujan, D
Markus Ullmann, D
Jaap van Ekris, NL
Marja Visser, NL
Maria Wimmer, I

List of Contributors

Bernhard K. Aichernig
Technical University of Graz
Institute for Software Technology (IST)
Münzgrabenstr. 11/II
A-8010 Graz, Austria

Doo-Hwan Bae
Department of Computer Science,
Korea Advanced Institute of Science
and Technology, 373-1, Kusong-dong,
Yusong-gu, Taejon 305-701, Korea

Yun Bai
School of Computing and Information
Technology
University of Western Sydney Nepean
Australia

P. G. Beerthuizen
Fokker Space B. V.
Dept. ERA
Newtonweg 1, P.O.B. 32070
2303 DB Leiden, The Netherlands

Alfredo Benso
Politecnico di Torino
Dipartimento Automatica e Informatica
Corso Duca degli Abruzzi, 24
I-10129 Torino, Italy

Cinzia Bernardeschi
Dipartimento di Ingegneria della
Informazione, Università di Pisa
Via Diotisalvi, 2
56126 Pisa, Italy

Antonia Bertolino
Istituto di Elaborazione della
Informazione, CNR
Via S. Maria, 46
56126 Pisa, Italy

K. Bhattacharjiee
Reactor Control Division
Bhabha Atomic Research Centre
Mumbai 400 025, India

Jean-Paul Blanquart
LIS / LAAS-CNRS
7 avenue du Colonel Roche
31077 Toulouse Cedex 4, France

Andrea Bobbio
Dipartimento di Scienze e Tecnologie
Avanzate, Università del Piemonte
Orientale "A. Avogadro" - C.so
Borsalino 54 – 15100 Alessandria, Italy

José-Carlos Campelo
Department of Computer Engineering,
Technical University of Valencia
Camino de Vera s/n, 46022 – Valencia
Spain

Paul Caspi
VERIMAG
2 rue de Vignate
F-38610 Gières, France

Suong-Deok Cha
Department of Computer Science,
Korea Advanced Institute of Science
and Technology, 373-1, Kusong-dong,
Yusong-gu, Taejon 305-701, Korea

A. Chiappini
Ansaldo Segnalamento Ferroviario
Via dei Pescatori
16100 Genova, Italy

Ester Ciancamerla
ENEA – CRE Casaccia
Via Anguillarese, 301
00060 Roma, Italy

A. Cimatti
IRST, Istituto per la Ricerca Scientifica
e Tecnologica
Via Sommarive
Povo 38050 – Trento, Italy

Tim Clement
Adelard
Coborn House, 3 Coborn Road
London, E3 2DA, United Kingdom

Pierre Corneillie
CR2A-DI
25 quai Gallieni
92158 Suresnes cedex, France

Ian Cottam
Adelard
Coborn House, 3 Coborn Road
London, E3 2DA, United Kingdom

Yves Crouzet
LIS / LAAS-CNRS
7 avenue du Colonel Roche
31077 Toulouse Cedex 4, France

Ireneusz Czarnowski
Gdynia Maritime Academy
ul. Morska 83
81-225 Gdynia, Poland

Gustav Dahll
Institute for Energy Technology
P.O. box 173
N-1751 Halden, Norway

Rogério de Lemos
Department of Computer Science
University of Newcastle upon Tyne
NE1 7RU, United Kingdom

Yves Deswarte
LAAS-CNRS
7 avenue du Colonel Roche
31077 Toulouse Cedex 4, France

S. D. Dhodapkar
Reactor Control Division
Bhabha Atomic Research Centre
Mumbai 400 025, India

David Eames
ASACS Safety and Standards Unit
RAF
United Kingdom

Chin-Feng Fan
Department of Computer Engineering
and Science, Yuan-Ze University
135 Far East Road
Chung-Li, Taiwan

Alessandro Fantechi
Dipartimento di Sistemi e Informatica
Università di Firenze
Via S. Marta, 3
50139 Firenze, Italy

Lucia Vilela Leite Filgueiras
Escola Politecnica da Universidade de
Sao Paulo
C.P. 61548
05424-970, Sao Paulo, SP, Brazil

Peter Froome
Adelard
Coborn House, 3 Coborn Road
London, E3 2DA, United Kingdom

Pedro Gil
Department of Computer Engineering
Technical University of Valencia
Camino de Vera s/n 46022 – Valencia
Spain

Stefania Gnesi
Istituto di Elaborazione della
Informazione, CNR
Via S. Maria, 46
56126 Pisa, Italy

John Goodson
Admiral Management Services Limited
Kings Court
91-93 High Strett Camberley
Surrey GU13 3RN, United Kingdom

Monika Heiner
Brandenburgische Technische
Universität Cottbus
Institut für Informatik
D-03013 Cottbus, Germany

Maritta Heisel
Otto-von-Guericke-Universität
Magdeburg, Fakultät für Informatik
Institut für Verteilte Systeme
D-39016 Magdeburg, Germany

Gordon Hughes
Department of Computer Science
University of Bristol
Woodland Road
Bristol BS8 1UB, United Kingdom

Andrew Hussey
Software Verification Research Centre
The University of Queensland
Brisbane, Qld, 4072, Australia

Yoon-Kyu Jang
Department of Computer Science
Korea Advanced Institute of Science
and Technology 373-1, Kusong-dong
Yusong-gu, Taejon, 305-701, Korea

Piotr Jedrzejowicz
Gdynia Maritime Academy
ul. Morska 83
81-225 Gdynia, Poland

Chris Johnson
Department of Computer Science
University of Glasgow
Glasgow, G12 8QQ, United Kingdom

Claire Jones
Adelard
Coborn House, 3 Coborn Road
London, E3 2DA, United Kingdom

Mohamed Kaâniche
LAAS-CNRS
7 avenue du Colonel Roche
31077 Toulouse Cedex 4, France

Tim P. Kelly
Department of Computer Science
University of York
Heslington York, YO10 5DD
United Kingdom

Tai-Yun Kim
Department of Computer Science &
Engineering, Korea University
1, 5-Ga Anam-Dong Seongbuk-Gu
Seoul 136-701, Korea

Heinrich Krebs
TÜV Rheinland
Am Grauen Stein
D-51105 Köln, Germany

W. Kruidhof
Fokker Space B. V.
Dept. ERA
Newtonweg 1, P.O.B. 32070
2303 DB Leiden, The Netherlands

Silke Kuball
Department of Computer Science
University of Bristol
Woodland Road
Bristol BS8 1UB, United Kingdom

Yong-Rae Kwon
Department of Computer Science
Korea Advanced Institute of Science
and Technology 373-1, Kusong-dong
Yusong-gu, Taejon, 305-701, Korea

Sung-Min Lee
Department of Computer Science &
Engineering, Korea University
1, 5-Ga Anam-Dong Seongbuk-Gu
Seoul 136-701, Korea

Gaetano Lombardi
Ericsson Telecomunicazioni SpA
Roma, Italy

Eda Marchetti
Istituto di Elaborazione della
Informazione, CNR
Via S. Maria, 46
56126 Pisa, Italy

John May
Department of Computer Science
University of Bristol
Woodland Road
Bristol BS8 1UB, United Kingdom

Christine Mazuet
Schneider Electric
Usine M3
F-38050 Grenoble Cedex 9, France

John A. McDermid
Department of Computer Science
University of York
Heslington York, YO10 5DD
United Kingdom

Sang-Yoon Min
Department of Computer Science
Korea Advanced Institute of Science
and Technology 373-1, Kusong-dong
Yusong-gu, Taejon, 305-701, Korea

Michele Minichino
ENEA – CRE Casaccia
Via Anguillarese, 301
00060 Roma, Italy

Raffaela Mirandola
Dipartimento di Informatica, Sistemi e
Produzione
Università "Tor Vergata"
Roma, Italy

Swapan Mitra
Lloyds Register of Shipping
20 Wellesley Road
Croydon CR0 2AJ, United Kingdom

Jin Mo
LIS / LAAS-CNRS
7 avenue du Colonel Roche
31077 Toulouse Cedex 4, France

Jonathan Moffett
Department of Computer Science
University of York
Heslington York, YO10 5DD
United Kingdom

John D. Musa
Software Reliability Engineering and
Testing Courses
39 Hamilton Road
Morristown, NJ 07960-5341, USA

Algirdas Pakstas
University of Sunderland
School of Computing Engineering and
Technology, Chester Road
Sunderland SR1 3SD, United Kingdom

Yiannis Papadopoulos
Department of Computer Science
University of York
Heslington York, YO10 5DD
United Kingdom

Fabio Paternò
CNUCE – CNR
Via S. Maria, 36
56126 Pisa, Italy

Emilia Peciola
Ericsson Telecomunicazioni SpA
Roma, Italy

Peter Popov
Centre for Software Reliability
City University of London
Northampton Square
London EC1V OHB, United Kingdom

Luigi Portinale
Università del Piemonte Orientale "A.
Avogadro"
C.so Borsalino, 54
15100 Alessandria, Italy

C. Porzia
Ansaldo Segnalamento Ferroviario
Via dei Pescatori
16100 Genova, Italy

Ewa Ratajczak
Gdynia Maritime Academy
ul. Morska 83
81-225 Gdynia, Poland

Maurizio Rebaudengo
Politecnico di Torino
Dip. di Automatica e Informatica
Corso Duca degli Abruzzi, 24
I-10129 Torino, Italy

Antonio Rizzo
Multimedia Communication Laboratory
University of Siena
Via dei Termini, 6
53100 Siena, Italy

Philippe Robert
ISOscope
8, rue Maryse Hilsz
F-31500 Toulouse, France

Francisco Rodríguez
Department of Computer Engineering
Technical University of Valencia
Camino de Vera s/n 46022 – Valencia
Spain

Laurence Rognin
Interaction Design Centre
Foundation Building
University of Limerick
Ireland

Alexander Romanovsky
Centre for Software Reliability
University of Newcastle-upon-Tyne
Newcastle upon Tyne NE1 7RU
United Kingdom

G. Rotondo
Ansaldo Segnalamento Ferroviario
Via dei Pescatori
16100 Genova, Italy

Amer Saeed
Department of Computer Science
University of Newcastle upon Tyne
NE1 7RU, United Kingdom

Rym Salem
VERIMAG
2 rue de Vignate
F-38610 Gières, France

Carmen Santoro
CNUCE – CNR
Via S. Maria, 36
56126 Pisa, Italy

Erwin Schoitsch
ARCS
A-2444 Seibersdorf, Austria

R. Sebastiani
IRST, Istituto per la Ricerca Scientifica
e Tecnologica
Via Sommarive, Povo
38050 Trento, Italy

Kaisa Sere
Department of Computer Science
Turku Centre for Computer Science
Lemminkaisenkatu 14 A
FIN-20520 Turku, Finland

Juan-José Serrano
Department of Computer Engineering
Technical University of Valencia
Camino de Vera s/n 46022 – Valencia
Spain

Sanjit Seshia
School of Computer Science
Carnegie Mellon University
Pittsburgh PA 17217, USA

Igor Shagaev
Institute of Control Sciences
Profsoyuznaya St. 65
Moscow, Russia

R. K. Shyamasundar
School of Technology & Computer Science
Tata Institute of Fundamental Research
Mumbai 400 005, India

Gerald Sonneck
ARCS
A-2444 Seibersdorf, Austria

Matteo Sonza Reorda
Politecnico di Torino
Dip. di Automatica e Informatica
Corso Duca degli Abruzzi, 24
I-10129 Torino, Italy

Lorenzo Strigini
Centre for Software Reliability
City University of London
Northampton Square
London EC1V OHB, United Kingdom

Mark Sujan
Inst. f. Rechnerentwurf und
Fehlertoleranz
University of Karlsruhe
Germany

Sophie Tahmassebi
Centre d'Etudes de la Navigation
Aérienne
Avenue Édouard Belin 7
31055 Toulouse Cedex, France

P. Traverso
IRST, Istituto per la Ricerca Scientifica
e Tecnologica
Via Sommarive, Povo
38050 Trento, Italy

Elena Troubitsyna
Department of Computer Science
Turku Centre for Computer Science
Lemminkaisenkatu 14 A
FIN-20520 Turku, Finland

Gilles Trouessin
CNAMTS / CESSI
14 place St-Etienne
31000 Toulouse, France

Vijay Varadharajan
School of Computing and Information
Technology
University of Western Sydney Nepean
Australia

A. Villafiorita
IRST, Istituto per la Ricerca Scientifica
e Tecnologica
Via Sommarive, Povo
38050 Trento, Italy

Daniel Weber
Schneider Electric
Usine M3
F-38050 Grenoble Cedex 9, France

Maria Wimmer
Multimedia Communication Laboratory
University of Siena
Via dei Termini, 6
53100 Siena, Italy

Swu Yih
I&C Department
Institute of Nuclear Energy Research
P.O.Box 3-11
Lung-Yang, Taiwan

Pedro Yuste
Department of Computer Engineering
Technical University of Valencia
Camino de Vera s/n 46022 – Valencia
Spain

Table of Contents

Invited Talk

Assessment and Certification

Safety Assessment and Human Factors (Poster Session)

Human Factors

Safety Assessment

Design for Safety (Poster Session)

Verification and Testing

Design for Safety

Dependability Analysis and Evaluation

Formal Methods and Security (Poster Session)

Formal Methods

Security

Software Reliability Engineering in Industry

John D. Musa

Software Reliability Engineering and Testing Courses

Abstract. Software reliability engineering has recently been playing a rapidly increasing role in industry [1]. This has occurred because it carefully plans and guides development and test so that you develop a more reliable product faster and cheaper. In this paper we will first describe what software reliability engineering is. Then we will discuss the current state of the practice; that is, how industry is using it. The current "best" way of practicing software reliability engineering will be discussed. Finally, we will outline some of the important open research questions; solutions to these problems hold great promise for further advances.

1.   Introduction

Software reliability engineering (SRE) is a practice for quantitatively planning and guiding software development and test, with emphasis on reliability and availability [2,3,4,5,6]. We define reliability as the probability a system or a capability of a system functions without failure for a specified time or number of natural units in a specified environment. Natural units are units other than time related to the output of a software-based product, such as pages of output, transactions, telephone calls, or jobs. Availability is the probability that a system or a capability of a system is functional at a given time in a specified environment.

SRE quantifies expected use by function and uses this information to make product development and test more efficient. It matches major quality characteristics (reliability, availability, schedule, cost) to user needs more precisely by setting quantitative objectives for reliability and/or availability as well as schedule and cost. Then it engineers project strategies to meet the objectives. Finally, it tracks reliability during system test against each objective as one of the release criteria.

2.   State of the Practice

SRE is a proven, standard, best current practice that is widely applicable, low in cost and schedule impact, and widespread in use.

As an example of the proven value of SRE, consider the development of a release of the AT&T International Definity PBX [7, pp 167-8]. When SRE was applied to this

M. Felici, K. Kanoun, A. Pasquini (Eds.): SAFECOMP'99, LNCS 1698, pp. 1-12, 1999

release, the project experienced a reduction in customer-reported problems by a factor of 10, a reduction of system test interval by a factor of 2, a reduction in total development time of 30%, and no serious service outages in 2 years of deployment. As the result of experiences like this on a number of projects, SRE was proposed as a candidate to become an AT&T best current practice. Qualification as an AT&T best current practice requires use on several (typically eight to 10) projects with documented large benefit/cost ratios, as well as a probing review by two boards of high-level managers. Some 70 project managers also reviewed the practice of SRE before it received approval in May 1991. Standards for approval as an AT&T best current practice are high; only five of 30 proposed best current practices were approved in 1991.

AT&T's Operations Technology Center in its Network Computing Services Division applied the SRE best current practice in a large fraction of its projects. It was the primary software development organization for the AT&T business unit that won the Malcolm Baldrige National Quality Award in 1994. In addition, four of the first five software winners of the AT&T Bell Laboratories President's Quality Award used SRE.

The American Institute of Aeronautics and Astronautics approved SRE as a standard in 1993, and IEEE standards are under development. McGraw-Hill and the IEEE Computer Society Press recently recognized the rapid maturing and standardization of the field, publishing a handbook on the topic [7]. The IEEE Computer Society's Technical Committee on Software Reliability Engineering is growing very rapidly and currently has a membership of more than 1,000 [8,9].

SRE implements perhaps the most significant concept of the higher levels of the Software Engineering Institute's Capability Maturity Model: that you need to measure the results of the software development process and use this information to optimize it. By providing a means for measuring process results, it provides a way to help evaluate the effectiveness of methodologies and tools that are being considered as possible standards. Thus it can help rationalize the many quality standards efforts that are currently under way.

SRE requires no changes in architecture, design, or code. Technically speaking, you can apply SRE to any software-based product, beginning at start of any release cycle. Economically speaking, SRE is also applicable to virtually all software-based products, although it may be impractical for small components (involving perhaps less than 2 staff months of effort), except perhaps in abbreviated form, unless you use them in a large number of products. Thus particular promise may lie in applying SRE to certify object libraries. Although object-oriented concepts have made better modularization possible, the promise and benefits of reuse are not being fully realized because developers (and probably rightly so) strongly resist using objects whose reliability they cannot vouch for.

Investment cost is low, involving no more than 3 equivalent staff days per person in an organization, including presenting an overview and a course to everyone and allowing for planning. Note also that you should actually write the investment cost off over multiple projects. Table 1 shows life-cycle operating cost as a function of project size.

Schedule impact of SRE is low, as most of its activities involve only a small effort that can parallel other software development work. The only significant critical path activity is 2 days of training.

Users of SRE include Alcatel, AT&T, Bellcore, CNES (France), ENEA (Italy), Ericsson Telecom, Hewlett Packard, Hitachi, IBM, NASA's Jet Propulsion Laboratory, Lockheed-Martin, Lucent Technologies, Microsoft, Mitre, Nortel, Saab Military Aircraft, Tandem Computers, the US Air Force, and the US Marine Corps. SRE has been applied to systems ranging from 5,000 to 10,000,000 lines of source code. Known applications include telecommunications, medical imaging, knowledge-based systems, a wide area network-based education system, a capital management and accounting system, a compiler, terminal firmware, instrument firmware, military systems, and the space shuttle [2]. Tierney [10] reported the results of a survey taken in late 1997 that showed that Microsoft has applied SRE in 50 percent of its software development groups, including projects such as Windows NT and Word. More than 50 *users* of SRE had published articles describing their experiences as of late 1997, and this number was growing rapidly ([2], pp. 371 - 374).

Table 1. Life-cycle operating cost of SRE.

Project Size (staff years)	Percent of Project Cost
5	3
10	2
20	1.5
50	0.7
100	0.4
200	0.22
500	0.1

3.   Current Best Practice

SRE involves six major activities, as shown in Figure 1. The SRE process follows a spiral model, in a manner analogous to the software development process. Iteration occurs frequently. Figure 1 represents an "unwound coil" of this model. We will outline the process here; for a detailed description, see [2].

In this paper, I will describe SRE in the context of an actual project at AT&T, which I call Fone Follower. I selected this example because the project was small (total staff less than 10, extra effort required for SRE about 1 staff month) and it relates to a function that most people can easily understand. The selection in no way implies that SRE is limited to small projects or to telecommunications systems. I have changed certain information to keep the explanation simple and to protect proprietary data.

Fone Follower is a system that lets telephone calls "follow" subscribers anywhere in the world (even to cell phones). Subscribers dial into a voice-response system and enter the telephone numbers (forwardees) to which calls are to be forwarded on the basis of time. Incoming calls (voice or fax) that would normally be routed to a subscriber's telephone are then sent to Fone Follower, which forwards them in accordance with the program entered. If there is no response to a voice call and the subscriber has pager service, Fone Follower pages. If there is still no response or if the subscriber doesn't have pager service, Fone Follower forwards calls to the subscriber's voice mail.

List Associated Systems. The first activity involves listing which of the associated systems of the product we will test. Possible systems include the product and its major variations, supersystems that include the product, and acquired major components of unknown or questionable reliability. Note that it may be feasible to separately test small components (such as objects) that are used in multiple applications.

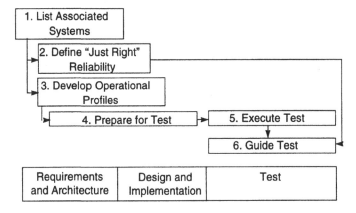

Fig. 1. The major activities of SRE and the corresponding development life-cycle stages.

Define "Just Right" Reliability. Defining the "just right" reliability consists of four parts:
1. Establishing failure severity classes and defining failure for each.
2. Choosing a common measure for all failure intensities.
3. Setting the system total failure intensity objective (FIO) for each associated system.
4. For any software you develop, finding the developed software total FIO and engineering project software reliability strategies to meet it.

A *failure* is a departure of program behavior during execution from user requirements; it is a user-oriented concept. Thus, when you define failures you are implicitly expressing users' negative requirements for program behavior. A *fault* is the defect in the program that causes the failure when executed; it is a developer-oriented concept. A *severity class* is a set of failures that each affect users to the same degree. The severity is often related to the criticality of the operation that fails. Common classification criteria include impacts on human life, cost, and capability. In general, classes are widely separated in impact because you can't estimate impact with high accuracy. Table 2 shows the severity classes for Fone Follower; they are based on capability impact. The failure definition process consists of outlining the negative requirements in a system-specific fashion for each severity class.

Table 2. Failure severity classes for Fone Follower.

Severity Class	Definition	Example
1	Key operation(s) unavailable	Calls not forwarded
2	Important operation(s) unavailable	Phone number entry inoperable
3	Operation(s) unavailable but workarounds exist	System administrators can't add subscribers from graphical user interface but can use text interface
4	Minor deficiencies in operations	System administrators' graphical interface screen doesn't display current date

Failure intensity is the number of failures per natural or time unit. We must choose which type of unit we will use, and select the particular natural unit if that is the type chosen.

To set the system total failure intensity objective (FIO) for each associated system, first determine whether users need availability or reliability or both. If at all possible, analyze the needs and expectations of users to arrive at the objectives. If not, use guidelines such as those in Table 3. If user needs are expressed in terms of availability, compute the FIO from the availability.

To find a developed software total FIO, determine and sum the failure intensities of the acquired hardware and software components and subtract the sum from the system failure intensity objective. There are three principal reliability strategies: fault prevention, fault removal, and fault tolerance. *Fault prevention* uses requirements, design, and coding technologies and processes, as well as requirements and design reviews, to reduce the number of faults introduced in the first place. *Fault removal* uses code inspection, unit test, and reliability growth test to remove faults in the code once it is written. *Fault tolerance* reduces the number of failures that occur by detecting and countering deviations in program execution that may lead to failures. Engineering these reliability strategies means finding the right balance among them to meet each developed software total FIO and schedule objective with the lowest development cost.

Table 3. Reliability Guidelines.

Failure Impact	Typical FIO (Failures/ Hr)	Time Between Failures
Hundreds of deaths, more than 10^9 cost	10^{-9}	114,000 years
One or two deaths, around 10^6 cost	10^{-6}	114 years
Around $1000 cost	10^{-3}	6 weeks
Around $100 cost	10^{-2}	100 hr
Around $10 cost	10^{-1}	10 hr

Develop Operational Profiles. Before discussing operational profiles, we must first define a few terms. An *operation* is a major system logical task of short duration (usually at least thousands per hour), which returns control to the system when complete, and whose processing is substantially different from that of other operations. An operation is actually a logical rather than a physical concept, in that it can execute over several machines in noncontiguous time segments. Some examples of operations are a command a user activates, the processing of a transaction sent from another system, a response to an event occurring in an external system, and a routine housekeeping task your own system controller invokes. Illustrations from Fone Follower include Enter forwardees, Process fax call, and Audit section of the phone number data base. An *operational profile* is simply a set of operations and their probabilities of occurrence. Table 4 shows a segment of an operational profile for Fone Follower and how we obtained it from the occurrence rates of individual operations.

The procedure to develop an operational profile is as follows:
- *Identify the initiators of operations.* Users are most commonly the initiators of operations, but initiators can also be external systems or the system's controller. To identify the users, you first determine the expected customer types on the basis of information such as the system business case and marketing data for

Table 4. Operational profile for Fone Follower.

Operation	Operations/hr	Occurrence Probability
Process voice call, no pager, answer	18,000	0.18
Process voice call, no pager, no answer	17,000	0.17
Process voice call, pager, answer	17,000	0.17
Process fax call	15,000	0.15
•		
•		
•		
Total	100,000	1

relatedsystems. You can then analyze the customer types for the expected user types or sets of users who will tend to use the system in the same way. User types are often highly correlated with job roles.

- *List the operations each initiator produces.* The system requirements are perhaps the most useful source of information for this task. Other sources include work-process flow diagrams for various job roles, draft user manuals, prototypes, and previous versions of the system. Direct discussions with "typical" expected users are usually highly enlightening and highly recommended.
- *Determine the occurrence rates of the operations.* Many people using SRE for the first time expect this task to be very difficult; our experience generally indicates it is much less difficult than expected. Frequently, field data already exists for previous versions of the same or similar systems. If not, you can often collect it. If the operations are event driven, you can often simulate the environment that determines event frequency. Finally, even if there is no direct data, there is usually some related information that lets you make reasonable estimates.
- *Determine the occurrence probabilities.* To do this, you divide the occurrence rate for each operation by the total operation occurrence rate.

You can apply operational profiles in many ways. Some of them are:
- Cut schedules and costs by finding alternatives to implementing low use noncritical functions (Reduced Operation Software or ROS)
- Plan a more competitive release strategy (operational development)
- Precisely focus resources on the most used and/or most critical functions or modules [applications: requirements development, design, opportunities for reuse, requirements and design reviews, coding, code inspection, unit test, change triage (limiting a necessary change such as handling the year 2000 problem)]
- Make test more effective by creating test environment that realistically represents field conditions

Figure 2 shows how to use operational profiles to plan a more competitive release strategy. Usually a small proportion of operations represent a large proportion of the use of a product. Implement these operations in Release 1 on an accelerated schedule, providing customers with most of what they need before your competitors do. Deliver the large proportion of operations that represent most of the development work with whatever delay is necessary to accommodate the accelerated schedule.

Proportion of operations developed

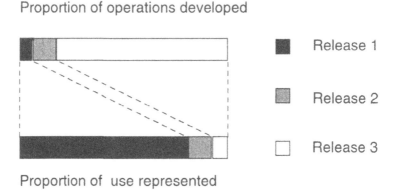

Release 1

Release 2

Release 3

Proportion of use represented

Fig. 2. Operational development.

Prepare for test. The activities in this step consist of specifying the test cases and test procedures. In specifying test cases, you use the operational profile to allocate test cases to operations. For example, for Fone Follower, you allocate 15% of the test cases to the Process fax call operation. You then detail the test cases within the operation by selecting from possible choices with equal probability. An example of detailing would be to specify a test case for the Process fax call operation in which the call is forwarded within the local calling area. Specifying the test procedures involves specifying the operational profiles that will invoke test cases during load test.

Execute test. This activity entails allocating test time, invoking test, and identifying failures and recording when they occurred.

You allocate test time among the associated systems, types of test, and operational modes. Types of test include feature test, load test, and regression test. *Feature test* is test that executes all the new test cases of a release independently of each other, with interactions and effects of the field environment minimized (sometimes by reinitializing the system). *Load test* is test that executes all test cases together, with full interactions and all the effects of the field environment reproduced as realistically and thoroughly as possible. *Regression test* is test that executes some (including all critical operations) or all test cases after each system build with significant change; it is designed to reveal failures caused by faults introduced by program changes. An *operational mode* is a distinct pattern of system use and/or environment that needs separate test because it is likely to stimulate different failures.

You first invoke feature test and follow that with load test. Regression test is typically done after each build that involves significant change. Identify all failures and record the natural or time units of failure occurrence or number of failures per interval of natural or time units.

Guide Test. In the last activity, you apply the failure data you have gathered to guide test. The application is different for reliability growth test and certification test. In reliability growth test, the goal is to track progress by examining the present failure intensity / failure intensity objective (FI/FIO) ratio. It is generally used for software developed in your own organization. In certification test, the goal is to determine if you should accept or reject a software component or system, with limits on the risks taken in making that decision. Certification test does not involve debugging. There is no attempt to "resolve" failures you identify. Certification test typically comprises only load test. It is generally used for software you acquire, including off-the-shelf or packaged software, reusable software, and software developed by an organization other than your own. If your customer is conducting an acceptance test of your product, you may follow reliability growth test with a certification test as a rehearsal. For reliability growth test, we apply failure data at fixed intervals; for certification test, after each failure. Testers track the FI/FIO ratio to determine any corrective actions to the test process that they should take and to guide release.

In reliability growth test, you can estimate the FI/FIO ratio from the natural or time units of failure events or the number of failures per interval of natural or time units, using reliability estimation programs based on software reliability models and statistical inference, such as CASRE (Computer-Aided Software Reliability Estimation) [7]. Figure 3 shows a FI / FIO trend for Fone Follower. Examination of the plot helps you identify "at risk" schedules or reliabilities and lets you take appropriate and timely corrective actions. If the FI / FIO ratio is very large with regard to the scheduled release, consider deferring features, rebalancing objectives for major quality characteristics, and increasing test and debugging resources. If there is a significant upward trend in the FI/FIO ratio, determine and correct the causes, which may be system evolution (change control may need improvement) or varying test selection probabilities for the operations (improvement in test execution may be needed).. Consider releasing the system when FI / FIO = 0.5. Although in theory testing could be terminated at FI/FIO = 1, in practice we wait until 0.5 to allow for errors in statistical estimation.

Certification test uses a reliability demonstration chart, such as that in Figure 4. Fone Follower applied a similar chart to certifying its operating system. You normalize failure data by multiplying them by the failure intensity objective. You can then plot each failure as it occurs on the chart. Depending on the region in which it falls, you may accept or reject the software being tested or continue test. In Figure 4, the test resulted in three failures. Each of the first two indicates that testers should continue test. The third falls in the accept region, indicating that sufficient data has finally been collected to demonstrate that the software can be accepted at the risk levels for which the chart was constructed. You can build reliability demonstration charts for different levels of consumer risk (the risk of accepting a bad program) and supplier risk (the risk of rejecting a good program).

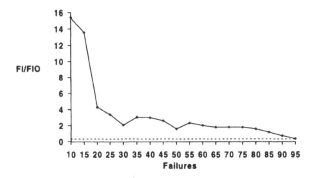

Fig. 3. Example of a failure intensity / failure intensity objective trend.

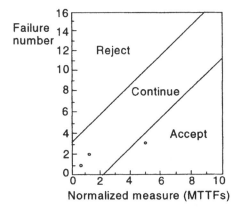

Fig. 4. Reliability demonstration chart for Fone Follower.

4.   Important Open Research Questions

One of the most potentially fruitful areas for research is the possibility for improving testing efficiency. SRE provides a clear numerical criterion for doing this, based on the relative importance of major quality characteristics, as indicated by software users: maximizing the relative failure intensity reduction rate with respect to execution time. SRE also simplifies the task by defining and quantifying usage by means of the operational profile, which lets us control a major source of variation.   Two very promising areas present themselves, equivalence partitioning and control of replacement of test cases.

An equivalence partition is a set of test cases that have the same failure behavior, such that one run can represent many, reducing the number of test cases that must be executed per failure exposed. The research needed is to find systematic and hence automatable ways of defining equivalence partitions that are as large as possible in occurrence probability covered but still minimize the risk of them having more than one failure mode.

Another promising area is the control of replacement of test cases, which is applicable to load test. Currently, load test is executed with replacement of test cases, as a test case is never executed twice under exactly the same conditions. However, it appears that conditions probably are not changing fast enough for two successive executions of the same test case to stimulate different failure behavior with high probability. Thus there is a clear opportunity to improve test efficiency by instituting some sort of controlled replacement, such as replacement after a time delay. The research needed is to find what this delay should be for maximum test efficiency under various conditions.

Software reliability engineers need improved methods of software reliability prediction. Software reliability prediction involves determination of software reliability from parameters of the product and the process, as contrasted to software reliability estimation, which involves determination from failure data. The prediction is needed for two different purposes; hence two different approaches may be needed:
1. Making tradeoffs in setting objectives for major quality characteristics
2. Engineering reliability strategies to meet objectives for major quality characteristics

There is also a need to estimate software reliability over a greater period of the life cycle than test so that appropriate development actions can be taken. There is some indication that software reliability models might be applicable to failure analogs prior to execution: for example, inspection failures vs inspection hours during requirements inspections, design inspections, or code inspection.

Finally, we expect increasingly to build systems from components or object that have known failure intensities. We want to be able to simply determine the resulting system failure intensities. This can be done most easily if the components are independent, noninteractive, and interchangeable, as is often the case with hardware. Initial work in establishing design rules and methodologies for developing such components (Professor Denise Woit, Ryerman University) is looking very promising.

5. Conclusion

SRE provides a powerful way to engineer development and testing so you can be confident in the availability and reliability of the software-based product you deliver as you deliver it in minimum time with maximum efficiency. Hence it is a vital skill for software developers and for companies for being competitive. There is considerable promise in several research areas for making SRE even more valuable.

References

1. Software Reliability Engineering website: overview, briefing for managers, bibliography of articles by SRE users, course information, useful references, Question of the Month:
http://members.aol.com/JohnDMusa/

2. Musa, J. D., Software Reliability Engineering: More Reliable Software, Faster Development and Testing, ISBN 0-07-913271-5, McGraw-Hill, 1998.
3. Musa, J.D., A. Iannino, and K.Okumoto; Software Reliability: Measurement, Prediction, Application, ISBN 0-07-044093-X, McGraw-Hill, 1987.
4. Musa, J. D., "More Reliable, Faster, Cheaper Testing with Software Reliability Engineering," Software Quality Professional, December, 1998, pp. 27-37.
5. Musa, J. D., "Software-Reliability-Engineered Testing," Computer, November, 1996.
6. Musa, J. D., "Software Reliability Engineering," Duke Distinguished Lecture Series Video, University Video Communications, 415-813-0506.
7. Lyu, M. (Editor), Handbook of Software Reliability Engineering , ISBN 0-07-039400-8, McGraw-Hill, 1996 (includes CD/ROM of CASRE program).
8. IEEE Computer Society Technical Committee on Software Reliability Engineering (publishes newsletter, sponsors ISSRE annual international conference): membership application at:
   http://www.tcse.org/tcseform.html
9. Electronic mailing list: send email to:
   sw-rel@computer.org
   To subscribe, put ONLY "subscribe" in body of message. To post (you must first subscribe), put text to be posted in body.
10.Tierney, J. 1997. "SRE at Microsoft." Keynote speech at 8th International Symposium on Software Reliability Engineering, Albuquerque, NM, November 1997.

John D. Musa currently creates and teaches courses and consults in software reliability engineering and testing. He has been involved in SRE since 1973 and is generally recognized as one of the creators of the field. Recently, he was Technical Manager of Software Reliability Engineering at AT&T Bell Laboratories, Murray Hill. He organized and led the transfer of SRE into practice within AT&T, spearheading the effort that defined it as a "best current practice." Musa has also been actively involved in research to advance the theory and practice of SRE. He has published more than 100 articles and papers, given more than 175 major presentations, and made several videos. He is principal author of Software Reliability: Measurement, Prediction, Application (McGraw-Hill, 1987) and author of Software Reliability Engineering: More Reliable Software, Faster Development and Testing (McGraw-Hill, 1998).

Musa received an MS in electrical engineering from Dartmouth College. He has been listed in Who's Who in America and American Men and Women of Science for many years. He is a fellow of the IEEE and the IEEE Computer and Reliability Societies and a member of the ACM and ACM Sigsoft. Contact Musa at 39 Hamilton Rd., Morristown, NJ 07960; j.musa@ieee.org.

For software reliability engineering course information, contact http://members.aol.com/JohnDMusa/.

A Systematic Approach to Safety Case Maintenance

T.P. Kelly and J.A. McDermid

Department of Computer Science, University of York
Heslington York, YO10 5DD, UK
tim.kelly@cs.york.ac.uk

Abstract. A crucial aspect of safety case management is the ongoing maintenance of the safety argument through life. Throughout the operational life of any system, the corresponding safety case can be challenged by changing regulatory requirements, additional safety evidence and a changing design. In order to maintain an accurate account of the safety of the system, all such challenges must be assessed for their impact on the original safety argument. This is increasingly being recognised by many safety standards. However, many safety engineers are experiencing difficulties with safety case maintenance at present, the prime reason being that they do not have a systematic and methodical approach by which to examine the impact of change on safety argument. This paper presents an approach that begins to address these difficulties by defining a process, based upon the principles of goal structuring, for the systematic impact assessment of safety case challenges.

1 Introduction

In the first instance the safety case argument will typically be constructed and presented (e.g. to a regulatory authority) prior to the system operating for the first time. The argument is often therefore based on estimated and predicted operational behaviour rather than observed evidence. For this reason alone, even in the absence of changes to the system or the regulatory environment, it is almost inevitable that the safety case will require updating throughout the operational lifetime of the system. Operational experience must be reconciled with the predictions made in the initial safety argument.

The system operators, as the 'owners' of the safety case, are typically responsible not only for its initial production but also for its maintenance throughout the lifetime of the system. There is growing recognition in the standards that appropriate mechanisms must be in place for the ongoing maintenance of the safety case. For example, the U.K. Railways (Safety Case) Regulations 1994 states in Regulation 6(1) that,*"A Person who has prepared a safety case persuant to these Regulations shall revise its contents whenever it is appropriate..."*. Similarly, for developers of defence related systems in the U.K., the Ministry of Defence Safety Standard 00-55 [1] states in section 4.7.1. that, *"After the preparation of the operational Safety Case, any amendments to the deployment of the system should be examined against the assumptions and objectives contained in the Safety Case."*

Although standards, such as those mentioned, demand appropriate and adequate revision of safety cases, they offer little advice on how such operations can be carried

M. Felici, K. Kanoun, A. Pasquini (Eds.): SAFECOMP'99, LNCS 1698, pp. 13-26, 1999

out. The safety case is a complex web of inter-dependent parts: safety requirements, argument, evidence, design and process information. As such, a single change to a safety case may necessitate many other consequential changes - creating a 'ripple effect'. The difficulty faced with current safety cases lies in discerning those consequential changes through the morass of poorly structured documentation. The level of assurance as to how well a safety case has been updated in the light of a change depends largely on the degree to which the document has been understood. There is little guarantee that all changes have been dealt with equally and systematically. Subjectivity plays a greater role in safety case maintenance than is desirable.

2   Current Problems in Safety Case Maintenance

Working from the published literature on this topic and from discussions with Rolls-Royce safety engineers the key problems currently being faced in safety case maintenance have been identified as the following:

- **Difficulty in recognising (importance of) challenges to the safety case**
  Some changes, such as a minor operational role change, may seem innocuous at first when given superficial consideration, but actually have a significant impact with respect to the context and argument of the safety case.
- **Difficulty in identifying the indirect impact of change**
  Safety arguments are a web of dependencies: it is necessary to identify the indirect ('knock-on') as well as direct (obvious) effects of changes. However, the dependencies within safety cases are often inadequately presented, or are obscured in current text-based safety arguments.
- **Lack of assurance / justification of the change process**
  Faced with a potential challenge to the safety case, those responsible for the maintenance of the safety case must decide on an appropriate response. The decisions about the level and nature of response made to a particular challenge must be expressed explicitly and justified in order to have confidence in the ongoing validity of the safety case.
- **Insufficient information recorded to support the change process**
  The previous problems have addressed the *quality* of the information recorded in the safety case. However, there is also a problem concerning the *quantity* of information recorded. If information (such as the assumptions and context surrounding safety claims) simply isn't recorded in the safety case then recognition of the impact of any changes requires a significant amount of detective work!

Together these problems result in an informal and often subjective change management process where even a basic level of repeatable and systematic impact analysis cannot be guaranteed. Given that the safety case should be maintained as a living argument that always correctly portrays the safety of a system, this informality is a serious concern.

3   Application of GSN to Change Management

A fundamental concern underlying the problems of safety case maintenance identified in the previous section is the poor perception of the individual elements of conventionally structured safety cases and of the interdependencies that exist between them. The Goal Structuring Notation provides a clear conceptual model of the safety case – representing its elements and interdependencies explicitly. Using the framework GSN provides as a basis for establishing a configuration model for safety cases, we illustrate that is possible to formulate a systematic approach to reasoning about and handling change.

The safety case can be considered as consisting of the following four elements:

- **Requirements** – the safety objectives that must be addressed to assure safety
- **Evidence** – information from study, analysis and test of the system in question
- **Argument** – showing how the evidence indicates compliance with the requirements
- **Context** – identifying the basis of the argument presented

These elements are obviously inter-dependent. Figure 1 illustrates the macro-dependencies that exist between these four elements.

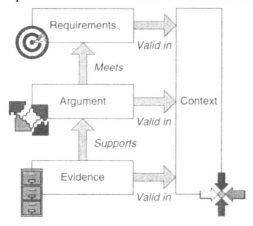

Fig. 1. Dependencies between elements of Safety Cases

This is a simplification of the dependencies that exist between these elements. Dependencies could also exist, for example, between pieces of evidence – e.g. between component failure modes and rates in a Failure Modes and Effects Analysis and basic events in Fault Tree Analysis. Figure 1 however, communicates those dependencies that exist through the *intentional* relationships of the *safety argument*. Recognising these dependencies helps to highlight where consistency must be maintained when handling change.

The Goal Structuring Notation [2, 3] has been specifically defined to model the entities and relationships shown in Figure 1. *Requirements* are represented in the notation as top level *Goals*. *Evidence* is represented in the notation as *Solutions*. *Contextual information* is represented in the notation as *Context*, *Assumption*, *Justification* and *Models*. *Argument* is communicated through the structuring of *Goals* supported by *sub-goals*. Figure 2 illustrates how a goal structure can be divided into the four essential elements – requirements, context, evidence and argument.

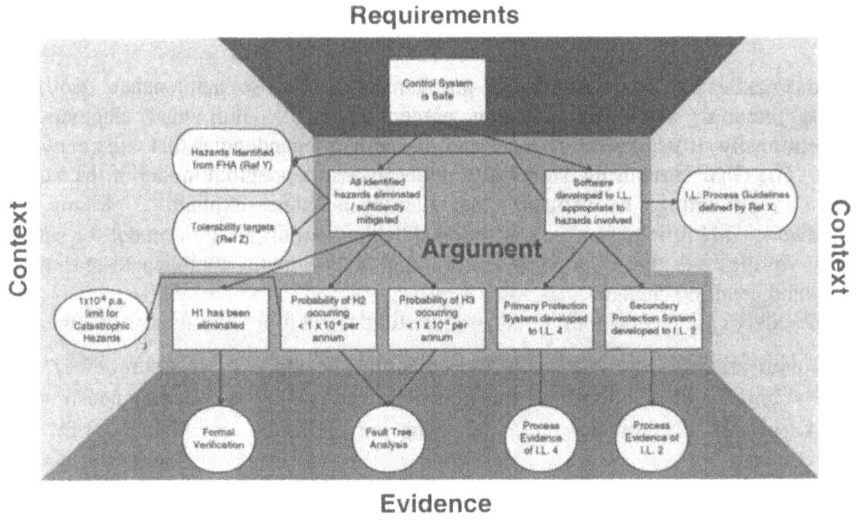

Requirements

Fig. 2. Relationship between safety case elements and the GSN

Through the explicit links of a goal structure, such as those shown in Figure 2, traceability is provided between the elements of the safety case argument. The following relationships are communicated:

- How requirements are supported by argument claims
- How argument claims are supported by other (sub) argument claims
- The context in which argument claims are stated
- How argument claims are supported by evidence

Such relationships are also present in conventional text-only safety cases. However, it is rare that they are communicated as clearly and explicitly as in a goal structure.

This paper proposes an approach that helps engineers to ask specific and structured questions regarding the impact of change on the safety case through utilising the documented dependencies presented in a goal structured safety argument.

4   A Safety Case Change Process

The safety case change activity can be thought of as consisting of two phases:

- The **Damage** Phase – Where a change is assessed for its impact on the safety argument of the safety case
- The **Recovery** Phase – Once the damage has been identified, the process of identifying a recovery action and following though the consequences of that action in recovering the safety argument.

There is an iterative (and potentially concurrent) relationship between these two phases. The action identified to *recover* the damaged part of the safety case may also result in *damage* to other parts of the safety case. For any one change, several iterations of the damage and recovery activities may be necessary to arrive again at a consistent and correct safety case. This highlights the importance of having an efficient and systematic process for carrying out these activities.

Using a goal structured safety case it is possible to provide a systematic structure to the activities carried out in these two phases. This structure is shown in Figure 3.

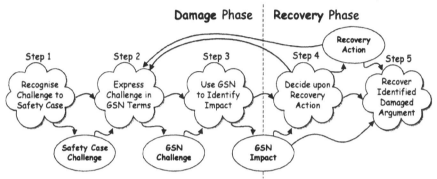

Fig. 3. A Process for Safety Case Change Management

The following sections describe how using GSN as a configuration model can support the five steps identified in Figure 3.

4.1   Step 1: Recognise Challenges to the Validity of the Safety Case

An important aspect of the through life maintenance of the safety case is awareness of challenges that could potentially render the safety case argument invalid – i.e. being aware of the vulnerability of the safety case argument to external change.

Using the model of the safety case proposed in Figure 1 – the role of the safety argument within the safety case is to establish the relationship between the *available evidence, safety objectives* and *contextual information* (such as design information). These three elements can be viewed as the 'givens' of the safety argument. Challenges to the validity of a safety argument will arise through challenging one of these givens, i.e. something in the 'real-world' context (outside of the safety case) will challenge the basis of the safety case presented.

The safety case will have been produced initially to present a valid safety argument with respect to the regulations, evidence and contextual information appropriate at the time. The difficulty in safety case maintenance is that any or all of these three elements may *change over time*. For example:

- An additional regulatory requirement may be added following an operational incident. An example of this from the civil aerospace domain would be the addition of a regulation regarding inadvertent thrust reverser deployment [4] following the Lauda Air thrust reverser deployment in flight accident.
- The design of a system may be changed for perfective, corrective or adaptive maintenance reasons or through technology obsolescence. Hogberg, in [5], describes responding to unanticipated *problems* with the design of a class of nuclear reactors.

- Assumptions regarding the operational lifetime of a system also form an important part of the safety case context. Such assumptions may be challenged by a desire to extend plant life beyond the originally intended period. Clarke, in [6], describes such a case for the life-extension of the U.K. civil Magnox nuclear reactors.
- Operational experience may challenge the evidence used as the basis of the original safety argument. For example, the safety case may estimate that a certain failure mode of a component will occur at a certain rate. This rate may be brought into question by operational data.

The start point of a systematic change process is the identification and acknowledgement of such changes on a routine basis (as recognised in many of the safety standards such as the HSE Civil Nuclear Safety Assessment Principles [7] and Defence Standard 00-55 [1]).

4.2   Step 2: Expressing Challenge in Goal Structure Terms

Step 2 is concerned with expressing an identified potential challenge in terms of a challenge to elements within the goal structure representation of the safety case argument.

There is a correspondence between the types of change introduced and the elements of a typical goal structure. A 'GSN Challenge' will be expressed always in terms of a challenge to elements of the notation representing the requirements, evidence or context. Figures (4-6) illustrate the mappings shown in the above table by providing sketch examples of requirements, evidence and context challenges expressed in GSN terms. (The convention introduced to denote that a GSN element or relationship is challenged is to place a cross (×) over that item.) The concern of this step is to express the *initial* challenge to a goal structured safety argument (i.e. the start point of impact assessment), rather than the total impact (which will be explored in Step 3).

Figure 5 illustrates a requirement change that translates into a challenge to a context reference made within a goal structure. The HSE Safety Assessment Principles are given as context to a strategy that bases its arguments upon them. If these principles change (e.g. are revised or added to) the basis of the existing argument is challenged.

Figure 4 depicts a real-world evidence change that translates directly into a challenge to a solution given within a goal structure. In this case, a fault tree is used to satisfy the probability claim for Hazard X. If the fault tree is called into question (e.g. through operational experience contradicting the basic fault event probabilities used or the implicit claims of independence) the role of this piece of evidence as a solution in the safety argument is challenged.

Figure 6 shows a real-world context change that translates directly into a challenge to a context reference made within a goal structure. In this case, the claim of operational safety is defined only within certain operating limits. If these operating limits were exceeded for any reason, the basis of the claim is challenged.

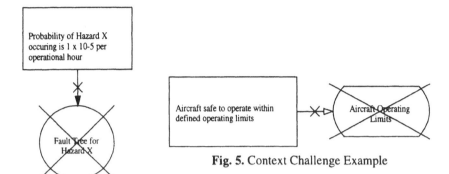

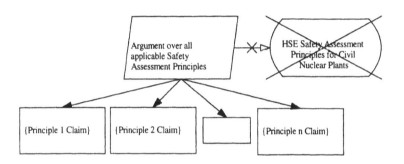

Fig. 5. Context Challenge Example

Fig. 4. Evidence Challenge
Example

Fig. 6. Requirements Challenge Example

4.3   Step 3: Using the Goal Structure to Identify Impact of Challenge

If a solution item is challenged (as shown in Figure 4) it challenges its *role* as a solution to all goals relying upon it through the *SolvedBy* relationship (shown by the lines headed with solid arrows). Equally, if a context item is challenged (as shown in Figure 5) it challenges the relationship with all goals previously expressed in the context of that item using the *InContextOf* relationship (shown by the lines headed with hollow arrows).

It is the challenge to the *structure* of the safety argument that must be explored (propagated) to determine the ultimate impact of any challenge on the *claims* of the safety argument. Based upon the semantics of the notation, the rules for the propagation of change within a goal structure are provided within the following sections.

4.3.1   Propagation of Challenges to Goals, Strategies and Solutions

Changing a goal, strategy or solution (G) within a goal structure challenges the following relationships within the goal structure:

- The role of G as a solution of parent goals or strategies (i.e. items higher up the goal structure). This is not a concern for the top goals of a goal structure.
- The role of G as a parent (objective) of supporting elements (i.e. to items lower down the goal structure). This is obviously not a concern for the solution elements of a goal structure.
- The relationship between G and its declared context - the GSN elements depicted on the left and right of the core argument, e.g. between the strategy and context shown in Figure 5.

4.3.2   Propagation of Challenges to Context, Models, Justifications and Assumptions

The effect of changing a context element is made more complicated that of changing a goal, strategy or solution owing to the *inheritance* of context elements implied by the semantics of the notation. Changing a context element challenges not only the most immediately associated goal or strategy but also *all* of the child goals and strategies underneath that item within the goal structure.

Changing a context element (C) challenges the following elements within the goal structure:

- All goals, strategies and solutions (G) that introduce C as context (through the *InContextOf* relationship).
- All goals, strategies and solutions which inherit C as context (i.e. all children of *G*).

When a goal, strategy or solution is challenged by a context change, the rules of change propagation for these elements (defined in the previous section) apply.

4.3.3   Potential vs. Actual Change Effect – The Role of the Safety Engineer

It should be noted that the rules described for the propagation of change over a goal structure define the *potential* change effect rather than necessarily the *actual* change effect. The approach taken is *pessimistic*. The role of the safety engineer responsible for maintaining the safety argument is then to examine each of these potential areas of impact to decide which require further investigation and which can be ignored (i.e. where the change can be considered *benign*).

The impact of any change will typically be explored to the point at which a (believed) appropriate recovery action can be determined.

4.4   Step 4: Deciding Upon Action to Recover Damaged Argument

Recovery is the process of returning the safety argument to a correct, consistent and complete state. The impact of a change (identified in Step 3) may mean that claims made within the safety argument (e.g. concerning the meeting of regulatory or customer requirements) are no longer supported. In such cases, the safety argument must be 'repaired' in order to bring the safety argument back to the original state of supporting the claims.

It is necessary to decide upon an appropriate action to recover the safety argument. This decision is set in the context of, and should be focused by, the impact that has been identified. For example, if after Step 3 it is found that the claim that 'No single point of failure can lead to hazard' can no longer be supported, then appropriate action should be taken towards *re*-supporting this objective – e.g. by making a design change that introduces redundancy.

In deciding how to recover the argument the following questions should be considered:

- **Can the requirements of the safety argument be altered (e.g. weakened) such that the safety argument still holds?**
- **Can the context of the safety argument be altered (perhaps restricted) such that the safety argument still holds?**
- **Can additional evidence be found / created such that the safety argument still holds?**

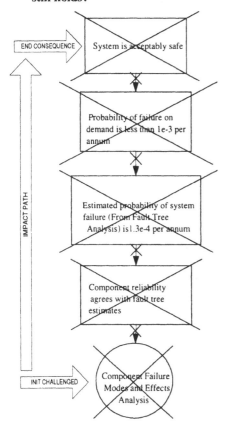

Fig. 7. An Example Impact Path

The particular action to recover from a challenge can only be decided on a case-by-case basis. However the impact history recorded from Step 3 will offer useful information. Consider the impact path shown in Figure 7.

In Figure 7 a general safety claim can no longer be supported **because** a supporting system reliability claim has failed. This claim has failed **because** a supporting fault tree claim has failed. This claim has failed **because** a component reliability claim has failed. This claim has failed **because** a supporting Failure Modes and Effects (FMEA) solution has been challenged (e.g. by operational experience).

The overall consequence of this change is that the general safety claim fails. However, the impact path communicates to the safety engineer that more reliable components are required in order that the FMEA evidence can once again support the component reliability claim. The fault tree can then be updated to continue to support the system reliability claim, and the latter can then continue to support the general safety claim.

4.4.1   Side-Effects of Recovery Action

The motivation for identifying and taking recovery action is the need to repair that part of the safety argument identified as damaged (as a result of Step 3). However the recovery action may itself necessitate further change to the safety argument. For example, a design change proposed in response to a challenge to one part of the safety argument may well challenge evidence used in another part. The impact of the recovery action must be assessed and managed in the same manner as the initial challenge.

4.5   Step 5: Recover Identified Damaged Argument

Damaged claims were identified at the end of step 3. In the damage process the effects of change are identified through the extent to which they impact, bottom-up, the claims made in the safety argument. The recovery process however works in the opposite direction – top-down – starting from the most fundamental claim challenged (i.e. the claim that is highest in the goal structure) and recovering the argument step-by-step downwards until the claims can be related back to the available evidence.

5   An Illustrative Example

This section illustrates the application of the impact assessment process to part of the safety argument for a nuclear reactor trip system (derived from details given in [8]). Figure 8 shows the structure of claims made regarding the timeliness of the trip system response.

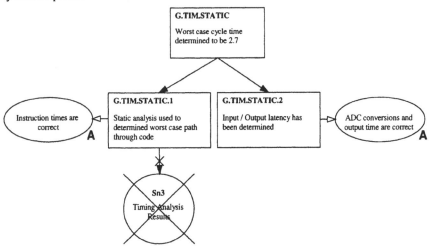

Fig. 8. Challenging the Trip System Timing Analysis Results

(**Step 1**) After initial acceptance of the safety argument, it is later recognised that there was a flaw in the static timing analysis tool used to determine the worst case response time. (**Step 2**) After examining the peripheral (context, solution and top requirement) elements of the safety argument, it is identified that this challenge directly concerns *Sn3 – Timing Analysis Results as* shown in Figure 8. (**Step 3**) The challenge to **Sn3** damages the claim **G.TIM.STATIC.1.** Damaging **G.TIM.STATIC.1** potentially damages the claim **G.TIM** (as shown in Figure 9).

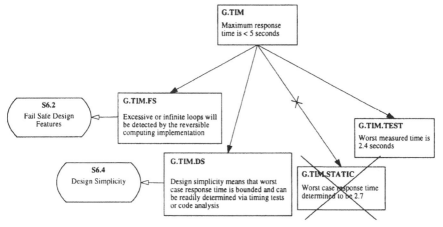

Fig. 9. Challenging the Trip System Timing Analysis Claim

At this point, one observes that a diverse argument has been applied in the quantitative claims put forward in support of **G.TIM**. Both analysis and test have been used. Even though **G.TIM.STATIC** is questioned, there is still the test claim **G.TIM.TEST** claim to support **G.TIM**. One observes also that a safety margin exists between the **G.TIM** and **G.TIM.TEST** claims, which increases confidence of **G.TIM.TEST** being able to support **G.TIM**. (**Step 4**) Given the diversity of the argument, it is possible to decide simply to accept the damage created by challenging the timing analysis results. However, the remaining argument would be weaker and more questionable. Another possibility would be to batch the change, and recover from the timing analysis challenge at a later point in time.

If responding to the change immediately, the safety engineer must identify an approach that will recover the damaged leg of the argument (i.e. the damaged **G.TIM.STATIC, G.TIM.STATIC.1** and **Sn3** elements). The decision could be to throw it away and replace it with a completely different supporting argument – i.e. prune back the argument to **G.TIM** and start again. Alternatively, the engineer could decide to replace 'like for like' and reinstate the argument in a form similar to that used already. Given that the challenge was due only to a flaw in the tool, reinstating the argument in the same form, after reworking the analysis on the corrected version of the tool, is probably the most effective option.

The safety engineer must now consider whether this action has any undesirable side effects on the rest of the argument, in addition to recovering the damage already identified. (**Step 2**) An examination of the peripheral elements of the safety argument shows that the recovery action of reworking the analysis does not necessarily damage any other element of the argument. However, the search does highlight the assumption **A10** (shown in Figure 8) that the instructions timings used in the analysis are correct. This assumption must be preserved as the analysis is reworked. **(Step 5)** After reworking the timing analysis, the safety engineer is in a position to recover the damaged argument. Working top-down from **G.TIM**, he or she needs to question whether the damaged **G.TIM.STATIC** goal must be restated. For example, if the new results were to show a new worst case response time of 2.9 seconds, **G.TIM.STATIC** would need to be restated accordingly. When **G.TIM.STATIC** has been recovered, the engineer must next examine **G.TIM.STATIC.1** and consider whether this also needs to be restated. It does not, and so **G.TIM.STATIC.1** can also be recovered. **Sn3** must now be examined to see whether it needs to be redefined. In fact **Sn3** must be altered to refer to the *new* timing analysis results.

6   Safety Argument Design *for* Change

Having considered a number of change scenarios over various goal structures, we have been able to identify and assess a number of strategies that can help safety arguments to improve their ability to withstand the effects of change. In particular, we have recognised the usefulness of the following two approaches:

- Safety Margins
- Diverse Evidence / Argument

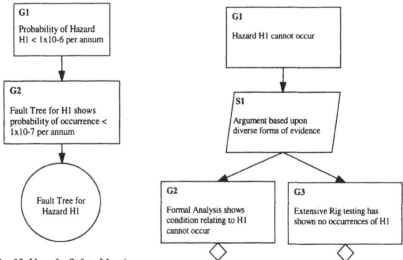

Fig. 10. Use of a Safety Margin within a Goal Structure

Fig. 11. Use of a Diverse Argument within a Goal Structure

A safety margin is created wherever a sub-goal or solution not only satisfies a parent goal, but also *exceeds* the requirement, thus providing a *safety margin*. By doing this, confidence is increased in the satisfaction of the parent and there is a 'margin for error' if the claims put forward in support of the parent goal are weakened at any future occasion (e.g. when the claim is challenged by operational data).

Figure 10 shows an example use of a safety margin within a goal structure: In Figure 10 the goal G2 exceeds the requirement set out by G1. The margin acts as a 'crumple zone'. Change can propagate through a goal structure up to G2. The margin between G1 and G2 absorbs the change and prevents further propagation, thus protecting the argument above G1.

Figure 11 shows an example use of a diverse argument within a goal structure. A diverse argument exists wherever a number of *individually sufficient* claims or evidence are put forward to support a particular parent goal. By doing this, confidence is increased in the satisfaction of the parent. For increased 'robustness' the individual arguments should ideally be based upon *independent* forms of evidence.

7   Limitations of the Approach

The following are the principal limitations of the approach described in this paper:

* Reliance upon correspondence between safety argument and safety case
* Influence of dependencies external to the safety argument

A brief explanation of each of these limitations is provided here.

The change impact assessment approach described in this paper is couched in terms of a safety argument recorded as a goal structure. The ability of the approach to express accurately and fully the impact of changes on the safety case depends on the degree to which the goal structured safety argument corresponds to the documented safety case. The usefulness of the approach in helping to maintain the safety case document depends on how well the relationship between the goal structure and document is understood. Employing document references with the goal structure (e.g. labelling a goal with the document section where that requirement is expressed) can explicitly draw out such links and improve this situation.

There are dependencies other than those shown in Figure 1 that can exist between the safety case elements of *requirements, evidence* and *context,* e.g. between pieces of safety case evidence. Goal structures record a subset of the dependencies that exist between the safety case elements. In order to get a complete model of dependencies between the elements, additional models are required to record the remaining dependencies. For example, evidence to evidence dependencies could be recorded through a data model such as that presented by Wilson, Kelly and McDermid in [3].

8   Conclusions

This paper presents a systematic approach to the management of safety case change. Starting from a goal structured representation of the safety argument, we have shown how it is possible to use the recorded dependencies of the goal structure to follow through the impact of a change and (having decided upon a corrective action or actions) recover from change. Observed successful strategies that can be employed in the production of safety arguments to mitigate the effects of change have been presented. Although there are recognised limitations to the approach presented, the principal benefit is that it provides a structured and systematic approach to reasoning about the effects of change where previously very limited support was available.

9   Acknowledgements

The authors would like to acknowledge the financial support given by the EPSRC and Rolls-Royce plc for the work reported in this paper.

10   References

1.   MoD, "00-55 Requirements of Safety Related Software in Defence Equipment," Ministry of Defence, Defence Standard August 1997.
2.   T. Kelly and J. McDermid, "Safety Case Construction and Reuse Using Patterns," presented at 16th International Conference on Computer Safety and Reliability (SAFECOMP'97), York, 1997.
3.   S. Wilson, T. P. Kelly, and J. A. McDermid, "Safety Case Development: Current Practice, Future Prospects," presented at Safety and Reliability of Software Based Systems - Twelfth Annual CSR Workshop, Bruges, Belgium, 1997.
4.   JAA, "Joint Airworthiness Requirements JAR-E: Engines (Change 8)," Civil Aviation Authority May 1990.
5.   L. Hogberg, "Shutting Down 5 Reactors: Reasons Why and Lessons Learnt," *Nuclear Europe Worldscan*, vol. 14, pp. 42-43, 1994.
6.   A. W. Clarke, "Magnox Safety Review: Extending the Life of Britain's Work Horses," *Nuclear Energy*, vol. 28, pp. 215-220, 1989.
7.   HSE, "Safety Assessment Principles for Nuclear Plants," Health and Safety Executive, HSE Books 1992.
8.   P. Bishop, R. Bloomfield, L. Emmet, C. Jones, and P. Froome, *Adelard Safety Case Development Manual*. London: Adelard, 1998.

11   Appendix: Key to Goal Structuring Notation (GSN) Symbols

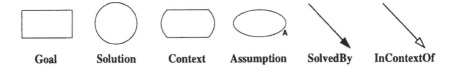

| Goal | Solution | Context | Assumption | SolvedBy | InContextOf |

SQUALE Dependability Assessment Criteria

Yves Deswarte[1]*, Mohamed Kaâniche[1], Pierre Corneillie[2] and John Goodson[3]

[1] LAAS-CNRS, 7 avenue du Colonel Roche
31077 Toulouse cedex 4, France
{Yves.Deswarte, Mohamed.Kaaniche}@laas.fr
[2] CR2A-DI, 25 quai Gallieni
92158 Suresnes cedex, France
pcorneil@cr2a-di.fr
[3] Admiral Management Services Limited, Kings Court, 91-93 High Street
Camberley, Surrey GU15 3RN, United Kingdom
goods_j@admiral.co.uk

Abstract. The aim of the SQUALE project is to develop assessment criteria to obtain a justified confidence that a system will achieve, during its operational life and its disposal, the dependability objectives assigned to it. The SQUALE criteria differ from traditional evaluation methods (security evaluation criteria, standards for the design, development and validation of safety critical systems), by: 1) their independence with respect to the application domains and industrial sectors, 2) their ability to address all dependability attributes, and 3) their progressiveness as a function of more or less strict requirements.

Introduction

The increasing use of computers in all industrial sectors leads to the need to specify and design computing systems which could fulfill the requirements of the targeted applications at the lowest cost. Various requirements have to be taken into account, whether functional (accuracy of the results, response time, ease of use...) or dependability requirements such as availability, confidentiality or maintainability [1]. It is then of great importance to know if a given system, COTS or developed specifically, is able to achieve all these requirements. It is widely recognized that ensuring system compliance to functional requirements is not an easy task due to the fact that it is not always possible to check the system behavior in all possible conditions that may occur during its operational life. This is even more difficult for the dependability aspects, since it is generally not possible to exercise the system in all faulty situations for which requirements have been defined, considering not only physical faults, but also design faults, human interaction faults or malicious faults [1].

For critical applications, i.e. those for which computing system failures could cause catastrophes, it is possible to gain a sufficient confidence in the system behavior by imposing well-suited development and validation methods that are specified in sector-specific standards: railways (CENELEC EN 50126 [2], EN 50128 [3] and ENV

---

* Yves Deswarte is currently on sabbatical at Microsoft Research, Cambridge, UK.

M. Felici, K. Kanoun, A. Pasquini (Eds.): SAFECOMP'99, LNCS 1698, pp. 27-38, 1999

50129 [4]), nuclear power (IEC 60880 [5]), avionics (ARP 4754 [6] and DO 178B [7] standards), etc. These different standards share many common characteristics, which shows the need for a generic evaluation approach, such as the one considered in the IEC 61508 standard [8]. In the same way, when considering computing system security, there are evaluation criteria such as the TCSEC [9], ITSEC [10] or Common Criteria [11] that can help to assess the system ability to face possible threats. But all this concerns only two aspects of dependability, namely safety and security. However, it is often necessary to take into account other dependability attributes such as availability or maintainability. For instance in air or railway transportation systems, if passenger safety is essential, availability is also critical for the system profitability. It is thus of great importance to be able to check if the system achieves all its dependability requirements, not limited to safety or security.

The approach presented here has been developed within SQUALE[1] (*Security, Safety and Quality Evaluation for Dependable Systems*), a European research project which is part of the ACTS program (*Advanced Communications, Technologies and Services*). The aim of this project was to develop assessment criteria which would make it possible to gain a justified confidence that a given system will satisfy, during its operational life and its disposal, the dependability objectives assigned to it. These criteria are generic in the sense that they do not aim at a particular application sector but on the contrary they have to be general enough not to require supplementary work for the system to be evaluated and certified according to the domain standards.

1   SQUALE Criteria Overview

The SQUALE assessment framework and criteria incorporate some basic concepts from the security criteria and safety standards. Particularly:
- the roles of the different parties involved in the assessment process are defined: sponsor, developer, assessor;
- the notion of "target of dependability assessment" (TDA) is introduced to specify the boundaries and the scope of the assessment;
- a process oriented assessment framework defines *confidence providing activities* which aim at giving the system the functionality and the quality necessary to fulfil its dependability objectives;
- different levels of confidence are defined to grade the importance of the dependability attributes and define the objectives to be satisfied with respect to each dependability attribute;
- different levels of rigor, detail and independence are specified for the confidence providing activities as a function of the confidence levels to be achieved with respect to each dependability attribute.

---

[1]   Current SQUALE project partners are CR2A-DI (F), prime contractor, Admiral (UK), IABG (Germany), LAAS-CNRS (F), Matra Transport International (F) and Bouygues Telecom (F).

2   The Dependability Assessment Framework

SQUALE criteria application takes into account the whole system life cycle (from the definition of concepts and initial needs to the system disposal), but it does not rely on a specific life cycle model. The SQUALE assessment framework takes into account the traditional system decomposition into subsystems and components (from the definition of the high-level requirements to the realization of system components, the assembling of these components according to the architecture, and finally the integration of the overall system into its operational environment). It is noteworthy that the system development should also include the definition of system installation, operation, maintenance and decommissioning procedures. Figure 1 summarizes the main tasks to be performed at a given level of system decomposition process considered in the SQUALE assessment framework model and the *confidence providing processes* to be implemented.

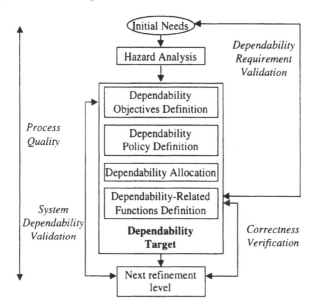

Fig. 1. SQUALE assessment framework and confidence providing processes

This framework is applied recursively at each refinement level of the system construction process up to the final implementation of system components and their integration. Each step of the refinement process has to start with a hazard analysis activity that consists in identifying the set of undesirable events (i.e. failures, threats, faults, etc.) that potentially have unacceptable consequences. The outputs of the hazard analysis activity should lead to: 1) the definition of the dependability objectives to be satisfied, 2) the specification of the dependability policy to be implemented to satisfy these objectives, 3) the allocation of dependability objectives to each subsystem (human, hardware, software, etc.), and finally 4) the definition of the dependability related functions to be accomplished by each subsystem.

Four *confidence providing processes* are distinguished in this general framework: dependability requirement validation, correctness verification, system dependability validation and process quality.

- *Dependability Requirement Validation* aims to ensure that at each level of system decomposition the threats and hazards of a TDA: 1) have been properly identified, 2) are covered by the respective dependability objectives, the dependability policy and the dependability related functions, and 3) comply with the initial needs of the systems.
- *Correctness verification* aims to ascertain that each level of the system implementation meets its validated requirements. One of its objectives is to check that the planned measures to prevent, tolerate, remove and forecast faults have been taken all along the development cycle and implemented correctly.
- *System Dependability Validation* checks the suitability of the dependability-related function implementation, including the effectiveness of the mechanisms implemented to counter the hazards, the ease of use of the system, the validation of fault assumptions and the analysis of side effects of the implemented system which may lead to critical situations.
- *Process Quality* aims to ensure the correct application of the methods, tools and procedures which have to be used during all the development process, the operation and the maintenance of the system, as well as those prepared for the decommissioning phase, in order to achieve a sufficient level of quality.

3   Dependability Target

To be assessed according to the SQUALE criteria, the system (or more precisely that part of the system which has to be assessed, i.e. the *Target of Dependability Assessment*, TDA) has to be described in a document called *Dependability Target* (similar to the Security Target document in the ITSEC). This document is intended to serve as a reference for the dependability assessment. In its initial version, the Dependability Target is developed in the earliest stage of the development process, before starting the main assessment activities. In the case of complex systems, this document has to be refined at each level of decomposition.

The Dependability Target contents are:

- the description of the system and its environment, including the system interface description (interfaces with other systems, interfaces with the physical environment, man-machine interfaces, interfaces to the organization, etc.) and the hazard-related assumptions concerning the environment, i.e. identifying the hazards which are eliminated by the environment conditions;
- the results of the hazard analysis, identifying what the system must protect and against what the system has to be protected; this analysis produces a list of threats and hazards for the system and its environment that shall be taken into account; it includes the assumptions made for each hazard in the analysis and the overall rating of the severity of each hazard with a description of the rating method;
- the definition of a set of objectives for each dependability attribute (safety, availability, confidentiality...); this activity consists in comparing the level of risks

(associated to the identified hazards and threats) with what is acceptable for the system; objectives are then defined to reduce the risks to an acceptable level;

- the definition of the dependability policy which describes how to fulfill dependability objectives through high level measures which are implementation independent; these measures are composed of rules and statements that the system has to enforce; this definition produces a set of regulations, standards, practices and procedures that should be used to achieve the dependability objectives, e.g. design diversity, partitioning, fail-stop processors, etc.
- the identification of the dependability-related functions, and their specifications;
- the dependability allocation, which defines the dependability objectives and policy for each dependability-related function; its purpose is to specify the role of each subsystem (human, hardware, software, other technologies) in the enforcement of the dependability policy and objectives;
- the definition of the required *dependability profile* (see Section 4) for each dependability-related function and component;
- the dependability plan, describing confidence providing activities and methods appropriate for the TDA; the methods are chosen according to the component dependability attributes, the expected confidence level and the life cycle phase.

4   Dependability Profile

For a given system, the non-functional requirements may apply to some or all of the dependability attributes (availability, confidentiality, reliability, integrity, safety and maintainability [1]). Moreover the importance of the attributes in a particular application may not be uniform. For instance, a safety-critical system may have safety and maintainability requirements, but the safety requirements are more significant than the maintainability requirements. In the SQUALE criteria, each attribute is assigned an expected confidence level, varying from 1 to 4, 1 being the lowest confidence level and 4 the highest one (see Table 1). A level 0 is also defined to indicate that nothing is required concerning this attribute. For instance, a system may be deemed to have a *dependability profile* A1, C0, R3, I3, S3, M2 which corresponds to confidence levels 1, 0, 3, 3, 3 and 2 respectively for availability, confidentiality, reliability, integrity, safety and maintainability.

Table 1. Confidence levels

Availability	A1-A4
Confidentiality	C1-C4
Reliability	R1-R4
Integrity	I1-I4
Safety	S1-S4
Maintainability	M1-M4

5   Confidence Providing Activities and Assessment

The assessment consists in checking that the confidence providing activities have been selected and carried out properly to achieve the requested confidence levels, and possibly in completing them. The assessment activities are thus organized according to the four main Confidence Providing Processes (CPPs) (Figure 1). For each CPP, a set of Confidence Providing Activities (CPAs) are defined together with appropriate methods that can be used to reach the objectives of these activities:

- The CPAs corresponding to the *Dependability Requirement Validation* include the preliminary hazard analysis, the probabilistic quantitative evaluation and the common cause analysis.
- For *Correctness Verification*, static analysis, behavioral analysis, formal methods and proofs, testing and traceability analysis can be used.
- *System Dependability Validation* includes penetration analysis, covert channel analysis and experimental evaluation.
- *Process Quality* is implemented by the quality assurance activities.

For each activity, the criteria define different levels for rigor (RL), detail (DL) and independence (IL). Each of these levels may take three values, from 1 (the lowest level) to 3 (the highest level), according to the confidence level identified in the dependability profile.

The rigor level determines how the activity has to be done (e.g. from informally to formally, from manually to automatically, etc.), the degree of justification to be provided to the assessor (e.g. suitability of methods, evaluation of tools, etc.), and the kind of evidence required (e.g. test coverage).

The detail level indicates the scope of the CPA such as whether it addresses: 1) parts or all of the system, 2) one or many refinement levels, 3) all the properties or only a subset.

The independence level specifies the organizational links between those carrying out the activity and the developers[2]. In most cases, IL1 indicates that they are independent persons, IL2 indicates independent departments, IL3 indicates independent organizations.

For each confidence providing activity, the SQUALE criteria provide a precise definition of each of the RL, DL and IL levels, as well as the relations between these levels and the confidence levels of each dependability attribute.

6   Complex Systems

6.1 Decomposition

Complex Systems are normally broken down into several subsystems, which themselves may be broken down further into sub-subsystems, and so on. Such a decomposition is necessary to:

---

[2] As indicated in Section 1, the assessors should always be independent from the developers and from the sponsor.

- control the complexity of the system,
- isolate certain types of functionality (e.g. confidentiality) in a few components rather than spread it thinly throughout the system,
- allow different types of component (e.g. hardware or software) to be developed by different teams,
- allow the development of some components to be subcontracted out,
- allow some components to be implemented using Commercial Off The Shelf (COTS) products.

As a system is decomposed into components and those components are further decomposed, decisions will be taken about the allocation of requirements to each component and the design of each component. As an integral part of this process, the Dependability Framework will be applied recursively to each component. Thus, the Dependability Target will be updated with the Dependability Target information for each component. This will involve the determination of the Dependability Profile for each component. These Dependability Profiles can be (and should be) different from the system Dependability Profile. It is good practice to isolate critical functionality in a part of the system, so that its implementation can be separated from other parts of the system.

Figure 2 shows an example of a system (with a partial Dependability Profile of S4, C3, ...) decomposed into 2 major components, A and B. The safety related functionality has been confined to A, and the confidentiality functionality has been confined to B, as demonstrated by their respective partial Dependability Profiles of S4, C0, ... and S2, C3, ... Component B has been further decomposed into components B1 and B2. B1 is slightly safety-related and confidentiality irrelevant (partial Dependability Profile of S1, C0, ...) and B2 implements all the confidentiality functionality (partial Dependability Profile of S1, C3, ...).

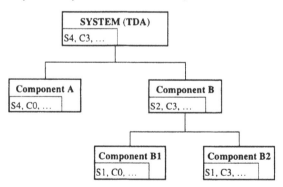

Fig. 2. Example of System Decomposition

In such an example, strong arguments must be provided to justify the separation of the components and demonstrate that:
- B cannot affect the safety functionality of A
- A cannot affect the confidentiality functionality of B
- B1 cannot affect the confidentiality functionality of B2
- etc.

If these arguments can be presented then consideration of the critical functionality can be confined to the relevant parts of the system. In the example shown, the activities needed for the development of a confidentiality related component can be confined to B, B2, ignoring A and B1.

6.2 CPAs Application

During the system decomposition process, a hierarchy of Dependability Profiles might be defined with a Dependability Profile associated with each component. The Dependability profiles of the sub-components corresponding to a given hierarchical level, together with the associated Dependability Objectives and Dependability Related Functions should be validated taking into account the Dependability Profile, Dependability Objectives and Dependability Related Functions of the corresponding component belonging to the immediately superior hierarchical level. The validation of the dependability refinement and allocation will be based on the CPAs defined in the criteria with levels of Rigor, Detail and Independence corresponding to the dependability profile of the latter component.

If we take the example of components B, B1 and B2, the CPAs should be applied as follows:

- Use CPAs with levels of Rigor, Detail and Independence corresponding to (S2, C3) to ensure that the decomposition of B with (S2, C3) into B1 with (S1, C0) and B2 with (S1, C3) is correct and valid (i.e., satisfies the dependability requirements of component B).
- Use CPAs with levels of Rigor, Detail and Independence corresponding to (S1, C3) for B2 and (S1, C0) for B1, respectively to ensure that each component satisfies its allocated requirements.

In all cases, the CPAs must be applied with respect to each Dependability Attribute at the confidence level for that attribute. For instance, in the above example, Correctness Verification testing of component B2 needs to be performed at Confidence Level 3 for confidentiality functionality and at Confidence Level 1 for safety functionality. Nevertheless, The developer would not be prevented from performing a CPA at a higher Confidence level than that required by the Criteria if it was thought to be more efficient. For example, in the case of component B2, the developer might decide to perform one hazard analysis at Confidence Level 3 and address both safety and confidentiality.

6.3 Subcontractors

The development of a component may be subcontracted by the developer of the system (prime contractor) to another organization. That organization can be either a separate company with a formal contractual relationship or a different department or team within the same company. In the former case there will be a formal contractual relationship and in the latter case at least an implicit contract. In either case, we can regard the organization implementing the component as a subcontractor.

Irrespective of whether there is a formal contract, it is crucial that the requirements for the component are correctly and completely described. The dependability requirements will be expressed in the Dependability Target for the component.

It may or may not be possible to perform Dependability Requirements Validation and Dependability Validation against the system Initial Needs etc. depending on the prime contractor's relationship with the subcontractor. Figure 3 illustrates the two possibilities.

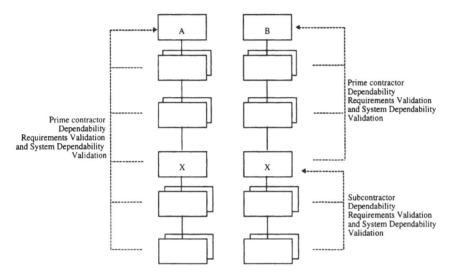

Fig. 3. Subcontracted Component

For system A, component X has been subcontracted but the prime contractor and subcontractor both have access to all the relevant information about the system. In this case, Dependability Requirements Validation and Dependability Validation can be performed for parts of the system (including X) against the Initial Needs etc. for the system.

For system B, again component X has been subcontracted but the relationship between the prime contractor and the subcontractor is such that:
- the prime contractor does not have access to the design etc. of X
- the subcontractor does not have access to the design etc. of the system outside component X.

This is a less desirable situation than with system A. Wherever possible, the prime contractor should try to ensure that he has sufficient access to the design etc. of X.

In this case the prime contractor can perform the Dependability Requirements Validation and Dependability Validation only on the components for which it has information. Specifically, the subcontractor can perform Dependability Requirements Validation and Dependability Validation only on the components for which it has information. Specifically, the Dependability Requirements Validation and Dependability Validation for the components of X can be performed only against the Initial Needs etc. of X, not of the system. It is most important to ensure that the requirements for X (which are imposed on the subcontractor) are correct and complete with respect to the system Initial Needs etc. Any errors or omissions will result in a component X that is not suitable for use in the system.

In each case, system A or system B, a Dependability Target is required for component X.

6. 4 COTS Products

There is often a need (or wish) to include COTS products in a system, for instance as component B2 in Figure 2. In order for this to happen a number of conditions must be fulfilled:

- the COTS product must provide the dependability (and other) functionality that is required of component B2;
- the COTS product must not provide too much unwanted functionality that could provide additional hazards;
- there must be sufficient confidence that the COTS product does provide just the necessary dependability functionality in the environment in which it will be used within the system;
- it must be possible to check that the previous conditions are fulfilled.

There must be a description of the COTS product identifying the functionality provided by the product and the environment(s) within which it will provide that functionality. Ideally this description will be in a Dependability Target, but it must exist, otherwise it will not be possible to check whether the product's functionality matches the requirements of the component it is to replace.

If the system component (B2 in our example) has some dependability requirements then it will have a Dependability Profile. This shows that there are some confidence requirements that have to be satisfied by the product and these confidence requirements can be obtained only by some form of assessment. There are a number of possibilities:

- the product has been subjected to an assessment against the SQUALE Criteria - there will be a certificate and assessment reports giving the results of the assessment and these results (achieved Dependability Profile, assessed functionality and environment) can be checked against the requirements for the component B2;
- the product has been assessed against some other criteria - this is similar to the previous case but it is also necessary the decide to what extent the other assessment method is equivalent to a SQUALE assessment;
- the product has not been assessed - the product cannot be used until it has been assessed either as a separate product or as part of the system assessment.

Conclusion

The SQUALE assessment criteria have been designed to address all attributes of dependability rather than only security (like the TCSEC or the ITSEC) or safety (like the DO178B or IEC 1508). Thus, they should be useful to guide the design, development and assessment of a large range of future systems whose requirements will spread over several dependability attributes. For instance, future avionics systems should take into account malicious threats (and thus security concerns) rather than only accidental threats such as design faults, hardware failures and human errors. The same concerns apply to large infrastructure survivability. In other domains such as banks or transactional systems, security and availability are the main dependability requirements.

With respect to existing and future safety, security and quality standards, it should be easy to adapt the SQUALE criteria so that an assessment according to these criteria should be sufficient to satisfy the standard requirements, or only a little complementary effort should be needed to meet these requirements.

Moreover, the SQUALE criteria aim to be progressive: for moderate dependability requirements, the cost of the confidence providing activities and of assessment activities should be a small percentage of the development costs, and the cost of these activities should grow progressively with the dependability level to be achieved.

In order to validate and refine the first draft of the SQUALE criteria, an experiment has been carried out to evaluate the control subsystem of a new automatic subway transportation system, METEOR. Based on the results of this experiment, improvement of the SQUALE draft criteria has been undertaken towards more flexibility and efficiency. A new draft of the criteria has been published [12] and another experiment has started on a very different system: rather than an already implemented system, it is a system currently being defined by Bouygues Telecom. Moreover, the dependability requirements are much less strict for this system than for METEOR, and should concern more the security aspects than the safety aspects. We are confident that this second experiment will confirm the progressiveness and flexibility of the SQUALE criteria.

References

1. J.-C. Laprie (ed.), Dependability: Basic Concepts and Terminology, Springer-Verlag, Dependable Computing and Fault-Tolerant Systems Series, vol.5, ISBN 3-211-82296-8, 1992.
2. CENELEC EN 50126, Railway Applications: The Specification and Demonstration of Reliability, Availability, Maintainability and Safety (RAMS), European Committee for Electrotechnical Standardization (CENELEC), 1997.
3. CENELEC EN 50128, Railway Applications: Software for Railway Control and Protection Systems, European Committee for Electrotechnical Standardization (CENELEC), 1997.
4. CENELEC ENV 50129, Railway Applications: Safety Related Electronic Systems for Signalling, European Committee for Electrotechnical Standardization (CENELEC), 1998.
5. IEC 60880, Software for Computers in the Safety Systems of Nuclear Power Stations, International Electrotechnical Commission (IEC), 1986.
6. Certification Considerations for Highly-Integrated or Complex Aircraft Systems, ARP 4754, Society of Automotive Engineers (SAE), Nov. 1996.
7. Software Considerations in Airborne Systems and Equipment Certification, DO178B/ED12B, Radio Technical Commission for Aeronautics (RTCA), European Organization for Civil Aviation Electronics (EUROCAE), December 1992.
8. IEC 61508, Functional Safety of Electrical/Electronic/Programmable Electronic Safety-Related Systems, Parts 1 to 7, International Electrotechnical Commission (IEC), 1998-1999.
9. TCSEC: Department of Defense Trusted Computer System Evaluation Criteria, U.S. Department of Defense, 1985.
10.ITSEC: Information Technology Security Evaluation Criteria, Office for Official Publications of the European Communities, Luxembourg, 1991, ISBN 92-826-3004-8.

11.Common Criteria for Information Technology Security Evaluation, Common Criteria Implementation Board, Version 2.0, CCIB-98-026, CCIB-98-027, CCIB-98-027A, CCIB-98-028, 1998.
12.P. Corneillie, S. Moreau, C. Valentin, J. Goodson, A. Hawes, T. Manning, H. Kurth, G. Liebisch, A. Steinacker, Y. Deswarte, M. Kaâniche, P. Benoit, SQUALE Dependability Assessment Criteria, LAAS Research Report n°98456 (revised), ACTS Project AC097, Jan. 1999, 190 pages, (also available at <http://www.research.ec.org/squale/>).

Acknowledgements. This work has been partially supported by the European Commission as part of the ACTS Programme under project AC097. The authors are grateful to the many other participants in the SQUALE project who contributed to the work presented here, and in particular Sylvain Moreau and Claudine Valentin from CR2A-DI, Alan Hawes and Tim Manning from Admiral, Helmuth Kurth, Götz Liebisch and Angelika Steinacker from IABG, and Paul Benoit from Matra Transport International.

Assessment and Certification of Safety - Critical Digital Architectures - The ACRuDA Project

Gerald Sonneck, Erwin Schoitsch

ARCS, A-2444 Seibersdorf, Austria
{gerald.sonneck, erwin.schoitsch}@arcs.ac.at

Abstract. ACRuDA (Assessment and Certification Rules for Digital Architectures) is a project partly funded by CEC. Its objective was to develop an assessment and certification method for safety critical digital architectures for use in the guided transport industry. The assessment process and the criteria were tested in three case studies. This paper gives an overview on the underlying principles of two of these and discusses how the assessment according to the ACRuDA framework promotes the cross-acceptance of certificates.

1   Introduction

The objective of the ACRuDA project (Assessment and Certification Rules for Digital Architectures) was to develop an assessment and Certification method for safety critical digital architectures for use in the guided transport industry. The project was partly funded by the Commission of the European Communities (CEC), DG VII, under the Fourth Framework Programme on Rail Transport (RA-96-SC.231) and comprises a consortium of MATRA Transport International (France - Project Leader), Ansaldo S.F. (Italy), ARC Seibersdorf (Austria), INRETS (France), Lloyd's register (UK), RATP (France), SINTEF (Norway), SNCF (France) and TÜV Rheinland (Germany).

The need for this project arose from the current situation in the certification of railway safety critical systems in Europe: today there are different practices in operating trains and railway lines, different technologies and different cultures; certification follows national practices and is based on historical practices. This results in problems for the operator, the interoperability, and the manufacturer. For the operator it is difficult to have confidence in systems developed, assessed and certified in another country, as there are major differences in the certification practices, and no or little mutual recognition for certificates between the countries. The interoperability is expensive today, as can be seen from the example of the Thalys TGV, which is equipped with several different signalling systems. Last but not least the manufacturer has difficulties to export his products and systems.

The ACRuDA consortium has formulated an assessment procedure and criteria for safety critical architectures and proposed a certification framework for these systems to facilitate cross-acceptance of the certificates thereby supporting the progress of the harmonisation of assessment approaches and the mutual recognition of certificates.

M. Felici, K. Kanoun, A. Pasquini (Eds.): SAFECOMP'99, LNCS 1698, pp. 39-45, 1999
© Springer-Verlag Berlin Heidelberg 1999

The ACRuDA assessment procedure and criteria are a set of rules and guidelines for planning and conducting an assessment of vital computers, i. e. both hardware and software. They have been tested and improved by conducting three case studies:

- DIGISAFE, a single channel architecture developed by MATRA Transport International and based on the coded monoprocessor,
- ELEKTRA, a dual channel architecture using safety bag techniques, developed by ALCATEL Austria, and
- S.A.R.A., a modular, distributed processing, hierarchical layered control system developed by ANSALDO Trasporti.

Apart from the principles mentioned above the way to realise them is also quite different. For signalling, e. g., the ELEKTRA system is designed to operate track-side signalling, while DIGISAFE and S.A.R.A. operate via a balise system to give information in the cab.

So ACRuDA's task was rather ambitious: to achieve cross-acceptance for such a wide range of systems is not trivial.

This is illustrated by the description of the underlying principles of the first two case studies, DIGISAFE and ELEKTRA, which forms the following part of this paper. The third part discusses the assessment and certification method proposed by ACRuDA.

2   DIGISAFE

DIGISAFE (MATRA Transport International) is based on the coded monoprocessor [1], [2], which is used in the train protection of line A of the RER express metro in Paris (1988), the POMA system in Laon (1989), the MAGGALY system in Lyon and in the fixed automatic pilot of the VAL in Chicago.

The basic principle of this single channel architecture consists of coding all the variables of the programme. So every variable X is composed of the pair (Xf, Xc), where Xf is the value part and Xc is the "control part" of the variable.

The programme instructions are designed to deal with these encoded variables: both the input and the output is in encoded form.

The used code consists of the following types of codes:

- An arithmetic code with the key A (a prime integer; if it has 48 bits, A (1014) to detect computing errors (errors of carry over, errors of shift, etc.). The code (Xf, Xc) of the variable X is a word of the code if and only if the following is true:
  2k Xf + Xc (0 (modulo A), where k is a fixed integer.
- A signature (static signature) to detect addressing errors (operand error, operator error, variables confusion). To each of the variables X and integer Bx is associated, which is called the signature of X and is independent of the value Xf of X. This signature is superimposed on the above arithmetic code. In this way X = (Xf, Xc) is a word of the code if and only if the following is true:
  2k Xf + Xc (Bx (modulo A).

The signatures of the intermediate variables and of the outputs are determined by the input signatures and the operations performed. The signatures of all outputs are independent of the input values and the execution paths followed; they are pre-calculated with a signature predetermination tool.

- A timing signature (dynamic signature) to detect dating errors (unwanted storage, incorrect number of loops, etc.). Every processing cycle is characterised by its proper date D, which is incremented at every loop. So $X = (Xf, Xc)$ at the time D is a word of the code if and only if the following is true:

  2k Xf + Xc (Bx + D (modulo A).

- A sequence signature (called "tracer") to protect against certain sequencing and branching errors. This tracer is updated after every instruction and can be computed by the predetermination tool. So finally $X = (Xf, Xc)$ is a word of the code if and only if the following is true:

  2k Xf + Xc (Bx + D + Tr (modulo A) = Sf (final signature).

In a fail-safe dynamic controller this final signature is compared with the pre-calculated signature.

3   ELEKTRA

ELEKTRA (ALCATEL Austria) [1], [3], [4], [14] is an electronic interlocking system with more than 40 installations in Austria, Hungary and Switzerland, a bigger one being Salzburg with more than 150 switches.

The system structure consists of three functional levels:

- Operator level with man/machine interface including the Visual Display Units (VDUs)
- Logic and safety processing level (realised on the central processors)
- Peripheral control level.

As the requirements to achieve high safety and high availability are partly contradicting each other, ELEKTRA has separate and different mechanisms for safety and availability.

To attain the safety requirements, all actions relevant to safety are processed on a two channel basis with diverse software (see below). For this purpose, the system (both hardware and software) is split up into a logic channel and a safety channel, the so called "Safety Bag". An operator's command input in the logic channel is checked against operating and safety conditions and if the result is positive, the output at the external field elements is prepared. Before output, however, there is a check back to the safety channel to verify whether the result determined by the logic channel would not lead to a dangerous operational condition ("Safety Bag" Procedure). Only when this procedure shows a positive result, will both channels, independently of each other, issue the required operating commands to the relay interface (software voting). In the relay interface, again, both commands undergo hardware-based comparison (hardware voting), before, finally, the external field elements are operated. If any of these comparisons detects a hazardous disagreement between the logic channel and the safety channel, the system goes into the safe status: all signals are set to STOP and a reboot is initiated (fail safe).

Additionally discrepancies between the channels will be detected by the operator, as the control of the colour VDUs, carried out with two separated serial inputs from the two channels, is displayed alternately at a frequency of about one Hz. In trouble-free operation, a static monitor picture will appear due to the congruency of the two pictures. In case of a fault in one of the two channels, the respective symbol will flash in the rhythm of picture switching, which will be recognised immediately by the operator (fail safe principle).

All this satisfies the safety requirements; any single hardware failure, however, would also trigger the fail safe mechanism.

For availability reasons it is therefore necessary to provide the processing channels with fault tolerant processor systems. For this purpose all central processors are tripled with majority voting (2 out of 3) in a software layer called VOTRICS (Voting Triple Modular Computing System), which is distributed in redundancy, so that also the voting process is no single point of failure.

The peripheral processors, such as Video Control Computers and Peripheral Control Computers are doubled. They operate in Hot Standby, which means, that one of the processors is active while the other is only fed with the actual information and does not participate in the processing itself. If the active processor fails, the redundant processor, waiting in the background but fully ready for service, will take over the processing, without any interruption of service.

The basic principle of the safety relevant system architecture is software diversity. Here ELEKTRA does not just use "n-version programming", diversity is engineered into the system. To achieve a maximum of design diversity it has been carefully specified, at which items the diversity is established. An example are the different specifications for the two channels, another one is the use of different languages: the logic channel is performing its task (e. g. setting routes, signals or switches) using programmes written in the procedural real-time language CHILL (CCITT High Level Language) based on the functional specification, while the safety channel (the "safety bag") implements the knowledge and experience of the signal man and station master using a rule-based approach programmed in PAMELA (Pattern Matching Expert System Language), a real-time expert system, which comprises around 700 rules.

4   Assessment and Certification

The main objective of the assessment process is to prepare an impartial report giving enough information on the safety of the product to demonstrate that the product meets the safety requirements specification and to support the certification of the product.

In order to avoid to repeat the assessment process each time an existing product or system is to be installed in another country, cross-acceptance of certificates is necessary. The three European Council Directives [5], [6], and [7] are the base for the definition of a new European model for assessment and certification in the railway field to achieve a situation, where certification bodies and certificates will be recognised by all licensing authorities throughout Europe.

To support these directives the ACRuDA project proposed an Assessment and Certification Methodology for Digital Architectures [8]. It is based on results from the CASCADE project, European Standards (especially [9], [10], [11], and [12]), relevant

European Council Directives, best practices in assessment and the experience of the ACRuDA Partners.

4.1   Assessment Method

The ACRuDA assessment method has been formalised in a set of high level assessment criteria, which will guide the assessor to arrive at a set of detailed criteria for his assessment target. This methodology has been updated already once taking into account the ACRuDA case studies' results and it must be updated regularly as the practice evolves in Europe.

The ACRuDA methodology deals with the basic architecture, which includes hardware and software, is railway generic and can be used in different railway applications. The basic architecture corresponds to the generic product in [11].

As the safety of a product is achieved by both technical measures and procedural measures (such as supplier organisation, staff, or experience), the assessment criteria must take into account the development process as well as the product.

This is realised already in the ACRuDA Assessment Activities, which begin with the identification of the safety requirements and continue with the assessment of the safety management, the quality management, the capability of the organisation to administer safety procedures, the development phase, the safety plan and the safety case.

The criteria are presented in the form of process and product properties. They state the requirements for the life-cycle processes and products; each requirement is devised to address a specific set of hazards. With each set of criteria a table of relevant techniques and measures is attached, which will generally satisfy the requirements. If other techniques or measures are used, they should be fully described and justified.

The assessment criteria cover the following:
* Process/project
* Requirements
* Design
* Validation and off line testing
* Fault and failure analyses
* Operation, maintenance and support
* Software
* Hardware

There are two main concepts for the assessment: the assessment of conformity and the assessment of effectiveness. Conformity is the degree to which a given implementation corresponds to the requirements; effectiveness is the degree to which the safety measures taken actually meet the desired results. Therefore the assessment of effectiveness consists of in the assessment of the safety functions, mechanisms and measures chosen to satisfy the safety requirements specification of a product, i. e. to look if the scenarios are complete, if the functions, mechanisms and measures are suitable, if all the functions operate together in a good way, and to consider the risks of failures as well as the tools, methods and the organisation of the supplier.

To show the importance of these concepts an example is given which refers to the cases studies described above:

In the criteria for design the techniques/measures for the architecture include:

- Single digital channel based on reactive fail-safety
- Dual digital channels based on composite fail-safety with fail-safe comparison
- Diverse digital channels with fail-safe comparison.

From the description above it is clear that both DIGISAFE and ELEKTRA conform to these criteria: DIGISAFE to the first and ELEKTRA to the two others. The assessment of effectiveness will look, how well these techniques are implemented. For DIGISAFE one item to be assessed will be the size of the code word, an important item for ELEKTRA will be the way, how the diversity is engineered into the development lifecycle (requirements, design, coding, testing, etc.).

4.2   Certification Method

From the above it is evident that cross-acceptance of certificates also needs a European certification framework. This defines the roles of supplier, sponsor, notified body, assessors, accreditation body, authority of a EU member state and the European Union in the certification process:

- The supplier designs, develops and validates the product according to current European Standards and Directives. He demonstrates the safety of the product according to the defined Safety Integrity Level (SIL) in the safety case
- The sponsor orders the assessment to demonstrate, that the product or system meets the safety requirements specification. He may choose a notified body from any European country [5].
- The notified body performs the assessment and certification of a product or system. It defines the procedures and means to fulfil the assessment and may use external assessors to perform parts of the assessment work [5], [6]. It maintains and publishes a list of assessment requests (past and present), refused and delivered certificates. The notified body must be accredited by an accreditation body.
- The assessors are bodies of proven technical competence, integrity, independence and confidentiality [5], [6]. They must be accredited by an accreditation body.
- The accreditation body gives the accreditation to the notified bodies and to the assessors according to [13]. It regularly monitors that they comply with this standard. The accreditation body is established by a member state authority.
- The authority of a EU member state appoints the notified bodies and establishes the national accreditation body. It regularly monitors their competence and independence [5], [6].
- The European Union defines the directives and standards as well as the European policy for assessment and certification, i.e. the procedures, methods, rules and criteria, for all the countries. The European Union gives an identification number to each notified body, keeps the official list of notified bodies and publishes all the information on the notified body in the Official Journal of the European Communities.

5   Conclusions

The cross-acceptance of certificates for safety-critical digital architectures in the railway sector is an important issue for the interoperability as well as for owners/operators and suppliers of such systems. The assessment method proposed by ACRuDA promotes the cross-acceptance by its assessment and certification methodology, which has been shown to be fair and applicable to the wide range of existing digital architectures.

References

1. ACRuDA Deliverable D1: State of the Art, Safety Architectures Synthesis, 1997
2. Martin, J. ; Wartski, s.: Vital coded processor: the new safety for transit system. IFAC IFIP, Wien, 1989
3. Doppelbauer, J.: ELEKTRA - Sicherheits- und Zuverlässigkeitsmechnismen (Mechnisms for Safety and Reliability). Paper presented at the 1st German-Austrian ENCRESS Workshop. Salzburg, 28 June 1995
4. H. Steinbrecher, H.: The ELECTRA System, The system for more than just electronic interlocking. IRSE, ASPECT91, London, 1991
5. Council Directive 96/48/EC: Interoperability of the European High Speed Train Network, 23 July 1996
6. Council Directive 93/465/EC: Modules related to the different phases of assessment procedures of conformity and rules of affixing and using CE mark, intended to be used in the technical harmonisation directives, 22 July 1993
7. Council Directive 90/531/EEC: Procurement procedures of entities operating in the water, energy, transportation and telecommunication sectors, 17 September 1990
8. ACRuDA Deliverable D3: The Proposed Assessment and Certification Methodology for Digital Architectures, 1998
9. prEN 50126, CENELEC: Railway Applications: The specification and demonstration of dependability, reliability, availability, maintainability and safety (RAMS), June 1997
10. prEN 50128, CENELEC: Railway Applications: Software for Railway Control and Protection Systems, June 1997
11. prENV 50129, CENELEC: Railway Applications: Safety Related Electronic Systems for Signalling, Version 1.0, January 1997
12. IEC 61508: Functional Safety: Safety Related Systems, Draft 1998
13. EN 450001: General Criteria for the Operation of Testing Laboratories, 1989
14. Schoitsch, E.; Dittrich, E.; Grasegger, S.; Kropfitsch, D.; Erb, A.; Fritz, P.; Kopp, H.: The ELEKTRA Testbed: Architecture of a Real-Time Test Environment for High Safety and Reliability Requirements. In Daniels, B.K., ed.: Safecomp'90, Proceedings of the IFAC/EWICS/SARS Symposium, Gatwick, UK, Pergamon Press, 1990.

Safety Evaluation of a Train Leader Telephone System

Gustav Dahll

Institute for Energy Technology,
P.O. box 173 N-1751 Halden, Norway
E-mail: gustav.dahll@hrp.no

Abstract. The paper describes methods used in a safety evaluation of a train leader telephone system. These methods include Fault Tree Analysis of the system in its environment to identify possible hazards, HazOp analysis based on the user interface, to identify faulty operator information which can cause these hazards, and FMECA based on Message Sequence Charts to identify possible computer failures which can lead to this faulty information. Emphasis is put on drawing conclusions on the general applicability of these methods.

1   Introduction

A computer based telephone system (TLT) which organises telephone contact between train drivers and train leaders has been implemented in the Train Leader Central in Oslo. The task of the train leaders is to supervise and control the complete railway net in Norway. A particular assignment to a train leader is to permit, via telephone, a train to bypass a red signal, in the case of a failure in the signalling system (which switch all signals to red as a fail safe state). This action is of course safety relevant, and thereby also the telephone system. This paper describes some of the methods that were used, and experience gained that may be of general interest.

A Preliminary Hazard Analysis was performed, consisting of two tasks. The first was to view the TLT system in the context of its environment, viz. the railway system, and identify potential severe accidents. One such accident was identified and used as a top event in a fault tree analysis (FTA). This is discussed in section 2.1. The second task was to look into the functioning of the system. A short, and simplified, description of the system, from the user's point of view, is made in section 2.2.

The further step was to perform a System Hazard Analysis based on a more detailed, technical, description of the system. This description is made in the form of message sequence charts (MSC). This is discussed in section 3.1.

Each of the MSCs were used as basis for a Failure Mode, Effect and Criticality Analysis (FMECA). This is discussed in section 3.2. The *objective* of this was to identify critical failures which potentially can lead to a hazard. To prevent the occurrence of these failures, particular safety tests, in addition to the planned factory acceptance tests, were suggested and performed. Also, some additional safety check to

M. Felici, K. Kanoun, A. Pasquini (Eds.): SAFECOMP'99, LNCS 1698, pp. 46–57, 1999
© Springer-Verlag Berlin Heidelberg 1999

prevent these failure to occur or to jeopardise safety were suggested to be implemented into the system. This is discussed in section 3.3.

Finally, the paper discusses how the lessons learned from this project can be utilised in safety evaluation of other systems.

2   Preliminary Hazard Analysis

2.1   Fault Tree Analysis

The event identified as most critical, and which is used as top event in the fault tree, is when a train drives into an obstacle. This obstacle may be another train, a large object which blocks the line, ongoing repair work etc. There may also be other critical events which could be considered, e.g. that the driver want to require an ambulance over the telephone in case of an accident, and that this information fails to come through to the train leader. This possibility was, however, not included in the analysis, as there are other means to communicate this, e.g. via a standard mobile telephone.

We also assumed that the train leader is informed about this obstacle. Otherwise he would have no possibility to decide whether it is safe for the train to drive into an area. Based on this, a fault tree was constructed as shown on fig. 1.

In the fault tree there are listed 11 (from 0 to 10) different root causes. However, not all the root causes are relevant for the analysis of the TLT system:

- Cause 0 includes all faults which are not directly connected to the communication between train leader and driver.
- Causes 1, 2 and 9 are human errors, and not considered in this analysis.
- Causes 4 and 7 are faults in other information systems than the TLT system.
- Cause 5 is caused by bad oral communication, possibly due to a bad telephone line. It is anyhow considered to be outside the TLT system.
- Cause 6 means that an outsider, e.g. a hacker or a saboteur breaks into the system with the intention to give either the train leader or the driver incorrect information. This was, however, considered so unlikely that it was not included in the subsequent analysis.

This leaves us with the three causes which relate to the TLT system and need to be further investigated:

- Root cause 4: Train leader gives permission due to wrong identification of train location
- Root cause 8: Permission given to wrong train due to wrong coupling of telephone
- Root cause 10: Two train leaders permit separately two trains to enter the same area.

The two first can be illustrated in fig. 2a: The train leader talks to train B but thinks he talks to train driver A, where there are no obstacle, so he gives permission to continue past the signal.

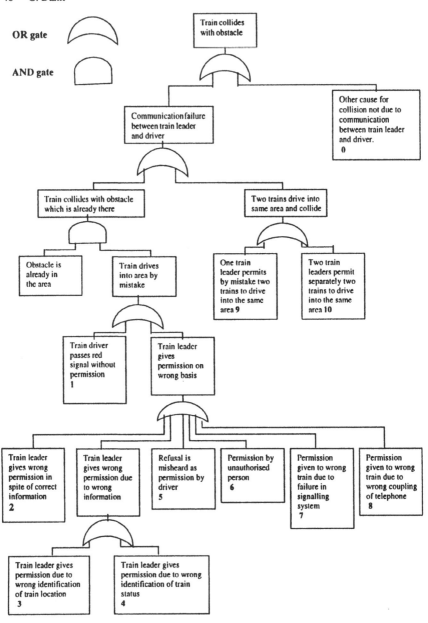

Fig 1 Fault tree for train collision.

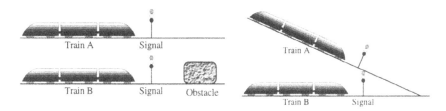

Fig. 2a Collision between train and obstacle   **Fig. 2b** Collision between two trains

The third can be illustrated in fig. 2b: Train leader a talks to train A and train leader b talks to train B. Both train leaders think they are responsible for this area of the rail net, and both give permissions to continue past the signal.

It should be emphasised that the fault tree is based on a fairly high level functional description of the TLT system, viz. that this system shall conduct the communication between train leaders and train drivers, and that the former shall, through this system, be able to safely give the train drivers permission to pass red light signals.

2.2   Functional Description of the TLT System

This section gives a short and very simplified functional description of the TLT system. As this system essentially is a communication system between train leader and train driver, the man-machine interaction on both sides determines the functioning of the system. In the train leader central there is a set of terminals for the train leaders, each equipped with a screen, a keyboard (and mouse) and a telephone. On the train drivers side there are different types of terminals, but in this paper we will, for simplicity, only deal with the simplest one, which was analysed first, viz. a set of fixed telephones, located at each signalling post between Oslo and Gardermoen. Through these the drivers may call up the train leader central and be directed to the train leader responsible for that area.

The train leader gets information about the calls via his/her screen (for the rest of this paper we will, for simplicity, use masculine form, even if several train leaders and drivers are women). This screen is divided into three fields (see fig. 3). One is a over-view of which train leaders are responsible for each of the rail areas (the 'responsibility window'). The second is a list of requested telephone calls (the 'request window'), and the third contains information of an actual dialog (the 'dialog window').

The latter has the same structure as one line in the request window, and contains information about telephone number, geographical location (in text form), a status indication, and other auxiliary information. Actually the screen layout is more complex than this, but as we in this report want to emphasis the principle and methods used in the analysis, we will try to simplify as much as possible, and concentrate on what is essential to explain this.

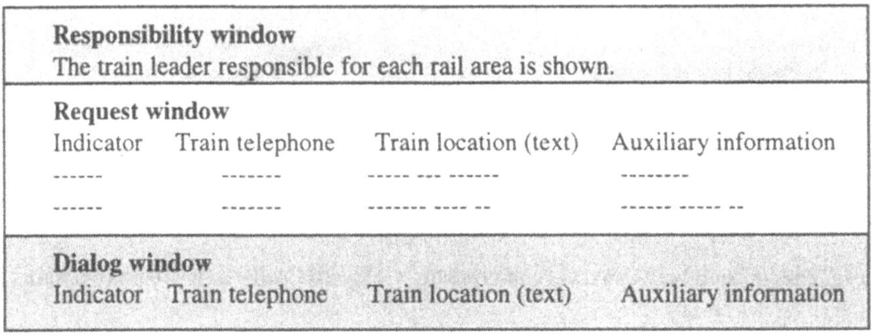

Responsibility window			
The train leader responsible for each rail area is shown.			
Request window			
Indicator	Train telephone	Train location (text)	Auxiliary information
------	-------	----- --- ------	--------
------	-------	------- ---- --	------ ----- --
Dialog window			
Indicator	Train telephone	Train location (text)	Auxiliary information

Fig. 3. Train leader's screen

When a train driver wants to call the train leader he lifts off the telephone receiver. This call is entered into the 'request list'. The train leader can pick any request from the list to make a connection. When this connection is made, the same information is shown in the 'dialog window', with an indication (made by colour shift) in the corresponding line in the request window. The train leader can now lift the receiver off the hook, and start talking.

Another function a train leader can make is to 'take over' the responsibility over a rail area from another train leader. Following this, the 'responsibility window' will change in his and all other train leaders' screens.

There are several other functions, but they will not be described here.

2.2   Hazard and Operability Analysis

A Hazard and Operability (HazOp) analysis looks at possible disturbances in the functioning of a system, rather than failures in the system components. The TLT system is essentially a human-to-human communication system and the HazOp analysis was performed on the interfaces between humans and the system, viz. the screen, the keyboard and the telephone itself. The two latter are well tested components so the HazOp analysis was concentrated on the information presented on the screen, which is particularly designed for the TLT system, and is based on software. The disturbances considered in the HazOp analysis were deviations from the intended information displayed on the screen.

In general terms, a HazOp analysis is performed as a kind of 'brain storming' activity: An analysis team is gathered, consisting of different experts, and headed by a HazOp leader. The team leader prepares in advance a so called 'HazOp form'. This form identifies a set of 'objects' and a set of 'guidewords' about these objects. At the analysis meeting the HazOp leader puts forward each object and corresponding guidewords, and asks the team to openly discuss the objects on the basis of the guidewords. A HazOp session was performed with participants from the users (a train leader), the developer (Alcatel) and the safety consultants (IFE, Scandpower).

One lesson learned from this experience is the importance of participation from the practical users (the train leaders) in such a session. Based on experience with the existing system, the train leader participant will reason about how a train leader would use the information presented, and how he would react to any incorrect information, e.g. by verifying this against information other information sources.

All the items of information which can occur on the screen constitute a set of objects. The guidewords concerned deviations from correctness in each of these items. Another type of objects are the processes which can change the screen information.

Questions asked were:

1. What can go wrong?
2. What could be the causes of this?
3. Which consequences could this possibly lead to (hazards)?
4. Can any of these consequences lead to any of the three root causes identified in the fault tree analysis?
5. If so, are there any countermeasures which can prevent this from happening?

An example is given for illustration:

Object: The train location field in the dialog window.

1. It can contain the location of another train which is in the request window.
2. Two identity numbers are mixed somewhere in the process.
3. The train leader may think he have connection to another train than he actually has.
4. If he does not check the corresponding line in the request window, or if this line has the same fault, this may lead to root cause 1.
5. The usual procedure for such calls, viz. that the train driver tells over the phone which location he calls from.

3   System Hazard Analysis

3.1   MSC Diagram Description

A System Hazard Analysis is an analysis based on a more detailed system description. The TLT system is essentially a communication system and the analysis was based upon the Message Sequence Chart (MSC) method [Z.120], to show how information, in the form of messages , is communicated between the different parts of the system. The MSC diagrams describe scenarios of interactions between the system and its environment. A diagram consists of a set of *processes* which can perform *actions* and exchange *messages* with each other and with the environment. The receiving of a message by a process can activate an action and sending of a message. A process will often be directly connected to a physical module, but it may also represent more abstract process or data modules. The actual choice of processes in an MSC is therefore not unique, but can be made in a way that best suits the purpose. An MSC diagram also has a time axis (going downward).

In the complete safety case for the TLT system, 16 different scenarios were described by MSCs, and altogether 19 processes were included in these diagrams. As this paper emphasises the principles of the methods used, we will concentrate on one MSC, viz. 'Call from train driver to the train leader central'. An excerpt of the MSC is shown in fig. 4a.

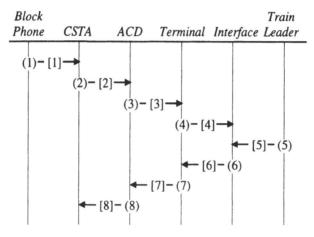

Fig 4a. Excerpt from MSC diagram

(1)	Train driver picks up the block telephone.
[1]	The block telephone number (BN).
(2)	A Call Identification (CI) number is generated for later identification of that particular call.
[2]	{BN,CI}.
(3)	ACD identifies, from a responsibility list, which train leader has the responsibility for the train area where the call comes from. A time stamp (t_0) is set, and the call is added to the request queue of the responsible train leader terminal (TT).
[3]	{ BN,CI,TT,t_0}
(4)	When the terminal receives a message on a request call, it search for BN in a catalogue to find associated text information (TI), such as geographic location etc. It generates a request text string (RT) which shall be written to the request window in the terminal screen. This information is also stored in a *request list*.

Fig 4b. Explanation of the processes and messages.

For simplicity the number of processes is limited to the essential ones, excluding design details of the system. The processes in this MSC are:

- The block telephone, i.e. the telephone permanently located at a signal point, from where the driver calls.
- Computer Supported Telecommunication Applications (CSTA) system
- Automatic Call Distribution (ACD) system.
- The train leader terminal.
- TLT's interface to the train leader (screen, keyboard, telephone)
- The train leader.

Numbers in parentheses and in square brackets identify actions and messages respectively. Thus the first line means that process 'Block-tlph' performs action (1) and sends message [1] to process CSTA. Fig. 4b explains some of the actions and messages. The content of a message is included in curly brackets.

MSCs are mainly used in the specification and design phase of system development. Even if this method for system development was used in some cases within the TLT project, it was not used for the system development related to the scenarios relevant for the safety analysis. The construction of the MSCs was therefore made in a retrospective analysis.

3.2   Failure Mode, Effect, and Criticality Analysis

Failure Mode Effect and Criticality Analysis (FMECA) is an analysis which concentrates on the potential failures of individual components. An IEC standard for FMEA and FMECA is given in IEC publication 812 [IEC812]. The basis for an FMECA analysis is a functional description of the system to be analysed, the target system, in terms of its components. For each of the components in the system, the aim is to identify all potential modes of failure..

This type of analysis has traditionally been applied to hardware components, even if it in recent years also have been applied to software modules. In this project, however, it was applied on the actions and messages in the MSCs. The intention was to ask the following questions for each action and message, based on the FMECA framework:

- what can go wrong? (*failure mode*)
- how can this occur? (*failure cause/mechanism*).
- which consequences will this have on the further actions and messages (*failure effect*).
- can any of these consequences potentially lead to any of the root causes described in section 2.1? (*failure criticality*)
- are there any internal failure detection mechanisms in the system which can detect this failure which can prevent, or reduce the possibility, that this failure will lead to a critical consequence (*failure detection*)
- if a safety critical failure could be caused by a software fault, which test procedure should be followed to detect this potential fault (*fault detection*)

Notice that even if the questions are very similar to the ones used in the HazOp analysis, they are applied on different objects. In the HazOp analysis they were applied on the user interface, and the analysis was made from the user's view, to identify failures in the information which could lead to hazards. In the FMECA they are applied on details in the internal functioning of the system, intended to identify potential dangerous (software) failures in the system.

An example from Message [2] of the MSC in fig. 4 is given for illustration:

failure modes:
1.   BN is corrupted
2.   CI is corrupted

Further analysis of failure mode 1:
*   *failure cause/mechanism:*
    1.   a transmission error (hardware failure)
    2.   a fault in the CSTA program which processes the receiving and sending of messages.
*   *failure effect:* The wrong block-telephone number will be processed further, and may eventually present wrong information about the call to the train leader.

*   *failure criticality* Depending on the failure in the information on the terminal, the train leader may be mislead to believe he talks to another train driver than he actually does. This corresponds to the safety critical root cause 4 in the fault tree.

*   *failure detection* An error checking mechanism could be able to detect certain failures, in particular random transmission errors. However, certain systematic failures caused by program faults may be difficult to detect, and may therefore be critical.

The initial intention was to perform such an analysis for all actions and messages, but because the total number of failure modes became too large, time did not allow a complete analysis. It was therefore necessary, wherever possible, to analyse sequences of actions and messages as one unity. Another problem was to identify possible failure mechanisms and effects based on the documentation alone. The method was, however, very useful as a framework for a systematic analysis.

3.3   Safety Enhancement

One objective of this analysis was to identify activities which could be done to enhance the confidence in the system as well as in the safety analysis. One can distinguish between three types:
1.   Testing the correctness of the system
2.   Checking the robustness of the system by fault injection
3.   Proposal of adding new features to the system which increase the reliability and robustness

In addition to an extensive factory acceptance test, a set of special *safety tests* were required to check that there program contains no faults that can jeopardise safety. As the number of possible test cases for the TLT system is too large for an exhaustive test, the testing was concentrated on the actions which the analysis identified potential hazardous failures.

The second type, i.e. the checking of the robustness, was performed by perturbing certain messages, and observing how this was handled by the system. This was partly done to test the internal failure checks, and partly to see whether the train leader would get warnings or redundant information which could prevent him from drawing wrong conclusions.

This leads to the third type mentioned above, viz. to propose to include simple new features in the system which could reduce the possibility of a hazard. Several such proposals were made. As an example, an alarm, visual and/or audible, should be given if a discrepancy between information in different windows were detected. This should increase the likelihood that the train leader becomes aware of the situation, and prevent him from drawing wrong conclusions about which block telephone he is connected to.

4   Conclusions and Lessons Learned

An important aspect for a research institution is whether one can make more general conclusions from observations and experiences made in practical projects. This is therefore the objective of this chapter.

4.1   The System

The TLT system is essentially a human to human communications system. The communication is, however, not symmetric. The train driver sends a request which is processed by the TLT system to produce information to the train leader. Based on this information, together with auxiliary information from other sources, the train leader sends a message back to the train driver. The correctness of this message can be safety critical. It is therefore essential that the train leader gets correct information through his terminal, and that he sends his message to the right address. It is of course also important that the train driver understands the message correctly, but this is a spoken message through a telephone, and not included in this analysis.

These considerations show a striking similarity to a process supervision and control system, as e.g. a control room system. Here the train driver corresponds to the process whereas the train leader is the operator. The process instruments send messages to the control and supervision system which transforms this into comprehensible information for the operator. Based on this information the operator shall make a decision on an action, which may be safety relevant, and send signals to the process to perform this action. Thus, the experience made in the TLT safety analysis is also relevant for a safety analysis of a human-machine interaction system.

4.2   Fault Tree Analysis

The use of a FTA to put the TLT system into a larger context was very useful, and has a general applicability. When a new control and supervision system shall be implemented, one should always investigate whether this could have any impact on safety. One should start with the identification of the process hazards and use them as top events in fault trees, and work downwards to see if one hits root causes which are due to failures in the target system. One should however use common sense and engineering judgement to disregard top events and prune off fault tree branches which can not be influenced by the target system.

The set of root causes which are due to failures in the system constitute a target for the further analysis, i.e. one will in the further safety analysis search for, and try to eliminate, faults and weaknesses in the systems which can lead to these failures, or show, by testing or other means, that such faults do not exist.

4.3   HazOp Analysis

As the system is essentially a human-to-human communication system where the interfaces between humans and the system is made via the screen, the screen information was chosen as the basis for the HazOp analysis. The disturbances in this connection were deviations from the intended information on the screen. This method could be applied to man-machine interaction systems in general.

The method is to list all the fields in the information display, and systematically go through this list with a HazOp group consisting of representatives for the users (important!), the developer and HazOp experts. The question should be: what would happen if the information in this field is wrong? Is this information essential for a correct decision. May a wrong decision here lead to any of the root causes identified in the FTA?

One experience made during the HazOp session was that it is difficult to design the HazOp form in advance. In the analysis of the HazOp log, an alternative, and simpler, form was found to be more adequate. A more general framework for this type of HazOp analysis, with emphasis on the communication and user interface between a system and an operator, could be useful.

4.4   System Hazard Analysis Based on MSC Diagram Description

The MSC methodology is a well established method for system specification and design, in particular of communication systems. It would have been a great advantage, both for the development and the safety evaluation of the TLT system, if this method had been used from the beginning. In the present case, however, the method was used retrospectively, with the possible error sources this may include. Even so, the use of MSCs was a very good way of communicating between the developers and the safety assessors, improving the understanding of the functioning of the system.

The advantages of applying FMECA on the actions and messages in the MSC diagrams are that the method is (in principle) systematic, and that it aids the identification of faults that are potentially safety critical. Having identified these faults, one can concentrate the further investigation on these. This is particularly useful if software can cause these faults, because communication systems are in general so complex that an exhaustive test and verification is incomprehensive. In the present case, this helped to reduce the number of safety tests considerably.

The method also is useful to identify robustness tests, i.e. tests on whether a random (hardware) failure may lead to a hazard. From knowledge about the system one may reason about where such failures may possibly occur. These can be simulated by corrupting messages identified in the diagrams.

A disadvantage with this method is that it is rather tedious and time consuming. There were, and are in general, many actions and messages, with a multitude of possible failure modes. In the assessment it was necessary to make shortcuts to complete the analysis in reasonable time. Another aspect, which is not of general nature, but relevant for this analysis, is that the method was developed along the way, with several iterative modifications. A future research task could therefore be to develop this method further including supporting tools.

Acknowledgement.

I want to acknowledge the persons who participated in this project, in particular Harald Thunem from IFE, Rune Winther from Scandpower and Olaf Wikesland from Alcatel.

References

IEC812   "Analysis Techniques for Systems Reliability - Procedures for Failure Mode and Effects Analysis (FMEA)", IEC publication 812, 1985.

Z.120   Recommendation of the Z.120 - Message Sequence Charts (MSC), ITU, 1996.

BDP97   S. Bologna, G. Dahll, G. Picciolo and R. Taylor: "Safety Application of Computer Based Systems for the Process Industry". Report for the ESSI project 21542 ENCRESS, June 1997

Lev95   N.G. Leveson: "Safeware", Addison Wesley Publishing Company 1995.

Safety Analysis Techniques for Validating Formal Models During Verification

Rogério de Lemos and Amer Saeed

Department of Computing Science
University of Newcastle upon Tyne, NE1 7RU, UK
{r.delemos, a.saeed}@newcastle.ac.uk

Abstract. The increased interest in the use of automated safety analysis is supported by the claim that safety analysis based on traditional techniques (predominantly manual) is error-prone, costly and not necessarily complete. It is also claimed that traditional techniques are not able to deal with the inherent complexities of software intensive systems. However, we show in this paper that a transition (from manual to automatic approaches) in the assessment process and technologies is accompanied by an inherent risk of obtaining false confidence, unless safeguards are provided. The safeguard presented in this paper integrates traditional deductive and inductive analysis techniques with model checking, a form of formal verification. The aim is to provide the safety analyst with a rigorous approach for the validation of formal models.

1. Introduction

The current trend has been to claim that traditional safety analysis techniques (predominantly manual) are error-prone, costly and not necessarily complete, moreover, it is also claimed that they are not able to deal with the inherent complexities of software intensive systems. In this paper, we claim that it is not sufficient to replace traditional techniques for automated counterparts which seem more effective in dealing with highly complex systems, unless the principles and rationale behind the traditional safety analysis techniques are preserved. Moreover, any change (i.e. the transition from manual to automatic) in the practice of conducting safety analysis is vulnerable to the inherent risk of obtaining false confidence.

Over the years, traditional safety analysis techniques have provided an effective means by which analysts are able to generate, in a rigorous manner, failure scenarios that might affect safety. These techniques have evolved to enable an analyst to acquire a deep understanding of the intricacies that affect the safety of complex systems. One of the merits of traditional safety analysis techniques is the methodological rigour that forces the analyst to focus on issues related with system safety. On the other hand, there are automatic safety analysis approaches, that lack the methodological rigour which enforces the safety analysts to have a comprehensive understanding of system

M. Felici, K. Kanoun, A. Pasquini (Eds.): SAFECOMP'99, LNCS 1698, pp. 58–66, 1999

safety (in terms of faults and their possible consequences). Furthermore, the formal models which provide the basis for the automatic approaches (the "raw material" of the automated tools) are often impenetrable to checks on their accuracy, hence are usually considered as "black boxes" by the safety analyst. In these circumstances, there is a change of emphasis from ensuring the completeness of the safety analysis to confirming the accuracy of the models subjected to safety analysis.

Automated tools might be effective in dealing with some of the inherent complexities of software based systems, for example dependencies of many failure modes of system components. However if support is not provided to enable the analyst to understand the rationale behind key safety-related decisions, then the effectiveness of these tools is limited. In our opinion, to reduce the risk of obtaining false confidence, the application of automated tools should be supported by a deductive and inductive analysis of the formal models subject to automated analysis. In this paper we present an approach which uses safety analysis techniques for validating the formal models required for model checking. The domain of application is safety-critical control systems, particularly those systems which are real-time and hybrid in their nature.

The paper is structured as follows. Section 2 provides an overview on model checking and the concept of abstractions, and describes the risks associated with model checking as a safety analysis technique. In Section 3 we describe how deductive and inductive analysis can be integrated with model checking in order to attain higher levels of confidence for the models being analysed. Finally, Section 4 concludes with a discussion evaluating our contribution and indicating directions for future work.

2. Model Checking

Model checking is a formal verification technique based on state exploration. Given a state transition system and a property, model checking algorithms exhaustively explore the state space to determine whether the system satisfies the property. The result is either a claim that the property is true (provision of *evidence*) or a counter-example in terms of a sequence of states that falsifies a property (guidance for *risk reduction*) /Chan 98/.

The diagram of figure 1, schematically represents the basic steps of model checking. The property-based and operational representations of the concrete model of the system are: $prSS_c$ and $opSS_c$. Concrete models might include, for instance, non-linearities which the model checking algorithms are unable to analyse. Hence the need to translate into linear models, by applying abstractions, to obtain the property-based ($prSS_a'$) and operational ($opSS_a'$) descriptions of an abstract model.

Abstract interpretation is a technique for the systematic translation of a concrete model to an abstract one (using conservative approximations), and can be used either for improving the efficiency for analysing a discrete system by reducing the state explosion /Clarke 94, Heitmeyer 98/, or for approximating nonlinear hybrid systems

/Henzinger 95a/. For both cases, existing approaches may rely on more that one method for obtaining efficient and precise representations, hence the multiple abstraction levels shown in figure 1. For example, for reducing the state space, *variable restriction* and *variable abstraction* can be used, respectively, to remove irrelevant variables and to replace detailed variables with more abstract ones /Heitmeyer 98/.

In model checking, a key relationship between an abstract model and the concrete model, from which its is derived, is preservation of properties (essentially invariants) across the models. Ideally an abstract model ($prSS_a$, $opSS_a$) developed for a concrete model ($prSS_c$, $opSS_c$) should be both *sound* (i.e. if $prSS_a$ is a property of $opSS_a$, $prSS_c$ is also a property of $opSS_c$) and *complete* (i.e. if it is sound, and $prSS_c$ is a property of $opSS_c$, $prSS_a$ is also a property of $opSS_a$). Methods have been proposed for abstraction that aim to preserve soundness and completeness.

One approach proposed for hybrid automaton /Henzinger 95a/ is to provide general algorithm's for the transformation of a concrete (nonlinear) model to an abstract (linear) equivalent. Two schemes are proposed. *Clock translation*, the resultant abstract model is both sound and complete, however the scheme can only be applied in the presence of strict conditions. *Phase-portrait approximation*, although this can be applied to any hybrid automaton the resultant model is sound but not complete. Another approach proposed for interpreted finite state machines /Heitmeyer 98/ is to provide methods for the derivation of an abstract model to support the analysis of a particular property, in the presence of certain conditions. This results in abstract models that are sound, but may not be complete. In summary, these methods enable an analyst to obtain confidence (directly from the process of translation) that the results obtained from model checking the abstract model are applicable to the concrete model.

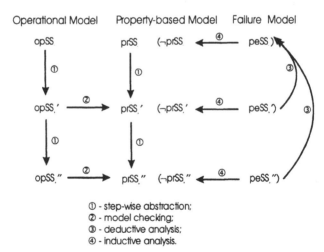

① - step-wise abstraction;
② - model checking;
③ - deductive analysis;
④ - inductive analysis.

Fig. 1. The basis for model checking

2.1. Model Checking and Safety Analysis

A typical approach for the application of model checking to safety analysis is: to represent the safety property that the system has to satisfy, usually associated with the negation of the system hazard, as the the property-based model, and the operational model would represent the system being designed, including the possible failures of the components of the system. For model checking to be effective as a safety analysis technique, it should support risk reduction and provide evidence for safety. In terms of risk reduction, model checking can identify the possible causes for the violation of the properties associated with the model; once causes are identified the model can be modified to eliminate or mitigate the risk (if both the property and model cannot be modified then risk remains unchanged). In terms of evidence, model checking can show that despite failures in the components of the system, the safety properties of the system are not affected (or if affected the risk associated with the failures is acceptable).

As with any modelling technique, the confidence that can be attributed to the results obtained from model checking is dependent on the accuracy of the models, hence property-based and operational models should be validated to confirm they are accurate representations of the actual system. Although it is relatively easy to check whether the operational model satisfies the specified properties, there are several error sources in the process of modelling. For example, either the property-based or operational models might have a mis-representation (inappropriate parameter which defines states/transitions of the automata, or flawed initial conditions) that allow a property to be confirmed for the model despite it being inappropriate for the real system. In particular, an analogy can be made with testing when applying model checking as a safety analysis technique: model checking is able to confirm the presence of faults in the model, but not their absence. Moreover, while testing is able to probe the actual product being developed, model checking is only restricted to probe a representation of the actual product. Hence, additional assurance should be provided that either the model being checked is an accurate representation of the system, or that all the exposed inaccuracies between the model and the actual system do not impact system safety.

In terms of abstract interpretation, although the actual methods for either reducing the state explosion or for approximating nonlinear hybrid systems might be sound and complete, the process of applying these methods is still error prone. During the transformation of a concrete specification into a more abstract one certain details of the models are discarded, these could eliminate some of the causes for a hazardous state. Although the abstract model might be proven to be safe, there are cases in which it cannot be claimed that the concrete model is also safe - when the abstract model $(prSS_a, opSS_a)$ is not a sound abstraction of the concrete model $(prSS_c, opSS_c)$.

In this paper we do not claim that model checking should be avoided as a safety analysis technique. On the contrary, our claim is that model checking is an effective technique when used with caution, as investigated for the model checker SMV (Symbolic Model Verification /McMillan 92/) for conducting fault analysis of chemical plants. Over confidence on the capabilities of model checking without balancing its inherent risks might lead to some unexpected and undesired situations. An approach for the validation of abstract interpretations using safety analysis techniques is presented. Instead of validating both the property-based and the operational models, the focus is on the property-based model. Otherwise the complexity of the proposed approach would be proportional with the number of states of the operational model.

3. Vulnerability Analysis for Abstraction

The aim of vulnerability analysis (VA), when applied to model checking, is to provide evidence to support the claim that safety properties of the abstract model are reflected in the concrete model, and to complement the results obtained from model checking. The mechanics for checking for potential vulnerabilities are based on the application of traditional deductive and inductive analysis of the property-based representations.

- *Deductive analysis*, in terms of safety analysis, starts with a hazard and proceeds backwards, seeking possible failures that can lead to the hazard. An example of a method which supports deductive analysis is Fault Tree Analysis (FTA).
- *Inductive analysis*, in terms of safety analysis, starts with a set of failure events and proceeds forward, seeking possible consequences (i.e. hazards) resulting from the events. Typical examples of methods which support inductive analysis are Failure Modes and Effect Analysis (FMEA) and Event Tree Analysis (ETA).

The approach being proposed is a safeguard against obtaining false confidence from model checking, or following inappropriate guidance for risk reduction in the system. Although the transformation methods can be sound/complete, it is possible that these methods are not applied in accordance with their guidelines. Moreover, there are situations in which existing methods for the abstract interpretation of concrete models are not suitable for a particular application, the analyst is forced to employ ad-hoc approaches to derive an abstract model. In these cases, although it might not be possible to find an alternative transformation which is sound/complete, it might nevertheless be effective to conduct the model checking of a correspondent abstract model, to obtain evidence that the risk is acceptable.

To incorporate deductive and inductive analysis into model checking, the original dual language (property-based and operational) description of systems has to include a third description related with the set of primitive events that lead to the violation of safety properties. The model of the system is then represented as a triple ⟨opSS, prSS, peSS⟩, which also includes the failure model (peSS) a predicate that characterises a set of primitive events (denoted by **peSS**) that refer to failures in the system components, or violations in the system behavioural assumptions.

The complete framework for model checking, including the representation of failure behaviours, is shown in figure 1. From this framework we can infer the following logical relations. The first two relations establish the cause-consequence relationship between the occurrence of primitive events and the violation of a safety property. The occurrence of a primitive event in the concrete model $peSS_c$ (abstract model $peSS_a$), is a sufficient condition for the violation of the safety property $prSS_c$ (resp. $prSS_c$):

$$peSS_c \Rightarrow \neg prSS_c \qquad\qquad peSS_a$$
$$\Rightarrow \neg prSS_a$$

The following relation is a term of a refinement relation which also includes safety assumptions and unsafe states /de Lemos 98/, and states that the violation of an abstract safety property implies the violation of the correspondent concrete safety property:

$$\neg prSS_a \Rightarrow \neg prSS_c$$

During the deductive analysis the aim is to identify and compare the set of primitive events of the concrete and abstract models which can lead to the violation of the safety property. This enables a comparison between the failure properties of two different models of the same system /Cepin 97/, and can lead to several possibilities. In terms of safety, the most relevant cases are those in which model checking of the abstract model leads to inconclusive results: when there is a subset of excluded primitive events ($peSS_c^* = peSS_c - peSS_a$) which are part of the concrete model, but not part of the abstract model. In these cases, model checking of the abstract model is not able to identify counter-examples which demonstrate that the safety property can be violated on the concrete model. Once these excluded primitive events are identified, the role of the inductive analysis is to establish the sequence of events that can lead to a system hazard. The outcome of this analysis will provide the basis to mitigate or eliminate the risk associated with a primitive event. This provides a complementary means for conducting safety analysis when model checking the concrete model is not possible. In terms of the diagram of figure 1, the deductive analysis is conducted by comparing the primitive events of a concrete model with its correspondent abstract interpretation, and the inductive analysis is conducted by identifying the sequence of events that lead to the violation of a safety property, once an excluded primitive event occurs.

The integration of safety analysis techniques with the abstract interpretation of concrete models is based on similar work which integrated deductive and inductive analysis with the process of decomposing and refining safety specifications /de Lemos 98/. For refinement, the main concern is to check what is the impact in terms of system safety when detailing a specification: new hazards can be introduced, and new assumptions have to be identified. Although the process of abstraction is quite different from the refinement of specifications (in the sense that detail is actually removed from the specifications rather being added), the safety analysis techniques which have shown to be effective for refinement can also be applied with minor modifications to abstraction.

3.1. Deductive Analysis

During the deductive analysis the aim is to confirm that the failure properties of the abstract model are consistent with those of the concrete model. The process to achieve this consists of two stages:

- a *causal analysis* of the concrete (and abstract models) to determine the causes for the violation of a safety property $prSS_C$ (respectively $prSS_a$) in the context of its operational specification $opSS_C$ ($opSS_a$);
- a *comparison* between the causes for the abstract and concrete models.

The starting point for the causal analysis is to identify the hazard characterized by the negation of the safety property (i.e. $\neg prSS_C$). The next step is to identify sources of failures which define the causes, known as primitive events, that lead to the hazard. In this paper, FTA is advocated for the deductive analysis, since it constraints the analysis by identifying only those behaviours that lead to the violation of specification $prSS_C$.

The comparison of $peSS_C$ and $peSS_a$ can result in five cases. Two extremes are: *identical* sets (i.e. $peSS_C=peSS_a$), the results of model checking are applicable to risk reduction and provision of evidence; *disjoint* sets (i.e $peSS_a \cap peSS_C=\{\}$), nothing can be inferred about the safety properties of the concrete model. The other three (more typical) cases are discussed in detail.

- *Event inclusion* - the primitive events of the concrete model are a subset of those obtained from the abstract model (i.e. $peSS_C \subset peSS_a$). Evidence is obtained from model checking, however guidance for risk reduction (i.e. counter- examples) for the abstract model may not be applicable to the concrete model.
- *Event exclusion* - the primitive events of the concrete model are a superset of those obtained from the abstract model (i.e. $peSS_C \supset peSS_a$). Guidance provided for risk reduction by model checking the abstract model can be used to modify the concrete model, however evidence that a safety property holds for the abstract model may not be applicable to confirmation for the concrete model. Two strategies can be adopted, to overcome the deficiencies in model checking for this case. In a first strategy, the impact of the excluded primitive events $peSS_C^*$ on system safety can be determined by inductive analysis. An alternative strategy is to define an additional property $prSS_a^*$, for which the corresponding $peSS_a^*$ will include $peSS_C^*$. In this case confirmation (by model checking) of both $prSS_a$ and $prSS_a^*$ can be used to confirm $prSS_C$.
- *Event overlap* - the intersection of the primitive events is a strict subset of the events of the concrete and abstract models (i.e. $pe=peSS_C \cap peSS_a$, $pe \subset peSS_C$ and $pe \subset peSS_a$). In this case both the evidence and guidance for risk-reduction, obtained from model checking, may not be applicable for the concrete model. The two strategies proposed in the event exclusion case can also be applied here. For event overlap these strategies enable the results to be treated as for event inclusion

(within an identified level of risk), or identify other properties over the abstract model to mimic event inclusion.

3.2. Inductive Analysis

Starting from the occurrence of a primitive event the role of inductive analysis of safety specifications is to determine the sequence of events which can lead to the violation of a safety property. The aim of the inductive analysis is to complement the safety analysis conducted using model checking by probing the primitive events of the concrete model which are not part of the set of primitive events of the abstract model.

This analysis is necessary for the cases of event exclusion and event overlap, to analyse the impact of excluded primitive events ($\mathbf{peSS_c}^*$). The identification of the sequence of events that leads to the violation of a safety property establishes potential deficiencies that the concrete model might have. These deficiencies need to be rectified to mitigate or eliminate the risk associated with a particular primitive event, unless the risk associated with them is acceptable. In this paper, the use of ETA is advocated for conducting the inductive analysis.

4. Conclusions

Although the model checking literature provides techniques which are sound and complete for obtaining abstract interpretations from concrete models, nevertheless the application of these techniques are still error prone (when not applied appropriately). Means to validate these abstract interpretations are necessary in order to obtain the required confidence that the abstract models obtained are indeed sufficiently accurate. In this paper we have presented an approach based on deductive and inductive analysis for the validation of the abstract models. We recognize the fact that the application of these techniques in complex systems is limited, however if the usage of these techniques is restricted to the property-based representations then we are able to scope their complexity. Furthermore, the traditional safety analysis techniques could have the same role as the dependency graph browser of the Software Cost Reduction (SCR) method /Heninger 78, Heninger 80/, in automatically removing irrelevant variables from the model.

Another aspect that might hinder the utilization of model checking as a safety analysis technique is the lack of a methodological support for guiding its use when conducting safety analysis. Testing, for example, is a validation technique which relies on a wide range of strategies, such as black box testing, and random testing, to ensure that the risk associated with a particular system is acceptable. Once similar methodological support is defined, confidence can be placed on model checking as a safety analysis technique. The feasibility of the approach has been illustrated by application to the industrial press case study /de Lemos 99/, in the context of the HYTECH model checker /Henzinger 95b/. Future work will focus on providing methodological support for the application of safety analysis techniques for the validation of formal models.

Acknowledgements

The authors would like to acknowledge the financial support of EPSRC/UK ADAPT and SafeGames projects.

References

/Cepin 97/ M. Cepin, R. de Lemos, B. Mavko, S. Riddle, A. Saeed. "An Object-Based Approach to Modelling and Analysis of Failure Properties". *Proceedings of the 16th International Conference on Computer Safety, Reliability and Security (SAFECOMP'97)*. York, UK. September 1997. Ed. P. Daniel. Springer-Verlag. Berlin, Germany. pp. 281-294.

/Clarke 94/ E. Clarke, O. Grumberg, and D. Long. "Model Checking and Abstraction". *ACM Transactions on Programming Languages and Systems (TOPLAS) Vol. 15(5)*. ACM. September, 1994.

/Chan 98/ W. Chan, et. al. "Model Checking Large Software Specifications". *IEEE Transactions on Software Engineering Vol. 27(7)*. IEEE Computer Society. July 1998. pp. 498-520.

/de Lemos 98/ R. de Lemos, A. Saeed, and T. Anderson. *On the Integration of Requirements Analysis and Safety Analysis for Safety-Critical Software*. Technical Report Series No. 630. Department of Computing Science, University of Newcastle upon Tyne, UK. May, 1998.

/de Lemos 99/ R. de Lemos, and A. Saeed. Validating Formal Verification using Safety Analysis Techniques. Technical Report Series No. 668. . Department of Computing Science, University of Newcastle upon Tyne, UK. May, 1999.

/Heitmeyer 98/ C. Heitmeyer, et. al. "Using Abstraction and Model Checking to Detect Safety Violations in Requirements Specifications". *IEEE Transactions on Software Engineering Vol. 27(11)*. IEEE Computer Society. November 1998. pp. 927-948.

/Heninger 78/ K. L. Heninger, J. Kallander, D. L. Parnas and   J. E. Shore. *Software Requirements for the A-7E Aircraft*. NRL Memorandum Report 3876. November 1978.

/Heninger 80/ K. L. Heninger. "Specifying Software Requirements for Complex Systems: New Techniques and their Applications". *IEEE Transactions on Software Engineering Vol. SE-6 (1)*. January 1980. pp 2-13.

/Henzinger 95a/ T. A. Henzinger, and P.-H. Ho. "Algorithmic Analysis of Non-Linear Hybrid Systems". *Proceedings of the Computer-Aided Verification (CAV'95)*. LNCS 939. Springer-Verlag. Berlin, Germany. pp. 225-238.

/Henzinger 95b/ T. A. Henzinger, and P.-H. Ho. "HYTECH: The Cornell HYbrid TECHnology Tool". *Hybrid Systems II*. Lecture Notes in Computer Science 999. Eds. P. Antsaklis, et. al. Springer-Verlag, Germany. 1995. pp. 264-293.

/Stauner 97/ T. Stauner, O. Müller, and M. Fuchs. "Using HYTECH to Verify an Automative Control System". *Hybrid and Real-Time Systems*. Ed. O. Maler. LNCS 1201. Springer-Verlag. Berlin, Germany. 1997. pp. 139-153.

/Turk 97/ A. L. Turk, S. T. Probst, and G. J. Powers. "Verification of Real Time Chemical Processing Systems". *Proceedings of the International Workshop on Hybrid and Real-Time Systems*. Lecture Notes in Computer Science 1201. Ed. O. Maler. Grenoble, France. March 1997. pp. 257-272.

Evaluating the Contribution of DesktopVR for Safety-Critical Applications

Chris Johnson

Department of Computing Science, University of Glasgow, Glasgow, Scotland, G12 8QQ.
Email: johnson@dcs.gla.ac.uk, http://www.dcs.gla.ac.uk/~johnson

Abstract. Desktop virtual reality (desktopVR) provides a range of benefits for training and visualisation tasks in safety-critical environments. Users can exploit conventional keyboards and mice to manipulate photo-realistic images of real-world objects in three dimensions using QuicktimeVR. Other approaches, such as the Virtual Reality Mark-up Language (VRML), enable users to navigate through three dimension models of virtual environments. Designers can exploit these techniques in training tools. They provide users with an impression of environments that are either too dangerous or too expensive to allow direct interaction during familiarisation exercises. DesktopVR also supports the visualisation of safety-critical information. For example, it can be used to provide engineers with an overview of the increasingly large and complex data sets that are being gathered about previous accidents and incidents. However, it is also important to balance the appeal of these techniques against a longer-term requirement that they actually support the tasks for which they are being developed. This paper, therefore, describes the problems that arose when two design teams attempted to validate the claimed benefits of desktopVR as a training tool for a regional fire brigade and as a visualisation tool for accident statistics.

1. Introduction

DesktopVR techniques are being introduced into an increasing range of safety-related applications [1]. However, it is difficult to determine whether these presentation techniques actually support users' needs [2]. The following sections illustrate this argument by focussing on the problems that arose during the evaluation of desktopVR in two safety-critical applications. The first focuses on the use of QuicktimeVR within a training package for a regional fire brigade. The second case study concentrates on the use of VRML to support the visualisation of events leading to major accidents. These are appropriate examples for this paper because they illustrate two radically different applications of desktopVR to support safety. In the former case, three-dimensional presentation techniques are being used to provide fire fighters with practical skills in the operation of specialist rescue equipment. In the later case, desktopVR techniques provide a more abstract overview of systems failure and human error during major accidents. In spite of such differences, it is possible to identify a number of common problems that arose during the evaluation and testing of these interfaces: it is hard to identify benchmarks that can be used to assess the

M. Felici, K. Kanoun, A. Pasquini (Eds.): SAFECOMP'99, LNCS 1698, pp. 67–78, 1999
© Springer-Verlag Berlin Heidelberg 1999

usability of desktopVR in safety-critical systems; it can be difficult to identify the specific user groups and tasks that are to be supported by desktopVR in safety-critical systems; it is difficult to measure the contribution of desktopVR because it, typically, only forms part of a larger interface design within a complex safety-critical system. These issues are not unique to desktopVR interfaces. Summative evaluation and benchmarking complicate the design of many other interactive systems. However, the consequences of failing to support user tasks make these problems particularly severe for safety-critical interface design. The risks of failure are also compounded by the lack of design guidance that developers can call upon during the application of desktop virtual reality.

2. The Fire Brigade Case Study

The training of Fire Officers is intended to provide both practical and theoretical skills. For example, they must learn how to operate breathing apparatus during fires. They are also expected to have specialised technical knowledge. Officers must know how to apply the latest foam technology to combat a range of different fires. Computer Aided Learning (CAL) tools are perceived by many in the Fire Brigade as a cost-effective means of delivering technical knowledge and practical skills. They are particularly appropriate for an organisation whose members are scattered amongst many different stations.

Fire fighters are often characterised by activist learning styles. It has been argued that they learn more effectively through direct experience than through the mediation of books or lectures [3]. DesktopVR techniques, therefore, provide important benefits for the development of CAL in the fire brigade. Fire fighters can learn by interacting with objects in virtual environments rather than by passively listening to conventional lectures. Figure 1 shows how desktopVR techniques were applied to a Heavy Rescue Vehicle (HRV) training package. These vehicles contain specialist lifting and cutting equipment that may be necessary to extricate people from major road traffic accidents. The photo-realistic facilities of QuicktimeVR provide a three-dimensional representation of the storage area inside the HRV. Individual items of equipment can be found by exploring the desktopVR view, shown in the middle panel of Figure 1, or by selecting an item from the list on the right.

The HRV package also provided detailed information about the equipment on the vehicle. Hypertext was used to provide electronic access to existing technical notes. Video clips were used to show the equipment "in action". Figure 2 shows how QuicktimeVR also enabled fire fighters to manipulate individual items of equipment. An important point about these models is that they provide three-dimensional views of items of equipment that are too heavy or cumbersome for an individual to lift. They are also available at times when fire officers cannot have direct access to the HRV itself.   In our case study, the HRV had to be available to respond to emergencies for almost 24 hours each day.   This implied that individual fire officers had almost no time to familiarise themselves with its equipment before they were actually involved in an incident.

Fig. 1. The Heavy Rescue Vehicle Training Package

Fig. 2. Object Rotation of Lucas Cutters on the Heavy Rescue Vehicle

3. The Accident Reporting Case Study

The previous section described how desktopVR provides fire fighters with an initial introduction to the equipment stored on an HRV. In contrast, the second case study focuses on the application of desktopVR to support the visualisation of more abstract safety-critical information. Most accident investigation agencies now place their reports on the World Wide Web. This is a relatively cheap means of disseminating information to companies and regulators [4]. However, we recently conducted an international survey to assess the effectiveness of these web sites. The questionnaire can be accessed on: http://www.dcs.gla.ac.uk/~snowdonp/quest.html

The results were disappointing [5]. Most readers found that web-based accident reports were poorly structured. Many found them harder to read than previous paper versions. Such reactions arise because most investigation authorities simply convert paper-based reports into html or pdf format. Few agencies exploit the novel presentation techniques that are supported by today's communications networks. In contrast, Figure 3 shows how an imagemap can be integrated into the Sheen report on the sinking of the Herald of Free Enterprise. Users select the relevant sections of the image to view all sections of the report that relate to the car deck, the bridge and so on. It is important to stress that these techniques are not intended to replace prose descriptions of major accidents. They do, however, provide relatively low cost means of augmenting the information in a manner that actually supports the readers' comprehension of the events leading to human 'error' and systems 'failure'. Figure 4 illustrates how desktopVR techniques can be used to extend such visualisations into three dimensions. These images show the layout of a cockpit using QuicktimeVR. Hypertext links again provide means of connecting objects in these environments with more detailed textual descriptions. This helps readers to gain a much more direct impression of the physical context in which particular events occur. Current work with the UK Health and Safety Laboratory is extending this approach from accident reports to more general litigation. Juries can be shown three-dimensional models of an accident scene to help them follow the legal arguments that are presented during court cases.

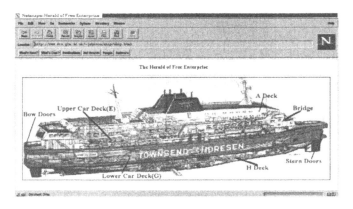

Fig. 3. Integrating Imagemaps into Accident Reports

The approach, illustrated in Figure 4, helps users to view location dependent information. It is less good as a means of viewing the course of human error and systems failure over time. Figure 5 illustrates a three-dimensional timeline that avoids this limitation. It contains markers that indicate the actions and events that occurred at particular moments during an accident. The user can walk along the line in three dimensions to view events from the start of the accident looking forward into the future. They can also look at the events from any other perspective to gain a better view of the things that happened immediately before and after that moment in time. Flags are used to represent the events leading to the accident. If a flag is planted into the line then an exact timing is available. A flag that has not been planted indicates that the exact time is not known.

Fig. 4. QuicktimeVR model for Aircraft Evacuation/Cockpit Familiarisation/Seat Booking

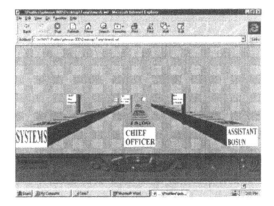

Fig. 5. Using VRML to Visualise Events in Major Accidents

4. The Problems of Validating DesktopVR

The previous section briefly how desktopVR can be used to support two very different safety-critical applications. This section goes on to describe the problems that arose when we tried to assess the usability and the utility of these systems.

4.1 Problem 1: Establishing Benchmark Criteria for DesktopVR

The first problem in evaluating any system is to determine the criteria that can be used to assess "usability" [6]. This immediately raised problems for the first case study because we were developing an entirely new system. At the start of the project, the fire fighters did not have access to any CAL applications. None of them had used or even heard about desktopVR. This created considerable problems because we had no means of establishing the "benchmark" criteria against which to evaluate the new interfaces. The best that we could do was to issue a questionnaire to assess the fire fighters' attitudes about existing training techniques. Figures 6 and 7 present the results for 27 fire fighters from two different stations within the same region. These results guided the development of our desktopVR system. In particular, we strove hard to avoid the negative reaction towards passive lectures, shown in figure 7.

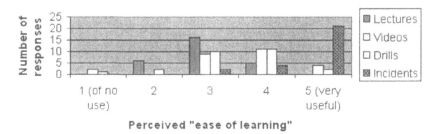

Fig. 6. Perceived "Ease of Learning" in the Fire Brigade Case Study

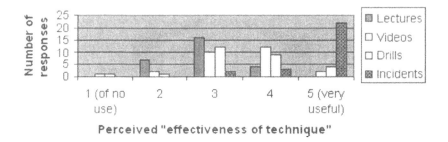

Fig. 7. Perceived "Effectiveness of Learning" in the Fire Brigade Case Study

Our problems began when we attempted to show that the new desktopVR system was better than the previous approaches. We were particularly concerned to show an improvement over conventional lectures and videos; the CAL system was not intended to reduce the amount of drill work or real incidents that the fire fighters were exposed to. Initially, we decided that we would re-issue the questionnaire. This would enable us to assess the fire fighter's attitudes towards lectures, videos, drills, incidents AND the new CAL tools. However, this raised a number of objections. The fact that this project had support from the highest levels of the fire brigade made it difficult for us to judge whether we were receiving unbiased responses to questions about the utility of desktopVR within a training tool. Similarly, it was less important for the fire brigade to show that our novel presentation techniques were effective than it was to ensure that the overall application satisfied their training objectives. The scores from a comprehension test were less important than the fire fighters' performance during real incidents. This created a number of practical problems. It can be extremely difficult to identify objective criteria for real-world performance in safety-critical tasks.   For instance, the time that it takes to extract a casualty is affected by many different contextual factors ranging from the make and condition of their vehicle through to the medical condition of that casualty.   Of course, more qualitative criteria can be applied but this raises the problem of validating and recording those assessments in a manner that supports effective, long-term comparisons between subjects.

The average length of service amongst the users of our system was fifteen years. Any subjective assessment after a few months access to the new technology would provide a poor impression of the long-term effectiveness of desktopVR. Such evaluation exercises can be complicated by the fire fighters exposure to real-world incidents. During the evaluation of our system, one group was asked to use some of the theoretical material during a real incident.   In balanced experimental techniques, half of this group should have been exposed to the CAL tool and half should have been exposed to conventional lectures.   This would then have enabled us to make valid comparisons between these two different training techniques.   It was impossible to achieve such a balance.   In a longitudinal study, these problems raise further ethical problems because they imply that some fire fighters should be deprived of a training resource over a prolonged period to measure the effect of the absense of that resource on their performance.

4.2 Problem 2: How to Identify Users and their Tasks?

The second case study focuses on the application of desktop virtual reality to support the presentation of accident reports over the World Wide Web. VRML timelines enable users to 'walk' into a model of systems failures and operator errors immediate before and after a particular point in an accident.   However, it remains an open question as to whether this novel interaction technique actually supports the tasks that people want to perform when they read an accident report. We, therefore, conducted an empirical evaluation in order to determine whether or not the techniques in Figures 3 and 4 were actually an improvement over paper based presentation techniques.   A randomised procedure was used in which investigators were provided with one of three possible versions of an accident report: a paper-based document; an image map interface based on figure 3 and a more abstract VRML interface based on figure 4. They were then asked to perform five tasks using the version of the report that they had been allocated.   These tasks were as follows:

1. When did the Chief Officer leave the Mess Room to return to the Bridge.

2. What important events happened at 18:28?

3. Write down the key events that happened on the bridge at approximately 18:23?

4. Write down the time that the Assistant Bosun returned to his cabin.

5. The Chief Officer gave conflicting evidence as to the time at which he left G deck to go to the Mess Room, write down the page reference where these conflicting statements are highlighted.

The first and fourth tasks tested the reader's ability to find the timing of critical events. The second task tested the reader's ability to locate information about a particular time in an incident.   Task three linked both location and timing information.   The final task tested higher level reasoning using the accident report. The results of an initial trial with five users performing these tasks are presented in the following figure.

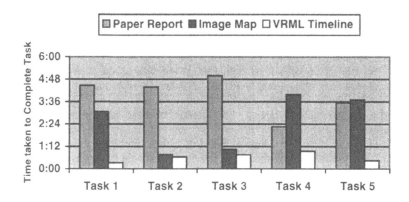

Fig. 8. Task Performance for the use of DesktopVR in Accident Reports

Figure 8 illustrates the strengths and weaknesses of empirical tests for the use of desktopVR in safety-critical applications.   Such studies provide useful comparisons between alternative presentation techniques for well-specified tasks.   However, the reliability of those results depends entirely upon the tasks being performed.   Such evidence can be entirely misleading if the tasks do not provide valid examples of the sorts of activities that the readers of an accident report might want to perform with a new system.   Of course, this is a general problem for the application of empirical techniques in user interface design.   However, there are particular differences that make these limitations more acute in the context of desktopVR for safety-critical systems:

1. It is more difficult to identify representative users and tasks for desktopVR applications than it is for other forms of interactive system. For instance, the interfaces illustrated in Figures 3 and 4 were specifically intended to improve the presentation of accident reports.   In order to validate these designs through tests, such as those used in Figure 8, we first had to identify the potential readers of an accident report.   This proved to be a non-trivial exercise.   An initial survey identified the potential audience as including: regulators (both within an industry and from other industries); lawyers; academics in a wide range of disciplines; systems engineers; human factors engineers; project managers, journalists, politicians, trades union officials etc.   Each of these user groups had a different set of tasks and priorities that they associated with the accident report.   This diversity led us to question the validity of the tasks that were used in our initial evaluation.

2. The consequences of using atypical tasks to establish the suitability of a human computer interface will be much greater in safety-critical systems than in other applications. One of the issues that emerged during our tests on the visualisation of accident and incident reports was that novel presentation techniques might actually bias the reader's view towards particular conclusions. This is dangerous because it might lead them to ignore potential causes of human 'error' or systems 'failure'. In particular, the visual appeal of accident simulations can persuade people to believe one particular version of events. This hypothesis is the focus for on-going research [5]. However, it underlines the point that changes to the presentation of safety-critical design information may have unexpected and potentially dangerous consequences.

Our experience has revealed that the problems of user and task diversity affect many other safety-critical applications of desktopVR. For instance, we were subsequently involved in the development of a QuicktimeVR model of a Boeing aircraft, shown in Figures 5. The intention was to use this model to show evacuation routes following a major accident. However, the product was also used to train passengers and fire-crews in evacuation procedures. It was then used by airlines to sell particular seats within the body of the aircraft. Sections of the model were also used to introduce psychologists and ergonomists to different cockpit configurations etc. This diversity of users and tasks affects much of the software industry. However, our experience is that it particularly affects desktopVR applications. The exploratory nature of these environments, combined with their superficial appeal, can create a large number of potential uses for this technology. Each of these users has particular informational needs and requirements. This creates further problems for the development and evaluation of safety-critical systems. The way in which an initial model can be marketed to diverse groups makes it difficult, if not impossible, for the designers and engineers who developed it to be certain that it actually supports the activities for which it is eventually being sold.

4.3 Problem 3: Assessing the Contribution of DesktopVR

Even if designers can identify particular user groups with particular tasks, it can be difficult to validate the contribution that desktopVR systems make to safety-critical interaction. For example, there is a danger that by focusing on particular training tasks, designers may overlook the broader context of VRML and QuicktimeVR applications. This point can be illustrated by Laurillard's [7] conversational model illustrated in Figure 9. The right-hand components of the diagram represent the iterative process by which users modify their view of the concepts that are being taught. They adapt their descriptions (activities 4 and 9) and modify their actions (activities 8 and 10) as they learn from their tutor's feedback. The left-hand components of Laurillard's model describe the iterative process that informs the teacher's interaction with their class. Tutors modify the tasks that they set in response to a group's initial attempts to fulfil those tasks (activities 11 and 12). This is important within the context of safety-critical training because tutors must assess whether their class actually understands the critical points that are being communicated. If they do not then the tutor will have to modify their approach if safety is to be preserved.

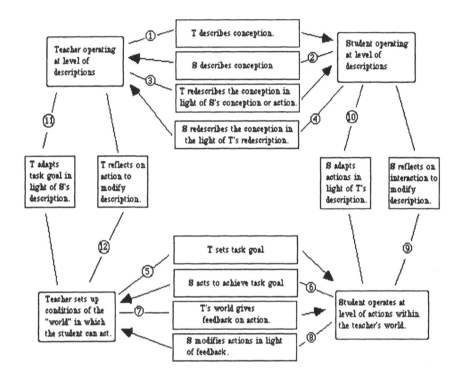

Fig. 9. Laurillard's Conversational Model for Effective Education.

Laurillard's model is important because it shows how the success or failure of desktopVR systems in safety-critical environments can depends upon a much wider range of training activities. In other words, VRML and QuicktimeVR techniques can only play a small role within the wider training activities of most complex organisations. In retrospect, the HRV tool failed to address many of the fundamental concerns raised by Laurillard's model. It supported the presentation of material, embodied in stage 1 of the model. It did not support stages 4-8. These activities focus on the use of tasks and exercises to provide students with feedback about their understanding of key concepts. These stages also provide the tutor with feedback about the need to improve their delivery techniques. Figure 10 presents a self-assessment tool that was, therefore, developed to accompany the HRV package. This screen implements a photographic multiple-choice question. Fire fighters are provided with feedback after each selection and are encouraged to provide further input if they make an incorrect selection.

Similar problems affect the documentation of accident reports. A reader's understanding of an accident report is only partially determined by their access to the information contained in desktopVR interfaces, such as those shown in Figures 4 and 5. Their analysis can be biased by previous experiences of human error and systems failure. Their interpretation can also be influenced by organisational pressures to

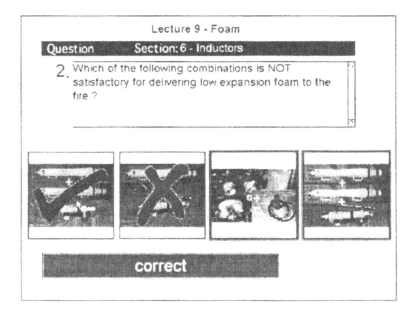

Fig. 10. A Photographic Multiple Choice Question

accept a particular version of events. Such biases cannot easily be rectified. They are compounded by the lack of evaluation both for desktopVR techniques and for conventional, paper-based accident reports. Many regulatory authorities neglect stages two and five of Laurillard's model; they make no attempt to assess the readers' interpretation of the reports that they publish. Until this omission is addressed, there seems little prospect that novel presentation techniques will address the shortcomings of many accident reports.

5. Conclusions

At present, most desktopVR systems are being developed to support what can be called "secondary" safety tasks. They do not support direct interaction with safety-critical processes but they are being used to train operators about safety-critical tasks. They are also being used to support the visualisation of safety-critical information. This paper has described a number of practical problems that have arisen during initial attempts to validate this new generation of interactive systems:

- it is hard to identify benchmarks that can be used to assess the usability of desktopVR in safety-critical systems;

- it can be difficult to identify the specific user groups and tasks that are to be supported by desktopVR in safety-critical systems;

- it can be difficult to measure the contribution of desktopVR because it, typically, only forms part of a larger interface design within a complex safety-critical system;

The paper has, therefore, moved from the specific problems of assessing particular desktopVR interfaces to the general issues of evaluating desktopVR within complex organisations. It is discouraging that we are faced by so many problems and so few solutions.

Acknowledgements

Thanks are due to the members of Glasgow Interactive Systems Group (GIST). In particular, Brian Mathers, Anthony McGill, Pete Snowdon, Alan Thompson all helped with the design, implementation and testing of the systems described in this paper. This work is supported by EPSRC grants GR/L27800 and GR/K55042.

References

[1] C.W. Johnson, *The Problems of Validating DesktopVR*. To appear in People and Computers XIII: Proceedings of HCI'98, Springer Verlag, Berlin, 1998.

[2] K. Kaur, A. Sutcliffe and N. Maiden *Improving Interaction with Virtual Environments*. In IEE Colloquium Digest 98/437, 1998.

[3] C.W. Johnson, *Why 'Traditional' HCI Design and Evaluation Techniques Fail With DesktopVR*. In IEE Colloquium Digest 98/437, 1998.

[4] C.W. Johnson, *Ten Golden Rules for Video over the Web*. In J. Ratner, E. Grosse and C. Forsythe (eds.) Human Factors for World Wide Web Development. 207-224. Lawrence Erlbaum, New York, United States of America, 1997.

[5] P. Snowdon and C.W. Johnson, Results of an International Survey into the Usability of Accident Reports. To appear in IEE Conference on People in Control, 1999.

[6] R.S. Kalawsky, *New methods and techniques for evaluating user performance in advanced 3D virtual interfaces*. In IEE Colloquium Digest 98/437, 1998.

[7] D. Laurillard, *Rethinking University Education: A Framework for the Effect ive Use of Educational Technology*, Routledge, London, 1993.

Human Performance Reliability in the Design-for-Usability Life Cycle for Safety Human-Computer Interfaces

Lucia Vilela Leite Filgueiras

Escola Politecnica da Universidade de Sao Paulo,
C.P. 61548, 05424-970, Sao Paulo, SP, Brazil
lfilguei@usp.br

Abstract. This paper proposes a method for integrating Human Performance Reliability Analysis techniques and the design-for-usability life cycle, so that human performance reliability can be assimilated in the design of Human-Computer Interface component of safety interactive systems. The benefits of this approach are an interface designed to reduce human errors in addition to a set of documents that allows application of human reliability analysis in licensing.

1 Introduction

Significant progress in development of human-computer interaction techniques has made no longer true the assertion that human factors are overlooked in system design. In fact, software industry has been allocating a considerable share of its efforts in research and development of usable, attractive user interfaces, as usability is acknowledged as a chief factor for system acceptance.

This effort has resulted in many guidelines and methods for human-computer interface (HCI) development. One of the most widely used methods now is Usability Engineering, as proposed in Nielsen [1], Nielsen and Mack [2] and Hix and Hartson [3] works. This method is based on acknowledgement that early consideration of user needs contributes both for system suitability and for reducing development costs, since it decreases significantly the number of requirement changes in lifetime.

One could expect that Usability Engineering should be successfully applied to the development of safety system HCIs, in order to reduce human error probability. Human operators have avoided a very larger number of incidents and mitigated consequences of many others, and this is due to human ability to solve new problems. Now, automatic systems succeed in behaving as programmed due to high investments on system reliability and fault-tolerance. Nevertheless, human errors keep on happening, this time associated to the bad coupling between human information needs and system capacity to provide them, as well as mismatch between human commands and system status [4]. When interacting with computers, human-induced faults can be consequences of poor HCI design. If human error was not consistently avoided during HCI design, overall system reliability and fault tolerance may have been overestimated.

M. Felici, K. Kanoun, A. Pasquini (Eds.): SAFECOMP'99, LNCS 1698, pp. 79-88, 1999
© Springer-Verlag Berlin Heidelberg 1999

Human Reliability Analysis (HRA) techniques have been developed in order to predict human error probability in a given mission. HRA tools have been used in post-accident evaluation and in Probability Risk Assessments in safety systems, to estimate quantitatively how well the human performs his mission in given condition. This means that HRA tools assume an existing system, and have been useful in *a posteriori* basis.

These considerations conduct to the need of developing HCI that supports human reliable performance. The proposed answer to this need is a design method that considers human reliable performance besides other engineering variables during design life cycle, so that resulting HCI can improve human performance and tolerate human errors. Consequently, design process also results in documentation that allows formal application of HRA tools for licensing purposes.

In order to present this method, Section 2 presents some comments on human error with computer interfaces; Section 3 defines the HCI for reliable human performance. Section 4 describes the proposed method.

2   Human Error with Computer Interfaces

One of the main reasons to employ computers in safety systems is the need to deal with complexity. Human interaction with these interfaces is distinct from other machine interaction mainly in the intellectual level of performed tasks. HCI can implement perceptual-motor activities, but is mostly used as decision aid. In addition, human computer interaction can manipulate abstract concepts. Another important aspect is that humans are not all time the agents - the computer can also be an agent and sometimes the human will only supervise the automatic actions.

Knowledge built into software - that Hollnagel [5] calls "artificial cognition" - plays the role of an agent that behaves in a way unknown to the operator. In this case, human errors will be related to wrong predictions about automatic behaviour and competition of conflicting goals.

Another dimension of complexity is navigation: operators have to move through information space to find out resources required to complete their task. Due to the increasing availability of data, information retrieval can be very time-consuming, besides the cognitive load to process all data found.

A third kind of error is associated to automation of human tasks, which substitutes manual, continuous work for an intellectual, intermittent work. This last error manifests in the following ways:
– Error in the perception of important events, that should trigger human actions. In general, lack of attention is due to long supervisory periods, without any physical activity.
– Loss of ability to perform, due to insufficient practice.

In addition to these, human erroneous performance can assume an incredible number of other forms that may lead to undesired consequences. Therefore, human error should be kept in focus during HCI design. Next section states desired characteristics for a HCI to support reliable human performance.

3 HCI for Reliable Human Performance

No method is useful if its goals are not known precisely. In order to design for reliable human performance, it is important to establish desired characteristics of the HCI. Notice that designing human-computer interfaces comprises not only the design of computer displays and interaction resources, but also the design of human tasks themselves.

HCI for reliable human performance must comply with the following requirements:

1. HCI must feed human mental model with adequate data, to guarantee that human is kept aware of process status. It is important also to consider that the interface should present not only process data, but also clues on automatic behaviour, to avoid mismatch between human actions and automatic responses.
2. Human tasks should be triggered whenever necessary by clear data presentation or by attention-calling devices. The interface should provide all data required to accomplishment of these tasks.
3. Interface should possess adequate action resources, so that the human can control the process and intervene in automatic behaviour, through manipulation of interface set of objects.
4. Interface should require the proper amount of human attention, so that human workload is placed out of the limits of boredom and extenuation.
5. Interface should be capable of indicating clearly an erroneous human action, and even reject it.

Next sections will propose a design method in order to achieve stated requirements.

4 Designing HCI for Reliable Human Performance

The proposed method, called APIS ("Analise e Projeto de Interfaces de Seguranca", Portuguese for Analysis and Design of Safety-purpose Interfaces) is based on the following two premises:

– Reliable human performance depends on proper transportation of operational goals to the interface functional specification process. As Norman [6] states: "The designer expects the user's mental model to be identical to the design model. But the designer doesn't talk directly with the user - all communications take place through the system image. If the system image does not make the design model clear and consistent then the user will end up with the wrong mental model."
– Human performance reliability is the adopted metric to evaluate transportation efficiency and should be iteratively collected, during the interface development cycle.

APIS is not an innovative method, but is rather a new reading of the design-for-usability life cycle using HRA techniques in some definite steps. APIS objectives are the design of the HCI for reliable human performance as described in Section 3, along with producing documentation intended to support formal HRA techniques for licensing purposes.

APIS steps are depicted in Fig. 1.

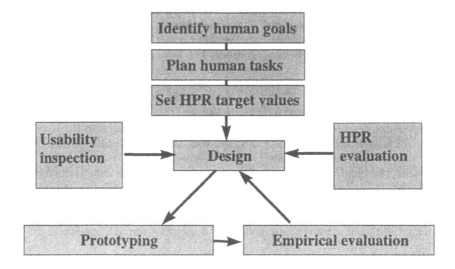

Fig. 1. APIS development cycle for human reliable performance

4.1 Design-for-Usability Life Cycle

Usability life cycle, as described in mentioned works, is currently the most widely used method to incorporate user needs to the HCI. Usability is a quality parameter and is decomposed into other attributes like ease of learning the interface concepts and commands, user performance, time retention or recall ability, error rate and user subjective satisfaction.

These attributes are set in the requirements analysis phase and evaluated iteratively during the life cycle, until established values are met. There are at least three evaluation types: analytical evaluation uses human performance models like GOMS [7]; usability inspection examines HCI usability by a human-interaction expert. Finally, empirical evaluation observes real users over prototypes.

The iterative development cycle must be controlled by cost-benefit analysis over the usability attributes, to define which changes to the human-computer interface will effectively contribute to user performance improvement.

However, usability is not reliability, although a usable system will induce a more reliable human performance. Systems that require human reliable performance should care of human error, establishing desired values for human performance reliability, based on mission criticality, and proceed design to meet this parameter.

4.2 Human Reliability Analysis Techniques

HRA techniques intend to predict human performance in a given mission. Today, there are several techniques with different requirements and different applications.

First generation techniques can produce human performance reliability as a function of human task and context variables. THERP, the most widely used technique, is based on task decomposition and probability compounding techniques. Due to scarcity of data to feed in the models, some techniques use expert judgement as an aid to calculate probabilities.

Although the application of different prediction methods may produce different results for one given system, they are still valuable tools to be used in the design of human interfaces, because second-generation methods are still under research.

It is beyond the scope of this paper to describe HRA techniques in detail. Many publications can direct the reader to these techniques [8], [9], [10]. However, application of most of these techniques requires a common method, as presented below.

First step is to determine situations in which human error can lead to undesired system status. This definition may come from traditional safety assessment methods, such as HAZOP (Hazard and Operability Study), and FMEA (Failure Mode and Effect Analysis), as well as from observation of real situations.

Second step is task analysis, when human tasks are detailed. Task analysis inspects not only human activities but also the organisational, physical and psychological environment in which activities are performed.

Human error analysis comes in sequence. Possible error situations are identified, as well as their causes, consequences and recovery possibilities.

Quantification can be performed as the next activity. Each HRA technique use different ways to estimate successful task performance, usually based on (scarce) historical data from similar tasks.

Last step is error reduction, in which some changes are proposed to the system, in order to avoid most critical errors.

Simple examination of the activities sequence makes evident that HRA requires a considerable effort. Most times, comprehensive studies have been justifiable only in high-risk systems. If system operation were critical enough to require HRA to be performed, a considerable amount of effort would be saved if system design process provided documentation on human task specifications and supporting HCI resources.

4.3 APIS Phases

This section details APIS phases, as shown in Fig. 1.

4.3.1 Identify Human Goals

APIS starts when system functions are attributed to humans and machinery. Qualitative and quantitative allocation techniques are generally used to support this activity, based on inherent characteristics of each component. Human goals constitute the missions where human performance reliability may be important. Criticality of each mission should be established in this step.

4.3.2 Plan Human Tasks

Task planning is an iterative refinement process that departs from human goals in each operational scenario and progresses on characterising human action and information requirements.

Task planning is a critical step in HCI development, because designers, who are responsible for correspondence between the operator's and system models, are seldom application specialists. User involvement in task planning process may overcome this problem.

For each task, designers must address the following aspects, in order to characterise completely each human task for HRA purposes:

- Identify task trigger events, which are system or environmental clues that indicate the opportunity of task accomplishment.
- Recognise information requirements and action resources for task completion, both from process data and from automatic functions.
- Determine maximum time to initiate task after trigger event, and required time to complete the task.
- Identify environmental factors that may affect human performance.
- Determine task parallelism, that is, which tasks can be executed concurrently by the same human.
- Establish conditions for task interruption or transitory suspension.

Task planning must address normal operation tasks, frequent or rare system failure recovery procedures and postulated accidents.

Application of task planning may have two different approaches: if the system being designed is a completely new one, the procedure is top-down. The designer departs from the required system goals and required system performance to detail human tasks.

In contrast, when the design intends to replace an existing system, then task analysis must go bottom-up. It may be necessary to extract goals from existing tasks. When the system is old, this may represent an additional burden on designers, because new generation workers may know what to do, but ignore the original reasons behind the tasks. In this case, new task design to enhance human performance will be possible only after actual goals have been identified.

For each one, a general event tree as the one shown in Fig. 2, adapted from Moieni, Spurgin and Singh [11], should be used to scrutinise possible human errors and their consequences. The designer should provide answers to the following questions:

- Could the human miss the trigger event (perception error)?
- Could the human identify a different task for the same environment clues (goal selection error)?
- Could the task be accomplished too early or too late (timely response error)?
- Could the human miss the moment to stop task execution (final condition detection error)?

In this phase of HCI design, system knowledge is insufficient for questions on execution errors. They will be explored later in design phase.

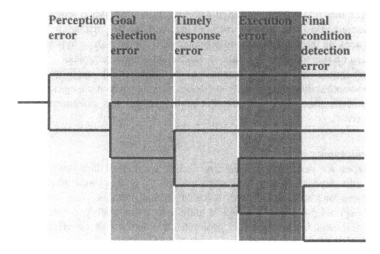

Fig. 2. General event tree for human operation

All errors considered relevant should then be planned for recovery. Human error recovery should address the following aspects:
− Information required in HCI to make human error evident.
− HCI resources to recover human error.
− Time frame in which recovery procedures are effective.

Documentation on this task planning process should provide applicable data to task analysis step in HRA procedures.

4.3.3 Set HPR Target Values
HPR target values should be established if demanded by each human mission criticality, based on requested system reliability. Values for other usability parameters can also be stated in this phase. These target values will be pursued during design phase.

4.3.4 Design
Information requirements obtained in task planning process will be part of requirement specification for HCI design. Vicente and Rasmussen ecological design concept suggests processing and organising information to fit directly into human cognitive level required by task planning. Filgueiras and Melnikoff [12] describe a method for the conversion of task planning results into an object-oriented model for human-computer interface design.

After HCI have been defined, human tasks can origin detailed operating procedures. Again, designers should investigate possible human error modes that may lead to the operation scenario not to complete successfully.

In the keystroke level of interaction, designer should consider the occurrence of slips and lapses. Design should avoid these errors by, for instance, introducing feedback or creating recovery functions that make the error harmless.

Mistakes that may happen in diagnostic and decision-making activities must also be considered. Designer should include mechanisms for decision aid whenever consequences of these mistakes compromise HPR stated value: hypotheses testing, information on rule validity and hints for rule selection are examples.

Design should be a cycle controlled by cost-benefit analysis over human performance reliability and usability attributes, defining which changes to the human-computer interface would effectively contribute to the enhancement of user performance.

4.3.5 Prototyping

Prototypes are necessary in usability design cycle, and they range from simple drafts of displays on paper or transparencies, to demos implemented in visual programming languages or even sophisticated simulation tools.

Designers should not expect to observe human errors in prototype evaluation. As an illustration, task time measured in prototype evaluation can be affected by stress distortion of time perception in actual operation. However, prototype evaluation can result in important clues about human performance, as Section 4.3.8 will show.

4.3.6 Usability Inspection

Inspection should be accomplished by an experienced specialist, checking HCI design rules, ergonomic recommendations and applicable standards.

In addition, usability inspection should guarantee that HCI implementation meets information requirements for each task planned, and for each defined human error recovery procedure.

4.3.7 HPR Evaluation

For those critical tasks, for which HPR values were postulated, HRA techniques should be used to calculate HPR. In these cases, HPR evaluation considers that human errors can happen in three distinct phases of task performance. In the first phase, from trigger event detection to task selection, human diagnosis and decision-making are chiefly perceptive and cognitive activities. Second phase corresponds to task execution, and this is dominantly a motor and automatic activity. Third phase, corresponding to final condition detection, is again a cognitive activity. So HPR can be calculated from two components:

- Reliability of human cognition, related to perception, diagnosis and decision making activities to start and end task execution.
- Reliability of human action, dependant on a given implementation of the HCI for supporting task execution.

In experiments with this method, expert judgement and THERP were used to calculate HPR. However, it is important to note that there may be no sufficiently precise data to perform a human reliability calculation as an absolute number.

In the other hand, those tasks that did not require a value for HPR can also be evaluated in a very simplified yet efficient manner. In these cases, an absolute value for HPR is less important than directing engineering resources to those design solutions that can minimise human error. In order to select between design alternatives, experts could judge task plans and HCI design to rate probability of each error mode and recovery procedures. Consequences severity should also be rated as a relative number, for instance, between 1 and 10.

A very simplified formula could be used to derive due designer attention:

$$\text{Attention} = P \text{ (unrecovered human error)} * \text{consequence severity} . \qquad (1)$$

Comparing resulting attention values can direct designers efforts to those enhancements that will favour reliable human performance. This approach is simple enough to allow for use as a parameter for controlling the design cycle. Clearly, attention results are useless for HRA purposes.

4.3.8 Empirical Evaluation

Empirical evaluation employs real users in scenario rehearsing. Tasks planned in previous APIS phases should be tested by a system operator using a prototype version. Human error conditions and their recovery should also be simulated. During rehearsal, operator must talk through his or her thoughts; all doubts and reactions should be recorded for later evaluation.

Rehearsals should first test single task execution, but as prototype grows, tests that are more comprehensive should evaluate decision aspects of the interface.

The most realistic prototype is still different from a full-scale simulator or real operation, and it is not expected that human errors committed during prototype evaluation be of the same nature as in true operation. However, usability attribute evaluation tests have a different dimension in a safety-purpose HCI.

Ease of learning can be measured from a learning curve that plots error rate versus time of user exposition to the interface. Ease of learning is associated to the derivative of this curve; that is, the HCI is easier to learn as steeper the curve drops to zero. In a safety-purpose system, operators will surely require intensive training before they can operate the process efficiently. Therefore, high exposure to system compensates any learning curve. However, tests with an operator who has not been exposed to the system can reveal adherence of HCI to user's conceptual model. Ease of learning, then, can be an indirect measure of interface consistency.

Errors show deviations from designed behaviour. It is important to verify **causes** of these errors, to identify HCI unsuitability to the operator conceptual model or perceptual/motor conditions. Errors during in the beginning of exposition to the system are useful to reveal operators conceptual model, for they will try to find in the HCI the objects needed to complete the task. On the other hand, errors after some acquaintance time indicate unsuitability of interaction dialogue or of recovery procedures. Hesitations are also important clues, for they reveal an error that could have happened.

Performance is another important usability attribute that can be measured in empirical tests. It is defined as the time the evaluator uses to carry out a specified task with the HCI, after some training. Performance tests evaluate minimum time, free from context influence. This time can be compared to the time requested in task planning phase. Performance empirical evaluation can also identify time components for a task:

− Time to prepare for action, that implies in thinking and alternative selection;
− Time to navigate in the interface, searching for required information;
− Time to activate interface controls

- Time to execute support activities, e.g., manipulating documents
- Time to communicate with other crew members

Time composition analysis may result in important results to improve the interface.

5 Conclusion

Previous sections of this paper presented a method to use human performance reliability as a metric for HCI development. Human performance reliability with computer interfaces is complexity dependent. Complexity can be handled by interface design, providing adequate tools for information handling and error avoidance. Design-for-usability methods can be useful to enhance human performance and avoid errors. Human reliability evaluation can be added to usability in order to design for human reliable performance.

Application of the proposed method can result in some sub-products: task planning can be useful to establish training scenarios; design evaluation can point to special technological solutions to aid human performance.

Further research should be directed to develop design environments that can automate application of this method. Once application is made easier, this method could be applied to non-safety human operated devices, in order to avoid human errors. This consideration is especially important because designers can be legally responsible for injuries or harm caused by customer misuse of such devices.

References

1. Nielsen, J.: Usability Engineering. Academic Press (1993)
2. Nielsen, J., Mack, R.: Usability Inspection Methods. John Wiley and Sons. (1994)
3. Hix, D., Hartson, H. R.: Developing User Interfaces - Ensuring Usability Through Product & Process. Wiley. (1993)
4. Evans, B.: Cockpit automation: The Good, the Bad, and the Ugly. Avionics Magazine. May 1998, pg 34-38.
5. Hollnagel, E.: Human Reliability Analysis - Context and Control. Academic Press. (1993)
6. Norman, D. A.: The design of everyday things. Currency-Doubleday. (1990)
7. Card, S. K., Moran, T. P., Newell, A.: The psychology of human-computer interaction. Lawrence Erlbaum Asssociates. (1983)
8. Dougherty, E. M., Fragola, J. R.: Human reliability analysis - a system engineering approach with nuclear power plant applications. John Wiley& Sons. (1988)
9. LaSala, K. P.: Human Reliability: a Brief Historical Perspective. In: IEEE Transactions on Reliability (1998)
10. Lee, K. W., Tillman, F. A., Higging, J. J.: A Literature Survey of the Human Reliability Component in a Man-Machine System. In: IEEE Transactions on Reliability, Vol. 37, No. 1 (1988)
11. Moieni, P., Spurgin, A. J., Singh, A.: Advances in human reliability analysis methodology. Part I: Frameworks, models and data. In: Reliability Engineering and Systems Safety, vol. 44. (1994)
12. Filgueiras, L. V. L., Melnikoff, S. S. S.: APIIS: a method for analysis and prototyping interaction-intense software, 6th. IFAC/IFIP/IFORS/IEA Symposium on Analysis, Design and Evaluation of Man-Machine Systems. (1995)

The Impact of Different Media on Safety and Usability of Interactive ATC Applications

Fabio Paternò[1], Carmen Santoro[1], and Sophie Tahmassebi[2]

[1] CNUCE-C.N.R., Via S. Maria 36, 56126, Pisa, Italy
{F.Paterno, C.Santoro}@cnuce.cnr.it
[2] Centre d'Etudes de la Navigation Aérienne, Avenue Édouard Belin 7,
31055 Toulouse Cedex, France
tahmasse@cenatoulouse.dgac.fr

Abstract. This paper identifies and discusses a set of criteria relevant to assess the impact of using different media in the design of user interfaces for safety-critical systems. An evaluation of different options concerning the allocation of such media during the design of an application in the Air Traffic Control domain is shown to illustrate and clarify our approach. Particular attention is paid on how different choices in allocating tasks among air traffic controllers affect usability and safety of operators' interactions.

1 Introduction

In spite of increasing development and availability of new communication technologies, little work has been dedicated to analyse more deeply the concepts which drive the choice and use of interaction media in the design of user interfaces for safety-critical systems. To this end we believe that, instead of completely relying on late empirical testing, it can be useful to perform an evaluation of different media and task allocation choices [1] according to appropriate criteria, to discard meaningless possibilities and to focus on problematic parts of the design.

In current applications the co-existence of more than one technology is getting more and more common, so there is a need to deeply understand nature and constraints of each medium and its appropriateness with respect to the user tasks and environments to evaluate which technology provides the best support.

The issue of allocating media is getting particularly demanding in current safety-critical systems where many studies have shown that accidents have been often caused by human error [2]. In such systems two contrasting trends seem to exist at the same time: on the one hand the belief that the more advanced technology used, the better in terms of performance and reliability; on the other hand, the indisputable reluctance and difficulty to introduce a new technology because its impact (especially in terms of safety and usability) is not always known and in the worst case it may threaten human life. An example of the latter issue is given by applications in a highly cooperative system [3] as the Air Traffic Control (ATC) area, where many problems have still to be solved. Number and duration of delays show that ATC systems are not always able to cope with passengers' demand; the growing air traffic increases the possibility of accidents; several incidents occurred because of the undesired effects of

M. Felici, K. Kanoun, A. Pasquini (Eds.): SAFECOMP'99, LNCS 1698, pp. 89-102, 1999
© Springer-Verlag Berlin Heidelberg 1999

operators' interactions or the lack of efficiency in current systems, requiring more sophisticated techniques for its management. Previous attempts have tried to introduce more advanced user interfaces for the controllers [4] or to provide them with an augmented reality environment [5] to make faster and more natural their activity, but unfortunately these approaches are remained at a prototype's stage and have not been followed by real utilisation.

Furthermore, the increases in air traffic have begun to highlight the potential bottleneck of radio channels which can become saturated during high levels of traffic, thus several solutions are going to be envisaged. Datalink (a technology allowing electronic exchanges of data [6]) is a solution that seems to overcome the main limitations of traditional communication systems. However, adding this technology in the system impels to understand its impact on User Interface (UI) design issues.

In the next sections, we introduce our approach giving at first a general overview of ATC system in terms of tasks [7] [8] that controllers have to support, with special care to media and tools provided by both VHF and datalink technologies. Then we select two design options on how to allocate interaction media to different users, defining the criteria we found relevant to estimate advantages and disadvantages of each considered option. Finally an assessment of the two choices is given according to the selected criteria. The discussion is focused on a case study in the ATC domain, however, the method proposed can be applied to other interactive safety critical systems where the interactive part has to be redesigned to support new requirements.

2   The Current ATC System Based on Vocal Communication

In this section we roughly describe the controllers' tasks during the en-route phase in the current French ATC system (other countries may present slight differences).

The civil airspace is divided into various control centres and, within each centre there are basically two controllers: the *executive* controller, who is due to maintain appropriate separation between aircraft in the sector, and to hold communications with pilots; and the *strategic* controller, who is in charge of co-ordinating transfer of aircraft from sector to sector with other strategic colleagues.

In addition, both controllers perform "in background" surveillance tasks. Thus, three kinds of communications can be distinguished (numbers refer to those in Fig. 1):

1. Between strategic and executive controllers of the same sector, (for example vocal and "elbow" communications to attract attention);
2. Between strategic controllers of two neighbouring sectors involved in a flight sector exchange (phone communications);
3. Between the executive controller of each sector and pilots currently in the sector (radio communications);

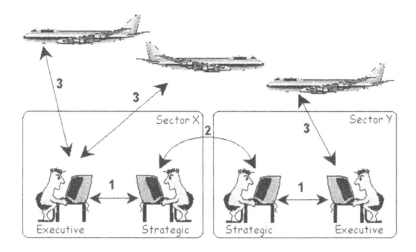

Fig. 1. The communications occurring between en-route controllers

Today, most of air/ground communications are conducted by voice over Very High Frequency (VHF) radio channels. At any time *many* pilots are in competition for speaking with *one* controller as only one speaker (controller or pilot) can broadcast over the radio, so the resulting "sharing" especially penalises pilots who sometimes have to wait because the frequency is kept busy by another communication.

However, the so-called "party line" (the fact that on a given frequency a pilot can listen to all the messages exchanged on that frequency —even the messages not addressed to him) has proved to be useful because pilots are able to check the exchanged information (avoiding possible misunderstandings of vocal communications), and to build their own mental traffic's representation. In addition, the party line contributes to enhance pilots situation awareness, as pilots can obtain advance knowledge of events and situations that can affect their flight (e.g. traffic congestion, delay report, weather conditions). In this way they can perform a better decision-making process, and possibly anticipate future controller's instructions offering to do some actions to speed up the traffic management in the sector.

Thus, the main advantage of the current R/T (Radio/Telephony) is that it allows rapid communications between pilots and controller being voice the most natural medium of human communication. Besides, an R/T message contains not only the message itself, but also some subjective information (stress, emotion, anger, humour, courtesy) which are relevant to pilots and controllers. However, the process of communicating by voice is prone to human error, because its transient nature might easily introduce mis-understandings and confusions. In addition communications exchanged through radio channels are generally concise (following the standard aeronautical phraseology) in order not to long occupy the frequency so they can not be considered really "natural" communications. Thus, the main limitations suffered by the current R/T channels can be either:

- *Technical,* channel congestion, limited range, simultaneous transmissions on the same frequency, amplitude modulation susceptible to weather interference or
- *Human,* mis-understandings due either to the poor quality of the communication, or transient nature of voice, difficulties to understand a non native language or accent, workload, confusion due to the party line effect.

In order to overcome most limitations of the current system, different alternatives have been proposed. One of the most promising is the adoption of datalink as additional medium of communication between controller and pilot, and we address the UI-related issues in the following sections.

3 Towards the New System

The current system seems to have reached limits of its capability and to be really short of efficient solutions, so increasing interest has been devoting to the possibility that conventional radio communications can be *augmented* with a new communication media called datalink, which electronically transfers digital messages to computer on the ground and in the aircraft. Initial considerations on human factors have already suggested that it could increase controllers' efficiency in the management of traffic and reduce potential communication errors, anyway special care has to be paid on its impact on the system, particularly in terms of variations to how controllers perform their tasks.

With regard to the latter point, three main differences are identified moving from the current system to an "augmented" one where both media are available:

1. *Change of task allocation between human and machine*: for instance, in datalink environment some tasks become automatically performed (e.g. the update of the ground system);
2. *Change of task allocation between human operators:* for example strategic-pilots datalink communications can occur as well;
3. *Change of artefacts manipulated by interaction tasks*: electronic flight strips are an example of "new" artefacts that can affect how tasks are performed.

More generally, these changes should carefully be analysed whenever a new application, supporting different interaction techniques and media, is designed. Furthermore, a number of factors related to how tasks are carried out must be considered when making comparisons between the design options. For instance, technological changes can have the effect of transforming control tasks into vigilance and monitoring tasks at which people are often less effective [9]. Similarly, design and task allocation decisions can have a significant impact on the workload of individuals and the range of responses to workload demands that are available to participants.

4 Supported Tasks

In this section we define more precisely activities that have to be performed by controllers in en-route ATC applications, using a task "granularity" refined enough to reason about pros and cons of each arrangement. In the following table the identified tasks (together with domain objects manipulated by) are listed.

Table 1. The Controllers' tasks

Task	Explanation	Domain objects
Monitoring Radar	Controllers have to check continuously the information provided by the radar	Flight traffic
Negotiation about Transfer Parameters	The strategic controllers have to negotiate about the best transfer flight parameters of flights which are going to change sector	Flight level
Annotate Strips	The controllers annotate flight strips to keep the "history" of traffic evolutions in the sector	Flight level, Route, Speed, Destination
Update Ground System	Both controllers —but generally only the strategic—update the ground-based computer system to reflect changes to flight data.	Flight level, Route, Speed, Destination
Detect Problem	The controller *identifies* a possible conflict in the current air traffic situation	Routes, flight level, lack of separation
Solve Problem	The cognitive process of *finding a solution* to solve a conflict or to give more regularity to the traffic flow	Current and foreseen air traffic
Send Clearance to Pilot	The task of sending instructions to aircraft	Flight plan, clearance
Send Information to Pilot	The task of sending information to aircraft	Weather information, delay reports
Handle First Contact	The task of replying to the first communication from a pilot who has just entered in the sector	Flight identifier, Frequency
Handle Last Contact	The task of sending the frequency to communicate with the controller of the next sector	Frequency
Inform Other Controller of Problem	One controller informs the other that something has been detected or something has to be done	Conflicts, conflicts' solutions

Note that in the table above we do not specify *which controller* actually performs a specific task, as the analysis of how to allocate tasks among the controllers (and the impact on the user interface design) is putting off until next sections.

5 Changes in Task Performance with the Introduction of DataLink

Fig. 2 shows an example of user interface for en-route controllers in a datalink environment: in the window, the radar data blocks of aircraft currently in the sector are recognisable, together with their associated electronic strips listed and displayed on the left-bottom part of the window. The controller is allowed to send instructions to an a/c either from the associated electronic strip or from its radar data block via a pop-up menu. Once the pilot replies with a positive answer *(Wilco* message), the ground system is automatically updated.

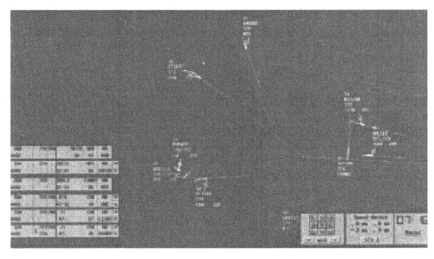

Fig. 2. An Example of Controller's User Interface in a Datalink Environment

In the current system, when the controller receives the affirmative answer from pilot s/he looks for the correspondent callsign on the radar screen, finds the associated strip in the rack, annotates it and updates the ground system. This activity is quite demanding as the information is "spread" over different supports (radar, paper flight strips), needing a high eye/hand co-ordination ability from the controller to blend them. The latter issue is an important safety concern, being assured that every information source which causes diversion of controller's attention focus is highly undesirable and should be avoided as much as possible.

In the new environment, first of all the controller is alleviated from keeping trace of traffic evolutions in the ground system as it is automatically performed. In addition, even if s/he does not have to annotate but just read the strip (to check conformance with a/c current position on the radar), now both pieces of information are on the screen, reducing necessary eyes' movements and resulting controller's fatigue.

6   The Analysed Options for Media and Task Allocation

In the following sections, we consider different options of allocating media and tasks between executive and strategic controllers as far as it concerns the communications controller-pilot(s). Each option will be evaluated on the basis of several criteria, ranging from the time of task performance, the balancing of the workload among controllers, to potential conflicts in accessing to shared objects and number of possible hazardous situations.

Before going forward into the proper analysis, it is better to define the hypothesis that we are going to keep unchanged for both options. First of all, the co-existence of different information sources of audio type (telephone, radio), peculiar constraints related to its own transient nature, and the high level of safety-criticality connected to communications exchanged through them, claims the need of allocating in a "dedicated" way only one audio medium to each controller (telephone to strategic, radio to executive). In this way all the assumptions where the strategic controller has to communicate with pilots on the frequency as well are discarded: in fact, if the strategic is already busy on the telephone with another colleague in order to negotiate some sector's change parameters, s/he cannot perform equally well (or equally quickly) the critical task of hearing and replying to pilots that would want to speak with him/her. In addition, as in every safety critical system the decision-making process is a decisive point we decided that both controllers have to monitor the traffic situation, but only the executive is in charge of deciding what the best solution is to solve a problem and act upon consequently. Initially, we started considering the three options graphically summarised in Fig. 3:

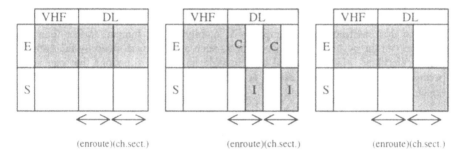

Fig. 3. A tabular overview of the three different options

Each table in Fig. 3 is split into two rows —one for each controller, executive (E) and strategic (S) and two columns —one of each media used for controller-pilot communications, voice (VHF) and datalink (DL). In addition the "DL" column is divided in two sections: the "ch.sect." section (communications needed to manage a sector change, namely the pilot's first contact, the controller's last contact and the consequent answers to these communications) and the "enroute" section (all the other tasks that have to be carried out during the en-route phase). In one case the DL section is split in turn into two subsections, clearance (C) and information (I), to distinguish the kind of messages that can be transmitted.

As you can see from the first table in Fig. 3, under the first option we suppose the executive controller handling both vocal and datalink communications with pilots then the whole row associated to him/her is shaded, whereas in the second and the third tables datalink communications are handled by both the controllers, with different arrangements. For the purposes of our analysis, we decided to discard the second option because it is really a small variation of the first one as the changes are rather minimal as well as their effects on the way to interact with the application.

7   Criteria for Integrated Evaluation of Usability and Safety

Currently, there is a lack of general agreement about the aspects that should be taken into account in allocating media, as well as guidelines that should evaluate this allocation process. Traditional approaches consider only the nature of information (e.g. urgency), the technical characteristics of the used media (constraints and limitations) and, of course the overall performance of the system. However, especially in safety-critical systems a more complete analysis has to focus a little more on the role of the human in order to prevent incorrect user interactions that can threaten human life. These incorrect behaviours are not necessarily totally wrong actions but also right actions performed at the wrong time: particularly in the ATC system, controllers are very sensitive concerning the "right time" to perform actions, as a too late action might transform a fairly difficult problem into a very difficult one. In order not to miss the right time for delivering an instruction, controllers monitor exact positions of aircraft, continuously refreshing them until the right moment arrives, switching from time to time on different situations in traffic, and this activity is a quite demanding task for them.

As in this environment the emphasis is mainly on the human, (rather than the machine and the system), interactive aspects such as tasks performed by the human, his/her workload, skills requested and possible hazardous situations that can arise because of incorrect human action or behaviour become key points. Finally, we selected the following criteria:

1. *Fair allocation of work between operators*: although this parameter is difficult to estimate from a quantitative point of view, we tried not to have completely unbalanced allocation of controllers' activities between the two operators.
2. *Possible hazardous situations*, as this aspect is really crucial in every safety-critical system. We use a HAZOP-like method [10][11] to analyse possible hazardous situations caused by "deviations from design intent" in the interactions between system components.
3. *Conflicts on shared objects between operators*: the maximum sharing between the controllers is desirable to minimise inconsistencies between the views of the two controllers and to maximise their concurrent activities. Higher the sharing, higher the accuracy with which the interface should be designed to avoid that (not well designed) concurrent accesses might cause conflict situations.
4. *Time of task performance*: improvements to the overall system's performance derive mainly from improvements to controllers' tasks performance, thus it is essential to identify bottlenecks and defeats in controllers' activity making up for them as much as possible.

It is worthwhile to stress that the aim of identifying such criteria is not to provide specific measurable parameters that can distinguish in a quantitative way between the options, but instead to suggest criteria that form a framework in which we may explore what the differences between the options are.

8 Evaluation

This section is devoted to evaluate pros and cons of each option according to the aforementioned criteria.

8.1 Case 1: Both Communication Media Allocated to the Executive

In Table 2 we divided tasks with respect to the human operator who performs them under the first option. For example, in the executive's column we list all the tasks that the executive controller is expected to perform when all communication media (datalink and radio) are allocated to him/her.

Table 2. Task allocation with communication media allocated to the executive

Strategic	Executive
Monitor Radar	**Monitor Radar**
Negotiate Transfer Parameters	
Annotate Strips	**Annotate Strips**
Update Ground System	**Update Ground System**
Detect Problem	**Detect Problem**
	Solve Problem
	Send Clearance to Pilot
	Send Information to Pilot
	Handle First Contact
	Handle Last Contact
Inform Controller of Problem	

In Table 2 four tasks (highlighted in bold) appear in both executive and strategic columns, seeming that some "redundancy" occurs in the system. Actually, two of them (namely the *Monitor Radar* task and the *Detect Problem* task) are really performed in a parallel way because both controllers are always in charge of monitoring the traffic flow and possibly detect problems (it is reasonable because of the high level of safety criticality of such tasks). The *Update Ground System* is normally performed by the strategic because the executive is generally too busy (of course, we refer to updates concerning non-datalink equipped a/c, otherwise they are automatically performed).

As far as it concerns the *Annotate Strips* task for each strip generated by the system, once the strategic possibly modifies the strip, s/he passes it to the executive controller who starts to use it when s/he receives the first contact from the pilot (annotating it to keep track of the flight evolution within the sector). When the flight associated to the strip is still in the sector, the strategic controller could have to annotate the strip again, because of a negotiation with the strategic controller of the sector which the flight is going to enter (this is a situation of "strip sharing" between the strategic and the executive controller).

8.1.1   Hazardous Situation

In the method that we have developed [12] based on the HAZOP approach, the procedure for identifying "deviations" (excursions of a value outside its normal operating envelope) from the design intent is performed by applying a number of *guidewords* referring to a specific type of deviation. The results of the analysis is recorded in a tabular form with the following elements: *task* the activity which is being analysed), *guideword* (the type of considered deviation), *deviation* (the specific detected problem or how the guideword is interpreted in the context of the task), *cause* (hypotheses on how the problem might arise), *consequence* (possible effects of the deviation for the system as a whole), *protection* (indicating how —within the current design—it is possible to protect from the deviation), *recommendations* (suggestions for an improved design).

Just to give an example of how it works, in this section we examine possible deviations in the executive's task of communicating the frequency of next controller to a pilot (using datalink messages and under the assumptions of the first option).We consider the "*Other Than*" guideword applied to *Handle Last Contact* task, indicating that the controller's last contact sent to a pilot (with a datalink message) results to be different from that intended: "different" because either wrong flight has been selected, or a wrong frequency has been sent, or the pilot has mis-read the correct message. Of course, for the same communication other guidewords could be examined as well (e.g. *None*: no communication occurs; *Early*: the communication occurs too early, *Late*: the communication occurs after the right time, and so on).

With this type of analysis, one hazardous situation that could appear using datalink messages to communicate the new frequency to a pilot is when the controller makes a mistake in identifying the a/c callsign on his/her interface and then s/he sends the command to a wrong flight. In addition, even if the controller is good at identifying and pointing with mouse the right a/c, s/he has to select the right command and the appropriate parameters: another possible deviation is to select a wrong frequency value. In order to avoid (reduce at least) possible errors performing these tasks the user interface should be designed in such a way to bound properly the range of possible values, to ensure that UI never stays in an "undefined" mode —for example the controller has selected the command and the parameters but s/he actually forgets to send the instruction: the user interface should take care either of avoiding these situations at all (for example by means of modal windows) or warning properly the controller about them.

For the purposes of our analysis it is meaningful to analyse the different role that each controller plays under these assumptions: the strategic controller's role is mainly devoted to support the executive's work, checking and monitoring his/her activity, therefore the need of providing the strategic with a proper feedback of executive's actions as far as it concerns the (silent) datalink communications. This feedback — differently from the VHF communications easily heard by the strategic as s/he stays very close to the executive— has to explicitly be provided on the strategic controller's user interface and carefully designed. On the other hand, the executive handles different media and tools to manage the traffic, increasing the possibility of incorrect interactions using them: thus, the likelihood that hazardous situations occur is **high**.

8.1.2   Possible Conflicts Derived from Shared Objects

Under this assumption the controllers have to manage really different tasks and actually they have to share only the strips and only if the strategic controller wants to update a flight parameter while the associated flight is still in the sector (and then under the control of the executive). The level of sharing is **low**.

8.1.3   Fair Allocation of Work

The executive controller has a bigger workload compared to the strategic's, because of many factors:

1. *Number of tasks*: the executive has to support all the communications with pilots and, at the same time, s/he has to think of the best solution to the problems as they unpredictably appear. The strategic controller has to negotiate with other strategic controllers and s/he has to update the ground system for all the non-datalink equipped planes in the sector (for datalink-equipped planes the update of the system is performed in an automatic way).
2. In addition, the executive's work is more stressful, because of more pressing *time constraints* which are, as the task of resolving problems and communicating with pilots have to be performed as soon as possible. On the contrary, the strategic can "organise" his/her work more freely than the executive colleague can: for instance, s/he does not have to update the system each time s/he receives a positive answer from a pilot, but it is enough that s/he updates the system until ten minutes before the flight crosses the sector boundaries (so that an updated strip is printed in the other sector).
3. The *type of skill requested*, because the task of quickly resolving an unforeseeable conflict in the traffic flow is obviously more demanding compared to the strategic controller's work of updating the ground system (that is a "routine" task above all).

The considerations above allow us to state that under this option there is an **unfair allocation of work** between the executive and the strategic controller.

8.1.4   Time of Task Performance

Consider the actions needed to perform a VHF communication from a controller to a pilot: first of all, as his/her communication is heard by all the pilots currently in the sector, s/he has to identify the flight with which s/he wants to communicate, so s/he at first reads the a/c identification and then s/he sends to the pilot the proper order, clearance or information, following the aeronautical phraseology. The concerned pilot has to read-back the instruction to declare that s/he is going (or not) to execute the order, possibly starting to do it.

The datalink technology allows controllers to have point-to-point communications, so first of all the controller has to identify on his/her interface the right a/c representation, pointing it with the mouse and then selecting menu allowing him/her to use the datalink capabilities. Then s/he selects the right command and (if requested) the appropriate parameters and s/he sends the instruction. The pilot's system sends to the controller's system the acknowledgement that the message is ready to be displayed on the pilot's interface, but only when the pilot looks at the message and replies with a "*Wilco*" message it means that s/he is able to perform the order.

Considering how a communication is supported by using datalink technology keep in mind that every datalink communication is always delayed because of normal transmission delays, so the VHF technology allows to gain shorter performance times being definitely more immediate. However, being the executive controller due to keep all the communications with pilots, especially in high traffic situations the global time needed to support them could get worse just because of the executive's bottleneck who can fulfil only one pilot's request at a time (**low performance with high traffic**).

8.2 Case 2: The Flight-State Dependent Data-Link Allocation

In this situation, all datalink-equipped a/c have to interact with both controllers, depending on the different phases of flight (with strategic controller when the flight changes the sector, otherwise with the executive). In the table below we summarise the tasks' arrangement:

Table 3. Task allocation in the flight-state dependent datalink allocation

Strategic	*Executive*
Monitor Radar	**Monitor Radar**
Negotiate Transfer Parameters	
Annotate Strips	**Annotate Strips**
Update Ground System	**Update Ground System**
Detect Problem	**Detect Problem**
	Solve Problem
	Send Clearance to Pilot
	Send Information to Pilot
Handle First Contact	
Handle Last Contact	
Inform Controller of Problem	

8.2.1   Hazardous Situations

In this option the strategic controller can send order to pilots, so it is possible that his/her orders can conflict to executive's, leading to possible hazardous situations. For example, the flight level requested for an a/c by the strategic controller could be different from that expected by the executive controller, so a dangerous situation could arise when the flight's control passes from one controller to the other one.

Along the lines of our analysis of the task examined in the previous section (send the new frequency to a pilot) all the issues continue to be valid with the exception of exchanging the executive's role with the strategic's one, being now the latter controller in charge of sending datalink messages to pilots approaching to change sector (*Handle First Contact* and *Handle Last Contact* tasks in Table 3).

It is worth noting that under this option the roles of the two controllers are more balanced (the strategic controller is not only a help for the executive controller), but s/he plays an active role in the sector traffic management, looking after part of datalink communications. Thus, the coordination and mutual awareness between the two controllers has to be augmented with respect to the previous option (because for example the strategic has to exactly know at what time the handover of a flight has to be performed with the executive and so does the executive). In addition, the strategic controller's activity of checking and supporting the executives work could get less effective. Therefore, under this option **controllers' mutual awareness and cross-checking are the most critical conditions for obtaining a low number of hazardous situations.**

8.2.2   Possible Conflicts Derived from Shared Objects
Under this option the aspect of "shared objects" is a bit more critical. It can happen that both controllers want to perform an action on the same a/c as they both can access to appropriate tools, thus it is relevant to take care of the incorrect behaviours that could occur if the actions are not well serialised. A good user interface highlighting when it is the right time to pass the control from the executive controller to the strategic and vice versa, (e.g. avoiding that the strategic decides to send a "last contact" instruction to a pilot whereas at the same time the executive controller wants to have other communications with the same a/c) should limit the number of conflicts that is **potentially high.**

8.2.3   Fair Allocation of Work
The workload between controllers is more distributed, either in terms of number of tasks, as in terms of type of task: in fact, while in the other cases the strategic had to perform all "routine" activities, now his/her activity can have a direct impact on the global system, as all flights going into the sector or leaving the sector have to communicate with him/her. Under high traffic situations it could happen that some flights perform the first contact but the strategic could be already occupied in other matters, so in this case the strategic can feel heavier his/her activity. The allocation of work seems to be **fair**.

8.2.4   Time of Task Performance
In this case the overall system's performance (often depending on the controllers' skills in anticipating conflicts) can benefit from an executive controller a bit more focussed on the flow in the sector because has been freed from several routine's communications (such first/last contact often are), so s/he can spend more time monitoring system, allowing him/her to be more ready to reply to pilots in order to prevent/solve conflicts. Of course, all these advantages can be exploited only if other co-ordination problems between the strategic controller and the executive controller are not added because of badly-designed user interface that does not take into account the need of mutual knowledge and awareness between controllers. Therefore, under this option, **if conflicts are resolved, the best performance is reached**.

9   Conclusions and Future Work

In this paper we discuss how different media can affect —in terms of safety and usability— the work of human operators in this type of applications. Besides, we show how the proposed criteria can be applied in the Air Traffic Control field.

The proposed approach starts from the assertion that the user interface design is a complex process, which has to consider several different aspects, especially when intended for a safety-critical application as in the air traffic control example considered in the paper (although the same issues can be applied to other areas). In this case the high co-operation requested between different users claims that possible changes in users' way of working have to be carefully analysed before introducing them in the system, as the effects of erroneous users' interactions can be easily propagated within such system with critical consequences.

Therefore, our work represents an attempt to structure all various aspects into a more organic approach which starts identifying the possible options in allocating media and tasks, analysing the resulting changes of environment, artefacts, and interactions between the different involved human agents and between the human and the system. The next step is to evaluate the options according to different criteria that we found relevant in the assumed environment: in our experience this qualitative evaluation can provide useful guidelines to assess pros and cons of each option.

According to the developed analysis, we plan to obtain a new system prototype for managing en-route air traffic with data link support that should satisfy selected safety and usability criteria. Further work on formal reasoning about safety and usability properties of this multi-users environment, with support of model-checking techniques, is also foreseen.

References

1. Leathley, B.A., HAZOP Approach to Allocation of Function in Safety Critical Systems, in Proc. Of the 1st International Conference on Allocation of Functions
2. Hollnagel E., Human Reliability Analysis, Academic Press, 1993
3. Paternò, F., Santoro, C., Tahmassebi, S. Formal Models for Cooperative Tasks: Concepts and an Application for En-Route Air Traffic Control. In *Proc. DSV-IS '98*, pp.71-86, Springer Verlag, Abingdon, U.K., June 1998.
4. Chatty, S., Lecoanet, P., Pen Computing for Air Traffic Control, in Proceedings of CHI'96, April 13-18, 1996 Vancouver, British Columbia, Canada
5. Mackay, W.E., Fayard, A.L., Frobert, L., Médini, L., Reinventing the familiar: exploring an augmented reality design space for air traffic control, in Proceedings of CHI'98, April 18-23, 1998, Los Angeles, CA USA
6. Operational Requirements for Air Traffic Management (ATM) Air/Ground Communications Services, Appendix A: Glossary and Abbreviations. Available from http://www.eurocontrol.be/projects/eatchip/odiac/document/apa_10.doc
7. Diaper, D., Task Analysis for Human-Computer Interaction, Chichester: Ellis Horwood.
8. Paternò, F., A Model-based approach to the design and evaualuation of interactive application, Springer-Verlag, 1999.
9. Hopkin, V.D. Air Traffic Control. In E. L. Wiener and D. C. Nagel, Eds. *Human Factors in Aviation*. Academic Press, 1988. Pages 639-663.
10. McDermid, J.A. and Pumfrey, D.J. A Development of Hazard Analysis to aid Software Design. Proc. COMPASS'94, IEEE Press. ftp://ftp.cs.york.ac.uk/hise_reports/safety/develop.ps.Z
11. Burns, D.J. and Pitblado, R.M. A Modified HAZOP Methodology For Safety Critical System Assessment. F. Redmill and T. Anderson, Ed. Directions in Safety Critical Systems —Proceedings of the Safety-Critical Systems Symposium, 1993, Springer-Verlag
12. Fields, B., Paternò, F.,.Santoro, C, Analysing User Deviations in Interactive Safety-critical Applications, Proceedings DSV-IS'99, Springer Verlag, June'99, Braga, June'99

Patterns for Safer Human-Computer Interfaces

Andrew Hussey

Software Verification Research Centre
The University of Queensland
Brisbane, Qld, 4072, Australia
ahussey@csee.uq.edu.au

Abstract. Design patterns have been widely touted as a potential solution to the difficulty of expressing and sharing software design expertise. Patterns have also recently been suggested as a basis for capturing the characteristics of "usable" user-interfaces. We propose that patterns may also be useful for guiding development of human-machine interfaces for safety-critical systems. We consider usability in the context of system safety and present a pattern language for developing safe human-machine interfaces.

1 Introduction

This paper is concerned with some of the issues that arise when developing human-computer interfaces for safety-critical systems. In particular, our aim is to provide rules for assuring the safety of the resulting system, compromising usability only where necessary.

We express our rules as "patterns". Each pattern is a "(description of) a recurring structural or behavioural solution" [16]. Patterns for software design (e.g., [6]) are now commonly used in industry and have been widely touted as a way to capture and share design expertise. Patterns are richer than just a set of guidelines; a pattern describes the context in which a solution applies and how the current context alters the required solution [4]. Patterns provide several benefits to system developers:

Communication: a common language for discussing design issues and for communicating principles of design;

Documentation: a common basis for understanding a system;

Reuse: a storehouse of available solutions for common design scenarios.

Mahemoff and Johnston [9] describe how patterns for usability might be constructed based on an overriding design philosophy and desirable design properties. Each pattern investigates how low-level guidelines may be directed toward supporting a particular recurrent task.

Many of the forces that make patterns a good solution for capturing usability design expertise are also active when the goal of development is safety. In particular, patterns are a good means of capturing the diversity of experiences needed for successful design of safety-critical user-interfaces. Patterns guide designers

M. Felici, K. Kanoun, A. Pasquini (Eds.): SAFECOMP'99, LNCS 1698, pp. 103-112, 1999

who often may lack formal training in developing safety-critical systems and for whom no common perspective, set of practices, or theoretical orientation can be assumed.

This paper gives the core of a pattern language for developing user-interfaces for safety-critical systems. We reformulate and summarise Leveson's [8, Ch.12] and Reason's [14] guidelines for developing user-interfaces for safety-critical systems as patterns. The approach taken in this paper focuses on recurring design solutions and is closer to that taken by Alexander [2] and by Gamma et al. [6], as opposed to that of Mahemoff and Johnston.

Each pattern that we present consists of four elements:

Intent: summary of the solution presented and the type of problem it solves;

Motivation: perspectives or facets of the problem (forces) that the solution addresses;

Applicability: a summary of the class of problems;

Solution: solutions to assuring safety for the class of problems are given in terms of guidelines. The solutions provided are based on the guidelines of Leveson and of Reason; they are an extension and summary of the existing guidelines.

In Sect. 2, we consider how both usability and safety goals can co-exist in the development of a safety-critical human-computer interface. Section 3 gives a pattern language for usability and safety. In Sect. 4, we discuss the *Druide* air-traffic control (ATC) system and consider how the patterns given in Sect. 3 are reflected in the design of Druide. We suggest improvements to Druide using our patterns as a guide. Section 5 considers the outcomes of this paper and future work.

2   Safety and Usability as Design Goals

2.1   What is Usability?

Shneidermann [15, p.8] emphasises the need for understanding of the community of users and the tasks to be accomplished, and the need for a commitment by developers to serving users. Those who design systems need to know how to think in terms of the eventual users' tasks and how to translate that knowledge into an executable system [5, p.1]. Correctness is of concern when the consequences for the user of incorrect actions or inaction are sufficiently undesirable.

Requirements for usability are frequently expressed in terms of guidelines e.g., [15, Ch.2]. For example, Mahemoff and Johnston [9] summarise the Macintosh, Windows 95, Motif, OpenLook and IBM Common User Access guidelines and extract several usability principles:

Task efficiency: the software should assist users of varied skill levels to accomplish tasks efficiently and effectively;

Reuse of knowledge: interaction techniques learned in one part of an application should be consistent with those used elsewhere in the application;

User-computer communication: information needs of the user are supported and expression of user operations is straight-forward;

Robustness: the software should prevent serious user errors but if errors do occur, there should be easy paths to recovery;

Flexibility: the software should be adaptable to each user's unique requirements.

2.2   What is Safety?

Safety has been defined by Leveson as "freedom from accidents and harm" [8, p.182]. A system is safe when the risk of a system hazard arising and leading to harm is acceptably low. Unlike usability, where the focus is only on the user, safety is also concerned with the consequences of user actions and inactions on, and the corresponding risk to, the community within which the user's work takes place; for example, this may be a factory, aircraft or warship. In safety-critical systems, such consequences are (by definition) more serious than for non-safety-critical systems. For safety-critical user-interfaces there is heightened concern with assuring correct user actions and inactions.

In essence, Task Efficiency, Reuse of Knowledge and Flexibility are not primary goals of safety-critical interactive system development. The primary goals of such a development are User-Computer Communication and Robustness. These latter two principles are concerned with the correctness of user actions and inactions. Where possible, task efficiency, reuse of knowledge and flexibility may be accommodated provided safety is not compromised. This section gives design patterns that assist a developer in enhancing User-Computer Communication and Robustness.

2.3   Safety First!

For safety, our primary concern is to ensure that user error is minimised. Safety favours correctness of user actions (or inactions), although efficiency may also become a safety concern if poor efficiency can lead to user inaction when action is necessary to avert a hazardous situation leading to an accident. Because usability is also concerned with correctness and because correctness, efficiency and user comfort are not necessarily mutually exclusive goals, guidelines for usability and for safety exhibit significant overlap. If a balance cannot be achieved so that a safety-critical system is both safe and enables sufficient productivity (efficiency and comfort are adequate), then the system may not be viable.

3   A Safety-Oriented Pattern Language for User-Interfaces

In this section, we discuss patterns for safe user-interface development. We give descriptions of eight example patterns based on guidelines for safety-critical user-interfaces provided by Leveson and by Reason.

The patterns provide an ontology for the design guidelines, grouping the guidelines with accompanying justification. As new guidelines are included, they can be incorporated in suitable existing patterns or, if appropriate, new patterns may be added. To remain concise, we do not give examples for each pattern individually, rather a single example applying the patterns is given in Sect. 4.

3.1 Undo

Intent: Tolerate user errors by enabling the user to return the system from an unsafe to a safe state.

Motivation: In many safety-critical systems risk can be reduced sufficiently and more economically by external controls on use of the system, such as operational procedures. Further, for many such systems, not all unsafe states can be prevented or avoided because the characterisation of a state as safe or unsafe depends on the external context of the system. For example, an automatic syringe cannot be economically provided with logic to determine when a dose is unsafe because this may depend on a multitude of factors and requires a doctor's expertise. In this situation the designer must provide the user with the opportunity to correct their error before an unsafe state becomes an accident.

Applicability: Use this pattern when an interaction error cannot be prevented or avoided.

Solution: Enable the user to undo effects of errors by (a) making errors observable (provide feedback about actions and the state of the system), (b) making the boundaries of acceptable performance visible to the users while their effects are still observable and reversible, (c) providing time to reverse errors and (d) providing multiple compensating (reversing) actions. An "undo" function should return the system to a clearly defined and recognisable state and it should be obvious that the undo has been completed successfully. Provide support for self monitoring of performance to enable error detection and correction. Safety-enhancing actions should be easy and robust; stopping an unsafe event should be possible with a single action. Conversely, safety-critical operational steps should be incremental, so that the consequence of interaction error is commensurately lower.

3.2 Error Prevention

Intent: Prevent the user from placing the system in an unsafe state.

Motivation: Ideally, unsafe states can be identified in advance and the system can be designed such that the unsafe state is impossible. Such preventative measures are referred to by Norman [12] as "forcing functions". Forcing functions prevent the potential consequences following an unsafe state being entered by removing that state from the valid states in which the system may exist.

Applicability: Use this pattern when an unsafe state can be identified and it is believed that the unsafe state identified does not provide the only path from other (more serious) unsafe states to safe states.

Solution: Provide interlocks to prevent inadvertent, potentially dangerous human actions. If safety interlocks are overridden, their status should be displayed and normal operation should not be permitted to resume until interlocks have been restored. See also patterns 3.3 and 3.6; if an error cannot be avoided then reduce its likelihood and provide a warning to the user.

3.3   Warning

Intent: If the system has entered a hazardous state, the user should be notified of the state that the system is currently in and the level of urgency with which the user must act.

Motivation: In most safety-critical systems, the user responds to system exigencies, preventing hazards from arising and if hazards do arise, preventing accidents occurring. To perform this role effectively, the user must be informed of the state of the system. In particular, the user needs to be specifically alerted when a hazard arises.

Applicability: Use this pattern when an interaction error cannot be prevented or avoided.

Solution: Make warnings brief and simple. Limit the number of alarms to a minimum and replace alarms by automation where possible [10]. Safety critical alarms should be distinguishable from routine alarms. The form of the alarm should indicate the degree of urgency and which condition is responsible for the alarm [13]. Minimise spurious signals and alarms (else, operators may become accustomed to ignoring warnings). Operators should be provided with straightforward checks to distinguish hazards from faulty instruments. The system should distinguish the override of safety-critical and non-safety-critical error or hazard indications. See also pattern 3.7; warnings should also be clearly displayed.

In [7], we give full descriptions for the following additional patterns. In this paper we only give their applicability and solution:

3.4   Knowledge-based Reasoning Supported

Applicability: Use this pattern whenever the rules that a user may apply in engaging with the system require individual judgement and consequently knowledge-based reasoning is anticipated.

Solution: Reduce the chance of interference between possible competing "mental models" by supporting memory with some externalised schematic of these alternatives. By externalising the mental model the burden on memory required for causal reasoning is reduced. Provide external memory aids to support the retention of items, acts and data that are not part of the current operational situation. Aid recovery from errors due to lack of cognitive resources by using the available data to simultaneously present information that is suitable for skill, rule and knowledge-based processing. An example of such a knowledge-based reasoning aid that we consider further in Sect. 4 is the paper strips used by air-traffic controllers to record flight details. See also pattern 3.8; independent information and interrogation are a valuable adjunct to knowledge-based reasoning.

3.5   Operator Awareness Maintained

Applicability: Use this pattern when the operator must monitor the state of the system (e.g., when the safety-critical system is largely automated) and there is a risk of operator skill shedding and lowered awareness.

Solution: Critical actions should be integrated into tasks so that activities requiring passive actions are minimised; tasks should be varied and encourage operator experimentation (without hazardous consequences). Because passive activities imply loss of operator skills, operators of such systems should be trained regularly [3]. The system should provide feedback on the system state [11]; if important information changes in a very short interval before or after the operator issues a command, the changes should be brought to the operator's attention (see pattern 3.3). The operator should be informed of any anomaly, the existing actions taken and the system configuration. Obsolete information should be flagged rather than removed.

3.6 Slip Reduction

Applicability: Use this pattern when a slip cannot be prevented or avoided.

Solution: Reduce the probability of a user generated error by addressing the causes of slips. Slips [12] are user errors that are concerned with automatic behaviour at the physical execution level. Minimise attentional capture by providing overview displays that the user can monitor at the fringe of consciousness. Provide cues for actions, e.g., design control panels to mimic the physical layout of the plant or system and minimise activities requiring repetitive actions. Encourage experimentation (without hazardous consequences) by the user to optimise sensorimotor skills. See also pattern 3.1; if slips occur, users should be able to undo the effects.

3.7 Clear Displays

Applicability: Use this pattern when there is a requirement that a safety-critical system displays information to a user.

Solution: Do not overload the operator with too much information; instead provide ways for the operator to get additional information. Avoid displaying absolute values, instead show changes and use analogue rather than or as well as digital displays. Provide references for judgement. Minimise the semantic distance between interface displays and mental models and the articulator distance so that physical actions mimic their meanings. See also pattern 3.3; warnings require special treatment.

3.8 Independent Information/interrogation

Applicability: This pattern is fundamental to the development of safety-critical systems because hazards may arise other than by user errors.

Solution: If the operator is to monitor automatic systems, provide independent information on the state of the system. Provide alternative sources of critical information in case the computer display fails; instrumentation meant to help operators deal with a malfunction should not be able to be disabled by the malfunction itself.

4   An ATC System Case Study

To illustrate using the patterns introduced in the previous sections, we describe an ATC (air-traffic control) user-interface and consider which aspects of the design of the user-interface are reflected in our patterns. We also consider how, by applying our patterns, the safety of the user-interface could be improved. The system examined is a prototype under development by the French aviation authorities, CENA (Centre d'Études de la Navigation Aerienne). The prototype has formed the basis for a CHI workshop on designing user-interfaces for safety-critical systems [1]. Our analysis of Druide in this paper is based on the descriptions of Druide given in [1].

4.1   The Druide System

The Druide ATC system is based on a data-link channel that is accessed from a menu-driven graphical user-interface, a radar screen annotated with flight information for each aircraft (call-sign, speed, heading and next beacon on its route) and paper strips that describe the flight plan for each aircraft. The paper strips are originally produced from flight plans submitted by the airlines. A controller is responsible for a sector of airspace including maintaining separation between aircraft. When changes are made to the flight plan for an aircraft in a sector, the changes are recorded on the corresponding paper strip. When an aircraft enters a sector, its pilot must communicate with the controller. The controller manages that aircraft while it is in their sector before "shooting" the aircraft to a new sector (notifying the next controller of the handover of control). Managing an aircraft involves communicating via the radar view and manipulating the paper strips. The controller may request that an aircraft change altitude, beacon, frequency, heading or speed.

A typical instantiation of the interface for Druide is shown in Fig. 1. The user is shown communicating a new altitude (CFL or Current Flight Level) to an aircraft. The selected aircraft with which the user is communicating is displayed in a distinguishable colour (because the picture is greyscale in this paper, we have circled the selected aircraft for ease of identification); selecting an aircraft produces a pop-up menu. When the operator clicks on the "CFL" entry in the menu, a further menu of altitude possibilities appears. The user selects from this menu and then clicks the "SEND" button (alternatively, if a mistake has been made, the user may click "ABORT").

The Druide system illustrates several of the patterns discussed in Sect. 3. User errors when choosing information from the system's menus can be undone by clicking "CNC" (i.e., a single action). The inclusion of a "SEND" button (and corresponding "ABORT" button) ensures that safety-critical actions are incremental. Hence there is some system tolerance of user error (pattern 3.1). Specifically, errors are observable (the system provides feedback about actions and the state of the system), there is time to reverse errors and there are multiple compensating (reversing) actions. Clicking "CNC" or "ABORT" returns the system to a clearly defined state (as reflected by the displayed attributes for each aircraft). A forcing function (behavioural constraint) is imposed on message content by limiting choice of revised flight segment information from menus

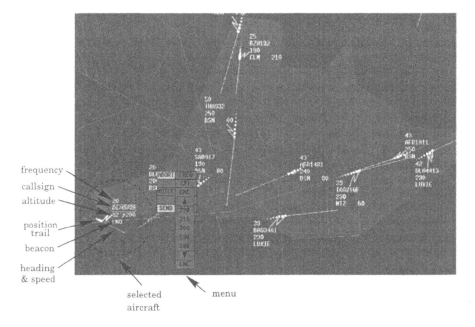

Fig. 1. The Druide radar display

(pattern 3.2). "Description" errors (in which messages are mistakenly sent to the wrong aircraft) are reduced by using the radar depiction as the basis for user-interaction with the system (pattern 3.6) rather than by voice communication; with the data-link system errors cannot occur as a result of human error at the recipient (pilot) end of the communication. In a non-data-link ATC system (i.e., instructions are communicated to aircraft by radio), errors may be concerned with description because aircraft are not adequately identified by the controller in the communication. In addition, by separating "ABORT" and "SEND" in the menu, "capture" errors such as sending when an abort is intended (because sending is more common) are reduced. The use of a radar display and trails showing where aircraft have been and their relative speed reflect part of the intent of pattern 3.7. Specifically, changes are shown for aircraft position, rather than absolute values, and the use of an active radar display reduces the semantic distance between interface displays and mental models and the articulator distance for selecting aircraft with which communication is to occur. Similarly, the ability of the operator to use radio to communicate directly with the aircraft directly applies pattern 3.8. Finally, the paper strips are a memory aid that supports knowledge-based reasoning (pattern 3.4).

4.2   Improving Druide

Our patterns suggest several additional improvements to Druide, as it has been described in [1], that would enhance the safety of the system. We discuss why each pattern is applicable to Druide and how it would be applied to improve the system.

The consequence of a loss of separation of aircraft is very serious; hence it is not unreasonable to expect that user errors should be prevented wherever possible. To prevent user errors that would lead to loss of separation, Druide could be an intelligent system, suggesting potential problems with messages that the operator formulates, e.g., messages that *may* result in violation of minimum separation if implemented by the aircraft to which the message is sent and preventing messages that *would* violate separation (i.e., applying patterns 3.2 and 3.3). Distinctive warnings would be provided to the user when a violation was anticipated or detected; for anticipated violations of separation the warning would be less urgent. The warning would be moded (i.e., operators would be forced to acknowledge the warning before proceeding) and would remain displayed in a non-obtrusive window (e.g., at the base of the screen) following acknowledgement. However the proposal potentially reduces task efficiency and therefore may not be viable in an operational setting. To counter interaction errors concerned with operator *inaction*, the system could actively seek user resolution of perceived conflicts (e.g., separation); such a strategy would be an application of pattern 3.5 which applies when the operator must monitor the state of the system. The operator would be informed of any anomaly, the existing actions taken and the system configuration. Again, this approach would also apply pattern 3.3), because reducing errors arising from user inaction is not possible, except by automating the air-traffic control system (generation of messages to aircraft for resolution of separation violations and satisfaction of aircraft flight plans). In addition, Druide could provide an "undo" operation to undo the effect of a message that has been erroneously sent to an aircraft (applying pattern 3.1). Specifically, such an undo operation would return the system to a clearly defined and recognisable state and it would be obvious that the undo had been completed successfully (e.g., each attribute for the aircraft would revert to their former value). In addition, there is opportunity for improvement of Druide's display (applying pattern 3.7). The pattern is clearly applicable because the amount of information displayed by Druide to the user is non-trivial. If Druide's display were three-dimensional, information relating to separation could be displayed directly and the operator could directly manipulate the display to alter aircraft separations. Such an approach would minimise the semantic distance between interface displays and mental models and the articulator distance.

5   Conclusions

Patterns can be used to create an ontology of design solutions for building user-interfaces for safety-critical systems. The content of the patterns has been compiled from existing guidelines for safety-critical user-interfaces. The patterns may be used with similar patterns for enhancing the usability of user-interfaces.

Usability can be characterised as the extent to which a system supports goals including correctness, task efficiency and flexibility. Building user-interfaces for safety-critical systems requires that additional attention be paid to assuring correctness of user actions, perhaps even at the expense of task efficiency and flexibility.

Our confidence that the patterns in this paper are useful to developers and enhance safety stems from their source in existing guidelines for developing safety-critical user-interfaces. Our future work is also concerned with validating the patterns by reference to existing safety-critical user-interfaces. This validation process may expose new patterns that should be added to the pattern language in this paper. We are also interested in experimentally determining whether applying the patterns during development of a user-interface enhances the safety of the resulting system.

References

1. CHI'98 Workshop (5) on Designing User Interfaces for Safety Critical Systems. ACM SIGCHI Conference on Human Factors in Computing Systems: "Making the Impossible Possible", 1998.
2. C. Alexander, S. Ishikawa, M. Silverstein, M. Jacobson, I. Fiksdahl-King, and S. Angel. *A Pattern Language.* Oxford University Press, New York, 1977.
3. L. Bainbridge. *New Technology and Human Error*, chapter 24, pages 271–283. John Wiley and Sons Ltd., 1987.
4. K. Beck and R. Johnson. Patterns Generate Architectures. In M. Tokoro and R. Pareschi, editors, *Proceedings of European Conference on Object-Oriented Programming, ECOOP'94*, pages 139–149. Springer-Verlag, 1994.
5. A. Dix, J. Finlay, G. Abowd, and R. Beale. *Human-Computer Interaction.* Prentice Hall, 1998.
6. E. Gamma, R. Helm, R. Johnson, and J. Vlissides. *Design Patterns: Elements of Reusable Object-Oriented Software.* Addison-Wesley, 1994.
7. A. Hussey. Patterns for Safety and Usability in Human-Computer Interfaces. Software Verification Research Centre TR99-05, The University of Queensland, January 1999.
8. N. G. Leveson. *Safeware, system safety and computers.* Addison-Wesley, 1995.
9. M. J. Mahemoff and L. J. Johnston. Principles for a Usability-Oriented Pattern Language. In P. Calder and B. Thomas, editors, *Proceedings of 1998 Australasian Computer Human Interaction Conference - OZCHI'98*, pages 132–139. IEEE Computer Society, 1998.
10. R. C. Mill, editor. *Human Factors in Process Operations.* Institution of Chemical Engineers, 1992.
11. D. Norman. The 'problem' with automation: inappropriate feedback and interaction, not 'over-automation'. *Philosphical Transactions of the Royal Society of London, Series B*, 327(1241):585–593, 1990.
12. D. A. Norman. *The Psychology of Everyday Things.* Basic Books, 1988.
13. R. D. Patterson. Auditory warning sounds in the work environment. *Philosphical Transactions of the Royal Society of London, Series B*, 327(1241):485–492, 1990.
14. J. Reason, editor. *Human Error.* Cambridge University Press, 1990.
15. B. Shneidermann. *Designing the User Interface: Strategies for Effective Human-Computer Interaction.* Addison-Wesley, 1992.
16. P. Viljamaa. The Patterns Business: Impressions from PLoP-94. *Software Engineering Notes*, 20(1):74–78, January 1995.

Impact of Communication on Systems Dependability: Human Factors Perspectives

Laurence Rognin[1], Jean-Paul Blanquart[2]

[1] Interaction Design Centre, Foundation Building, University of Limerick, Ireland
Laurence.Rognin@ul.ie
[2] LIS (LAAS-CNRS), 7 av. du colonel Roche, 31077 Toulouse Cedex 4, France
Jean-Paul.Blanquart@laas.fr

Abstract. Dependability of many complex and critical systems strongly relies on human operators, both through human reliability, and human ability to adequately handle unexpected events. This paper focuses on ergonomic field studies of air traffic control activities, and more specifically on the analyses of communication within teams of controllers. We show how operators spontaneously use the natural redundancy and diversity of human communication (multimodality, addressing characteristics, ...), so as to successfully maintain mutual awareness. This is the key for reliable cooperation, for the sake of global system dependability which rests on mechanisms such as error detection, recovery, and prevention (by anticipation and regulation). This study helps providing specifications for the design of systems efficiently supporting both human cooperation, and human ability to contribute to dependability.

1. Introduction

Modern technology allows more and more complex systems to ensure more and more critical functions. However, in most critical systems a significant role is still ensured by human operators, and especially teams of operators. In many work settings, humans have to maintain continuously a precise knowledge, of the state of the technical system and of the environment on the one hand, and of the actions, intentions and knowledge of their colleagues on the other hand. This is the key for their ability to handle appropriately unexpected events: detection of errors (due to human or technical components), diagnosis, and selection of an appropriate sequence of actions. Up to a large extent, the global dependability of many socio-technical systems thus depends on the efficiency of teamwork.

Cognitive ergonomics, as a discipline, provides methods and tools aimed at understanding how humans actually behave, act and interact in work situations, and at identifying how given work settings constrain or improve human capabilities. Therefore, it can contribute significantly to the overall design and exploitation process of critical socio-technical systems.

This paper reports on our approach and the results gathered for several years on various domains (nuclear, space, air-traffic control, etc.). These are illustrated here on our most recent ergonomic field studies, conducted in an Irish Air-Traffic Control Centre. Air-Traffic controllers work in cooperation with colleagues (other controllers

M. Felici, K. Kanoun, A. Pasquini (Eds.): SAFECOMP'99, LNCS 1698, pp. 113–124, 1999

in the same or in adjacent centres, pilots) and use the support of a computerised system, so as to provide a critical service, ensuring both the traffic handling (availability concerns) and the collision avoidance (safety concerns).

The paper focuses on the influence of the work settings on the cooperation, especially through the supports provided to an efficient and reliable communication. It is advocated that multimodal communication within a shared workspace is an efficient support to reliable cooperation, through the elaboration and updating of shared knowledge and mutual awareness, which in turn contribute to the global system dependability.

This paper is composed of seven sections. Sections 2 and 3 present the theoretical framework (cognitive ergonomics) and the methods guiding our study. Section 4 outlines the main characteristics of air-traffic control activities in Ireland. Section 5 describes the collaborative dimension of these activities and points out the importance of the shared workspace in communication. Section 6 shows how communications impact on the system reliability, in enabling controllers to implement loops of controls. Finally, Section 7 concludes and outlines some directions for future work.

2.   Theoretical framework: Cognitive ergonomics

Even though it is difficult to characterise it as a theory, cognitive ergonomics rests on a specific set of assumptions and views of the world.

Initially interested in the analysis of people at work, it is now defined more widely as the analysis of people interacting with their environment. The primary focus of ergonomics is the understanding of working conditions, in order to improve them (and originally reduce human pain and injuries). Close to the Anglo-Saxon "human factor" approach, cognitive ergonomics is still more than anthropometrics, as it does not only focus on the physical aspect of work. Last of all, ergonomics analyses are design-oriented in the sense that analysts aim to understand working situations in order to improve them (through design, modifications, or training)

The main assumption in cognitive ergonomics is the difference between the *task* defined by the organisation (what people are expected to do) and the *activity* observed in real work environments (what people really do).

This distinction is based on the observation that whatever the rules and procedures are, they can not be guaranteed complete, efficient and correct in any circumstances. So, usually in real-time situation, operators have to adapt these rules and procedures to the constraints of the situation [5]. These constraints can be as diverse as technical failure, weather problem, human error, strike, etc.

One quality of the ergonomics approach is the emphasis put on the role of people in adapting their task to the specific requirements of the situation. Indeed, observations in the workplace highlight the limits of tasks description, and the modifications required in real situations. Taking into account the differences between task and activity enables the analysts to identify the limits of the procedure, and provides a better understanding of human capabilities and adaptive competencies [4].

This justifies the importance put by ergonomics on field work. The work rests on the analyst's integration within the workplace [6]. What motivates this, is the idea that, only in the workplace analysts will grab what work is really about. Interviews with workers about their real work provide important information related to their vision and their perception of the way *they think* they perform their work. It is then obvious, that certain aspects can not emerge through interview, due to two main reasons: first, actions are not always conscious, and second, complex sequences of actions are not perceived as a set of simple actions.

What ergonomics proposes is an external, objective description of what is taking place in the working environment. Using techniques as diverse as note-taking, sketches, photographs, interviews and video-recordings, ergonomics bases the analysis of the work practices on the description of the real performance of work, within its real context[1].

In the next section, the method used in the context of the Air-Traffic Control (ATC) analysis is presented.

3. Field work

In Air-Traffic control, people deal with a highly complex and safety-critical system. As described in the previous section, cognitive ergonomics insists on the necessity to perform field studies. In such a safety-critical context, where temporal constraints are important, the methodology used to approach the working situation and collect data has to be very carefully prepared and implemented.

The observation and analysis of Air-Traffic control activities performed in the Irish control centre aimed to describe and understand the work practices of controllers. We expected this study to reflect not only the performance of formal tasks, but also the contribution of controllers to system dependability through adapting their actions to the requirements of the situation. Thus, it aimed to analyse the collective activities, highlighting the use of environmental resources (people, tools and documents) and the role of communication in systems dependability.

As stated before, the ergonomics approach emphasises the importance of field studies. In Air traffic control, we clarified that we planned to be in the control room, observing people, taking notes and from time to time even video recording activities. Our second request was in terms of controllers' availability, as we needed their explanations, comments and feedback, in order to validate our understanding of their work.

It was performed with respect to basic ergonomic "principles"[2]. Thus, it followed two distinct steps, a first one focusing on the specified tasks (through reading documents and observing the work settings), the second on the real performance of work, usually called the activity (through observation of and interviews with controllers).

Our analysis of people work practices focused on the verbal and non-verbal communications, cooperative mechanisms (help, mutual adjustment, awareness, regulation), use of tools, documents and procedures.

From these observations, we identified features, which we considered relevant in the context of our study. Before discussing them in the next sections, let us first present the activity of ATC in Ireland.

---

[1] This latter point refers to the fact that some could suggest a simulation of the activity in a laboratory. However, this would unfortunately eliminate external (and often unexpected) factors.

[2] Actually, in accordance with our ethic, we did clarify with controllers various points, such as their anonymity, the use of video-recording and the objectives and constraints of the study.

4.   Air-Traffic control in Ireland

Air Traffic Control is the service provided to airlines, and ensuring that aircraft fly safely from one place (departure) to another one (arrival). Closely related to the temporal organisation of flights (air-traffic management), ATC is restricted to actions on aircraft from their taking off to their parking on airports areas. It aims at avoiding collisions between planes and managing the daily traffic.

ATC is usually decomposed in three main activities, called tower, approach and en-route control (see fig. 1).

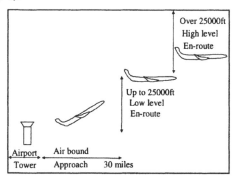

Fig. 1. From tower to en-route control. Case of departing aircraft.

Tower control deals with the landing and take-off, as well as the parking of planes. This means that in addition to the control of aircraft, the controllers are in charge of the safety of the ground area (runway and parking). Theoretically, the aircraft is handed over from tower to approach control once it is air-bound, or conversely when it is positioned over the runway (usually between 3 and 5 miles away from the airport, depending on the speed of the aircraft).

Approach control refers to the movements of planes approaching or leaving the airports (up to 30 miles distance). Approach control does not only ensure the separation of aircraft, but could rather be described as the integration of aircraft within existing flow, with high constraints, especially in the case of landing.

En-route refers to the control of traffic within the airspace, at a minimal distance of 30 miles from the airport. In Ireland, en-route is split between low level (between ground level and 25000ft) and high level (above 25000ft).

The controlled airspace is divided into volumes called sectors. Each sector is managed by two controllers (radar and planning controllers), accountable for all the traffic crossing their sector. Besides the control of aircraft already in a given sector, their task consists also of anticipating forthcoming aircraft as well as informing other sectors which will later accept the aircraft leaving their sector.

ATC is strongly based on co-ordination between sectors. Co-ordination occurs both between similar sectors (en-route), but also between different types of sectors (en-route and approach or approach and tower control).

The activity of controlling the air-traffic differs according to the geographic area (near an ocean versus in the middle of a continent) as well as the location of planes in the air space (low level, high level, close to the border with another sector, close to an airport).

In Ireland, approach and tower control centres are located all over the country, in every airport. Shannon is the only Irish en-route control centre, combining the three types of control described earlier on.

In spite of a quite small air space (i.e., quickly flown over), Shannon plays indeed a very important role among the European ATC centres, due to its location at the Western European Point. This leads it to deal with all the "oceanic" traffic, composed of flights both arriving from and going to the American continent. The controllers have to deal successively with two different types of activities: a- welcoming flights after their oceanic journey, making sure their separations are correct and integrating them safely into the European traffic, and b- organising the succession of planes, so that they all fly safely over the ocean (where no control is ensured). In addition, the Shannon controllers are also in charge of European traffic flying to, from, and within Ireland.

5.   Collaborative activities involved in ATC

The tasks of controllers are described extensively in official documents. The objectives of ATC are to "ensure the separation standards between aircraft". Despite an explicit description of each function, the air-traffic control is considered as a joint task, in the sense that close cooperation between the two controllers is required. The planning controller is described as the "radar's assistant". The control of aircraft is considered as a "combined team effort between a radar and a planning controller". The planning (or procedural) controller's task is described as "to assist the radar controller to the fullest extent in the control of aircraft operating within the area of responsibility of the sector".

These descriptions focus on the responsibility of the controllers, but without explicitly mentioning how these responsibilities (or missions) have to be honoured. Moreover, even in the official documents, the organisation anticipates the need for real-time adaptation, and specifies clearly that "nothing in these duties precludes a qualified controller from using his own discretion and initiative in any particular circumstance".

Working closely together, the controllers have to integrate various sources of information in order to co-ordinate their actions in the global mission consisting in transporting efficiently and safely human beings and goods from one point to another. For example, when an airport is facing unexpected problems (strike, weather conditions, accident), the controllers have to integrate the information in their strategy, in order to choose an appropriate solution.

In the remaining parts of this paper, we exclusively focus on the activities of controllers in charge of **en-route**, and more specifically, **high level sector**.

In the next section we consider the pair of controllers as an entity, and describe how it cooperates with external actors (inter-cooperation with pilots, other sectors, etc.). Then we describe the intra-cooperation within this entity.

5.1.   Inter-cooperation: Co-ordinating activities

In accordance with Suchman's descriptions [15], each working position can be identified as a co-ordination centre, which continuously co-ordinates its activity with other people's activity. Each sector appears as a node within a complex network, in charge of co-ordinating various actions and decisions.

The network is composed of people involved in the control of planes, while they are in a specific sector. These people are pilots, controllers from adjacent sectors, co-ordinator and data assistants.

The different agents in interaction with en-route controllers may either:

• be mutually dependent without sharing operative goals (e.g., cooperation between high level and approach, which are not directly related, but might affect one another),

• cooperate directly in order to achieve shared goals (e.g., cooperation between two adjacent sectors about a same plane, still in one sector, but soon to enter the next one).

Each aircraft requires co-ordination between sectors, at least when the aircraft is handed over. This co-ordination is usually implicit, as controllers use shared resources (as described in the next section) in order to anticipate the entrance of an aircraft in their sector. There is also explicit and indirect co-ordination, mediated by pilots, who are first told to change their radio frequency (by the sector they leave), and then are in charge of contacting the new sector.

Co-ordination between sectors is direct, explicit and verbal when a specific aircraft might cause problems. In this case the sector foreseeing a problem contacts the adjacent sector in order to agree jointly on a decision.

Controllers have the possibility to access multiple sources of information and knowledge such as observations, heuristics, diagram of the installation, indicators, and evolution of parameters. This gives them the opportunity to confront their observations and then combine the various sources of information. As stressed in [13], multiple points of view on a similar aspect are essential, especially in situations such as problem solving (conflict resolution in the case of ATC).

In this context, as we will see later in the paper, the two controllers in charge of a given sector need to share an updated representation of the situation.

5.2. Intra-cooperation: Working in a shared space

In addition to co-ordination between sectors, and with pilots, ATC is a highly collaborative activity, which requires two controllers to work jointly on a same airspace for the efficiency and safety of the traffic control.

In order to make decisions, controllers need to be aware of the current situation, in terms of the features of each aircraft (destination, speed, altitude) as well as the features of the traffic in the sector. It is interesting to observe that in this situation, the system is aimed to provide information, not only to one controller, but to both of them.

The physical workspace functions as a common information space [1] in which agents cooperate, communicate and exchange information in order to control the technical system. This shared workspace (called a suite) is not only an open space within which information is exchanged, but also a medium in the sense that each component of the environment functions as a resource in providing itself information [10].

The suite is composed of a radar screen, a strip progress board (full of strips[3]), an electronic data display (EDD), a printer, various keyboards and track balls (connected to the radar, the EDD and the radio), and notepads. Headphones enable controllers to communicate with pilots (radio) and other control centres (telephone).

If we focus on a specific suite, we notice that its design takes into account the collective dimension. Most of the information supports, even if individual, are accessible to both controllers. The controllers share visual as well as audio resources. Lastly, thanks to their proximal location, they can monitor one another's position and movements (figure 2a and b).

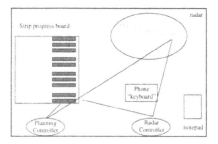 

Fig. 2a and b. Visibility of information in the shared workspace. Each controller has visual access to his/her colleague supports of information (sketch left, picture right).

The co-located agents have the opportunity to observe each other, distributing and acquiring explicitly as well as implicitly information, through verbal messages, visual observation of other agents and of informational supports such as the radar screen, the strips progress board, the radio or the notepad. Thus, the working position provides some cues and informs about the current and the planned actions and usually enables co-operators to infer their colleague's current intentions and strategies.

Yet, the availability of information is not sufficient to ensure dependability, it has to be validated. The system is designed in order to provide both controllers with information related to the same events, but presented under different formats. Actually, if you consider the radar screen and the strip, they both inform about aircraft, but some information are given to one controller, and inferred by the other. For example, the planning controller reads on the strips the direction of the aircraft, while the radar controller infers it from the image. Similarly, the expected times are written on the strips, but only inferred from watching the radar: here, the radar controller infers from the current location and speed where an aircraft will be in the next few minutes.

These redundant data contribute to the quality and diversity of the available information, allowing the team members to elaborate a rich and shared representation of the situation, to know the current actions and potentially to detect errors, thus contributing to the system dependability.

---

[3] The strips are paper documents presenting various features of flights (departure, destination, expected times, level, speed). Planning controllers organize them accordingly to these features in order to represent a dynamic image of the air-space.

5.3.   Multimodal / artefactual cooperation

Cooperation in shared workspaces is mediated both by human and technical supports. We do consider as "communication" every attempt made by one person to distribute or/and acquire information. This involves both the production and the reception of messages. Once we define communication as an exchange taking place between people, then most of cooperative acts (talking to someone, pointing at a device) work as communication [9]. Therefore, in this section we illustrate various modalities of communication observed in the case of ATC.

As stressed by [2], communication supports the confrontation of experiences, the creation and updating of knowledge, the elaboration and circulation of norms and the negotiation of working domains.

The communications observed within and without the control room are either verbal messages (spoken communication), written ones (paper documents, information on screen, location of strip), or "gesture-based" (other's position or actions within the space and/or on the environment).

Physical behaviour (movements, deictic), para-verbal signs (pitch, rhythm of verbal messages) and environmental resources are used to give information or to acquire others' attention).

So, the co-location enables controllers to use both audio and visual channel to transmit and acquire information. For example, the planning controller can take into account the direction of the look (part of the screen, strip board, other sector in the same room), the reactions to instructions (stress, humour, concentration) and the gestures (actions) and the artefacts acted upon.

The arrangement of the work space influences the communication pathways, which can be either:

• Explicit and face-to-face within the shared space: the radar controller informs the planning controller of a request just received from the previous sector (an aircraft is already put on its clearance level).

• Explicit and mediated between the shared space and other areas: due to the situation, all communications between controllers and pilots, or between sectors are mediated either by radio or by telephone. Thus, all instructions given to pilots, or information transmitted to other sectors are mediated, but direct and explicit. For example, "climb to level 370".

• Implicit within the shared space: the planning controller can hear the direct communication addressed by a radar controller to a pilot or to another sector. In this case, we talk of implicit communication, in the sense that it is not addressed, but available due to the public nature of information in the shared workplace. Similarly, when a planning controller updates a flight strip, he/she makes it public that he/she knows that a modification occurred.

The various modes of communication are complementary and enrich one another, usually enabling the success of communication through taking away ambiguity and supporting error detection.

6.   From communication to dependability

We saw in the previous section that the controllers, seated side by side, are able to access, use and act on shared resources. Their proximal location enables them to see what the other is doing (or watching), to hear what is said or done, to modify the other's environment, to perform the other's task, or to emphasise what should be done. Multimodal and direct communications are extensively used.

In this section, we draw a line between communication and dependability in showing that i) communication is basically used to inform people, ii) this information enables people to develop a mutual awareness and iii) this awareness is the main support for human reliability and finally global system dependability.

6.2. Communication informs

The basic and most obvious function of communication in the workplace is information. Controllers communicate in order to exchange information, both verbally and non verbally. The latter refers to the fact that sometimes actions on artefacts provide information about what the actor is doing and inferences about what he/she is up to. When a radar controller is pointing at the radar screen, even without a word, he/she is then not only attracting the other's attention, but also giving information about a specific aircraft, which has to be monitored.

The information can be direct or indirect. For example, when a radar controller informs a pilot about turbulence or weather conditions in a specific area, we can consider the information as given explicitly and directly. From the planning controller's point of view, the heard communication provides information about what the pilot knows, or what he/she is supposed to do. So, in this case, we consider that the communication, even though non-addressed to the planning controller, still contains information relevant to his/her own activity.

The communication can be described at various levels: information about the current situation (weather conditions), about the sharing of knowledge (pilots are aware of these conditions) and last of all about the impact these shared information have on the pilots' actions and preferences. Of course, this last level is based on the combination of the real-time information and controllers past experiences. Indeed, from past experiences, controllers expect certain information to have specific impact on pilots or on other controllers' decisions and actions (for an example, see [8]).

6.2. Information provides awareness

Cooperation between controllers requires them, first to share an understanding of the current situation, and second, to know that they do share this understanding. In other words, they need to be mutually aware of the situation (including both the process and their respective knowledge). Mutual awareness is a large concept, referring to individual knowledge of a shared situation. We talk of mutual awareness when people are not only aware of each other's activities, but also aware of their reciprocal awareness. The supports for awareness in ATC are audio (radio, telephone, paraverbal signs) and visual (observing gestures, actions, as well as data on the radar and strips).

Awareness can be related to the actors, the system, the availability and location of people and resources, the current objectives, actions, tasks, the context (normal vs. incidental), the situation and the current state of the process (e.g., in Shannon, West bound vs. East bound). It is enhanced by many means, from a shared training and experience to the access to real-time data. Let us illustrate this with a few examples, associating means with the awareness they enhance:

• *Awareness about who is talking*: supported by watching the communication keyboard (as a specific button lights up according to the caller, and indicates the sector), by listening to a conversation and identifying its topics, by observing what the speaker is watching, or where he/she is oriented to.

- *Awareness about the availability of the other*: supported by observing the physical posture, by listening if they are engaged in communications, by observing their actions.
- *Awareness about current actions*: supported by watching which planes are acted upon, by listening to comments from actors while they work, by listening to the instructions they give, by observing their physical behaviour.
- *Awareness about current situation*: supported by observing the position of strips, the sequences of aircraft on the radar screen, by listening to the pitch and tone of discussions.

In ATC, controllers have to monitor the others' performance and provide information related to their on-going activity. Each member of the team is then facing an extra activity on the top of the defined one (i.e., controlling the traffic). The real activity then consists in performing the task itself, acquiring information about related actions and functions and making one's task visible.

Let us now point out how these extra activities directly contribute to human reliability and therefore to system dependability.

6.3.   Awareness supports human reliability

As defined in [3], the dependability of a system is the trustworthiness of the service it provides to its users. Dependability must be addressed considering the impairments, which could prevent the system from providing its service, and the means allowing to cope with these impairments.

In ATC, we identified as safety-critical both technical components (radar, radio, data links) and human processes (perception, communication, information processing, actions). The main dependability attributes in the situation are the availability (both have to be ready to intervene efficiently) and the safety (collision avoidance).

In relation with the object of this paper (human factors), we now focus on the controllers' dimensions (dependability attributes and means, as defined above).

The organisation ensures the availability of controllers in planning roasters, enabling peripheral listening and the sharing of resources (both enabling people to quickly notice when their help is required). People enhance this in accepting this informal extension of their task (as described in [5]).

The main means used by the controllers are the *prevention* and the *tolerance* of faults. Part of these means are introduced by the organisation, while others are implemented spontaneously by the controllers.

Prevention refers to the anticipation and avoidance of faults (or of errors caused by humans). In Air-Traffic Control, the organisation provides redundant and overlapping information (radar and strips), as well as requires regular cross-checking (inter-sectors, and with pilots). Controllers at work regularly infer and assess the other's intentions, observe their actions (both verbal and non-verbal), anticipate their needs (contacting pilots, modifying plans) and regulate each other's activity (taking in charge each other's tasks). All these mechanisms are made possible by the availability of information (shared and accessible resources) and by the existence of an updated mutual awareness.

Tolerance refers to the fact that a service can be provided, a mission ensured despite the presence of faults in the system. This can be described in terms of error detection and recovery (or compensation) and is enabled by the existence of redundancies and loops of control in the system. In ATC, the organisation provides multiple sources of information, allows the real-time reorganisation of teams (opening new sectors, providing an extra controller at a specific position). Controllers detect errors because they are sharing information, they continuously monitor each other's actions (peripheral vision and listening) and they are mutually aware of what is going on (this enabling them to detect unexpected and doubtful decisions or instructions). Recovery is supported by the fact that both controllers can talk with pilots, and each controller can take in charge the other's activity, as well as modify the other's actions. This last point is facilitated by the organisational documents[4].

7.   Conclusion

This study, focusing on collaboration between air-traffic controllers, stresses the specificity of collaboration in a shared workspace, where people can share visual and audio information. It illustrates how actors involved in the work use these multimodal sources of information to collaborate. Communications provide information on current activities, supporting the elaboration and updating of shared knowledge and mutual awareness. These human activities enhance the dependability means introduced at the design stage by the organisation.

The field studies reported here, which benefited from the support of the controllers and their management, have been conducted over a period of 3 months. They enabled the collection of rich and diverse data, thanks to the fact that the theoretical background and the methodology have been previously implemented in other complex and critical domains. We used the study as an opportunity to validate and generalise the existence of collaborative mechanisms previously observed in these other situations (described extensively in [7]).

Based on the field studies reported in the present paper, a new collaboration just started with the Irish Aviation Authority. The objectives of the project are to integrate human factor issues in the design of new controllers working positions, and therefore benefit from the results presented in this paper.

In our current work we also address from another perspective, the understanding, assessment and generalisation of the basic cooperation mechanisms and of their relations with dependability. An initial comparison between our observations and studies in air-traffic control within Europe [11, 12] highlights differences at various levels (task distribution, available resources, conventions in work practices). Our objective is to investigate these differences and understand how, despite such diversity, controllers achieve similar objectives (ensuring regular and safe flow of aircraft). We especially intend to understand how, in different environments, very similar basic cooperative mechanisms emerge. The underlying hypothesis is that the identification of the basic and natural cooperative mechanisms, along with their conditions of emergence and their global impact on the system behaviour, provides the necessary clues to design socio-technical systems benefiting as much as possible from their positive impact on dependability.

---

[4] These documents, as we mentioned earlier say that "nothing [...] precludes a qualified controller from using his own discretion and initiative in any particular circumstance".

Acknowledgements

The present work was supported by the EU-TMR project COTCOS. The authors wish to thank the personnel from the Shannon control centre for their help and availability. The authors wish to associate Evelyne Morvan to this paper, thanking her for her support and collaboration.

References

1. Bannon, L. & Bodker, S. (1997). Constructing Common Information Spaces. In J.H.e. al (Ed.), *Fifth European Conference on Computer Supported Cooperative Work,* (pp.81-96). September 7-11, Lancaster, England: Kluwer Academic Publishers.
2. Lacoste, M. (1983). Des situations de parole aux activités interprétatives. *Psychologie Française, 28 (3-4)*, pp.231-238.
3. Laprie, J.-C. (1993). Dependability: From Concepts to Limits. In *Symposium on Safety of Computer Control Systems (SAFECOMP'93.)*, pp.157-168. Poznan, Poland: Springer-Verlag.
4. Leplat, J. (1990). Relations between task and activity: elements of elaborating a framework for error analysis. *Ergonomics, 33*, pp.1389-1402.
5. Morvan, E., Rognin, L., & Spérandio, J.-C. (1996). Reshaping Task Contents: Operators' Contribution to Systems Reliability. In *Eighth European Conference on Cognitive Ergonomics - ECCE'8*, pp.35-40. Granada, Spain, September 10-13.
6. Pougès, C., Jacquiau, G., Pavard, B., Gourbault, F., & Champion, M. (1994). Conception de collecticiels pour l'aide à la prise de décision en situation d'urgence : la nécessité d'une approche pluridisciplinaire et intégrée. In B. Pavard (Eds.), *Systèmes coopératifs : de la modélisation à la conception* (pp.351-375). Toulouse : Octarès.
7. Rognin, L. (1996) *Coopération humaine et sûreté de fonctionnement des systèmes complexes.* PhD Dissertation. Université Paul Sabatier, Toulouse, France.
8. Rognin, L. (1998). Working in Control Rooms. Cooperation and Communication in Shared Workspaces. In F. Darses & P. Zarate (Ed.), *Third International Conference on the Design of Cooperative Systems*, pp.99-109. May 26-29, Cannes, France.
9. Rognin, L. (1999). Handling complexity in control room. Modes and functions of communication in shared workspaces. In T.H. Benchekroun & P. Salembier (Eds.), *Cooperation and Complexity.* Springer-Verlag.
10. Rognin, L. & Bannon, L. (1997). Constructing Shared Workspaces through Interpersonal Communication. In E. Fallon, M. Hogan, L. Bannon, & J. McCarthy (Eds.), *ALLFN'97, Revisiting the Allocation of Functions Issue*, pp.227-239. Galway, Ireland, October 1-3.
11. Rognin, L., Salembier, P., & Zouinar, M. (1997). Latent Organisational Reliability. In E. Fallon, M. Hogan, L. Bannon, & J. McCarthy (Eds.), *ALLFN'97, Revisiting the Allocation of Functions Issue*, pp.63-71. Galway, Ireland, October 1-3.
12. Rognin, L., Salembier, P., & Zouinar, M. (1998). Cooperation, Interactions and Socio-Technical Reliability: the case of Air-Traffic Control. Comparing French and Irish settings. In *Proceedings of ECCE 9*, pp.19-24. August 24-26, Limerick, Ireland.
13. Schmidt, K. (1994). *Modes and Mechanisms of Interaction in Cooperative Work. Outline of a Conceptual Framework* No. Risø-R-666(EN)). Risø National Laboratory, Roskilde, Denmark.
14. Schmidt, K. & Bannon, L. (1992). Taking CSCW Seriously: Supporting Articulation Work. *Computer Supported Cooperative Work (CSCW). An International Journal, 1 (1-2)*, pp.7-40.
15. Suchman, L. (1993). Technologies of Accountability. Of lizard and aeroplanes. In G. Button (Ed.), *Technology in Working Order: Studies of Work, Interaction and Technology* (pp.113-126). London: Routledge.

A Method for Operator Error Detection Based on Plan Recognition*

Jin Mo and Yves Crouzet

LIS / LAAS-CNRS
7, avenue du Colonel Roche
31077 TOULOUSE Cedex 4, France
Yves.Crouzet@laas.fr

Abstract. In man-machine systems, operator errors represent an important source of system failures. Therefore, the human dimension must be taken into account in the development of these systems. The methods of prevention usually used, that consist in eliminating as much as possible the occurrence of operator error, have proved to be insufficient.
This paper describes a complementary approach which consists of tolerating the occurrence of operator error, while avoiding its undesirable consequences. We specifically focus on a method of operator error detection by a software man-machine interface that constitutes an important part of the implementation of operator error tolerance. This method is based on the recognition and the verification of plans executed by the operator during his interactions with the technical system. The main phases of operator error detection are examined. The proposed method of operator error detection is then applied to an air traffic control system, called CAUTRA.

1 Introduction

The procurement of dependability in complex systems (air traffic control, nuclear power plant, etc.) has resulted in a dramatic reduction of failures of these systems caused by faults likely to remain (or occur) in hardware or software components. Owing to this, the dependability of such critical systems become more sensitive to the errors of humans in charge of operating these systems (**operators**). Furthermore, technical progress has induced major changes in the content and methods of work carried out by operators. While the operator is increasingly relieved of manual tasks, he is required to carry out ever more complex mental tasks. This shift in the operator's tasks explains the many accidents in aviation, power plants and process controls due to human errors [13]. In [8], the author rated human errors as a primary cause of about 80 % of all major accidents in aviation, power production and process control.

---

* This work was partially supported by the French Research Center for Air Traffic Control.

M. Felici, K. Kanoun, A. Pasquini (Eds.): SAFECOMP'99, LNCS 1698, pp. 125–138, 1999
© Springer-Verlag Berlin Heidelberg 1999

For critical systems where human acts as an operator (**human-machine systems**), it is, therefore, important to consider impairments involving humans in addition to all hardware- or software-related faults. This observation has led to a significant amount of work to tackle the problem of lack of human reliability in the exploitation of complex systems. These studies aim primarily at reducing the occurrence of human errors using preventive methods by trying to eliminate the conditions likely to induce operator errors. An adequate task allocation between humans and the machine [12, 4], and the ergonomic design of human-machine interfaces considering the user criteria [2] are examples of potential methods for reducing human errors.

While the use of such preventive methods is an important factor to increase the dependability of a human-machine system, the complete elimination of operator errors is not realistic. A more realistic view consists in accepting the occurrence of human operator errors while preventing their consequences on system dependability (i.e., the **fault tolerance** approach). This approach comes as a complement to those aiming to reduce the occurrence of operator errors [11].

Most methods for tolerating operator errors are now based on human contribution used as a support for tolerance, either by the operator alone [10], or by the pool of operators [5]. The approach proposed in this paper aims to use the human-machine interface as a support to the tolerance of operator errors.

The remainder of the paper is composed of seven sections. Section 2 presents the conceptual framework. Section 3 describes the case study supporting the development of our approach. In Section 4, the basic hypotheses considered, and some general principles used for the detection of the operator errors, are presented. Section 5 is devoted to the formalism retained for the description of the operator tasks. Based on this formalism, Section 6 describes the method proposed for the detection of operator errors. Section 7 details the implementation of detection principles on the case study given in Section 3. Finally, Section 8 concludes the paper.

2 Conceptual Framework

To improve the dependability of human-machine systems with respect to operator errors, we propose that the human-machine interface be transformed into an error confinement barrier. To fulfill this objective, the interface must ensure early detection of the operator's erroneous actions before they reach the technical system (hence before being executed). Operator's errors not confined by the interface (i.e., non-detected errors) can propagate as errors into the technical system and thus result in failures of the overall human-machine system (Fig. 1).

To prevent an erroneous operator action from directly affecting the technical system, the actions of the operator are first analyzed at the interface by specific error processing mechanisms built into the interface. As is now common practice in dependable computer systems, the processing of operator errors can be decomposed into two steps: error detection and error recovery. The approach retained for the detection step constitutes the main theme of the paper and is addressed in depth in the remainder of the paper. Error recovery relies on cooperation between the operator and the interface. In our view, the purpose of the error processing features mechanisms included in the interface should not be to stop every erroneous action, but rather to assist the operator in his activity. It is considered that the operator does not

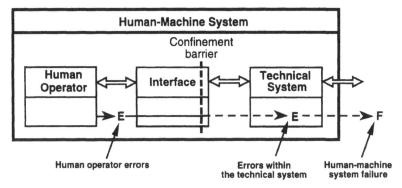

Fig. 1. Confinement of errors by the human-machine interface

deliberately execute erroneous actions on the system, and that he must remain fully in control of the system to be able to cope with any unexpected event.

3 Case Study

The case study considered for developing the proposed approach concerns the operational maintenance of a subset of the French Air Traffic Control System referred to as CAUTRA [9]. CAUTRA is a system that allows traffic controllers to control the air traffic flow. Therefore, a high level of availability and reliability is required. To reach these objectives, CAUTRA is based on a redundant system composed of three computers (DG1, DG2 and DG3) supporting several replicas of the two main CAUTRA applications: Flight Plan Processing (FPP), and Radar Data Processing (RDP). One of the replica acts as the operational version of the application (noted OPE), while the two other are used as backup versions (noted SEC and TST respectively). SEC is the secondary replica corresponding to a hot spare (automatic reconfiguration); TST provides a warm backup (manual reconfiguration).

The high level of availability required for CAUTRA (e.g., less than 5 minutes of unavailability per year for the RDP application) requires that the failure of one system component be processed on-line by the maintenance operators[1] (CAUTRA operators).

The work assigned to these operators consists in **tasks** that can be decomposed into a set of **actions**. An error made by a CAUTRA operator during his tasks may result in a degradation of the system availability.

4 Hypotheses and General Principles

The method proposed to detect operator errors draws on the knowledge of both the operator activity and the technical system. It is based on reasonableness checks of (i) the pertinence of the actions undertaken by the operator relative to the state of the

---

[1] These are the operators considered in this paper (not the air traffic controllers)

system, and (ii) the consistency of successive actions. The implementation of the operator error detection process relies on three main hypotheses:

Hypothesis 1: The operator's activity is described by **procedures**.

The fact that the activity of an operator can be expressed by the execution of predefined procedures (or **plans**), corresponding to a consistent series of elementary actions, allows for a check of consistency between the various actions required to be carried out.

Hypothesis 2: The detection process must not disturb the normal activity of the operator, except for the error recovery phases.

The implementation of the detection process could have been facilitated by asking the operator to explicitly specify each plan when it is started. Indeed, it would have then been sufficient to control that the actions carried out by the operator complied with the specified plan. For simple cases, where the operator's plans can be easily expressed, such a solution is technically feasible. However, this approach can hardly be implemented as, in practice, situations are more complex. Accordingly, we preferred not to alter the regular activity of the operator and opted for a solution in which the operator's plans are derived by the human-machine interface via the observation of the operator's actions (**commands**).

Hypothesis 3: The operator can suspend execution of an initiated procedure to carry out a more urgent one, following the occurrence of some specific event in the technical system.

Hence, the detection process must take into account the fact that the operator can start a new plan before the on-going one is completed.

The application of this strategy for detecting an operator's error encompassing (i) plan recognition and (ii) plan execution check, requires the use of a formalism to precisely express the operator's plans. The next section describes the formalism used to represent plans.

5   Representation of Operator Plans

Among the formalisms suitable for representing the operator plans, such as SADT and Petri nets [1], blocks of knowledge [3], and UAN (User Action Notation) [7], the Method for Analytical Description of tasks (MAD) [14] matches best our representation needs. The formalism used is based on an adaptation of the MAD formalism as described in the next subsection.

5.1 Plan Structure

The MAD formalism utilizes a graphical representation to describe a plan. A plan is regarded as a hierarchical tree in which each entity (the plan itself and the constituting actions) is identified by a name and a number. Basic entities are actions (commands) carried out by the operator at the interface; they constitute **elementary actions**. A set of elementary actions can be grouped together, at an upper hierarchical level, as a **composed action** that corresponds to a structured sequence of less complex actions, called **sub-actions**. Recursively, a composed action can be defined from composed actions of a lower level. Links between entities of a considered level and the composed entity of the upper level are defined by constructors indicating how entities of the considered level are arranged to form the composed entity.

Fig. 2 illustrates the use of the MAD formalism for the description of a plan made up of 8 elementary actions distributed among three hierarchical levels.

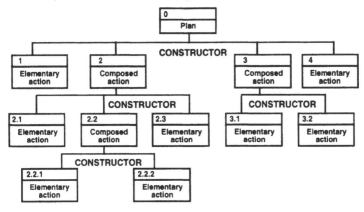

Fig. 2. Hierarchical description of the structure of a plan

To describe the operator plans, we have selected the following three types of constructors:

- **SEQ**: sub-actions (elementary or composed actions) listed under the constructor must be executed sequentially from left to right;
- **PAR**: all sub-actions have to be executed, but the order of execution is not predetermined;
- **ALT**: only one of the sub-actions must be executed; therefore, it indicates that a plan or a composed action can be executed according to several alternatives.

To allow enhanced flexibility in the definition of plans, we have also considered three attributes supplementing these constructors so as to be able to account for some specific features, in particular when dealing with composed actions: contextual actions, interruptible actions (i.e., actions that can be interrupted), and optional actions. These attributes are:

- **"Contextual"** (CONT): This attribute specifies that the execution of the action (composed or elementary) depends on a condition (predicate) relating to the context (status) of the technical system. The action is to be executed if the predicate is true and not executed in the opposite case.
- **"Interruptible"** (INT): Although the execution of a composed action has already started, it can be interrupted by another action linked to the same constructor. Such an attribute applies only to composed actions described by an ALT or PAR constructor. The execution of a composed action without this attribute can not be interrupted by another action linked to the same constructor.
- **"Optional"** (OPT): All actions (composed or elementary) must not necessarily be executed. This attribute accounts for the fact that although the action is explicitly included in the plan, it is valid to skip it however.

To adequately describe a plan, the necessary **conditions** for executing it and, as well as the actions that form it, have to be specified. For a plan, these conditions are characterized both by **pre-conditions** and **post-conditions**. The former specify the necessary conditions for the plan to be launched; if they are not fulfilled, the plan cannot be initiated. Post-conditions of a plan express the state of the technical system reached at the end of the plan execution. As in the case of a plan, an operator action is also characterized by pre-conditions. These conditions must be met to allow for the action to be executed.

Given below is the formalism used to describe one of the procedures related to the case study considered: it deals with the procedure for restarting the operational version (OPE) of the FPP application on the (warm) backup computer (TST). For sake of clarity, the procedure shown in Fig. 3 is a simplified version of the actual procedure.

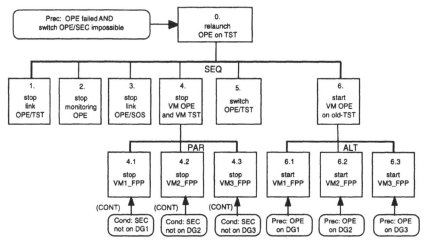

Legend: Prec   → pre-conditions associated with an action or a plan
           Cond   → condition associated with an action with the attribute "Contextual execution"
           VM   → Virtual Machine
           OPE   → Operational version of the FPP application
           SEC   → Secondary replica of the FPP application (hot back-up)
           TST   → Test version of the FPP application (warm back-up)
           SOS   → Secondary replica of the RDP application (hot back-up)

Fig. 3. Example of representation of a reconfiguration procedure

5.2 Overall Structure of a Set of Plans

Fig. 4 shows an example of the overall structure of a set of plans; the example is limited to two plans.

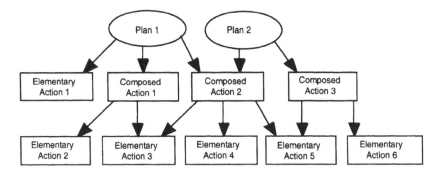

Fig. 4. Overall structure of a set of plans

The error detection process relies on this structure to try to relate the elementary action undertaken by the operator and one of the known plans. The structure depicted in Fig. 4 shows that it is not always easy to link an elementary action to a specific plan, as a single action can belong to several plans. Indeed, if the operator undertakes an action that belongs to the set of elementary actions {3, 4, 5}, it will not be possible to identify unambiguously the plan these actions actually belong to. Thus, in the following, these actions will be called **conflicting** actions with respect to the recognition of the plans. Furthermore, from hypothesis 2, we exclude the (simple) case where the operator is explicitly asked to specify the intended plan. As a result, the identification of this plan must be carried out by the detection process.

5.3 States of Plans

In addition to the structural description introduced in the previous subsection, it is also necessary to define the state of a plan to adequately describe its dynamic evolution. Four states have been defined for a plan (Fig. 5): inactive, active, inactive in conflict and active in conflict.

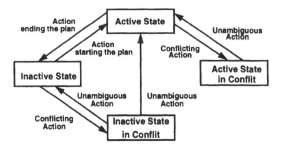

Fig. 5. Possible states for a plan

The two main states of a plan are inactive and active. A plan remains inactive as long as its execution has not been initiated; it enters the active state when the operator undertakes an action that can start its execution, and it becomes inactive again when an operator's action completes it.

It is worth pointing out again that according to the hypothesis 3, the operator may execute several plans in parallel; therefore, several plans can be active at the same time. Thus, plan recognition alone cannot always link the action being executed to a single plan. Hence, two additional "**conflict**" states have been considered. The plan enters a conflicting (inactive or active) state whenever the operator action is conflicting (see Sect. 5.2). The plan shifts from a conflict state to a no conflict state when the operator attempts an action that makes it possible to lift the ambiguity (unambiguous action). When in the inactive conflict state, the plan enters the active state if the non ambiguous action allows the execution of the plan to proceed, otherwise it returns to the inactive state.

6   Detection of Operator Errors

Before describing the error detection process, we briefly define first the related terminology we will use hereafter.

An **attempted** action (command being applied on the interface) is always an elementary action. Such an action is said to belong to a plan if it is a terminal node of the tree that describes the plan.

An action will be considered as an **allowed** action, if it allows a plan to be started or continued, on the basis of (i) the plan structure that defines the scheduling of the action and of (ii) the related attributes. Otherwise, the action is considered as **unexpected**.

An action will be termed as **valid**, if it is allowed and if, furthermore, its precondition (possibly those of the plan itself in the case when the action is the first action being executed for a plan) are verified. Otherwise the action will be termed as **erroneous**.

The detection process proposed is based on the gradual recognition of the plan capable of justifying the attempted action (i.e., the operator command being applied at the interface). Two main features characterize the detection process:

1. Checking that the attempted action is a valid (non erroneous) action to either start or continue at least one plan.
2. Managing the conflicts between plans if more than one plan contain the attempted action.

6.1   Checking for the Validity of an Action

After a command has been applied (attempted action), the checking process will first determine those plans including this action. For each plan including the attempted action, the latter has to be combined with both the current state of the technical system and the preceding operator actions to identify the plan(s) for which this action is valid. In the sequel, we describe the algorithm used to check the validity of an attempted action.

6.1.1   Algorithm for Checking the Validity of an Action. Fig. 6 summarizes the principle of validity checking. When an action is undertaken by the operator, the process carried out by the human-machine interface is characterized by two main steps:

1. For each plan containing the attempted action, check whether the action allows the plan to be started or continued.
2. Assess the pre-conditions of the action (as well as the pre-conditions of the plan for an inactive plan).

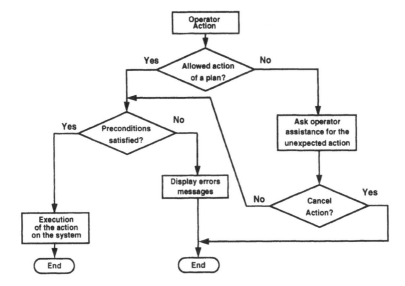

Fig. 6. Principle for Checking the Validity of an Action

Identification of an action not allowed results in a message being sent to the operator to warn him of such an event. Again, the operator should be given the possibility of maintaining the action under exceptional circumstances. The error detection/recovery phase that follows identification of an unexpected action makes it possible to cope with the operator's execution errors. If the operator confirms the action despite the warning, it is assumed that he is aware of the consequence of his action provided this action does not impair the dependability of the system.

After an operator action has been identified as allowed, the algorithm checks its consistency with respect to the status of the technical system. To ensure that, some of the operator's actions are associated with conditions regarding the status of the system that are aimed at preventing their execution when the latter conditions are not met. These conditions are represented by pre-conditions specific to an action or to the launch of the plan. Actual execution of an action for which pre-conditions would not be fulfilled may seriously jeopardize the safety or availability of the system.

An action is executed by the interface on the technical system only if it verifies all the pre-conditions (of the action and possibly of the plan). This restriction remains valid if the operator confirms the action despite the warning message received from the interface.

We will now present the principle used for determining the list of allowed actions for a plan and illustrate it with an example.

6.1.2   Determination of the List of Allowed Actions. Determination of allowed actions is carried out by exploring the hierarchy of the plan starting from the top, i.e., starting from the actions of the highest level. First, the allowed actions are determined among the set of actions of the highest level. These actions depend on (i) the constructor connecting them to the plan, (ii) their organization within the plan, and (iii) the associated attributes. Actions identified as allowed are included in the allowed actions list of the highest level. The same processing is repeated for each composed action in this list; thus, for each allowed composed action, we determine among the sub-actions of the next lower level, those actions that are allowed to start or to continue it. The process is repeated until all allowed elementary actions are identified. Thus, each allowed composed action of the plan has a list of its allowed sub-actions, and all elementary actions included in these lists of allowed actions constitute the final set of allowed actions for the plan. Fig. 7 examplifies the principle of determination of allowed actions; for simplicity, we only consider actions without attributes.

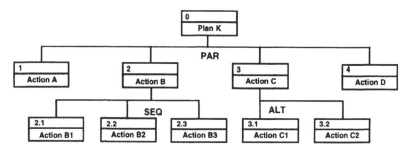

Fig. 7. Example of determination of allowed actions

Let us assume that plan K is in an inactive state. In other words, no action belonging to the plan has been executed. According to the definition of the PAR constructor, the four actions of the highest level (A, B, C, D) belong to the list of allowed actions. Among these, actions B and C are composed actions. To start action B, the only allowed sub-action is B1 (due to the SEQ constructor). However, for the composed action C defined by the ALT constructor, the allowed sub-actions are actions C1 and C2. In brief, actions A, B1, C1, C2 and D are the allowed elementary actions to begin plan K.

As an example, let us assume now that the operator executes action C1. The interface has thus to determine the new set of allowed actions. Among the actions of the highest level, only actions A, B and D are allowed, as the execution of the composed action C is already completed. Consequently, action B is the only allowed composed action. Because the only allowed sub-action of action B is B1, the new list of allowed actions for plan K contains now actions A, B1 and D.

6.2 Handling of Conflicts between Plans

When an attempted action can either activate or continue more than one plan, a conflict arises between plans to identify the one actually executed by the operator. Nevertheless, despite the conflict, the attempted action is deemed correct, and therefore, immediately executed by the human-machine interface.

Conflict resolution consists in identifying the suitable plan by using additional information provided by the next actions of the operator. To do that, we carry out a virtual evaluation rather than real evaluation of allowed actions for conflicting plans. Thus, future allowed actions can be determined for each conflicting plan. As long as the following action of the operator does not enable the ambiguity to be lifted, because it is also allowed for the conflicting plans (e.g., a single composed action pertaining to several plans), the allowed actions of the conflicting plans are further virtually evaluated. When the operator executes an action allowed in one conflicting plan only, the conflict is solved.

7 Implementation of a Prototype Interface

A prototype interface of CAUTRA, integrating the principle presented in this paper, has been developed to validate the proposed approach for operator error detection. The prototype utilizes a simulation model of CAUTRA and illustrates the proposed approach for the tasks of the CAUTRA on-line maintenance operator.

7.1 CAUTRA Simulation Model

To be able to carry out experiments in the lab, we first developed a simulation model of CAUTRA using the Statecharts formalism [6].

System components are characterized by a set of five states: Off, Initialization, Nominal operational mode, Degraded operational mode, Failed. Transitions between the different states are generated either by the system's internal events or by the operator's commands undertaken on the human-machine interface (labels beginning with c_). By way of example, Fig. 8 shows the Statechart modeling the behavior of a CAUTRA computer.

7.2 Description of the Tasks of the CAUTRA Operator

Among the CAUTRA operator tasks, we mainly focused on those designed to recover from CAUTRA component failures. Indeed, these are the main tasks allocated to the CAUTRA maintenance operators. Furthermore, their completion is much more critical. Additionally, they are particularly interesting for the first application of our error detection method. Indeed, the number of actions being limited, these tasks are relatively simple: they rely on procedures and are, therefore, easy to be modelled under the form of a plan structure. Finally, they make use of the human-machine interface as the main medium for intervention and action to maintain and restore the

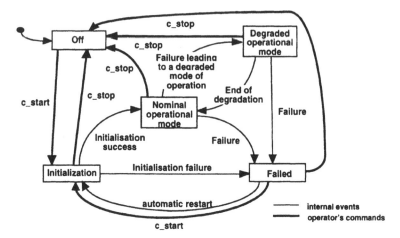

Fig. 8. Model of a computer

system. Based on the formalism presented in Section 5, we modeled 20 on-line maintenance procedures.

To implement the plan recognition process independently of the operator tasks, the algorithmic part of this process has been separated from the description of the operator plans. The latter are thus described as a data structure implemented in C language. The structure selected is hierarchical and recursive, thereby allowing for the plans and constituting actions to be easily defined. Only sub-actions of the highest level have been defined in the structure of a plan or of a composed action. Actions of the lower level are coded as child structures by using the same structures.

Fig. 9 shows how a plan is defined as a C language structure. On this figure, we have included only the main elements used to describe a plan.

Operator actions are described using a similar structure. As for a plan, the structure is recursive, thereby allowing for a composed action to define only sub-actions of the highest level.

```
struct plan {
  char *name;                       /* name of the plan */
  int state;                        /* state of the plan */
  int type;                         /* type of constructor */
  struct action girls[MAX];         /* actions of the highest
                                       level */
  struct action *act_ allow[MAX];   /* allowed actions list */
  int fac[MAX];                     /* indication of optional
                                       actions */
  struct cond *prec;                /* pre-conditions */
} ;
```

Fig. 9. Definition of a plan

8 Conclusions

In this paper, we have described an approach aimed at using a human-machine interface as a support to the tolerance of operator errors. In particular, the means allowing error detection have been detailed. The proposed solution focuses on procedural activities for which the description of the operator's activity can rely on plans corresponding to a consistent set of elementary actions. The considered detection method is based on the recognition and verification of the plans executed by the operator. This has led us to propose a hierarchical description of the operator's plans.

The proposed detection method has been applied to a real case: the on-line maintenance of the air traffic control system CAUTRA. So as to complement our theoretical study, we drew up a prototype interface to concretize the proposed detection mechanism. To make experimentations possible on this prototype interface, we developed a behavioral model of CAUTRA using Statecharts formalism. So, the feasibility and usefulness of the proposed error detection technique could be exemplified.

The approach must now be assessed further for situations close to real ones. To do so, we plan to proceed with the development of the prototype by including all the procedures of the CAUTRA operator. Then, broader experiments will become feasible so as, on the one hand, to assess the proportion of detected errors, and on the other, to assess the disturbance to the operator provoked by false alarms.

Acknowledgements

The authors would like to thank Jean Arlat and Corinne Mazet for their helpful suggestions during drafting.

References

1. M. Abed, J.M. Bernard and J.-C. Angué, "Task Analysis and Modelization by using SADT and PETRI Network", Proc. *10th European Annual Conference on Human Decision Making and Manual Control*, Liège, Belgium, 1991.
2. J.M.C. Bastien and D.L. Scapin, "Ergonomic Criteria for the Evaluation of Human-Computer Interfaces", INRIA, Report 156, 1993.
3. G. Boy, "The Block Representation in Knowledge Acquisition for Computer Integrated Documentation", Proc. *4th AIAA-sponsored knowledge acquisition integrated documentation for knowledge-based systems workshop*, Banff, Canada, 1989.
4. Y.Y. Chu and W.B. Rouse, "Adaptive Allocation of Decision Making Responsibility between Human and Computer in Multitask Situations", *IEEE Transactions on Systems, Man, and Cybernetics*, vol. 9, no. 12, pp. 769-778, 1979.
5. G. De Terssac and C. Chabaud, "Modeling and Reliability in Human-Machine Systems", Toulouse-Mirail University, France, Report 11.226/CP, 1988 (in French).
6. D. Harel, "STATEMATE: A Working Environment for the Development of Complex Reactive Systems", *IEEE Trans. on Software Engineering*, vol. 16, no. 4, pp. 403-414, 1990.

7. H.R. Hartson, A.C. Siochi and D. Hix, "The UAN : A User-oriented Representation for Direct Manipulation Interface Design", *ACM Transactions on Information Systems*, vol. 8, no. 3, pp. 181-203, 1990.

8. E. Hollnagel, "Human Reliability Analysis: Context and Control", In B.R. Gaines & A. Monk (Eds.), Computers and People Series, London: Academic Press, 1993.

9. K. Kanoun, M. Borrel, T. Morteveille and A. Peytavin, "Modeling the Dependability of CAUTRA, a Subset of the French Air Traffic Control System", in *26th IEEE Int. Symp. Fault-Tolerant Computing, (Sendai, Japan)*, pp. 106-115, 1996.

10. J. Leplat, "Error Analysis, Instrument and Object of Task Analysis", *Ergonomics*, vol. 32, no. 7, pp. 813-822, 1989.

11. C. Mazet and H. Guillermain, "Error Tolerance and Man-Machine Cooperation", Proc. *3rd International Conference on Probalistic Safety Assessment and Management (ESREL'96-PSAM-III)*, Crete, Greece, pp. 406-411, 1996.

12. C.A. Rieger and J.S. Greenstein, "The Allocation of Tasks between the Human and Computer in Automated Systems", Proc. *IEEE 1982 International Conference on Cybernetics and Society*, New York, pp. 204-208, 1982.

13. W.B. Rouse and N.M. Morris, "Conceptual Design of a Human Error Tolerant Interface for Complex Engineering Systems", *Automatica*, vol. 23, no. 2, pp. 231-235, 1987.

14. D.L. Scapin and C. Pierret-Golbreich, "Toward a Method for Task Description: MAD", Work with Display Units 89 (L. Berlinguet et D. Berthelette, Eds.), Elsevier, Amsterdam, pp. 371-380, 1990.

Hierarchically Performed Hazard Origin and Propagation Studies

Yiannis Papadopoulos and John A. McDermid

Department of Computer Science, University of York, YO10 5DD, UK
{yiannis, jam}@cs.york.ac.uk

Abstract. This paper introduces a new method for safety analysis called *HiP-HOPS (Hierarchically Performed Hazard Origin and Propagation Studies)*. HiP-HOPS originates from a number of classical techniques such as Functional Failure Analysis, Failure Mode and Effects Analysis and Fault Tree Analysis. However, it extends, automates and integrates these techniques in order to address some of the problems currently encountered in complex safety assessments. The method enables integrated assessment of a complex system from the functional level through to the low level of component failure modes. It mechanises and simplifies a large part of the analysis, the development of fault trees, and can guarantee the consistency of results. HiP-HOPS is currently supported by a tool called the Safety Argument Manager (SAM). In this paper we introduce the method and we show how it has helped us analyse and improve the safety of a distributed brake-by-wire system for cars.

1. Introduction

Classical safety analysis techniques such as Functional Failure Analysis (FFA) [1], Hazard and Operability Studies (HAZOP) [2], Failure Mode and Effects Analysis (FMEA) [3] and Fault Tree Analysis (FTA) [4] have demonstrated their value in a variety of contexts over the years, and they are still widely practised by safety engineers. These safety studies still form the spinal element of the safety case, and provide a frame for the interpretation of the results from other, more localised, verification activities such as testing and the application of formal methods. As the complexity of modern programmable electronic systems increases, however, the application of classical techniques is becoming increasingly more problematic.

The first problem that can be observed is inconsistencies in the results from the various safety studies of the system which mainly arise from the selective and fragmented use of different methods at different stages of the design lifecycle. Classical techniques assume different design representations which reflect different levels of abstraction in the system design. While, for example, FFA requires only abstract functional descriptions, HAZOP and FMEA require architectural designs of increasing detail and complexity. The problem is that these different design representations are often inconsistent. One of the causes of inconsistency is that different notations are employed at different stages of the lifecycle. Perhaps more importantly, abstract designs are not always kept updated, and they don't reflect changes made in lower level designs. Inevitably, the analyses that are based on

M. Felici, K. Kanoun, A. Pasquini (Eds.): SAFECOMP'99, LNCS 1698, pp. 139–152, 1999
© Springer-Verlag Berlin Heidelberg 1999

inconsistent designs become themselves inconsistent. One significant conclusion that in our view can be drawn from this discussion is that if we wish to *address the problem of inconsistencies in the analyses then we must find ways to guarantee the consistency of the design as this evolves in the course of the lifecycle.*

A second problem in classical safety analysis is the difficulty in relating the results of the various safety studies between them and back to the high-level functional failure analysis. The problem here lies in the difficulty that analysts encounter in drawing a coherent and complete picture of how low level component failures contribute to hazardous system malfunctions. Although fault trees are built for this purpose, the traditional process of constructing these fault trees relies almost exclusively on expert knowledge, and lacks a systematic or structured algorithm which the analyst can apply on a system model in order to derive the tree. In complex systems this process becomes tedious, time consuming and error prone, and the resultant fault trees are large, but more importantly, difficult to interpret and verify.

In consequence, safety analyses are in practice not only voluminous but also fragmented and inconsistent. Such analyses, however, are difficult to interpret and do not always provide a useful resource in the design of the system. But, is it not precisely the aim of safety analysis to improve the system design? And *does the fragmentation of classical techniques not compromise this aim?* To address this and some of the other questions that we have raised in this section, we propose a new method for safety analysis which, we believe, improves classical safety analysis techniques.

The new method is called *Hierarchically Performed Hazard Origin and Propagation Studies (HiP-HOPS).* The method enables the integrated assessment of a hierarchically described complex system from the functional level through to the low level of component failure modes. To ensure the transferability of the practical experience that classical analyses incorporate, we have founded the new method on a number of well-established techniques such as FFA, FMEA and FTA. At the same time we have *modifed, automated* and *integrated* these techniques to overcome some of the difficulties that we have already discussed. The method *mechanises* and *simplifies* a large and traditionally problematic part of the analysis, the development of fault trees. It also integrates classical hardware safety analysis with software hazard analysis and guarantees the consistency of the results from the assessment. HiP-HOPS draws from previous work on new safety assessment techniques, more specifically, the work on the Failure Propagation and Transformation Notation [5] and a technique called Failure Logic Analysis for System Hierarchies [6].

In this paper we introduce the method and demonstrate its application on a distributed programmable electronic braking system for cars. This system is a research prototype that has been developed in the context of a European Commission funded project called Time Triggered Architectures (TTA-ESPRIT Project 23396). The system provides a design concept for future brake by wire applications in the automotive industry. It is implemented over a network of six programmable electronic nodes which communicate using TTP/C [7], a Time Triggered communication Protocol. Two of these nodes, the pedal nodes, are physically located near the braking pedal. Their function is to continuously read and broadcast the braking demand on two replicated busses. On the receiving end of communication, there are four wheel nodes which calculate and apply the final braking pressure on the four wheels of the car.

2. HiP-HOPS

In HiP-HOPS all safety studies are performed on a consistent hierarchical model of the system. The method places constraints on the notations used, and introduces some additional notation for describing levels of design. The notation allows complex systems to be modelled as system hierarchies (Fig. 1). At each level of the system hierarchy, flow diagrams are used to describe the operation of the system and its subsystems. At plant level such flow diagrams can be derived, for example, from engineering schematics or piping and instrumentation diagrams. At lower levels, data flow diagrams (e.g. MASCOT diagrams) can be used to describe the design of software and hardware components.

2.1 Functional Failure Analysis

The safety analysis process starts with exploratory functional failure analysis (FFA) of a conceptual design of the system. At this stage an abstract functional model of the system is used in order to identify *single and plausible combinations of multiple functional* failures and assess their effects and criticality. The functional model is constructed as a functional block diagram which identifies the system functions and their dependencies in terms of material and energy flows or data.

Each function in this model is systematically examined for potential failure modes is a number of failure classes which include the loss of function, the unintended delivery of function and malfunctions such as early or late deployment. For each such failure the analyst has to determine the effects, criticality and the potential for detection and recovery. Once we have identified all the single functional failures, we can then identify and list plausible combinations of multiple failures and, in a similar way, examine the effects and criticality of such failures.

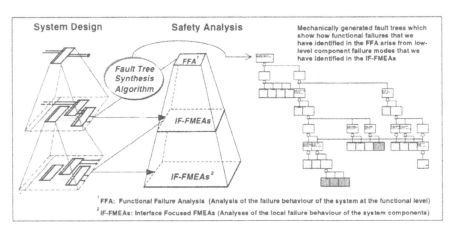

Fig. 1. Overview of Design and Safety Analysis in HiP-HOPS

The first objective of this study is to identify critical functional failures of the system, in other words functional losses or malfunctions which lead to severe or catastrophic effects. The second objective is to identify, and remove early any *avoidable* dependencies between different functions that can lead to common mode failures, in other words conditions where more that than one function fail as a result of a single initiating event. The results of the study are recorded in a tabular form and provide early in the design process a comprehensive picture of the ways that the system can fail.

2.2 Analysis of the failure behaviour of components

As the design decomposition and the refinement of the hierarchical model proceed, we identify basic hardware and software components. The failure behaviour of these components is analysed using an extension of FMEA.

Traditional FMEA examines the *origins* of failure within the component itself. In other words, it examines the failure behaviour of the component considering only internal malfunctions (possibly caused by the environment). The function of a component in the failure domain, however, is much more complicated. A component does not only generate failure events. It can also detect (or not) and respond (or not) to failure events generated by other components which interface to the component inputs.

A component, for example, may detect disturbances of its input parameters, e.g. the absence of a power signal, or a value that is out of range. In turn, the component can *mitigate* the propagation of such failure events. It may, for example, replace a detected invalid input value with a correct default value. It can also fail to detect input failures and *propagate* these failures to other components. Finally it may *transform* a certain input failure event, to a different type of output failure. An example of this is a component which detects a timing failure to one of its inputs and, in response, fails silent (e.g. the TTP/C protocol communication controller [9]).

To capture these additional aspects of the behaviour of the component, we propose an extension of FMEA, called IF-FMEA (*Interface Focused-FMEA*). IF-FMEA is a tabular technique. It can be used in a similar way to traditional FMEA in order to examine component failure modes caused by internal malfunctions. Beyond that however, the method provides a systematic way to examine the *detection, mitigation and propagation* of failure across the component *input* and *output interfaces*.

The method is applied to each component and generates a failure model (represented as a table) for the component under examination. An IF-FMEA table provides a list of component failures modes as they can be observed at the component outputs. For each such failure the analysis determines the causes as a logical combination of un-handled internal malfunctions and un-handled deviations of the component inputs. Beyond hardware safety analysis, IF-FMEA can also be used for software hazard analysis. An example of a software IF-FMEA is given in Table 1. The table presents the IF-FMEA of the pedal task which is located on the pedal node of the brake by wire system.

Table 1. IF-FMEA of PEDAL task

Output Failure Mode	Description of output failure	Input Deviation Logic	Component Malfunction Logic	λ (f/h)
O-PEDAL1. Driver_msg	Omission of PEDAL1 output (braking demand). It can be caused by task malfunction or out of range failures of both pedal sensors	(V>max-PS1.value | V<min-PS1.value) & (V>max-PS2.value | V<min-PS2.value)	PEDAL1.task_ malfunction	1.00E-07
Vs_0- PEDAL1. Driver_msg	PEDAL1 output (braking demand) stuck at 0. It can be caused by memory stuck at 0 failures, or by stuck at minimum failures of both pedal sensors.	Vs_min-PS1.value & Vs_min-PS2.value	PEDAL1.memory_ stuck_at_0	2.00E-07

The task reads the braking demand provided by two pedal sensors, detects invalid (out of range) measurements and provides as output the average of the valid sensor readings. The output of the pedal task is the driver message that is send over the bus to the wheel nodes. Table 1 examines two potentially hazardous failure modes of this output.

The first such failure is an omission of the driver message. The analysis shows that this event can arise from a task malfunction with a probability of 10^{-7}f/h. Such a malfunction can be caused, for example, by a failure of the processor or the operating system. The output event can also be caused by deviations of the inputs that the task receives from the pedal sensors. Indeed, if both sensor readings are out of the valid range of measurement, the task is unable to produce the driver message.

The second hazardous output failure examined in the table is a condition where *the value of the driver message is stuck at zero* and does not represent the actual pedal stretch. This condition can be caused by stuck at zero failures of the memory elements used by the task with a probability of 2×10^{-7}f/h. In addition, the analysis shows that the condition will also occur if both sensor inputs are stuck at the minimum of the normal measurement range

Clearly, an IF-FMEA of a component shows how the component reacts to failures generated by other components. In addition, it determines the failure modes that the component itself generates or propagates. Such a table, we believe, can be usefully employed by the designer of the system in order to improve the failure detection and mitigation mechanisms of the component under examination and other components in its periphery.

2.3 An Algorithm for the Mechanical Synthesis of Fault Trees

IF-FMEA tables contain expressions which describe the causes of output failures as logical combinations of internal component malfunctions and deviations of the component inputs. The formal grammar of these expressions is given in Figure 2.

The grammar recognises parenthesised logical expressions which contain conjunction (&) and disjunction (|) operators and other tokens representing *component malfunctions* or *input deviations*. Such tokens are recognised as *component malfunctions*, unless if they contain a hyphen (-) in which case they are recognised as *input deviations*. The part preceding the hyphen is interpreted as the *failure class* ('O' for omission, 'C' for commission, 'Vs_0' for value stuck at zero etc.) while the remaining part of the string is interpreted as the name of the component input.

Figure 2 shows the parse tree generated when, for example, the expression "(fmode.A | fmode.B)&O-power" is processed using the foregoing grammar. By a depth first traversal of the parse tree we can generate, and evaluate (using the failure rates given in the IF-FMEA table) an equivalent fault tree for this expression. In HiP-HOPS this mechanism is used as part of an algorithm for the automatic synthesis of fault trees.

Fault trees for hazardous functional failures are constructed by traversing the hierarchical design of the system moving backwards from the final elements of the design (actuators) towards the system inputs (sensors). In the course of this process, we parse the expressions contained in the IF-FMEAs of the components that we encounter during the traversal, and progressively substitute the input deviations received by each component with the corresponding output failures propagated by other components.

We have recently completed the development of a tool which implements the proposed fault tree synthesis algorithm (see Figure 3). This tool is an extension of the Safety Argument Manager (SAM) [8] tool that has been developed by the University of York to support the production of safety cases. SAM allows the user to conduct a wide range of classical safety analysis, and relate the results from individual studies to an overall safety argument about the system. Beyond facilitating classical safety analyses, SAM now also allows the development of hierarchical models, component safety analysis using IF-FMEA, and the mechanical synthesis of fault trees.

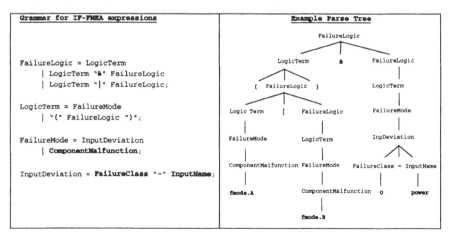

Fig. 2. Formal grammar for IF-FMEA expressions and example parse tree

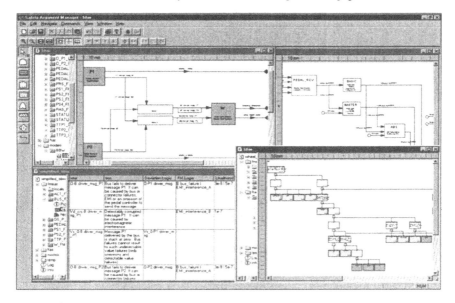

Fig. 3. Tool support for HiP-HOPS within SAM

The fault trees which are automatically constructed and displayed by the tool show how functional failures at the outputs of the system or its sub-systems arise as a result of lower level functional failures and component malfunctions. These fault trees link in a consistent manner the results from the functional failure analysis to low-level IF-FMEAs and the design representation. SAM allows direct navigation between nodes of the fault tree and system models so that we can always trace easily the origins of failure back to the system design. Branches of the fault tree that contribute more to the overall failure probability point out directly areas where the design can be improved. Such design iterations do not pose problems to the mechanical synthesis of fault trees since a new fault tree can be automatically constructed after each design iteration.

3. Case Study

We have used HiP-HOPS and SAM to assess a prototypical distributed brake-by-wire (BBW) system for cars. Our analysis of this system starts at the functional level, and proceeds all the way down the design hierarchy to examine the failure behaviour of low-level hardware components (such as sensors, actuators, processors, busses and communication controllers) and software components (such as the tasks running on the nodes of the distributed architecture). A detailed discussion of the results from this case study is clearly out of the scope of this paper. Drawing from these results however, we will attempt to illustrate how the proposed method can help to address problems of classical techniques, improve the system design and achieve consistent and meaningful safety cases.

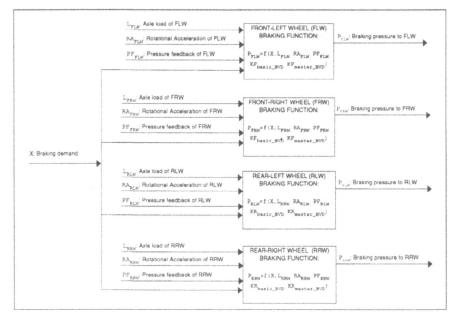

Fig. 4. Abstract Functional Model of the Brake by Wire System

The functional failure analysis of the BBW system was carried out early in the design process. Although it was based on a conceptual design of the system, it has helped us to determine ways in which the system can fail beyond the obvious loss of braking, and to consider detection and recovery mechanisms for these failures. Figure 4 illustrates the abstract functional model of the BBW system which provided the basis for the analysis.

The model shows the four braking functions delivered by the system (one on each wheel), their input parameters and their outputs. Our first observation on the model is that the *four braking functions are dependent* since they rely on the same physical input, the *braking demand* provided by the driver. This dependency is essential and it cannot be removed. The implication for the design is that the braking demand must be carried in a reliable manner from the driver's pedal to the wheels. We have, therefore, decided early to replicate the pedal nodes which capture the braking demand and use a dual bus for carrying this information to the wheel nodes

Our model also shows that the four braking functions are almost identical. They perform identical calculations on identical *types* of input data (braking demand, axle load, wheel rotational acceleration, pressure feedback) and generate identical types of output (braking pressure to the wheel). Their only difference is defined by the parameters KF and KR which determine the distribution of braking between the front and rear axle of the car (the ratio *front:rear* is approximately *2:1*). The symmetry of this functional design across the longitudinal axis of the car made it possible to examine only two out of the four braking functions in the course of the FFA.

The first part of the FFA identifies *single* functional failures of the *front-left and rear-left wheel* braking functions. Each of the two functions has been systematically examined for potential failures in a number of failure classes which include the loss of function, the unintended delivery of function and malfunctions such as early or late deployment. For each failure that we have identified, the analysis records the effects in terms of the impact on three parameters of the car: stability, steerability and braking capacity. The severity of each failure is described using the standard four severity classes of IEC-61508 [10] (catastrophic, critical, marginal, insignificant).

Our analysis shows that certain functional failures can be mapped to other types of failures. *Late and less braking,* for example, can be seen as temporary *loss of braking* with obviously less severe effects. Table 2 summarises the four most severe failures of each braking function. It can be noticed that in this type of distributed system there is no *catastrophic* single functional failure and that all single functional failures are tolerable (*critical*). There are also possibilities for detection and recovery from a number of failures. Some of the effects of a permanently locked wheel on the stability of a car, for example, can be compensated by a recovery function which in response to the initial failure locks the diagonal wheel (see Table 2:FL7).

Table 2. Main functional failures of a wheel braking function

Failure	ID	Effects on System	Severity	Detection	Recovery	Recommendation
OYB: Loss of Braking (omission) when there is braking intention	FL3	The car tends to drift to the side -30% stability -18/-32% braking -15% steerability In the worst case the drift is opposite to the drivers intention	Critical	Locally, using feedback from pressure sensor Remotely, by the status reporter and monitor tasks	Not Possible	In addition, the failure can be detected by a global rotational acceleration sensor. An Electronic Stability Program device may handle the problem (this is out of the scope of this BBW system)
CNB: Unintended Braking (Commission) when there is no braking intention	FL4	The car tends to drift to the side	Critical	It is possible in certain cases by comparing the state of the pedal with the pressure sensor feedback from the wheel	Release actuator	Detection algorithm should be sufficient to detect pedal sensor failures and internal corruption of the pedal messages. There should be provisions to keep commission failures temporally limited
LYB: Permanently Locked Wheel When there is braking intention	FL7	-30% of stability -1/-2% of braking -65% steerability In the worst case the drift is opposite to the drivers intention	Critical	It is possible, by using feedback from the rotational sensor	Release pressure until wheel unlocked If for any reason the wheel remains locked then, lock the diagonal wheel	Incorporate an ABS algorithm, to prevent permanent locking of wheel. In addition implement a detection mechanism for ABS failure and a recovery mechanism at system level (locking of diagonal wheel)
LNB: Permanently Locked Wheel when there is no braking intention	FL8	Equivalent to FL4 but more severe since maximum braking is applied	Critical	It is possible, see FL4 and additionally by using feedback from the rotational acceleration sensor	See FL4	See FL4

In the second part of the FFA we have considered combinations of multiple (two, three and four) functional failures. The first step here was to identify the plausible combinations of such failures. The system has four braking functions and each function has four major failure modes (see Table 2). Although the number of the possible combinations of those failure is large, a systematic examination of those combinations has shown that the number of *unique* combinations is relatively small. One reason is the symmetry in the functional design of the BBW system. In addition, certain combinations are impossible because they can only occur in different and mutually exclusive modes of system operation (braking/no braking).

The analysis has shown that, with the exception of loss of rear axle braking, the loss of two or more braking functions is intolerable (severity=*catastrophic*), mainly because of unacceptable loss of braking capacity. Recovery is impossible and, therefore, such multiple failures should be prevented by design, for example by taking measures against common cause failure. The analysis also indicates that the commission of two or more functions (unintended braking) can be tolerable if it is temporally limited, in other words if it is a result of short transient failures or if there is rapid detection and release of the braking actuator.

Finally, the analysis points out some interesting conclusions concerning the treatment of other multiple failures. While, for example, the severity of a single locked wheel is *critical*, the severity of two locked diagonal wheels becomes *marginal*. We can, therefore, use the intentional locking of the diagonal wheel as a mechanism that can compensate some of the negative effects of a single wheel locking failure. In addition, the analysis confirms that the locking of four wheels is less severe than the locking of three or, in some cases, two wheels (e.g.: rear axle). Thus, the intentional locking of all wheels can be used as a compensatory mechanism against certain more serious locking failures.

This high level FFA equipped us with a comprehensive view of the ways in which the system can fail, and helped the design of the initial architecture of the system. To ensure consistency between the analyses, all the remaining aspects of safety assessment were performed on a consistent *hierarchical model* of this architecture. The hierarchy was developed during the design decomposition process. The process involved the decomposition of the system into sub-systems, and then further decomposition of each sub-system into more basic modules. The hierarchical model that we have developed in SAM is precise and is based on the actual hardware and software implementation of *one* braking function over two pedal nodes and one wheel node.

Figure 5 illustrates the top level architecture of this model. It can be noticed that the pedal nodes (P1, P2) and the wheel node (W) are marked as sub-systems. Each such sub-system in the model has a subordinate hierarchical level which describes the architecture of this sub-system. This decomposition process is repeated until we reach the low levels of the hardware and software implementation.

As the hierarchical model of the system evolved, IF-FMEAs contributed further to its improvement. Sensor IF-FMEAs, for example, provided lists of sensor failure modes as these can be observed at the sensor outputs (e.g. output stuck, biased, out of range, exhibiting non-linear drift etc.). These IF-FMEAs have directly supported the design of hardware redundancy schemes and averaging or voting algorithms for the detection and masking of sensor failures. IF-FMEA has also helped us to analyse software architectures.

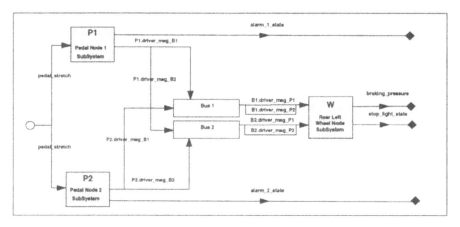

Fig. 5. Top level of the hierarchical model of the BBW system

It has helped us, for example, to identify a condition that could make an early version of the generic *peak detection* algorithm of the BBW system fail with possibly severe consequences for the system. The peak detection algorithm is applied to sensor readings in order to detect and remove transients that violate the normal dynamic behaviour of the physical parameter. The average of the k last valid readings (vm$_1$.. vm$_k$) is calculated in every cycle of measurement. If the current reading (m) deviates from this average more than a maximum allowable limit (ε), i.e. if

$$| m- (_{i=1}\Sigma^x \ vm_i) / k | > \varepsilon,$$

then it is considered invalid and is discarded.

The model of a software task that uses such a mechanism is illustrated in Figure 6. The task performs peak detection on the input value (m). When the input value does not violate the peak detection criterion, it is copied to the task output (o). In the opposite case the output carries the average of the last k valid values (a). During the IF-FMEA analysis of the task and as we systematically examine the task output (o) for potential failure modes, we will have to consider the possibility of the output being *stuck at* a certain value. Part of the examination process is to identify deviations of the input (m) that can cause the *stuck at* failure at the output.

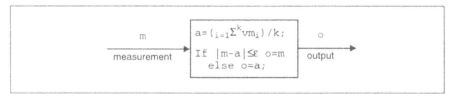

Fig. 6. Simplified Model of the Peak Detection and Removal Task

An obvious case of such a deviation is the *omission* of input. For as long there is an omission of input, the output will be stuck at a value defined by the average of the k last valid measurements. More importantly the *stuck at* failure may persist following the end of a temporary omission. Indeed, *if the omission is long enough* to create a deviation between the restored measurement and the last valid average which is greater than ε, *then all new measurements will be discarded as invalid.*

Let us now assume that the task is part of the wheel node implementation. The task input is the pedal message arriving through the bus and the task output is the braking pressure applied to the wheel. Our analysis has shown that if there is a *temporary omission* of the pedal message at the early stages of braking (e.g. due to electromagnetic interference), the output might be *permanently stuck at zero or at a low braking value* which will cause *a failure to brake.*

Once we have determined the failure behaviour of all the components in the hierarchical model, we can then proceed to the final stage of the analysis where we determine the structure of the fault propagation process in the system. At this stage, we determine how the functional failures that we have identified in the exploratory FFA arise from combinations of the low-level component failure modes that we have identified in the IF-FMEAs. As we have explained, in HiP-HOPS this is achieved *mechanically* with the aid of a *systematic algorithm* for the *synthesis of fault trees.*

In the course of the BBW case study we have used the method and the tool to mechanically generate, regenerate and evaluate a number of such fault trees. Figure 7 illustrates, for example, the fault tree that SAM has synthesised for the event "loss of wheel braking". Using assumptions about component failure rates that we have made in the IF-FMEAS, SAM has calculated the likelihood of the top event to be 8.08×10^{-7} f/h. We must point out that some of these assumptions may not be realistic. In addition, the design of the system has changed since we have last analysed it. For those reasons the number that we have calculated does not provide a realistic failure rate prediction for the brake by wire system.

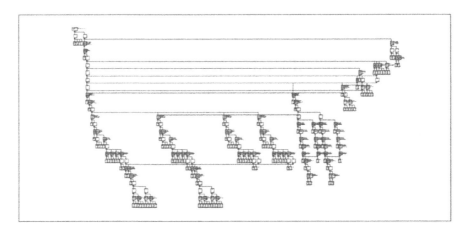

Fig. 7. Distant view of the fault tree that SAM generated for the event "Loss of wheel braking"

In our view though, it indicates that HiP-HOPS can rationalise the development and maintenance of large fault trees, and, in that sense, can alleviate some of the problems currently encountered in the quantitative aspects of complex safety assessment. It is equally important to point out that the synthesis algorithm cannot generate such fault trees if there are inconsistencies in the hierarchical model or between the analyses. In such cases the algorithm simply points out the inconsistencies. Synthesised fault trees, therefore, link in a consistent manner the results from the various analyses to each other and back to the high-level functional failure analysis, and hence guarantee the consistency of the safety case.

4. Conclusions

Safety analysis techniques are evolving to deal with the complexity of modern safety critical systems, for example via the use of functional approaches to safety assessment. However, two significant problems still arise in the assessment of complex systems using classical safety analysis techniques: inconsistencies in the results from the different safety studies of the system and a difficulty in relating the various analyses between them and back to the functional hazard assessment.

In this paper, we have shown one way to address these problems by extending, automating and integrating a number of classical techniques into a new method for safety analysis called HiP-HOPS. We have described the method and demonstrated its application on a distributed brake by wire system for cars.

In HiP-HOPS, the analysis of a complex system starts at the functional level and proceeds all the way down to the low levels of the hardware and software implementation. The method assumes a consistent hierarchical model of the system and can guarantee the consistency of results. HiP-HOPS integrates hardware safety analysis with software hazard analysis. It also introduces a new algorithm for the synthesis of fault trees which mechanises and simplifies a large part of the safety assessment process, the development of fault trees. The method has helped us to improve the failure detection and recovery mechanisms of the brake by wire system. It has also helped us identify subtle errors in the design of certain software algorithms.

Our limited experience from the application of the new method has been very positive. More work is, however, required to further evaluate the practicability of the method, and to determine its potential and limitations. Currently, for example, HiP-HOPS is only suitable for the analysis of complex electromechanical systems which have limited interaction with human operators. But, would it be possible to apply the method on more interactive systems where operator errors contribute significantly to the failure of the system? This is one of the questions that we will attempt to address in the near future.

Acknowledgements

The authors wish to thank Pete Fenelon and Giuseppe Mauri from the University of York. Their earlier work on new techniques for safety assessment [5][6] has influenced several of the principles that underlie HiP-HOPS. We also wish to thank all our colleagues at the Technological University of Vienna and Daimler Chrysler Research in Berlin who have helped us understand the technology involved in the TTA project. This work would not have been possible without the infrastructure that Pete Kirkham and Steve Wilson have developed in SAM and upon which the algorithms of HiP-HOPS have been implemented. Special thanks also go to Ralph Sasse from Daimler Chrysler who has provided us with an insight to the mechanics of brake by wire systems.

References

[1]Society of Automotive Engineers, ARP-4761:Aerospace Recommended Practice: Guidelines and Methods for Conducting the Safety Assessment Process on Civil Airborne Systems and Equipment, 12th edition, SAE, 400 Commonwealth Drive Warrendale PA United States, 1996.

[2]Kletz T., HAZOP and HAZAN: Identifying and Assessing Process Industry Standards, 3rd Edition, Hemisphere Publishers; ISBN: 1-560-32276-4, 1992.

[3]Villemeur A., Reliability, Availability Maintainability and Safety Assessment, John Willey and Sons , ISBN 0-471-93048-2, 1992.

[4]Vesely W.E., et al, Fault Tree Handbook, US Nuclear Regulatory Committee Report NUREG-0492, pages X.15-18, US NRC Washington DC United States, 1981.

[5]Fenelon P., McDermid J.A., Nicholson M. and Pumfrey D.J, Towards Integrated Safety Analysis and Design, ACM Applied Computing Review, 2(1):21-32, 1994.

[6]Mauri G., McDermid J.A., Papadopoulos Y., Extension of Hazard and Safety Analysis Techniques to Address Problems of Hierarchical Scale, IEE Colloquium on Systems Engineering of Aerospace Projects, London, IEE Digest No: 98/249, pages. 4.1/4.6, IEE, 1998.

[7]Kopetz H., Real-time Systems, Design Principles for Distributed Embedded Applications, ISBN 0-7923-9894-77, Kluwer Academic Publishers, 1997.

[8]McDermid J.A., Support for Safety cases and Safety Arguments Using SAM, Reliability Engineering and System Safety, 43:111-127, Elsevier Science, 1994.

[9]International Electrotechnical Commission 65A/179-185, IEC-61508: Functional Safety of Electrical/Electronic/Programmable Electronic Safety-related Systems, IEC, 3 rue de Varembé CH 1211 Geneva Switzerland, 1997.

[10]Kopetz H., Grunsteil G., TTP: A Protocol for Fault Tolerant Real-time Systems, IEEE Computer, 27(1):14-23, 1994.

Hardware Redundant Vital Computers - Demonstration of Safety on the Basis of Current Standards

Heinrich Krebs [1] and Swapan Mitra [2]

[1] TÜV Rheinland, Am Grauen Stein, D-51105 Köln
Fax: Int +49 221 806 2581, E-Mail: bahn-tuev@iseb.com
[2] Lloyds Register of Shipping, 29 Wellesley Road, Croydon CR0 2AJ
Fax: Int +44 181 681 4839, E-Mail: swapan.mitra@lr.org

Abstract. A 2 out of 2 computer is used as an example to discuss the safety strategy of hardware redundant vital computers. One prerequisite for safety is a short fault disclosure time. A maximum fault disclosure time is standardised in ENV 50129. ENV 50129 contains a note which recommends a measure how to fulfil the standard's requirement. This paper analysis whether the standard's requirement is consistent with the safety target or not, and whether the measure is suitable to meet the requirement. Alternative requirements and measures are recommended.

1. Introduction

This presentation is a result of the European Project ACRuDA (RTD Programme RA-96-SC.231). ACRuDA dealt with „Assessment and Certification Rules for Digital Architectures" in transport guided systems. An important part of ACRuDA was to develop an assessment method and certification scheme for vital computers. The assessment method had to be based on the relevant standards, e.g. ENV 50129 [1], IEC 61508 [2]. A critical interpretation of these standards was therefore unavoidable.

2. Objectives

Hardware redundant vital computers can have different structures, e.g. 2 out of 2, 2 out of 3, 3 out of 5 structures. The theory of these m out of n systems is well founded and the knowledge wide spread. To choose and realise these global structures serious problems do not occur. Serious problems occur in the details of the design and assessment process. These problems are common for all m out of n structures. We will therefore confine our presentation to one representative structure. For reasons of simplicity this will be the 2 out of 2 (short 2/2) vital computer.

The main objective of our presentation is, to describe problems and how to overcome these problems in creating and assessing the safety case. We therefore do not strive for completeness in description. We will confine our considerations to problematical

M. Felici, K. Kanoun, A. Pasquini (Eds.): SAFECOMP'99, LNCS 1698, pp. 153-162, 1999
© Springer-Verlag Berlin Heidelberg 1999

parts of doublechannel vital computers. Some of these problems have a technical character other problems exist only in connection with the current standards.

3.   The Main Properties on Which the Safety of a Doublechannel Vital Computer Relies [3]

As described in chapter 2 our considerations confine on the 2/2 vital computer. Fig. 1 demonstrates how this structure works.

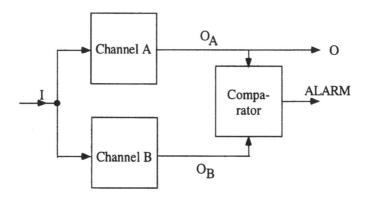

Fig. 1. 2/2 vital computer. $O = f(I)$; $ALARM = (O_A \neq O_B)$

As long as the comparator function is available, the system according to Fig. 1 is completely safe against a one channel fault. If one of the channels A or B is faulty and if, as a consequence one of the output signals O_A or O_B is false, the comparator will detect and negate this state. IF the channel fault does not cause a false channel output, the comparator will not detect this fault. As long as the fault is not activated by an appropriate input, the fault will be without consequence to the output and remains latent. This latency time can have a remarkable value, in which a fault in the other channel can occur.

A double fault, that means one fault in channel A and one fault in channel B, can lead to a hazardous event. The hazardous event occurs if the faults in channel A and B are activated simultaneously and cause identical false outputs $O_A = O_B$. The comparator has no effect against such a double fault. Short disclosure times for single faults have to reduce the probability of hazardous double faults to a tolerable value. Measures which ensure short fault detection times, and which prove sufficient short fault detection times are central problems in the design and assessment of multichannel vital computers.

Another hazardous state can be caused by the unavailability of the comparison function. If the comparator is not available, a false output O_A already causes the hazardous event. There are two different approaches for fail safe comparators.

1. Hardware-Comparator
   The comparator is a hardware unit with inherent fail safe properties.

2. Two Channel Software Based Comparator
   A comparison program is implemented in each of the two channel computers.
   Channel computer A executes the comparison and generates the comparison result
   $ALARM_A$. Channel computer B generates $ALARM_B$ in an analogous way. A
   simple intrinsic fail safe hardware unit concatenates the two alarms to the output
   signal ALARM.

Summarising we state. The safety of a 2/2 computer depends
1. On the reliability of the channels A and B.
2. On the fail safe behaviour of the comparison function
3. On short fault disclosure times.

4.   Calculation of the Failure Probabilities for the 2 out of 2 Vital Computer [4]

4.1   Calculation on the Basis of the Standard's Disclosure Time t_o

The standard ENV 50129 specifies for 2/2 vital computers a maximum fault
disclosure time t_o.

$$t_o = \frac{1}{1000 \cdot 2 \cdot \lambda} \tag{4.1}$$

where λ is the failure rate of one channel.
Interpretation of t_o:
t_o is the maximum duration for which a fault could exist. In actuality the fault duration
is distributed between 0 and t_o. We assume the equal distribution for the disclosure
time. So the mean of the disclosure time will be

$$M(t_o) = t_o/2 \tag{4.2}$$

At this moment we do not want to discuss how to fulfil this „standard requirement".
Our primary intention is to find out whether t_o, according the equation (4.1), leads to
acceptable safety properties of 2/2 vital control computers. To keep the following
calculations more generic we want to introduce the general fault disclosure time t_d. t_d
has the same character than t_o , but can take on different values. A short fault
disclosure time t_d is required to reduce the probability of a double fault to a tolerable
value.
In the following we will use the linear approximation instead of the exponential
function. The probability of fault in channel A of a given 2/2 computer during the
interval t is $\lambda_A \cdot t$. The mean duration of a fault in channel A is $t_d / 2$. During the

time $t_d / 2$ channel B will fail with the probability $\lambda_B \cdot t_o / 2$. The probability for a double fault during the interval t is therefore

$$Q_D(t) = \left(\lambda_A \cdot t\right) \cdot \left(\lambda_B \cdot t_d / 2\right)$$

$$Q_D(t) = \lambda_A \cdot \lambda_B \cdot t \cdot t_d / 2 \tag{4.3}$$

The result (4.3) is independent of the sequence of events (fault in A before fault in B or vice versa). With the assumption $\lambda = \lambda_A = \lambda_B$ we get in (4.4) the probability for a double fault in a 2/2 vital computer.

$$Q_D(t) = \lambda^2 \cdot t \cdot t_d / 2 \tag{4.4}$$

$Q_D(t)$ according (4.4) does not take into account faults in the comparator.

2/2 vital computers are designed in a way that $\lambda_{comperator} \ll \lambda$, so (4.4) can be regarded as a reasonable approximation. In many cases the external comparator is an inherent fail safe device which do not contribute to the failure probability of the vital computer.

Not every double fault leads to a hazardous event. The hazardous event occurs when the fault in channel A and the fault in channel B will be activated by the same input, and the false outputs O_A and O_B will be equal. Only a ratio of total double faults are hazardous. We call k, defined in (4.5), „Ratio of Hazardous Double Faults".

$$k = \frac{hazardous \quad double \quad faults}{all \quad double \quad faults} \tag{4.5}$$

The ratio of hazardous double faults is difficult to assess, therefore designers and assessors tend to assume conservatively k = 1, as long as they can afford such an assumption. The real value of k depends on many properties of a 2/2 vital computer. The assessment of k will not be discussed in detail in this presentation. For 2/2 control systems however with multidigit outputs a ratio k between 0.1 and 0.01 can be assumed.

To demonstrate the effect of k, we will provisionally take k = 0.01. With the ratio k we can formulate the hazardous fault probability Q_H.

$$Q_H = k \cdot Q_D \tag{4.6}$$

Applying (4.6) on (4.4) we get (4.7)

$$Q_H(t_d, t) = k \cdot \lambda^2 \cdot t \cdot t_d / 2 \tag{4.7}$$

Replacing t_d by t_o according the equation (4.1) we get (4.8) the probability of a hazardous fault for a 2/2 computer which is based on the standard's requirement for the fault disclosure time.

$$Q_H \left(t_o, t \right) = \frac{k \cdot \lambda \cdot t}{4000} \qquad (4.8)$$

With k = 0.01 and $\lambda = 10^{-5} h^{-1}$, a demanding requirement, we get (4.9).

$$Q_D \left(t_o, a \right) = 2.2 \cdot 10^{-7} \qquad (4.9)$$

The result of (4.9) is not really satisfactory for vital computers of Safety Integrity Level 4 (SIL4). But more alarming is the fact, that the standard ENV 50129 does not require any values for λ or k. The standard does not even confine the specified fault disclosure time according (4.1) to a certain Safety Integrity Level.

4.2   Introduction of a Calculated Disclosure Time t_{oc}

The standard ENV 50129 requires that a 2/2 vital computer has a fault disclosure time t_o which is smaller than or equal to $1 / \left(2000 \, \lambda \right)$. We do not know how the required standard disclosure time t_o was determined by the standardisation committee, and there was no way to obtain this information. We would like to introduce in this chapter, in contrast to the "standard disclosure time" t_o, the "calculated disclosure time" t_{oc} for the 2/2 vital computer.
The chosen criterion for the "calculated fault disclosure time" t_{oc} is the following:

> t_{oc} has to be determined in a way so that the probability for a hazardous double fault $Q_H \left(t_{oc}, t \right)$ equals $t \cdot THFR.$.

Where *THFR* is the Tolerable Hazardous Failure Rate.

We assume that the calculated fault disclosure time is equally distributed between the values *0* and t_{oc}. The derived formula (4.7) describes the probability of a hazardous double fault in a 2/2 vital computer with the generic disclosure time t_d. Replacing t_d in (4.7) by the „calculated fault disclosure time" t_{oc} we get Formula (4.10) the probability for the hazardous double fault for a computer with a fault disclosure time t_{oc}.

$$Q_H \left(t_{oc}, t \right) = k \cdot \lambda^2 \cdot t \cdot t_{oc} / 2 \qquad (4.10)$$

Equation (4.11) represents the chosen criterion for t_{oc} in analytical form

$$k \cdot \lambda^2 \cdot t \cdot t_{oc} = 2 \cdot t \cdot THFR \qquad (4.11)$$

$$t_{oc} = \frac{2 \cdot THFR}{k \cdot \lambda^2} \qquad (4.12)$$

t_{oc} according (4.12) is finally the calculated fault disclosure time, which meets the chosen criterion.

4.3   Survey and Discussion of the Calculated Results

Equation (4.1) shows the maximum fault disclosure time for 2/2 vital computers according ENV 50129.

$$t_o = \frac{1}{2000 \; \lambda} \tag{4.1}$$

We are not satisfied with this standard fault disclosure time t_o because it is not suitable to achieve the top safety target. We proposed a different fault disclosure time t_{oc}, which meets the top safety target for 2/2 vital computers.

$$t_{oc} = \frac{2 \cdot THFR}{k \cdot \lambda^2} \tag{4.12}$$

On the basis of these two different fault disclosure times t_o and t_{oc} we calculated two different probabilities $Q_H (t_o, t)$ in (4.8) and $Q_H (t_{oc}, t)$ in (4.13) for a hazardous double fault in a 2/2 computer.

$$Q_H (t_o, t) = \frac{k \cdot \lambda}{4000} \cdot t \tag{4.8}$$

$$Q_H (t_{oc}, t) = THFR \cdot t \tag{4.13}$$

The two equations (4.8) and (4.13), which describe two different vital computers, are linear functions of t. These two computers can be therefore described by their constant Hazardous Failure Rates $HFR (t_o)$ and $HFR (t_{oc})$:

$$HFR (t_o) = \frac{k \cdot \lambda}{4000} \tag{4.14}$$

$$HFR (t_{oc}) = THFR \tag{4.15}$$

$HFR (t_o)$ is a hazardous failure rate of a 2/2 computer, which is designed according the standard's requirement. That means its fault disclosure time is $t_o = 1/2000 \; \lambda$. $HFR(t_{oc})$ is a hazardous failure rate of a 2/2 computer, of which the fault disclosure time has the value $t_{oc} = 2 \cdot THFR / (k \cdot \lambda^2)$. Table 1 gives an overview of values for 6 representative examples. $THFR$, λ and k are independent variables of the 2/2 computer. An effective fault disclosure time shall be a function of these independent variables. t_{oc} is really a function of $THFR$, λ and k. t_o however only depends on λ. The main safety characteristic of a vital computer is its hazardous failure rate HFR. The hazardous failure rate depends on the fault disclosure time. According to the two different fault disclosure times t_o and t_{oc}, Table 1 contains two different hazardous failure rates $HFR(t_o)$ and $HFR(t_{oc})$. The last line of the table contains the quotient $HFR(t_o) / HFR(t_{oc})$. For examples, for which this quotient is approximately 1, the standard fault disclosure time leads to acceptable results. In the worst case of these 6 examples this quotient reaches the value 2500.

Table 1. Dependency of the Hazardous failure Rate and of the Fault Disclosure time on the independent variables $THFR$, λ and k

THFR: Tolerable Hazardous Failure Rate of the 2/2 computer (Safety Target)
λ: Failure Rate of one computer channel
k: Ratio of Hazardous Double Faults
t_o: Maximum Fault Disclosure Time according standard ENV 50129
t_{oc}:   Calculated Maximum Fault Disclosure Time, which meets the Safety Target
HFR (t_o):   Hazardous Failure Rate of the 2/2 computer as function of t_o
HFR (t_{oc}):   Hazardous Failure Rate of the 2/2 computer as function of t_{oc}

k	0.01					
$THFR$	10^{-12} h^{-1}		10^{-10} h^{-1}		10^{-8} h^{-1}	
λ	10^{-3} h^{-1}	10^{-5} h^{-1}	10^{-3} h^{-1}	10^{-5} h^{-1}	10^{-3} h^{-1}	10^{-5} h^{-1}
$t_o = \dfrac{1}{2000\lambda}$	0.5 h	50 h	0.5 h	50 h	0.5 h	50 h
$HFR(t_o)=\dfrac{k\cdot\lambda}{4000}$	$2.5\cdot10^{-9}$ h^{-1}	$2.5\cdot10^{-11}$ h^{-1}	$2.5\cdot10^{-9}$ h^{-1}	$2.5\cdot10^{-11}$ h^{-1}	$2.5\cdot10^{-9}$ h^{-1}	$2.5\cdot10^{-11}$ h^{-1}
$t_{oc} = \dfrac{2\cdot THFR}{k\cdot\lambda^2}$	0.0002 h	2 h	0.02 h	200 h	2 h	20000 h
$HFR(t_{oc})=THFR$	10^{-12} h^{-1}	10^{-12} h^{-1}	10^{-10} h^{-1}	10^{-10} h^{-1}	10^{-8} h^{-1}	10^{-8} h^{-1}
$\dfrac{HFR(t_o)}{HFR(t_{oc})}$	2500	25	25	0.25	0.25	0.0025

5.   How to Realise the Required Disclosure Time?

5.1   The General Problem

The standard ENV 50129 tolerates for 2/2 vital computers a maximum fault disclosure time t_o according (4.1). We criticised this standard requirement in section 4.1 as not appropriate to the top safety target for a 2/2 vital computer. We derived „Calculated Fault Disclosure Time" t_{oc} according (4.13) which meets the top safety target perfectly. Up to now it has not been discussed how to fulfil the requirement for a certain fault disclosure time. This is in fact the most complex problem in design and assessment of vital computers.

The discussed fault disclosure times t_o and t_{oc} have the character of „Tolerable Fault Disclosure Times" (TFDT). Every vital computer has its „individual Fault Disclosure Time" (FDT). This is one of the most important properties of the vital computer. The designer has to fulfil the criterion (5.1).

$$FDT \leq TFDT \qquad (5.1)$$

It is a great problem to determine the FDT for a concrete computer. The problem is even much greater to determine FDT for an abstract computer. We were not able to provide in ACRuDA a perfect solution to this problem. However ACRuDA describes relations between the fault disclosure time and certain safety measures and reveals an old, wide spread and dangerous misunderstanding which is additionally disseminated by the standard ENV 50129.

5.2   What Does the Standard ENV 50129 Recommend?

The first foot note in the section B.3.3 of ENV 50129 reads:

> *NOTE: The fault detection time is the test interval in the case of detection by the equipment itself, or the maintenance interval in the case of detection by staff. In the extreme case it is the installed lifetime of the system. In the case of equipment in storage, it is the interval between periodic testing by maintenance personnel.*

We are going to analyse the notes first sentence, which is of highest importance for the practical use.

> *"The fault detection time is the test interval in the case of detection by the equipment itself."*

Interpretations of this sentence:
ACRuDA's Interpretation: *"For those faults, which will be detected by the cyclic test, equals the fault detection time the test interval".*

We hope that the standardisation committee interprets its own text in the very same way. In that case we highly recommend replacing the standard's note by a text, which gives no chance of misinterpretation.
False, but most common Interpretation: *"The fault detection time equals unconditionally the test interval".*

This false interpretation is wide spread. An huge majority of engineers believe in this false interpretation and they design and assess systems on the basis of this interpretation. These engineers have good reasons for their misinterpretation. A remarkable number of older publications have treated self checks as a most important measure to reduce the fault disclosure time to a tolerable limit. Calculations were made, to determine a maximum test interval to meet a certain assumed safety criterion. These publications and especially these calculations dated from the time were coverage factors of self checks were not known or this knowledge was not wide spread. The publications assumed, at least implicitly, a test coverage factor c = 1. The coverage factors of computer self checks are actually from one far away.

The traditional explanation of the safety of a 2/2 Vital Computer reads:
The 2/2 computer is safe against one fault. Whether this single fault will be activated and detected, depends on the stream of inputs. It can last by chance very long before the input will occur, which activates the fault in question and gives the comparator the chance to detect this fault. To reduce this long, input dependent fault detection time of the comparison process, the self check was introduced, which has an input independent ability to detect fault. This theory led in the past to the opinion that the test interval t_i equals the maximum fault disclosure time t_o. This belief has today still a lot of believers.
An assumption that a 2/2 system is after the self check as good as new, is not realistic. Every self check has a limited coverage factor c. The coverage factor is usually defined

$$C = \frac{n_{det}}{n_{total}} \qquad (5.2)$$

n_{det}:   number of single faults which can be detected by the test
n_{total}:   number of all possible single faults
We do not want to go into detail in the sophisticated test theory, but to evaluate an assessment approach we have to know at least some rough results. The greatest problem is to test a CPU. For a CPU we have to expect coverage factors between 0.7 and 0.8. The easiest is to test a ROM; here we expect c = 0.999. The coverage factor for a RAM depends very much on the testing time the designer wants to spend. Let us expect c = 0.98. For the ROM and RAM test it is assumed, that the CPU is intact. For our basic considerations we will therefore choose for the whole computer as an example c = 0.8.
Now we want to consider the effectiveness of cyclic self checks. Cyclic check means, exactly the same test will be repeated. One fundamental property of a cyclic self check is, that a fault which was not detected by the previous self check, will not be detected by all following self checks. The probability for one fault in a self checked one channel computer can be calculated as follow.

All faults: $Q(t) = \lambda \cdot t$

Detected faults: $Q_d(t) = c \cdot \lambda \cdot t$

Undetected faults: $Q_u(t) = (1-c) \cdot \lambda \cdot t$

Reduced failure rate: $\lambda_u = (1 - c) \cdot \lambda \qquad (5.3)$

λ_u according (5.3) describes the „rate of undetectable faults". Replacing λ by λ_u the effect of selfcheck is completely taken into account. For our basic considerations we can choose c=0.8 as a realistic example. So the whole effect of the selfcheck can be substituted, concerning the safety, by a reduction of the failure rate by 80%. Much higher coverage factors than 0.8 are not possible for computers.

The standard ENV 50129 contains no requirements concerning self check coverage factors. The standard has no requirements concerning a maximum failure rate λ. Other parameters or safety measures, which influence the fault disclosure time, are also not mentioned in the standard.

As a conclusion we can state: The standard ENV 50129 gives very little help in how to realise the required small fault disclosure time. The text of the NOTE in B.3.3 causes misinterpretations by the majority of the readers. These misinterpretations very often lead to vital computers which are far from meeting the safety target, the Tolerable Failure Rate of the vital computer.

5.3   General Recommendations

The following brief recommendations are a kind of emergency program. These recommendations are determined for those whom we destroyed an illusion. The illusion namely, that a frequent selfcheck alone can fulfil the requirement: *„the fault disclosure time shall be smaller than the tolerable fault disclosure time"* In case you are not able to demonstrate in a sound mathematical way that your vital computer meets the above requirement, you can always follow the state of the art. I.e. you have to demonstrate that your vital computer is at least as good as the great number of computers which represent the state of the art. But even for this simplified approach you must know what is relevant for a small fault disclosure time.

We presume you have a conventional 2/2 computer, i.e. without diverse software and without random online tests. In this case your computer has only one mean to detect a fault which remained undetected by the selfcheck. This is the comparison process. You have to take care that your comparison process will be as good as possible or at least as good as the state of the art. The following measures can be chosen:

1. Compare process results
2. Compare process results and intermediate results
3. Compare all data on the two busses

The more the comparator compares, the sharper is the test. The chance to detect a latent fault grows from 1. to 3.

4. Take special measures for protection computers
5. Take care that a detected fault will be always removed.

References

1. CENELEC ENV 50129:1998 Railway applications: Safety related electronic systems for signalling
2. IEC Functional safety of electrical / electronic / programmable electronic safety-related systems; especially Part 2: Requirements for electrical / electronic / programmable electronic safety related systems; 1997-02-01
3. El Koursi, Meganck (ed.): ACRuDA Deliverable D1; State of the Art – Safety Architectures Synthesis; ACRuDA/INRETS/MK-PM/WP1/D1/97.12/V2
4. Krebs, Mitra: Fundamentals of Multichannel Vital Computers in ACRuDA Deliverable D7: Synthesis and Conclusion; TÜV Report No.: 947/T 98/130, 25 September 1998

System and Software Safety Analysis for the ERA Control Computer

P.G. Beerthuizen and W. Kruidhof

Fokker Space B.V., dept. ERA,
Newtonweg 1, P.O.B. 32070,
2303 DB Leiden, The Netherlands.
e-mail: {p.beerthuizen | w.kruidhof}@fokkerspace.nl

Abstract. The European Robotic Arm (ERA) is a seven degrees of freedom relocatable anthropomorphic robotic manipulator system, to be used in manned space operation on the International Space Station, supporting the assembly and external servicing of the Russian segment.

The safety design concept and implementation of the ERA is described, in particular with respect to the central computer's software design. A top-down analysis and specification process is used to down flow the safety aspects of the ERA system towards the subsystems, produced by a consortium of companies in many countries; the user requirements documents and the critical function list are the key documents in this process. Bottom-up analysis (FMECA) and test, on both subsystem and system level, are the basis for safety verification. A number of examples show the use of the approach and methods used.

1   The European Robotic Arm (ERA)

As a prime contractor to ESA, Fokker Space are responsible for the design and development, integration and testing of the European Robotic Arm.

Its operational capabilities include the manipulation of large size payloads (including space station segments), replacement of small and large equipment boxes (orbit replaceable units), space station inspection services, and support of cosmonauts during extra vehicular activities.

The symmetrical design (figure 1) with a complete three degrees of freedom wrist and shoulder, and a general purpose end effector on both sides, allows ERA to relocate to different operating locations, by grappling a new base point and releasing the previous one. To this end, the space station provides an infrastructure supporting ERA consisting of a network of base points and related wiring for power, video and data communication.

M. Felici, K. Kanoun, A. Pasquini (Eds.): SAFECOMP'99, LNCS 1698, pp. 163–176, 1999
© Springer-Verlag Berlin Heidelberg 1999

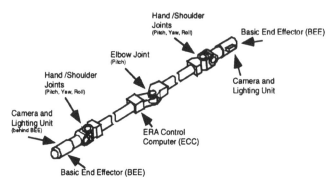

Fig. 1. ERA symmetrical design

The ERA will be commanded and monitored by a cosmonaut, either internal or external to the space station, in several real-time control modes from the control panel Man Machine Interface (MMI). It must be capable of manoeuvring without a direct cosmonaut view on the scene, and with limited operator supervision due to the general availability of only two space station crew members. Therefore ERA is designed to operate both fully automatic (by means of pre-defined "Auto Sequences"), or manually. These modes of operation are well depicted in the schematics of figure 2, which can be found in chapter 2 of [1].

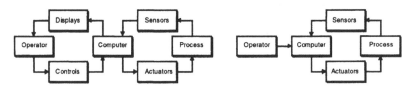

Fig. 2. The role of the computer in the ERA operation, ref. [1]

ERA can be commanded in one of several modes, of which the following are of interest to this paper:
- in *stand-by* mode ERA is able to communicate and receive commands, but the joint brakes are still on, and there is no movement yet;
- in *active* mode all ERA functions are enabled, and the system is ready for operation.

The control design of the ERA is implemented as three types of motion:
- free space motion, for large moves, using feed forward control;
- proximity motion, using camera supported optical target feedback, to prepare for:
- compliant motion, using torque/force control, when ERA comes into physical contact with its environment.

The computer and software operate in a safety critical environment.

Each motion type has a *hold* state as its default state, while different types of *moves* can be commanded either from Auto Sequences (automatic operation) or from the MMIs (manual operation). Figure 3 shows the control state diagramme.

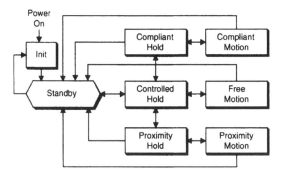

Fig. 3. ERA control state diagramme

The software-system architecture, largely based on Ada tasking with some 25 active tasks, is built basically on a hierarchical structure:

- the application layer has ERA supervisory and safety related tasks, and contains control of the ERA configuration, modes of operation, and mission handling;
- the service layer provides action execution control, subsystem interaction services and databus scheduling; it also contains a number of motion related safety checks;
- the operating system layer provides device drivers for the I/O-devices (mainly Mil-Std 1553B controllers), and basic software services contained in the Ada runtime.

Application and service layer together are called "application software". The software runs on the ECC hardware, consisting of the hardware processor layer provided by a RISC processor (ERC32), and separate Mil-1553 I/O-controllers for the bus protocols.

The software has been developed applying HRT-HOOD [2] for the architectural design, and applying the principles of Deadline Monotonic Scheduling.

The software, based on the Aonix AdaWorld compiler environment for the ERC32, is developed by three subcontractors: Tecnospazio SpA (Italy) is responsible for the application layer, TERMA Elektronik AS (formerly CRI, Denmark) for the service layer, Daimler Chrysler Aerospace (Germany) for the operating system layer software.

2 The Safety Requirements Baseline

As the ERA customer the European Space Agency has defined the system FMECA and Hazard Status Sheets to be among the basic safety analysis documents, in addition to safety testing.

The system requirements define four severity classes for the consequences of a failure in the system, with increasing level:

- Minor;
- Major: inability to complete a mission or to achieve the specified performance;
- Serious: injury, or major damage to the ERA and/or the space station;

- Catastrophic: loss of life.

The requirements are formulated as:

- No single subsystem or human failure shall lead to Catastrophic or Serious consequences;
- No second subsystem failure, independent from the first, shall lead to Catastrophic or Serious consequences.

Failure of functions with Serious or Catastrophic severity are called *safety critical functions*. These functions are required to be safe after two consecutive independent failures on subsystems. The (manual) interaction of the cosmonaut is not allowed as a safety barrier for automatic ERA operation; cosmonaut interaction is also considered too slow in many such occasions. For manually controlled operations the cosmonaut is actively monitoring and interacting with the sytem.

The software development is performed according to the ESA PSS-05-0 [3] including the guidelines, and the additional ERA software standard, as class B software. Class A software design is required when a single software function is safety critical in itself; through the chosen safety approach, it was possible to avoid these occurrences, thereby being more cost and time efficient without compromising the system safety.

Through this approach it was also possible to avoid significant impact on the software safety mechanisms, despite significant changes in the ERA functional requirements [4].

3   General Safety Strategy Considerations

The approach is based on a top-down strategy based on past experiences in fault tolerance techniques in aircraft and satellite attitude/orbit control system design, and published fault tolerance and safety techniques (most notably [1] with respect to the software; [5] describes the principals used in the ERA safety approach). A strict distinction was made between safety and reliability, and the methods related to these two different things.

The general principles used in the approach are briefly mentioned hereafter.

The general techniques, eventually applied in the ERA project, comprise the Hazard and Operations Analysis, Fault Tree Analysis (FTA), definition of safety requirements and operational constraints, Failure Modes/Effects and Criticality Analysis (FMECA), common-cause/mode analysis, hardware-software interaction analysis, detailed analysis of specific cases, and testing. Much attention is paid to the methods and techniques of software development, analysis and testing; this emphasis is specified in the ERA project specific software standard.

The approach starts top-down, from the system level aspects, and results in system level hazard protection mechanisms specified towards the different hardware and software subsystems. A balance between hardware and software safety mechanisms was introduced in order to obtain the maximally possible separation of safety barriers against hazards. In addition, data security, lockout, lockin and interlock mechanisms were specified and designed (refer e.g. to [1] for a description of these techniques), to guard against accidental and unintended behaviour of the arm.

The functional analysis of ERA provides the inventory of the functions which must be represented in the ERA design in order to fulfil the ERA mission.

The hazard and fault tree analyses of ERA provide the inventory of the safety barriers that are needed to prevent hazards with Serious or Catastrophic consequences from occurring.

The output of the functional analysis and the hazard analysis has been used as an input for:

- the design of the ERA onboard software; with respect to the software the required functions are defined in the User Requirements Document (cf. [3]);
- the system functional FMECA; this is a functional level analysis document, i.e. the ERA functions are defined as the input elements for the analysis. The failure modes of the ERA application software have been analysed in a dedicated section of the ERA system level FMECA.

The main hazards for the ERA were analysed to be related to:

- impact of the arm (and payload) velocity;
- collision (position and orientation related, fragility);
- forces exerted by the ERA on extra vehicular activities and/or on equipment.

From the system level FMECA the Critical Functions List (CFL) has been derived, which, similar to the ERA System level FMECA, contains a section dedicated to the ERA application software.

The CFL is a primary input document for the software developing subcontractors, in addition to the User Requirements Documents, to analyse the software safety. It defines the severity of the analysis items, and indicates barriers that have been specified within the total scope of the ERA design.

Therefore it can be used to limit the effort required to design safety barriers, since all developing subcontractors have the full view on the available system barriers; without this information it would be difficult, if not impossible, for the subcontractor to assess which safety barriers are required, which can easily lead to superfluous and even deleterious barrier implementations on a local subsystem level.

For the software, the entry items of the CFL are mainly the interface calls of software functions, with emphasis on the following aspects:

- the function is not executed;
- the function is incorrectly executed, analysed for different cases if necessary;
- the function is executed at a wrong point in time.

In the ERA project safety is crucial importance. So it is also of the utmost importance that the safety critical functions are correctly identified and that the associated safety provisions are correctly implemented on lower levels. Therefore the CFL is extensively discussed with the subcontractors, in order to verify that the failure modes are properly understood both by the prime and the subcontractor, and to ensure that the defined safety barriers are indeed adequate.

When it is identified that insufficient or inadequate safety barriers are present for a certain entry, on the functional level, then additional barriers will be specified by the prime contractor.

Provisions have been made in the ERA project to keep the software developer FMECA focused on safety :

- the safety critical functions have already been identified on system level;
- for the so-called SR-FMECA, on software requirements level, the software developer is authorised to limit his analysis to the safety critical functions contained in his software;
- with respect to the development of checks which are needed as safety barriers against the failure modes of safety critical functions, the software developer has been provided with the information on the barriers that were already defined on ERA system level;
- the subcontractors are required to identify in their FMECAs (by referring to the applicable CFL-entry number) to which system level failure mode a software function and its related severity correspond.

In order to facilitate the exchange of data, the ERA standard FMECA table format has been imposed on the software developer. The subsystem FMECAs (including the SR-FMECAs) are fed into the system level FMECA, in order to verify completeness and correctness of the system FMECA, throughout the (sub)system and software development phases.

SR-FMECAs are in several cases supported by fault tree analyses on software requirements level, for the CFL-entries.

The safety barriers are, in many instances, checks specified for and implemented in the ECC software. These checks are required to be independent from the critical function which they are intended to protect. This independence must be analysed to the appropriate level.

Using the traceability between the Software Requirements Document and Architectural Design Document, the critical function and associated checks are identified in the architectural design. Based on this, it is determined whether or not new, unintended dependencies have been introduced in the design. For each pair/triple of critical functions and/or checks, the result may either be: *dependent*, *independent*, or *insufficient information*; the latter category denotes situations where more information is needed in order to determine dependencies. Where dependencies exist, suggestions for design changes will be made. The emphasis of the AD-FMECA, on architectural design level, is therefore on common-cause/mode failures.

For the *insufficient information* cases in the AD-FMECA, the detailed design is analysed with the aim of determining the actual dependencies in the final design. Again, if dependencies are discovered, changes to the design are suggested.

In the ERA approach this process can be proceeded onto code level, if required, for which the software fault trees according to Leveson [6] were chosen to be applied; in practice this level was not needed in the followed approach.

The solving of software dependencies in the architectural design and lower levels of the development are no longer included in the User Requirements Documents, except for those cases where a solution on system level or in another software layer appeared to be more effective or efficient.

In the annex the system level FMECA, the CFL, and the SR-FMECA for the software are compared with respect to their entry items.

4   Software Level Checks

For failure modes with may have Serious or Catastrophic consequences, it is required to implement the two fail-safe requirement in the ERA design in such a way, that there are at least two mechanisms which are able to detect the failure mode concerned. The mechanisms are chosen to be in hardware and/or software.

Upon detection of an anomaly, the checks ensure that the ERA is immediately brought into a well defined safe state. This safe state is always the Standby mode (figure 3), whereby the active control of the joints is stopped, and the arm fully braked.

When a (safety-critical) function fails (first failure) and one of the checks fails (second failure), the last check or another safety mechanism will still ensure the safe state of ERA to be reached. This approach is valid under the strict condition that the checks are independent of the function they monitor, and that the checks are independent of each other.

At the start of the project, checks may not have been defined in sufficient quantity or quality, either due to the completeness of the design or due to the impossibility to detect the failure mode on system level, at that moment. Some adjustments to the safety analyses and/or the specifications were therefore required in the course of the project, but they appeared to be quite limited. Only one large adjustment was necessary to the collision detection check, but this originated in a customer requirement in relation to added functionality of the arm.

The specified checks are applicable to different modes of operation of the arm (figure 3), e.g.:
- a target validity check is active in proximity motion control, to avoid that incorrect or inadvertent target images (e.g. due to sunlight or space station surface mirroring) control the arm in the wrong direction;
- a torque/force deviation check is active in compliant motion control, to ensure the validity of torques and forces used;
- a path deviation check is active in all control modes, to check that the interpolated trajectory, between start and end poses of the arm, is followed with sufficient

accuracy (note, that e.g. excentric payload mass might cause a temporary deviation of the intended path, due to the mechanical flexibility of the arm);

- a path interpolator check, which is actually resulting from common cause/mode failure analysis, checks whether the calculated path (by the ECC), which is used by the path deviation check, is to be trusted. This check is implemented using the inverse algorism of the path deviation check;
- a singularity check protects in Cartesian free motion control against accidentally getting too close to kinematic singularity conditions;
- a collision detection check is active during free motion control and in a more limited way also during proximity motion control. The collision detection check uses models of the space station contained, the ERA, payloads and obstacles, in the ECC, to calculate in real-time the safe distance between the ERA (with payload) and the space station, and between the ERA (with payload) and itself.

This list is not exhaustive.

The design of the arm includes a variety of lockout, lockin and interlock mechanisms, as well as provisions to guard against data corruption (hence high reliability of the mechanisms underlying the safety provisions).

Since the Standby mode is inherently safe, while Active mode with active control raises the potential for unsafety, the transition to Active mode is guarded with a dual unlock mechanism through the commanding from the MMI, and configuration checks on both hardware and software to ensure that all required functionality is available. The Standby mode is also the basic fall-back mode, in case of failure detection.

All commanding has been made state-dependent, i.e. commands are accepted by the ECC's Command_Handler software when making sense, otherwise commands are rejected; in parallel, the MMIs also have their guards and state dependency to avoid issuing inadvertent commands.

Different software objects (implemented as Ada tasks) in the software keep track of configuration information: e.g., the control algorisms require that the correct set of joints is unbraked and available, while the complementary set is not; meanwhile, another object keeps track of the overall commanded configuration, and reacts if there is a difference (irrespective of the cause). In case of identifying a difference, the system will be put in safe mode. As an example, the rigidisation state of the torque/force sensor is checked in certain states to allow calibration to zero torque and force before actual use; the accidental use of an uncalibrated sensor can thereby be prevented, which would cause excessive build-up of torques and forces in compliant control (instead of controlling them to zero).

Rendering the arm into a safe condition is performed on software level through the Event_Handler object (Ada task). This is the highest priority task in the system, continuously watching the so-called Event_Buffer (which is a *protected object*). All tasks in the software have independent access to the Event_Buffer for reporting any anomaly, and return to nominal where applicable; three classes of events are used: *nominal*, *caution* and *danger*. Caution events only result in a message to the operator. Danger events are interpreted by the Event_Handler to result in a

Soft_Emergency_Stop (SES), i.e. all active control is stopped, a watchdog communication between the ECC and all subsystems (most notably the joints) is stopped which results in autonomous de-activation (braking, as it concerns the joints), and autonomous fall-back to the Standby mode.

Although the approach does not foresee checks on top of the execution of other checks, there is one specific deviating case. The proper execution of a SES is again checked by a check which verifies the correct state after the SES has been performed (within a time limit); if this state is not reached, then (through the communication with the MMI) a request to the operator for a Hard_Emergency_Stop is performed, i.e. the operator is required to cut the power to the system as a last resort. The possible incapability of the link between ECC and MMI to transmit such a request is separately safeguarded by a periodic alive protocol between the two on the same channel; failure of this protocol independently causes a MMI-request to the operator for immediate action, and causes the ECC to independently execute a SES (due to a danger event).

The checks for the software are basically all specified in the User Requirements Documents for the software subcontractors. In some cases it was required in a later increment to add some details or make small adaptations. But the requirements stability has shown to be remarkably good for the checking sections, despite the very big functional changes that had to be introduced in the other sections in the course of the project.

Several other safety mechanisms in the other subsystems, will not be described here; an extensive example can be found in [7].

It is further noted, that many checks must be inhibitable, for contingency operation purposes; this is an explicit requirement from the customer. The default state of the checks is however *enabled*, and disabling requires again a double action. It is also checked that the actual check-enabling state is consistent with the commanded state; if this fails, then a danger event will be raised and the (not-inhibitable) Event_Handler will force a Soft_Emergency_Stop.

5   Some Examples

In the following chapters examples of the software safety implementation are presented, which are by no means exhaustive or complete, but still show in sufficient detail the steps performed in the safety analysis and design.

5.1   Deviation from a pre-defined trajectory

Automatic moves in Cartesian free motion control are prepared and checked in advance on ground, and executed through an Auto Sequence by the ECC. In case a move is incorrectly executed, the ERA may deviate from the planned trajectory, potentially resulting in SER or CAT consequences in case of collision with an obstacle such as the space station, or a cosmonaut (figure 4).

The path, along which the ERA moves, is characterised by a start pose and a commended end pose of the move; pose here means both position and orientation of the point of reference on the arm with or without a payload attached. In order to reach the desired end pose, the ECC path interpolation software generates a sequence of setpoints in time for each of the individual to be controlled joints, and subsequently sends these setpoint data to the joints. The subsequent joint setpoints cause the ERA to move over a desired fraction of the path.

The path deviation check uses joint angular information to calculate the actual path along which the point of reference actually moves; this actual path must be within a defined boundary from the interpolated path. When this condition fails, a danger event is raised (resulting in a SES).

The path interpolator check uses the initial pose information and calculated path fractions to check whether the arm has actually moved the desired fraction of the path.

Through the analysis on software requirements level, it showed that both the move and the path interpolator check will be affected if the desired fraction is calculated wrongly. To eliminate this problem a *fraction consistency check* was divised on software level (though not visible in the User Requirements Document), and the potential common mode failure is added to the AD-FMECA for the service layer software; the fraction consistency check is added in the fail-safety column of the FMECA. The fraction consistency check is automatically activated at the start of the move, and cannot be inhibited.

Similarly, with regard to the path deviation check a *frame consistency check* was introduced on software level to avoid that wrongly generated control frames would be used, which are common to both the control calculations and the path deviation check. The frame consistency check is further analysed in the DD-FMECA, on detailed design level, to ensure that the control frames used by the controller and path deviation check are correct. If a controller frame is faulty, both the move and the path deviation check will fail. So the analysis verifies that no errors are introduced when control frames are derived from the database control frames. An Ada source code review was undertaken, and no common mode failure has been identified on code level.

At this level the analysis on the service layer software (similar analysis was performed on the other software in the ECC), which narrowed down from an over 200 page document on software requirements level to a 10 page document on detailed design level, was stopped.

5.2   A move is stopped prematurely

A typical example of where the severity could easily be misjudged is the case that, while moving correctly along a planned path, a Cartesian move is terminated too early (figure 4). The desired end pose is then not fully reached. This fault could be due to wrong execution of the software, but also other causes, like a cosmonaut manually interrupting the move and not finishing the move afterwards, can be viewed in the same way.

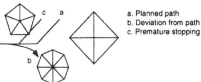

a. Planned path
b. Deviation from path
c. Premature stopping

Fig. 4. Errors in Cartesian motion control

At a first glance this seems to be a safe case, with at most Major consequences because ERA is still on the planned path and is not moving. Missions are executed involving the subsequent execution of moves, e.g. first along a straight line in one direction and then, in order to avoid an obstacle in a different direction. A move, following a move which has ended in a wrong pose, may result in a collision with an obstacle which otherwise would have been avoided. Hence the severity must be Serious or Catastrophic, instead of Major. This condition is depicted in figure 4.

When this information would not have been made visible to the software subcontractor (through the CFL), safety criticality would not have been evident, and the analysis in the software FMECAs might be stopped on a too high level, thereby failing to provide the feedback needed to define the correct design of the software.

A behaviour as described above can be characterised as performing a robotics action at a *wrong moment in time*. These failure modes are usually the hardest to cope with, because it is very difficult to design a safety barrier against it.

A suitable safety barrier can only be found when going sufficiently deep in the architectural (and detailed) design of the software, because only on these levels the individual elements of which the software is composed, and their interaction, become clearly visible.

One of the checks to particularly guard against this type of errors is the *collision detection check*. This software check uses a software model of the space station and obstacles including potential payloads and of the arm itself, in a database within the ECC, to perform real-time collision potential within pre-defined boundaries. Collision potential is checked also with respect to hitting the arm itself, since the wrist part (particularly with a payload grappled) could collide with the upper arm limb. These calculations are performed in all free motion control states (because of the potentially large movements). For proximity motion control only the potential of colliding with the arm itself is checked. The general collision detection is of course of no value in compliant motion control, since it is the purpose of the arm then to be in contact with the space station's payload mounting units.

The correctness of the collision detection database models for the ECC is performed on-ground, in the mission preparation activities. This ground system makes use of the

RobCAD models, and generates an ECC model which can be used by the application layer software in the ECC. Verification of the ECC database models is done by taking that representation, and re-creating a separate RobCAD model with the reverse algorism; both the original and the model derived from the collision detection database are compared, where the latter must be inspected to be always be the envelope of the original. In the ground preparation a hardware model of the ECC with all its software contained is used in the mission verification.

5.3   State consistency checking

The Command_Handler, the motion control software, and the different checks have been deliberately made independent by using different tasks. In the detailed software level a common cause failure between the momentary setting of the controller state for motion commands and the associated motion checks was detected.

What at first sight looks to be a timing problem, i.e. the Ada tasks do not all reach the desired state in exactly the same moment in a concurrent system, can also be described as the occurrence of an unauthorised transition from one controller state (related to *motion*) to another (related to *stop*).

Since such a transition is normally only performed on command, the desired state (linked to the command issued) can be compared to the actual state which should be the result of the command; this is implemented as the *state consistency check*.

Any discrepancy will result in a danger event being generated, upon which a Soft_Emergency_Stop will bring the ERA into a safe state.

6   Conclusions

The User Requirements Documents and Critical Functions List have been successfully used to ensure consistency in the safety approach and analyses both at ERA system level and at (software) subcontractor level.

By the co-ordinated application of these documents, duplication of subcontractors' analyses on system level and among each other could be avoided to a very large extent. Furthermore they support:

- transferring the system level knowledge on the consequences of erroneous behaviour of ERA (severity) to the subcontractors;
- allowing the subcontractor to concentrate on the analysis specifically of safety critical functions, thereby providing their feedback needed to define the architectural and detailed design;
- allowing the subcontractor to identify, on his level, for which failure modes of safety critical functions checks (additional to the checks defined on system level) are required, and implement these in the most optimal way.

Limiting the FMECA of the subcontractor to the safety critical functions consequently keeps the size of the SR-FMECA and the AD- and DD-FMECAs to a (safe) minimum. Thereby it helps the subcontractor to keep a good overview of his analysis and helps him to concentrate on the identification and reduction of common cause/mode failures which are crucial to the system safety.

By keeping the User Requirements Documents and the Critical Functions List in line with each other throughout the software development process, they facilitate the correction of any deficiencies that may be found on lower level.

This applies both to system level and to software level:

- as the maturity of the design grows and the lower level information is fed back into system level, any open points to be solved on system level will become visible;
- on software level, the common cause/mode failure modes of safety critical functions and their checks become visible, to be dealt with as close as possible to the source(s) from which they originate.

One essential common cause/mode failure is still unsolved in the system. The Ada runtime, although of course extensively tested by the manufacturer, is not available to be analysed either on design or source code level, due to property rights. Since the (tasking) design of the system was largely established long before the final choice of the processor and Ada compiler suppliers were defined, there is little to do about this crucial point. Since the ERC32 and AdaWorld compiler environment are a main choice by ESA for their space projects, the analysis of the runtime kernel is assumed further to be outside the safety analysis responsibility of the ERA project.

References

1. N.G. Leveson, *Safeware: System Safety and Computers*, Addison Wesley, 1995
2. A. Burns and A.J. Wellings, HRT-HOOD: A Structured Design Method for Hard-Real_Time Ada Systems, Elsevier, 1995
3. European Space Agency, *Software Engineering Standards*, PSS-05-0, issue 2
4. C. Maegaard and P. Beerthuizen, *Development of a Hard_Real_Time System in a World of Changes*, Proceedings of the Data Systems in Aerospace Conference, DASIA'98, Athens, Greece, May 1998
5. P. Beerthuizen, C. Maegaard and A. Rusconi, *ERA Safety Strategy*, Proceedings of the Data Systems in Aerospace Conference, DASIA'98, Athens, Greece, May 1998
6. N.G. Leveson, et al, Safety Verification of Ada Programs Using Software Fault Trees, IEEE Software 8(4), pp.48-59, 1991
7. R.A. Bosman and J.F.T. Bos, *Control of the Joint Runaway Hazard for the European Robotic Arm*, ESREL 98, Trondheim (N), June 1998

Annex

Table 1. The entry items of the ERA system level FMECA are compared to the items in the Critical Functions List and in the software requirements level FMECA, for the ECC application software.

Entry	System level FMECA	CFL	SR-FMECA
Entry number	-	Identical to system level FMECA entry nr.	-
Item	Subsystem / software	Identical to System level FMECA	-
Function	-	Identical to System level FMECA	Combined with item
Cause	Link to SR level FMECA entries provided	Not included in CFL	Information provides link to lower level in software
Failure Mode	-	Identical to System level FMECA	Failure mode in Software (SR level)
Consequences	Consequences on System level	Not included in CFL	Consequence on s/w level, with reference to entry nr. of CFL / System FMECA
Severity S/W class	SER or CAT for safety critical functions	Identical to System level FMECA	Identical to System level FMECA
Operational phase / mode	-	Identical to System level FMECA	Identical to System level FMECA
Observable Symptoms	Observable symptoms on System level	Not included in CFL	Observable symptoms on software level
Fail-safety	Contains checks (originating from Hazard Analysis), for failure mode analysed	Identical to System level FMECA	Contains System level safety checks and checks on s/w level
Fail-Operational	Contains information on diagnosis and recovery	Identical to System level FMECA	Contains information on diagnosis and recovery on s/w level
Remarks	E.g. reference to end-to-end test on System level	Identical to System level FMECA	Remarks on s/w level, e.g. reference to test of the s/w function analysed

Safety Markup Language: Concept and Application[1]

Chin-Feng Fan[1] and Swu Yih[2]

[1] Department of Computer Engineering and Science
Yuan-Ze University, 135 Far East Road, Chung-Li, Taiwan
csfanc@saturn.yzu.edu.tw
[2]I&C Department, Institute of Nuclear Energy Research
P.O. Box 3-11, Lung-Tang, Taiwan

Abstract. This paper proposes a method to expedite hypertext construction and improve document reading efficiency by using meaningful tags. Hazard Life Cycle is proposed as the common semantic framework for documents in safety engineering practice. Under this framework, we developed Safety Markup Language (SML) to annotate the major concepts in software-related nuclear regulation. A computer tool has been constructed to convert these SML tags into desired hyperlinks for review purpose. This approach reduces the manual effort in hyperlink construction, and supports information retrieval in a concept unit, which is closer to human cognition than that obtained from a conventional approach. Potential improvements achieved by this SML-based method include efficient checking of information completeness, tracing of review issues, and reduction of clerical work in license review.

1. Introduction

Document reading has become a more and more important activity for safety engineering practitioners in such tasks as licensing review, accident investigation, and product liability argument. Safety engineers can handle documents of simple systems effectively, but for complex systems like nuclear power plants, the huge amount of inter-related documents has become an enormous burden for those who have to read and process them. In certain cases, the overwhelming documents have created an unbalanced situation between document load and safety engineers' document processing capability. Such an unbalanced situation not only deteriorates safety engineers' performance but may also jeopardize safety of the target equipment. Effective document handling tools and techniques are urgently needed.

Computer supported hypertext is promising in enhancing people's document reading capability. It provides a structure better matching human reading and cognition process than conventional paper-based documents. However, current hypertext approach is mostly address-based, and the constructing of address-based hyperlinks is very tedious and time-consuming. This paper proposes an efficient way to expedite hypertext construction by using meaningful tags. The rationale is that

[1] This work was supported in part by National Science Council, Republic of China, under the grant no. NSC87-2218-E-155-014-NU and NSC88-2213-E-155-002.

M. Felici, K. Kanoun, A. Pasquini (Eds.): SAFECOMP'99, LNCS 1698, pp. 177-186, 1999
© Springer-Verlag Berlin Heidelberg 1999

since the contents of each document is composed of inter-related domain concepts, these concepts can be organized into a semantic framework. This framework is shared by all concerned documents. Therefore, we can assign names/tags to these domain concepts, and then hyperlinks can be established among document paragraphs that have the same or related tags. Furthermore, the constructed hypertext system can be retrieved in a concept unit; thus, the presentation mechanism is closer to human cognition mechanism than that of a conventional approach. A computer tool assisting to realize this approach will be needed to help safety engineers to cope with complicated documents. The unbalancing problem between overloaded documents and people's reading capability will then be alleviated.

In this paper, a Safety Markup Language (SML) is defined to represent the elements and dependency relations of the common semantic framework of software-related nuclear regulation. Application-specific processing of the SML tags will then be applied to form an efficient hyper-document. In the following, we will first discuss related background, and then present our approach, followed by the case study in software-related nuclear regulation. Improvements achieved by this SML-based approach are also discussed.

2. Background

This research uses markup to construct hyperlink and provides efficient reading. Thus, we will discuss hypertext and markup in this section. Hypertext refers to electronic documents in which information is arranged and accessed in a nonlinear fashion [1,3,6]. The interconnection between chunks of documents is usually defined by pre-defined, address-based hyperlinks. However, the creation of address-based hyper-links among various documents is usually tedious and needs to be done manually.

Markup traditionally refers to the annotation or instructions for formatting or typesetting. The names for the annotation are called tags. Such formatting languages include Unix nroff and troff. Later on markup languages become more general; besides formatting, they can provide annotation for text syntactical structures such as title and paragraph. SGML[4], XML[2] are such general markup languages. HTML, providing formatting markup, is a subset of SGML and popular in constructing homepage on WWW. There are a few famous domain specific markup languages, such as Chemical Markup Language (CML)[7] and Mathematical Markup Language (MathML)[5].

3. Concept-Based Approach

To enhance reading efficiency, we have investigated human reading and identified key factors affecting reading efficiency. The top portion of Fig. 1 shows the typical reading process. The underlining process is the concept transfer process from the writer to the reader. If the writer's concepts can be represented explicitly and flexibly, then reading efficiency can be enhanced. The key tasks are how to *extract*, *present*, and then *manage* the concepts as well as their dependencies. Our approach to these key tasks is shown in the lower part of Fig. 1. To extract the concepts to transfer, we

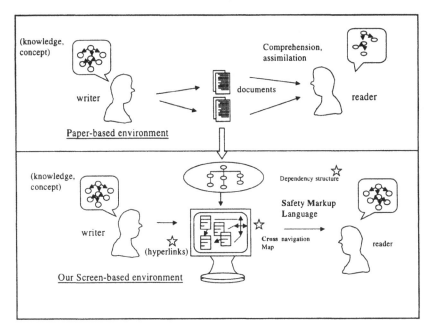

Fig. 1. Document reading process

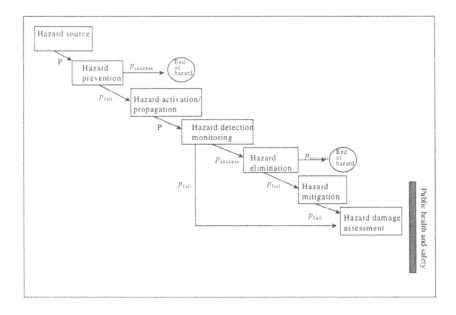

Fig. 2. Hazard life cycle

first identify the common semantic framework for safety engineering practice. To present the major concepts, we annotate them in a Safety Markup Language; to manage these concepts and their dependencies, appropriate tag processing and tools will then be developed. The presentation and management of the extracted concepts will be discussed in Sections 4 and 5, respectively.

The core activities of safety engineering deal with hazards. Thus, we identify *hazard life cycle* as the common semantic framework for safety engineering practice. When a hazard occurs, hazard prevention measures in the target system may succeed and end the hazard. However, when prevention fails, the hazard may be activated and propagated; while, hazard detection and monitoring schemes in safety practice may detect it and then eliminate such a hazard; if hazard elimination does not work, then mitigation methods will be required. If all fail, an accident may occur. This hazard life cycle is shown in Fig. 2.

4. Safety Markup Language (SML)

Since major activities of safety engineering practice interact with the hazard life cycle, we propose to derive the semantic concepts in safety documents under this hazard life cycle framework. Markup will be used to represent the key features of this framework. Each safety engineering domain (for example, nuclear plants, oil industry, and aviation) has its own general-agreed explicit and tacit knowledge. Domain expertise is needed to derive such knowledge of how domain concepts are organized and manipulated so as to form a domain-specific markup language. In this research, we chose nuclear software regulation as our case study, and developed a Safety Markup Language (SML) for its domain concepts and concept dependency structures. Similar approach can be used for deriving concept markup languages for other application domains in safety engineering. These meaningful markup tags not only reflect domain concepts, but they can also be further converted to links to connect related chunks of documents. Thus, SML facilitates further processing to enhance reading efficiency.

Our case presented here is narrowed down to documents dealing with the digital Reactor Trip System (RTS). The themes of these documents involve *hazard life cycle*: the concept of *hazards* occurs first, followed by its prevention, detection, and elimination; all rely on developers' safe designs and regulators' safety determination; while both the developers and the regulators need to comply with nuclear software regulation. *Hazards, Safeguard, Criterion, Developer's assessment, and Regulator's assessment* are thus the major concepts extracted. These concepts are expanded into lower level concepts. Safety assessment needs to provide trustworthiness evidence, and thus, concepts "*Assessment*" and "*Trustworthiness*" are also needed. Moreover, related properties or mechanisms to support trustworthiness are addressed in the regulation. These properties or mechanisms include *reliability, testability, independence, redundancy, diversity, defense-in-depth, single-failure,* and *fail-safe.* All these concepts are included as tags in SML. Finally, the concept "*Developer's Assessment*" should include complied criteria and the developer's assessment. Also, the concept "*Regulator's Assessment*" includes the reviewer's safety determination of the developer's safety report. The proposed Safety Markup Language (SML) structure is shown in Fig. 3. Figure 4 is the SML in SGML format.

SML is then used to mark nuclear software standards and regulatory codes. However, besides content knowledge, the knowledge of text presentation sequence also helps readers' comprehension process. Therefore, we may also add syntactical tags, such as *introduction, scope,* and *description.*   Such syntactical tags can be generated in a traditional way. Fig. 5 shows an example of a mixture of syntactical and semantic tags. In these examples, domain concepts are annotated in SML, shown in bold face letters. Such combination of semantic and syntactical tags is highly desirable and useful; further complex computer processing is possible.   Figure 6 shows fragments of marked document instances.

5.   Application and Tool Support

After domain concepts and concept dependencies have been extracted and represented in markup tags, we need to manage these tags to form a desired hypertext system so as to support efficient and flexible document reading process.

Nuclear software regulation is a complex system with intricate cross-references. A navigation tool is designed to organize and navigate through it. Generally, there exist two kinds of natural association in a document system: the association among different documents, and the association within each document. For nuclear I&C software regulation, the association among the documents is abstract-versus-concrete association: documents range from abstract law to specific industrial standards. For example, 10CFR (Codes of Federal Regulation, Chapter 10) and RG1.7 (Regulatory Guide) are high level regulation; SRP 7.2 (Standard Review Plan, Section 7.2) [8] is more concrete guidance; while IEEE 603 is a specific industrial standard.   On the other hand, the association within each document is cause-consequence association; namely, the hazard life cycle.   Therefore, we propose a *cross structure* for representing the association:

- *Vertical* axis expresses abstract-versus-concrete association.
- *Horizontal* axis represents cause-consequence association.

This is shown in Fig. 7; this cross structure acts as a navigation map. SML tags are shown in overlapped square boxes, which can be expanded to show lower-level information by mouse clicks.   After documents are marked in SML, application-specific processing will then convert these SML tags into links in a pre-agreed way. The agreed processing for review process may be to link the paragraphs marked by the same tags in related documents. This is shown in Fig. 8.

We have developed a computer tool for supporting document review process. The tool is written in Microsoft Visual Basic 5.0 under Chinese environment, using mdb database format which is provided by Access 97.   The tool establishes the appropriate indexing structures in the database for tags marked on documents. Documents can be tagged and added into this system at different time though the editing mode of the tool; these tags will be converted into appropriate links by this tool.   Thus, this approach reduces the manual effort in creating address-based hyper-links among documents.   Figures 9 and 10 show the navigation map and browsing windows.

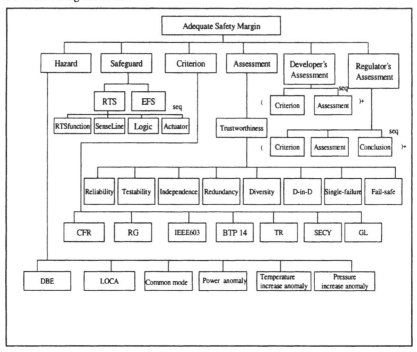

Fig. 3. Safety Markup Language structure

Safety Markup Language

<!ELEMENT AdequateSafetyMargin --(Hazard I Safeguard I Criterion I Assessment I
    DeveloperAssessment I RegulatorAssessment)* >
<!ELEMENT Hazard --(DBE I LOCA I CommonMode I TemperatureIncrease I
    PowerAnomaly I PressureAnomaly) >
<!ELEMENT Safeguard -- (RTS I EFS)>
<!ELEMENT RTS --(RTSfunction, SenseLine, Logic, Actuator) >
<!ELEMENT Criterion-- (CFR I RG I IEEE I BTP I TR ISECY IGL I #PCDATA) >
 <!ATTLIST Criterion Type (atHazard I atSafeguard I atTrustworthiness I atTMIReq)
    "atSafeguard" >
<!ELEMENT Assessment -- Trustworthiness>
<!ELEMENT Trustworthiness -- (Reliability ITestability I Independence I Redundancy I
    Diversity I DefenceInDepth I SingleFailure I FailSafe) * >
<!ELEMENT DeveloperAssessment -- (Criterion, Assessment) +>
<!ELEMENT RegulatorAssessmen-- (Criterion, Assessment, Conclusion) +>
-- all unspecified elements are #PCDATA --
<!ELEMENT DBE -- (#PCDATA) > ....<!ELEMENT Conclusion -- (#PCDATA) >

Fig. 4. SML in SGML

```
<!ENTITY    %doctype "SRP7.2" -- Standard Review Plan Sec. 7.2 Reviewers'
    Guideline -- >
<!ELEMENT        %doctype;  --  (ReviewArea,  Criterion+,  ReviewProcedure,
    RegulatorAssessment, Implementation, Reference) >
<!ELEMENT ReviewProcedure -- (ReviewTask , ReviewIssues) >
<!ELEMENT ReviewIssues -- (Criterion |Hazard | Trustworthiness ) + >
```

Fig. 5. SML and structural tags

```
SRP 7.2 Acceptance Criteria
<Criterion type="atTrustworthiness" > <CFR> 10 CFR 50.55a(a)(1), "Quality
    Standards." <\CFR> <\Criterion>
......
<Criterion type="atTMIReq" ><CFR>10 CFR 50.34(f), "Additional TMI-Related
    Requirements," or equivalent TMI action requirements imposed by Generic
    Letters. <\CFR><\Criterion >
```

Fig. 6. Marked instances

6. Discussion

We have performed experiments in using this tool in part of license review process of Lung-Men Nuclear Power Plant in Taiwan. The preliminary results show that the proposed approach can efficiently retrieve relevant information and reduce clerical work in review process. The potential improvements can be achieved by the SML-based approach are listed below:

1. Checking information completeness: In general, regulatory codes prescribe only the required information items for licensing review, but they give applicants the freedom to arrange these items into different documents for applicants' convenience [9]. However, it becomes the reviewer's nightmare to identify required information, which spreads over multiple documents. Safety Markup Language can alleviate this problem. For example, it used to take weeks for just checking whether the submitted documents have all the required information items, such as sections and paragraphs; while with appropriate tags, most of the checking can be done in seconds.
2. Reducing clerical work: Before licensing review, reviewers have to spend time in collecting and preparing relevant documents; during the review process, reviewers have to go back and forth between paragraphs of regulatory documents and the applicant's documents. With hyperlink-based documents, such traversal can be accomplished within one or two mouse clicks. The saved time can be devoted to analytical work to improve the review quality.
3. Tracing review issues: Tracing of safety issues is a major task during licensing process. When concern of safety is raised by reviewers, the applicant needs to resolve the concern. It becomes a question-and-answer process between reviewers and the applicant; sometimes the concern may expand and evolve into several complicated issues. It is troublesome for both reviewers and applicants to track the

history of these evolved issues. Now such issues and relevant information can be organized by using safety markup, and thus they can be retrieved as hyper-documents.

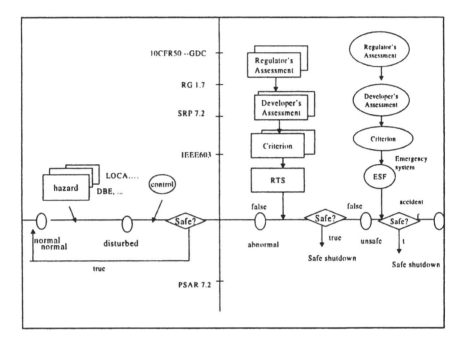

Fig. 7. Cross logical structure as a navigation map

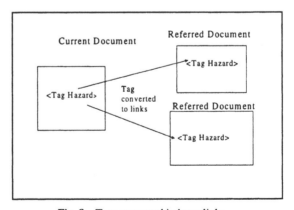

Fig. 8. Tags converted in hyperlinks

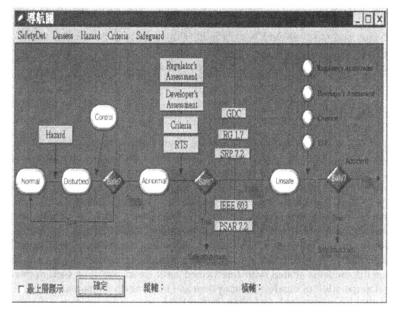

Fig. 9. Navigation map

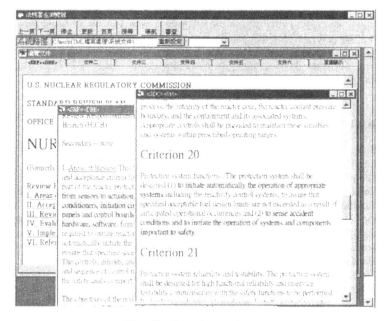

Fig. 10. Browsing mode

Compared with previous manual-based review experience, the hyper-document-based review is much more efficient and effective. The only problem is that in order to develop and maintain such a system, developers need to be familiar with both the markup language and nuclear regulatory codes. Technology transfer courses and procedures are desired to train more safety engineers to adopt this technique.

7. Conclusion

Anyone who once used hyperlink-based documents will be impressed by the powerful jumping feature and will agree that hyperlink-based documents can provide a more effective and flexible way of reading than paper-based documents. Since document reading plays an important role in safety engineering practice, it is desirable that safety related documents can be presented in hyperlink format, and then safety engineers' performance could be greatly enhanced.   But in reality hyperlink documents have not .been widely used in safety practice due to time-consuming hyperlink creation bottleneck. This paper proposes a concept-based tagging technique for constructing hyperlink documents. Some application domains need to manipulate multiple documents shared with intertwined basic concepts. For such domains, the logical association of the document system and underneath domain knowledge should be explicitly represented and then utilized for improving reading efficiency and support sophisticated processing. We proposed to use a cross navigation map to capture the logical structure or association of the nuclear software regulation system. We have defined a Safety Markup Language to represent domain concepts and their structures.   The pre-agreed processing of these tags can then be performed. This technique has been applied to part of software review process of Lung-Men Nuclear Power Plant with satisfactory results. The presented technique can also be applied to other domains besides safety practice, such as ISO quality system documents (ISO 9000) or software development life cycle document (IEEE 12207) to improve the efficiency of document review process.

References

1.   Bush, V., *As We May Think, Atlantic Monthly*, 176 (1945) 101-108
2.   Connonlly, D. and Bosak, J. "Extensible Markup Language (XML)," http://www.w3.org/XML/ (1997)
3.   Conklin, J., "Hypertext: An Introduction and Survey," *IEEE Computer* (1987) 17-41
4.   Goldfarb, C. F., *The SGML Handbook*, Oxford Univ. Press (1990)
5.   Ion, P. and Miner, R., "Mathematical Markup Language," W3C Working Drafte, http://www.w3.org/pub/WWW/TR/WD-math (1997)
6.   Jonasses, D. and Mandle, H., edited, *Designing Hypermedia for Learning*, Spring-Verlag (1989)
7.   Murray-Rust, P. "Chemical Markup Language (CML)," Version 1.0, http://www.venus.co.uk/omf/cml/ (1997)
8.   USNRC, NUREG 0800, *Standard Review Plan*, Chapter 7, "Instrumentation and Control"
9.   USNRC, BTP 14, *Acceptance Criteria for Digital I&C Software Review Process*

Extendable Ground-to-Air Communication Architecture for CoDySa

Algirdas Pakstas[1] and Igor Shagaev[2]

[1]University of Sunderland, School of Computing, Engineering and
Technology, Chester Road, Sunderland SR1 3SD, England
a.pakstas@ieee.org
[2]Institute of Control Sciences, Profsoyuznaya St. 65, Moscow, Russia
ish@ipu.rssi.ru

Abstract. Existing structure of the System for Objective Checking provides only passive safety of flying vehicles. CoDySa (Concept of Dynamic Safety) principles are based on analysis of operating cycle of aircraft. Implementation of CoDySa in practice presumes completing of the steps to modernize existing system. This paper presents further development of the CoDySa principles, namely ground-to-air communication architecture. Possibilities to upload safety-enhancing software components (*safelets*) are discussed together with scenarios of their use.

1 Introduction

Safety provision for vehicles such as aircraft, spacecraft, trains, ships, cars, etc. is of special importance because any serious technical failure could result in catastrophic consequences including loss of human life.

The existing Systems of Objective Checking (SOC) of aircraft and their related controls are normally based on the assumption that the greater is the amount of data about safety-critical devices, the better its in-flight conditions can be evaluated and correct recommendations worked out from post-flight logistic analysis. Some real accidents, however, indicate that in spite of extensive information concerning aircraft state and on-board events such as leakage, engine troubles, and pilot's errors, there was no way of avoiding them. Thus, organization of the collecting, registration, storing and processing of the flight control information is a problem that requires special attention.

Recent projects developed by EUROCONTROL such as Datalink [1] and Human Machine Interface for the Air Traffic Controllers [2] are addressing mainly on-ground activities as well as ground-to-air *message communication* in a standardized but fairly limited way. The real need, however, exists for systems that will be able to assist the pilot in more active ways, and when failure takes place will either tolerate it or assist graceful degradation to the appropriate (acceptable) state. Moreover, pilots in

M. Felici, K. Kanoun, A. Pasquini (Eds.): SAFECOMP'99, LNCS 1698, pp. 187-201, 1999
© Springer-Verlag Berlin Heidelberg 1999

complex cases are unable to provide correct recovery of the system after fault manifestation.

A Concept of Dynamic Safety (CoDySa) has been developed during 1990-1996 primarily targeting improvement of aircraft safety [3]. A working prototype of the system has been developed and tested on aircraft.

This paper is devoted to the further development of the CoDySa principles, namely ground-to-air communication architecture. Section 2 discusses role of the SOC in aircraft operation cycle. Sections 3 and 4 briefly present CoDySa principles here in order to introduce its most important features. Possibilities to upload Java *safelets* are discussed in the Section 5 while scenarios of their use are shown in the Section 6.

2. Role of SOC in The Aircraft Operation Cycle

Let's consider the operation cycle of the aircraft to which extremely strict safety requirements are applied. Flight cycle can be briefly divided into the following stages: take-off, flight proper, and landing. In terms of reliability, provision/ improvement of aircraft safety, obviously, means actions for successful completion of the operation cycle as shown in Fig. 1.

In existing aircraft SOCs (System of Objective Checking, Fig. 2) sensors are sending information to the control system and also, sometimes in a processed form, to the flight recorder.

The SOC system for railways is generally built in similar ways. The main SOC functions in these and similar systems are oriented to *collecting, registration* and *storing* of information on safety-critical devices *during* their mission.

The trend today in building SOC is to employ *flight recorders* featuring a greater volume of stored data, reduced size and weight, and higher environmental tolerance. It might be well to underscore that sequential data recording with mechanically translated carrier imposes on the SOC system certain functions and structure.

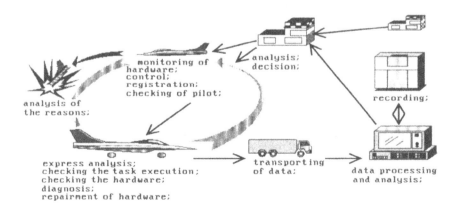

Fig.1. Model of the information flow in the flight cycle

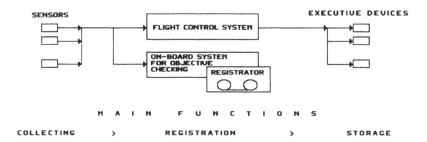

Fig.2. Basic structure and functions of the on-board System
for Objective Checking (SOC)

Fig. 3. Challenger case

In some extremely complicated systems such as Shuttle and test SOCs, the on-board information is sent to the ground-based part of the system where it is again tape-recorded!

According to the available information on the Challenger accident, owing to this SOC system organization, nothing was undertaken to save the situation, although all necessary data on the state of the spacecraft and its systems were available well before the explosion (Fig. 3).

The experience gained in Russia indicates that the time required for jettisoning a fuel tank and/or a stage is 0.1 sec at most, that for cabin with crew, 0.2 sec. Therefore, one could have benefited from the *10 seconds that were left before the explosion.*

Thus we come to the following conclusions concerning the structure of future SOCs:

(1) The major sources of faults and accidents with the vehicles are as follows: mechanical elements (body, engine, wings, fuselage, car suspensions, etc.); control systems and their components (electronic equipment; software; human operator, e.g. pilot or locomotive driver).

(2) The flow of SOC information in terms of safety is *basically incorrect and requires re-design.* In fact, the objective checking systems as are operated within the modern aviation environment are intended to cover manufacturers, flight administration etc. against liability claims rather than to save pilots and their crews, passengers, and environment from accidents and their consequences.

(3) To ensure safe operation of a flying vehicle, the flow of data must be *real-time processed* so that number of accidents can be minimised, and consequences reduced. The flying vehicle itself (or any other vehicle) should be designed so that its safety checking facilities are supported by adequate facilities for elimination of the causes of undesirable effects such as blocking, equipment reconfiguration, and restoration of vehicle operability.

(4) The human operator can be assisted in his decisions by the active support from the base with the help of additional information which may not be available on the vehicle at all or was not available before start of the mission. Thus, the *ground-to-air communication system* must be designed in order to deliver to the pilot essential information in an easy understandable form.

Thus, strictly speaking, the term SOC is obsolete for such a system. In its new role let us call this system on-Board Active Safety System (BASS). Notably, BASS will not replace control systems and pilot controls, but supports dynamically maximal flight safety.

3. BASS Structure

In order to make SOC *active* there are two essential steps:

(1) Replace tape-based memory to RAM-based storage (Fig. 4).

(2) Add processing facilities for compression of the flight data, analysis and forecast of the future trends, as well as prevention of possible undesirable effects (Fig.5).

(3) Design and develop safety systems more reliable than control systems.

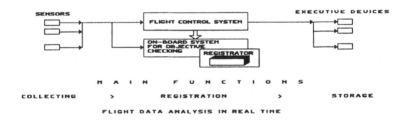

Fig. 4. Step1: replacing tape recorder by the RAM

For the identical size, magnetic tape capacity exceeds that of RAM by the factor of 3 to 4. Nevertheless, RAM-based devices can be regarded as acceptable because average compression ratio for the flight data varies between 9 and 12 what effectively eliminates factor of capacity from the criteria list. Additionally, RAM-based SOC devices will allow real-time access to the flight data stored in it. Replacement of the tape-based SOC devices to RAM-based would also enable higher frequency of the sampling of analogous signals which will give effect to the accuracy of the stored

Fig. 5. Step 2: adding processor

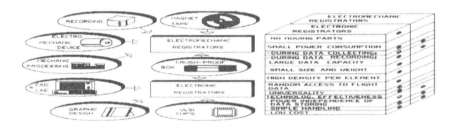

Fig. 6. Technological features of the design of the on-board flight recorders

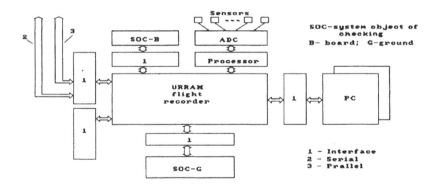

Fig. 7. BASS structure

data. The technical features involved in design and production of RAM-based storage are shown in the Fig. 6.

BASS prototype system has been designed and produced with factory testing during 1990-1994. The existing BASS comprises three ARINC boards, two boards of electronics and one of universal adaptive power supply. As any on-board unit, BASS is logically divided into two major zones (Fig.7), *active* and *passive*.

The *active* zone contains the processor and interfaces with the purpose to input and process the flight data. The structure of the *passive* zone is extremely regular [4], [5], [6].

4. Dynamic Safety System

For provision of the safe operation of the existing, intensively operated aircrafts, a ground-board safety system may be implemented as shown in Fig. 8.

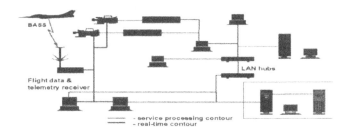

Fig. 8. CoDySa-based ground-board safety system.

It has coupled rings of two local area networks at the aerodrome enabling fast in-flight state analysis of the aircraft, automated flight preparation and servicing, and also, if using the available software and hardware simulators, profound analysis of the aircraft state, pilot's actions, etc. Real-time tasks will require use of the powerful workstations but off-line support (information and administration activities including personnel training) can be allocated to the more ordinary PCs. This combination enables reasonable cost/performance parameter for total system to be achieved.

5. Upploadable Safelets

On-board avionics systems are proprietary and no standardisation is expected in the foreseeable future. The various microprocessors employed dramatically vary in their performance. Motorola 68X2X, PowerPC 603, R4000, and 486DX2 those mentioned here. Thus, in the case where additional information (preferably in easily understandable visual format!) needs to be delivered to the pilot by uploading it from the ground station, there is an obvious need for a platform-independent solution. There are the following two ways to implement it:

- Add some additional equipment especially dedicated to receiving this extra information.
- Use the same processing facilities which already exist but provide software which will be able to accept some sort of standard document format.

The first method has the advantage that it can be totally isolated from control contours and it can be standardised in the same way as radio communication and navigation systems. However, it requires additional hardware on-board and it must be fitted in the same weight/space limits devoted to the avionics system. Additionally, since the nature of this equipment is to provide assistance to the pilot in special situations, it may never be used at all during the aircraft life. This consideration significantly reduces attractiveness of the first approach. The second method requires the choice of a standard format accepted by all aircraft manufacturers (also true for the first method!) and to implement a software system for every processor on-board to handle uploaded information.

There is one example of this in the computer industry where the PostScript format is used by many printers in order to produce pictures while printers are built using different microprocessors. In this case each printer type is equipped with the PostScript-interpreter.

Thus, functionally such upplodable agents (applets) will upgrade on-board avionics systems during the flight for achieving better safety. We will call these uploadable components *safelets*.

In a search for a platform-independent solution a *standard format* and either *interpreter-oriented* or *on-the-fly code-generation run-time system* will be investigated. We will discuss two possible solutions for implementation of safelets, namely Java and Juice.

Since safelets are sort of computer viruses which are added to the on-board systems, there is always the *hazard* that they are not authentic but are sent by irresponsible "jokers", or in case of the military aircraft, directly by enemy forces. Thus, security issues are raised as well.

5.1 Java

Why Java? Let's look at the three main reasons which make Java potentially suitable for safelet implementation.

First Reason: It is a programming language (i.e. *standard format*) which was specially designed for creation of platform-independent software. It works in such a way that every computer which wants to run Java-code, must be equipped with the *interpreter* and support libraries to implement necessary calculations or visualisation tasks.

Second Reason: Java has proved to be a feasible solution in the heterogenous computing environments *with dynamic uploading* of the information according to the user requirements.

Third Reason: Java applets are very much suitable for implementation of *the visualisation and animation* tasks which are important for time-constrained situations.

Java's distribution format is a sequence of so-called byte-codes. The inventors of Java thought up an "ideal" processor designed specifically for running Java programs and used the instruction set of this ideal processor as the "intermediate language" in which Java programs are shipped. It is entirely conceivable that the ideal Java processor can actually be implemented in hardware, and Sun has actually already announced such processors.

To summarise, Java includes the following features [7]: object-oriented language with data-centric model, native multi-threading support, garbage collection, no pointers, no macro support, compiler-generated symbolic byte code (interpretable), restricted access to run-time environment, runtime verification of code integrity, digital signature, encryption.

Critics against Java. Let's now discuss the arguments against Java.

Java is not real-time: This is the most obvious argument to reject Java for implementation of the mission-critical software. This argument, however, is based on the presumption that all avionics software must be hard real-time software. This is, in our opinion, not very applicable to safelets because most likely they will not be directly used to control aircraft but rather will try to assist the pilot by providing additional information. Finally, if it is still needed, there is already a published proposal [8] for a real-time dialect of Java which was enthusiastically evaluated by the developers of both kinds of applications – embedded systems and ordinary Java applications. Thus, we can expect a stable version of the real-time Java fairly soon.

Java applications are slow: This issue is related to the previous one and it is pretty much true because of the nature of the Java Byte Code interpretation. But in the majority of situations it should not cause a problem because uploadable information does not always have to be animated. Possible scenarios are discussed below.

Java is not safe: A number of security flaws, discovered in early implementations of Java, received a lot of publicity [9]. Needless to say these errors were corrected as soon as they were discovered.

The *Byte Code Verifier, Class Loader* and *Security Manager* has been discussed [10] as the means to ensure Java applet security.

Applying the verifier requires data-flow analysis and a partial repetition of the compiler's integrity checks. For each machine instruction, it must examine all possible paths leading to the instruction to ensure that the registers hold values of the appropriate type. This analysis requires structural information about the program that is not immediately available in a sequential virtual-machine instruction stream. Extracting the required structural information from such a "flat" representation is a time-consuming task whose complexity grows faster than linear program size. Thus, this feature indirectly makes Java less attractive for implementation of the critical real-time safelets.

There is also the possibility to sign applets with the user's digital signature [10]. Cryptography functions added to the Java Developer Kit are not sufficient for use worldwide because the U.S. federal government does not allow strong encryption tools to be included in software exported or used outside of the country.

Thus, the question is whether Java-safelets are secure enough to be used in serious applications. For aircraft with high security demands (such as military), Java is not recommended because the trade-off between the security aspects and its power is not good enough. But in aircraft where security is not a key issue, Java offers benefits along with acceptable security risks. Java applets are still a much better alternative than Microsoft's ActiveX, which does not include sufficient security mechanisms.

5.2 Juice

Origins of Juice. Juice [11] is a new technology for distributing executable code across the World Wide Web and in this respect, it is similar to Java. However, Juice differs from Java in several important aspects that allows it to outperform Java in many applications.

Juice grew out of a research project headed by Niklaus Wirth. His aim was to invent a language that was at once *simple* and *safe to use*. The new language should also support the *object-oriented programming paradigm*, be *efficiently compilable*, and applicable to a wide range of programming tasks from systems programming to teaching. A language with these properties was defined by Wirth in 1988 and given the name Oberon [12]. The overview of the Oberon implementation can be found in [13].

Oberon vs. Java. Oberon looks a lot like Pascal, and Java looks a lot like C. A closer comparison of Oberon and Java shows, however, many similarities:

- both languages are strongly typed while permitting the definition of "extended" types that are backward-compatible with their ancestors,
- both prohibit pointer arithmetic and mandate the presence of a garbage collector in their run-time environment, and
- both provide the notion of modular "packages" that are compiled separately and dynamically linked at run-time

The type paradigm applied by Java and Oberon has important consequence for the type-safety of the applets and will be discussed in more detail below. Here we just note that both languages are fully type-safe, and hence both are equally suitable for applet-programming.

Juice is to the Oberon language what the *Java Virtual Machine* is to the Java language: the means of distributing portable software.

Juice encompasses three key components:

- an architecture-neutral software distribution format,
- a compiler that translates from Oberon into the Juice portable format, and
- a plug-in that enables Netscape and Microsoft Internet Explorer browsers to run Juice applets.

Thus, Juice has a very similar application domain as Java and shares with the Java the same reasons (see above) which make it potentially suitable for safelet implementation.

Juice Outperforms Java. The most notable difference between comparable Juice and Java applets is probably that the Juice version of any applet is likely to run a lot faster than its Java counterpart [11]. Rather than being interpreted, as Java applets normally are, Juice always compiles each applet into the native code of the target machine before it begins execution [14]. Once an applet begins executing, it runs at the full speed of compiled code. Juice's on-the-fly compilation process is not only exceptionally fast, but it also generates object code that is comparable in quality to commercial C compilers. In contrast, even the latest just-in-time compilers for Java that have been announced by major vendors are not yet trying to compete with regular compilers.

Juice Compressed Tree Code vs. Java Byte-Code. The effectiveness of Juice largely depends on its software distribution format [11]. This distribution format (called *slim binaries)* is far more complex than Java byte code. It is based on a tree-shaped program representation as is typically used transiently within optimizing compilers. Rather than containing a linear code-sequence that can be interpreted byte-by-byte, a Juice-encoded applet contains a *compressed tree* that describes the actions of the original program [15], [16]. The tree preserves the control-flow structure of the original program, which makes it much easier to perform code optimization while the tree is translated into the native instruction set of the target machine.

In the actual Juice implementation, tree compression and linearization are performed concurrently, using a variant of the classic LZW data-compression algorithm [17]. Unlike the general-purpose compression technique described by Welch, however, the algorithm applied in Juice is able to exploit domain knowledge about the internal structure of the syntax tree being compressed. Consequently, it is able to achieve much higher information densities (Figure 9)

It appears that there are no conventional data-compression algorithms, regardless of whether applied to source code or to object code (for any architecture, including the Java virtual machine), that can yield a program representation as dense as the slim binary format [18].

Thus, users with slow (e.g. wireless) connections (or in emergency flight situations) save time by transmission Juice applets rather than Java applets of the same functionality.

In fact, the time saved by the faster downloading normally more than compensates for the on-the-fly compilation phase.

Juice's Enhanced Security. As it is noted in [18] the topic of mobile-code security is independent of the choice of programming language that a mobile program is written in, and also independent of the representation that is used in transporting applets to target machines. A minimum requirement is that *type-safety* is maintained.

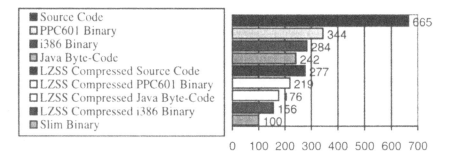

Fig. 9. Relative Size of a Representative Program Suite in Various Formats

However, absolute type-safety requires more than just compile-time checking because an attacker could hand-craft a malicious applet directly in the mobile code representation without passing it through a compiler, thereby circumventing the type-safety of the source language. As a consequence, mobile code needs to be scanned and verified *prior to execution* even if it is based on a "safe" language [19].

Juice tree-based encoding avoids many of the security issues that are difficult to solve in any environment based on a virtual-machine similar to Java [11]. By the very definition of the tree-encoding scheme, it is impossible to encode a tree that violates scoping rules of the source language. Such an "illegal" program cannot even be constructed by hand. Java's byte-code instructions, on the other hand, are at a much lower semantic level.

As discussed earlier, most of the existing implementations of Java provide code verifier for incoming mobile code [10]. Juice currently does not includes a code verifier. However, as it is stated by the Juice authors [18] this is simply a restriction of the current implementation of the Juice system, and does not mean that Juice's intermediate representation is less well suited for verification than Java's.

The tree-based Juice distribution format in effect makes this particular data-flow analysis unnecessary. It also allows for highly efficient load-time integrity checking, as every node in the encoded tree is fully typed.

The advantages of Juice are even more obvious for the large applets. Java, on the other hand, has an advantage in the area for which it was originally invented: embedded applications in consumer electronics and household appliances.

6. Scenarios for Using of Upploadable Information

As discussed earlier, human operators can be assisted with the help of additional information provided from the base. Let us look at the possible scenarios of using uploadable information.

6.1   Aircraft Emergency Landing

One obvious situation when such additional information can be extremely important is aircraft emergency landing. Civil aviation pilots are normally provided with maps and other important navigation sources but with certain limits imposed by the vehicle purpose (weight, space, etc.). Also, since nobody can be sure where and when an emergency landing will occur, even the most precise navigation sources, while helpful during the ordinary flight can be outdated or not detailed enough in the particular place where the landing must be fulfilled.

Examples of such additional information are location and other important parameters of the new bridges (possible obstacles), highways (possible landing lane), tower control information (avoiding conflicts with other aircraft in the sector).

Such information delivered by the safelets can be either static (e.g. drawings or maps) or dynamic (updatable map of the flights in the segment).

By all means this information must be much more clear and easy to understand and operate than current simple radar displays. Figure 10 shows a typical view of the current Air Traffic Control (ATC) system. Operation procedures there are based on manipulating the paper strips (or similar format electronic forms) with essential flight information.

6.2   Integration of Ground and On-board Air Traffic Control (ATC) Systems

There are already efforts to create a universal co-ordination system allowing transfer of aircraft Centre to Centre and sector to sector by means of predefined messages (SYSCO). However, this system is addressing only activities of control towers but is not directly intended to assist pilots. Work to create a paper-strip-less Human Machine Interface (HMI) for the next generation of ATC Systems is under way [2]. This HMI can easily be integrated within CoDySa in order to assist the pilot and provide him/her information which the air traffic controller will see on his/her display.

Fig. 10. Radar Display of the Current ATC

Figure 11 shows an example of the radar display from the Medium Term Conflict Detection System (MTCD) which is a part of the EATCHIP Phase III project. This is a system looking for potential conflicts along the 4D trajectories of all aircraft taking into account the clearances given to the aircraft by the control tower.

A potential conflict means that the trajectories of the aircraft involved are predicted to come closer than the allowed minimum distance. The route through the sector is displayed, starting from the actual position with segments of it coloured to show the conflict and its seriousness. The route for the other flight(s) involved is displayed with a dotted line to the area of conflict. After the conflict segment the route is not displayed.

Any potential conflict between *the Cleared Flight Level (CFL)* and the *Transfer Flight Level (TFL)* is displayed in yellow, meaning that the ATC clearance given will not lead to a conflict but the planned flight levels for the involved flights will lead to a conflict if the clearance to that level is given.

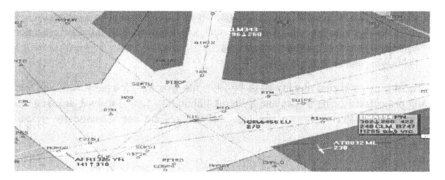

Fig. 11. Radar display of the future ATC system.

Any potential conflict between *the Actual Flight Level (AFL)* and the CFL is displayed in red, meaning that with the clearance given there will actually be a separation violation between the involved flights. All traffic not relevant to the subject aircraft is displayed in a grey colour.

The most attractive feature of this approach is that the HMI prototype is implemented in Java and this fact alone is a step towards a definition of the structure and contents, as well as the development of the standard class libraries for visualisation of the air traffic information. This experience could be useful in the Juice-based approach.

Conclusions

A new Concept of Dynamic Safety (CoDySa), the principles and approaches to its implementation are intended to modernize existing Systems for Objective Checking (SOC) which currently provide only *passive* safety of flying vehicles.

Use of the uploadable safelets for bringing important safety information to the pilot is suggested as a further development of the CoDySa.

There are following problems which should be solved before introducing safelets:

- Introducing regulations for the types of information uploadable to the aircraft. Set of messages defined in the HMI project [2] gives us a clear guideline for the selection of the appropriate information.
- Clarification of the status of the safelet in the process of making the decision by the pilot (information only, advice, strong advice, direct instruction from the control tower, etc.).
- Security mechanism for authentication of the safelets should be built in order to avoid hazards of the Trojan Horse.
- Finally, building infrastructure for uploading of safelets. This can be done gradually starting from pilot-project zones and extending experience worldwide.

Implementation of safelets (both for real-time and not) will need development of:

- Industry-standard, reusable and extendable software component library (classes).
- Development tools for various purposes such as human–machine interface generators, validation tools for Datalink messages, etc.
- Debugging and monitoring tools.

Having in mind that already back in 1996 the Boeing Company was beginning R&D project at Boeing's Airplane Systems Laboratory (ASL) to look at using Java for real-time projects, we can conclude that safelets are not nonsense for aviation industry after all.

References

1. ODIAC - Operational Requirements for Air Traffic Management (ATM) Air/Ground Data Communications Services, EUROCONTROL 1998.
    (http://www.eurocontrol.be/projects/eatchip/odiac/)
2. EATCHIP PHASE III Human Machine Interface (HMI). EUROCONTROL, 1998
    (http://www.eurocontrol.be/projects/eatchip/hmi/)
3. Shagaev, I., Pliaskota, S. BASS: on Board Active Safety System. Active Control of Safety. Flight Review, No. 7-8 (1996)
4. Shagaev, I. Yet Another Approach to Classification Of Redundancy. In: IMEKO Congress, Helsinki, Finland (1990) 117-124
5. Shagaev, I., et al. Fault Tolerant RAM With Extremely High Reliability, Part 1. Automatic and Remote Control, No.3 (1992)
6. Shagaev, I., et al. Fault Tolerant RAM with Extremely High Reliability, Part2. Automatic and Remote Control, No.2 (1993)
7. The Java language: a white paper. Sun Microsystems (1995) http://java.sun.com/
8. Nilsen, K. Real-Time Java (v.1.1) Iowa State University, Ames, Iowa (1996)
    www.newmonics.com

9. Dean, D., Felten, E. W., and Wallach, D. S. Java Security: From HotJava to Netscape and Beyond. In: Proceedings of the 1996 IEEE Symposium on Security and Privacy, Oakland, California (1996) 190-200
10. Niinimaki P., Markkanen P., Kajava J. Java Applets and Security. In: Databases and Information Systems, Proc. 3rd IEEE International Baltic Workshop, April 15-17, Riga, Latvia, Vol. 2 (1998) 125-136
11. Franz, M., Kistler, T. Introducing Juice. Irvine: University of California (1996) http://caesar.ics.uci.edu/ juice/index.html
12. Wirth, N. The Programming Language Oberon. Software – Practice and Experience, Vol.18, N 7 (1988) 671-691.
13. Brandis, M., Crelier, R., Franz, M., and Templ, J. The Oberon System Family. Software - Practice and Experience, Vol.25 No12 (1995) 1331-1366
14. Franz, M. Code-Generation On-the-Fly: A Key to Portable Software. Zürich: Verlag der Fachvereine, ISBN 3-7281-2115-0 (1994)
15. Franz, M., Kistler, T. Slim Binaries. Communications of the ACM, Vol.40, No 12 (1997) 87-94
16. Franz, M. Adaptive Compression of Syntax Trees and Iterative Dynamic Code Optimization: Two Basic Technologies for Mobile-Object Systems. In: Vitek, J. and Tschudin, C. (Eds.), Mobile Object Systems: Towards the Programmable Internet, Springer Lecture Notes in Computer Science, No. 1222 (1997) 263-276
17. Welch, T. A. A Technique for High-Performance Data Compression. IEEE Computer, Vol. 17, No 6 (1984) 8-19
18. Franz, M. Open Standards Beyond Java: On the Future of Mobile Code for the Internet. Journal of Universal Computer Science, Vol. 4, No:5 (1998) 521-532
19. Yellin, F. Low Level Security in Java. In: Fourth International World Wide Web Conference, World Wide Web Consortium, Boston, Massachusetts (1995) http://www.w3.org/pub/Conferences/WWW4/Papers/197

Hierarchical Reliability and Safety Models of Fault Tolerant Distributed Industrial Control Systems[1]

J.C. Campelo, P. Yuste, F. Rodríguez, P.J. Gil, and J.J. Serrano

Fault Tolerant Systems Group - Department of Computer Engineering
Technical University of Valencia – Camino de Vera s/n 46022 – Valencia. Spain
{jcampelo, pyuste, prodrig, pgil, juanjo}@disca.upv.es

Abstract. In order to study different configurations of distributed systems hierarchical models are needed. Hierarchical models are suitable to friendly and easily study the influence of different parameters in distributed systems. In this paper a hierarchical modelling approach of a distributed industrial control system is presented. In this sense, different fault tolerant techniques to be used are evaluated and different possible system configurations are studied. Two fault tolerant architectures for the distributed system nodes are explained and their influence in the whole system is evaluated. Also the benefits of using checkpointing techniques are presented. In order to do the hierarchical models we use stochastic activity networks and the UltraSAN tool.

1 Introduction

When distributed industrial control systems are designed, one of the aspects demanded in many cases goes through determining the reliability and safety obtained. In this sense, when different options and different fault tolerant techniques can be applied, it is desirable to model the system with each proposal to obtain the results for the dependability attributes.

In distributed industrial control systems, improvements concerning the dependability can be outlined in three different ways: at first level, different fault tolerant architectures can be used. At application level, checkpointing techniques based on recovery points can be also applied. Also, at network level different network application levels with fault tolerant capabilities can be used [5]. With the previous fault tolerance levels, distributed systems design implies some questions: How much reliability and safety can be obtained with different architectures? how are reliability and safety improved if recovery points are used? To study these aspects, it is interesting to have a distributed system model that can be easily changed to friendly determine the number of nodes, their architectures, number of networks, whether or not to use recovery points, etceteras.

---

[1] This work is supported by the Spanish *Comisión Interministerial de Ciencia y Tecnología* under project CICYT TAP96-1090-C04-01

M. Felici, K. Kanoun, A. Pasquini (Eds.): SAFECOMP'99, LNCS 1698, pp. 202–215, 1999
© Springer-Verlag Berlin Heidelberg 1999

The previous paragraphs justify the development of hierarchical models in order of easily change the basic modules of the whole system. In the related bibliography some complex models can be found. These models study different hardware systems and the hardware--software interactions [12][13][14][15].

In order to model the distributed system, we decided to use UltraSAN, a tool based on stochastic activity networks [1][2][3][9] and with the capability of doing composed models from simpler models.

The Fault Tolerant Systems Group (GSTF) of the Technical University of Valencia has developed different fault tolerant architectures for the distributed system nodes. In this sense, we are interested in analysing the system reliability and safety accomplished with these architectures and quantifying the benefits of using recovery points.

This paper is organised as follows: after the introduction, stochastic activity networks (SANs) and UltraSAN are presented. In section three the different fault tolerant architectures of the system nodes are analysed and their models are presented. After that, the hierarchical model is presented and the different configurations studies are described. Finally the results, conclusions and future work are presented.

2 Stochastic activity networks and UltraSAN

Stochastic activity networks (SANs), developed by Meyer and Sanders [1][2][3][9][10][11], are extensions to timed Petri nets. SANs are comprised of activities, places and input and output gates. The places, represented by a circle (just as in Petri nets), store tokens, and are used to represent the system resources or system states.

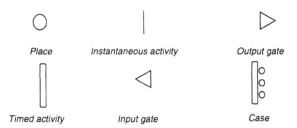

Fig. 1. Stochastic activity networks basics blocks

Two types of activities can be distinguished: timed activities and instantaneous activities. Timed activities represent delays by a probabilistic distribution. If the time to complete an operation is insignificant, then it can be modeled by instantaneous activities. Cases are used to model uncertainty about what happens upon completion of an activity.

Activities are enabled when the preceding places have any mark or also when a gate enables them. Gates serve to connect places and activities. Input gates provide flexibility in specifying enable conditions for activities. On the other hand, output gates, specify how the marking is updated upon the completion of an activity. Input gates are composed of a predicate and a function. Output gates only have an associated function. The input gate predicate is a boolean expression. Thus, when the predicate is true, the gate is enabled. This gate enabling causes that the activities connected to it are activated. So, when the time associated to activities elapses, the function associated with the input gate will be executed. The gates predicate and function can be represented by all the instructions of the C programming language.

To specify the model, UltraSAN offers a graphical interface (X-Window) under UNIX and LINUX operating systems. One of the most interesting features of this tool is the possibility of doing hierarchical designs, using the UltraSAN composed model option. Under this name the join and replicate primitives appear to make more complex models (Fig. 2) from independent and simpler models (Fig. 2: memory, E/S and CPUs). Join and replicate primitives communicate through a set of places identified as common among the SANs.

Rate rewards and impulse rewards are the formalism used in UltraSAN to define the variables to measure. Rate rewards are associated with the marking of the SAN while impulse rewards are associated to the expiration of the activities. In this sense a reward can be associated to some system state or states that result meaningful to determine how much time does the system spend in those states.

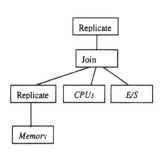

Fig. 2. Composed model example

3 Node architectures

In this section two different architectures for the nodes of the distributed system will be explained. More detailed information about these architectures can be found in [4].

3.1 Architecture-I

The architecture-I has as its main objective reliability and safety improvements with a low cost. This node architecture is shown in Fig. 3. It consists of two communication networks, two microcontrollers, one for communication tasks (8-bit microcontroller) and other for the execution of the control algorithms (16-bit microcontroller with on-chip CAN interface), and a dual-port RAM.

Commonly in industrial applications different nodes could accomplish similar functions. This is due to the fact that they can be connected to the same set of sensors and actuators. So, checkpointing techniques can be used to allow recovering of failed nodes. To do this, an important aspect is to store the state of each node in the dual-

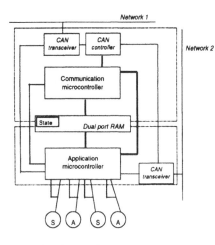

Fig. 3. Architecture I

port RAM and to update it periodically. Thus, in case of failure in the application microcontroller, the communication microcontroller can send the state to other node that could continue its function (if it is connected to the same set of sensors and actuators). To do this, an important aspect is to reach a high error coverage, mainly for the application microcontroller (the most complex component). In order to obtain a high error coverage, the communication microcontroller fulfils, also, functions of watchdog processor. In this way, the communication microcontroller can detect errors in the other processor and inhibit possible outputs to the actuators and possible error messages to the network (this is known as fail-silent behaviour).

3.2   Architecture II

The second node architecture has as main objective to obtain better reliability (Fig. 4). This is due to the fact, that when is not possible (physically) to connect sensors and actuators to several nodes we need a structure which offers better reliability. So, this architecture continues its function in presence of a permanent failure in one of the application microcontrollers (in addition to transient failures).

Architecture II modifies the previous one slightly with the addition of a second 16-bit microcontroller for the application (spare), so the system can recover from a permanent failure. If the communication microcontroller detects a failure in the application microcontroller will stop it and run the spare.

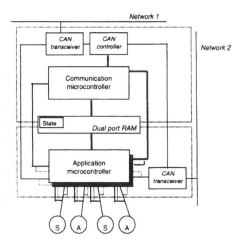

Fig. 4. Architecture II

3.3 Dependability models

Architecture-I model. The model that represents a single node with architecture-I is shown in Fig. 5. In this model each place represents a state of the system and is the direct conversion of the Markov model for reliability and safety [4].

Activities between places represent the transitions from one state to another. In Table 1, the expressions of these transitions are shown.

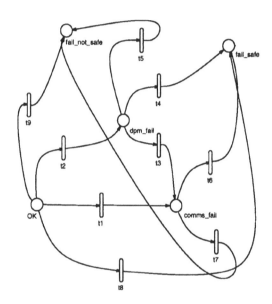

Fig. 5. Architecture I: SAN model

Table 1. Activity time distributions for SAN model

Activity	Expression
t9	$\lambda_{cpu}(1-C_{cpu})P_p + \lambda_{mdp}(1-C_{mdp})P_p + \lambda_{ic}(1-C_{ic})P_p + \lambda_{cpu}(1-Ct_{cpu})(1-P_p) + \lambda_{mdp}(1-Ct_{mdp})(1-P_p) + \lambda_{ic}(1-Ct_{ic})(1-P_p)$
t8	$\lambda_{cpu}C_{cpu}\,P_p$
t4	$\lambda_{cpu}C_{cpu}P_p$
t5	$\lambda_{cpu}(1-C_{cpu})P_p + \lambda_{ic}(1-C_{ic})P_p + \lambda_{cpu}(1-Ct_{cpu})(1-P_p) + \lambda_{ic}(1-Ct_{ic})(1-P_p)$
t2	$\lambda_{mdp}C_{mdp}\,P_p$
t1	$\lambda_{ic}C_{ic}\,P_p$
t3	$\lambda_{ic}C_{ic}\,P_p$
t6	$\lambda_{cpu}C'_{cpu}\,P_p$
t7	$\lambda_{cpu}(1-C'_{cpu})\,P_p + \lambda_{cpu}(1-Ct'_{cpu})(1-P_p)$

In table 2 the meaning of the different factors that we can see in the transition equations is explained.

Table 2. Meaning of the factors

λ_{cpu}	Application microcontroller failure rate
λ_{ic}	Communication microcontroller failure rate
λ_{mdp}	Dual port memory failure rate
C_{cpu}	Permanent errors coverage of the application microcontroller
C_{mdp}	Permanent errors coverage of the dual port memory
C_{ic}	Permanent errors coverage of the communication microcontroller
C_{tcpu}	Transient errors coverage of the application microcontroller
C_{tic}	Transient errors coverage of the communication microcontroller
C_{tmdp}	Transient errors coverage of the dual port memory
$C_{t'cpu}$	Transient errors coverage of the application microcontroller when the communication microcontroller (*watchdog processor*) is faulty.
C'_{cpu}	Permanent errors coverage of the application microcontroller when the communication microcontroller (*watchdog processor*) is faulty.
P_p	Permanent failures probability.
$(1-P_p)$	Transient failures probability.

Architecture-II model. The second node architecture considered is the double-node. It is a node in which the main microcontroller is replicated and, in case of a failure, it can be switched off and recovered.

The model for this node is thus based on the previous, but considering the following cases (Fig. 6):

- There are two microcontrollers.
- One of them has failed and the system has recovered. What we have now is the same as in the single node case.
- The spare microcontroller has failed and the error has not been detected. The node will keep working but any failure in the application microcontroller will make it crash.

3.4 Nodes dependability results

We have obtained reliability and safety results of the node architectures solving the previous models. The values showed in table 3 have been chosen for the models.

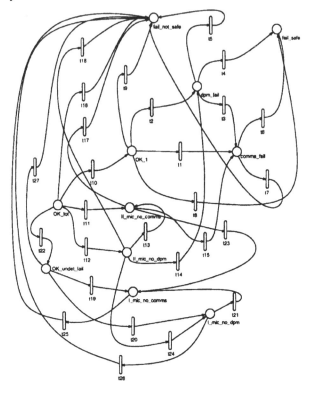

Fig. 6. Architecture-II SAN model

Table 3. Parameters for models resolution

Application microcontroller failure rate	1e-05
Communication microcontroller failure rate	1e-04
Dual port memory failure rate	1e-04
Permanent errors coverage of the application microcontroller	0.99
Permanent errors coverage for the application microcontroller when the communication microcontroller (watchdog) is faulty.	0.5
Permanent errors coverage of the dual port memory	0.999
Permanent errors coverage of the communication microcontroller.	0.8
Transient errors coverage of the communication microcontroller.	0.8
Transient errors coverage for the dual port memory	0.999
Transient errors coverage for the application microcontroller.	0.75, 0.80, 0.85, 0.90, 0.95, 0.99, 0.999
Permanent failure probability -- Time	0.2 -- 10000 h

In Table 4 the node reliability and safety results can be seen (for both architecture I and II).

Table 4. Nodes reliability and safety

	Reliability (I)	Safety (I)	Reliability (II)	Safety (II)
Ct=0.75	0,9588465	0,97822869	0,977663573	0,9780142
Ct=0.80	0,96268653	0,98210725	0,98155103	0,9819305
Ct=0.85	0,966554194	0,9860013	0,98548202	0,98586249
Ct=0.9	0,97041281	0,98991089	0,98942875	0,98981024
Ct=0.95	0,97741949	0,99383611	0,9933913	0,99377381
Ct=0.99	0,97429918	0,99698756	0,99657277	0,99695688
Ct=0.999	0,97812293	0,99769802	0,99729001	0,99767351

4. Distributed system model

Now, that the dependability attributes of a node are known, new questions arise about the distributed system. These questions are: what about the dependability of the distributed system? How are reliability and safety improved if recovery points are used? In order to study these aspects a distributed system model is presented.

We are assuming a distributed industrial control system composed by six fault tolerant nodes as described in the previous section. We are interested in analysing different configurations of the system. These configurations are:

1. Configuration 1: six fault tolerant nodes -architecture I- without using checkpointing.
2. Configuration 2: six fault tolerant nodes -architecture I- using checkpointing. In this case, due to the process to control node 3 can continue node 4 jobs and vice-versa. The same behaviour also applies for nodes 5 and 6. Node 1 and node 2 can not be recovered by any other.
3. Configuration 3: same configuration of case 2, but using architecture-II for nodes 1 and 2.
4. Configuration 4: six fault tolerant nodes -architecture II- without using checkpointing.

4.1 Modelling approach

In order to develop a hierarchical model of the distributed system, we are going to do a composed model. This composed model will be based in different and independent blocks. In first place, as it can be seen in Fig. 7, we have a module to represent the communication networks.

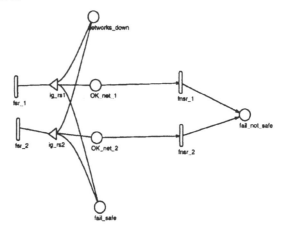

Fig. 7. Net submodel

In the beginning there is one mark for each working net, in place "OK_net_X", when a net crashes its mark goes to place "networks_down" where there will be a mark for each failed net. In this system we are using only a maximum of two copies of resources (networks), but this concept of a place keeping the account of failed units can be easily extended to a higher amount just by changing the number of allowable failed units of the resource before a system failure occurs taking the system to the "fail_safe" state.

It is remarkable that this will work only for covered errors, when the system detects the error and reconfigures itself to work with less units, because any uncovered error will directly take the system to the "fail_not_safe" state.

Activities represent an exponentially distributed variable with a rate equal to the expected failure rate of the corresponding component. In this model there are four activities modelling the networks behaviour.

Activities "fnsr_X" have a rate of: $(\lambda n) * (1- (Pp)) * (1- (Cn))$, where:

- λn is the network failure rate.
- Pp is the probability of the failure being permanent.
- Cn is the network error coverage, that is, the probability of the error being covered by the error detection mechanisms in the system.

This means that all non-permanent, uncovered network errors will take the system to the "fail_not_safe" state. Activities "fsr_1" and "fsr_2" have a rate of: $(\lambda n) * (Pp)$. This means that all permanent network errors will be detected and if the system is unable to reconfigure itself (if there are no spare networks left) it will go to "fail_safe" state. Input gates are in charge of deciding when activities are enabled and what to do upon completion of the activity.

Following with our example of network failures, activities "fnsr_X" will be enabled as long as there are marks in places "OK_net_1" and "OK_net_2" respectively. This means that as long as there is any network running, there is the possibility of one of them failing and taking the system to the "fail_not_safe" state. Gates "ig_rs1" and "ig_rs2" enable activities "fsr_1" and "fsr_2" when there are marks in "OK_net_1" and "OK_net_2". So far this works the same way, the difference comes when this activities complete. If there is no mark in place "networks_down" the mark in the failed net goes to this place. When the spare net fails there will already be a mark in "networks_down" so with no network left the whole communications system will fail. The piece of code that defines input gate "ig_rs1" in UltraSAN is:

```
Predicate:
  MARK(OK_net_1)>0
Function:
  MARK(OK_net_1)=0;
  if(MARK(networks_down)>0)
              MARK(fail_safe)=1;
      else  MARK(networks_down)++;
```

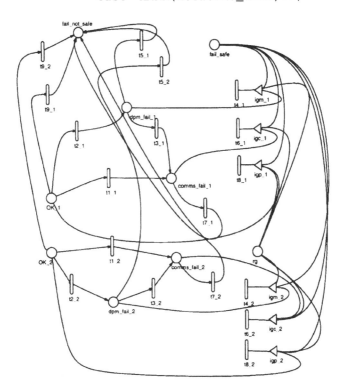

Fig. 8. Two-node cluster

In second place we have the module that implements the nodes that can not be recovered by anyone else (Fig. 5 or 6). If nodes can be recovered by another one, a third block is needed. As it can be seen in Fig. 8, it is necessary to develop a new model to represent the interactions between two nodes. It is based on two single node subnets but considering a resource place in which there are as many marks as failed nodes. It works the same way as the communication networks subnet of the previous model.

The place that accomplishes this job is place "rg". The places "fail_safe" and "fail_not_safe" are common among all the models that compose the hierarchical model. If three or more nodes can be recovered, only a new submodel needs to be done to model this behaviour and joined with the rest of the model.

For nodes that can not be recovered by any other, we are considering using, as it has been said, architecture II (Fig. 6) to compare the results with the ones obtained with architecture I nodes. In the following figures the hierarchical models are presented.

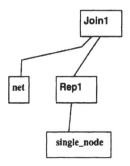

Fig. 9. Six architecture-I nodes without checkpointing

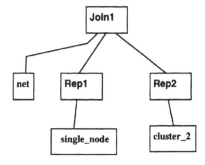

Fig. 10. Six architecture-I nodes with checkpointing in four of them

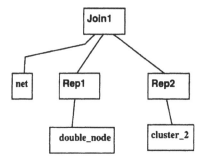

Fig. 11. Two architecture-II nodes and four architecture-I nodes with checkpointing

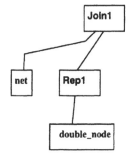

Fig. 12. Six architecture-II nodes without checkpointing

As it can be seen in the previous figures, by changing the hierarchical structure we can study different configurations. So, in Fig. 9, Rep1 indicates 6 replicas of the single node model whereas in Fig. 12 changing only the node subnet (double_node) allows us to study another system configuration in which we have architecture-II nodes. In Fig. 10 and 11, Rep1 are two replicas of the node subnets (architecture-I or II) and Rep 2 are two replicas of the recoverable cluster (Fig. 8) composed by two architecture-I nodes each with checkpointing.

4.2   Results

In order to obtain the reliability, rate rewards in the places of the model named "Fail_not_safe" and "Fail_safe" are used. In these places the predicate is MARK(Fail_not_safe) > 0 || MARK(Fail_safe) > 0 and the function associated is equal to 1. So, this metric represents the non-reliability of the system (1-reliability). For safety, the rate reward is only associated with the "Fail_not_ safe" place. In this case, the predicate is MARK(Fail_not_safe) > 0 and the function associated is equal to 1. Therefore, this metric represents the non-safety of the system. These rewards have been measured on fail safe and fail not safe places of net subnet. In order for these places to represent the marking of the full system, fail safe and fail not safe places in all subnets must be made common.

In Fig. 13 and 14 reliability and safety results of different configurations are shown. These results have been obtained with a transient error coverage equal to 0.75 (a realistic value from fault injection campaigns), a network failure rate equal to the application microcontroller failure rate and the rest of variable settings as shown in Table 3.

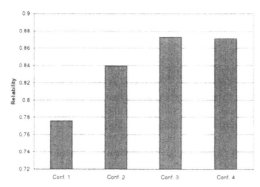

Fig. 13. System reliability

In Fig. 13 the improvements due to the use of checkpointing technique (configuration 1 versus configuration 2) can be seen. In the same figure, configurations 3 and 4 versus 1 and 2, show the benefits of the inclusion of architecure-II nodes. Also, from the reliability point of view, using 6 architecture-II nodes without checkpointing does not improve the results obtained with configuration 3, in which we have two architecture-II and four architecture-I nodes with checkpoints. From the safety point of view, little difference can be seen (Fig. 14). This is due to the close results of node safeties (Table 4). As in the nodes, configuration 4 (composed by six architecture-II nodes) shows the worst (relatively) safety results. This is due to the higher complexity of architecture II.

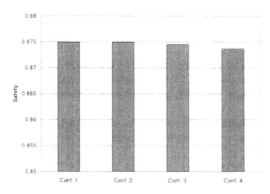

Fig. 14. System safety

5   Conclusions

In this paper a modelling approach to study the reliability and safety of a distributed system has been presented. This model is based on the models of the fault tolerant nodes in the system. A hierarchical approach of distributed system modelling has been presented. With the distributed system model we can study the influence of different fault tolerant techniques.

Although a hierarchical distributed industrial control system model has been presented, this modelling approach is applicable to generic distributed systems. As it can be seen in the results, from the reliability point of view, checkpointing techniques are a suitable option to avoid the need for a more complex and expensive architecture. Obviously, a performance study is also necessary to evaluate the performance degradation due to checkpointing. This study is going to be done in near future. Also, network failure rate influence, common mode faults and other configurations are going to be studied.

6   References

1. Meyer, J.F., Sanders, W.H.: Specification and construction of performability models. Proceedings of the Second International Workshop on Performability Modelling of Computer and Communication Systems, Mont-Saint-Michel, France (1993)
2. Sanders, W.H., Meyer, J.F.: Reduced base model construction methods for stochastic activity networks. IEEE Journal on Selected Areas in Communications, vol. 9, (1991) 25-36
3. Meyer, J.F., Movaghar, A., Sanders, W.H.: Stochastic activity networks: structure, behaviour and application. Proceedings of the International Conference on Timed Petri Nets. Torino, Italy. (1985) 106-115
4. Campelo, J.C., Rodríguez, F., Gil, P.J., Serrano, J.J.: Dependability evaluation of fault tolerant architectures in distributed industrial control system. 2nd IEEE International Workshop on Factory Communication Systems, Barcelona, Spain. (1997) 193-200.
5. Campelo, J.C., Rubio, A., Rodríguez, F., Serrano, J.J.: Fault tolerance in distributed industrial control systems. 1998 Western Multiconference on Computer Simulation, San Diego, USA. (1998) 87-92
6. Campelo, J.C., Yuste, P., Rodríguez, F., Gil, P.J., Serrano, J.J.: Dependability evaluation of fault tolerant distributed industrial control systems. Seventh International Workshop on Parallel and Distributed Real-Time Systems (WDPRTS 1999), San Juan, Puerto Rico. (1999) 384-388
7. Prodromides, K.H., Sanders, W.H.: Performability evaluation of CSMA/CD and CSMA/DCR protocols under transient fault conditions. IEEE Transactions on Reliability, vol. 42 (1993) 116-127
8. Prodromides, K.H., Sanders, W.H.: Performability evaluation of CSMA/CD and CSMA/DCR protocols under transient fault conditions. Proceedings of the Tenth Symposium on Reliable Distributed System, Pisa, Italy (1991) 166-176
9. Sanders, W.H., Obal, W. D.: Dependability evaluation using UltraSAN. 23th International Symposium on Fault Tolerant Computing, Toulouse, France. (1993) 674-679

10. Sanders, W.H., Obal, W. D., Qureshi, M.A, Widjarnako, F.A. UltraSAN version 3: architecture, features, and implementation. Technical report 95S02, Center for reliable and high-performance computing. Coordinated science laboratory. University of Illinois at Urbana-Chanpaign. (1995)

11. UIUC: UltraSAN users manual version 3. Center for Reliable and High Performance Computing, Coordinated Science Laboratory, University of Illinois at Urbana-Champaign (1995)

12. Borrel, M.: Interactions entre composants matériel et logiciel de systèmes tolérants aux fautes. Caractérisation, formalisation, modélisation. Applicacion á la sûreté de fonctionnement du CAUTRA : Thèse. Laboratoire d'Analyse et d'Architecture des Systèmes du CNRS (LAAS) Rapport LAAS n. 96001. (1996)

13. Kanoun, K., Borrel, M., Morteveille, T., Peytavin, A.: Modelling the dependability of CAUTRA, a subset of the French air traffic control system. 26ᵗʰ Symposium on Fault-Tolerant Computing. Sendai, Japan. (1996) 106-115

14. Kanoun, K., Borrel, M.: Dependability of fault-tolerant systems: explicit modelling of the interactions between hardware and software components. Proceedings of the IEEE International Computer Performance and Dependability Symposium (IPDS'96) (1996).

15. Nelli, M., Bondavalli, A., Simoncini, L. : Dependability modelling and analysis of complex control systems: an application to railway interlocking. Dependable Computing - EDDC2-. Second European Dependable Computing Conference. Taormina, Italy. (1996) 93-110

The Development of a Commercial "Shrink-Wrapped Application" to Safety Integrity Level 2: The DUST-EXPERT™ Story

Tim Clement, Ian Cottam, Peter Froome, and Claire Jones

Adelard, Coborn House, 3 Coborn Road, London, E3 2DA, UK
pkdf@adelard.co.uk

Abstract. We report on some of the development issues of a commercial "shrink-wrapped application"—DUST-EXPERT™—that is of particular interest to the safety and software engineering community. Amongst other things, the following are reported on and discussed: the use of formal methods; advisory systems as safety related systems; safety integrity levels and the general construction of DUST-EXPERT's safety case; statistical testing checked by an "oracle" derived from the formal specification; and our achieved productivity and error density.

1 Background and Introduction

The DUST-EXPERT advisory system was developed by Adelard from detailed requirements [1]—including new engineering theory—produced by the UK Health and Safety Executive (HSE).

DUST-EXPERT advises on the safe design and operation of plant that is subject to dust explosions. It is related to, but not directly based on, the prototype of the system developed by Dr Sunil Vadera and colleagues at Salford University. The Salford software is now referred to as the "research version" to distinguish it from Adelard's commercial version. HSE successfully used the research version for some time but realised that, if the technology was to become more widely used, a fully quality assured version was needed. Similarly, it would be necessary to develop the system to some appropriate SIL—Safety Integrity Level—as defined by IEC 61508 [2]. Of course, this standard does not exactly apply to an advisory system such as DUST-EXPERT, as there is no "equipment under control" as such, but we followed the requirements of Part 3 of the standard so far as practicable.

The DUST-EXPERT application provides:

- *general advice* on preventing dust explosions, via the familiar Microsoft Windows™ Hypertext Help system (both general help and also context dependent)
- *user-extensible databases* containing properties of over a thousand types of dust and a few sample properties of construction materials
- *decision trees* that are used in determining which approaches (such as fitting an explosion relief vent, or suppression) are appropriate for the plant under investigation

M. Felici, K. Kanoun, A. Pasquini (Eds.): SAFECOMP'99, LNCS 1698, pp. 216–225, 1999
© Springer-Verlag Berlin Heidelberg 1999

- *calculation methods* for quantitative analysis of, for example, the size of vents needed to control the effect of explosions and the strength of typical vessels

The system was originally specified to run under DOS/Windows 3.1 but also runs on Microsoft's 32-bit operating systems, and has been extensively validated for the original Windows 95 release.

2   The Safety Integrity Level of an Advisory System

To some people the idea of an advisory system being safety related is akin to saying a book (such as [3] in this case) is safety related. Others observe the way in which numbers produced by computer-based systems are taken as gospel and are rarely double-checked, certainly unlike reading a point off a graph in a reference text.

In order to determine the appropriate SIL, we conducted a fault tree analysis from data of reported explosions, the ratio of injuries to fatalities, etc. (see for example [4]). Briefly, we concluded that assuming the failure of explosion relief vents led to 1 death/100 000 workers/year, the vent is at SIL 1, and DUST-EXPERT—as a potential contributing factor—should be developed to SIL 2.

3   The Development Process

The project team put together for DUST-EXPERT had the structure illustrated in Fig. 1.

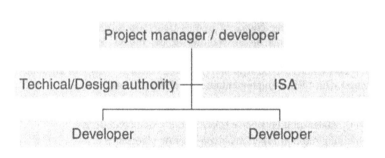

Fig. 1. The team structure

ISA stands for Independent Safety Assessor; he was an Adelard employee but was otherwise independent of the development team. Within the development team there was some sharing of roles: for example, the project manager switched from development to testing as the project progressed, and the technical design authority assisted the two main developers.

The overall shape of the development process was of the type known as the "V with prototyping" model. That is, a traditional approach is taken with diversions, in parallel, to produce input for downstream activities, the main one being to build a dummy system in order to carry out user interface acceptability trials. Prior to Adelard's involvement, HSE had also used the research prototype in order to construct a solid and complete requirement specification. That effort was the main factor in Adelard being able to select a low risk, standard V-model for the development of the commercial, quality assured version.

We chose to build the model of the system in a standard formal specification language (VDM [5]) for the following reasons:

• VDM is a rich and expressive notation for expressing design models.
• Compared with the obvious choice of direct modelling in the main implementation language (Prolog), we gained a strong type system with explicit operation domains, a collection of abstract data types such as sets and maps, and a powerful notation for expressing functions and state changing operations (especially useful for modelling both the database feature and the Windows' interface).
• The IFAD VDM toolbox was available for both type checking of the model and also animating it (where theoretically possible); this latter feature was used both in validating the model and downstream as an oracle against which we could check the results of the pseudo-randomly generated test cases.
• We gained greater confidence in the design than if, say, we had employed some pseudo-code notation without a formal semantics.
• We were able to carry out a software Hazops on the VDM model itself as well as using it for structuring reviews.
• The standard VDM proof obligations allowed us to check the requirements for consistency, although for cost reasons we only carried out these checks informally.

The entire functionality was modelled; the most novel aspect of which is the formal model of the user interface. A separate description of this has recently been published [6].

Once we had an acceptable model of (at least the vast majority of) the requirements, we faced the choice of how to transform this model into code (Prolog) whilst retaining confidence in the validity of the model. We chose to carry out a refinement within VDM to a level where we could define one-to-one transliterations from the VDM features to corresponding Prolog features. This was all done by hand[1] with reviews. Our "VDM implementation level model" has:

• sets and maps implemented as lists
• Windows' states split between explicit and implicit conditions
• the remaining implicit functions given definite algorithms

The transliteration to Prolog was first described in a written procedure and then checked in reviews. This step was probably the most error prone in the development as clerical errors are extremely difficult to spot by review and Prolog compilers are,

---

[1] It is worth noting that in the meantime the IFAD VDM toolbox feature of being able to generate C++ code from (most of) a VDM model has matured, and that that approach, which we rejected because of its immaturity at the time, should be considered for other developments.

by definition, forgiving of such mistakes. Still, our final error density was pleasingly low (see Section 4 below).

C++ code was developed by making simple correspondences between, for example, "add element to list" with "add new information line to window".

4   Productivity and Other Metrics

DUST-EXPERT consists of 15 820 lines[2] written in Prolog and 17 554 lines in C++. The Prolog is relatively complex compared to the C++ code used for the user interface, and yet is shorter. A number of factors are at work here: Prolog is at a higher level of abstraction than C++ and much of the C++ code was generated from tools or was simply textually replicated as necessary.

Our productivity was above industry norms with the Prolog being "produced" at approximately half the rate of the C++. This, again, has to do with complexity and the much more rigorous way in which the core Prolog was generated compared with the C++ code; doubtless human and other factors played their parts too.

At the conclusion of statistical and path coverage testing there were 31 known faults, spread across both the Prolog and C++. This amounts to less than 1 per KLOC (thousand lines of code). Of these discovered faults most were minor and only one could be regarded as remotely safety related; through a coding slip from VDM to Prolog it was possible to circumvent the security of the password protected database partitions.

Since release a further small number of faults have come to light, none of which are safety related, and our error density is still just under 1 per KLOC.

There are some 70+ formal reviews recorded in the project database. These are of various kinds: documents, code, progress, etc. They average out at approximately one per week over the development period.

5   User Interface Prototype

The research version of DUST-EXPERT was a DOS application and had very limited facilities for data entry. This had been identified by HSE as a weakness in the system. As the use of Windows allowed a much richer interface, we proposed to develop a prototype program to demonstrate to the client, and test on potential users, the acceptability of the interface design. Furthermore, we wanted the interface to be as intuitive as possible for users to prevent possibly dangerous misunderstandings.

The user interface prototype had no functionality for actually calculating values, but merely allowed the user to enter values through a calculation screen, navigate a single decision tree and use the Windows' help. We consulted with a user-interface expert on the initial design and then carried out trials with some typical users at our site; other users were sent disks to install the prototype on their own systems and a

---

[2] All lines of code are measured as non-blank, non-comment lines. The Prolog also follows our VDM style of naming and layout, which produces (perhaps unusually) wide lines of code.

questionnaire to fill in for feedback. This resulted in several useful changes to the screen layouts, which were then demonstrated to the Project Board.

The DUST-EXPERT user interface design is regarded as very successful. It is believed to have completely changed the attitude towards Windows and Windows-based software of some of the application's champions and early adopters within HSE.

6   Safety Case

The safety claims applicable to DUST-EXPERT are listed in the following table.

Table 1. Safety claims

	Safety claim
1	Functional correctness
2	Accuracy (the results are sufficiently accurate when calculated using finite-precision arithmetic, and numerical instability should be detected)
3	Security (appropriate steps are taken to prevent malicious and accidental changes to methods and data)
4	Modifiability (the chance of maintenance-induced errors is minimised)
5	Fail safety (there is a low probability of unrevealed failures)
6	Usability (the system makes it hard for users to make errors)

A case that would justify Safety Integrity Level 2 was necessary. After some further study, the Adelard project team concluded that we could use several of the techniques usually associated with SIL 3 developments at either manageable or no extra cost.[3] Two examples are the use of formal specification techniques, rather than say structured methods, and a somewhat larger amount of statistical testing than is actually predicted as strictly necessary by the theory for a confidence level of 95%. Provided costs can be kept to acceptable levels, this approach is clearly a good one as it helps to overcome the inevitable level of uncertainty present in the underlying assumptions.

A full Safety Case was produced as a so called "living document" (i.e. there were initial, interim and operational versions) to justify the development, based on:

- a formal specification (the model) of the entire system, including the user interface, in ISO Standard VDM
- identifying and carrying out informal, hand proofs of safety properties on the formal model
- execution of an appropriate subset of the formal model as an "oracle" to aid in verification and validation

---

[3] Because, for example, the project team members were all familiar with formal modelling techniques.

- implementation in Prolog where possible (being semantically close to the VDM used in the model) and otherwise in C++ for maximum flexibility in the user interface
- a significant quantity of testing of the integrated system
- a "design for safety" approach where design features were adopted to support the safety arguments

The structure of the safety case follows Def Stan 00-55 [7] recommendations and also Adelard's own (emerging at that time, now published [8]) safety case development methodology. Statistical testing is dealt with in some detail (Section 7) below. Here we summarise just a few of the other safety arguments applied to DUST-EXPERT.

6.1   Interval Arithmetic

There is a possibility that the underlying hardware—which will vary from user to user—may contain faults and give rise to occasional errors. These may not be detected by the test cases, or may be a feature of the chipset on the PC of a particular user. Furthermore, the calculation methods may be unstable for certain input values. We therefore implemented an "interval arithmetic" virtual machine for DUST-EXPERT. For each method, this carries three values of each variable through the calculations in a systematic way: the actual value, a value slightly below it, and a value slightly above. Generally, the size of the interval is the default precision of the variable, although the user can override this. If the interval at the end of the calculation is greater than 3% of the final value, it is displayed along with the result.

The use of interval arithmetic supports a claim of numerical accuracy of methods, modifiability (since instability in new methods will be detected) and fail safety (many numerical errors should be revealed).

6.2   Design Diversity

DUST-EXPERT contains some design diversity that should reveal certain faults.

A hard-copy log is produced of the methods that have been used and their results, including the source of data (by user input, from the databases, or by subsidiary calculation). This is independent of the graphical user interface (GUI), and therefore provides a defence against display errors. Input values are displayed in a particular colour (red by default) when they are first entered on the GUI. When the focus moves (e.g. because the user presses Tab or Enter) the value is read and then all the data values on the current screen are rewritten from the Prolog bindings in a different colour (green by default). This provides a defence against the use of stale data and many types of display error.

This use of design diversity supports a claim of fail safety for the methods and GUI.

6.3   Analytical Reasoning

Formal proof is not required by [2] or [7] for SIL 2 software. However, we carried out two sets of hand proofs of safety properties to give confidence that a sample of the subsidiary safety properties hold of the formal specification.

Since the identified safety properties have been shown to hold of the top-level VDM model by testing and by proof, the Prolog must preserve the safety properties provided the translation is correct. For a SIL 4 development, this argument would probably be by means of formal proof. The strength of this argument for lower level systems is a matter for engineering judgement, based on the predefined translation strategy.

The use of analytical reasoning supports a claim of functional correctness of the VDM and Prolog sources, to address residual doubt in the (statistical) testing.

6.4   Desk Checking

To enter the calculation methods into DUST-EXPERT, they are first translated to a special-purpose concrete syntax and then loaded into the underlying shell.

The concrete syntax form was checked against the requirements by hand. The internal form was checked by means of a specially written tool that:

- checks calculation method groups for: undeclared variables; variables in the group display lines that do not match the group variables; undeclared methods; and undeclared display line methods
- checks calculation methods for: undeclared variables; variables in the method display lines that do not match the method variables; undeclared options; undeclared display line methods; and local variables that are not defined before they are used

DUST-EXPERT has two databases: a database of dust properties; and a small database of materials properties for use in the Strength of Weak Vessels module.

The materials database was provided on disk to Adelard by HSE and no further checking was carried out. However, in view of its small size, it is reasonable to assume that the HSE would have detected any errors in their reviews of the system.

The following checking of the dust properties database was performed:

- The database was checked by HSE before being provided to Adelard in dBASE III format.
- A specially developed tool was used to print out the internal form of the database in the same format as the source book. This was then checked by hand against the source book. Some 70 errors were found, mostly misregistration of data in columns and single-digit errors. These were marked up on the printed copy.
- These were corrected, following discussions with HSE, in the dBASE III files.
- The tool was then used to print the database, and these were compared with the marked up printed copy. No errors were then detected.

This process also provides assurance of the database module read function. Approximately 1100 records, each containing 16 fields, were checked, giving a level of assurance of better than one error in 17 600 data values.

This use of desk checking supports a claim of accuracy of the calculation methods, databases and warning screens.

6.5   In-Service Data Recording

Arrangements have been set up to inform Adelard of in-service failures of the software. These arrangements should enable:

- the timely correction of any safety related failures
- the recording of data on the effectiveness of the software engineering process
- long-term assessment of the claims made in the safety case

7   Statistical Testing

Probabilistic or statistical testing is a technique for verifying and validating the integrated system, i.e. treating it as a black box. It therefore helps to provide safety assurance in the presence of faults in the various issues of Microsoft Windows and even in lower level software and hardware. Contrariwise, changing one of these components—such as moving to Windows 98 or NT from Windows 95—involves, as a minimum, running all the test cases again in the new environment.

A definition of the statistical approach is:

"The black box sampling of a system with *sufficient* and *representative* pseudo-randomly generated data to assure correctness to some desired *level of confidence.*"

The first issue is how to judge that one's test data is representative. We were in the fortunate situation of having the HSE's experiences with the research prototype, as well as their expert judgements as to which calculation sets (e.g. for vent sizing) are normally used and which only exceptionally. This translated into an order of magnitude more tests for the so-called Basic Calculations Group than for each of the seven more specialised groups, all of which are equally likely and therefore share the same number of generated test cases.

The second issue is how to know if a generated answer is correct. Here we used a subset of the VDM model and executed it under the control of the IFAD VDM toolbox. That is, the test case generator we built (see later) could output a test case in one of two syntaxes: in Visual Basic for Microsoft VisualTest, for testing the application running in its intended environment; and in the VDM command language of the IFAD toolbox, for consulting the oracle. Ideally the oracle and the application should be completely independent to avoid common-mode failures. For the DUST-EXPERT development this was not the case as the application was (partly) the systematic transformation of the VDM model. However, to mitigate potential common-mode failures due to the hardware or software platforms, we made the environments that the oracle and the application ran under radically different (see Table 2).

Table 2. Oracle versus application environments

Oracle	*Application*
486 processor	Pentium processor
Linux operating system	Windows 95
Linux C runtime libraries (e.g. for crucial floating point calculations)	Microsoft C and LPA Prolog libraries (e.g. for crucial floating point calculations)

The question remains, from our definition of this approach, how many test cases are sufficient? A very informal summary of the theory, which can be found in, e.g., IEC 65108, is:

- we know from our safety analysis that DUST-EXPERT must be responsible for no more errors than 1 in (a little under) 1000 demands
- 1000 successful test cases would then tell us that the application was equally likely to be right as wrong (50% confidence)
- applying the formula that the statisticians have given us [9] tells us that 3500 test cases executed successfully would mean that we could have 95% confidence that the application was generating the correct numbers
- to compensate for the risk that out underlying assumptions were less than perfect[4] we increased this figure slightly to 3800

We pseudo-randomly generated 2400 tests for the Basic Calculation Group and 200 each for the remaining seven specialised groups, making our total of 3800. In addition, over 1000 directed tests were executed, some from HSE's supplied acceptance suite and some generated independently by Adelard. In the case of these tests the oracle varied, from the VDM model, to prototype models in C (for an iterative ducting calculation), through the research prototype (where the requirements had not changed significantly), to the use of a conventional desk calculator. The vast majority of these directed tests are also coded in Visual Basic for VisualTest and thus can be rerun with little inconvenience. Statistically speaking they are biased (we chose them all for some reason), but their successful execution certainly added to the development team's confidence in the system's correctness. They also covered the entire system rather than just the critical calculation parts.

Pleasingly, all 3800 statistical tests gave the result the oracle predicted. We did uncover one fault: if approximately 160 calculation windows were opened in one session the application crashed. The problem was diagnosed as an overflow of an integral subrange variable in the user interface code. There were also two surprise results where the application produced negative answers. This was diagnosed as predictable—our oracle told us to expect them—from the poor choice of constraints on the calculation methods concerned.

It is worth noting that the fabled UNIX toolset still has a place in our Windows dominated world. The generators and checkers needed were constructed in a few days as UNIX-based Shell scripts, and were small enough to have their validity checked by inspection.

---

[4] An example is the assumption that any value from the possible range of input values (as defined by HSE) was equally likely. In some cases we knew that HSE had made the input ranges infeasibly wide.

8   Conclusions

We produced a complex advisory system, on top of a reusable shell supporting constraint-based programming, and demonstrated its conformance to Safety Integrity Level 2. Several aspects of the safety case are at the high end of the SIL 2 band; this both strengthens our argument at this integrity level (because some assumptions are based on engineering judgement) and means that we could rack up the safety case to SIL 3, should it ever be necessary, at only a fraction of the overall development cost.

DUST-EXPERT is not claimed to be error free, but it is demonstrably safe with an enviably low fault density.

References

1. *ITT for Development of DUST-EXPERT,* ITT reference: version 5, issued 13-Feb-95, HSE.
2. International Electrotechnical Commission, *Functional safety of electrical/electronic/ programmable electronic safety-related systems.* IEC 61508.
3. Lunn G., *Guide to Dust Explosion Prevention and protection, Part 1 – Venting,* 2nd ed., Institute of Chemical Engineers, 1992.
4. Schoeff, R.W., News Release & Summary for 1994. Dust Explosion Statistics—USA. Europex Newsletter, May 1995.
5. Information technology—Programming languages, their environments and system software interfaces—Vienna Development Method—Specification Language—Part 1: Base language, ISO/IEC 13817-1, 1996.
6. Clement, T., *The formal development of a Windows interface,* Proceedings of the Northern Formal Methods Workshop, Ilkey, 1998.
7. *The Procurement of Safety Critical Software in Defence Equipment,* Def Stan 00-55 (Parts 1 and 2) / Issue 2.
8. Adelard, *ASACD: the Adelard Safety Case Development Manual,* Adelard, ISBN 0-95337710-5, 1998.
9. Littlewood B., Strigini, L., *Validation of ultra-high dependability for software-based systems,* Communications of the ACM, Vol. 36, No. 11, pp69–80, November 1993.

Safety Verification of Ada95 Programs Using Software Fault Trees

Sang-Yoon Min, Yoon-Kyu Jang, Sung-Deok Cha, Yong-Rae Kwon, and Doo-Hwan Bae

Department of Computer Science, Korea Advanced Institute of Science and Technology
373-1, Kusong-dong, Yusong-gu, Taejon, 305-701, Korea
{sang, ykjang, cha, yrkwon, bae}@salmosa.kaist.ac.kr

Abstract. Software fault tree is a graphical analysis technique that is based on the concept of axiomatic verification. A template-based approach to software fault tree analysis was proposed for Ada83 programs. For the past years since this approach, no noticeable extensions or revisions on the template-based software fault tree analysis have been proposed while the target language has been evolved into Ada95. In this paper, we examine the validness of the original Ada83 analysis templates to determine which of them are still applicable to Ada95 programs considering major changes from Ada83 to Ada95. In addition, we propose newly required templates as well as the necessary modification of the original Ada83 templates in order to cope with the changes. We demonstrate the use of our proposed templates with an example program.

1. Introduction

Software fault tree analysis is an intuitive graphical technique used for partially verifying system safety. The base mechanism of software fault tree analysis is an axiomatic verification where postconditions describe the hazardous conditions rather than the correctness conditions. A node in a software fault tree represents a condition(possibly a hazardous condition). Each non-leaf node in the tree has one or more child nodes that represent the preconditions of the non-leaf node. By building a software fault tree where the root node represents a hazardous condition to be checked, we can perform a backward analysis through traversing from top to bottom. More details of the analysis mechanism of software fault tree can be found in [1].

A template-based software fault tree analysis technique was proposed for Ada83 programs by Leveson et al.[1]. Along with the wide acceptance of Ada83 in safety critical domains, this template-based approach was recognized as a useful technique for the safety analysis of Ada83 programs.

With the steady need for Ada in industry, the language has evolved continuously. As a result, Ada95 has been introduced with some noticeable major changes. Contrary to the steady evolution of the language, much less research has been done in the area of software fault tree analysis of Ada programs. The original template-based approach to Ada83 programs has not been validated for Ada95 programs. In this paper, we are amending the original templates to cope with the evolution of Ada language. We

M. Felici, K. Kanoun, A. Pasquini (Eds.): SAFECOMP'99, LNCS 1698, pp. 226–238, 1999
© Springer-Verlag Berlin Heidelberg 1999

examine the original Ada83 templates to determine which of them are still applicable to Ada95 programs. In addition, we make some revisions on the existing templates and propose newly required templates for Ada95 programs. In Sect.2, we briefly mention the major changes from Ada83 to Ada95. In Sect.3, we discuss the original Ada83 templates to find their applicability to Ada95 programs. Then, we describe the revisions we made on the original templates. We also propose newly added templates for Ada95 programs. In Sect.4, we show a case study with the newly revised set of Ada95 templates. We also discuss some practical issues on Ada95 programming styles and software fault tree analysis. We draw conclusion and future work in Sect.5.

2. Primary Changes from Ada83 to Ada95

In this section, we briefly describe the characteristics of Ada95 comparing to those of Ada83. We referenced the Ada95 Rationale[2] and the Language Reference Manuals of Ada83 and Ada95[3,4] to find the major differences between those languages. We also referenced other Ada reference books[5,6] for the comparison of the languages. The major changes from Ada83 to Ada95 can be characterized in four factors: *programming by extension, class wide programming, hierarchical libraries*, and *protected types*. These changes are due to the strengthened object-oriented concept in Ada95.

Type extension in Ada95 is based on the concept of the existing derived types in Ada83. In Ada95, it is possible to declare a new type that refines an existing parent type. Inheriting, redefining, and adding new features in the components and the operations of the parent type are supported. In Ada95, types marked by the keyword *tagged* may be extended.

The introduction of a class wide type in Ada95 gives an effective means to manipulate any kind(in its type hierarchy) of a type. Each value of a class wide type has a tag which identifies its particular type from other types in the hierarchy tree at runtime. The runtime binding of appropriate procedure is called *dispatching*. Class wide type is used generally in two ways. First, an access type may be declared to refer to a class wide type to let the access be able to designate any value of the class wide type. Second, parameters of a procedure may be class wide types. This kind of procedures(or functions) is called *class wide subprogram*.

Ada95 also provides a hierarchical library structure containing child packages and child subprograms. When the hierarchical libraries in Ada95 collaborate with class wide type, they influence the construction of the fault tree template.

Ada95 provides a more enhanced mechanism for task synchronization than the simple rendezvous mechanism of Ada83 by introducing *protected type*. A protected-type object may have three forms of protected operations: a function, a procedure, and an entry. A procedure in the protected body can manipulate the private data whereas a function is only allowed to perform read access to the private data. Therefore, the simultaneous multiple calls of functions are allowed. The action of an entry call is supported by an entry with a barrier condition. This condition must be true before the execution of the entry body.

3. Newly Required and Modified Templates for Ada95

Leveson et al. have defined a set of failure mode templates for Ada83[1]. They constructed the templates focusing on the general statements of Ada83 such as assignment, if-then-else, procedure call, case, loop, select, rendezvous, exception, abort, block, code, delay, entry, exit, raise, and return statements.

Defining failure mode templates is analogous to defining the failure semantics of programming language statements. Thus, the original templates of Ada83 may be inappropriate for Ada95 since new statements have been added and the semantics of some existing statements have been changed. In this section, we revise some of the original templates for Ada83. To distinguish the revised parts of our proposed templates from the original Ada83 templates, we use italicized labels for those nodes which are newly added or have revisions on their child nodes. In addition, we propose some additional templates to cover the new features of Ada95.

3.1 Select Template

In Ada83, the select statement is used in timed entry calls, selective wait, and conditional entry calls. In Ada95, it can be also used in *asynchronous transfer of control* [2]. This enables an activity to be abandoned if a condition arises, and let an alternative sequence of statements to be executed instead. This gives the ability of performing mode changes without the introduction of an agent task (in Ada83, mode changes can be programmed by using an agent task.). Therefore, the template should be revised to handle the case that asynchronous transfer of control causes failure. We also modify 'or' relationship into ``mutually exclusive" relationship ('m-xor' operators in our templates) in the template to improve understandability and semantic consistency. The modified *select* template is shown in Fig.1.

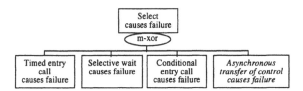

Fig. 1. Modified *Select* Template

3.2 Timed-Entry-Call and Conditional-Entry-Call templates

In the original Ada83 templates, no separate template is constructed to cover the case in which a timed entry call causes failure. They just show an expansion of the node 'timed entry call causes failure' in the original *select* template only considering two subcases of possible causes: 'rendezvous causes failure' and 'time out causes failure'. This expansion does not cover the cases of the failure occurring at the entry calls in task and protected type object.

The revised timed entry template is shown in Fig.2. The node 'entry call causes failure' can be expanded with the other templates proposed in the latter sections, and eventually cover the cases of the failure occurring at the entry calls in task and protected type object. The *conditional entry call* template for Ada83 has been revised in similar sense. Fig.3 shows its revised template for Ada95.

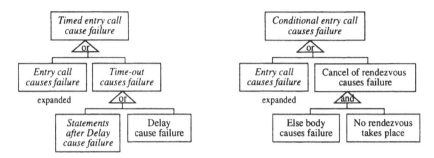

Fig. 2. Modified *Timed-Entry* Template   **Fig. 3.** Modified *Conditional-Entry* template

3.3 Exception Template

Although the semantics and syntax of the exception statement in Ada83 remain unchanged in Ada95, the exception template must be revised in order to agree more precisely with its semantics. In the original template, the failure in an exception caused by another propagating exception can not be identified. For example, when an exception x causes failure, it may be due to the failure occurred in the body of an exception y which propagated x. However, because the body of x does not cause any failure, the propagated failure is ignored(in Fig.4(a), the root node (1) becomes false when the node (2) is false even if the node (5) was true).

Furthermore, when an exception is called, its parameters may cause failure. This must be considered in the template. Fig.4(b) shows the revised *exception* template. In this template, the node 'A propagating exception causes failure' can be replaced recursively into 'Exception causes failure' in order to continue fault tree analysis. Then, this exception is considered as locally raised exception, and the analysis follows the left branch the template.

3.4 Asynchronous-Transfer-of-Control Template

In Ada95, asynchronous transfer of control is carried by a new form of *select* statement which comprises two parts: an abortable part and a triggering alternative.

As a simple example, consider Fig.5(a). The general underlying idea is that if the statement between *then abort* and *end select* do not complete its execution before the expiry of the delay, then it is abandoned, and the statements following the delay are executed instead. On the other hand, if the execution completes before the expiry of the delay, then the delay statement itself is abandoned. The statement that triggers the abandonment can alternatively be an entry call instead of delay statement: if the call

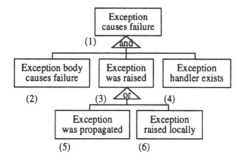

(a) *Exception* Template for Ada83

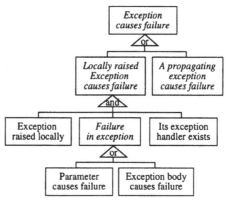

(b) *Exception* Template for Ada95

Fig. 4. Modified *Exception* Template

returns before the computation is complete, then again the computation is abandoned, and the statements following the entry call are executed instead.

Failures in asynchronous transfer of control may occur at the triggering alternative or the abortable part. A triggering alternative is either a delay statement or an entry call statement. Of course, the entry call can be made to a task or to a protected object. The situation in which a triggering alternative causes failure is one of two cases: time-out triggering alternative with a delay statement causes failure or entry call triggering alternative causes failure. Failure in time-out triggering alternative may occur at a delay statement or the statements after the delay statement. Failure in entry call triggering alternative may occur at the entry call or statements after the entry call. Analysis of an abortable part is straightforward because an abortable part is a sequence of simple or compounded statements. Fig.5(b) shows the failure mode template for asynchronous transfer of control.

```
select
    delay 5.0;                        -- triggering alternative
    Put_Line("Calculation did not complete");
then abort
    Invert_Giant_Matrix(M);    -- abortable part
end select;
```

(a) An example of asynchronous transfer of control

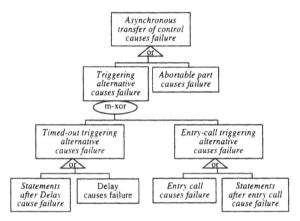

(b) *Asynchronous-Transfer-of-Control* template for Ada95

Fig. 5. *Asynchronous-Transfer-of-Control* Template for Ada95

3.5 Entry-Call Template

Since an entry call in Ada83 may occur only in tasks, the entry-call template for Ada83 considers only the entry call in tasks. Protected objects in Ada95 exhibits a new type of an entry call with barrier conditions. Therefore, the entry-call template should cover both the entry call in a task and the entry call in a protected objects. The revised entry-call template is shown in Fig.6(a). The node 'entry call in tasks causes failure' can be replaced with the corresponding template shown in Fig.6(b) which is similar to the original Ada83 template. Fig.6(c) shows the *entry call in protected objects* template. When the entry of a protected object is called, its barrier(*when* clause in the protected body) is evaluated; if the barrier is false, then the call is queued. At the end of an entry body(or a procedure body) of the protected object, previously queued entry calls (whose barriers are now true) take precedence over other calls contending for the protected object. The cases in which barrier condition evaluation causes failure or statements in entry body causes failure are considered in our template.

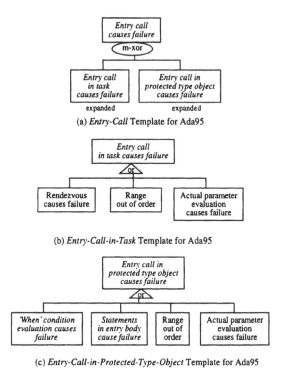

(a) *Entry-Call* Template for Ada95

(b) *Entry-Call-in-Task* Template for Ada95

(c) *Entry-Call-in-Protected-Type-Object* Template for Ada95

Fig. 6. *Modified Entry-Call* Templates for Ada95

3.6 Procedure-Call Template

Class wide types are used in order to choose the procedure of an appropriate type or the type of parameters in a procedure at runtime. We call the parameters in class wide type *class-wide-type parameters* and parameters in the other types *ordinary parameters*. We also classify procedures into *non-class wide subprogram* and *class-wide subprogram* according to their parameter types(class-wide type and the other types). Fig.7(a) shows the modified procedure call template. The template for a function call has the similar form with this template.

For the case in which failures may occur in non-class-wide subprogram call, class-wide type is used in only dispatching. We reflect this characteristic into the original *procedure-call* template. Fig.7(b) shows the revised new template.

Since class wide subprograms have both ordinary parameters and class-wide-type parameters, the case that ordinary parameter causes failure and the case that class-wide-type parameters causes failure must be considered together. In the latter case, when a type which was assigned to the parameter at runtime was wrong, a failure may occur. This is not a compiler error, but a logical error due to programmers' incorrect construction of inheritance hierarchy. Fig.7(c) shows the template for a class-wide-subprogram call.

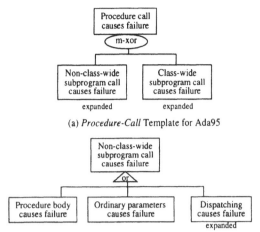

(a) *Procedure-Call* Template for Ada95

(b) *Non-Class-Wide Subprogram Call* Template for Ada95

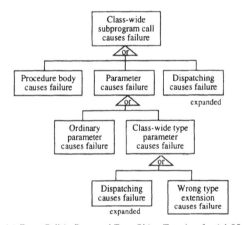

(c) *Entry-Call-in-Protected-Type-Object* Template for Ada95

Fig. 7. *Procedure-Call* Templates for Ada95

3.7 Dispatching Template

"Dispatching causes failure" means that an incorrect type is bound to the class wide type at runtime. It does not mean a compiler error but a logical error due to a badly constructed inheritance tree of the type. In the template for dispatching, all possible types which can be bound to a class wide type must be considered. For a class wide type T'Class, these are the union of all the types in the tree of derived type rooted at T.

Figure 8(a) shows an example type tree[1]. In this figure, a value of any of the Alert types can be implicitly converted to *Alert'Class*. In the Fig.8(b), we do not know which *Handle* procedure (we assume that a distinct procedure *Handle* is defined for each type.) will be called until runtime because we do not know which specific type the alert belongs to. When the appropriate procedure is determined, its parameters are implicitly converted to the specific alert type. Therefore, in fault tree analysis, we must consider the procedure *Handle*s of all types (*Alert, Low_Alert, Medium_Alert, Emergency_Alert,* and *High_Alert*) in the tree. Fig.8(c) shows the template for dispatching. *'T1', 'T2', ..., 'Tn'* are the set of types which a class wide type can be bound at runtime.

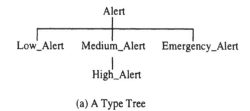

(a) A Type Tree

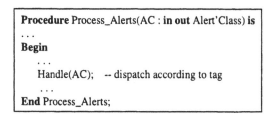

(b)An Example of Dispatching

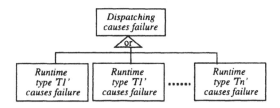

(c) Dispatching Template for Ada95

Fig. 8. An Example of Dispatching and Dispatching Template for Ada95

4. Case Study and Practical Issues

In this section, we show an example analysis of Ada95 program with the proposed templates. Leveson et al. used an Ada83 implementation of a traffic-light control system[1]. We also use the rewritten program of this example in Ada95. The requirements of the example system are as follows:

A traffic-light control system at an intersection consists of four identical sensors and a central controller. The sensors in each direction detect cars approaching the intersection. If the traffic light in its direction is not green, the sensor notifies the controller so the light will be changed. A car is expected to stop and wait for a green light. If the light is green, the car may pass the intersection without stopping. The controller accepts change requests from the four sensors and arbitrates the traffic-light changes. Once the controller changes the light in one direction (east-west or south-north) to green, it maintains the green signal for five seconds so other cars in the same direction may pass the intersection without stopping. Before the green light in any direction becomes red, it should remain in yellow for one second so any car in the intersection may clear. The light then turns to red while the light in the opposite direction turns green.

Before showing an example program for analysis, we need to discuss an issue on programming style of Ada95 language. We can implement the Ada95 program for the above requirements in different styles: we may define shared data as private type of a protected object or as global variables. In the above example, the candidate for shared data is traffic light.

In terms of object-oriented programming concept, declaring shared data as global variable are undesirable. Implementing shared data as protected type and supporting data sharing through message passing fit better to object-oriented concept. However, it is just a programming style.

In the aspect of task synchronization, implementing shared data as a protected type does not cause any race condition since the protected type has an inherent strong mechanism for task synchronization. However, using global variable may cause race conditions.

These two different programming styles also cause different system behaviors. Tasks requesting for reading or modifying protected type must be queued one by one while another task is in processing. This strong task serialization based on request arrival time may cause unwanted behavior of the system. For example, this excessive task serialization forces every individual car coming to intersection to pass the intersection one by one in the order of arrival time. For behavioral correctness, we must implement the traffic light as a global variable rather than protected type even if it is against to the object-oriented design concept. The following program shows the implementation of the procedure for our example problem.

```
1 procedure Traffic2 is
2    type Direction is (East, West, South, North);
3    type Color is (Red, Yellow, Green);
4    type Light_Type is array (Direction) of Color;
5    Lights : Light_Type := (Green, Green, Red, Red);   --the lights of the signal ( a global data)
6    Newcar : Character;
7    protected type Signaltype is              --a signal is defined as a protected object
8       entry Change(Newdir : in Direction);
9       private
10       Usage : Integer := 0;
11    end Signaltype;
12    task type Sensor_Task(Dir : Direction) is     --a sensor is a task
13       entry Car_Comes;
14    end Sensor_Task;
15    protected body Signaltype is
16       entry Change(Newdir : in Direction) when Usage = 0 is
17       begin
18          Usage := 1;
19          case Newdir is                   --changing the signal lights
```

```
20          when East I West =>
21              Lights := (Green, Green, Red, Red); delay 5.0;
22              Lights := (Yellow, Yellow, Red, Red); delay 1.0;
23              Lights := (Red, Red, Green, Green);
24          when South I North =>
25              Lights := (Red, Red, Green, Green); delay 5.0;
26              Lights := (Red, Red, Yellow, Yellow); delay 1.0;
27              Lights := (Green, Green, Red, Red);
28          end case;
29          Usage := 0;
30      end Change;
31  end Signaltype;
32  Mysignal: Signaltype;                          --instantiating a signal
33  task body Sensor_Task is
34  begin
35      loop
36          accept Car_Comes;
37          if(Lights(Dir) /= Green) then
38              Mysignal.Change(Dir);              --call to the protected type object, signal
39          end if;
40      end loop;
41  end Sensor_Task;
42  EastSensor: Sensor_Task(Dir => East);          --the sensor at east
43  WestSensor: Sensor_Task(Dir => West);          --the sensor at west
44  NorthSensor: Sensor_Task(Dir => North);        --the sensor at north
45  SouthSensor: Sensor_Task(Dir => South);        --the sensor at south
46 begin
47      while Newcar /= 'q' loop                   --the console codes simulating car comings
48          Text_Io.Get(Item=> Newcar);
49          if (Newcar= 'e') then
50              Eastsensor.Car_Comes;
51          elsif(Newcar = 'w') then
52              Westsensor.Car_Comes;
53          elsif(Newcar = 'n') then
54              Northsensor.Car_Comes;
55          elsif(Newcar = 's') then
56              Southsensor.Car_Comes;
57          elsif(Newcar = 'q') then ;
58          end if;
59      end loop;
60      delay 1.0;
61      abort NorthSensor;
62      abort SouthSensor;
63      abort EastSensor;
64      abort WestSensor;
65 end Traffic2;
```

In the procedure traffic95, since the variable *Lights* is a global variable, tasks' requests for reading and modifying the value of Lights may occur simultaneously. Eventually, race conditions may occur. One of the race conditions that may occur in the traffic light system is the case in which two cars traveling from the north and east are in the intersection simultaneously[1]. We illustrate the application of software fault tree analysis with the traffic95 program by analyzing the event occurring of this race condition. The analysis proceeds by finding the causes of the event and their relationships. Two cars traveling from north and from east can be in the intersection simultaneously in many ways. We use the case where the north car enters the intersection as the east car enters.

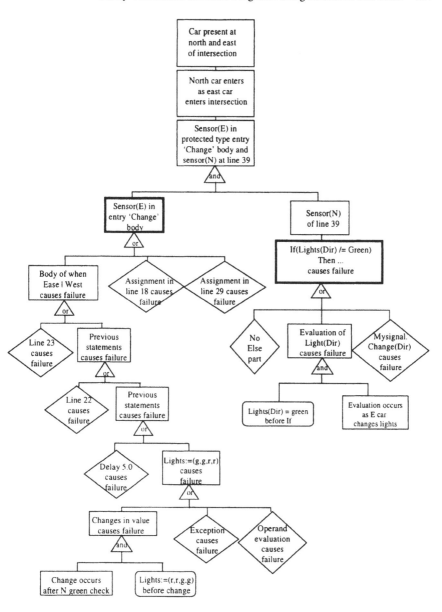

Fig. 9. Fault Tree for Procedure *traffic95*

Figure 9 shows the fault tree for a procedure traffic95. In this example, the above case describes the situation where *Sensor_task(E)* is in the body of the protected type *Signaltype* and *Sensor_task(N)* bypassed the entry call *Change* since the condition is not satisfied. This implies that the signal(N) was green when a car from the north approached to the intersection. It ,therefore, entered the intersection without stopping.

Since the immediately preceding statement of line 39 is an *if* statement, we apply original *If-Then-Else* template to line 37 through 39 for analysis. Since *Sensor(N)* does not issue a call to *Change* and no *else* clause exist, only the evaluation of *Lights(Dir)* must be considered. It is clear that *Lights(N)* is green since *Sensor_task(N)* bypass this point. Then, if *Sensor_task(N)* checks the color of lights as *Signaltype* changes the value of *Lights* at the request of *Sensor_task(E)*, a race condition will occur. The *"Sensor(E)* in entry *Change* body" event is analyzed by using the *Entry-call-in-Protected-Type-Object* template. Since *Sensor(E)* is in the body of the entry *Change*, the first, third, and fourth cases in the template are discarded. In the second case, because two assignment statements(lines 18 and 19) are not a direct cause of the event, we are only concerned with the case that body of *when East or West causes failure*. For the rest part, the analysis is similar to the Leveson's example and we have found the race condition[1]. This hazard occurs in the situation the Sensor(E) changes variable *Lights* and *Sensor(N)* reads the value of *Lights*(N is green) simultaneously.

5. Conclusion and Future Work

In this paper, we have defined the fault tree templates for the fault tree analysis of Ada95 programs. Our templates are based on the original templates proposed for Ada83 programs. We studied the differences between Ada83 and Ada95 in syntax and semantics. We examined the validness of the original Ada83 templates to determine which of them are still applicable to Ada95 programs, and revised some of the templates of Ada83 for Ada95 programs. In addition, we proposed additionally required templates for Ada95.

Since these templates are not defined for all syntactic statements of Ada95, the proposed templates are not comprehensive and complete. As future work, we need to revise them and define more templates if necessary. Also, more rigorous validation of the templates may need to be done.

References

1. Nancy G. Leveson, Stephen S. Cha, and Timothy J. Shimeall, "Safety Verification of Ada Programs Using Software Fault Trees," *IEEE Software*, July 1991, pp. 48-59.
2. *Ada95 Rationale*, Intermetrics, 1995.
3. *ADA83 LRM*, ANSI/MIL-STD-1815A-1983, DOD, 1983.
4. *ADA95 LRM*, ISO/IEC 8652:1995(E), Intermetrics 1995.
5. Grady Booch, Doug Bryan, and Charles G. Petersen, *Software Engineering with Ada*, The Benjamin/Cummings Publishing Company, Inc., 1994.
6. Michael B. Feldman and Elliot B. Koffman, *Ada95 Problem Solving and Program Design*, Addison-Wesley, 1996.

Programming Rule Static Verification for Reliable Software

Philippe Robert

ISOSCOPE, 8, rue Maryse Hilsz, F-31500 Toulouse - France
e-mail: philippe.robert@isoscope.com, http://www.isoscope.com

Abstract. The aim of this article is to present experimental results related to static verification of programming rules. The experiment reported bears on 10 industrial software projects. The source code (C and C++) has been statically analysed to check for conformance to a set of programming rules. The results show that a significant amount of the defects identified are actually software faults that may lead to failures during execution. This article explains the verification method used and discusses tools for such verification. It analyses the results and formulates the recommendation to perform static verification of source code in a systematic way.

1   Introduction

Programming rules are very often used in the context of software quality assurance. Requirements aiming at mastering all the phases of the software development process exist in most quality assurance standards such as ISO 9001. Applying these requirements to the coding phase lead to the elaboration of a set of programming rules that are referred to in the Software Quality Plan. The quality team is therefore usually in charge of verifying the actual application of these rules.

However, very little guidance exists in standards to select the rules to be applied. The objective in conducting the study reported here was to analyse the pertinence and the effectiveness of some programming rules. In order to focus the study, it has been limited to reliability issues in the context of C and C++ programming. However, the goal here is not to propose the *best* programming rules for reliable software, but to present experimental results for *some* rules related to reliability.

In the second section of this article, 10 software products on which the experiment has been conducted are presented. In section 3, 8 programming rules are presented. Then, the experimentation itself is reported, in section 4. This presentation discusses the verification method, the use of tools and provides the number of rule violations for each product as well as the number of actual faults identified. Finally, analyses of experimental results, conclusions and perspectives are proposed.

M. Felici, K. Kanoun, A. Pasquini (Eds.): SAFECOMP'99, LNCS 1698, pp. 239–249, 1999
© Springer-Verlag Berlin Heidelberg 1999

2   Experimentation Set

ISO**SCOPE** provides its customers with software product evaluation services. In this context, programming rule verification has been performed on the source code of many software projects.

Among these projects, ten featuring C or C++ source code have been selected as a representative set of varied application domains. These projects are characterised in table 1 below.

In this table, the following information is provided:
- the application domain,
- the size expressed in "lines of code" (LOC),
- the programming language,
- the fact that a programming standard had been imposed to the developers for the development project and
- the fact the project was considered as not fully validated when the verification was performed.

Table 1. Characterisation of products

Project Number	Application Domain	Size (LOC)	Prog. language	Prog. Std. imposed?	Already validated?
P1	Air Traffic Control	150 000	C	YES	NO
P2	Computer Aided Design in Civil Engineering	180 000	C++	YES	NO
P3	Data Management	300 000	C	YES	YES
		300 000	C++		
P4	Telecommunication	460 000	C	NO	YES
P5	Booking system	36 000	C	NO	YES
P6	Energy	210 000	C	NO	YES
P7	Energy	200 000	C++	NO	YES
P8	Aerospace	52 000	C	YES	YES
P9	Aerospace	36 000	C++	YES	YES
P10	Aerospace	33 000	C	YES	YES
	Total size	1 957 000			

3   Programming Rules

3.1   Defining of Programming Rules

Imposing programming rules is a very common practice when quality assurance is formalized in a software development project. Many standards, especially in the context of highly critical software development, require that programming rules be defined, documented and used. This is an obvious way to control the coding phase of the development process.

In practice, many sources exist that propose programming rules. For language C and C++, it is possible to cite many references as, for example, [1, 2, 3, 4]or textbooks as [5 or 6].

However, very little guidance is usually available to define and select appropriate rules. Therefore, what usually happens is that, when a programming standard is required, a pre-existing set of rules is referred to "as is" in the project software quality plan.

This practice may lead in many cases to extra costs and to poor application of the programming standard. The reasons for that may be poor or limited training of the development staff in the programming standard application and rejection by developers of rules that are not clearly understood.

One approach to overcome these issues is to select programming rules according to project objectives. Therefore, the number of rules is limited and the role of each of them is clearly identified. Training the development team is therefore easier since the justification of rules is clearly established and costs for verification are reduced. To implement this approach, one uses software product characteristics defined in ISO/IEC FDIS 9126-1: 99 [7], as a guide. This international standard defines the following characteristics: functionality, efficiency, usability, maintainability, portability and reliability. It is possible, using this standard, to identify pertinent objectives and select the programming rules accordingly.

3.2   Programming Rules for Reliability

In this paper, we concentrate on the software aspects of reliability. ISO/IEC FDIS 9126-1 defines reliability as *"The capability of the software product to maintain a specified level of performance when used under specified conditions"*. This means that everything that prevents the software product to behave as specified impairs its reliability. This is the case for programming errors.

Programming errors should be considered as software faults. According to [8], a **fault**, when it is activated, causes an execution **error** which, if it is not tolerated by the software product, may cause a **failure**.

Therefore, an approach to define programming rules related to reliability is to aim at reducing the error risks. The process should be to investigate causes of usual programming errors and to propose rules to control these causes.

The impact of programming rules is then twofold. On the one hand, rules, when they are adhered to, can be considered as contributing to **fault prevention**. On the other hand, verification of rules contributes to **fault elimination**.

The relation between programming rule verification and reliability is indirect. Verifying programming rules may lead to identify quality defects which, in some cases, can be diagnosed as actual faults that may lead to failure during software execution.

3.3   Programming Rules Experimented

In this section, we focus on 8 programming rules for C and C++ which are presented with an a priori justification of their relationship with software reliability. These rules are part of those that have been experimented in the study presented in this article.

R1. A default rubric shall always be used in a switch sentence: for the software stability and reliability it is recommended [1,2] that all switch statements should have a default case, which may be merely a "fatal error" exit. This rule demands that an abnormal situation treatment must be devised, even when the possibility of such a situation has been considered as improbable. Such a rule improves software fault tolerance.

R2. The break instruction shall always be used at the end of each branch of a switch: although the absence of a break may be used on purpose to obtain some optimization effect, the break instruction is sometimes just forgotten and this absence may cause the execution of undesired code.

R3. Constants shall be represented by symbolic constant if the same value is used several times: it allows maintaining the consistency of the program when the value is modified and, therefore, prevents errors.

R4. Testing the result of an affectation is forbidden: Despite the cases where they consist in coding optimization, testing the result of an affectation may often be a programming error (confusion between the affectation operator "=" and the comparison operator "==").

R5. Test instruction shall not be used out of control statement: although using a test instruction out of a structure of control is authorized by the compiler, it is often the result of a confusion between the "=" and "==" operator.

R6. Code duplication shall be avoided: it is necessary in order to avoid inconsistencies of the program when it is modified.

R7. Dead code shall be forbidden: here is only considered the code that is statically not accessible; it is indeed very often an error, due to the misplacement of return or break instructions, or of comment marks.

R8. The goto instruction shall not be used: goto statements lead to de-structured code that are difficult to master and that may cause errors (see [2]).

Of course, many other rules have been proposed in the literature that can be related to software reliability. The approach has been to select the rules that seemed most pertinent and for which results were available.

4   Experimental Results

4.1   Verification Method and Tools

In the experiment presented here, the verification of the conformity to programming rules has been performed on the whole of the software product source code. In order to do so, automatic verification tools have been used.

However, verification cannot be fully automated. Three steps are needed:

- automatic tools provide list of potential non-conformities;
- these potential non-conformities have to be qualified to determine whether they are actual non-conformities or whether they are to be considered as false alarms;
- then, when non-conformities are qualified, it is necessary to investigate whether they constitute a real risk of being a fault or not.

4.1.1   Use of Tools

Programming rules is quite a popular concept and many tools have been developed to perform their verification in an automatic way. Tools are available for a wide range of classic programming languages such as Fortran, Cobol, C, C++, ...

In this section we introduce a few tools for C and C++. It is to be noted that, in most cases, rules applicable to C programs are also pertinent for C++ programs. In many cases tools that verify rules for C++ are also able to perform verification on C ANSI code. This presentation is not an exhaustive tool survey and is here just to illustrate the existence of tools.

The following tools have been used to conduct this experiment:
- CodeWizard of Parasoft,
- ProLint of ISD.
- Logiscope RuleChecker of Verilog (C code only),
- CodeCheck of Abraxas.

References to the use of tools for programming rules verification can be found in [9 and 10].

The extensive practical experience on which this study relies lead to the following comments:
- tools with a predefined set of rules produce a large volume of non-conformities ; a filtering environment is needed in order to get rid of rule violations that were not selected in the project;
- significant effort and expertise is needed to develop the scripts implementing rules ; quite often the set of rules that are shipped with the commercial tools are limited or inadequate ; this is especially the case for several rules related to maintainability;
- while these tools are easy to operate on toy examples, they need significant practice and a dedicated environment to be run on large industrial projects.

4.1.2   Qualification of Potential Non-conformities

Automatic tools are not always able to identify only actual non-conformities. This comes from the fact that programming rules contain a certain amount of program semantics that are not attainable by automatic tools.

For example, several rules may be relative to the presence or not of justification comments, i.e. programmers are authorised not to respect the basic rule provided they justify it with a dedicated comment. This is often the case with the rule forbidding testing of the result of an affectation.

Another example is the rule related to code duplication. In this case, tools are able to suggest potential duplication. Tools used in this context are basic utility tools such as Unix's ls, diff, ... These tools combined with more sophisticated ones that perform source code measurements and exhibit the code control structure allow the identification of potential duplicates. This approach is rather similar to what is reported in [11], although this work is more orientated towards maintainability evaluation. Once potential duplicates are identified, manual inspection of the corresponding code is used to determine whether there is actual duplication or near-duplication.

4.1.3   Interpretation of Non-conformities

The third step of the method used in this experiment is to assess the impact of the validated non-conformities on reliability of the evaluated software product. This step may be performed together with the impact assessment on maintainability or portability, since some rules are related to several quality objectives.

When programming rules have been imposed in the software development process, all the validated non-conformities are to be considered as quality defects and recorded as such. However, they may not be actual faults, i.e. they may not have a direct negative impact on reliability. As it is the case for most of the rules expressed above, most non-conformities have a negative impact on maintainability because future modification may result in faults. In some other case, the assessment of non-conformities may lead to identify an actual fault in the software.

In many cases, it is possible to decide that a defect is not a fault without a knowledge of the software architecture. When this decision is not possible, the defect needs to be submitted to developers or maintainers. Then, with their intimate knowledge of the software product architecture or by testing the software, they can decide whether the quality defect identified is actually a software fault. Being a fault means the defect makes the software behave in disaccordance with its specification or its design.

On the basis of this assessment, actions can be recommended, either to modify the code just to improve software maintainability or actually to remove a fault.

4.2   Raw Results

The verification of programming rules has been performed on the ten software products introduced above. For each of these products, the number of validated non conformities has been identified for the rules presented above. In some cases, probable faults have been identified and have been submitted to the development team.

In the table below results are presented. In this table, the numbers provided indicate how many quality defects were identified, "na" means that the corresponding result is not available, "++" means that many defects were identified and the numbers within brackets indicate how many actual faults were identified and validated by the development team.

Table 2. Results of programming rule verification

	Rule (summary)	P1	P2	P3	P4	P5	P6	P7	P8	P9	P10
R1	default case mandatory	22	30	30	125	9	4	52	0	29	11
R2	break mandatory in switch cases	20 (1)	5 (4)	32 (7)	++ (7)	11 (1)	++ (1)	6	2	++	8
R3	symbolic constants mandatory	na	7	na	na	na	na	na	++	++	++
R4	affectation testing forbidden	1	9	2 (1)	19 (1)	2	na	na	0	1	0
R5	testing only in conditionals	2 (2)	na	1	13 (13)	na	na	na	0	0	0
R6	avoid code duplication	++	21	++	++ (1)	++	16	7	10	4	6
R7	dead code forbidden	5	1 (1)	9	20 (3)	3	2 (1)	1	na	3	na
R8	goto instruction forbidden	0	8	50	138 (1)	10	na	0	++	0	0
	Total number of faults : (45)	**(3)**	**(5)**	**(8)**	**(26)**	**(1)**	**(2)**	**(0)**	**(0)**	**(0)**	**(0)**

4.3   Examples of Qualification and Interpretation of Non-conformities

In this section, we provide two examples of interpretation of non-conformities.

The first proposed example is related to dead code. The verification tool identifies the following code as being unattainable.

```
      . . .
         break;
      Default :
         return(0);
         break;
      . . .
```

Due to a typing error, "Default" (because of the upper-case D) is considered as a label and not as the default case for the surrounding switch block. This is certainly a fault. It should be noted that such a fault is bearly identifiable through manual inspection. The only other way to detect it is dynamic testing.

If the typing error had not been made, the last break instruction would have been identified as dead code. However, that would have not been considered as a fault or even as a defect since it is there in application of rule R2.

In the following examples, the rule (R4) preventing the test of affectation result is breached twice. However, only in the first case, was a fault diagnosed. In the second case, we only see a quality defect.

```
        . . .
if (num_abc = -1)

        . . .
if (pfich = fopen(penv, "r"))

        . . .
```

5   Analysis of Results

5.1   Global Analysis

In order to be able to assess the efficiency of programming rule verification, it is necessary to have an estimation of the effort needed to perform this verification. Globally, the effort needed to verify the source of the 10 projects was about 50 person days. If this effort is related to the overall size of the programs verified, we end up with a verification rate of 40 000 lines of code verified per person day of effort, which is far higher than what can be achieved manually.

This effort is not proportional to the size of the source code verified. The effort can be distributed by the following steps (in the context of the verification performed by a third party):
– reception of the source code, which needs a significant effort, since include files (i.e. .h files) are very often missing,
– running of the appropriate tools,
– analysis of results, validation of defects and interpretation of their significance,
– elaboration of a report.
It should be noted that for this effort, quite often, more than the 8 rules presented here are verified. Moreover, the interpretation bears also on maintainability and portability.

The result of this effort is the identification of 45 faults. It is interesting to relate this result to other studies such as [12 and 13]. Formal comparison of these results is not direct. However, to use the same measurement unit as in [12], the verification reported here is performed at a rate of about 5000 LOC per hour (2 millions lines for 400 hours), to be compared to 125 LOC per hour. It should be noted that our size measure includes comments whereas Fagan's does not. Of course, manual inspections cover more than just formalised rules.

For highly critical software, one should consider using verification tools first and merging the validation of defects and interpretation of their significance with the objectives of manual inspection. The use of automatic tools would alleviate the burden of boring verification actions and allow the identification of faults not easily identifiable by manual inspections.

5.2 Detailed Analysis

5.2.1 Use of switch Instructions

Two rules are related to multiple choice instructions : the use of the default clause and the use of break instructions for each case.

The verification of the rule related to using a default clause did not allow the identification of faults. However, the contribution of this rule is more related to the notion of fault tolerance than to that of fault avoidance. It should also be noted that although this rule is most often present in programming standards, it is very often breached. This is significant of the limited acceptance of programming rules by developers.

On the contrary, verification of the rule imposing break instructions at the end of each branch of switch block lead to the identification of many faults: 21 for our experiment. However, the fact that it is breached many times results from its application in the default clause for which many practitioners consider the break instruction as not mandatory. It means, therefore, that finding a breach of this rule outside a default clause leads very often to the identification of a software fault.

5.2.2 Symbolic Constants

To impose the use of symbolic constants as opposed to literal constants results primarily from maintainability needs. The connection of this rule to reliability is indirect: when the product has evolved, the fact that this rule is violated may lead to inconsistent versions of constants denoting the same concept. It is not possible for an evaluator not directly involved in the development to really perform a fault diagnosis but exhibiting lists of literal constants can reveal faults to maintainers. Therefore, this verification is very helpful in the case of aging software.

Another finding relates to the fact that although it is imposed, this rule is very often not adhered to.

5.2.3 Affectation Testing

The rule that forbids the testing of affectation result is globally well respected. In two cases, it was identified as an actual fault in the software. This can be interpreted by stating that in most cases programmers understand clearly the risks with this construction and therefore identified breaches are often mistakes.

5.2.4 Testing Only in Conditionals

Apart from one case, all the defects identified relating to the rule forbidding test expressions outside control structure have been interpreted as actual software faults. The exception has been found within reused code of which developers had no precise knowledge. These findings make the systematic verification of this rule a very effective tool to identify faults.

It should be noted that most often, breaches of this rule are not voluntary; they rather result from typing errors.

5.2.5   Code Duplication

As for the use of symbolic constant, the avoidance of code duplication is remotely connected to software reliability. Risks exist when one instance is not modified like all the other instances. In this context, exhibiting closely related near duplicates allows developers to identify some faults resulting from incomplete maintenance actions.

5.2.6   Dead Code

In many situations, unattainable code results from the rule that imposes break instructions at the end of all branches of switch instructions. When a clause finishes by, for example, a return instruction, the following break instruction can be considered as dead code. However, in some other situations, the context allows in identify that, for example, important treatments have been forgotten when break or return instructions have been inserted in the code. These situations may lead to a fault diagnosis.

5.2.7   Unconditional Branches

The use of goto instructions has been for a long time a very hot topic [14]. Apart from one case where the specific context of the code was such that it was possible to diagnose a fault, the search for goto did not allow to the identification of software faults.

This does not mean that, especially when it is used in a way that de-structure the code, the use of goto is not harmful to maintainability.

6   Conclusions and Perspectives

The main conclusion of the study reported in this article is that automatic verification of programming rules completed with manual interpretation of the rule breaches allows the identification of a significant number of software faults that may impair software reliability. Of course, it is not possible to quantify the contribution to reliability improvement, since the frequency of activation of the detected faults is not known.

This approach has proved to be very cost effective, compared to manual inspection. Although it does not allow the identification of all the fault that manual inspection does, it can identify faults that are very difficult to find through manual inspection.

Although it is not claimed that the programming rules experimented in this study are the best ones, some of them have demonstrated their usefulness:

- a break instruction shall always be used at the end of each branch of a switch,
- testing the result of an affectation is forbidden,
- test instruction shall not be used out of control statement,
- dead code is forbidden.

Of course, these rules, as well as many others, are useful to perform an assessment of the software product maintainability or portability.

The issue of systematic versus sampling verification is also illustrated by the results of this study. Since many faults found are indeed non voluntary mistakes by the programmers (e.g. typing errors), sampling is not effective in identifying faults. The verification must be exhaustive to achieve the goal.

On the basis of this analysis, one may question the need to define programming standards: one approach could be just to perform the verification. On this point, experience shows that when programming rules have not been imposed or respected, the amount of possible non-conformities is very high which demands a significant effort to validate them. When rules have been imposed and respected, non-conformities are far less numerous and thus easier to interpret. Furthermore, in this situation, non-conformities are often typing errors and therefore likely to be actual faults.

Finally, several directions exist to pursue this work. One approach is related to rules that are specific to C++ programming such as rules related to default constructors or destructors and rules related to the redefinition of methods, for which verification scripts exist. Another direction would be to compare the faults found by rules verification before validation and the faults found by dynamic testing.

References

1. NASA, *"C style guide"*, Software Engineering Laboratory Series, SEL-94-003, August 94,.
2. Centre National d'Etudes Spatiales, *"Règles essentielles pour l'utilisation du langage C"*, MPM-53-00-06, 1 Mars 1995, Ed.2 - Rév.0.
3. Centre National d'Etudes Spatiales, *"Règles essentielles pour l'utilisation du langage C++"*, MPM-53-00-13, 16 juin 1996, Ed.1 - Rév.0.
4. Erick Nyquist & Mats Herricson, *"PROGRAMMING in C++ Rules and Recommandations"*, Ellemtel Telecom. Systems Laboratories, réf. M 900118 rév. C.
5. Kernighan, Brian and Dennis Ritchie, *"The C Programming Language"*, Englewood Cliffs NJ, 1978 (1st Ed.), 1988 (2nd Ed.), Prentice Hall.
6. Scott D. Meyers, *"Effective C++ : 50 Specific Ways to Improve Your Programs and Designs"*, Addison-Wesley, 2nd edition (September 1997), ISBN: 0201924889.
7. ISO/IEC, *"Software product quality - Part 1: Quality model"*, ISO/IEC FDIS 9126-1, 1999. See also ISO/IEC 9126:1991(E).
8. J.-C. Laprie, (Ed.), *"Dependability: Basic Concepts and Terminology"*, Dependable Computing and Fault Tolerance, Vol. 5, Vienna, Austria, Springer-Verlag, 1992.
9. Richard Bache et Gualtiero Bazzana, *"Software Metrics for Product Assessment"*, McGraw-Hill, 1993.
10. Rae, Robert and Hausen, *"Software Evaluation for Certification"*, International Software Quality Assurance Series, McGraw-Hill, ISBN 0-07-709042-X, 1995.
11. Mayrand et al., *"Evaluating the Benefits of Clone Detection in the Software Maintenance Activities in Large Scale Systems"*, Workshop on Emp. Soft. Studies, Monterey, Nov., 96.
12. M.E. Fagan, *"Advances in Software Inspections"*, IEEE Trans. on Soft. Eng., Vol. SE-12, N°7, July 1986.
13. Victor R. Basili, Richard W. Selby, *"Comparing the Effectiveness of Software Testing Strategies"* IEEE Trans. on Soft. Eng., Vol. SE-13, N° 12, December 1987.
14. Edsger W. Dijkstra, *"Goto Statement Considered Harmful"*, Com. of the ACM, March 1968.

Automated Black-Box Testing with Abstract VDM Oracles

Bernhard K. Aichernig

Technical University of Graz, Institute for Software Technology (IST),
Münzgrabenstr. 11/II, A-8010 Graz, Austria.
email: aichernig@ist.tu-graz.ac.at,
fax: ++43 316 873 5706

Abstract. In this paper the possibilities to automate black-box testing through formal requirement specifications are explored. More precisely, the formal method VDM (Vienna Development Method) serves to demonstrate that abstract requirement models can be used as test oracles for concrete software. The automation of the resulting testing frame-work is based on modern CASE-tools that support a light-weight approach to formal methods. The specification language used is VDM-SL, but the results are easily transferred into similar model oriented methods such as B, Z or RAISE.

1 Introduction

During the last few years the interest in formal software development has been growing rapidly. One of the main reasons for this is the availability of tools to assist the developer in using these formal methods. The author, too, has contributed to the growing repertoire of automated tools by an extension of a commercial tool [5]. However, formal methods are not often applied in industrial projects, despite the growing maturity of the theories and tools, and the need of a mathematical basis [6]. Several reasons can be identified for the absence of formality in the software development process: Too many different notations have been invented, the lack of integration into informal approaches, and the strong emphasis on formal proofs.

The last point needs clarification. Of course, the formal theory and hence the possibility of conducting formal proofs is the important attribute of a formal method. However, the advantage of a formal notation to specify requirements precisely and unambiguously should not be missed, even if formal proofs are not the project's focus.

Consequently, instead of promoting formal correctness proofs, we regard the automation of functional testing as the next step in a smooth integration of formal methods, to raise the level of reliability, after formal specification techniques have been introduced. To sum up, this work is a further contribution to the lately propagated light-weight approach to formal methods [19].

The ISO-standardized Vienna Development Method (VDM) [18, 11, 20] serves to demonstrate how a well-established formal method supports the automation

M. Felici, K. Kanoun, A. Pasquini (Eds.): SAFECOMP'99, LNCS 1698, pp. 250-259, 1999
© Springer-Verlag Berlin Heidelberg 1999

of testing. VDM is one of the most widely used formal methods, and it can be applied to the construction of a large variety of systems. It is a model oriented method, i.e. its formal descriptions (specifications) consist of an explicit mathematical model of the system being constructed. Furthermore, VDM is supported by CASE-tools and even allows an integration into informal methods like UML or Structured Analysis, and so does our testing approach.

Previous work has shown how test-cases may be derived from formal specifications [9]. However, little attention had been given to the fact that formal models of software requirements are inherently abstract in the sense that detailed design decisions are not included. Consequently, the test-cases, derived (or even generated) from such an abstract model, are abstract too, and thus inappropriate for a direct automatic test of a target system. For that reason, a mapping between abstract and concrete test data is required.

The presented framework focuses on the usage of formal requirements specifications as test oracles for concrete implementations. The approach is based on the formal definition of abstraction as a homomorphism, called the retrieve function, which maps the concrete level into the abstract. If the retrieve function is implemented and the post-condition is executable, then the model may serve as a test oracle and specification as well. The approach is not limited to VDM, but can also be applied in other model oriented methods like B [1], Z [25] or RAISE [13].

After this introduction, the following Section 2 describes the general approach of using specifications as test oracles. Then, Section 3 explains three possibilities to automate the approach by using a commercial tool, the IFAD VDM-SL Toolbox. Finally, Section 4 contains some concluding remarks and the identification of possible directions to future work.

2   From Formal Specifications to Oracles

The Vienna Development Method provides the two needed concepts in order to support the presented testing process. First, the formal specification itself, which precisely defines what a function or operation should compute. Second, the concept of data-reification, that provides a formal definition of abstraction. In the following, both concepts are explained and their role in our testing approach will be clarified.

2.1   VDM-SL Specifications as Oracles

As already mentioned, in VDM a system is specified in terms of abstract mathematical models. VDM-SL, the general purpose specification language of VDM, provides mathematical objects, like sets, sequences, maps etc., to model a system's state. The functionality is formulated by imperative operations, which manipulate these abstract state representations or applicative functions. Two styles can be distinguished to define functionality: implicit and explicit definitions. An implicit operation defines *what* should happen by pre- and post-conditions. The pre-condition is a logical constraint on the input stating what must hold that the functionality is defined. The essential part is the post-condition, a relation between the input, the old state, the output and the new state.

The following example is inspired by an industrial project in which a voice communication system for air traffic control has been formally specified [16]. Here, an abstract view of the system's radio switch is modeled. The switch assigns frequencies to operator positions on which communication may be established. The VDM-SL model refers to frequencies and operator positions by the identifiers *FrqId* and *OpId*. The relation is modeled by a finite mapping from operator positions to a set of frequencies. A map can be interpreted as a two-column tabular whose left- and right-side entries can be accessed by the domain (*dom*) and range (*rng*) operators.

The set of frequencies represents frequency coupling, which means that communication is forwarded to all frequencies in the set. A requirement of the switch is that a frequency must not belong to two different coupling sets. This is expressed by means of a data-invariant, stating that for all two frequency sets, with more than one element, they may not have frequencies in common.

$$Switch\text{-}a = OpId \xrightarrow{m} FrqId\text{-set}$$

$$\text{inv } s \triangleq \forall fs1, fs2 \in \text{rng } s \cdot \text{card } fs1 > 1 \wedge \text{card } fs2 > 1 \;\Rightarrow\; fs1 \cap fs2 = \{\}$$

A function *couple-frequency*, defined by pre- and post-conditions, adds frequencies to an operator position. The pre-condition says that if the operator position has already a frequency associated, then no frequency set with a cardinality greater than two must exist that already contains the frequency to be added. This would lead to violation of the system's invariant.

The post-condition establishs the following relation between the input (f, op and s) and the resulting output r. If the operator position has already a frequency associated, then the resulting map equals the old one with the input frequency added to the existing set of frequencies of the operator position. This is expressed by overriding (†) a map entry. In case of a new operator position, the result equals the old switch with the new map entry.

$$couple\text{-}frequency \,(f : FrqId, op : OpId, s : Switch\text{-}a) \; r : Switch\text{-}a$$
$$\text{pre } \; op \in \text{dom } s \;\Rightarrow\; \neg \exists fs \in \text{rng } s \cdot f \in fs \wedge \text{card } fs > 1$$
$$\text{post if } op \in \text{dom } s$$
$$\qquad \text{then } r = s \dagger \{op \mapsto s\,(op) \cup \{f\}\}$$
$$\qquad \text{else } r = s \dagger \{op \mapsto f\}$$

From a testers perspective, the post-condition serves as a test oracle. In general, an oracle is any program, process or data that specifies the expected outcome of a set of tests as applied to a tested object [7]. Here, the oracle is a predicate, a Boolean function, which evaluates to true if the correct output is returned, with the premise that the pre-condition holds. The signature of the post-condition oracle above is:

$$post\text{-}couple\text{-}frequency : OpId * FrqId * Switch\text{-}a * Switch\text{-}a \rightarrow \mathbb{B}$$

The two arguments of type *Switch-a* define the relation between the old and new value of the switch. Note that pre-conditions define the input values for 'good' tests, where valid outputs can be expected.

However, the system's model and consequently the oracle is abstract and cannot be directly used as a test-oracle for a test on implementation level. What is needed, is a link between the abstract level and the concrete level. In VDM, and other formal methods, this link is provided by a precise definition of abstraction.

2.2   The Definition of Abstraction

The M in VDM is based on a refinement of an abstract specification to a more concrete one, which usually is carried out in several steps. Refining the data model is called data-reification, which is correct if it establishs a homomorphism between the abstract and refined, more concrete, level. In Figure 1 our notion

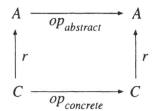

Fig. 1. The morphism of abstraction.

of abstraction is represented by a commuting diagram, where operations (op) are viewed as functions from input to output states. The abstract operation $op_{abstract}$ manipulates an abstract state representation of type A. The concrete operation $op_{concrete}$ incorporates detailed design decisions and maps a refined input state to an output state. Examples for such data-refinement would be to implement a set through a balanced binary-tree, or the other way round, to view a data-base system as a set of data. The relationship between the abstract and the concrete is defined by a a function r mapping a concrete state to its abstract counterpart. The diagram shows that the retrieve function r is a homomorphism for which the following formula holds:

$$\forall \ in : C \cdot op_{abstract}(r(in)) = r(op_{concrete}(in))$$

Using an implicit function definition on the abstract level, the formula for a correct implementation (refinement) is:

$$\forall \ in : C \cdot pre\text{-}op_{abstract}(r(in)) \ \Rightarrow \ post\text{-}op_{abstract}(r(in), r(op_{concrete}(in)))$$

This simply means that the abstract post-condition must hold for the concrete input and output, mapped to the abstract level by r, if the pre-condition is satisfied.

Modern tools allow the interpretation of explicit VDM-SL definitions. If the retrieve function and the post-condition predicate are defined explicitly, the formula above can be evaluated and thus provides a testing frame-work inside VDM-SL. However, to test functionality implemented in a programming language like C++, the language gap between programming languages and the specification language has to be overcome. In the following it is shown how modern tools provide these bridges and help to automate the approach.

3 Automated Test Evaluation

The combination of the notion of abstraction and the possibility to use specifications as test oracles leads to a testing framework with abstract oracles. Modern tools like the IFAD VDM-SL Toolbox [17] allow the interpretation or even code-generation of such pre- and post-conditions which leads to an automated test evaluation through post-condition oracles. In Figure 2 the data-flow of the new testing scenario is presented. An implementation is executed with a concrete

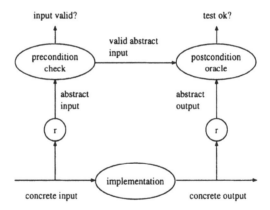

Fig. 2. DFD of the testing scenario.

test input (state). An implemented retrieve function maps the concrete input and output to its abstract representations. A pre-condition check validates the input and feeds it into the oracle which checks the relation to the produced output. If the post-condition evaluates to true, the test passed. The advantage of the approach is the automation of black-box testing by the usage of structural test-data. Another possibility would be to code the reverse of r in order to test with abstract test-data derived from the specification.

In the following, the possibilities for automation by using the IFAD tools are explained in more detail.

3.1   Code-Generation of Oracles

The IFAD Toolbox provides a C++ code-generator, which translates explicit VDM-SL specifications to C++ source code, using a VDM library. With this tool the post-condition functions, like in our Switch example, can be automatically translated to C++ . Even the pre-condition with its quantors over finite sets can be code-generated. Below the generated C++ code for *post-couple-frequency* is shown:

```
Bool post_couple_frequency(int f, int op, Map s, Map r) {
  Bool varRes;
  Bool cond;
  cond = (Bool) s.Dom().InSet(op);
  if (cond.GetValue()) {
    Map var2;
    Map modmap;
    Set tmpVar2;
    Set var2;
    var2 = Set().Insert(f);
    tmpVar2 = (Set) s[op];
    tmpVar2.ImpUnion(var2);
    modmap = Map().Insert(op, tmpVar2);
    var2 = s;    var2.ImpOverride(modmap);
    varRes = (Bool) (r == var2);
  }
  else {
    Map var2;
    Map modmap;
    modmap = Map().Insert(op, f);
    var2 = s;    var2.ImpOverride(modmap);
    varRes = (Bool) (r == var2);
  }
  return varRes;
}
```

What remains to implement manually is the retrieve function. Special C++ generator functions in the VDM library facilitate the conversions of C++ types into VDM objects.

3.2   Interpretation of Oracles with the Dynamik Link Facility

Another approach is to use the Toolbox interpreter in order to evaluate the oracle inside VDM-SL. The dynamik link facility may be used to call the C++ functions to be tested from inside the Toolbox [12]. The dynamik link facility enables a VDM-SL specification to execute parts written in C++, during interpretation.

It is called dynamik link facility because the C++ code is dynamically linked together with the Toolbox.

In order to access the implementation, a *dlmodule* has to be defined which contains the function's declaration. For our example that would be

dlmodule *CPP*

  exports

    functions *couple-frequency-ext* : $\mathbb{Z} \times \mathbb{Z} \times \mathbb{Z} \xrightarrow{m} \mathbb{Z}$-set $\rightarrow \mathbb{Z} \xrightarrow{m} \mathbb{Z}$-set

end *CPP*

, if we model frequencies and operator positions as integers ($\mathbb{Z}$). In order to test *couple-frequency* in this case two functions are to be implemented. One mapping the input to the implementation representation and calling *couple-frequency*, and the retrieve function which converts the output back to the abstract VDM-SL data-type.

With this approach abstract VDM-SL test-cases are fit into the implementation. Hence, here the following must hold for a correct implementation $op_{concrete}$:

$$\forall\, in : A \cdot pre\text{-}op_{abstract}(in) \;\Rightarrow\; post\text{-}op_{abstract}(in, r(op_{concrete}(rep(in))))$$

, where the function $rep : A \rightarrow C$ maps the abstract input to its concrete representation.

3.3   CORBA Oracles

A third elegant way to bridge the language gap is CORBA, the Common Object Request Broker Architecture [22]. The VDM-SL Toolbox provides a CORBA based API through which a program can access the Toolbox [27]. The CORBA interface of the VDM-SL Toolbox is defined in IDL, the interface definition language of CORBA. The language mapping is done by the IDL interface through which the full functionality of a running toolbox may be invoked.

This includes the loading of a specification and the starting of the interpreter. With this technique a post-condition oracle can be accessed and evaluated through the API. Since CORBA is a distributed object architecture the Toolbox may even run on a different (test-)server providing the oracles. Since CORBA IDL converts different programming languages, the test approach can be applied to as many programming languages as IDL mappings have been implemented, e.g. C++ and Java.

4   Concluding Remarks

In this paper we have presented an approach for automated test evaluation through VDM-SL oracles. We have shown the general strategy and presented more details how the resulting test approach can be automated. The three presented solutions for automation are based on the commercial tool IFAD VDM-SL Toolbox.

To our present knowledge, only one automated black-box testing approach has been based on an explicit mapping from an implementation level to a formally specified and abstract post-condition oracle [8]. In this early work, the post-condition oracle had to be translated manually into Prolog. Of course, other formal model oriented approaches to testing have been published, but they differ in two aspects: First, the focus rather lies on test-case generation, than on oracle generation and automated test evaluation [21, 9, 26, 15, 24, 10, 2, 23]. Hence, the abstraction problem is not considered at all. Second, explicit specifications serve as active oracles which calculate and compare the specified output to the program under test [14, 3, 28]. In contrast to our passive oracles, these solutions cannot handle non-deterministic results.

Our idea has been presented in [4] the first time. This work could also be extended with test-case generation techniques in order to automate the whole test process. However, the automated test evaluation especially supports random testing.

In future we envisage an instrumentation of objects with post-condition oracles. Objects can be instrumented through inheritance without changing the actual code. Then, testable objects inherit the functionality from its superclass and provide additional retrieve and oracle functions as testing methods.

We feel that the application of both, formal specifications and formal development tools to testing, as presented here, will be a powerful combination. However, more case studies are needed in order to evaluate the approach formally.

Acknowledgments

The author would like to thank IFAD's team for their support concerning the VDM-tools. Many thanks belong to Peter Lucas and the members of our formal methods group for the stimulating discussions. Finally, the three anonymous referees are acknowledged for their comments on an earlier version of this paper.

References

1. J.-R. Abrial. *The B-Book, Assigning programs to meanings.* Cambridge University Press, 1996. ISBN 0521 49619 5(hardback).
2. Lionel Van Aertryck. *Une méthode et un outil pour l'aide à la génération de jeux de tests de logiciels.* PhD thesis, Université de Rennes, January 1998.
3. Sten Agerholm, Pierre-Jean Lecoeur, and Etienne Reichert. Formal specification and validation at work: A case study using VDM-SL. In *Proceedings of Second Workshop on Formal Methods in Software Practice, Florida, Marts.* ACM, 1998.

4. Bernhard K. Aichernig. Automated requirements testing with abstract oracles. In *ISSRE'98: The Ninth International Symposium on Software Reliability Engineering, Paderborn, Germany*, pages 21–22, IBM Thomas J.Watson Research Center, P.O.Box 218, Route 134, Yorktown Heights, NY, USA, November 1998. Ram Chillarege. ISBN 3-00-003410-2.

5. Bernhard K. Aichernig and Peter Gorm Larsen. A proof obligation generator for VDM-SL. In J. Fitzgerald, C.B. Jones, and P. Lucas, editors, *FME'97: Industrial Applications and Strengthened Foundations of Formal Methods*, volume 1313 of *Lecture Notes in Computer Science*, 1997.

6. Bernhard K. Aichernig and Peter Lucas. Softwareentwicklung — eine Ingenieursdisziplin!(?). *Telematik, Zeitschrift des Telematik-Ingenieur-Verbandes (TIV)*, 4(2):2–8, 1998. ISSN 1028-5068.

7. Boris Beizer. *Software Testing Techniques*. Van Nostrand Reinhold, New York, 2nd edition, 1990.

8. R.E. Bloomfield and P.K.D. Froome. The application of formal methods to the assessment of high integrity software. *IEEE Transactions on Software Engineering*, SE-12(9):988–993, September 1986.

9. Jeremy Dick and Alain Faivre. Automating the generation and sequencing of test cases from model-based specifications. In J.C.P. Woodcock and P.G. Larsen, editors, *FME'93: Industrial-Strength Formal Methods*. Springer-Verlag, April 1993.

10. Michael R. Donat. Automating formal specification-based testing. In Michel Bidoit and Max Dauchet, editors, *TAPSOFT '97:Theory and Practice of Software Development, 7th International Joint Conference CAAP/FASE*, volume 1214 of *Lecture Notes in Computer Science*, pages 833–847. Springer-Verlag, April 1997.

11. John Fitzgerald and Peter Gorm Larsen. *Modelling Sytems, Practical Tools and Techniques*. Cambridge University Press, 1998.

12. Brigitte Fröhlich and Peter Gorm Larsen. Combining VDM-SL specifications with C++ code. In Marie-Claude Gaudel and Jim Woodcock, editors, *FME96, Industrial Benefit and Advances in Formal Methods*, Lecture Notes in Computer Science, pages 179–194. Springer, March 1996.

13. Chris George et al. *The Raise Development Method*. The BCS Practitioner Series. Prentice Hall, 1995.

14. Andrew Harry. The value of reference implementations and prototyping in a formal design and testing methodology. Report 208/92, National Physical Laboratory, Queen's Road, Teddington, Middlesex TW11 0LW, UK, October 1992.

15. Steffen Helke, Thomas Neustupny, and Thomas Santen. Automating test case generation from Z specifications with Isabelle. In *ZUM'97*, 1997.

16. Johann Hörl. Formal specification of a voice communication system used in air traffic control. Master's thesis, Institute for Software Technology (IST), Technical University Graz, Austria, December 1998.

17. IFAD. IFAD's homepage. http://www.ifad.dk/.

18. Cliff B. Jones. *Systematic Software Development Using VDM*. Prentice-Hall International, Englewood Cliffs, New Jersey, second edition, 1990.

19. Cliff B. Jones. Formal methods light: A rigorous approach to formal methods. *IEEE Computer*, 29(4):20–21, April 1996.

20. P. G. Larsen, B. S. Hansen, H. Bruun, N. Plat, H. Toetenel, D. J. Andrews, J. Dawes, G. Parkin, et al. Information technology — Programming languages, their environments and system software interfaces — Vienna Development Method — Specification Language — Part 1: Base language, December 1996. International Standard ISO/IEC 13817-1.

21. Janusz Laski. Data flow testing in STAD. *The Journal of Systems and Software*, 12(1):3–14, 1990.

22. OMG. The common object request broker architecture and specification, revision 2.0. Technical report, OMG, 1996.

23. Jesper Pedersen. Automatic test case generation and instantiation for VDM-SL specifications. Master's thesis, Department of Mathematics and Computer Science, Odense University, September 1998.

24. J. Peleska and M. Siegel. Test automation of safety-critical reactive systems. *South African Computer Journal*, 19:53–77, 1997.

25. J. M. Spivey. *The Z Notation*. Series in Computer Science. Prentice-Hall, 1989.

26. Philip Alan Stocks. *Applying formal methods to software testing*. PhD thesis, The Department of computer science, The University of Queensland, 1993.

27. Ole Storm. The VDM Toolbox API users guide. Technical report, IFAD, 1998.

28. H. Treharne, J. Draper, and S. Schneider. Test case preparation using a prototype. In *B'98 — Second B-Conference*, 1998.

Towards Statistical Control of
an Industrial Test Process

Gaetano Lombardi[1], Emilia Peciola [1], Raffaela Mirandola[2],
Antonia Bertolino[3], Eda Marchetti[3]

[1] Ericsson Telecomunicazioni SpA, Roma, Italy
{teiloga, E.Peciola} @rd.tei.ericsson.se
[2] Dip. di Informatica, Sistemi e Produzione Univ. "Tor Vergata", Roma, Italy
mirandola@info.uniroma2.it
[3] Istituto di Elaborazione della Informazione, CNR, Pisa, Italy
{bertolino, e.marchetti} @iei.pi.cnr.it

Abstract. We present an ongoing experience aimed at introducing statistical process control techniques to one crucial test phase, namely Function Test, of a real world software development process. We have developed a prediction procedure, using which, among other things, we compare the performance of a Classical model vs. a Bayesian approach. We provide here the description of the prediction procedure, and a few examples of use of the models over real sets of data. However, far from aimed at identifying new statistical models, the focus of this work is rather about *putting measurement in practice*, and in easy and effective steps to improve the status of control over test processes in a soft, bottom-up approach. The experience described has started quite recently, and the results obtained so far, although limited in scope, are quite encouraging (as well as exciting for the involved team), both in terms of predictive validity of the models and of the positive response got from development personnel.

1 Introduction

*It is only in the state of statistical control that statistical theory provides
with a high degree of belief, prediction of performance in the immediate future*

W. Edwards Deming

In this paper we report about an ongoing experience at Ericsson Telecomunicazioni S.p.A. in Rome (TEI in the following) aimed at applying statistical process control techniques to the Function Test process.

We discuss here the objective of this study and the starting point. In the next section we outline the approach taken. In Sections 3 and 4 we briefly describe two statistical estimators used for data analysis, from a Classical and a Bayesian viewpoint, respectively. Section 5 then gives a few examples, and Section 6 provides the conclusions.

M. Felici, K. Kanoun, A. Pasquini (Eds.): SAFECOMP'99, LNCS 1698, pp. 260-271, 1999
© Springer-Verlag Berlin Heidelberg 1999

1.1 Objective

Within the frame of the company-wide Ericsson System Software Initiative (ESSI), regular assessments are being performed at all Ericsson Software Design Centers according to the Capability Maturity Model (CMM) for software, Version 2 draft C [1]. Main objectives of ESSI are to identify key areas for process improvement and to propose a framework for subsequent improvement actions. An assessment has been recently performed at TEI organization covering the AXE10 (multi-application, open-ended digital switching product for public telecommunications networks) software development area. The software processes at TEI were found to be at the Defined level of maturity (level 3). Although this result was very satisfying, TEI is now going to initiate some of the level 4 practices. The organization intends to improve its capabilities in statistical process control and in prediction methods. As it is not economically justifiable to apply statistical process control techniques to all processes, a set of processes has been selected according to the business objectives of the organization. One of the selected processes is Function Test, that is one of the four test phases in TEI test strategy, namely:

1) Basic Test, testing the smallest module (test object) in the system. The goal is to verify design specification;
2) Integration Test, testing a functional area: all modules in that area are integrated;
3) Function Test, verifying system functions;
4) System Test, verifying system performance and architectural requirements.

Function Test has been identified as strategic in meeting the commitments to customers with respect to quality objectives, for the following reason. One of the TEI objectives is reducing of a determined amount the fault density figures that are obtained by monitoring the first six months of operation of released products. Fault density is measured by the ratio between the cumulative number of failures observed in those six months and the product size, expressed in lines of code. Root Cause Analysis (RCA) of reported failures is routinely performed, to track back failures to the phase in which they have been originated. An important finding of RCA for TEI products was that a high percentage of failures (48%) corresponded to software faults that could have been discovered during the Function Test phase. Therefore, one of the actions proposed to reduce fault density figures is related to reducing the failures slipping through from Function Test to operation. The failures slipping through, that is one of TEI GPC quality objectives, is measured as the ratio between the number of failures found during first six months, and the sum of failures found during Function Test and first six months.

In this paper we apply statistical techniques taken from the literature to the Function Test process in order to put under control its effectiveness in failure detection.

1.2 Starting Point

Currently, Function Test is performed along a function test specification, with the goal of testing conformance of the target function to its specifications. Test cases are derived manually by testers, by making a systematic analysis of the specification documentation and trying to cover all the specified functionalities (or use cases). It means that the test cases are deterministically chosen by examining the functional specifications and altogether before test execution starts (which implies that the number of tests to be executed is decided in advance).

Function Test execution is organised in a specified number of stages. The tests are not executed continuously, but only during the working days (i.e., five days in a week) and 8 hours per day. All the failures discovered within a stage are logged and reported to software designers, who trace failures back to code and correct them. A new software version is then released, which is resubmitted to test in the next test stage. For each project, the information registered consists of the start and end dates of the test phase, and of the calendar day (but not the day time) of discovery of each failure. Test execution (CPU) times were not recorded.

Function Test stops when all the test cases defined in the test case specification have been successfully performed, either at first try or after suitable fault repair. Specific exit criteria related to the measured rate of failures detected over the testing period are not explicitly considered in test process, and no estimation of achieved remaining number of faults is currently performed.

2   The Approach

Measurement provides an assessment of an entity under observation (more precisely, of some attributes of this entity [2]). However, the specific objectives for doing any measurement must be clearly stated within a well-defined measurement programme. In fact, only when the objectives are explicitly identified, by interpreting the results of measurement we can take appropriate decisions, and put these into useful actions [2].

2.1 Measurement Objectives

In this study the final objectives are: to put under statistical control the Function Test phase and to investigate the feasibility of introducing testing exit criteria according to remaining faults prediction.

One of the attributes to measure to achieve these goals is the *effectiveness in failure detection* during Function Test, i.e., the rate of failures detected over a fixed period of testing. In particular we use the failure data observed in the first part of the test process to *predict* the expected cumulative number of failures over the planned period of Function Test. A very important property of prediction system is the speed of convergence of estimates. On this respect, we are currently comparing the performances of different estimators (see section 3 and 4).

However, using the predictions provided by the estimators requires insight and knowledge of the process which goes well behind the statistical analyses described here. For instance, suppose that measurement brings to our attention an unexpectedly low number of failures with respect to standard figures. This can be due to an ineffective test process (bad news), or instead to a very good development process (good news).

How the presented estimators are used in project control and management and how historical data through several projects are used to set reference/target measures is outside the scope of the present paper.

2.2 Data Model

As a first step in this investigation, we analysed the typology of data available to lay down an appropriate data model. We could access sets of failure data collected over several projects during the phase of Function Test.

We decided to adopt a data model close to the current logging procedures, as it would be difficult and expensive to change them. As the failure reports are registered on a daily base, we decided to group the failure data into *test intervals* (TIs), each one a day long. A TI in which at least a failure is observed is called a *failed test interval* (FTI), otherwise it is said a successful TI. Quite obviously, anyhow small a test interval is chosen, until this remains larger than a single test there will always be a chance to observe more than one failure within it.

Hence, our model estimates the expected number of failures in two subsequent steps: first we predict N_{FTI}, i.e., the expected number of FTIs; then, from this number, we derive the expected number of failures N_F. To do this, we define a random variable Q to denote the probability that the next TI is failed. Then, over a NTI long period of test intervals, using a valid estimate $\hat{Q}$ of Q, we easily obtain:

$$N_{FTI} = NTI \bullet \hat{Q} \tag{1}$$

Once a value for N_{FTI} is so estimated, the total number of failures clearly will depend on how many failures on average are observed within a FTI. We again introduce a random variable F to represent the number of failures observed within a FTI, and then derive N_F from N_{FTI}, with:

$$N_F = N_{FTI} \bullet \hat{F} \tag{2}$$

As concerns the estimation of $\hat{F}$, we decided to adopt the classical estimator $E[F]$, based on the *sample mean* (also called *arithmetic mean*) of the observed failures over the number of observed FTIs. The choice of the sample mean lies on the observation that, for the projects considered, it soon stabilizes. Furthermore, for large samples it shows the property of consistency and unbiasedness [3].

2.3 Prediction Procedure

The statistical control procedure is based on the following main steps:

- Consider the test intervals assembled in groups of 5 TIs (corresponding to one calendar week of testing) and assign to each group an increasing identification number k with $k = 1,..., \dfrac{NTI}{5}$.

- After observing the k-th (current) group of failure data derive values of:

  2.1) the cumulative (i.e., from group 1 to group k inclusive) number of FTIs

2.2) the cumulative number of failures

- Using the observations of step 2) derive:

  3.1) an estimate $\hat{Q}$ of Q, based on statistical models (Sect. 3 and 4)

  3.2) an estimate $\hat{F} = E[F]$ of F

  3.3) predictions of global N_{Fn} and global N_F over a future period testing, based on formulas (1) and (2)

- By use of classical statistical techniques (e.g., confidence interval, relative error) evaluate the accuracy of the estimates obtained at steps 3.1), and 3.2)

- If the estimates $\hat{Q}$ and $\hat{F}$ do not reach the desired level of accuracy, wait for the data relative to another group of 5 TIs, increment k and repeat Steps 2 through 4.

- Check the model, i.e., evaluate if the proposed model and the substantive conclusions fit the data and how sensitive are the results to the modelling assumptions.

In the next sections we describe two different estimators used in step 3.1). Specifically, Section 3 shows a model based on the Classical (frequentist) approach, while Section 4 presents a model based on the Bayesian approach.

3 Using a Classical Approach

A classical approach to derive the probability Q that the next TI is failed, given a sample of NTI, is based on the *maximum likelihood* estimate [3, 4]. The idea underlying the maximum likelihood estimate of a parameter that characterizes a random variable Q, is to choose that parameter value that makes the observed sample values $Q_1, Q_2, ..., Q_n$ the most probable.

In our case the sample to be analysed is formed by sets of test intervals of size n (with $n=5, 10, ..., $ NTI), and we want to predict, as early as possible, the proportion Q of FTIs. We can visualize the sample as a sequence of Bernoulli trials with probability Q of failure on each trial (note that in such a way we are assuming independent TIs, which is reasonable for the approach followed in test selection). Thus, if the observed number of failed TIs is f, then the likelihood function l is given by [3, 4]:

$$l(Q) = Q^f (1 - Q)^{n-f} \qquad (3)$$

The *maximum likelihood* estimate of Q is that value of Q that maximizes the likelihood function l, or its logarithmic form. Solving for Q yields the maximum likelihood estimate:

$$\hat{Q} = \frac{f}{n} \qquad (4)$$

It can be proved [3] that such $\hat{Q}$ is an unbiased, consistent, and the minimum variance unbiased estimator of Q.

To complete the statistical control procedure, we associate to each $\hat{Q}$ its *confidence interval*, that is a probability judgement about the accuracy of the estimate delivered. We are dealing with a random variable, so we cannot predict with certainty that the true value of the parameter, Q, is within any finite interval. We can, however, construct a confidence interval, such that there is a specified confidence or probability that the true value Q lies within that interval. For a given confidence level, of course, the shorter the interval, the more accurate the estimate.

It can be proved [3] that, for a sample of large size n, an approximate $100(1-\alpha)\%$ confidence interval for the Bernoulli parameter Q is given by:

$$\hat{Q} - z_{\alpha/2}\sqrt{\frac{\hat{Q}(1-\hat{Q})}{n}} < Q < \hat{Q} + z_{\alpha/2}\sqrt{\frac{\hat{Q}(1-\hat{Q})}{n}} \tag{5}$$

where $\hat{Q}$ is obtained by (4) and values for the parameter $z_{\alpha/2}$ are found in statistical reference tables [4].

Therefore fixed a confidence level (90%) according to the producer exigencies, we associate to each $\hat{Q}$ estimate after n TIs, $\hat{Q}(n)$, the relative confidence interval.

The study of the confidence intervals leads us to determine that, after a certain number n^* of TIs, the desired level of accuracy is reached. Therefore we can use the estimate $\hat{Q}(n^*)$, obtained after n* TIs, to make predictions about the number of FTIs after (n*+5), (n*+10), ..., NTI test intervals. In other words, after NTI test intervals, the number of failed test intervals N_{FTI} can be simply obtained by $N_{FTI} = NTI \bullet \hat{Q}(n^*)$ (see Eq. (1)).

To complete the prediction procedure, we can now apply Eq. (2) to obtain the global number of failures expected at the end of Function Test.

To assess whether the model inferences seem adequate we check, a posteriori, the obtained predictions against the real outcomes of several projects. Some examples of application are illustrated in Section 5.

The main limitation of this approach lies on the fact that a large amount of data is necessary to derive significant confidence intervals. Consequently the value n* of TIs guaranteeing the desired level of accuracy can result quite high.

4   Using a Bayesian Approach

The method described in the previous section has a broad field of application. We can use it whichever is the behaviour of the product under test. But this is also a limitation of the method, because it is not able to exploit the evidences of historical data collected over other TEI projects and which could contribute to better predict the cumulative number of failures.

For this reason, we investigated other methods which could be correlated to the behaviour of the product under test, with the purpose of reaching more accurate estimates or, more importantly, of anticipating the moment in which the predictions can be trusted. In this section, we report the application of a Bayesian approach.

We chose this kind of approach after an accurate analysis of the failure behaviour of several products. We observed in fact that every realization of the random variable

Q can only take discrete values of the form $\frac{1}{i}$ within an interval $\left[\frac{1}{M},1\right]$ (where M is a maximum fixed value). Precisely, for each i within $[1, M]$, the associated discrete distribution, or probability mass function (pmf) of Q, $p_Q\left(\frac{1}{i}\right) = P\left(Q = \frac{1}{i}\right)$, gives the probability that the next FTI will be observed after $(i\text{-}1)$ successful TIs. In particular, and more notably, we observed that *for all products* considered the pmf of Q always concentrated for most of its realizations on three same consecutive values, while took very rarely the other possible values. We thought that a Bayesian approach was the most effective way to exploit this knowledge (in the spirit of the approach described in [5]).

In the Bayesian framework [6], probabilities are meant to describe an observer subjective knowledge of yet-unknown events. This knowledge continuously evolves as new events are observed: inferences are drawn by combining the pre-existing knowledge with the new evidence collected through observation.

In our context, the observed behaviour of Q in the projects considered constitutes an important starting point to model a tester's subjective belief about the rate of failure detection during TEI Function Test. We express this knowledge through an appropriate modelling of $p_Q\left(\frac{1}{i}\right)$, the *prior* pmf. During the performance of Function Test, the realization of a sequence of test intervals with and without failures is observed. Thanks to this evidence, the tester's knowledge about *this specific product* evolves and a new distribution for the pmf of Q, called the *posterior* pmf, can be derived.

Denoting by F_n the sequence of observed outcomes (failed/successful) for the first n TIs, the posterior pmf for Q, denoted by $p'_{Q,n}\left(\frac{1}{i}\right)$, then gives $P\left(Q = \frac{1}{i} \mid F_n\right)$, i.e., it is the update of $p_Q\left(\frac{1}{i}\right)$ after having observed the sequence F_n.

Applying Bayes' formula we have:

$$p'_{Q,n}\left(\frac{1}{i}\right) = P\left(Q = \frac{1}{i} \mid F_n\right) = \frac{P_{prior}\left(Q = \frac{1}{i}\right) P\left(F_n \mid Q = \frac{1}{i}\right)}{\sum_{j=1}^{M} P\left(F_n \mid Q = \frac{1}{j}\right) P_{prior}\left(Q = \frac{1}{j}\right)} \tag{6}$$

in which the term $P\left(F_n \mid Q = \frac{1}{i}\right)$ is usually called a *likelihood function*.

With f denoting the number of FTIs observed in the sequence F_n, the likelihood function can be derived as a binomial distribution with parameters n and $\frac{1}{i}$.

Substituting, the posterior distribution $p'_{Q,n}\left(\frac{1}{i}\right)$ hence is:

$$p'_{Q,n}\left(\frac{1}{i}\right) = \frac{P_Q\left(\frac{1}{i}\right) \cdot \left(\frac{1}{i}\right)^f \left(1 - \frac{1}{i}\right)^{n-f}}{\sum_{j=1}^{M} P_Q\left(\frac{1}{i}\right) \cdot \left(\frac{1}{j}\right)^f \left(1 - \frac{1}{j}\right)^{n-f}} \tag{7}$$

In the step 3.1 of our prediction procedure (Sect. 2.3), we use this updated pmf to derive $E_n[Q]$, i.e. the posterior expectation of Q after n TIs. This is taken as the estimator $\hat{Q}$ in Eq. (1) to derive $N_{FTI,n}$, i.e., the predicted number of FTIs expected after NTI test intervals, based on the test outcomes collected during the first n test intervals, *and* on the prior expectation about Q. From $N_{FTI,n}$ the expected number of failures can then be derived in the usual way.

In the next section we provide some examples in which this Bayesian model is compared with a Classical approach.

5 Examples and Discussion

We have so far presented a "textbook", Classical approach for predicting the expected number of failures in Section 3, and an alternative, Bayesian approach in Section 4. The second model was introduced not because it is claimed to be better than already existing methods, but because we hope it can prove more suitable to assess the specific TEI Function Test process. In particular, we think that since it exploits the prior available knowledge about the rate of occurrence of FTIs it needs fewer data to obtain valid predictions.

Indeed, deriving a prior distribution for the probability of interest is in general a difficult task, which also generates some perplexity towards the usefulness and applicability of Bayesian inference methods. In this case, the data available from several projects submitted to the same testing process conducted easily to an empirical distribution in which the rate of occurrence of FTIs concentrates within a strict interval.

In this section we provide a few examples of results obtained from use of the two described estimators. In the following figures we report the results obtained by applying the models to different data sets coming from the Function Test phase of large telecommunication systems. The size of the software varies from project to project (minimum 50 kloc, maximum 150 kloc), and the failures in the data sets considered were classified as priority B[1] (major failures).

In the following diagrams, on the horizontal axis we put the number of elapsed groups of TIs. On the vertical axis we put the cumulative number of failures over

---

[1] A failure is classified as priority B if it implies:
- large restart with or without reload;
- small restart;
- the function required for the operation and maintenance of the change is out of order;
- traffic disturbance on a single route, or for a few subscribers;
- a dominant PCB (printed circuit board) has a significantly higher failure rate than predicted;
- increased priority from level C for commercial reasons.

completion of the scheduled test period (for confidentiality reasons, we have to omit the actual numbers). We report a dashed curve for the Classical predictions, and a continuous curve for the Bayesian ones. When a prediction becomes acceptable (according to step 4 of the prediction procedure), we fix it and the curve becomes a straight line. The model check (step 6) is presented in the figures below by showing the actual number of failures observed at the end of the test period (the dotted horizontal line) (of course this knowledge is used in no way to make the prediction). The strip marked with vertical segments around the latter signs the zone where the relative error of the prediction would be below 10%.

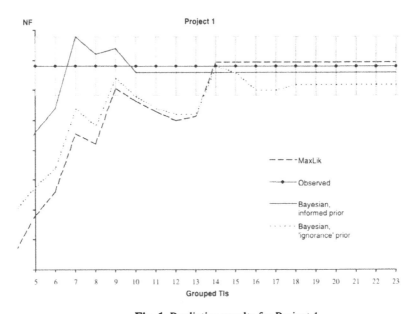

Fig. 1. Prediction results for Project 1

In Fig. 1 we show the results for Project 1. The maximum likelihood method produces a valid prediction after 14 groups of TIs. The light gray curve, labelled Bayesian "ignorance" prior, would be the output from the Bayesian model using as a prior pmf a uniform distribution, i.e., not exploiting any specific knowledge from the test process under observation. We see that with this uninformed prior we gain no particular advantage in using the Bayesian model; on the opposite, the prediction stabilizes only after 18 groups of TIs. However, considering the output from the same model with the informed prior pmf, the prediction is anticipated of as much as four groups relatively to the Classical model, that is a very good result from the manager's point of view. With regard to the outcome of prediction, both models produce accurate estimates.

In the second project considered (Fig. 2), the Bayesian prediction stabilizes three groups in advance with respect to the Classical method, and in addition we see that for this project the estimate produced with the latter is outside the 10% error strip.

But unfortunately the Bayesian model does not consistently work better for any data set. In the third example (Fig. 3), we see that the Classical model reaches first a stable prediction.

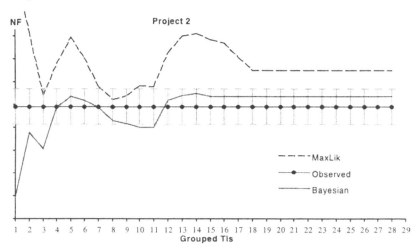

Fig. 2. Prediction results for Project 2

So, the idea is that we can apply both estimators in parallel, and use that one that first gives a valid prediction. We believe that in most cases this should be the Bayesian. However we are still collecting more data to continue the model validation.

The empirically found prior pmf for Q is a very useful result in itself. In particular, we believe it can provide testers with a very rough estimate of lower and upper bounds for the cumulative number of failures expected even before the Function Test phase starts. The quite regular typologies of behaviour showed by TEI projects under Function Test in fact permits us not only to know which will be the interval $\left[\frac{1}{i}, \frac{1}{i+1}\right]$ that includes the actual value of $E[Q]$, but also to establish a good approximation value for $E[F]$. These numbers used in the formulas (1) and (2) provide us with rough bounds for the cumulative number of failures. For instance, considering a certain class of projects and if the Function Test process is planned to last for 100 TIs, we can estimate prior to starting the test process that the expected cumulative number of failures at the end of the test will be within [38, 50]. With evidence collected over more projects, we expect to be able to decide historical failure effectiveness densities, to be used as reference in process control.

6 Conclusions and Future Developments

We have presented an ongoing experience aimed at introducing statistical control over TEI Function Test processes. So far we have outlined the procedures for failure data collection, and the statistical models for interpreting the data. In particular, we

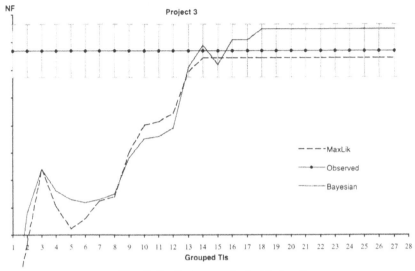

Fig. 3. Prediction results for Project 3

have introduced a Classical approach, based on the maximum likelihood estimate, and a Bayesian model, incorporating empirically defined prior distributions for the rate of detection of failures. We have already examined both models on several projects in a preliminary study, and now plan to introduce the models within the standard test processes, so to make a more comprehensive validation. A key aspect in the definition of the models was not to require any unnecessary additional work from testers, and viceversa to adapt as much as possible the models to the existing procedures.

The objective of introducing statistical control techniques within TEI is to achieve the capability to take decisions and then actions with desirable and predictable effects. We have discussed the application of statistical models to predict the expected number of failures over the planned period of Function Test. From our perspective, such models provide the project management team with an effective and not expensive means to take corrective actions when causes of variation are identified with respect to the Function Test process performance baselines (e.g., minimum and maximum fault density computed on historical data in the same product line), and with respect to meeting TEI slipping through objectives.

The implementation of appropriate corrective actions (such as executing extended Basic Test in parallel to Function Test, or postponing the end date of Function Test) can mitigate the risk of failures slipping through Function Test to first six months in operation, thus reducing rework and maintenance cost. Pilot projects to identify the most effective analysis technique, and to perform cost benefit analysis for the mitigation risk strategies connected to the application of the model are planned. In fact, no extra costs are required to collect data and apply the statistical models, as data collection is executed according to the standard procedure. To allow the easy use of statistical models within projects, a tool to be incorporated in the test environment will be developed.

The pilot projects will be managed according to a *Function Test Measurement Plan*. The Measurement Plan has the purpose to transfer baseline, models, practices approved by the organisation to the projects and then to bridge project's performance to organisation's capability. Very briefly, this plan includes:

- organisation objective and capability baseline,
- analysis technique and tools to be used,
- database where to store project's measurement collection,
- mitigation risk strategies according to objective uncertainty guideline,
- Return on Investment analysis.

References

1. Paul, M.: CMM v2.0 draft C, 22 October 1997
2. Fenton, N.E., Pfleeger S.L.: Software Metrics A Rigorous and Practical Approach. International Thomson Computer Press (1998)
3. Allen, A.O.: Probability, Statistics, and queuing theory with computer science applications. Academic Press (1990).
4. Loyd,E.: Handbook of Applicable mathematics: Statistics. Vol. III, IV, John Wiley & Sons (1987.)
5. Bertolino, A, Strigini, L.: Predicting software reliability from testing taking into account other knowledge about a program. In Proc. Quality Week '96. San Francisco (1996).
6. Gelman, A., Carlin, J.B., Stern, H.S., Rubin, D.B.: Bayesian data analysis. Chapman & Hall (1995)

Choosing Effective Methods for Design Diversity
- How to Progress from Intuition to Science

Peter Popov[1], Lorenzo Strigini[1], and
Alexander Romanovsky[2]

[1]Centre for Software Reliability, City University, Northampton Square,
London EC1V OHB, U.K.
{ptp,strigini}@csr.city.ac.uk
[2]Centre for Software Reliability, University of Newcastle-upon-Tyne,
Newcastle upon Tyne NE1 7RU, U.K.
Alexander.Romanovsky@newcastle.ac.uk

Abstract. Design diversity is a popular defence against design faults in safety critical systems. Design diversity is at times pursued by simply isolating the development teams of the different versions, but it is presumably better to "force" diversity, by appropriate prescriptions to the teams. There are many ways of forcing diversity. Yet, managers who have to choose a cost-effective combination of these have little guidance except their own intuition. We argue the need for more scientifically based recommendations, and outline the problems with producing them. We focus on what we think is the standard basis for most recommendations: the belief that, in order to produce *failure* diversity among versions, project decisions should aim at causing "diversity" among the *faults* in the versions. We attempt to clarify what these beliefs mean, in which cases they may be justified and how they can be checked or disproved experimentally.

1 Introduction

This paper is a preliminary discussion of the main hitherto un-addressed questions in achieving effective design diversity, i.e., producing diverse-redundant systems with low probability of common-mode failures of the channels.

Developers of critical systems often employ diversity between redundant channels. Redundancy protects the system against physical failures of the individual channels, but leaves it vulnerable to design faults which, if repeated in them all, can cause common-mode failures. So, in applications such as nuclear plant protection it is common to employ parallel, diverse channels. Each channel separately inputs and processes plant data and can trigger a safe shut-down if it detects indications of unsafe conditions. Two current trends are increasing the interest for design diversity: increased reliance on off-the-shelf products, which may lack complete documentation

M. Felici, K. Kanoun, A. Pasquini (Eds.): SAFECOMP'99, LNCS 1698, pp. 272–285, 1999
© Springer-Verlag Berlin Heidelberg 1999

of quality development procedures, and the practical disappearance of non-software based alternatives (e.g., non-smart sensors) for many functions.

For software, design diversity is sought by having two or more separate teams develop variants (often called *versions*) of a program. It is hoped that, if one version fails, the other[s], being internally different, will not fail at the same time: if they contain bugs, these will not cause failures in exactly the same circumstances in all versions. The versions must exhibit the same functional (externally visible) behaviour. The two or more versions are then run in a redundant configuration, so that failures in a subset of the versions may be masked or at least detected. More refined arrangements are possible, e.g. with some version only performing a monitoring or auditing function on others which have active control functions [1, 2]. Other benefits are also sought from implementing multiple versions, e.g., "back-to-back" testing provides a cheap, though imperfect, oracle for automated testing.

An important problem with design diversity (as with most other techniques for reducing or tolerating design faults) is that the reliability gain that it produces is difficult to evaluate. We know that one cannot assume diverse versions to fail independently, and all other techniques for assessing high levels of reliability are no less problematic for multiple-version than for ordinary software. For a summary of research results on this problem readers can refer to [3-5].

The other important question is how best to achieve effective diversity, i.e., a low probability that the versions will fail together. A project manager can indirectly control this by various decisions. To preserve diversity, the teams developing the versions are typically not allowed to exchange information about the development. Considering that people engaged in similar activities often make similar mistakes, they may also be given explicit directives for diversifying the internal structures of their products (e.g., using different algorithms). However, how do we know that these decisions will actually improve the delivered multi-version product?

The existing literature, and even standard documents, contain lists of such decisions that a design manager can apply to pursue diversity, which can be seen as "common-sense" advice (e.g., [6] gives developer-oriented advice, [7, 8] give customer-oriented requirements). For brevity, we shall call them "DSDs", for "diversity-seeking decisions". A complete list of plausible DSDs would span the whole development process, from team selection, to using different development environments, different tools and languages at every level of specification, design and coding, implementing each function with different algorithms, applying different V&V methods, etc. Some DSDs (like choice of algorithms) will be specific to an individual product.

But how can a project manager choose from such a "shopping list"? One may think that the more DSDs are applied, the better. But most of them have a cost: duplication of activities, added co-ordination effort, need for staff with specific skills. How many DSDs are enough for the desired level of assurance against design faults, or what is a cost-effective set of DSDs? There is currently no scientific answer to this question. We are not even sure that the advantages from various DSDs add up. We could think, for instance, that a DSD (say, specifying diverse algorithms for the various versions) produces benefits by giving a team a "scrambled" version of the problem seen by another team, so that they are not likely to make the same mistakes. However, perhaps there is a point beyond which further "scrambling" produces no further advantage: the problems seen are already as different as they can be. Then, applying a second DSD (say, using very different design methods for the various versions), possibly just as effective as the first one when used alone, would not give any additional advantage when used in combination with it.

In short, to decide which DSDs should be applied in a given project one needs to answer questions about their effectiveness (individually and in combinations). Then, a rational choice would become possible, considering known costs and other practical constraints. But the effectiveness of the various, plausibly useful DSDs is unknown. Instead, a project manager or system-level designer now has little to rely on except intuition, guided by personal experience. Experience is a poor guide for drawing general laws on how to avoid problems that are very rare in the first place; and intuition has been shown repeatedly to fail on these matters: the issues with diversity are subtle, and difficult even to define properly. For instance, some developers maintained that design-diverse channels would obviously fail independently, until this was proven wrong by theory and experiments alike. Even now, the assumption is often made that "functional diversity" (in which the channels perform similar system-level functions, but using different input data, different actuators and generally different techniques) guarantees independence of failures, a view that is refuted in [9].

In this paper, we examine how the technical community can gain better understanding of how useful diversity is generated, and thus projects can better choose among DSDs. The first step is to define more clearly the questions to be asked and recall what is known about the answers (Section 2). Next, we will examine what evidence can be produced of the efficacy of a DSD (Section 3). In Section 4, we detail the most common form of intuitive argument in favour of a DSD, which is based on its presumed efficacy in causing "diverse" development errors and/or "diverse" defects in the versions. In Section 5, we try and formalise these arguments via models that could be used in practice: we describe situations in which the empirical data could give a strong scientific basis for trusting a DSD. Section 6 contains our conclusions.

2   What Is Useful Diversity and What Is Known About It

2.1   Essential Terminology

We first need to define a few terms. We will say that a version (or a system) *fails* when its behaviour deviates from what it should be. We will say that a failure is caused by a *defect* or *fault* in the code. Any human error that caused the defect to be in the code as executed will be called a *mistake* (although this term is often given a more specialised meaning in psychology [10]). A mistake could be, for instance, mis-stating or omitting to state a required function in a requirement document; failing to notice a defect in a specification document during an inspection; accidentally using the wrong variable as target of an assignment statement, during coding; omitting to test under a certain condition that would reveal a fault.

To keep things simple, we will always refer to the simplest diverse-redundant configuration: two versions in a "1-out-of-2" configuration, in which proper operation of one version is sufficient for the whole system to function properly.

Most discussions about diversity use the terms "diversity" and "independence" in a rather informal way. We need to clarify their meaning, if we wish to learn more about them by scientific methods. First of all, the term "diversity" may designate several concepts (Fig. 1). DSDs produce "process diversity". They presumably cause the versions to be visibly different in their structure and internal operation ("product diversity"). They also cause -one hopes- the versions to be less likely to contain identical defects than if the DSD were not employed in the first place ("fault diversity"). And finally, if successful, they reduce the probability that the versions will fail in the same way on the same demands ("failure diversity"). Failure diversity is the actual goal of DSDs. All the rest are means to this end, and without more analysis we cannot even be sure that they are necessary means, rather than unnecessary side-effects.

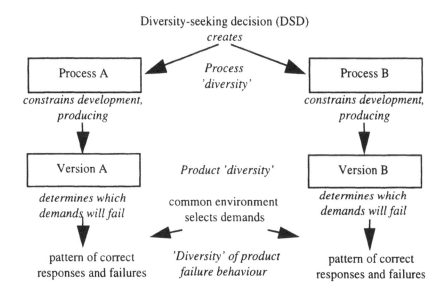

Fig. 1. The causal links from DSDs to failure diversity

"Independence" of failures between two versions means simply that the probability of the two failing together on a demand is the product of their individual probabilities. Many practitioners and some standards [7, 8] advocate (or prescribe) that versions be developed "independently" to achieve effective diversity. Strict separation between the teams seems the solution. However, modelling has shown [3] that even if we can achieve this perfect "causal independence", we should expect, on average, positive correlation between version failures; while "forced diversity" may in theory achieve lower correlation between version failures, including independence or even negative correlation. "Forced diversity" means, in the terminology of this paper, applying *some* DSD[s]; and those demanding "independent development" would usually agree that it is desirable. However, DSDs may actually impose more common constraints on the developments, and generally mean that the developments are not "statistically independent" (as one attempts to achieve negative correlation between some characteristics that are deemed important). So, the word "independence" is applied to development to mean a form of statistical dependence; while it is applied to failures in the statistical sense.

2.2   Modelling Diversity: the Need for Probabilities

The explanation of the modelling results quoted above [3, 4] is that one can see the development of a version as an uncertain process. The versions actually produced are, in practice, picked (independently, by assumption, when modelling perfectly independent developments) from a distribution of versions that *could have been* produced. The problem that they have to solve is the same for them all. Presumably, some of the demands pose a more difficult problem than others, in the specific sense that versions are more likely to fail on the former than on the latter. The mathematics then shows that this uneven distribution of "difficulty", common for all versions, causes, on average, positive correlation among their failures, when averaged over the profile of demands to which the versions will be subjected. However, by forcing diversity, i.e., by DSDs that cause process diversity, one might cause two teams to encounter different distributions of "difficulty": the demands that are especially difficult for the team using one process may be the easier ones for a team using the other process. This of course decreases the risk of common failures.

The conclusion is that forcing diversity - by adopting a DSD - is certainly beneficial (on average) if the DSD creates two process variants that offer the *same* guarantees of reliability. When this is not true, we have to trade off the degree of diversity between versions against the risk of lower reliability in the version developed with the worse method. Consider for instance an organisation that uses two languages, A and B. Suppose that experience has shown that the choice of language does not seriously affect program reliability. Having to develop a two-version system, the right choice is then to develop one version in language A and the other in B. However, if this organisation had found language A to produce generally more reliable programs than B, deciding whether the two-version system should be an A-A or an A-B system would require far more information (see [3] for details).

This leads to another consideration about any search for effective DSDs: effectiveness is judged in terms of future results, but these will vary among projects that apply a given DSD. So, effectiveness must be stated in terms of probabilities. As for measures of effectiveness, many choices are possible. A DSD could be judged effective enough if it reduces by 1/2 the probability of common failures among two versions (in a project of a certain type); or if it reduces by 1/2 the probability of common failures being more likely than 10^{-3}; and so on. The choice depends on one's requirements. The problem in arriving at such statements is one of *prediction*. As usual in engineering, one can only decide how to *achieve* certain results by *assessing* the effects that the means proposed will have on the products "in general". In other words, by deciding how much the use of a certain DSD should increase one's confidence in the product delivered, before the product is actually built. So, the prediction is about the statistical effects of the DSD on the products that *may* be developed for a given requirement, without the benefit of information about the individual product of interest. The fact that precise predictions are probably infeasible should not discourage us: for decision-making it is usually sufficient to know whether a certain decision is "substantially better than" (or even simply "at least as good as") another one.

2.3 Empirical Evidence

We know very little about the general efficacy of any specific DSD. Experiments [2, 1] have seldom been analysed from this viewpoint (attempts are presented in [11, 12], and some interesting considerations in [13]). In any case, they only provide anecdotal evidence: each experiment only developed multiple versions of one program, leaving open the doubt whether a DSD that appeared beneficial would be so when developing another program. In addition, most experiments have developed toy programs in artificial, non-industrial environments. Industrial examples exist, and companies publicise the DSDs they use. For instance, the CBI railway signalling system uses C and assembly language for diverse channels [14]; Airbus has used a specialised process control specification language with a code generator side by side with a conventionally developed version [15]; software in the ELEKTRA railway signalling system [16] has a "conventional" primary channel side by side with a rule-based safety-monitoring channel. But published failure data from these products only indicate that they are very reliable. Reasoning about whether different DSDs (or none at all) would have produced much different reliability would require detailed analysis, which, though worth attempting, risks being inconclusive when based on a handful of failures or of defects. On the other hand, even if all channels in such products were perfectly fault-free, this would not mean that the DSDs used by these companies were useless (an argument occasionally heard is "if diversity has not prevented any accident, why not drop it and save the extra cost?"). The purpose of DSDs is to ensure that *even if* the versions contained faults (which developers try to make unlikely anyway, but cannot make impossible), these faults would be less likely to cause system failures. In practice, observing an association between a DSD and high system reliability will not be enough to argue that one caused the other, unless we understand the causal mechanisms by which the DSD promotes high reliability.

3 Demonstrating the Efficacy of a Development Decision

Suppose we wish to decide whether a certain DSD is likely to be effective enough to be employed in our next 2-channel system. For the sake of concreteness, imagine the DSD is the use of the Ada language in one version and of C in the other. To convince ourselves that a certain DSD is sufficiently effective for a certain use, we can in theory proceed in different ways:

1. since the only measure that matters is the reliability of 2-version systems, we could collect reliability data about many pairs of versions developed with the Ada-C DSD, and many pairs which did not employ it (i.e., used either Ada only or C only). Statistical analysis would allow us to filter out the effects of other factors (general quality and effort spent in the various projects, for instance). Clearly, this approach is not generally practical: Pairs of programs performing essentially the same functions exist, but they are produced under so many different conditions that the data filtering exercise would be close to hopeless, even if the organisations concerned could provide the data in comparable formats. Two-channel systems are rare; separate programs that perform similar functions in different systems may be subject to different demand profiles, so that failure data may not be comparable. For programs of very high quality, failures might be so rare that we could not estimate the advantage brought by diversity.
   We could produce multiple pairs via controlled experiments, but costs would limit us to toy programs or non-professional developers. To believe that whatever results we obtain extend to real industrial developments, we would need first to understand the cause-and-effect chains via which the DSD affects reliability, so well to believe that they are the same in the lab and in an industrial environment.

2. we could use the models described in [3, 4]: by estimating how "difficulty" varies among demands for versions developed with either Ada or C. However, "difficulty" is not defined here in terms of the likelihood that developers make mistakes when dealing with certain design problems, i.e., something of which we may have direct experience from the past. It is defined in terms of the probabilities that these mistakes cause failures on certain demands, weighted with the probabilities of those demands. To confidently evaluate our DSD, we would need hard empirical evidence. But to collect it, we would have the same problems indicated above, of scarcity of data, multiplied by the fact that we would need detailed reliability data for individual demands (which is impossible) or classes thereof (which is demanding), rather than for the whole operation of each program.

3. last, we could try and refine the common intuition that "a DSD in some sense causes 'fault diversity'; 'fault diversity' in some sense causes 'failure diversity'" (we are using "fault diversity" as shorthand for "tendency of versions to exhibit qualitatively different fault patterns"). If we can model these two cause-effect links, we could then try and demonstrate their existence separately. In particular, the "fault diversity" effect of a DSD may be relatively easy to measure. Practitioners have experience of the relative frequencies of different kinds of defects in different development processes. Besides, some DSDs make some types of fault impossible in one of the versions. Psychologists have studied human error [10], and their knowledge could be applied either to argue that our DSD should indeed cause "fault diversity", or to design economical experiments to check such conjectures.
   There is less evidence for a link between fault diversity and failure diversity. Last but not least, what we wish to be able to demonstrate is that the two links of the

chain, if both proven, combine to prove the property of interest, i.e. that the DSD causes failure diversity. For a start, this requires one to define "fault diversity" in a similar way for both links, and this definition to be such that "fault diversity" and its effect on failure diversity can be measured by feasible experiments. One also needs a mathematically tractable model of how they would combine.

This third, two-step method of demonstrating the efficacy of a DSD is appealing as it would allow greater reuse of knowledge than the other two. If we could show that a certain kind of 'fault diversity' has a useful effect on 'failure diversity' as a general rule, we could evaluate a DSD without expensive measurements on failures, as required by methods 1 and 2. We would only need evidence about the 'fault diversity' it causes, and even this could in some cases be based on general psychological knowledge about the effects of different problem-solving constraints on human error. The rest of the paper is devoted to studying method 3 in more detail.

4 The Fault-Failure Chain: Informal Discussion

In this section, we describe difficulties with the intuitive notion that diversity "propagates" down the fault-failure chain. This appealing notion cannot be taken for granted. The similarity of the terms "failure diversity" and "fault diversity" is misleading. Failure diversity refers to "failing on different demands" (or "failing with different failure behaviours albeit on the same demand"), and specifically high failure diversity means a low probability that both version will fail equally on the same demand. Fault diversity is a subtler concept: a *tendency* of versions to exhibit qualitatively different faults. When we compare the faults in two programs, we can decide whether we think they are different from some viewpoint, e.g., because they seem to be caused by qualitatively different mistakes (a programmer's typo vs misinterpreting the specifications) or they cause different failure behaviours (e.g., a memory violation trap vs taking a wrong branch). However, we are now interested in how a DSD affects the *potential for* diversity among the *unknown* faults that *may* remain in a pair of versions when deployed.

Our problems in linking fault diversity to failure diversity arise from:

1. the difficulty of linking faults (defects in the code) to the specific demands on which they would cause failures;
2. the fact that the importance of a fault depends on the *probability* of those demands on which it causes failures.

About item 1, we notice that a fault can be identified in two ways (neither method guarantees unique identification - i.e., that all analysts will agree on the list of the faults in a given product- but we can neglect this difficulty for the time being):

- as a code defect, defined by its position in the code and its type. This presents a difficulty. Two defects in diverse versions, which use different variable identifiers, and possibly different languages, will hardly ever look identical, even when they

would cause common failures. So, versions may always have "different" faults, and useful metrics of "how different" they are become difficult to define;
- as the set of demands on which the defect causes the version to fail (a "failure region" in the "demand space"). This is a less common view, but with it one can decide objectively whether two failure regions are disjoint, overlapping (and by how much) or coincident, and from this information define measures of diversity.

Unfortunately, there is no general, intuitive law linking failure regions to the defects that create them. Defects that appear similar either in type or location may never cause failures on the same demands, while defects that are different in appearance and caused by different mistakes may produce failures on the same demands.

Since two versions may be such that recognising faults as identical between the two may be impossible, and yet a pair of faults (one per version) that affected overlapping sets of possible demands would of course cause system failures, "fault diversity" must somehow be referred to "types of faults", or "positions of faults" rather than to individual faults. Many schemes for fault classification are in use (e.g. [18]), so that statistics are available about the frequencies of the various types. Whether these data can be used for our investigation is yet to be seen.

Different considerations apply to diversity in the *location* of faults. If we can create a mapping between the parts of code that perform similar functions in the two versions, we can in principle measure the frequency with which a certain pair of processes (a DSD) creates defects in the same parts of the two versions. A lower frequency would be an indication of a more effective DSD. Intuitively, the reason for considering this form of "fault diversity" desirable is that defects that affect "corresponding" parts of the code in two versions are more likely to cause failures on the same demands than defects affecting "non-corresponding" parts. This cannot be taken for granted, but is plausible and can be studied empirically.

5 The Fault-Failure Chain: Special Cases

We have argued that if one chose a DSD at random from those that are commonly advocated as useful, one would be hard put to produce a convincing argument that it is indeed so. We now consider a related question: are there special (and plausible) circumstances that would demonstrate that a certain DSD is useful? We are not looking for an exemption from scientific rigour. Few useful engineering techniques have been found by working from first principles. More simply, engineers have demonstrated that a specific technique worked, and then adopted it. So, if researchers can state a set of verifiable, sufficient conditions for a DSD to be practically useful, they will have given practitioners a chance of confirming that a specific DSD is useful (or perhaps that it is not) in their circumstances, though no guarantee that they can reach such definitive judgements on all possible DSDs.

5.1   First Scenario: Relying on Experience of Mapping between Fault Classes and Failure Classes

Suppose that experience has shown that (for the class of software considered) the vast majority of failures are due to faults that affect (for each version) disjoint sets of demands, and these sets are the same for all versions. An example could be those faults that are due to misinterpreting the specified response for some particular class of demands. We could then define the set of all possible faults, $\{F_1, F_2, ..., F_N\}$, and similarly index the sets of demands on which each fault causes failures (*failure regions*): $\{R_1, R_2, .., R_N\}$. Our DSD creates two development processes, A and B. These determine the probabilities of each fault being present in versions produced with either process: $P_A(F_1)$, $P_A(F_2)$, ..., $P_A(F_N)$ and $P_B(F_1)$, ..., $P_B(F_N)$. The operational environment will determine the probabilities of demands that belong to the various regions: $P(R_1)$, $P(R_2)$, ..., $P(R_N)$. If the two versions are developed "truly independently" (i.e., if the only commonalities between the development efforts for these two versions are in the problem to be solved, which would affect *any* development of versions for this system, rather than being due to interactions between these two specific development efforts), the probability of failure is:

$$\sum_{i \in [1, N]} P_A(F_i)\, P(R_i) \qquad \text{for a single version produced with process A}$$

$$\sum_{i \in [1, N]} (P_A(F_i))^2\, P(R_i) \qquad \text{for 2 versions, both produced with process A}$$

$$\sum_{i \in [1, N]} P_A(F_i)\, P_B(F_i)\, P(R_i) \qquad \text{for 2 versions, produced with processes A and B}$$

It can be shown that if both processes give the same average reliability, an A-B system is better, on average, than either an A-A or a B-B system. If, say, process A gives the higher average reliability, then a B-B pair should be avoided, but the choice between an A-A and an A-B pair depends on the values of all the individual probabilities in the formulas. Since we would not know the detailed set $\{F_1, F_2, ..., F_N\}$, we could not decide on this basis. However, we may well know the relative frequencies of different *classes* of faults observed with process A and with process B in the past, and thus have estimates for their relative frequencies in the current project. It is conceivable that we know that different *classes* of faults typically affect different sets of possible demands. For instance, perhaps initialisation defects and defects concerning the sequencing of concurrent activities tend to affect different kinds of demands. But even with this one-to-one mapping between defects in the code and subsets of the demand space, theorems in [5] show that predicting the overall failure rate requires the unknown parameters (probabilities of individual faults and of the demands that would trigger them) to satisfy special conditions. In conclusion, one cannot use this form of argument about the fault-failure chain without first proving by experiment several rather strong laws governing software development in the environment of interest.

5.2   Second Scenario: Relying on Probability of No Faults

Another possibility may present itself for organisations with a high-quality process: it may turn out that a given process (say, A) can be trusted with a certain probability (say, $1-P_A(i)$) completely to avoid faults that would affect a given category of demands, i. In this case, a basis for dependability assessment could be the probability of having any failure at all during the lifetime of a two-version system. A certain probability of no faults of a given category is a lower bound on the probability of none of the failures that they might cause happening over the whole system lifetime (see [19] for a detailed discussion). So, for instance, in the simple scenario below the decision would clearly be that an A-B pair is to be preferred to an A-A pair, although process A produces on average better versions.

| | | upper bound on prob. of failure | | |
class of demands	probability of demand class	process A	process B	minimum
demand class 1	0.7	1%	10%	1%
demand class 2	0.3	5%	3%	3%
upper bound on probability of system failure:		0.022	0.079	0.016

5.3   Third Scenario: Diversity in the Positions of Faults

We now switch to the apparently more promising, alternative measure of "fault diversity" in terms of differences in the *positions* of the faults (cf end of Section 4). An interesting shortcut now appears possible for collecting empirical evidence of the efficacy of a DSD. The main intuitive basis for believing that defects affecting different parts of the code are likely to give low probability of common failure is the belief that these different parts of the code will often be invoked by different demands. It is then apparent that we could directly try and measure the effects of DSDs on the probabilities of non-null intersections between failure regions in different versions. The costs of experiments would still be high, but there is an interesting simplification compared to procedure 1 in section 3. If the failure regions in two versions have null intersection, the two versions will never fail together, *no matter* what distribution of demands they are subjected to. So, experimenters would not need to test the versions with realistic demand profiles, and be concerned that different profiles would invalidate the experimental results. An analysis of the "static" characteristics of failure regions would be substituted for a "dynamic" measure of failure probabilities. Such experiments could at least demonstrate the efficacy of a DSD at the "programming-in-the-small" level (e.g. at the level of individual procedures). If this were proven, then a separate study could examine how failure diversity "in the small" is related, if at all, to failure diversity at the system level.

6 Discussion

We have shown that there are traps in the intuitive ways of reasoning about the effectiveness of diversity-seeking decisions (DSDs) in project management, and there is room for progress towards more scientific decision-making. Our first contribution is simply to point out the possible pitfalls in intuitive reasoning: this knowledge in itself is a safeguard for the decision maker.

We have explored the intriguing possibility of giving a scientific basis to the common belief that - at least in some cases - failure diversity can be expected as a result of "fault diversity". If this could be shown for specific DSDs, decisions could be based to some extent on general laws of human error behaviour instead of having to be re-validated for every combination of processes and product requirements. There is no guarantee of success, but we are working on specifying experiments to provide more empirical evidence. Initial experiments and analysis of existing data should aim at excluding un-promising theories and concentrate effort on those that may give practically useful rules for project decisions.

As for the example models in Section 5, the first two scenarios are unlikely, but we conjecture that the main theorems we used would still be true under less restrictive assumptions: we are working on mathematically tractable models for more general and realistic classes of situations. For instance, the formulas in Section 5 assume that all failure regions are fully disjoint. Yet, it is clear that similar formulas should apply if failure regions are *usually* disjoint, and a way of defining this "usually" should be adopted that can be verified by practical statistical observations. The third scenario (in 5.3) is much more plausible, though making it a practical possibility would still require much new experimental work.

The methods we have outlined for evaluating DSDs will be appropriate in those cases in which tractable models can represent the essential terms of the situation (all the important factors determining the probability of common failures for the specific system of interest, though not all factors), and parameters can be estimated with enough precision (the actual bounds on these estimates determine whether the method will show that the DSD is useful). There will certainly remain useful DSDs for which it will be impossible to prove their usefulness with the methods discussed here. Whether these will still be worth adopting will depend on the other evidence available and their costs.

This discussion has many limits. It is a preliminary discussion, about questions that have not been asked before in such detailed terms. For reasons of space, we have omitted considerations of several additional aspects of the problem which we believe to be ripe for investigation. For instance:

- we only talked about the average reliability to be expected from a certain DSD. In reality, it would be desirable to have an idea of the distributions of these probabilities - an idea of how likely we are to satisfy a given reliability requirement. We have shown elsewhere [20] that diversity may be seen essentially as a means for reducing the unavoidable *variance* in the results of software development. We are currently extending this line of research. However, even

indications about averages would be more help for the decision makers than what is now available;
- there are ways a DSD may affect failure diversity that we have not yet considered. For instance, differences in structure between two complex versions may imply that essentially similar defects, even if triggered by similar sets of demands, produce errors that propagate differently in the two versions, resulting in failure diversity;
- we do not know yet how to reason about *combinations* of multiple DSDs. For some practical situations, it would be sufficient to be able to demonstrate that combining two given DSDs is no worse than applying either one of them alone. This seems a plausible conjecture, but we intend to clarify which conditions must apply for it to be true.

In any case, the necessary research involves the collection of empirical evidence, guided by models determining which kinds of evidence are needed and what the statistics should be like in order to demonstrate usefulness (or lack thereof) of specific project decisions.

Acknowledgements

This work was supported in part by Scottish Nuclear under the DISPO project (DIverse Software PrOject, Contract No. PP/79405/MB), and by the U.K. Engineering and Physical Sciences Research Council under the DISCS project (Diversity In Safety Critical Software, grant GR/L07673).

References

1. Voges, U. (Ed.): Software diversity in computerized control systems. Springer-Verlag, Wien (1988)
2. Lyu, M.R. (Ed.): Software Fault Tolerance. Wiley (1995)
3. Littlewood, B., Miller, D.R.: Conceptual Modelling of Coincident Failures in Multi-Version Software. IEEE Transactions on Software Engineering SE-15 (1989) 1596-1614
4. Littlewood, B.: The impact of diversity upon common mode failures. Reliability Engineering and System Safety 51 (1996) 101-113
5. Popov, P., Strigini, L.: Conceptual models for the reliability of diverse systems - new results. In Proc. 28th International Symposium on Fault-Tolerant Computing (FTCS-28), Munich, Germany (1998) 80-89
6. Lyu, M.R., He, Y.: Improving the N-Version Programming Process Through the Evolution of a Design Paradigm. IEEE Transactions on Reliability R-42 (1993) 179-189
7. MoD 00-55 Def Stan 00-55, Requirements for Safety Related Software in Defence Equipment. U.K. Ministry of Defence, Issue 2 (1997)
8. MoD 00-56 Def Stan 00-56, Safety Management Requirements for Defence Systems. U.K. Ministry of Defence, Issue 2 (1996)
9. Littlewood, B., Popov, P., Strigini, L.: A note on reliability estimation of functionally diverse systems. Reliability Engineering and System Safety, to appear (1999)

10. Reason, J.: Human Error. Cambridge University Press (1990)
11. Lyu, M.R., Chen, J., Avizienis, A.: Experience in Metrics and Measurements for N-Version Programming. International Journal of Reliability, Quality and Safety Engineering 1 (1994) 41-62
12. Avizienis, A., Lyu, M.R., Schuetz, W.: In search of effective diversity: A six-language study of fault-tolerant flight control software. In Proc. 18th International Symposium on Fault-Tolerant Computing, Tokyo, Japan (1988) 15-22
13. Kersken, M., Saglietti, F. (Ed.): Software Fault Tolerance: Achievement and Assessment Strategies. Springer-Verlag (1992)
14. Mongardi, G.: Dependable Computing for Railway Control Systems. In Proc. 3rd IFIP Int. Working Conference on Dependable Computing for Critical Applications (DCCA-3), Mondello, Italy (1993) 255-277
15. Briere, D., Traverse, P.: Airbus A320/A330/A340 Electrical Flight Controls - A Family Of Fault-Tolerant Systems. In Proc. 23rd International Symposium on Fault-Tolerant Computing (FTCS-23), Toulouse, France, 22 - 24 (1993) 616-623
16. Kantz, H., Koza, C.: The ELEKTRA Railway Signalling-System: Field Experience with an Actively Replicated System with Diversity. In Proc. 25th IEEE Annual International Symposium on Fault -Tolerant Computing (FTCS-25), Pasadena, California (1995) 453-458
17. Bishop, P.G., Pullen, F.D.: Failure Masking: A Source of Failure Dependency in Multi-version Programs. In Proc. 1st IFIP Int. Working Conference on Dependable Computing for Critical Applications (DCCA-1), Santa Barbara, USA (1989) 53-73
18. Chillarege, R.: Orthogonal Defect Classification. In Lyu, M.R. (Ed.): Handbook of Software Reliability Engineering: Computing, McGraw-Hill and IEEE Computer Society Press, (1996) 359-400
19. Bertolino, A., Strigini, L.: Assessing the risk due to software faults: estimates of failure rate vs evidence of perfection. Software Testing, Verification and Reliability 8 (1998)
20. Popov, P., Strigini, L., Pizza, M.: The efficacy of diverse redundancy against design error: some practical considerations. In Proc. INucE Third International Conference on Control and Instrumentation in Nuclear Installations, Edinburgh, U.K. (1998)

A First Step Towards the Integration of Accident Reports and Constructive Design Documents

Chris Johnson

Department of Computing Science, University of Glasgow, Glasgow, G12 8QQ, UK.
Tel: +44 (0141) 330 6053 Fax: +44 (0141) 330 4913
http://www.dcs.gla.ac.uk/~johnson, EMail: johnson@dcs.glasgow.ac.uk

Abstract. Accident reports are intended to explain the causes of human error and system failure. They are based upon the evidence of many different teams of experts and are, typically, the result of a lengthy investigation process. They are important documents from an engineering perspective because they guide the intervention of regulatory authorities who must reduce the impact and frequency of system 'failures' and human 'error'. There are, however, a number of problems with current practice. In particular, there are no established techniques for using previous findings about human 'error' and systems 'failure' to inform subsequent design. This paper, therefore, shows how extensions to design rationale and contextual task analysis techniques can be used to avoid the weaknesses of existing accident reports.

1. Introduction

Given the importance of accident reports for the development of interactive systems, it is surprising that there has been relatively little research into the usability and utility of these documents [1]. The mass of relevant literature about safety-critical interface design [2, 3] and even the usability of design documents in general [4] is not matched in the field of accident reporting. There are some notable exceptions, for example, Prof. Van Der Schaaf heads an established group at the Technical University of Eindhoven. However, this work is very much the exception. The bulk of human factors research continues to focus upon techniques that can be used to analyse the causes of human error rather than upon the delivery mechanisms that publicise those findings to practising interface designers and systems engineers. This paper, therefore, presents techniques that use findings about previous failures to inform the subsequent development of interactive systems.

1.1 The Embley Case Study

A collision between the bulk ship River Embley and the Royal Australian Naval patrol boat HMAS Fremantle will be used to illustrate the remainder of this paper [5]. This accident has been chosen because it was the result of complex interactions between several different operators and several different systems. For instance, the crew of the River Embley were equipped with a GPS display, two radars, a gyro

M. Felici, K. Kanoun, A. Pasquini (Eds.): SAFECOMP'99, LNCS 1698, pp. 286–296, 1999
© Springer-Verlag Berlin Heidelberg 1999

compass and bearing repeaters, automatic steering systems and a course recorder plotter.   This collision was also the result of complex interactions between the various members of both crews.   These interactions were affected by their on-board systems but also by individual levels of experience and training within the crews. Finally, this accident typifies the many 'near-misses' that contribute most to our understanding of human 'error' and system 'failure'.   Nobody was seriously hurt and no pollution resulted from the collision.

At 21:00hrs on 13th March 1997, three patrol boats were approaching the Heath reef, part of the Great Barrier Reef, from the South.   The River Embley was a deep draught vessel and so was obliged to keep to the Eastern side of a two-way route off the reef.   VHF contact was established between the bridge of the HMAS Fremantle and the River Embley.   A few minutes after 21:00, the lead patrol vessel Fremantle crossed ahead of the Embley followed by the second patrol boat, in line.   The third vessel altered course to pass between the Embley and Heath reef.   HMAS Fremantle made a number of small alterations to her course and at about 21:08 the rudder was put 20¼ to starboard.   The patrol boat collided with the River Embley.

2. Analysing Human Error and Systems Failure

The purpose of the Maritime Incident Investigation Unit (MIIU) investigation 'is to identify the circumstances of an incident and determine its causes.   All reports of the investigation are published to make the causes of an accident known within the industry so as to help prevent similar occurrences' (http://www.miiu.gov.au).   This section, therefore, explains why it can be difficult for readers to identify the causes of human 'error' and systems 'failure' from conventional accident reports.

2.1 Locating the Evidence to Support an Argument

It can be difficult for readers to identify the causes of an accident because the evidence that supports a particular conclusion may be distributed over many different pages in a conventional accident report.   For instance, the MIIU found that:

"The reasons for HMAS Fremantle's actions...involve a complex chain of human factors, which include, but are not limited to:
    •incomplete passage and contingency planning;
    • being unaware of traffic on the reef;
    • lack of experience in traffic encounters within the Great Barrier Reef;
    • the decision to apply 20û of starboard helm based on incomplete and scanty information." (page 30)

The MIIU found that the Fremantle's crew lacked experience of encounters within the Great Barrier Reef.   The evidence for this conclusion is presented on pages 8 and 16 of the report.   The Fourth Officer was in charge in the run-up to the collision and he was undergoing watch keeping training:

"It (the Fremantle) normally operates with a crew of 23, but on 13 March the crew numbered 24.   This included the Commanding Officer, the Executive Officer, the Navigating Officer and the Fourth and Fifth Officers, both under watch keeping training." (page 8).

"The Commanding Officer remained on the bridge monitoring the Fourth Officer until 21:20 when the Patrol Boat was off Hay Island.   The Fourth Officer was fixing the ship's position every 6 minutes.   Satisfied that the Fourth Officer was in complete control of the situation the Commanding Officer went to his cabin, about three metres from a flight of eight steps that led from the main deck to the bridge." (page 16)

This distribution of analysis and evidence creates significant problems for interface designers who must exploit the recommendations of accident reports to guide the subsequent development of navigation systems and training procedures.   It is a non-trivial task to filter out the mass of contextual evidence presented between pages 8, 16 and 30 of the MIIU document.   Unless they can do this, however, it would be difficult to trace the connection between the working practices on the Fremantle and the causes of the accident as presented in the conclusions of the report.

2.2 Implicit Arguments

A further problem is that readers must often re-construct the implicit arguments that are embedded within accident reports.   For instance, the previous citation from page 30 argued that the Fremantle's crew was unaware of traffic on the Reef.   This is supported by evidence on page 18 of the report.   The Commanding Officer was unaware of the position of the Embley as he ordered the manoeuvre:

"The Commanding Officer asked what rudder angle had been ordered and the Fourth Officer told him 10 degrees, and the Commanding Officer advised him to increase the angle to 20 degrees.   At this time he became aware of the voices on the VHF.   Almost immediately the Commanding Officer saw a green light and became aware of a "great black wall".   He immediately issued direct orders to the helmsman of "hard to starboard" and full astern" (page 18).

This argument was never explicitly made in the MIIU report.   The reader is forced to infer a link between the evidence on page 18 and the conclusions on page 30.   In this instance, the inference seems well justified.   However, previous work has shown that many readers construct a mass of causal explanations and inferences that were never intended by the producers of an accident report [1].

2.3 Alternative Lines of Reasoning

It can often be difficult to identify alternative hypotheses about human 'error' and systems 'failure'.   For instance, the first of the following quotations presents the MIIU argument that the River Embley's crew might have used an Aldis lamp to alert the Fremantle.   The second quote is taken from the Master's submission to the MIIU in which he argues that the use of this signalling devices would not have helped to avoid the collision:

"With hindsight, it might have been better to use an Aldis lamp to attract the attention of the approaching vessel, under Rule 36.   The Aldis lamp would also have illuminated the ship side and the expanse of hull between the foremast and the mainmast." (page 26)

"As the risk of, or impending, collision had only been observed by either vessel crew immediately before impact, and the sound signals - whose use was close at hand - not by hurrying some 10 meters to the wing (lighting an Aldis light in the wheelhouse would destroy night vision, and be unacceptable both aboard and during an inquiry), were "completed at or just before the moment of collision", use of the Aldis lamp was inappropriate in those brief moments" (page 33).

The layout of many conventional reports makes it difficult for readers to view both sides of such arguments.   In our example, the MIIU analysis appears within the main body of the report while the Master's rebuttal is documented in an appendix after the conclusions of the report.   Such a separation makes it difficult for designers to accurately assess the best means of avoiding future failures either through improved training practices or through the development of additional systems support.

3 Using Conclusion, Analysis and Evidence Diagrams to Visualise the Argument in Accident Reports

The previous section has argued that a number of problems prevent designers from accurately assessing the causes of human 'error' and systems 'failure' as they are documented in conventional accident reports.   This section goes on to argue that a number of graphical techniques can be used to avoid these limitations.

3.1 Locating the Evidence to Support an Argument

Figure 1 uses a Conclusion, Analysis, Evidence diagram to represent the relationship between the MIIU's conclusions and the evidence that is presented within their report.

The MIIU report concluded that the Fremantle's crew made several human 'errors'. These mistakes included their failure to complete adequate contingency and passage planning.   This analysis is supported by evidence that the crew failed to identify the waters off Heath Reef as being restricted for deep draught vessels, see page 29 of the report.   The human errors also included a lack of awareness about the other traffic on the reef.   This is supported by evidence that both the Fourth Officer and the Commander assumed that the River Embley was some 2.5 miles away when they were, in fact, much closer.   This evidence is cited on page 18 of the report.   The Fremantle's crew also lacked experience of encounters within the Great Barrier Reef. This analysis depends upon two related pieces of evidence.   Firstly, that the Fourth office was on the bridge in the lead up to the collision **and** secondly that this officer

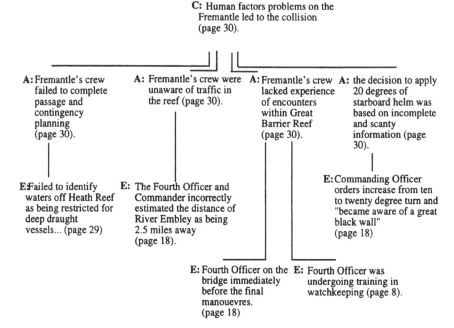

Fig. 1. Conclusion, Analysis, Evidence (CAE) Diagram for the Fremantle Collision

was undergoing training in watch keeping.   Finally, human factors problems led to the collisions because the decision to apply 20 degrees of starboard helm was based upon incomplete and scanty information.   The Commander's surprise at the consequences of his decision, cited on page 18 of the report, provide evidence for this assertion.

Figure 1 explicitly illustrates the way in which pieces of evidence contribute to an investigator's analysis of human 'error' and systems 'failure'.   The intention is not that CAE diagrams should replace conventional reporting techniques but that they should provide an overview and structure for the argument that these documents contains. They provide a road map for the analysis that is presented in an accident report.

3.2 Implicit Arguments

CAE diagrams can also help readers to identify the implicit inferential chains that are a common feature of many accident reports [6].   For example, the previous section argued that there is no clear link in the conventional report between the conclusion of human error and the evidence that supports this conclusion.   The following CAE diagram, therefore, shows how evidence on page 18 supports the claim on page 30 that the Fremantle's crew were unaware of other traffic on the Reef.

Not only is it important that accident reports explicitly represent the lines of analysis that support a particular conclusion, it is also important to record any evidence that might contradict such an argument.   This is illustrated by the dotted line in Figure 2;

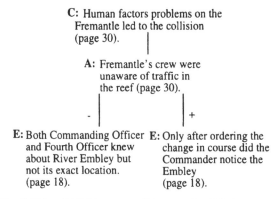

Fig. 2. Using CAE Diagrams to Represent Implicit Arguments.

there is evidence to suggest that the on-board systems did alert the crew of the Fremantle to the presence of the Embley but that the Fremantle's crew were unsure of its exact position. The following section builds on this argument to show how CAE diagrams can represent alternative lines of analysis and not simply contradictory evidence about operator 'error'.

3.3 Alternative Lines of Reasoning

CAE diagrams provide an overview of the arguments that both support and weaken particular conclusions. Figure 3 uses a dotted line to show the way in which the Master's argument about the use of the Aldis lamp called into question that of the MIIU investigator. In contrast to the conventional report, the relationship between these two lines of argument is explicitly represented within this diagram.

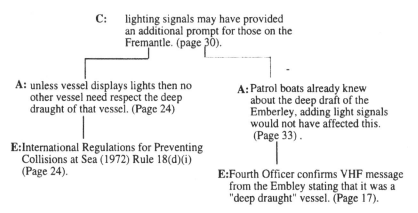

Fig. 3. Using CAE Diagrams to Represent Alternative Arguments

There are strong differences between CAE diagrams and other notations that have been used to support accident analysis, such as Fault Trees [1]. These formalisms are, typically, used to map out the timeline of operator 'error' and system 'failure' that leads to an accident.   In contrast, CAE diagrams represent the analytic framework that is constructed from the evidence about those events.   In this respect, our approach shares much in common with Ladkin, Gerdsmeier and Loer's WB graphs [7].

4. Literate Investigations

The previous section has shown how diagrammatic techniques can be used to support the presentation of accident reports.   This has important consequences for interface development.   Firstly, CAE diagrams encourage accident investigators to explicitly document the evidence that supports claims about 'operator error'.   Secondly, they help the readers of an accident report to trace and understand the arguments that lead to those claims.   Such benefits are of little value, however, if designers cannot exploit the products of accident investigations to support development.   This section, therefore, explains how techniques from design rationale [4] and contextual task analysis [8] can be used in conjunction with CAE diagrams to provide a link between the analytical techniques of accident investigations and the constructive techniques of interface development.

4.1 Design Rationale

CAE diagrams provide a graphical representation of the arguments that accident reports construct for the causes of human 'error' and systems 'failure'.   In contrast, design rationale notations provide a graphical overview of the arguments that support development decisions [9].   For example Figure 4 illustrates some of the design options that might improve situation awareness on the Reef.   The first option is to force all ships to notify their position to an existing monitoring system.   This is supported by the criteria that it would provide an external means of ensuring that crews comply with regulations.   The Reefrep system could monitor and log the reporting behaviour of each vessel.   The development of such a system is not supported by the affect that it would have upon crew workload.   The second design option is to use crew training procedures as a means of ensuring adequate levels of situation awareness.   This is not supported by the possibility of performing external checks.

A major limitation with the previous diagram is that it provides little or no indication of the status or source of the criteria that are represented.   In other words, we have no means of assessing the evidence that external checks are, indeed, difficult to perform on crew training practices.   Such problems can be avoided by integrating design rationale techniques, such as the QOC notation shown in Figure 4, with previous findings about human 'error' and system 'failure' during previous accidents and incidents.

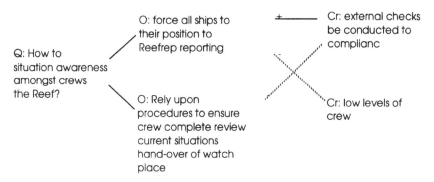

Fig. 4. Questions, Options and Criteria diagram shows design options for situation awareness.

4.2 Using Accidents to Provide Contextual Support For Development Decisions

Figure 5 integrates CAE and QOC diagrams for the Fremantle collision.   The CAE diagram represents the MIIU's finding that the crew were unaware of other ships in their vicinity.   A link is then drawn to the QOC diagram to show that this finding justifies designers in considering how to improve situation awareness amongst the crews in the Reef area.   It is important not to underestimate the benefits that such links provide.   For instance, it is relatively easy to provide well considered solutions to the problems that are addressed in safety cases.   It is less easy to know what problems should be anticipated during the development of safety-critical interfaces [3].   By linking development documents directly to the products of accident investigations, it is possible to ensure that designers base their subsequent development decisions at least partly upon those problems that have arisen with previous applications.

Further links can be drawn between the analytical products of accident investigations and the constructive use of design rationale.   For instance, evidence about previous operator 'errors' can be used to support particular lines of argument in a QOC diagram.   Figure 6 illustrates this approach   Relying upon improved training procedures, rather than a Reef reporting system, is not supported by the argument that external checks can be conducted to ensure compliance.   This argument is, in turn, supported by the CAE analysis that the Fremantle's training procedures left them unprepared for their encounters on the Reef.   Again, by integrating these two approaches, interface designers have an explicit means of demonstrating that the 'mistakes' of the past are being used to inform subsequent interface development.   In this case, improved training procedures may have to be supported by automation.

5. Conclusion and Further Work

Accident reports are a primary mechanism by which designers can learn from the mistakes of the past.   These documents analyse and explain the causes of human 'error' and systems 'failure'. Unfortunately, a range of recent work has identified

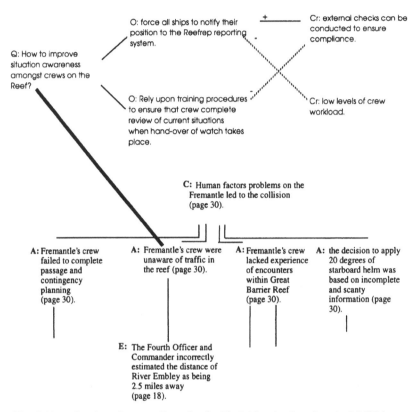

Fig. 5. Using Previous Operator 'Errors' to Justify Asking the Questions in QOC Diagrams.

limitations and weaknesses in conventional reporting techniques [1, 7].   It can be difficult for readers to locate the many different pieces of evidence that support particular arguments about operator 'error' and system 'failure'.   These items of information can be scattered throughout the many different pages of an accident report.   A second problem is that readers are often forced to reconstruct complex chains of inference in order to understand the implicit arguments that are embedded within accident reports.   Finally, it can be difficult to identify alternative hypotheses about human factors problems and systems failures given existing reporting techniques.

This paper has argued that the graphical structures of Conclusion, Analysis, Evidence (CAE) diagrams can be used to avoid the problems mentioned above. These explicitly represent the relationship between evidence and lines of argument. They also provide a graphical overview of the competing lines of argument that might contradict particular interpretations of human 'error' and systems 'failure'.   However, these diagrams do not directly support the subsequent development of interactive systems. In particular, previous work has not provided means of exploiting these diagrams within safety cases. We have, therefore, argued that design rationale techniques be integrated with the argumentation structures of CAE diagrams.   This offers a number

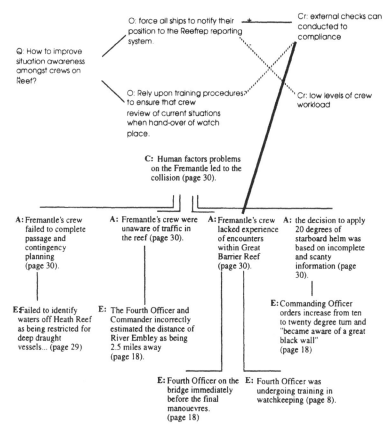

Fig. 6. Using Previous Operator 'Errors' to Justify Criteria in QOC Diagrams.

of benefits.   In particular, the findings of previous accident investigations can be used
to identify critical design questions for the subsequent development of interactive,
safety-critical systems.   Similarly, the arguments that support or weaken particular
design options can be linked to the arguments in accident reports.   Previous instances
of operator 'error' and systems 'failure' can be cited to establish the importance of
particular design criteria.   This helps to ensure that evidence from previous accidents
is considered when justifying future development decisions.

Much further work remains to be done.   We have empirical evidence to support the
use of design rationale by practicing designers with real-world design tasks [10].
However, these findings must be extended to support the integration of CAE
diagrams.   Doubts also remain about the syntax used in Figures 5 and 6.   We are
aware that the proliferation of hypertext links can lead to a complex tangle which
frustrates navigation and interpretation by interface designers and regulatory
authorities.   Similarly, more work needs to be conducted to determine whether it is
appropriate to constrain the semantics of the links between CAE and QOC diagrams.
Our initial development of this technique has exploited informal guidelines about the
precise nature of these connections.   However, it is likely that these guidelines may

have to be codified if the approach is to be used by teams of accident investigators and systems designers.   We have gone at least part of the way towards resolving these problems through the development of tool support [11].

Acknowledgements

Thanks are due to the Australian Department of Transport and Regional Development and their Maritime Incident Investigation Unit.   Their openness has greatly helped efforts to improve accident reporting. I would also like to acknowledge the support of the Glasgow Accident Analysis Group and Glasgow Interactive Systems Group. This work is supported by EPSRC grants GR/L27800 and GR/K55042.

References

[1] L. Love and C.W. Johnson, AFTs: Accident Fault Trees. In H. Thimbleby, B. O'Conaill and P. Thomas (eds), *People and Computers XII: Proceedings of HCI'97*, 245-262, Springer Verlag, Berlin, 1997.

[2] D. Norman, *The 'Problem' With Automation : Inappropriate Feedback And Interaction Not Over-automation*. In D.E. Broadbent and J. Reason and A. Baddeley (eds.), Human Factors In Hazardous Situations, 137-145, Clarendon Press, Oxford, United Kingdom, 1990.

[3] J. Reason, *Human Error*, Cambridge University Press, Cambridge, United Kingdom, 1990.

[4] T.P. Moran and J.M. Carroll (eds.), Design Rationale Concepts, Techniques And Use, Lawrence Erlbaum, Hillsdale, New Jersey, United States of America, 1995.

[5] Maritime Incident Investigation Unit, Investigation into the Collision Between the Australian Bulk Ship River Embley and the Royal Australian Navy Patrol Boat HMAS Fremantle off Heath Reef at About 22:09 on 13 March 1997, Report 112, Australian Department of Transport and Regional Development, Canberra, Australia, 1997.

[6] C.W. Johnson, Proof, Politics and Bias in Accident Reports. In C.M. Holloway (ed.), Proceedings of the Fourth NASA Langley Formal Methods Workshop. NASA Technical Report Lfm-97, 1997.

[7] P. Ladkin, T. Gerdsmeier and K. Loer, *Analysing the Cali Accident With Why?...Because Graphs*. In C.W. Johnson and N. Leveson (eds), Proceedings of Human Error and Systems Development, Glasgow Accident Analysis Group, Technical Report GAAG-TR-97-2, Glasgow, 1997.

[8] G. Cockton, S. Clark, P. Gray and C. W. Johnson, Literate Design. In D.J. Benyon and P. Palanque (eds.), *Critical Issues in User System Engineering (CRUISE)*, 227-248. Springer Verlag, London, 1996.

[9] S. Buckingham Shum, Analysing The Usability Of A Design Rationale Notation. In T.P. Moran and J.M. Carroll (eds.), Design Rationale Concepts, Techniques And Use, Lawrence Erlbaum, Hillsdale, New Jersey, United States of America, 1995.

[10] C.W. Johnson, Literate Specification, *The Software Engineering Journal* (11)4:225-237, 1996.

[11] C.W. Johnson, *The Epistemics of Accidents,* Journal of Human-Computer Systems, (47)659-688, 1997a.

A Holistic Design Concept to Improve Safety Related Control Systems

Maria Wimmer[1], Antonio Rizzo[1], and Mark Sujan[2]

[1]Multimedia Communication Laboratory, University of Siena, and Institute of Psychology, CNR, Rome, Italy
[2]Inst. f. Rechnerentwurf und Fehlertoleranz, University of Karlsruhe, Germany
wimmer@ip.rm.cnr.it, rizzo@media.unisi.it, sujan@ira.uka.de

Abstract. Every complex control process is formed by three types of resources. These Software, Hardware and Liveware resources interact with each other, they are mutually dependent, and they are embedded in a given Environment. However, one common pitfall of traditional design approaches is that they do not consider this systemic view appropriately. We propose a holistic design methodology based on this concept of SHEL for all phases of the design process: understanding the whole system, the activities performed, the criticality, and the knowledge that was created when breakdowns were encountered; and designing not just the artifacts to be introduced, but rather the complete work environment, including the processes, operators' jobs, formal procedures and training. Evaluation, iteration, and user participation are key characteristics of this holistic design approach.

1. Introduction

Information technology (IT) can substantially contribute to the dependability of complex systems such as train traffic control, air traffic control, aircraft cockpits, or chemical process control. Potential benefits include for example the balancing of manual workload and fatigue, relief from and more precise handling of routine operations, and the elimination of individual human differences. In several studies [1, 6] it has been reported, however, that the introduction of IT into workplaces and the automation of functions has led to serious safety problems or to costly system under-utilisation. Many of these problems have arisen from a lack of attention to the strong dependencies that exist among the individual components of a complex system and the neglect of the psychological demands of the humans working within the system.

The design of a complex process control system, which is safety related, and where reliability is an important factor, requires the careful consideration of all the components forming the control system. Here it is important to include also aspects like procedures or rules, which define the way in which the work is carried out, or social and communicational aspects. In order to achieve the desired goals a given process requires a combination of the available resources. This combination is changing over time, as no complex system can be considered static. Environmental influences, the learning of the humans within the system, or the degradation of hardware components render the complex system a highly dynamic entity.

M. Felici, K. Kanoun, A. Pasquini (Eds.): SAFECOMP'99, LNCS 1698, pp. 297–309, 1999
© Springer-Verlag Berlin Heidelberg 1999

The improvement of the overall system reliability requires more than the consideration of the reliability of the individual components. This becomes particularly obvious in abnormal situations, where humans, machines, and the organisation need to co-operate effectively and efficiently in order to respond adequately. The design needs to ensure that, when a given combination of the resources cannot support the process adequately anymore, it can be replaced quickly by more appropriate configurations. Therefore, the design of a more reliable system implies not only the consideration of the individual resources in isolation, but rather also the consideration of their smooth interaction and integration.

Traditional design philosophies put their focus on the efficient realisation of the support system to be designed, hence on the support tool in isolation. Their major drawback is that they do not consider the different system resources, the environment, the processes, and the objects to be acted on in an integrative way. Since it is hard to specify human behaviour in formal logical models, ergonomic issues have been accounted for only in the design of the user-interface, after the design of the supporting IT. For the same reason the implications of the introduction of new artefacts to the existing work system and to the human working practices in particular have often been neglected. Consequently, also user participation was deemed unnecessary and was conducted insufficiently.

In this paper we present a holistic design process to improve the operation and the reliability of complex control systems. The design builds on an understanding of the whole system, the activities performed, the criticality, and the knowledge that was created when breakdowns were encountered. It is directed towards the design of not just the artefacts to be introduced, but rather of the complete work environment, including issues like the jobs of the humans, the procedures and the training. To this end, we introduce a model to broaden the conception of a complex system to include all available resources (section 2). In section 3 we present the holistic design process and discuss the benefits and the necessity of user participation. The proposed design approach has been applied in a real-world case study in the railways sector and the results will be reported in section 4. Concluding remarks will be presented in section 5.

2. Systemic View: the SHEL Model

Every complex system is formed by three types of resources. The first, Hardware, concerns any physical and non human component of the system as equipment, vehicles, tools, manuals, signs and so forth. The second, Software, concerns the true computational code, the norms, rules, procedures, practices and any other formal or informal rule that define the way, in which the different components of the system interact among them and with the external environment. The third, Liveware, concerns any human components in their relational and communicational aspects. The arrangement of hardware, software and liveware resources operates always in a context defined by economical, political, historical, and social factors (Environment). However, environmental factors can only rarely be manipulated directly by designers. Even though they can shape and constrain the system under development, they may not reasonably be considered proper resources. The relationship between the components in the environment represents the systemic view of a complex system, which is referred to as the SHEL model (see Fig. 1, [4]).

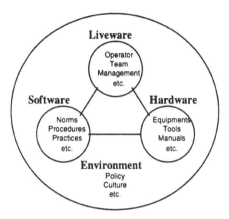

Fig. 1. Visualisation of a complex system according to the SHEL model. The lifeware component contains human aspects of the system, like the humans working in the system, the communities of practice they belong to or the social rules that govern their interaction. In the hardware component are grouped all artefacts like vehicles or signs. The software component finally comprises all the procedures and rules that determine how the work is carried out. The denominator SHEL is adopted from Edwards [4].

The systemic view proposed by the SHEL model is consistent with a long lasting and empirically well grounded theory of human cognition, i.e. the cultural-historical theory of Vygotsky, Luria and Leontev (for a review see [2]). This theory has recently received various attention and several authors in the field of man-machine systems have elaborated along the main ideas of Vygotsky's approach [5, 7, 14, 15]. The cultural-historical theory, its recent elaboration (e.g. Distributed Cognition, Activity Theory) and the SHEL model share the assumption that any complex process is always defined by a specific combination of hardware, software and lifeware resources. There is no exclusive combination of the resources to shape a specific process, yet a good performance and reliable operation of any process depends on an adequate combination of the different resources, which is dependent also upon the status of the environment and the dynamic system variables.

The systemic view helps to understand that any lack of resources in one dimension should be compensated by changes in the other dimensions, and that bad coupling of the resources prevents the accommodation needed to face variances. Indeed, the extensive literature on accident, incident, and near misses which occurred in safety critical systems [9, 17] stresses that both the weaknesses and the strengths of a system are in the interaction among the components. Individual components, as specific equipment or a specific computational code, or even a specific operator, engaged in well-defined activity, are likely to be assessed as highly reliable (especially for equipment and code). However, their reliability assessment for well-defined activities is not representative at all of the way, in which they will operate in real working systems [11]. In particular, evidence was provided that tight coupling of hardware and software components, and poor coupling of the human element within a given complex system, are the more important weaknesses of safety critical systems [17, 18].

The adoption of the systemic view has important implications for the way in which safety related systems have to be designed. In the next section we will present the holistic design process which is the result of our elaboration on the SHEL model.

3. Holistic Design

3.1. Design Philosophy

In accordance with the SHEL model, the philosophy behind the holistic design conceives a complex system as a dynamic entity, consisting of components which are closely connected and interdependent. The design or re-design of a complex system implies the creation or modification of a SHEL space. In general this involves the introduction of new artefacts or the modification of existing ones. Every artefact may be seen as mediation tool for intended actions. Hence, it may be viewed as the externalisation of knowledge which was formerly or is still possessed by humans. Therefore, designing a new system implies the redistribution of knowledge among the components.

As an illustration let us consider the programming of a VCR for recording a TV movie. With the early VCRs the process required a lot of human resources since the user had to collect information concerning the channel number, the date, and the schedule of the movie from TV magazines. These had then to be inserted into the VCR by a lengthy and error prone procedure. Often the user also had to estimate and program the VCR for some additional recording time to take into account possible advertisements during the show. In the second generation VCRs the process was re-organised by introducing a laser pen. The laser pen was able to read a bar code associated with each movie in TV magazines, which contained all the information concerning the schedule and the channel number of the movie. The user had to scan the bar code with the pen and then point it towards the VCR and download remotely the information. The required resources were thus shifted from the lifeware to the hardware (the laser pen) and to the software (a generally agreed rule to put into the bar code both the channel number and the schedule of the movies). However, also this process proved to be unsatisfactory, because the reading of the bar code was not always successful and because of the need of an additional, separate piece of hardware (laser pen). The latest generation of VCRs employ a numeric code associated with each movie. Like the bar code, also this numeric code contains all the required information. The user has to copy the numeric code from the TV magazine into a the VCR by a dedicated keyboard on the remote control or on the VCR body itself. In this way, resource requirements were shifted back from hardware to lifeware (a more active role of the user) and software. This organisation of the process seems to be the one offering the best chances for success and is commonly used.

Every process within a complex system is performed by a combination of the hardware, software, and lifeware resources. In response to environmental influences, or upon the breakdown of parts of a specific resource or its inability to support the process adequately, there needs to be a quick and efficient adaptation of the resources to reliably achieve an intended system state. In practice, this reconfiguration relies on the flexibility and creativity of the humans to compensate the lack or the inefficiencies of specific resources. Since the humans, i.e. the lifeware resources, are the most adaptive components of the complex system, the design needs to aim at supporting this adaptability and at enhancing the interaction of the lifeware and the other resources.

To enhance the adaptive capability knowledge should be distributed in such a way as to provide redundancy between the different resources, rather than relying on redundancy within a single resource. This implies that upon the breakdown of components, there should be alternative SHEL configurations to support the process. In particular, the humans should be enabled to perform their work in a variety of ways with different mediating artefacts. A consequence of this could be, for example, the continuous manual involvement of humans in routine tasks in order to keep this knowledge in the lifeware resource.

During the design of a system the distribution of knowledge must be fully understood. In order to achieve this, the involvement of the relevant stakeholders becomes a prerequisite and a valuable tool. They can provide direct information about how the work is being conducted. As the users acquire experience of using artefacts in context, as they make modifications to better suit their needs, they produce valuable knowledge which the design team must try to capture. Most importantly, the knowledge which the humans produce when they manage breakdowns of the other resources and adapt to unforeseen events needs to feed back into the organisation, as this is the basis for a successful learning and adaptation of the organisation. Indeed, if we consider the evolution of a complex system, it is easy to observe, that the same is not true for hardware resources, where the knowledge contained can only degrade with time (if they are not maintained by humans).

The necessity of user participation has become obvious, and there are further benefits to be gained by its application. It may serve to increase the feeling of collective ownership and may lead to a greater commitment to the projected changes. Likewise, the attitude towards the new work environment may be more positive and the feeling of trust users have towards supporting artefacts may increase by a considerable amount [13]. Most importantly, though, the direct involvement of the users may serve to further their feeling of responsibility, may increase user motivation and improve the overall level of communication. A lack of these affective factors can manifest itself in a variety of negative ways, like defective incident reporting, which was a major contributing factor in the Therac-25 accidents [12]. Eventually, system safety can only be substantially improved by providing a work environment which stimulates the feeling of responsibility of every individual instead of furthering the moving to-and-fro of responsibility in an anonymous crowd.

3.2. Design Process

The proposed holistic design is an evolutionary and multidisciplinary process. The evolutionary nature of the process, in combination with the active user participation, provides an effective means to minimising the risk that the system does not meet user requirements. The joint involvement of end-users and other stakeholders from the management aims to ensure that user needs and organisational requirements are both respected and consistent with each other. Preliminary design solutions can be tested against real scenarios and the results can feed back into the next iteration cycle. The holistic design process requires a variety of skills, which needs to be accounted for by the employment of multidisciplinary design teams which are sufficiently diverse to make appropriate design trade-off decisions. Among the different roles can be, for example, the end-users, the managers of the end-users, system analysts and system engineers, sales people, human-computer interaction specialists, human factors experts, and training and support personnel [8]. The activities carried out during the design process can be grouped as depicted in Fig. 2. As it is easy to note, the holistic design shares many methodological issues with other recent approaches for designing interactive systems, such as user-centred design [16] or Participatory Design [10]. However, the focus of the proposed approach is not on the user and its knowledge, but on the distribution of knowledge among the three basic resources and their interaction.

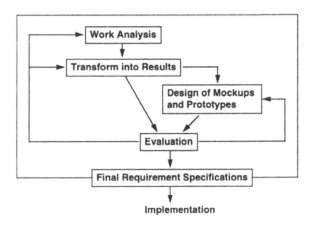

Fig. 2. The general concept of the applied holistic design approach

Indeed, the design process is based on analysis and design of all relevant system components. In the Work Analysis phase the key characteristics of the hardware, software and lifeware resources are studied in strong relation with the processes to be carried out. Work analysis aims at capturing the knowledge produced and its distribution within the complex system. The analysis starts with gathering knowledge of simple elements of the complex system, and receiving feedback about the correct understanding. Thereby, the users and the work context play a central role. Then, in an iterative way work analysis enlarges its focus in order to deal with the complexity of the system. Several analysis methods and tools need to be applied, as no single analysis method currently available would satisfy the required holistic consideration. Many task analysis methods would induce the bias of considering mostly the tasks related to the artefact considered relevant for the system to be designed, instead of considering the SHEL resources in their integrity.

The knowledge collected during the work analysis needs to be described and organised in documentation in order to provide a comprehensive description serving also as mediation tool for shared understanding. Reports and models like narratives, graphics, or scenarios are being produced, which are to be communicated about within the design team, with the users and other relevant stakeholders. These results are documents to be evaluated, and to be modified continuously during the evolution of the design. They serve as a basis for the design of mock-ups, prototypes, and for the definition of the final requirements specification.

The next stage is to create potential design solutions. Simulations, mock-ups and prototypes allow designers to communicate effectively with the users. Using these tools, several design options can be explored, and the feedback from the users can be incorporated from the beginning.

Evaluation is an integral part of the holistic design process. During each iteration it is important to receive feedback about the appropriateness of analysis results and mock-ups or prototypes. Early in the design the evaluation serves to a large extent to receive feedback from the users if the design team's understanding of the processes to be supported and the knowledge distribution was adequate and sufficient. In later stages the evaluation can assess if the goals and requirements have been met.

After satisfying analysis, design, and evaluation results, the requirements specification and the current mock-ups and prototypes form the final requirements specification. These documents are the input for the following implementation phase. This phase should be managed by adhering to an appropriate quality model and process.

4. Experiences from a Train Traffic Control (TTC) Case Study

4.1. Introduction to the Environment

The Italian National Railways (Ferrovie dello Stato, FS) provided a Case Study where the proposed holistic design approach has been applied and evaluated in a real work environment. The work concerned the control and reactive management of the train movements within a certain control zone of the FS-network. Both, the operators (Dirigente Centrale, DC) and the work environment were accessible for our analyses.

When performing their work the operators observe the train movements and compute the deviations of the real data from the planned time schedule. The overall goal of the operators in this case is to make decisions for rearranging the productive resources and objects based on their assessment of deviations in order to avoid or minimise inconveniences, or even incidents that may lead to economical damages or harm to humans. Thereby, the assessment of the deviations is based on the gravity of the deviations, formal rules, the experience of the DCs, and on other actually valid environmental and system variables. To react appropriately - especially in emergency cases - the DCs need to have in any moment an understanding of the dynamic system. Thereby, they use several artefacts for keeping the necessary knowledge alongside.

The DCs have the supervisory control of the train movements in their control zone. Yet, the direct responsibility and management of the different resources (e.g. train drivers, locomotives, wagons) is assigned to other departments as defined in the organisational structure of the FS. Hence, the DCs have to collaborate and co-ordinate with colleagues of other departments, when they need to allocate productive resources, which leads to highly interactive processes. Especially in the reactive management of the train movements most of the activities include interaction with other agents, regardless of what the content of the interaction is, be it information providing or acquiring, co-ordination of work, co-decision, negotiation, co-operation, etc.

The functions to be performed by the humans are cognitive demanding and often a large number of cognitive processes and interdependent entities have to be managed concurrently. Information may not be available at all or it may be ambiguous, requiring the human to actively search for the missing information. A non-exhaustive list of characteristics of the case study environment is given in Table 1.

Table 1. Characteristics of the Railways Case Study

Attribute	Characteristics
Work	- Already existing system with different levels of IT support - Multiple agents distributed over time - Multiple, probably non-overlapping / non-consistent internal representations - Information is ambiguous / incomplete / inconsistent / not available - Multiple conflicting targets / goals (e.g. passengers vs. cargo) - High impact of some potential errors - Tasks are cognitive demanding - Large number of cognitive processes have to be co-ordinated - Several entities have to be controlled concurrently - Strong interdependencies of the involved entities - Varying workload - Time pressure - Economical criticality - Safety related system - Work in context - Highly dynamic and low predictable system
Users	- Long experience - Highly skilled - Familiar with organisational and social structures - Mostly male
Working Conditions	- Noisy office environment - Shift work - Group and individual work
Organisational Structure	- Hierarchical - Divided into regional zones - Very large organisation

4.2. Experiences from the Roma - Grosseto Environment

The work analysis started by focusing on the basic processes and objects of the workplace. We chose the environment with the less advanced IT because the processes were more obvious than in the other cases where they had already been embodied in mediating artefacts. The initial knowledge acquired through videotapes and some explanations of objects by the operators was mapped into models. These knowledge representations have in turn been presented to the operators to get feedback about the correct understanding, to clear misunderstandings, and to provide a common awareness of what has been analysed. In several iterations of acquiring knowledge, filtering/transforming and evaluating it, the understanding of the work has been enlarged by broadening the focus of interest and enlarging the complexity. Further analysis methods which have been applied were interviews, audio-recordings, analytical methods, and, in a limited way, ethnography.

The result of the work analysis is a comprehensive mapping of the actual productive system into a model world by using different representations. Some results of the work analysis in the case study were descriptions of processes, of objects in use, of critical issues, of the mediation tools, scenarios, and interaction reports. The critical issues describe the problems and weaknesses of the actual work environment, which have been elicited via structured interviews.

Scenarios have been used to exemplify critical issues in certain processes, which elicited for example knowledge distributions which were not well defined, problems due to environmental factors, or problems in the use of or with the trust in the available mediation tools. Descriptions of emergency cases derived from stories and narratives of the operators have been reproduced in scenarios, too. In Fig. 3 a scenario with decision making and script based recording activity is presented, which illustrates some critical issues of the Roma - Grosseto environment.

TTC is a complex control process depending on the dynamic behaviour of the productive system. This dynamism can only be managed by intelligent agents capable of gathering the required knowledge, of allocating it in the right time, and of modifying it as necessary. The DCs are experts knowing how to perform the process, which artefacts support their activities and how reliable these tools are. They know about the weak points and critical issues in supporting the work, and they are well-trained, professional personnel. There exist of course standard procedures for how to react in certain emergency cases. But one cannot predict when they are needed and if they need modification. It is a central responsibility of the DCs to allocate the right procedure on demand. As yet humans are the only efficient component being able to deal with uncertainty cases in such a way that they can minimise eventually arising negative consequences of unforeseen events [3].

Considering other work environments at Roma Termini, the impact of advanced technology has been a reduction of human agents in the most advanced control zone: the station managers have been replaced by IT, and the DC operates directly on the line by setting remote junctions and signals through the switchboard on the work desk. Obviously, the job and the responsibility have changed for the operator.

Another interesting insight was that in case of breakdowns of the supporting artefacts the operators in the more advanced work environments have to proceed with the work as is done in Roma - Grosseto. A breakdown of the support system causes a lot of problems: communication becomes the most important critical factor, the operators are not used to proceed in an old way of process control any more, information about the actual status of the dynamic system has been lost, station managers have to be allocated to the stations, etc. The interdependencies of the SHEL components rise with the amount of technology. If there is no redundant possibility of resource combination for performing a process, a breakdown of the supporting artefact may end up in a safety critical situation.

Based on these insights and a comprehensive understanding of the workspace captured during the first round of work analysis a preliminary specification of requirements and general system architecture have been done. These were the starting

Scenario for Roma - Grosseto
Description of the situation:

Today is Thursday, 20 November, 1997. It is 11:20 in the morning. The train movement is as in scenario 1, with some time preceding. The DC realises that he will soon have to organise an overtaking of two trains, because the 515 (an Intercity) is faster than the 3259, which is a direct one. The two trains move as follows: 3259 from S. Marinella with 186 (minutes of delay) and should arrive at Ladispoli at 11:25 515 from S. Marinella with 14 and should arrive at 11:30 ... One DC controls the movements on the line. The other inserts data into the Ranger.

Description of the sequence of actions (the last two columns represent the links to processes and critical issues):

time	sequence of action	activity descr.	critical issues
11:25	The DC considers, where it would be the best to organise the priority activity. He controls the composition of the stations, which are graphically represented in front of him. He knows the lengths of the train no. 3259, which he has to park in a station at a side track. He realises that he has three possibilities: Palidoro, Maccarese or S. Pietro.	2.8	7.2, 5.x
11:26	The thoughts of the DC are the following: if he stops the 3259 at Palidoro or Maccarese he will loose around 10 minutes. Instead, if he does it at S. Pietro he will loose only 5 minutes, because there is already a planned stop and the trains are already near to each other.	2.8	7.2, 7.3
11:27	The DC decides to do the overtaking at S. Pietro and calls the station with the micro. While he is waiting for the response, the DC observes the whole map in order to update his overview of the whole control zone.	2.8	5.1
11:28	The station manager (DL) of Maccarese calls and communicates: 56603 at 9 with 70; 7380 at 21 22 in time. The DC registers. Meanwhile, S. Pietro responds, but the DC tells the DL to wait a moment. Then the DL of Maccarese continues the conversation and asks: how comes the 3259? The DC responds: with 186 left from S. Marinella. DL: and the 515? DC: with 14 left from S. Marinella. The DL understands that the two trains are very close and realises that there will be an overtaking to do. So he asks the DC: will you do it at my place? The DC responds: no, I'll do it at S. Pietro.	1.1, 2.3, 2.5	6.3, 6.4, manage comm., mutual awareness, info spreading, 8.1
11:30	The DC tells the DL of S. Pietro, who waited on the micro: Park the 3259 and let the 515 pass.	2.7	1.4, manage comm

Fig. 3. Scenario 2 of Roma - Grosseto describes problem solving to decide where to organise the necessary overtaking of the two involved trains. With the three possible stations the local community in the activity is formed by the DC, the station managers (DL) of S. Pietro, Maccarese and Palidoro, and the two involved train drivers. The supporting HW-artefacts are: 1) the time/station matrix, which provides an external support for the building and understanding of the dynamic system; 2) the M42, which is a written form informing the

operator about characteristics of the trains e.g. the length; 3) the graphical representation for the composition of the stations; and 4) the theoretical timetable. Some examples of SW-components are the procedure of how the DC communicates the priority decision to the DL of S. Pietro at 11:30, or the way in which the DL of Maccarese (at 11:28) communicates the train positions. As there are no tools available for the prediction of the future development, the knowledge for the decision making exists mainly in the mind of the DC. The reasoning is influenced by the actual situation, the experience and skills of the DC, and similar situations in the past. When the DC interacts with Maccarese also the DL understands the local situation. It shows that they are mutually aware of the problem. Yet, a weak point in the actual workplace is that only the station in charge of performing the overtaking gets informed about the decision the DC has taken.

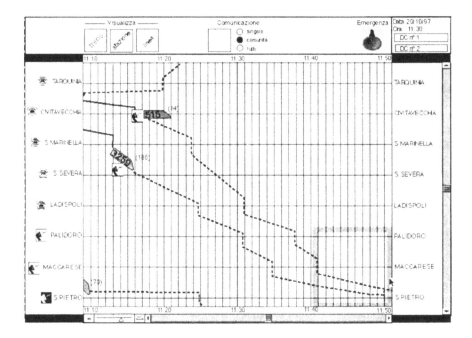

Fig. 4. Monitor 1 of mock-up 2 for Roma - Grosseto. Some critical aspects are addressed as follows: the extrapolation in the future is done by the system that knows the history of the trains, their characteristics and their theoretical time schedule. The predicted trajectory is visualised in dotted lines. The system recognises conflicts like the necessary overtaking between the 3259 and the 515 and alerts it to the DC, thus creating a local community between the two trains, the DC and the involved station managers (all 'objects' within the rectangle). The DCs can decide to let the system solve the problem (the system knows the rules about priority, and the characteristics of the trains and involved stations), they can co-operatively work on the problem, or they can solve the problem on their own. In any case, the system installs a communication channel to the involved agents and provides them with the information about the decision, which is highlighted with the active phone icons. The inverted icon at S. Pietro signifies that this is the main communication, whereas the others involved listen to the communication.

points for the design of mock-ups, which were based on simple scenarios. An example of mock-up corresponding to the scenario in Fig. 3 is shown in Fig. 4.

The mock-ups which were designed in the first two design iterations tried to address the issues instantiated in the scenarios. In particular they tried to redistribute the communication knowledge among the components since this was the most important critical issue reported by the DCs. It is important that in the proposed approach mock-ups can be seen as a kind of task model, which allows representing dynamic behaviour in a very simple, cheap and easy way to be understood and modified.

An impressive experience has been collected from the first round of evaluating the mock-ups. It puts forward the importance of user participation and the powerfulness of simple mock-ups. Assuming that there was no automatic train detection system available the operator had to manually insert the train positions, which he got from a station manager. In the first design iteration we did not focus on data entry. We just designed a form where the train, station, and time had to be selected and inserted via mouse click and keyboard. However, the DCs emphasised that this way of data entry is very time-consuming, and it is not adequate and conform with the communication practice. In fact, the DCs were quite faster in drawing the trajectory by hand on the paper matrix. This experience resulted in mapping the paper-and-pencil way of recording train movements to the system by selecting and clicking on the screen (mouse click, touch screen, etc.).

This simple example, even if not directly related to safety issues, shows how the soundness of a complex system is based on the interaction among components, and it makes clear that the system should be designed according to this principle starting from the most simple interaction.

5. Conclusions

Complex systems, like the TTC system presented in this paper, are highly dynamic entities, the success of which is strongly dependent upon a smooth integration and effective co-operation of the available resources. Breakdowns of individual components or of the interaction among the components may have critical influences on the safety of the system. It is important that such breakdowns can be compensated quickly by different resource allocations. Generally, the human component is responsible for the adaptive and creative behaviour in response to criticality.

The proposed holistic design is based on this conception and aims to design the components of the system and their interaction in an integrative way. Each single resource is designed and assessed both for its contribution to reach a given state and to support or compensate a lack of contribution from other resources.

User participation is a key characteristic of this design approach. Users can help in understanding the work environment and the knowledge distribution. They have created valuable knowledge, when they had to deal with abnormalities, which is not yet part of the organisation and which needs to be captured. User participation is a strong and necessary tool in improving the reliability of complex systems, because the adaptive capability of the human can be supported and their need for cognitive and affective support can be addressed directly.

The approach seems very promising and has been applied for evaluating already defined system requirements for the control centre of a new high-speed line in Italy. However, further investigation is needed for improvement and to develop support tools for managing the whole development lifecycle of the holistic design approach[1].

References

1. Clegg, C.W., Warr, P.B., Green, T.R.G., Monk, A., Kemp, N.J., Allison, G., Landsdale, M.: 'People and Computers: How to Evaluate your Company's new Technology'. Ellis Horwood, Chichester (1989)
2. Cole, M.: 'Cultural Psychology'. Cambridge, MA: Harvard University Press (1996)
3. Degani, A. & Wiener, E. L.: 'Procedures in Complex Systems: The Airline Cockpit'. In IEEE Transactions on Systems, Man, and Cybernetics - Part A: Systems and Humans, Vol. 27 (3), May 1997
4. Edwards, E.: 'Introductory overview'. In Wiener, E.L. & Nagel, D.C. (eds.): Human Factors in Aviation. San Diego: Academic Press (1988)
5. Engestrom, Y.: 'Developing thinking at the changing workplace: Toward a definition of expertise'. Technical Report 130. University of California San Diego. Center for Human Information Processing (1989)
6. Hornby, P., Clegg, C.W., Robson, J.I., MacLaren, C.R.R., Richardson, S.C.S., O'Brien, P.: 'Human and organisational issues in information systems development'. In Behaviour & Information Technology, vol. 11 (3), 1992, 160-174
7. Hutchins, E.: 'Cognition in the Wild'. MIT Press (1995)
8. ISO/DIS 13407: 'Human-centred design processes for interactive systems'. Draft International Standard (1997)
9. Kletz, T.: 'Lessons from disaster', Houston: Gulf Publishing Company (1993)
10. Kyng, M., Mathiassen, L., Beardon, C.: 'Computers and Design in Context'. MIT Press (1997)
11. Levenson, N.: 'Safeware'. Readings, MA: Addison Wesley (1995)
12. Levenson, N.G. & Turner, C.: 'An investigation of the Therac-25 accidents'. In IEEE Computer, 1993, 18-43
13. Lewis, M.: 'Designing for Human-Agent Interaction'. In AI Magazine, 19(2), 1998, 67-78
14. Norman, D. A.: 'The psychology of everyday things'. New York: Basic Books (1988)
15. Norman, D. A.: 'Things that Makes Us Smart'. Readings, MA: Addison-Wesley (1993)
16. Norman, D. A., & Draper, S. W.: 'User Centered System Design'. Hillsdale, N. J.: LEA (1986)
17. Perrow, C.: 'Normal Accident: Living with high-risk technologies'. New York: Basic Book (1984)
18. Rasmussen, J., Pejterson, A.M., Goodstein, L.P.: 'Cognitive Systems Engineering'. Wiley & Sons (1994)

[1] This work was carried out in the OLOS project, funded by the Human Capital Mobility Network program of the European Commission. We would like to thank the Italian Railways for their collaboration and support and we are deeply grateful to the operators and managers of the Santa Bibbiana plant for their lively participation to the study.

Comparing Fault Trees and Bayesian Networks for Dependability Analysis

Andrea Bobbio[1] , Luigi Portinale[1], Michele Minichino[2], Ester Ciancamerla[2]

[1] Dipartimento di Scienze e Tecnologie Avanzate,
Università del Piemonte Orientale "A. Avogadro" , C.so Borsalino 54 ,
15100 Alessandria, Italy
[2] ENEA - CRE Casaccia, Via Anguillarese 301,
00060 Roma , Italy

Abstract. Bayesian Networks (*BN*) provide a robust probabilistic method of reasoning under uncertainty. They have been successfully applied in a variety of real-world tasks and their suitability for dependability analysis is now considered by several researchers. In the present paper, we aim at defining a formal comparison between *BN* and one of the most popular techniques for dependability analysis: Fault Trees (*FT*). We will show that any *FT* can be easily mapped into a *BN* and that basic inference techniques on the latter may be used to obtain classical parameters computed using the former (i.e. reliability of the Top Event or of any sub-system, criticality of components, etc...). Moreover, we will discuss how, by using *BN*, some additional power can be obtained, both at the modeling and at the analysis level. In particular, dependency among components and noisy gates can be easily accommodated in the *BN* framework, together with the possibility of performing general diagnostic analysis. The comparison of the two methodologies is carried on through the analysis of an example that consists of a redundant multiprocessor system, with local and shared memories, local mirrored disks and a single bus.

1 Introduction

Fault Tree Analysis (*FTA*) is a very popular and diffused technique for the dependability modeling and evaluation of large, safety-critical systems [7,9], like the *Programmable Electronic Systems (PES)*. The technique is based on the identification of a particular undesired event to be analysed (e.g. system failure), called the *Top Event (TE)*. The construction of the Fault Tree (*FT*) proceeds in a top/down fashion, from the events to their causes, until failures of basic components are reached. The methodology is based on the following assumptions: *i*) -events are binary events (working/not-working); *ii*) -events are statistically independent; *iii*) -relationships between events and causes are represented by means of logical *AND* and *OR* gates. However, some *FT* tools relax the last assumption and allow the inclusion of the *NOT* gate and related (e.g. *XOR*) gates.

In *FTA*, the analysis is carried on in two steps: a qualitative step in which the logical expression of the *TE* is derived in terms of prime implicants (the minimal cut-

M. Felici, K. Kanoun, A. Pasquini (Eds.): SAFECOMP'99, LNCS 1698, pp. 310-322, 1999
© Springer-Verlag Berlin Heidelberg 1999

sets); a quantitative step in which, on the basis of the probabilities assigned to the failure events of the basic components, the probability of occurrence of the *TE* (and of any internal event corresponding to a logical sub-system) is calculated.

On the other hand, *Bayesian Networks (BN)* have become a widely used formalism for representing uncertain knowledge in probabilistic systems and have been applied to a variety of real-world problems [6]. *BN* are defined by a directed acyclic graph in which discrete random variables are assigned to each node, together with the conditional dependence on the parent nodes. Root nodes are nodes with no parents, and marginal prior probabilities are assigned to them.

Standard analysis of *BN* concerns the computation of the posterior probability of any given set of variables given some observation (the evidence) represented as instantiation of some of the variables to one of their admissible values. This general analysis may proceed along two lines. A forward (or predictive) analysis, in which the probability of occurrence of any node of the network is calculated on the basis of the prior probabilities of the root nodes and the conditional dependence of each node. A backward (diagnostic) analysis in which, given some evidence, the posterior probability of any set of variables that may cause the evidence is computed.

The aim of the present paper is to compare the modeling and the decision power of the *FTA* and *BN* methodologies in the area of the dependability analysis. First, an algorithm is presented to convert a *FT* into a *BN* and it is shown how the results obtained from a fault tree analysis can be cast in the *BN* setting. Subsequently, various modeling extensions, available in the *BN* language [1], are investigated. In particular, it is shown how the binary *AND/OR* dependence among components can be overcome, by introducing *noisy* gates and gates with *leak*. Moreover, *n*-ary (or multi-state) components can be easily accommodated into the picture, and various kinds of common-cause-failure dependencies can be taken into account.

At the analysis level, the *BN* methodology is able to compute a measure of the severity of each single component, or of any subset of components jointly considered, conditioned on the occurrence of the *TE*. Moreover, the quantitative effect of noisy *AND/OR* logic and common cause failures can be estimated.

The comparison of the two methodologies is carried through the analysis of an example. The example (taken from [10], consists of a redundant multiprocessor system, with local and shared memories, local mirrored disks and a single bus.

2 Bayesian Networks

Bayesian Networks [12] are usually defined on discrete random variables, even if some extensions have been proposed for dealing with some form of continuous random variables; in this paper, we will concentrate on the discrete case.

A Bayesian Network *(BN)* is a pair $N = \langle \langle V, E \rangle, P \rangle$ where $\langle V, E \rangle$ is a DAG (Directed Acyclic Graph) representing through edges E conditional dependences among (discrete) random variables $V = \{X_1, X_2, ..., X_n\}$ and P is a probabilistic distribution over V such that

$$P[X_1, X_2, ..., X_n] = \prod_{i=1}^{n} P[X_i \mid Parent(X_i)] \qquad (1)$$

In a *BN*, we can then identify a qualitative part (the structure represented by the DAG) and a quantitative part (the set of conditional probabilities). Variables are also called *nodes*. The qualitative part represents a set of conditional independence assumptions that can be captured through a graph-theoretic notion called *d-separation* [12]. This notion has been shown to model the usual set of independence assumptions that a modeler assumes when considering each edge from variable X to variable Y as a direct dependence (or as a cause-effect relationship) between the events represented by the variables.

Because of these assumptions, the quantitative part is completely specified by considering the probability of each value of a variable conditioned by every possible instantiation of its parents (i.e. by considering only local conditioning); variables having no parents are called "root variables" and marginal prior probabilities are associated with them. Such local conditional probabilities are usually defined using *conditional probability tables* (*CPTs*).

The basic inference task of a *BN*, consists of computing the posterior probability distribution on a set of query variables Q, given the observation of another set of variables E called the evidence, (i.e $P(Q \mid E)$). Particular attention has been paid to an instantiation of the above problem in which the query set Q is a singleton composed by just one variable and the problem is applied to each variable of the net (but the evidence ones). Different classes of algorithms have been developed that, given the evidence E, compute the marginal posterior probability $P(X \mid E)$ for each variable X in the *BN* outside the evidence. While this computation may be sufficient in several applications, there may be cases requiring the computation of the posterior joint probability of a given set Q of variables.

3 Mapping Fault Trees to Bayesian Networks

Given a *FT*, it is straightforward to map it into a binary *BN*, i.e. a *BN* with every variable V having two admissible values: *false* ($\overline{V}$) corresponding to a *normal* or *working* value and *true* (*V*) corresponding to a *faulty* or *not-working* value. For the sake of simplicity, let us for now consider *FT* having just *AND/OR* gates: the mapping can be obtained as follows:

- for each *leaf node* (i.e. basic system component) of the *FT*, create a *root node* in the *BN* having the same (prior) probability distribution as in the *FT*;
- for each *gate* of the *FT*, create a corresponding *node* in the *BN*;
- label the node corresponding to the gate whose output is the *TE* of the *FT* as the *Fault* node;
- connects nodes in the *BN* as corresponding gates are connected in the *FT*;
- for each node corresponding to an *AND* (respectively *OR*) gate create a *CPT* such that the node is true with probability 1 iff all incoming nodes are true (respectively

iff at least one incoming node is true) while it is false with probability 1 elsewhere[1].

The above mapping can be easily generalized to deal with fault trees having different kinds of gates (as for instance *k-out-of-n* gates); moreover, as we will see in the following, the specification of a complete *CPT* can be avoided in particular situations.

We will discuss this mapping through the following example concerning the redundant multiprocessor system shown in fig. 1 and taken from [10].

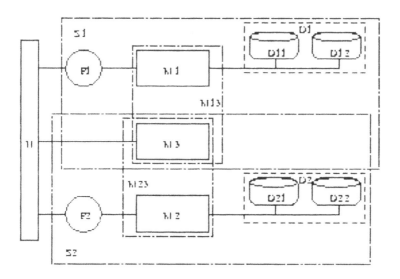

Fig. 1. A redundant multiprocessor system

Such a system is composed of a bus N connecting two processors P_1 and P_2 having access to a local memory bank each (respectively M_1 and M_2) and, through the bus to a shared memory bank M_3. Each processor is connected to a mirrored disk unit. If one of the disks fails, the processor can use the mirror and, at the same way, if the local memory bank fails, the processor can use the shared one. The whole system is functional iff the bus N is functional and one of the processing subsystems is functional. Fig. 1 also shows the partitioning into logical subsystems, i.e. the processing subsystems S_i $(i=1,2)$, the mirrored disk units D_i $(i=1,2)$ and the memory subsystems $M_{i3}(i=1,2)$. The *FT* for this system is shown in fig. 2(a) and the structure of the corresponding *BN* in fig. 2(b). As an example, in fig. 2(b) we have also shown the *CPT* entries for the node *Fault* and the node S_{12} corresponding to an *OR* and an *AND* gate, respectively. The fault probabilities of components are then assigned as

---

[1] This means that in this case, non-root nodes of the *BN* are actually deterministic nodes and not random variables.

prior probabilities of root nodes on the *BN*; for example, the probability of processor P_1 being faulty will be modeled as the prior probability $P(P_1)$ on node P_1 (with $P(\overline{P_1}) = 1 - P(P_1)$ being the probability of processor P_1 functional).

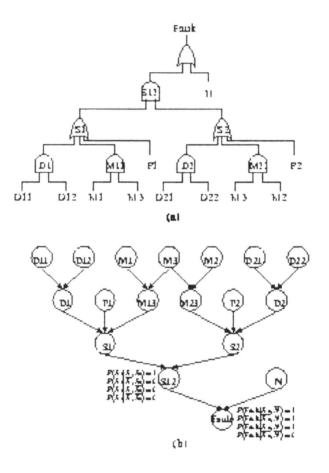

Fig. 2. Fault Tree (a) and Bayesian Net (b) for the multiprocessor system

4 Modeling Issues

The mapping procedure described in sect. 3 shows that each *FT* can be naturally described as a *BN*. However, *BN*'s are a more general formalism than *FT* 's; for this reason, there are several modeling aspects underlying *BN*'s that may make them very appealing for dependability analysis.

4.1 Noisy gates

The first issue concerns the nature of the dependence relations among variables in a *BN*: differently from *FT*, such relations are not restricted to be deterministic, but they may be probabilistic. This corresponds to being able to model uncertainty in the behavior of the "gates" that in a *FT* represent interactions between subsystems. Of particular attention for reliability aspects is one peculiar modeling feature often used in building *BN* models: *noisy gates*. As mentioned in sect. 2, when specifying *CPT* entries one has to condition the value of a variable on every possible instantiation of its parent variables, making the number of required entries exponential with respect to the number of parents; noisy gates can reduce this effort by requiring a number of parameters linear in the number of parents, while keeping the ability of modeling uncertain relations.

Consider for example the subsystem S_1 in fig. 1: it fails if either the disk unit D_1 or the processor P_1 or the memory subsystem M_{13} fail. Consider now the case that the logical *OR* interaction is *noisy* or probabilistic: even if one of the components of S_1 fails, there is a (possibly small) positive probability that the subsystem works. This corresponds to the fact that the system may maintain some functionality or may be able to reconfigure (with some probability of reconfiguration success) in the presence of particular faults.

BN can avoid the complete *CPT* specification by adopting the so-called *noisy-or model*. Given a binary variable Y having the set of parent binary variables $X_1, ..., X_n$, the noisy-or model requires to specify n parameters $p_1, ..., p_n$, where each p_i is interpreted as the probability of Y true given that X_i is true and all the other parents are false (i.e. $p_i = P(Y \mid \overline{X_1}, ... X_i, ... \overline{X_n})$). By assuming that each X_i influences Y independently from each other, the local model is completely specified if we further assume that Y is false if none of the parents is true. Indeed it can be shown [12] that if X is a particular instantiation of $X_1, ..., X_n$ and π_x is the set of true variables in X, then

$$P(Y \mid X) = 1 - \prod_{X_i \in p_x}(1 - p_i) \qquad (2)$$

Returning to the example, we may for instance model the fact that S_1 works with probability 0.01 even if the disk unit D_1 has failed. This means that $p_{D_1} = P(S_1 \mid D_1, \overline{P_1}, \overline{M_{13}}) = 0.99$; suppose now that the system can recover also if other components of S_1 fail, but with a smaller probability (e.g. $p_{P_1} = p_{M_{13}} = 0.995$). Then, we can for instance compute the probability of the subsystem S_1 failed when both D_1 and P_1 have failed and M_{13} is still working as $P(S_1 \mid D_1, P_1, \overline{M_{13}}) = 1 - (0.01 * 0.005) = 0.99995$. As one can expect, such a probability is larger than the probability of S_1 failed given that only D_1 has failed.

The above construct does not allow to model that fact that the subsystem may fail even if all its components are functional, since it assumes that $P\left(S_1 \mid \overline{D_1}, \overline{P_1}, \overline{M_{13}}\right) = 0$.

However, it is often necessary, in reliability modeling, to include causes of failure (usually referred to as *common causes*) that determine the system to go down even in the presence of components up. To this end, an extension of the noisy-or can be adopted, called *noisy-or* with *leak*. In this model, one assumes that there is a positive probability (called the *leak* or *background probability*) of having Y true even when all parents X_i are false. This can be modeled by thinking to the influence between X_i and Y as changed by adding an unknown parent L: the leak (or the common cause in reliability terminology). In this way $P\left(Y \mid \overline{X_1},..., \overline{X_n}\right)$ is interpreted as $P\left(Y \mid \overline{X_1},..., \overline{X_n}, L\right) = l$ and then equation 2 becomes

$$P(Y \mid X) = 1 - [(1-l) \prod_{X_i \in p_X}(1 - p_i)]$$ (3)

In the example, we may assign to S_1 a common cause failure probability $l_{cc} = 0.02$, even if all components are functional. This term accounts for the fact that we missed some unknown cause of failure, either because we do not know it precisely or because we do not deem appropriate to build up a finer representation for the system. In this case, if we still compute the probability of the subsystem S_1 failed when both D_1 and P_1 have failed and M_{13} is still working, we obtain $P\left(S_1 \mid D_1, P_1, \overline{M_{13}}\right) = 1 - [0.01 * 0.005 * (1 - l_{cc})] = 0.999951$ which is slightly larger than in the previous case when no leak probability was present.

Similar considerations can be done for variables corresponding to *AND* gates of the FT, by taking into account the *noisy-and model* (dual to noisy-or). The modeler has to specify the parameters $p_i = P\left(Y \mid X_1,..., \overline{X_i},...X_n\right)$ for getting

$$P(Y \mid X) = \prod_{X_i \in p_X} p_i$$ (4)

Consider for instance the mirrored disk subsystem D_1 that fails if both disks D_{11} and D_{12} fail. However, in a more refined view of the model, we can suppose that the mirrored connection is not perfect, and there is a small probability (e.g. 0.001) that the disk subsystem D_1 fails when a single disk is up: (i.e. $p_{D_{11}} = P\left(D_1 \mid \overline{D_{11}}, D_{12}\right) = p_{D_{12}} = P\left(D_1 \mid D_{11}, \overline{D_{12}}\right) = 1 * 10^{-3}$). We can then compute the probability of D_1 failing when both disks are functional as $P\left(D_1 \mid \overline{D_{11}}, \overline{D_{12}}\right) = 10^{-3} * 10^{-3} = 1 * 10^{-6}$.

Notice that the noisy-and gate is not appropriate to model the *coverage* [4] probability of the reconfiguration process in a redundant system (where the coverage c is defined as the probability that the reconfiguration process is able to restore the system in a working state when a redundant element fails). Suppose that in the memory subsystem M_{13} there is a small probability (e.g. $1-c$) that the subsystem M_{13} does not recover the failure of a single memory bank: (i.e. $p_{M_1} = P\left(M_{13} \mid \overline{M_1}, M_3\right) = p_{M_3} = P\left(M_{13} \mid \overline{M_3}, M_1\right) = 1-c$). The above assumption does not entail that M_{13} must have a positive probability of failure when both banks are functional, and the complete *CPT* must be specified in this case.

This kind of noisy-and model assumes that the subsystem certainly fails when all involved components fail. If this is not the case, the noisy-and can be generalized with a leak parameter as the noisy-or.

4.2 Multi-state variables

All the above considerations concerned binary variables. The use of *multi-state* or *n-ary* variables can be very useful in many applications, where it is not sufficient to restrict the component behavior to the dichotomy working/not-working. An usual case occurs when components manifest more than one failure mode (e.g. open/short) and the failure modes have a very different effect on the system operation (e.g. fail-safe/fail-danger).

Suppose to consider a three-state component whose states are identified as *working (w)*, *fail-open (f-o)* and *fail-short (f-s)*. In *FT* the component failure modes must be modeled as two independent binary events (*w/f-o*) and (*w/f-s*); however, to make the model correct, an *XOR* gate must be inserted between *f-o* and *f-s* since they are mutually exclusive events. On the contrary, *BN* can include *n-ary* variables by adjusting the entries of the *CPT*. A useful generalization of the noisy-gate construct is called *noisy-max*, and may be applied to *n-ary* variables, with the only constraint of having an order defined on the set of the admissible values of the variables (see for example [8] for more details).

4.3 Sequentially dependent failures

Another modeling issue that may be quite problematic to deal with using *FT* is the problem of components failing in some dependent way. In Fig. 2, the shared memory M_3 affects both subsystems, but we would like to model also a common dependence on the failures of basic components. For instance, the abnormal operation of a component may induce dependent failures on other ones. Suppose for instance that we refine the description of the multiprocessor system by adding the component *power supply (PS)* such that, when failing, causes a system failure, but it may also induce the processors to break down. A *FT* for representing this should add a new input *PS* to the *TE* of the *FT* of fig. 2 to represent a new cause of system failure as shown in fig. 3(a); however, modeling the dependence between the failure of *PS* and the failure of processor P_i (*i=1,2*) is not possible in the *FT* formalism.

Notice that, in the *BN* model one may be even more precise, by resorting to a multi-state model for the power supply; indeed, a more realistic situation could be the following: *PS* is modeled with three possible modes: *correct, defective* and *dead* where the first corresponds to a nominal behavior, the second to a defective working mode where an abnormal voltage is provided, while the last corresponds to a situation where *PS* cannot work at all.

Of course, *dead* mode will cause the whole system to be down, but we want to model the fact that when *PS* is in the *defective* mode the processors increase their conditional dependence to break down. This can be modeled in a very natural way, by considering the variable *PS* to have three values corresponding to the above modes and by setting the entries in the *CPT* in a suitable way.

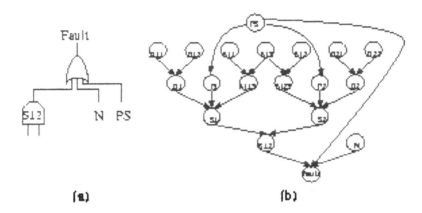

Fig. 3. Adding power supply: fault tree (a), bayesian net (b)

5 Analysis Issues

Typical analyses performed by fault trees involve both qualitative and quantitative aspects. In particular, any kind of quantitative analysis exploits the basics of the qualitative analysis, thus the minimal cut-sets computation. Minimal cut-sets are the prime implicants of the *TE* and are usually obtained by means of minimization techniques on the set of functions represented by the boolean gates of the *FT*. Given the set of minimal cut-sets, usual quantitative analysis involves:

? the computation of the overall unreliability of the system corresponding to the unreliability of the top event (i.e. *P(Fault)*);
? the computation of the unreliability of each identified subsystem, corresponding to the unreliability of each single gate;
? the importance of each minimal cut-set, corresponding to the probability of the cut-set itself by assuming the statistical independence among components.

In particular, if each component c_i has probability of failure $P(c_i)$, the importance of a cut-set *CS* is given by $P(CS) = \prod_{c_i \in CS} P(c_i)$. Notice that such a quantity refers to the a-priori failure probability of each component.

As shown in section 3, any *FT* can be mapped into a *BN* where non-root nodes are deterministic. Any analysis performed on a *FT* can be performed on the corresponding *BN*; moreover, other interesting kinds of analyses that are not possible in a *FT*, can instead be performed on the corresponding *BN*. Let us first consider the basic analyses of a *FT* and how they are performed in the corresponding *BN*:

? *unreliability of the TE*: this corresponds to computing the prior probability of the variable *Fault*, that is $P(Q|E)$ with $Q = Fault$ and $E = 0$;

? *unreliability of a given subsystem*: this corresponds to computing the prior probability of the corresponding variable S_i, that is $P(Q|E)$ with $Q = S_i$ and $E = 0$.

Differently from the computations performed on a *FT*, the above computations in a *BN* do not require the determination of the cut-sets. However, any technique used for cut-set determination in the *FT* can be applied in the *BN*: indeed, the boolean functions modeled by the gates in the *FT* are modeled by non-root nodes in the *BN*.

Concerning the computation of the cut-set importance, it is worth noting that *BN* may directly produce a more accurate measure of such an importance, being able to provide the posterior probability of each cut-set given the fault.

Related to the above issue is another aspect that is peculiar of the use of *BN* wrt *FT*: the possibility of performing *diagnostic problem-solving* on the modeled system. In fact, in many cases the system analyst may be interested in determining the possible explanations of an exhibited fault in the system. Cut-set determination is a step in this direction, but it may not be sufficient in certain situations. Classical diagnostic inference on a *BN* involves:

? computation of the posterior marginal probability distribution on each component;
? computation of the posterior joint probability distribution on subsets of components;
? computation of the posterior joint probability distribution on the set of all nodes, but the evidence ones.

The first kind of computation is perhaps the most popular one when using *BN* for diagnosis (see for instance DXpress [8] or MSBN [11] or HUGIN [2] tools). One advantage is that there exist well-established algorithms that can compute the marginal posterior probability of each node by considering this task as if it was a single query (i.e. it is not necessary to pose more queries of the type $P(Q|E)$, each time considering Q equal to the node for which we want the posterior distribution). Moreover, this kind of computation is very useful for determining the criticality of the components of the system, in case a fault is observed [1]. The main disadvantage is that considering only the marginal posterior probability of components is not always appropriate for a precise diagnosis [12]; in many cases the right way for characterizing diagnoses is to consider scenarios involving more variables (for example all the components). The other two kinds of computation address exactly this point.

5.1 Example

Consider the multiprocessor system of fig. 1; we assume an exponentially distributed failure time for all the components, with the following failure rates (expressed in *f/h* units): processors P_i : $1_{P_i} = 5*10^{-7}$; memory banks M_i: $1_{M_i} = 3*10^{-8}$; bus *N*: $1_N = 2*10^{-9}$; disks D_{ij}: $1_{D_{ij}} = 8*10^{-5}$. Let us evaluate the system behavior at a mission time $t = 5000$ hours. The evaluation of the prior probabilities on the *BN* of fig.2(a), at the mission time t and assuming the previous values for the failure rates, provides the following results: $P(P_i) = 25*10^{-4}$; $P(M_i) = 15*10^{-5}$; $P(N) = 1*10^{-5}$; $P(D_{ij}) = 0.32968$.

Forward propagation on the *BN* allows us to compute the unreliability of the *TE* as the a-priori probability of system failure, i.e. *P(Fault)*=0.012313.

If we observe that the system is faulty at time *t*, the marginal posterior fault probabilities of each component are then computed as: $P(P_i \mid Fault) = 0.02252$; $P(M_i \mid Fault) = 15*10^{-5}$; $P(N \mid Fault) = 81*10^{-5}$; $P(D_{ij} \mid Fault) = 0.98436$. This parameters may be useful to provide an indication of the criticality of each single component if the system is faulty; observe that the severity ranking based on posteriors is different from the one based on priors. We can also notice that the most critical component is in this case each disk. However, this information is not completely significant from the diagnostic point of view; indeed, by considering the disk units, the only way of having the fault is to assume that all the disks D_{11}, D_{12}, D_{21}, D_{22} have failed at the same time (indeed, it is the only minimal cut-set involving only disks). This information (the fact that all disks have to be jointly considered faulty to get the fault) is not directly derived by marginal posteriors on components. In fact, for diagnostic purposes a more suitable analysis should consider the posterior joint probability of all the components given the system fault as evidence. This analysis corresponds to search over the state space represented by all the possible instantiations of the root variables (i.e. components), the most probable state given the fault.

In this case, we can determine by means of *BN* inference that the most probable diagnosis (i.e. the most probable state given the system fault) is exactly the one corresponding to the faulty value of all the disks and the normal value of all the other components; in particular, we obtain:

$$P(\overline{N}, \overline{M}_1, \overline{M}_2, \overline{M}_3, \overline{P}_1, \overline{P}_2, D_{11}, D_{12}, D_{21}, D_{22} \mid Fault) = 0.95422$$

Notice that the above diagnosis does not correspond to the cut-set { D_{11}, D_{12}, D_{21}, D_{22}}, since the latter does not imply that the unmentioned components are working (i.e. assigned to the normal value); anyway, the posterior probability of the cut-sets can be naturally computed in the *BN* setting by a query on all the disk variables conditioned on the observation of the fault.

In a reliability context, it seems more reasonable to restrict the attention to root variables, only. However, an alternative way of characterizing diagnoses is to view them as complete assignments to all the variables but the evidence ones; this corresponds to search over the state space of all the possible instantiations of every variable in the *BN*. When the task consists in computing the most probable of such diagnoses it is called *MPE* computation [12] (where *MPE* stands for *most probable explanation*).

An interesting possibility offered by *BN* is that there exist algorithms able to produce diagnoses (either viewed as only-root assignments or all-variable assignments) in order of their probability of occurrence, without exploring the whole state space; they are usually called *any-time* algorithms, since the user can stop the algorithm at any-time, by getting an approximate answer that is improved if more time is allocated to the algorithm. For example, an algorithm based on the model described in [13] is able to provide the most probable diagnoses, given the observation of the fault, in the multiprocessor system at any desired level of precision. By specifying a maximum admissible error ε in the posterior probability of the diagnoses, the algorithm is able to produce, in order of probability, every diagnosis D with an estimate $P'(D|Fault)$ such that its actual posterior probability is $P(D|Fault)=P'(D|Fault) \pm \epsilon$

In the example, by requiring diagnoses to be root assignments and $\epsilon =1*10^{-6}$ the first 3 diagnoses are, in order:

$$d_1 : \left(N,\overline{M_1},\overline{M_2},\overline{M_3},\overline{P_1},\overline{P_2},D_{11},D_{12},D_{21},D_{22}\right)$$

$$d_2 : \left(N,\overline{M_1},\overline{M_2},\overline{M_3},\overline{P_1},P_2,D_{11},D_{12},\overline{D_{21}},\overline{D_{22}}\right)$$

$$d_3 : \left(N,\overline{M_1},\overline{M_2},\overline{M_3},P_1,\overline{P_2},\overline{D_{11}},\overline{D_{12}},D_{21},D_{22}\right)$$

The first one represents the already mentioned most probable diagnoses with all disks faulty, while the second and the third one are two symmetrical diagnoses: d_2 represents a fault caused by disk failures in the first sub-system and a processor failure in the second; d_3 represents a fault caused by disk failures in the second sub-system and a processor failure in the first.

Posterior probabilities are then computed within the given error level as:

$P(d_1|Fault)=0.954223$

$P(d_2|Fault)=P(d_3|Fault)=98.87*10^{-4}$

The algorithm guarantees that any further diagnosis will have a posterior probability smaller or equal than $P(d_2|Fault$). It is worth noting that this result is in general obtained without exploring the whole state space, that in this case is equal to $2^{10}=1024$ states, being 10 the number of components.

Similar results may be obtained for complete variable assignments.

6 Conclusions and Current Research

Bayesian Networks are becoming widely used for dependability analysis of safety critical systems as the Programmable Electronic Systems (PES). During PES lifecycle, dependability analysis is performed at different levels addressing hardware, software and the whole system. Here, we have dealt with *BN* versus *FT*, a very popular technique for hardware dependability analysis. *BN* versus *FT* can address interesting questions allowing both forward and backward analysis; moreover, *BN* are more suitable to represent complex dependencies among components and to include uncertainty in modeling. Due to the presence of a software component, there is a major concern on how the overall PES dependability is evaluated. Software faults and human errors introduce design faults in PES. Probabilistic analysis of software dependability is a formidable task, for which no proven method is available. *BN* seems to be promising for sounder assessment of software dependability [3]. Overall system dependability, due the impact of design faults, is not well understood. The evaluation of overall system dependability can be obtained by considering and combining all the different sources of relevant information (evidence), including software and hardware dependability analysis [5]. The possibility of use of *BN* to support the evaluation of overall system dependability along the acceptance process of safety critical PES is under exploration. Although the use of *BN* seems to be promising at different levels of PES dependability analysis, they do not provide a direct mechanism for representing temporal dependencies, that are well implemented in popular techniques for dependability analysis, such as Markov Chains and Stochastic Petri Nets.

References

1. G. Almond: An extended example for testing Graphical Belief. Technical Report 6, Statistical Sciences Inc. (1992)
2. S.K. Andersen , K.G. Olesen , F.V. Jensen , F. Jensen: HUGIN - A Shell for Building Bayesian Belief Universes for Expert Systems. In Proc. 11th IJCAI, Detroit (1989) 1080-1085
3. K. A. Delic, F. Mazzanti, L. Strigini: Formalising Engineering judgement on software dependabiility via Belief Networks. Technical Report , SHIP (1995)
4. J. Bechta Dugan, K. S. Trivedi: Coverage modeling for dependability analysis of fault-tolerant systems. IEEE Transactions on Computers (1989), 38 , 775-787
5. N. Fenton , B. Littlewood, M.Neil, L. Strigini, A. Sutcliffe , D. Wright: Assessing Dependability of Safety critical Systems using diverse evidence. Technical Report. EEC DATUM Project
6. D. Heckermann, M. Wellman, A. Mamdani (eds.): Real-world applications of Bayesian Networks. Communications of the ACM, 38 (1995)
7. E.J. Henley, H. Kumamoto: Reliability Engineering and Risk Assessment. Prentice Hall, Englewood Cliffs (1981)
8. Knowledge Industries. DXpress 2.0 (1996)
9. N.G. Leveson. Safeware: System Safety and Computers. Addison-Wesley (1995)
10..M.Malhotra, K.Trivedi. Dependability modeling using Petri nets. IEEE Trans, on Reliability, 44 (1995) 428-440
11. Microsoft Corp. Microsoft Belief Network Tools
12. J. Pearl: Probabilistic Reasoning in Intelligent Systems. Morgan Kaufmann (1989)
13. L. Portinale, P. Torasso: A Comparative Analysis of Horn Models and Bayesian Networks for Diagnosis. Proc. 5th Italian Conference on Artificial Intelligence, Springer Verlag (1997)

FlexFi: A Flexible Fault Injection Environment for Microprocessor-Based Systems

Alfredo Benso, Maurizio Rebaudengo, and Matteo Sonza Reorda

Politecnico di Torino
Dip. Automatica e Informatica
Corso Duca degli Abruzzi 24
I-10129 Torino, Italy
{benso, reba, sonza}@polito.it

Abstract. Microprocessor-based systems are increasingly used to control safety-critical systems (e.g., air and railway traffic control, nuclear plant control, aircraft and car control). In this case, fault tolerance mechanisms are introduced at the hardware and software level. Debugging and verifying the correct design and implementation of these mechanisms ask for effective environments, and Fault Injection represents a viable solution for their implementation. In this paper we present a flexible environment suitable to compute the fault coverage provided by hardware and software mechanisms existing in most microprocessor-based systems. The environment, called FlexFI, is flexible, since it allows the adoption of different solutions for implementing the most critical modules, which differ in terms of cost, speed, and intrusiveness in the original system behavior.

1. Introduction

Our society is facing an increasing dependence on computing systems, especially in areas (e.g., air and railway traffic control, nuclear plant control, aircraft and car control) where a failure can be critical for the safety of human beings. Safety-critical systems often incorporate levels of redundancy to guarantee the correct execution of the service in order to tolerate or simply signal the presence of possible faults that can cause system failure. Redundancy implies an additional cost in the overall system. Moreover, the design and production flow of these systems must be different from the traditional ones, and allow guaranteeing that the fault tolerance characteristics are correctly designed and implemented. For these reasons, new CAD tools and environments are required, which support the designer and production engineers in the task of producing truly reliable systems.

Unlike performance, fault tolerance and reliability can not be evaluated through the use of benchmark programs and standard test methodologies, but only by observing the behavior of the system (or of a model) when a fault appears. *Fault Injection* (FI), the deliberate insertion of faults into an operational system to determine its response, has been recognized [1] as a powerful technique that allows studying the effects of the faults in a system when executing application programs.

M. Felici, K. Kanoun, A. Pasquini (Eds.): SAFECOMP'99, LNCS 1698, pp. 323–335, 1999
© Springer-Verlag Berlin Heidelberg 1999

Several Fault Injection techniques have been proposed and practically experimented [2]; they can basically be grouped into *simulation-based* techniques [3] [4] [15], *software-implemented* techniques [5] [6] [7], *hardware-based* techniques [8], and *hybrid* techniques [16] where hardware and software approaches are applied together to optimize the performance.

None of the mentioned approaches seems to be a global solution, since they are generally targeted to a particular computer system or they consider only particular types of applications. Moreover, none of them is specifically targeted to embedded microprocessor-based systems, and they often exploit features (such as Operating System support) which are seldom available in these systems. Finally, the introduction of computer-based devices into safety-critical mass products (e.g., in the automotive area) requires new approaches to fault tolerance evaluation, characterized by a lower cost and an easier applicability.

The goal of this paper is to present a FI environment, called *FlexFI*, which can be easily customized to the specific needs of the design of most system designs. FlexFI includes different modules for Fault List Generation and Collapsing, Fault Injection, and Result Analysis. Most of the code for Fault Injection runs on a host computer, which orchestrates the experiments and is connected to the target system exploiting existing features, normally provided for debugging purposes. Three versions of FlexFI are presented, based on a pure software solution, on a hybrid hardware-software approach, and exploiting a debugging feature (BDM) existing in most of the recent Motorola microprocessors and microcontrollers. The three versions are briefly described (more details can be found in [9] and [10] respectively) and their characteristics compared: they provide a full range of choices for the fault tolerance evaluation of an embedded system.

Section 2 outlines the general assumptions and decisions underlying the organization of the FlexFI system, Section 3 describes its architecture, and Section 4 outlines the characteristics of its three different versions. Section 5 draws some conclusions.

2. Assumptions

Fault injection allows validating dependability measures of a target system constituted by a *hardware architecture* and a *workload software application*. An *injection campaign* is composed of elementary injections, called *experiments*. In a fault injection campaign the input domain corresponds to a set of faults and a set of input stimuli, while the output domain corresponds to a set of observation points of the faulty system behavior and a set of measures dependability measures obtained through the Fault Injection.

2.1 Faults

The fault model we selected is the transient single bit flip. This model is frequently used in fault injection tools [4] [6] since it is very similar to the faults occurring in real systems [Lala85]. Each fault is characterized by the following information:
- *fault injection time*: each fault is injected at the assembly level, before the execution of a machine level instruction. The fault injection time is thus expressed

in terms of number of instructions executed since the beginning of the application execution;

- *fault location*: the address of the memory location or the register where the fault has to be injected;
- *fault mask*: the bit mask that selects the bit(s) that has (have) to be flipped.

Therefore, each fault corresponds to flipping a single bit in a microprocessor register or in the memory area containing either the code or the data at a given time instant (e.g., executed instruction) during the program execution. A *golden run* experiment is performed in advance by executing the same code with the same activation trajectory, but without injecting any fault. The information gathered from the golden run experiment are used as a reference for fault list generation and collapsing.

The size of the fault list is a crucial parameter for any kind of Fault Injection campaign, because it dramatically affects the feasibility and meaningfulness of the whole campaign. For this reason, our environment includes a module for fault list collapsing, which is based on the techniques presented in [11].

The adopted approach aims at reducing the fault list size in a fault injection environment, by applying the set of Fault Collapsing rules presented in [11]. Those rules do not affect the accuracy of the results gathered in the following Fault Injection experiments, but simply aim at avoiding the injection of those faults whose behavior can be foreseen a priori. The validity of the collapsing rules is bounded to the specific Fault Injection environment which is going to be performed, and to the set of input data stimuli the target system is going to receive. Experimental results gathered with some benchmark programs show that the average reduction in the obtained fault list size thanks to the proposed collapsing techniques is about 40% [11].

2.2 Input Stimuli

Two important issues relate to this point:

- how to determine an input trajectory to be applied to the target system during each FI experiment; several proposals have been made to solve this general problem. In this paper, we do not deal with this problem, but we limit our interest to the techniques for performing the FI campaign, once the trajectory is known.
- how to practically apply the trajectory to the system; this issue is particularly critical when considering embedded systems, since they often own a high number of input signals of different types (digital and analog, high- and low-frequency, etc.). In general, the only viable solution requires setting up a suitable environment around the target system, able to excite it with the right stimula. This environment is often the same which is used for performing the behavioral and final testing of the system.

2.3 Faulty system behavior observation and classification

At the end of the FI campaign, a proper tool produces a report concerning the dependability measures. A major figure is the fault coverage computed with respect to the whole Fault List.

This information is obtained by observing the system behavior after fault injection, and identifying the differences with respect to the fault-free system behavior. By incidence, this requires implementing some time-out mechanism for the identification of faults forcing the system in endless loops. Note that all the operations involved by the observation task should also be minimally intrusive.

Fault coverage is defined with respect to some Error Detection Mechanism (EDM). Microprocessor systems usually provide some mechanisms to detect faults, such as:

- Hardware EDMs, i.e., system exceptions, built-in in the processor chip;
- Software EDMs, i.e., software checks, possibly inserted in the target application.
  Faults are classified into one of the following categories:
- *Fail-Silent* behavior: the fault does not produce any failure;
- *Detected by an EDM*: the fault triggers a system exception (such as *illegal instruction, divide by zero, address fault, access fault, bus error, privilege violation*) or a software EDM. Upon exception triggering, an *exception routine* is executed to possibly recover from the error or to halt the system.
- *Fail-Silent Violation* behavior: the target application terminates correctly but produces incorrect results;
- *Time-out*: the number of executed instructions exceeds a user-defined limit (e.g., because the target application entered into an endless loop).

3. The FlexFi Environment: overall architecture

The architecture of the FlexFI environment is shown in Fig. 1. The system is composed of the following main modules:

- the *Fault List Manager* generates the fault list to be injected into the target system;
- the *Fault Injection Manager* injects the faults into the target system;
- the *Result Analyzer* collects the results and produces a report concerning the whole Fault Injection campaign.

To minimize the intrusiveness into the target system, the FlexFI system uses a host computer, which is in charge of performing some of the tasks listed above. In particular, all the FI tasks which are not strictly required to run on the target system are located on the host computer, which also stores all the data structures (e.g., the Fault List, and the output statistics) required by the FI campaign. The host computer communicates with the target system, by exploiting the features provided by most systems for debugging purposes (e.g., the serial line handled by a ROM monitor which allows the debugging of most microprocessors).

This solution presents several advantages:

- The intrusiveness into the target system is minimal. Only a very small amount of additional code for FI is stored and executed on the target system. Moreover, almost no code modification is required on the target application.
- The overall environment is more robust; in fact, if any fault causes the target system to crash, the host computer can keep the control of the environment, reset the target system, and resume the execution of the experiment. In this way, the memory image of the target application is also stored in a safe place (i.e., the host computer memory) and can be easily restored in the target system before the ex-

Target System   Host Computer

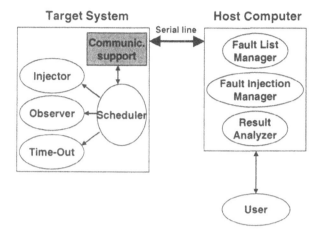

Fig. 1. Architecture of the FlexFI system

ecution of each FI experiment. Likewise, the fault list and the result information
are safe; they cannot be corrupted by a target system crash or by an error in the
memory area storing them.

• The user of the FI environment can enjoy a more usable and friendly interface
running on the host computer.

Care must be taken to limit the slow-down factor caused by the communication
operations performed through the serial interface.

3.1 Fault Injection Manager

The Fault Injection Manager (FIM) is the most crucial part in the whole Fault
Injection system. In fact, it is up to the FIM to start the execution of the target
application once for each fault in the list generated by the Fault List Manager, to
inject the fault at the required time and location, and to observe the system behavior,
recovering from any possible faulty behavior (e.g., from hardware generated
exceptions). The pseudo-code of the FIM is reported in Fig. 2.

During the target application execution, a *FI scheduler* monitors the advancement
of the target program, triggering other FI modules in charge of injecting the fault
(*Injector* module), observing variable values in order to classify the faulty behavior
(*Observer* module), or stop the target application when a time-out condition is
reached (*Time-out* module).

The pseudo-code of the FI scheduler module is reported in Fig. 3. Note that the
Observer module refers to an ad hoc data structure, which contains the list of
observation points; for each point, this data structure contains the name of the
variable, the time when the variable should be observed, as well as the value the
variable should have at that time. The list must be filled by the application
programmer based on the knowledge of the behavior of the application itself.

In order to allow the FIM to maintain the control over the FI campaign, a
mechanism has to be devised and implemented to handle the case, in which a hard-

```
void fault_injection_manager()
{
        campaign_initialization();
        /* Experiment Control Loop */
        for( every fault f_i in the fault list)
        {
          experiment_initialization(f_i);
          spawn(target_application() );
          spawn(FI_scheduler(f_i) );
          update_fault_record(f_i);
        }
        return();
}
```

Fig. 2. Fault Injection Manager pseudo-code

```
void FI_scheduler(FAULT f_i)
{
        instr_counter++;
        if (instr_counter==fault.time[f_i])
        trigger( injector());
        for( k=0; k<num_of_observation_points; k++)
            if (instr_counter==observation_time[k])
            trigger( observer( observed_variable[k],
value[k]));
        if (instr_counter > max_time)
        trigger( time_out());
}
```

Fig. 3. Scheduler module Pseudo-code

ware exception is activated, and the target application is consequently interrupted. The target system exception handling procedures have to be suitably modified for this purpose, so that they first communicate to the FIM the type of triggered exception, and then return the control to the FIM itself (instead of the interrupted instruction).

It is worth underlying the importance of the experiment initialization phase. The effects of the fault injected during an experiment should in no way affect the behavior of the target application when the following experiment is performed; for this reason, the FI system must restore the environment for the target application execution as a preliminary phase of each experiment: one safe (but slow) way to do so is to restore the full memory image of the application (code and data) and the values of all the relevant system variables. The main issue when implementing this restoring task is to limit its time duration as much as possible, in order to reduce the time requirement of the global FI campaign.

In the following, we will present different techniques for implementing these modules in an embedded system.

4. The FlexFI environment: specialized versions

After having described the general architecture of the FlexFI system, we now propose three different solutions for implementing it. The three solutions differ in terms of intrusiveness, speed, and cost, thus offering a full range of possible choices for dealing with fault-tolerant embedded systems:

- the *Software-based* version [9] is a software-based technique which exploits the trace exception mode available in most microprocessors; it represents a low-cost approach, whose main limitations are the time intrusiveness and the relatively high slow-down factor.
- the *Hybrid* version [10] is a hybrid technique in which faults are injected via software by means of an interrupt procedure triggered by an extra hardware board; time intrusiveness is very limited in this case, at the cost of developing a custom piece of hardware devoted to FI.
- the *BDM-based* version [12] exploits the Background Diagnostic Mode [Moto96] existing in most of the recent microprocessor and microcontroller kernels produced by Motorola. The advantages of hardware solutions are reached in this case by simply exploiting a feature provided for free by the processor.

Each of the three versions has been implemented in a prototypical tool to practically verify its characteristics. Details are provided on the resulting prototypical system.

4.1 Software-based version

This version exploits the Trace Mode facility existing in most microprocessors for implementing the FI scheduler: thanks to the trace mechanism, a small procedure (corresponding to the FI scheduler) can be activated after the execution of any application assembly instruction with minimum intrusiveness in the system behavior (apart from a slow-down in the application performance).

The *FI scheduler* procedure is in charge of counting the number of executed instructions and verifying whether any FI module reached its activation point. When proper, the procedure activates one of the following modules, each corresponding to a software procedure stored on the target system:

- the *Injector* module, which is activated when the fault injection time is reached.
- the *Time-out* module, which is activated when a predefined threshold in terms of number of executed instructions is reached, and stops the target application, returning the control to the FIM.
- The *Observer* module, which is in charge of observing the value of target application variables, thus checking whether the application is behaving as in the fault-free fashion or not. When differences are observed, these are communicated to the FIM through the serial interface. The observer module is activated at proper times, depending on the target application characteristics.

4.1.1 Prototypical tool
We implemented the software-based version of FlexFI for a commercial M68KIDP Motorola board [13]. This board hosts a M68040 microprocessor with a 25Mhz frequency clock, 2 Mbytes of RAM memory, 2 RS-232 Serial I/O Channels, a Parallel Printer Port, and a bus-compatible Ethernet card.

The Fault Injection Manager is composed of the scheduler procedure which amounts to about 50 Assembly code lines, of the modified exception handling routine which needs about 10 Assembly code lines more than the original one, and of the

Initialization procedure that is written partly in ISO-C and partly in Assembly language and globally amounts to about 200 source lines. Due to the high modularity of the FIM code, the task of adapting it to a new application program can easily be accomplished.

When run on some sample benchmark applications, this version of FlexFI showed a slow-down factor due to Fault Injection of about 25 times.

4.1.2 Comments

The software-based version of FlexFI is the most general one (the approach can be implemented on virtually any system) and does not require any special hardware, thus being very inexpensive.

On the other side, this approach has some drawbacks:

- there is some code intrusiveness, due to the need for storing the Scheduler procedure, as well as the Injector, Observer, and Time-out procedures, in the target system memory
- there is also some data intrusiveness, since some small data structures, such as the one for storing the information about the current fault and the observation points, must also be stored in the target system memory
- forcing the target system to work in Trace mode causes a serious degradation in the execution speed of the application program: this reduces the number of FI experiments that can be performed, and often prevents this approach from being used when real-time systems are considered.

4.2 Hybrid solution

This solution overcomes the major drawbacks of the previous software-based solution, at the cost of introducing some custom hardware. An external board is exploited during the Fault Injection experiment to implement the scheduler.

The board is equivalent to a low-cost and specialized logic-analyzer. It is connected to the target system bus and is able to count the number of executed instructions by monitoring the values of the *processor status pins*. When one of the pre-defined points is reached, the board activates an interrupt protocol and trigger the proper FI module. Running concurrently with the target processor, the board avoids the overhead introduced by the software-based version. Therefore, the execution speed of the target system is not changed during the FI experiment, and the environment can be effectively exploited for evaluating real-time applications.

The board can work in two different modes:

- in *off-line mode*, it acts as a peripheral device, and can properly receive and react to read and write commands from the target system CPU
- in *on-line mode*, it continuously monitors the processor status pins, and counts the number of executed instructions from the last start command; as soon as the instruction counter matches the *injection time*, the board sends an interrupt to the processor. The interrupt handling routine is in charge of injecting the fault.

During the experiment initialization phase, the host computer must program the board by sending it the following commands:

- `set_injection`: it defines the fault injection time, i.e., the number of executed instructions before the fault injection
- `set_timeout`: it defines the time-out threshold, i.e., the maximum number of instructions that can be executed before stopping the experiment
- `set_observation_point`: it defines an observation point, corresponding to a 3-tuple composed of an observation time (in terms of number of instructions), a variable address, and a variable value.
- `start`: the board begins to count the instructions executed by the processor
- `stop`: the board switches to off-line mode.

At the end of every fault injection experiment (no matter its result), the control returns to the Fault Injector Manager, which classifies the fault according to the observed system behavior and updates the statistics stored on the host computer.

4.2.1 Prototypical version
We implemented a prototypical version of the board, which is customized for a MC68040 microprocessor. The FI board has then been evaluated on the same commercial M68KIDP Motorola system used for the software-based version of FlexFI described in the previous subsection. In our implementation, the board is a memory-mapped device, thus allowing the CPU to program and control it through simple memory writes and read instructions. The board has been implemented using two Programmable Logic Devices, thus guaranteeing its re-programmability and flexibility. The board includes 2 Xilinx XC3130 FPGAs, a 256 K x 56 bits memory, and some glue logic. Its manufacturing cost is about 500 US $. Although in the current version the board has been customized for a MC68040 microprocessor, the same approach can be easily adapted to other families of microprocessors.

When run on sample benchmark applications, the hybrid version of FlexFI showed a slow-down which was exclusively due to the time required by the experiment initialization phase, and thus strongly dependent on the size of the memory image of the target application, and on the speed of the communication link between the target system and the host computer.

4.2.2 Comments
The intrusiveness of the fault injection process into the target system from the point of view of the execution speed is practically removed, so that this version of the FlexFI system can be adopted to deal with real-time embedded systems.

On the negative side, this solution requires the design and implementation of a hardware device which should match the characteristics of the specific target system.

4.3 BDM-based solution

The most recent Motorola microprocessors and microcontroller devices feature a special mode of operation called Background Debugging Mode (BDM) [14]. When enabled, this mode allows an external host processor to control the target microcontroller unit (MCU) and access both memory and I/O devices via a simple serial interface. BDM was originally introduced to easy code development and debugging, but can be also well suited for supporting the implementation of efficient and barely intrusive Fault Injection systems.

During the fault injection experiment, the application program is executed in debugging mode and BDM is in charge of resetting the system, downloading the application target program, executing the fault injection, and triggering a possible time-out condition. The method allows the injection of faults both in the memory image of the process (data and code) and in the internal registers of the processor.

To allow BDM to perform fault injection, the injection time is converted in the following format:

- *Instruction address*: the address of the instruction to be interrupted for fault injection
- *Instruction repetition*: the number of times *n* the considered instruction has to be executed before injecting the fault.

During the experiment initialization, the FIM sets a breakpoint at the instruction corresponding to the considered fault. Thanks to the above mentioned breakpoint, the *scheduler* process is activated at every execution of the instruction where the fault has to be injected. At its n-th activation, the scheduler activates the *injector*. Note that in this version the scheduler is a software module running on the host computer, while the injector corresponds to a single BDM command that modifies the memory location or user register determined by the content of the fault location field.

After the fault has been injected in the system, its behavior has to be observed, and the differences with respect to the fault-free system behavior have to be identified. When temporal constraints are not the main concern, this can be done by observing the values of some specified variables when a given point in the target program execution is reached. A suitable sequence of BDM commands has been included in the *observer* module. Preliminarily, a breakpoint is set each time a variable or register must be observed: every time one of these breakpoints is reached, the scheduler is activated, and issues a BDM command, which accesses the variable or register value and verifies whether it corresponds to the fault-free value or not.

Also the *Time-out* module is managed by BDM and programmed by the host processor. A BDM command sets the *watchdog* period to a time exceeding the one needed by the fault-free execution. If the program is still running when the watchdog period limit is reached, it is stopped, the fault is classified as "time-out", and the experiment continues by injecting the next fault in the list.

4.3.1 Practical Experience

A prototypical version of the described Fault Injection environment has been implemented on the commercial Evaluation Board LA-7902 produced by Lauterbach GmbH. This board hosts a MC68332 microcontroller with a 16Mhz frequency clock, 128 kbytes of RAM memory and a V.24 interface. The BDM interface is managed by the TRACE32-ICD commercial tool produced by Lauterbach GmbH. The host computer is an 80486 PC with a 33Mhz frequency clock, 16 Mbytes of RAM memory, running Microsoft Windows95 Operating System.

The whole Fault Injection system is composed of about 500 lines of BDM program written in the PRACTICE language and running on the host computer. Apart from the module implementing the *observer* module, the system can be easily adapted to deal with any target application program.

When running it on the usual benchmark applications, we observed two kinds of slow-down phenomena. The first one is due to the time required by the experiment initialization phase, and is dependent on the size of the memory image of the target application, which is downloaded on the target system before every FI experiment starts. The second one is due to the fact that forcing the microprocessor into the BDM mode causes its clock to slow-down by a factor equal to about 2 times.

4.3.2 Comments

The approach is minimally intrusive in terms of code modification: the only required modification on the application software is the one concerning the exception procedures. It is also easily portable from one system to another, provided that BDM availability is given.

A certain slow-down in the execution time of the target application can be observed, mainly due to the slow-down on the system clock forced by the activation of the BDM mode. Due to this fact, this approach requires special care in order to be exploited with real-time applications.

4.4 Summary

In this subsection we provide the reader with a comparative overview of the different versions of the FlexFI system, gathering the results of the practical experiences we made with our prototypical system.

First of all, Table 1 summarizes the ways in which the critical modules of the FIM are implemented in the three versions. FW stands for firmware, being the BDM commands implemented in the microcode of the processor. Experiment initialization mainly aims at rebuilding the proper environment for the fault to be injected, by downloading from the host computer the target application memory image in the system and setting up the system variables.

Table 1. implementation solutions for the main modules of the FIM.

	FI scheduler	Injector Observer Time-out	Experiment Initialization
SW-based	SW	SW	ROM Monitor
Hybrid	HW	SW	ROM Monitor
BDM-based	FW	FW	FW

Table 2 summarizes the main characteristics of the three versions in terms of cost (for equipment and for development), intrusiveness, and speed.

Table 2. comparing the characteristics of the three versions of the FlexFI system.

	Cost		Intrusiveness	Speed
	for equipment	for development		
SW-based	Low	High	High	Low
Hybrid	Medium	Medium	Low	High
BDM-based	Low	Low	Low	Medium

Table 2 shows that the three versions of the FlexFI system, although easily interchangeable within the environment, have complementary characteristics, thus providing the designer with a high flexibility in choosing the best suited solution to his needs.

5. Conclusions

When evaluating the fault tolerance mechanisms of microprocessor-based systems used in safety-critical applications, the designer needs a suitable environment allowing to effectively perform FI experiments.

The paper describes the architecture of the FlexFI system, which is particularly suited for microprocessor-based systems, and whose main characteristic is that it is customizable to the specific needs of the considered application. In particular, we presented three versions of FlexFI, which allow the designer to choose the best solution in terms of cost, intrusiveness, and speed of the FI experiments. Prototypical implementations of the three versions have been built to verify their feasibility and effectiveness, and a comparison between their characteristics has been reported.

Further work is currently being done to improve FlexFI from the point of view of user friendliness and ease of use, and to evaluate it on other applications.

6. References

1.   J. Clark, D. Pradhan, *Fault Injection: A method for Validating Computer-System Dependability*, IEEE Computer, June 1995, pp. 47-56
2.   M.C. Hsueh, T. Tsai, R.K. Iyer, *Fault Injection Techniques and Tools*, IEEE Computer, April 1997, pp. 75-82
3.   E. Jenn, J. Arlat, M. Rimen, J. Ohlsson, J. Karlsson, *Fault injection into VHDL Models: the MEFISTO Tool*, FTCS-24, 1994, pp. 66-75
4.   T.A. Delong, B.W. Johnson, J.A. Profeta III, *A Fault Injection Technique for VHDL Behavioral-Level Models*, IEEE Design & Test of Computers, Winter 1996, pp. 24-33
5.   J. Carreira, H. Madeira, J. Silva, *Xception: Software Fault Injection and Monitoring in Processor Functional Units*, DCCA-5, Conference on Dependable Computing for Critical Applications, 1995, pp. 135-149
6.   G.A. Kanawati, N.A. Kanawati, J.A. Abraham, *FERRARI: A Flexible Software-Based Fault and Error Injection System*, IEEE Trans. on Computers, Vol 44, N. 2, February 1995, pp. 248-260
7.   S. Han, K.G. Shin, H.A. Rosenberg, *Doctor: An Integrated Software Fault-Injection Environment for Distributed Real-Time Systems*, IEEE Int. Computer Performance and Dependability Symposium, 1995, pp. 204-213
8.   J. Arlat, M. Aguera, L. Amat, Y. Crouzet, J.C. Fabre, J.-C. Laprie, E. Martins, D. Powell, *Fault Injection for Dependability Validation: A Methodology and some Applications*, IEEE Transactions on Software Engineering, Vol. 16, No. 2, February 1990, pp. 166-182
9.   A. Benso, P. Prinetto, M. Rebaudengo, M. Sonza Reorda, "*A Fault Injection Environment for Microprocessor-based Boards*", IEEE International Test Conference, 1998, pp. 768-773

11. A. Benso, M. Rebaudengo, L. Impagliazzo, P. Marmo, *"Fault List Collapsing for Fault Injection Experiments"*, Annual Reliability and Maintainability Symposium, 1998, pp. 383-388

12. P. Prinetto, M. Rebaudengo, M. Sonza Reorda, *Exploiting the Background Debugging Mode in a Fault Injection system*, IEEE International Computer Performance and Dependability Symposium, 1998, pag. 277

13. Motorola Inc., *M68000 Family Programmer's Reference Manual - M68000PM/AD*, 1992

14. Motorola Inc., *A Background Debugging Mode Driver Package for Modular Microcontrollers*, by S. Howard, Motorola Semiconductor Application Note AN1230/D, 1996

15. A. M. Amendola, A. Benso, F. Corno, L. Impagliazzo, P. Marmo, P. Prinetto, M. Rebaudengo, M. Sonza Reorda, *Fault Behavior Observation of a Microprocessor System through a VHDL Simulation-Based Fault Injection Experiment*, EURO-VHDL'96, 1996, pp. 536-541

16. A. Benso, P.L. Civera, M. Rebaudengo, M. Sonza Reorda "*A low-cost programmable board for speeding-up Fault Injection in microprocessor-based systems*", Annual Reliability and Maintainability Symposium, 1999, pp. 171-177

Structural Software Reliability Estimation

Silke Kuball, John May, and Gordon Hughes

Safety Systems Research Centre, Department of Computer Science, University of
Bristol, Merchant Venturers Building, Woodland Road, Bristol BS8 1UB, UK,
{silke, jhrm, hughes}@cs.bris.ac.uk

Abstract. Structure is introduced to the process of software reliability estimation. An estimator for the overall software failure rate is constructed using estimators of subtask–failure rates. This is done for the case when testing reveals no failure. The obtained estimator depends on the number of subtasks present in the code and on the code structure. The model proposed covers sequential and simple branching structures.

1 Background

Methods for software reliability estimation become increasingly relevant with the growing routine use of computers in many safety–critical applications such as nuclear power plants, chemical process plants and aircraft. An assessment of the inherent risk associated with the use of computer–based systems is an important part of the licensing process. Safety–critical applications are becoming progressively sophisticated, and it appears to be an empirical rule of thumb that more sophistication requires greater system complexity with greater scope for systematic failure. Yet the literature does not contain any formal understanding of the implications of complexity for safety.

The most widely accepted and used models for the purpose of estimating systematic reliability are statistical system testing (SST) models. The aim of statistical system testing is the estimation of the system's failure rate which is interpreted as the probability of failure on demand. Estimation is performed based on the results of N independent test runs. A demand is an input generated by the software's environment. A test input is randomly generated according to the software's operational input distribution (OID). In this paper, the special case is considered where testing reveals no failure. A traditional and widely used approach for software failure rate estimation when testing reveals no failure is the Single Urn Model (SUM model) by Miller et al. [1]. In this model the Bayes theorem is used to derive a distribution for the software failure rate when N successful black–box tests have been performed. The strength of this model lies in the possibility to make use of prior information about the system's failure behaviour. However, constructing a prior density for a complex system is very difficult, and thus uniform prior functions are used in order to express the absence of specific prior functions. This does, however, not allow expression of

M. Felici, K. Kanoun, A. Pasquini (Eds.): SAFECOMP'99, LNCS 1698, pp. 336–349, 1999
© Springer-Verlag Berlin Heidelberg 1999

differences in complexity, for example differences in size, between different software versions. Therefore it cannot be used to explain the significance of system complexity for safety assessment. The literature contains few attempts to use system structure information in reliability estimation. Some most interesting exceptions include [2] [3] [4] [5]. However, the existing work in this field is diverse in nature and there is no consensus on a suitable approach, hence it is not widely used. There is therefore need for further research of which this is a first step.

This paper investigates how knowledge about software structure can be incorporated into the software reliability estimation process. It builds on the recently introduced *structural model for software reliabilty estimation* [May, Kuball and Hughes [6]] which extends fundamentally some earlier research [5] [7] [8]. This paper is a further significant extension of the work towards general software structures. After describing the basic principles of the structural model (section 2), this paper extends the structural model to deal with branching code (section 3.1). Examples are constructed that serve to investigate the influence of prior parameters on the overall software failure rate estimator (section 3.2). The main result of section 3 is given in Theorem 1. Section 4 contains the discussion of the new approach.

2 Methodology

2.1 Introduction

Assume a program P is split into two sequentially arranged disjoint components: C_1 and C_2. In considering a sequential arrangement of components we express the assumption that each component is executed for each input. In order to assess a reliability figure for P, the software is tested with N inputs generated according to its OID. No failure is observed. From the above assumption it is clear that C_1 receives the same number of tests as C_2, the same number as received by the whole program P. If applied to C_1, C_2 and P separately, the SUM-model with uniform priors results in the same estimator for C_1, C_2 and P, only depending on the number of successfully performed independent test runs, disregarding the length of the code executed, not to mention other aspects of structural complexity. This is counter–intuitive and as pointed out in [5], it is of general interest to investigate whether approaches to software reliability estimation which disregard software complexity provide realistic estimates at all since a potential underestimation of the software failure rate leads to an unknown level of risk. Another very important issue is that with a black–box SST approach, a prior for the overall system failure rate is required. Since, most likely, the system itself is newly developed, perhaps using Commercial–Off–the–Shelf (COTS) components, there exists no prior knowledge on the performance of this system. However, smaller subtasks of the same system have probably been used before in various contexts. For the components themselves, prior unit test data might be available. These different sources of information can only be adequately eploited when taking the internal software structure into account.

The estimation of the software failure rate as the probability of failure on demand is based on the observation of how the software performs once it is exposed to a simulation of its operational environment. It is conceivable that for a less complex software system N successful test runs might have a different implication on our belief about the system's integrity than they might have for a more complex software system. Size is one possible aspect of software–complexity since the amount of components interacting within the code influences the scope for failure occurrence. We conceive therefore that the number of components which constitute a software system and which might cause failure when interacting should influence the outcome of the failure rate estimation process.

2.2   Structural Model for Sequential Software

Assume the program P to be split into m sequentially arranged disjoint components, see Fig. 1. These components constitute the software P completely and they potentially induce failure of P when acting alone or when interacting with other components. Interaction between components exists when there is data–flow between them. In the case of sequentially arranged components it is assumed that the same components interact for all inputs.

It has to be observed that the components themselves could be fault free (correct relative to the behaviour intended for them) but still their combination faulty. In fact the situation frequently occurs where highly reliable units induce failure into a system when put into interaction with each other. A failure is an unintended input-output pair. A fault is regarded as a minimal sequence of components, which if replaced by non-faulty code can remove a failure.

Definition 1.   *1. Components are said to* **interact** *when there is data–flow between them. A sequence of interacting components (not necessarily adjacent) is called an* **interaction***.*
   2. An **admissible code–sequence** *is an interaction or a single component.*
   3. Let $\mathcal{P}$ *denote the set of all admissible code–sequences for program* P*. Let* n *denote the number of elements in* $\mathcal{P}$*.*

Let $P_i \in \mathcal{P}$ denote an interaction where the order in which the components appear in the sequence is fixed, as determined by the software's data–flow, and a component only appears once within each sequence, i.e. there are no loops. The failure behaviour of an interaction is defined as follows. Consider the interaction P_1 in Figure 1. Assume P_1 is an element of $\mathcal{P}$. We introduce the notion of **elemental failure** of P_1. Elemental failure of P_1 means failure of the interaction between C_1 and C_2 and C_3. Elemental failure of P_1 is traced back to a set of faults which when triggered by the test input causes the interaction of C_1, C_2 and C_3 to fail, but does not for example fail the interaction of only C_1 and C_2. The set of faults that cause P_1 to elementally fail can be described as the set of all faults causing failure within the code–part (C_1, C_2, C_3) minus the set of faults causing failure of the interaction between (C_1, C_2), (C_1, C_3), (C_2, C_3) or failure of the components C_1, C_2, C_3 themselves.

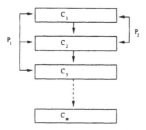

Fig. 1. Structural model with components C_i and example–subsequences P_1, P_2.

The set of faults causing elemental failure of P_1 is called **"elemental fault set"** for P_1. This means that although failure of a subsequence of $P_i \in \mathcal{P}$ will almost certainly imply failure of P_i, it does not imply elemental failure of P_i. Observing elemental failure of interaction for $P_1 \in \mathcal{P}$ and $P_2 \in \mathcal{P}$ (Fig. 1) is considered as two different events entirely. These events are based on two different sets of elemental faults respectively. Observing elemental failure or success of P_1 does not imply information on the set of faults contributing to elemental failure of P_2 and does therefore neither give information on whether P_2 fails or succeeds nor on the probability of elemental failure of P_2. The elemental failure behaviour of the interactions is therefore considered as a set of independent events. This leads to two statements:

Remark 1.   1. For each test run, let $X(P_i)$ be a random variable which indicates whether an elemental failure has occurred due to execution of $P_i \in \mathcal{P}, i = 1,\ldots,n$ (then $X(P_i) = 1$) or whether no elemental failure of P_i has been observed (then $X(P_i) = 0$). The random variables $X(P_1),\ldots,X(P_n)$ are assumed to be independent random variables.

    2. Let θ_i be a random variable describing the probability of elemental failure of $P_i \in \mathcal{P}$. $\theta_1,\ldots,\theta_n$ are assumed to be independent random variables. They are called elemental failure rates.

What effect do the above independence assumptions have when testing reveals no failure? It might be argued that observing N successful test runs for some of the interactions P_i implies high quality of the developing team and should be counted towards increasing the reliability of other interactions. Disregarding the updated confidence in P_i when assessing the posterior belief about the remaining interactions is conservative and can be accepted in order to investigate a first step of taking code size into account when assessing software reliability.

A prior density is assigned to each θ_i. For the case of sequential code, when testing is performed all N test runs proceed through all admissible code–sequences $P_i \in \mathcal{P}$. When no failure is observed, all admissible code–sequences $P_1,\ldots,P_n \in \mathcal{P}$ have been successfully tested N times. Confidence in each of the interactions and components is increased. Using Bayes' Theorem the prior belief in all $P_i \in \mathcal{P}$ will be updated according to the SUM–model using the test outcomes. Because of the above independence assumptions all priors will be updated independently from each other. The updated prior functions (posterior probability densities) are combined to produce a density function for the overall software failure rate θ of P. The following result for the posterior density of θ was derived in [6].

Assume a program P to consist of m sequential components. Assume the independence assumptions as described in Remark 1. Let n denote the number of admissible component–sequences $P_i \in \mathcal{P}$. Uniform $\beta[1,1]$–priors are asssigned to the elemental failure rates θ_i. If N tests are performed without revealing failure then the posterior probability density function for the overall program failure rate θ is

$$f^{struct}(\theta|0,N) = \frac{1}{(n-1)!} \cdot (1+N)^n \cdot (1-\theta)^N \cdot (-1)^{n-1} \cdot \ln^{n-1}(1-\theta).$$
$$Exp[\theta|0,N] = 1 - \prod_{j=1}^{n}(1 - Exp[\theta_i|0,N]) = 1 - (1 - \tfrac{1}{N+2})^n. \tag{1}$$

In the following the sequential structural model is extended to include branching of code. An estimator for the overall software failure rate θ is given in form of the posterior expected value of θ. The posterior variance of θ is given.

3 Structural Model with Branching Instructions

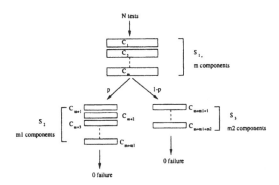

Fig. 2. Structural model with branching of code.

A program P is considered with underlying structure such as in Fig. 2. P consists of a part S_1 which is executed by all inputs and of branches S_2 and S_3 which are executed with probability p and $1 - p$ respectively. The software data–flow determines possible component–interactions. There is no interaction between components of S_2 and components of S_3. Interactions can occur within S_1, within S_2, within S_3, between components of S_1 and of S_2 and between components of S_1 and S_3.

Definition 2.   *1. Let $\bar{S}_i$, $i = 1, 2, 3$ define the set of admissible code–sequences (i.e. components and interactions) within code part S_i. Elements of $\bar{S}_i$ are called $P_j^{(i)}$, $i = 1, 2, 3$.*

2. *Let (S_1, S_2) denote the code part given by S_1 and S_2 executed in sequence. Let $\overline{S_1 S_2}$ denote the set of all admissible code–sequences in $(S_1 S_2)$.*

3. *$\overline{S_1 S_2} \backslash \bar{S}_1$ denotes the set of admissible component–sequences in code part (S_1, S_2) without those sequences belonging to $\bar{S}_1$. That means interactions between at least one component of S_1 and at least one component of S_2 and the admissible code–sequences of S_2. $\overline{S_1 S_3} \backslash \bar{S}_1$ is defined correspondingly. Elements of $\overline{S_1 S_2} \backslash \bar{S}_1$ are called $P_i^{(12-)}$, elements of $\overline{S_1 S_3} \backslash \bar{S}_1$ are called $P_i^{(13-)}$.*

The concept of elemental failure of the interactions as defined in the structural model for sequential code is adopted.

4. *The elemental failure rates of code sequences $P_j^{(i)}, i = 1, 2, 3$ are called $\theta_j^{(i)}, i = 1, 2, 3$. The elemental failure rates of $P_j^{(12-)}$ are called $\theta_j^{(12-)}$, the elemental failure rates of $P_j^{(13-)}$ are called $\theta_j^{(13-)}$.*

5. *$n_1 =$ number of elements in $\bar{S}_1$.*

6. *$n_2 =$ number of elements in $\overline{S_1 S_2} \backslash \bar{S}_1$.*

7. *$n_3 =$ number of elements in $\overline{S_1 S_3} \backslash \bar{S}_1$.*

Independent prior densities are assigned to all elemental failure rates. The independence assumptions (Remark 1) on the interaction's elemental failure behaviour carry over from the structural model for sequential code. Elemental failure of an admissible code–sequence occurs independently from elemental failure of any other admissible code–sequence. Especially in the case of branching code it is true that an input revealing success of any interaction or component in $\overline{S_1 S_2} \backslash \bar{S}_1$ does not contribute to our belief in $\overline{S_1 S_3} \backslash \bar{S}_1$'s reliability since it never enters any of the interactions or components in $\overline{S_1 S_3} \backslash \bar{S}_1$.

It is assumed that N randomly selected test runs are performed without revealing failure. For a given input observing no failure means that no failure is observed in $\overline{S_1 S_2}$ or no failure is observed for $\overline{S_1 S_3}$ depending on the input's path. An amount N_1 of tests will enter S_2, an amount $N - N_1$ of tests will enter S_3. After testing is complete, the code–sequences in $\bar{S}_1$ have been tested N times without revealing failure, the code–sequences in $\overline{S_1 S_2} \backslash \bar{S}_1$ have been tested N_1 times without revealing failure, those in $\overline{S_1 S_3} \backslash \bar{S}_1$ have been tested $N - N_1$ times without revealing failure. This information is now combined to estimate the overall software failure rate θ. Due to the independence assumptions all priors will be updated independently after the data have been observed. As in the sequential structural model this will be done using the SUM approach.

3.1   Estimation of the Overall Software Failure rate

For the above structural model with branching, θ can be expressed with the following equation.

$$\theta = 1 - \text{Prob}(0 \text{ failure in } P)$$

$$= 1 - \text{Prob}(0 \text{ failure in } \bar{S}_1) \cdot [p \cdot \text{Prob}(0 \text{ failure in } \overline{S_1 S_2} \backslash \bar{S}_1) \tag{2}$$

$$+ (1 - p) \cdot \text{Prob}(0 \text{ failure in } \overline{S_1 S_3} \backslash \bar{S}_1)] \,.$$

From the independence assumption on the sequences' elemental failure behaviour follows:

$$\theta = 1 - \prod_{j=1}^{n_1} (1 - \theta_j^{(1)}) \cdot (p \cdot \prod_{k=1}^{n_2} (1 - \theta_k^{(12-)}) + (1 - p) \cdot \prod_{h=1}^{n_3} (1 - \theta_h^{(13-)}). \tag{3}$$

A possible estimator for θ is given by the posterior expected value of θ given the observed data "N tests, whereby N_1 tests proceed through S_2 and 0 failures". When conditioned on the data, the elemental failure rates are still independent. The posterior expected value for the overall software failure rate θ can thus be calculated as follows.

$$Exp[\theta|0, N, N_1] = 1 - \prod_{j=1}^{n_1} (1 - Exp[\theta_j^{(1)}|0, N]) \cdot \Big[p \cdot \prod_{k=1}^{n_2} (1 - Exp[\theta_k^{(12-)}|0, N, N_1])$$

$$+ (1 - p) \cdot \prod_{h=1}^{n_3} (1 - Exp[\theta_h^{(13-)}|0, N, N - N_1]) \Big]. \tag{4}$$

The following statements will be used to calculate the posterior variance for θ.

Lemma 1. *Let X and Y be independent random variables whose first and second moments exist, let a, b be real numbers. Then*

i. $Var[X \cdot Y] = Exp^2[X] \cdot Var[Y] + Exp^2[Y] \cdot Var[X] + Var[X] \cdot Var[Y].$

ii. $Var[X + Y] = Var[X] + Var[Y].$

iii. $Var[a + b \cdot X] = b^2 Var[X].$

The posterior variance of θ is then obtained by the following formula.

$$Var[\theta|0, N, N_1] = Var \Big[\prod_{j=1}^{n_1} (1 - \theta_j^{(1)})|0, N \Big] \cdot \Big[p \cdot \prod_{k=1}^{n_2} (1 - Exp[\theta_k^{(12-)}|0, N_1]) +$$

$$(1 - p) \cdot \prod_{h=1}^{n_3} (1 - Exp[\theta_h^{(13-)}|0, N - N_1]) \Big]^2 +$$

$$Var \Big[p \cdot \prod_{k=1}^{n_2} (1 - \theta_k^{(12-)}) + (1 - p) \cdot \prod_{h=1}^{n_3} (1 - \theta_h^{(13-)})|0, N, N_1 \Big] \cdot$$

$$(\prod_{j=1}^{n_1} (1 - Exp[\theta_j^{(1)}|0, N]))^2 + Var \Big[\prod_{j=1}^{n_1} (1 - \theta_j^{(1)})|0, N \Big] \cdot$$

$$Var \Big[p \cdot \prod_{k=1}^{n_2} (1 - \theta_k^{(12-)}) + (1 - p) \cdot \prod_{h=1}^{n_3} (1 - \theta_h^{(13-)})|0, N, N_1 \Big]. \tag{5}$$

To assess $Exp[\theta|0, N, N_1]$ and $Var[\theta|0, N, N_1]$, the posterior distributions of the sequence elemental failure rates are required. To obtain these we apply the SUM model by Miller et al., [1] to each admissible code–sequence. In the SUM approach the likelihood of observing "0 failures in N test runs" given a software failure rate θ_i is modelled as Binomial$[N, \theta_i]$ distribution. Using a conjugate $\beta[a, b]$ prior for θ_i it then follows from the Bayes Theorem that:

$$f(\theta_i|0, N) = \frac{(1-\theta_i)^N \cdot (\theta_i)^{a-1}(1-\theta_i)^{b-1}}{\int_{\theta_i} (1-\theta_i)^N \cdot (\theta_i)^{a-1}(1-\theta_i)^{b-1} d\theta_i}$$

$$= \frac{1}{B[a, N+b]} \cdot \theta_i^{a-1}(1-\theta_i)^{N+b-1} = \beta[a, N+b]. \tag{6}$$

Hereby $B[a, N+b]$ denotes the complete Beta function. The posterior expected value and the posterior variance for θ_i are given by:

$$Exp[\theta_i|0, N] = \frac{a}{a+b+N}.$$

$$Var[\theta_i|0, N] = \frac{a \cdot (N+b)}{(a+N+b)^2 \cdot (a+N+b+1)}. \tag{7}$$

In order to evaluate (4) and (5), the prior–parameters a, b have to be specified for each elemental failure rate. In [1] a single prior for the failure rate of the whole program P is needed. The structural model however requires elemental priors which describe the failure behaviour of subtasks. Thus construction of priors is brought down to a more elemental level. A distinction is possible between more complicated tasks in the code and simple tasks, a distinction which is not feasible without including structure into the software reliability estimation process.

To make a start, the posterior expectation and variance will be calculated for the special case where all priors are given by the same set of parameters $a, b \in [0, 1]$.

Lemma 2. *Let $\theta_1, \ldots, \theta_m$ be independent random variables, all with the same marginal density function $\beta[a, b]$. Then*

$$Var[(1 - \theta_1) \cdot (1 - \theta_2) \cdot \ldots \cdot (1 - \theta_m)] = \sum_{j=1}^{m} (1 - \tfrac{a}{a+b})^{2(m-j)} \cdot \binom{m}{j} \cdot \left(\frac{ab}{(a+b)^2 \cdot (a+b+1)}\right)^j$$

$$= [Exp^2[(1 - \theta_1)] + Var[(1 - \theta_1)]]^m - Exp[(1 - \theta_1)]^{2m}.$$

Proof by induction, using the formulae for expected value and variance of the $\beta[a, b]$ distribution.

Theorem 1. *Let the independence assumptions as specified under the structural model with branching instructions hold. Assume a program P has been tested N times without revealing failure whereby N_1 test runs have proceeded through branch S_2. Let the elemental failure rate priors be $\beta[a, b]$ densities.*

A) *The posterior expected value for the overall program failure rate θ is given by*

$$\hat{\theta} = Exp[\theta|0, N, N_1] = 1 - (1 - \tfrac{a}{a+N+b})^{n_1} \cdot [p \cdot (1 - \tfrac{a}{a+N_1+b})^{n_2}$$

$$+ (1 - p) \cdot (1 - \tfrac{a}{a+(N-N_1)+b})^{n_3}].$$

B) *Let*

$$\Pi_1 = [(1 - \tfrac{a}{a+b+N})^2 + \tfrac{a(b+N)}{(a+b+N)^2(a+b+N+1)}]^{n_1} - (1 - \tfrac{a}{a+b+N})^{2n_1}.$$

$$\Pi_2 = [(1 - \tfrac{a}{a+b+N_1})^2 + \tfrac{a(b+N_1)}{(a+b+N_1)^2(a+b+N_1+1)}]^{n_2} - (1 - \tfrac{a}{a+b+N_1})^{2n_2}.$$

$$\Pi_3 = [(1 - \tfrac{a}{a+b+(N-N_1)})^2 + \tfrac{a(b+(N-N_1))}{(a+b+(N-N_1))^2(a+b+(N-N_1)+1)}]^{n_3}$$

$$- (1 - \tfrac{a}{a+b+(N-N_1)})^{2n_3}.$$

Then

$$Var[\theta|0, N, N_1] = \left[(1 - \tfrac{a}{a+b+N})^{2n_1} + \Pi_1\right] \cdot (p^2\Pi_2 + (1-p)^2\Pi_3)$$

$$+ \Pi_1 \cdot \left[p(1 - \tfrac{a}{a+b+N_1})^{n_2} + (1-p)(1 - \tfrac{a}{a+b+(N-N_1)})^{n_3}\right]^2.$$

Proof. Admissible code–sequences in S_1 have been N times tested without revealing failure. Under the specified prior assumptions their elemental failure rates have posterior density $\beta[a, N + b]$. Elements in $\overline{S_1 S_2}\backslash\overline{S_1}$ and $\overline{S_1 S_3}\backslash\overline{S_1}$ have been tested N_1 times and $N - N_1$ times respectively without revealing failure. The posterior densities of their elemental failure rates are therefore $\beta[a, N_1 + b]$ and $\beta[a, N - N_1 + b]$ densities respectively.

A) Using the specified independence assumptions, the formula for the posterior expected value follows from (4) and (7).

B) Under the given independence assumptions, Π_1, Π_2 and Π_3 follow from Lemma 2 and (7). Using (5) they can be combined to produce the posterior variance.

□

In the case where the priors have different parameters a_i, b_i, the formula for the calculation of $Var(\theta|0, N, N_1)$ becomes quite lengthy. But the principle stays the same, Lemma 1 i. is applied stepwise using (7) until the Variance in (5) is evaluated. In the case of identical parameters a, b, the formula could be simplified to yield the result of Theorem 1 B).

So far, a theoretical model has been developed to investigate the influence of structural characteristics on the overall software failure rate. It is necessary to understand the issues of the detailed mathematical model first. Then it will become clear how to approximate this model by a simpler model which is practically simpler to use. A first step to detect some interesting issues is to start off with a constructed example. This serves to detect sensitivity of the estimation result to prior assumptions by changing the priors for one subbranch consecutively while keeping the remaining priors constant. This is done in the next section and some initial results outlined. Starting from these initial insights, two paths of future work emerge. Firstly, theoretical work which aims to extend the model to comprise more complex cases, first of all the case of structures which fork and then join again. To deal with these structures, it is necessary to understand how to model the set of interactions for these structures and what the implications of N failure–free test runs are within the context of these structures. Research work is ongoing to formalize a valuable approach. Secondly, the models achieved so far need to be tested on real examples. We currently plan experiments to test this model on a real–life example provided by our sponsors. From the results we hope to gain insight on how to further develop the existing model with the long–term aim to generate a practically applicable tool.

3.2   Example

The overall software failure rate θ for a simple example program P, see Fig. 3 will be estimated using the structural model for branching software. The posterior expected value of θ as given in Theorem 1 is used as estimator. It is assumed

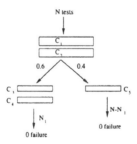

Fig. 3. Example for branching code with 5 components.

that all subsequences in (S_1, S_2) and (S_1, S_3) are *admissible* code–sequences. The aim in this section is to study the effect of assigning different levels of prior reliability to the elements of $\mathcal{P}$ or the elements of $\overline{S_1 S_3} \backslash \overline{S}_1$.

Five cases are examined and their results compared to the results obtained with the sequential structural model and the SUM–model respectively. In the following, the choice of prior parameters is described. Table 1 contains the estimation results.

In the first case, all elemental priors are set to be $\beta[1, 1]$. The prior expected value for each θ_i is then 0.5. In the second case we assume the following szenario.

Component C_5 has high complexity and is therefore given a prior failure rate density $\beta[2,1]$ to express that it incorporates a difficult subtask. For the same reason, interactions between S_1 and S_3 are assumed to be subject to low prior credibility. Assuming the same developing team for all components, the priors for elements in $\overline{S_1 S_3} \backslash \bar{S}_1$ are chosen as $\beta[2,1]$ priors, i.e. their prior expected value is approximately 0.7, their variance approxiamtely 0.06. All other priors are left as $\beta[1,1]$. In the third case, we assume that the component C_5 as well as its interactions with S_1 are well-known subtasks, the performance of which has been monitored as highly reliable in various other contexts. Hence, the elements of $\overline{S_1 S_3} \backslash \bar{S}_1$ are treated as a priori $\beta[1/99,1]$ distributed, i.e. the prior expected value is shifted to the smaller value of 0.01. Again, all other priors are left as $\beta[1,1]$ densities to observe the effect of just this change in prior assumptions. Case number four assumes $\beta[\frac{1}{99},1]$ priors for all interactions and components. This simulates the fact that all constituents of P and their interaction are a priori believed to have high reliability. In case five again the priors of $\overline{S_1 S_3} \backslash \bar{S}_1$ are now changed to $\beta[2,1]$ and all others remain $\beta[\frac{1}{99},1]$ priors. The influence of these different subsystem prior assumptions on the overall software failure rate estimator will be examined. It is to be expected that the existence of less reliable interactions and components in $\overline{S_1 S_3} \backslash \bar{S}_1$ increases the failure rate estimator according to the weight of these components in the whole software systen P, i.e. their usage and their number. If the same interactions and components are assumed to be a priori reliable and the observed data confirm this assumption, the effect will be as if failure of that part of the software was negligible, i.e. as if only failure of the sequence (S_1, S_2) mattered. Therefore it is to be expected that the resulting failure rate estimator will be similar to the result obtained with the structural model for sequential code for the system (S_1, S_2) with 4 components.

The formulae for the calculation of the posterior expected value and the posterior variance of θ when differing prior parameters are used are given below.

$$\hat{\theta} = 1 - (1 - \tfrac{a_1}{a_1+b_1+N})^{n_1} \left[p(1 - \tfrac{a_2}{a_2+b_2+N_1})^{n_2} + (1-p)(1 - \tfrac{a_3}{a_3+b_3+(N-N_1)})^{n_3} \right].$$

$$Var[\theta|0, N, N_1] = \left[(1 - \tfrac{a_1}{a_1+b_1+N})^{2n_1} + \Pi_1 \right] \cdot (p^2 \Pi_2 + (1-p)^2 \Pi_3)$$
$$+ \Pi_1 \left[p(1 - \tfrac{a_2}{a_2+b_2+N_1})^{n_2} + (1-p)(1 - \tfrac{a_3}{a_3+b_3+(N-N_1)})^{n_3} \right]^2.$$

The parameters a_i, b_i, $i = 1, 2, 3$ are the prior parameters assigned to $\theta_j^{(1)}$, $\theta_k^{(12-)}$ and $\theta_h^{(13-)}$ respectively, and they are used to calculate the values of Π_1, Π_2 and Π_3 as in Theorem 1 B). The following parameters are used for the computations.

1. Number of components in $S_1 = 2 \Rightarrow n_1 = 2^2 - 1 = 3$.
2. Number of components in $S_2 = 2 \Rightarrow n_2 = 2^4 - 2^2 = 12$.
3. Number of components in $S_3 = 1 \Rightarrow n_3 = 2^3 - 2^2 = 4$.
4. $p = 0.6$.
5. $N = 10^4$, $N_1 = 6500$.

Table 1. Posterior expected value and posterior variance for θ under varying model assumptions.

Model	Priors	$\mathcal{E}(\theta\|0,N)$	$\mathrm{Var}(\theta\|0,N)$
Structural Model	1. all priors $\beta[1,1]$	0.00187	$1.8\cdot10^{-7}$
with Branching	2. $\overline{S_1S_3}\backslash\bar{S}_1$ priors: $\beta[2,1]$	0.0023	$2.4\cdot10^{-7}$
	3. $\overline{S_1S_3}\backslash\bar{S}_1$ priors: $\beta[\frac{1}{99},1]$	0.0014	$1.3\cdot10^{-7}$
	4. all priors $\beta[\frac{1}{99},1]$	$1.8\cdot10^{-5}$	$1.8\cdot10^{-9}$
	5. prior for $\bar{S}_1$ and $\overline{S_1S_2}\backslash\bar{S}_1$: $\beta[\frac{1}{99},1]$, prior for $\overline{S_1S_3}\backslash\bar{S}_1$: $\beta[2,1]$	$9\cdot10^{-4}$	$1.05\cdot10^{-7}$
Sequential Structural Model	$\beta[1,1]$	0.001498	$1.49\cdot10^{-7}$
SUM–model	$\beta[1,1]$	$9.9\cdot10^{-5}$	$9.9\cdot10^{-9}$

Table 1 contains the results. It can be seen that existence of a priori unreliable subtasks has a noticeable influence on the posterior expected value and the posterior variance of the overall software failure rate. Especially when comparing cases four and five, an increase of the posterior expected value by almost a factor 100 can be observed. As discussed above, the assumption that elements in $\overline{S_1S_3}\backslash\bar{S}_1$ are a priori reliable if all others are given $\beta[1,1]$ priors (case 3) leads to a result very similar to that of the sequential structural model. However, the result is even smaller due to the fact that (S_1S_2) is only executed with probability 0.6. When compared to the SUM–model all cases except case four (all priors $\beta[\frac{1}{99},1]$) yield higher posterior expected values and variances than the SUM approach.

As seen in this constructed example, prior information of interaction failure behaviour influences the outcome of the failure rate estimation. This has two implications. Firstly, when disregarding information on subtask behaviour valuable information is discarded and the resulting estimators might be less realistic than estimators which make use of this information. Secondly, the sensitivity of the overall failure rate estimate to prior belief requires that prior evidence be a posteriori verified and continuously renewed once new evidence becomes available.

4 Discussion

In this paper the *structural model* for software reliability assessment has been extended to include both sequentially structured as well as branching code. For

$p = 1$ the results obtained for the case of branching code coincide with the posterior expected value and posterior variance obtained with the structural model for sequential code [6].

For the structural model with branching instructions the posterior expected value and posterior variance depend on the number of admissible code–sequences, the amount of successful testing of these sequences, the prior parameters for the elemental sequence failure rates as well as the probability weights of the program's branches.

The results obtained with the black–box SUM model vary with the system's failure rate prior and the amount of successful system testing. Both approaches would coincide if the SUM system prior expressed the exact same prior belief as would be obtained by 'merging' all component–based priors into one prior density by 'adding' up all possible failure sources according to their probabilty weight in order to constitute the system failure rate. This, however is not feasible within a black–box model, since such a clear prior conception of a system's failure behaviour can only be gained by considering the system's structure which is not done in a black–box approach. Even though the SUM approach and the structure based model can in theory result in the same estimator, it is hardly possible to achieve an informative system failure rate prior for the SUM model. But noninformative priors are not always the way to take. Even if they seemingly express ignorance, they still impose assumptions on the systems failure behaviour and must be treated with care. They can under certain circumstances even lead to an underestimation of the actual failure rate. The more likely disadvantage however lies in the fact that they discard actual information. Thereby they serve no purpose when trying to locate critical parts of a complex software system which distort the overall system reliabilty. The identification of critical system parts is however useful when carrying out cost–benefit analysis for the application of additional subsystem tests before starting system tests and this can be an important issue for COTS–based systems.

It should be emphasized that the aim here is not to replace one reliability estimation approach simply by another, based on different assumptions, but to establish a methodology for the assessment of software safety which is based on realistic information and allows to identify the influence of different system parts on the overall system reliabilty.

To summarize, these are the compelling reasons to understand the precise way in which system design impacts on systematic reliability estimation:

1. We expect that the extra information constituted by system design details leads to more realistic reliability estimates.

2. A structural approach is needed to study the reliability implications of COTS–based software. Here, the identification of critical system parts which distort the overall system reliability can be used to carry out cost–benefit analysis for the application of additional subsystem tests before putting the components into the context of overall system testing.

3. Structural models will allow the identification of designs which are inherently good for reliability estimation, and hence the first scientifically based guidelines on system design for systematic reliability.

Hence this work addresses three issues of commercial importance to system developers. Firstly, in the test planning and management phase. Developers have long needed a sensible means of determining an appropriate level of testing for a given system since testing is expensive. Secondly, the question arises how a given testing–budget should be spent in order to achieve the highest possible reliability estimate, i.e. how to most efficiently perform testing. The statistical approach discussed here can clearly act as a basis for these decisions if it can be developed to apply generally to real–life cases, which will be the next stage of this research.

The third issue has even wider implications. This approach to reliability estimation has the potential to provide feedback to software design, attacking one of the most fundamental questions in software engineering, namely, how to design demonstrably reliable software architectures.

Acknowledgement: This work was funded under the HSE Generic Nuclear Safety Research Programme and is published with the permission of the Industry Management Committee (IMC). The authors would like to thank the staff of British Energy and the Nuclear Installations Inspectorate involved in the Development of Dynamic Testing (DDT) project.

References

1. K.W. Miller et al., "Estimating the Probability of Failure when Testing reveals no Failures", IEEE Trans. Software Eng. **10**, No. 2 (1992) 33–43
2. B. Littlewood, "A Reliability Model for Systems with Markov Structure", Applied Statistics **24** (1975) 172–177
3. J.-C. Laprie and K. Kanoun, "X–ware Reliability and Availability Modelling", IEEE Trans. Software Eng. **18**, No. 2 (1992) 130–147
4. M.R.Lyu (ed.), Handbook of Software Reliability Engineering, IEEE Computer Society Press and McGraw–Hill (1996)
5. J.H. May and A.D. Lunn, "New Statistics for demand–based Software Testing", Information Processing Letters **53** (1995) 307–314
6. J.H. May, S. Kuball and G. Hughes, "Test Statistics for System Design Failure", Proceedings of the International Workshop for Reliability Modelling and Analysis, National University of Singapore, M. Xie and D.N.P Murthy (eds), The National University of Singapore, November 1998
7. J.H. May and A.D. Lunn, "A Model of Code Sharing for Estimating Software Failure on Demand Probabilities", IEEE Trans. Software Eng. **21**, No. 9 (1995) 747–752
8. J.H. May, G. Hughes and A.D. Lunn, "Reliability Estimation from Appropriate Testing of Plant Protection Software", Software Engineering Journal (1995) 206–218

Hazard Analysis in Formal Specification

Kaisa Sere and Elena Troubitsyna

Abo Akademi, Department of Computer Science,
Turku Centre for Computer Science,
Lemminkaisenkatu 14 A, FIN-20520 Turku, Finland
{Kaisa.Sere, Elena.Troubitsyna}@abo.fi

Abstract. Action systems have proven their worth in the design of safety-critical systems. The approach is based on a firm mathematical foundation within which the reasoning about the correctness and behaviour of the system under development is carried out. Hazard analysis is a vital part of the development of safety-critical systems. The results of the hazard analysis are semantically different from the specification terms of the controlling software. The purpose of this paper is to show how we can incorporate the results of hazard analysis into an action system specification by encoding this information via available composition operators for action systems in order to specify robust and safe controllers.

1 Introduction

The purpose of this paper is to show how to incorporate information about potential hazards obtained as a result of safety analysis in a formal system specification. Our target systems are reactive, i.e., usually concurrent systems that interact with their environment and respond to not only normal safe situations, but to the occurring hazardous situations as well. We often call this environment a plant. Examples of such systems are embedded control systems.

We use the action system formalism [2] as our main design technique. This formalism is a state based approach to system design. It provides a completely rigorous foundation for the stepwise development of system specifications and implementations. It has found many applications especially among parallel and distributed systems among which many are safety-critical [4, 14].

Formal methods like action systems give us techniques to formally specify the functionality of a system, to verify its correctness or to develop the system stepwise from an abstract specification to its implementation. However, these methods seldom interface well with the more informal techniques developed for example for safety analysis [10, 16]. The purpose of this paper is to develop a theory on how hazard analysis and risk analysis techniques are used hand-in-hand with action systems and how the results of the analysis are stepwise adopted by the specification in order to produce safe and robust systems, both hardware and software.

Hansen et al. [7] spotted the problem of the semantic gap between the abstract level of the hazard analysis and the way of software specification. They suggest using the results of Fault Tree Analysis as a source of the formulation of requirements which embedded software should meet. In their approach a description of fault trees is given

M. Felici, K. Kanoun, A. Pasquini (Eds.): SAFECOMP'99, LNCS 1698, pp. 350–360, 1999
© Springer-Verlag Berlin Heidelberg 1999

in terms of real-time temporal logic. Their goal is to obtain a safety invariant which embedded software should preserve. Another approach to incorporation of safety analysis methods in the software development process suggests to use safety analysis techniques (e.g. fault tree analysis) for assessing safety properties of software. This idea underlies works of Leveson et al. [8, 9]: giving an analysed program a fault tree semantics they show how to assess its safety. Wong and Joyce [19] show how safety-related hazard are expressed in terms of source code for embedded software in order to verify this with respect to the hazards. The approach proposed by Clarke and McDermid [5] is based on representing weakest precondition of a program as a fault tree – such a representation shows unsafe states which the program might reach. Our approach has an opposite view – rather than apply the fault tree analysis to already developed program we instead use its results as a guidance for developing software. Therefore, the approach we advocate in this paper is closer to that of Hansen et al. However, we not only obtain a safety invariant as they do, but in addition show how the identified hazards can be specified and handled by the controller software.

In our earlier work [13, 17] we have proposed methods to reason about the impact of probabilistic behaviour of components on the overall safety of a control system. We concentrated on the probabilistic extension of the specification language developing tools to reason quantitatively about the systems' safety. However, the systems which we considered were rather deterministic and moreover, we could not distinguish between different types of failures occurred in the system. Here we do not extend the language but rather use the available modularization operators, most notably the prioritising composition [15], to capture the idea of hazards. Priority is computationally more convenient to work with than probability since probabilities do not fit well with the inherently non-deterministic way action systems work.

The system itself is developed in a modular fashion, concentrating first on the normal behaviour of the system stating both the plant and the controller requirements within a single framework. Thereafter the different failure mechanisms are incorporated into the specification. Hence, we can separate the concerns, concentrate on parts of the system separately as well as use and state assumptions about the physical plant itself. This is an approach traditionally advocated by action systems [4,14]. We as well as other researchers [11] argue that only such an approach makes a formal analysis of a system feasible, easier adjustable and less redundant.

We proceed as follows: in Section 2 we briefly describe action systems concentrating on the language issues and refinement as well as defining the important composition operators. In Section 3 we outline the way control systems are specified in the action systems framework. In Section 4 we show how the results of the hazard analysis can be encoded into the formalism. We end in Section 5 with some concluding remarks.

2 Action systems

An action system $\mathbf{A}$ is a set of actions operating on local and global variables:

$$\mathbf{A} ::= |[\textbf{ var } a; \ A0; \textbf{ do } A1 \ []...[] \ An \textbf{ od }]|$$

The system $\mathbf{A}$ describes a computation, in which local variables a are first created and initialised in $A0$. Then repeatedly any of the enabled actions $A1, \ ..., \ An$ is non-deterministically selected for execution. The computation terminates if no action is enabled, otherwise it continues infinitely. Actions operating on disjoint sets of variables can be executed in any order or in parallel. The global variables of A are those mentioned in *A1, ..., An* but not declared locally.

Actions are taken to be *atomic*, meaning that only their input-output behaviour is of interest. They can be arbitrary sequential statements. Their behaviour can therefore be described by the weakest precondition predicate transformer of Dijkstra [6]: $wp(A,p)$ is the weakest precondition such that action A terminates in a state satisfying predicate p. In addition to the statements considered by Dijkstra, we allow pure guarded commands $g \rightarrow A$, non-deterministic choice A [] B between actions A,B, and non-deterministic assignment $v := v'.Q$ which assigns to variables v such a value v' that the predicate Q holds.

$$wp(abort, p)=false \qquad wp((A;B), p)=wp(A, wp(B, p))$$
$$wp(skip, p)=p \qquad wp((A[]B),p)=wp(A,p) \wedge wp(B,p)$$
$$wp(v:= e,p)=p[v:= e] \qquad wp((g \rightarrow A),p)=g \Rightarrow wp(A,p)$$
$$wp(v:= v'.Q,p)=(\forall v'.\ Q \Rightarrow p[v:= v'])$$

Generally, an action that establishes any postcondition is said to be miraculous. We take the view that an action is only enabled in those initial states in which it behaves non-miraculously. The guard of an action characterises those states for which the action is enabled:

$$gd\ A\ =\ \neg wp(A, false)$$

The body S of an action $A = g \rightarrow S$ is denoted by sA.

Let A and B be actions. The prioritising composition A // B selects the first operand if it is enabled, otherwise the second, the choice being deterministic.

$$A\ //\ B = A\ []\ (\neg gd\ A \rightarrow B)$$

The prioritising composition of two actions is enabled if either operand is.

$$Gd\ (A\ //\ B) = gd\ A \vee gd\ B$$

Let us now study different notions of refinement for action systems [3]. We say that action A is refined by action C, written $A \leq C$, if, whenever A establishes a certain postcondition, so does C:

$$A \leq C\ \text{iff for all}\ p:\ wp(A,p) \Rightarrow wp(C,p)$$

Together with the monotonicity of wp this implies that for a certain precondition, C might establish a stronger postcondition than A (reduce non-determinism of A) or even establish postcondition *false* (behave miraculously).

When carrying out refinement in practice one seldom appeals to the above definition. Instead certain pre-proven refinement rules are used. The following theorems give refinement rules that are especially useful when working with hazards as will be seen later:

Theorem 1. *For two actions A, B we always have that*

$$A\ []\ B\ \leq A\ //\ B$$

Theorem 2. *The prioritising composition of actions of the form*

$$g1 \lor g2 \to abort \, // \, g3 \to A$$

where A can be abortive, is refined by the prioritising composition of the form

$$g1 \to abort \, // \, g2 \lor g3 \to A$$

A variation of refinement is if A is (data-) refined by C via a relation R, written $A \leq_R C$. For this, assume A operates on variables a,u and C operates on variables c,u. Let R be a predicate over a,c,u:

$$A \leq_R C \text{ iff for all } p: R \land wp(A,p) \Rightarrow wp(C, (\exists a \bullet R \land p))$$

Data refinement allows the local variables of an action system to be replaced. We have the following theorems to prove data refinement between actions:

Theorem 3. $A \leq_R C$ *holds iff*
(i) $R \land gd \, C \Rightarrow gd \, A$
(ii)   for all $p: R \land gd \, C \land wp(sA,p) \Rightarrow wp(sC, \exists a \bullet R \land p))$

Theorem 4. $v := ? \leq_R w := w'.Q$ *if* $Q \land R \Rightarrow (\exists v'.R[v,w := v',w'])$
where $v := ?$ *stands for assigning to v any arbitrary value.*

Data refinement $\mathbf{A} \leq_R \mathbf{C}$ for two action systems holds if we in addition to the above refinement on actions can show that the initialisation in the two systems establishes R and that $R \land gd \, A \Rightarrow gd \, C$ [3] intuitively stating that the two systems terminate similarly.

3 Specifying Control Systems

Let us now sketch a way to specify control systems within action systems formalism. Rather than embody all the requirements in the initial specification, we introduce some of them in successive refinement steps. Usually, refinement is used as a way of verifying the correctness of an implementation with respect to a specification, but it can also be used as a way of structuring the requirements such that they are easier to validate [4, 14]. In this paper we develop mechanisms to handle failure situations by the refinement activity.

Our initial action system is intended to model the behaviour of the overall system, that is, the physical environment and the controller together. It allows us to use assumptions that we make about how the environment behaves. The initial specification of the system is very abstract. Usually it is build in such a way that all the details concerning interaction between the plant and the controller (via the sensors and the actuators) as well as details of failures representation are omitted.

Below the plant and the controller are modelled as working concurrently

$$\textbf{System} ::= |[\textbf{ var } v, fail, ...; \textbf{ do } P \, [] \, C \textbf{ od }]|$$

Both P and C are actions and they might share variables. This initial specification takes form of the interleaving between the plant action P

$$P ::= v, fail := ?,?$$

where v are the state variables needed to model the plant state, and the controller action C

$$C ::= Fail \, / \! / \, (Unit_1 \, [] \, Unit_2 \, [] \, ... \, [] \, Unit_M \,)$$

The controller consists of a prioritising composition of the action *Fail*

$$Fail ::= fail \rightarrow Emergency$$

which shuts down the system if some failure occurs, i.e., the action *Emergency* is equivalent to *abort*, and the actions $Unit_i$ $i=1..M$ which have the form

$$Unit_i ::= g_i \rightarrow control \; action_i$$

The variable *fail* models a global system failure. Each of the actions $Unit_i$ specifies the control required to operate a certain plant device (we call it a plant unit) in absence of failures. They can refer to the variables v, and normally some other variables too, denoted as ... above. Observe that we can be certain that there are no failures present when an action $Unit_i$ is executed as the prioritising composition between the faulty behaviour and the control actions ensures this. Without this operator, i.e., using the choice operator between these actions, the control actions would require a more elaborate guard, namely $g_i \wedge \neg fail$. This latter approach is taken for instance by Liu and Joseph [12].

In our initial specification **System** we assume that the state of the plant can be directly observed by the controller. At this stage the safety condition imposed on the system is formulated as a constraint on the physical parameters of the system, e.g. maintaining temperature, water level, pressure etc. in a predefined safe region. Safe operation of **System** can be expressed via a safety invariant *safety* on the state variables of the system.

$$safety ::= \neg fail \Rightarrow safety \; condition$$

Safety is checked within the weakest precondition calculus by ensuring that the initial state establishes *safety*, and that *wp(C,safety)* holds, i.e. the actions of the controller preserve *safety*. At the presence of more information on failures this invariant can be weakened by expressing this new information.

Further refinement of the initial specification leads to the introduction details of the implementation which make specification more realistic: the controller cannot observe a real state of the plant anymore but rather makes assumption about it on the base of the sensors reading. The control is performed by means of the actuators which, like the sensors, are modelled as state variables [4].

4 Including Hazards

In our previous work on action systems for safety-critical systems [4, 14] failure modes of the components together with the safety invariant imposed on the system were given. The task was to capture these requirements by performing refinement. In the industrial practice, however, a design of a safety-critical system assumes that this information is unavailable and should be obtained as a result of a safety analysis of the system. The controller should withstand faults appearing in the fault-prone units. To obtain the failure modes and safety invariant for the controlling program we investigate those faults and classify them. We rely on Fault Tree Analysis (FTA) [16] for performing hazard analysis.

FTA is a deductive safety analysis technique. It is a top-down approach applied during the design stage. Preliminary hazard identification provides information about functions of the system and possible failures. This information is taken as an input for the FTA. The result of the FTA is an identification of component faults that result in different hazardous situations. Each fault tree has a root representing a hazardous failure. The tree traces the system to the lower component level to reveal the possible causes of the failure.

We assume that a set of hazards **H** is obtained as a result of the hazard identification. For each hazard $H_i \in \mathbf{H}$ an appropriate fault tree FT_i is constructed. The obtained fault trees form a set **FT** which we analyse to obtain information facilitating performance of the next refinement step – an introduction of failure modes. Firstly, the set **FT** is a source of non-redundant information about the unit faults which are potentially dangerous. Secondly, each fault tree provides a logical representation of a failure in terms of faults of the plant units. Next, the set **FT** allows us to formulate a safety invariant for the embedded software. Finally, it serves as a basis for the identification of criticality (frequency and severity) for each hazard.

Analysing each particular tree we make a list of faults associated with each unit in the plant. For each unit $Unit_i$ for $i=1..M$, F_i is the set of faults associated with this unit

$$F_i ::= \{ F(i,1)...F(i,k_i) \}$$

here $k_i \in \mathbf{Nat}$ and $\forall i,j\colon \mathbf{Nat}.\ i \in 1..M \wedge j \in 1..k_i \bullet F(i,j) \in \mathbf{IF}$, where **IF** denotes the set of all faults.

For example, assume that as a result of the hazard analysis for some hypothetical safety-critical system two hazards H_1 and H_2 are identified. Furthermore, for each of them the fault tree is constructed, as shown in Fig. 1. There are two faulty units, *Unit1* and *Unit2*. The corresponding lists of faults

$$F_1 ::= \{\mathrm{F}(1,1),\ \mathrm{F}(1,2)\},$$
$$F_2 ::= \{\mathrm{F}(2,1),\ \mathrm{F}(2,2),\ \mathrm{F}(2,3)\}$$

indicate all potentially hazardous faults occurring in each unit. Those lists are non-redundant, since they contain only faults which lead to arising of the system failures. Note that in our example the failure $F(1,1)$ contributes in both hazards but is represented once in the list.

The identified faults *IF* are modelled as new state variables in the system specification

$$\mathbf{var}\ F(1,1),\ ...,\ F(1,k_1),\ ...,\ F(M,k_M) : \mathbf{Bool}$$

Hence, each hazard H_i is now formulated as a predicate over the identified component failures. For example, the hazards H_1, H_2 given in Fig. 1 are represented as follows:

$$H_1 ::= F(1,1) \vee (F(2,1) \wedge F(1,2))$$
$$H_2 ::= F(1,1) \wedge F(2,2) \wedge F(2,3)$$

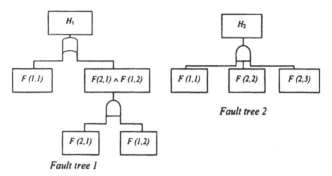

Fig. 1. Examples of Fault Trees.

On the base of the available quantitative information about component reliabilities or of expert knowledge for each hazard we calculate a frequency of its occurrence and its severity. This allows us to calculate the risk associated with the hazard. There are a number of methods and standards providing guidance for the classification of risks [16]. Without going into details we assume without loss of generality that there are three disjoint classes of hazards formed on the basis of the classification of risks associated with the hazards.

$$\begin{aligned}
&\textit{Class I:} && \{H1, ...Hc_1\} \\
&\textit{Class II:} && \{Hc_1+1, ...Hc_2\} \\
&\textit{Class III:} && \{Hc_2+1, ...Hc_3\}
\end{aligned}$$

Let us make this more concrete by giving a potential interpretation to the classes. Assume that on the base of the performed classification we formulate failure modes of the system to be designed. The system enters *Emergency* mode if any of hazardous situation from *Class I* occurred. Hence, these are the hazards that are intolerable and have a high risk associated with them. The mode *Rescue* is caused by hazards belonging to class *Class II*. These are less severe hazards but still critical. They should be avoided or their effect should be mitigated. An occurrence of a hazard from *Class III* transforms the system into the *Degraded* mode. Here the failures can be tolerated as the risks associated with the corresponding hazards are negligible.

Now we return to the specification of the system from the software point of view. The refinement step to be undertaken now should lead to a specification where the identified failures of units and failure modes are represented. The abstract variable *fail* denoting a global failure in the original system **System** is replaced by the new state variables $F(i,j)$ representing the individual failures in **IF** of the components. Hence, we are about to change the data representation of the systems and this calls for data refinement. The refinement relation R establishes a correspondence between the variables:

$$R ::= fail = (\vee H_i \, for \, i=1..c_3 \,)$$

Bearing in mind, that each of the predicates H_i, $i=1..c_3$, describes a corresponding hazard in terms of the state variables, $F(1,1)... F(M,k_M)$, we obtain the following intuitive formulation of the refinement relation R: *A failure occurred in the initial specification corresponds to the occurrence of one or a combination of the identified hazards in the refined specification.*

The plant action P is refined to the action P'

$$P' ::= v, F(1,1),...F(1,k_1),... F(M,k_M) :=$$

$$v', F(1,1)',...F(1,k_1)',... F(M,k_M)'.Q$$

which produces a "safe" state in case all of the variables $F(i,j)$ are assigned to *false* and "unsafe" state if some of the variables $F(i,j)$ is set to *true*. Different combinations of the variables representing failures being set to *true* represent different hazardous situations occurring in the system. The predicate Q is formed from studying the physical characteristics of the designed system. Besides the information about hazards, the safety analysis supplies information about the dynamics of the plant (e.g. rates of changing of controlled parameters) as well. We capture it at this refinement step. Intuitively, the predicate Q narrows the scope of possible values of v to feasible limits. To prove the refinement $P \leq_R P'$ we use Theorem 4 which amounts to proving

$$Q \wedge R \Rightarrow (\exists fail'. R[fail, v, F(1,1)...F(M,k_M) := fail',v', F(1,1)'...F(M,k_M)'])$$

An example of such a refinement can be found elsewhere [4].

To introduce the different failure modes in the specification we refine the action *Fail* with three actions *Fail1, Fail2, Fail3* which describe the different classes of hazards:

> $Fail1 ::= g1 \rightarrow Emergency$
> $Fail2 ::= g2 \rightarrow Rescue$
> $Fail3 ::= g3 \rightarrow Degraded$

The action *Fail1* specifies the reaction of the system on hazards from *Class I* which is *Emergency*, shut down of the system. The occurrence of a hazard or several of them is modelled by the guard of the action, which is defined to be disjunction of hazards from *Class I*:

$$g1 = \vee H_i \ for \ i = 1..c_1$$

The hazards belonging to *Class II* are specified by the action *Fail2*. Since a hazard from *Class II* does not lead to the imminent catastrophe, some actions to bring the system back to a non-hazardous state should be undertaken. Generally, the action has the form

$$Fail2 ::= H_{c1+1} \rightarrow Rescue_{c1+1} []...[] H_{c2} \rightarrow Rescue_{c2}$$

Here each of the individual actions becomes enabled if a corresponding hazard from *Class II* occurs. The body of each action is an invocation of some *Rescue* procedure, which models how to cope with the occurred hazard. The structure of the action *Fail3* is similar to the action *Fail2*, but has the hazards of *Class III* as the guards and corresponding corrective procedures as the bodies.

The refinement

$$Fail \leq_R Fail1 \ [] \ Fail2 \ [] \ Fail3$$

is proved by applying Theorem 3. To verify condition *(i)* we observe, that the guards of the actions *Fail2* and *Fail3* are disjunctions of the constituting inner actions. The condition

$$R \wedge (g1 \vee g2 \vee g3) \Rightarrow fail$$

holds since $g1 \vee g2 \vee g3 = (\vee H_i \ for \ i = 1..c_3)$.

Since, presumable, the corrective procedures in the bodies of actions do not change the values of failure-representing variables, the refinement between the bodies of the actions (condition (ii) of Theorem 3) is verified trivially. It is instructive to note, however, the contribution of the refinement activity in the safety aspect of the system. Namely, the identification of failures and failure modes allowed us to specify corrective actions which should be taken by the controller to withstand certain hazardous failures. It is a significant improvement compared to the initial specification which is intolerable to all failures.

Another safety requirement which we capture on this refinement step is a necessity to cope with the failures according to their criticality: we give priority to failures with high risks associated to them. Hence, *Fail1* should be executed immediately when enabled. Also *Fail2* and *Fail3* will be taken whenever enabled provided no action in a higher priority class is enabled. A normal control action $Unit_i$ is only taken when there are no failures detected in the system. Therefore, the most severe hazards – hazards belonging to *Class I* should be handled by the controller with highest priority. They form the class of highest priority in the specification of the controller. Consequently, the priority of the class decreases with increasing its priority index. The non-deterministic choice between the failure actions cannot guarantee this. The effect is obtained by refining the failure actions further appealing to Theorem 1:

$$Fail1 \; [] \; Fail2 \; [] \; Fail3 \leq Fail1 \; // \; Fail2 \; // \; Fail3$$

The refinement of C with the controller action C'

$$C' ::= Fail1 \; // \; Fail2 \; // \; Fail3 \; // \; (Unit_1 \; [] \; Unit_2 \; []... \; [] \; Unit_M)$$

is verified by additionally proving the termination condition

$$R \wedge fail \Rightarrow (g1 \vee g2 \vee g3)$$

which holds trivially in this case. We have now proved that **System**$\leq_R$ **System'** holds with

System' $::= |[\; \textbf{var} \; v, F(1,1), ... F(M, k_M), ...; \; \textbf{do} \; P' \; [] \; C' \; \textbf{od} \;]|$

Further refinement steps to be taken are concentrated on the introduction of fault tolerance and fault avoidance for the first two classes of the failures, i.e., further refining the *Emergency* and *Rescue* situations. Proof of such refinement is based on Theorem 2: the theorem justifies the transfer of actions belonging to the most critical classes to the less critical classes. This can be achieved by refining "definitely" abortive behaviour into non-abortive or less likely to be abortive.

Often safety conditions imposed on a system under construction are time dependent. Within the action system formalism time is usually modelled via a state variable which is updated at each iteration of the system, as illustrated by the development of the mine pump control system [18]. We show there that such a representation of time facilitates modelling of both occurrence and detection of failures (in [18] we were mostly concerned about sensor failures). We model the failure of a sensor by not updating the state variable representing a time stamp accompanying each sensor reading. Detection of the failure is performed by comparison of the current system's time with the time stamp accompanying a sensor reading.

5 Concluding Remarks

We have shown how the information about a hazardous situation occurring in a plant can be embedded in the specification of a control program. Via this embedding the hazardous situations are treated according to their criticality and urgency. This allows us to enhance safety of the overall system by ensuring that in case some marginal failure occurred simultaneously with a more critical failure the latter one will be treated with the highest priority.

We have chosen to model the plant with the controlling software within the action system formalism. The proofs justifying the correctness of our design were either rigorously carried out within the refinement calculus or were given as "generic" proof obligations, which have to be instantiated for each particular system. For instance, the predicate Q in the refinement of the plant action needs to be found as well as the actions modelling the *Rescue* and *Degraded* modes. The latter are formed together with modifying the *safety* invariant in such a way that $wp(C',safety)$ holds for the new predicate. This is demonstrated in an accompanying paper on a case study in the design of a mine pump control system [18].

Another merit of the chosen framework, is that there is mechanical tool support assisting in the design as it is possible to use e.g. the B Method [1] for action systems [14]. We omitted the description of modular reasoning with action systems, but we still kept modular-like style: each failure class as well as control of each plant device can be easily transformed into separate modules without running a risk to overlook subtle details of their interaction.

Acknowledgements. The work reported here was supported by the Academy of Finland.

References

1. J.-R. Abrial. The B-Book: Assigning Programs to Meanings. Cambridge University Press, 1996.
2. R. J. R. Back. Refinement calculus, Part II: Parallel and reactive programs. In J. W. de Bakker, W.-P. de Roever, and G. Rozenberg, editors, *Stepwise Refinement of Distributed Systems*, volume 430 of *Lecture Notes in Computer Science*, pages 67 - 93, Mook, The Netherlands, May/June 1989. Springer-Verlag, 1990.
3. R. J. R.Back and J. von Wright. Trace Refinement of Action Systems. In Proc. of *CONCUR94*, Sweden, August 1994. *Lecture Notes in Computer Science*. Springer-Verlag, 1994.
4. M. Butler, E. Sekerinski, and K. Sere. An Action System Approach to the Steam Boiler Problem. In Jean-Raymond Abrial, Egon Borger and Hans Langmaack, editors, *Formal Methods for Industrial Applications: Specifying and Programming the Steam Boiler Control*, Lecture Notes in Computer Science Vol. 1165. Springer-Verlag, 1996.
5. S.J. Clarke and J.McDermid. Software Fault Trees and Weakest Preconditions: A Comparison and Analysis, *Software Engineering Journal*, July 1993.
6. E.W. Dijkstra. A Discipline of Programming. Prentice Hall International, Englewood Cliffs, N.J., 1976.
7. K.M. Hansen, A. P. Ravn and V. Stavridou. From Safety Analysis to Software Requirements. In *IEEE Transactions on Software Engineering*, Vol.24, No.7, July 1998

8. N.G.Leveson. Software Safety in Embedded Computer Systems. *Communication ACM,* Vol.34, No.2, February 1999.
9. N.G. Leveson, S.S. Cha and T.J.Shimeall, Safety Verification of Ada Programs Using Software Fault Trees. *IEEE Software,* July 1991.
10. N.G. Leveson. Safeware: System Safety and Computers, Addison-Wesley, 1995.
11. N.G. Leveson, M.P.E. Heimdahl, H. Hildreth, and J.D. Reese. Requirements Specification for Process-Control Systems. In *IEEE Transactions on Software Engineering,* 1994.
12. Z. Liu and M. Joseph. Transformations of programs for fault-tolerance. In *Formal Aspects of Computing,* Vol 4, No. 5 1992, pp. 442-469
13. A. McIver, C. C. Morgan and E. Troubitsyna. The probabilistic steam boiler: a case study in probabilistic data refinement. In *Proc. of IRW/FMP'98,* Australia, 1998.
14. E. Sekerinski and K. Sere (Eds.). Program Development by Refinement - Case Studies Using the B Method. Springer Verlag 1998.
15. E. Sekerinski and K. Sere. A Theory of Prioritizing Composition. The Computer Journal, VOL. 39, No 8, pp.701-712. The British Computer Society. Oxford University Press.
16. N. Storey. Safety-critical computer systems. Addison-Wesley, 1996.
17. E. Troubitsyna. Refining for Safety. TUCS Technical Report No.237, February 1999.
18. E. Troubitsyna. Specifying Safety-Related Hazards Formally. In *Proc. of 17ᵗʰ International System Safety Conference,* Orlando, FL USA, August 1999. To appear.
19. K. Wong and J. Joyce. Refinement of Safety-Related Hazards into Verifiable Code Assertions. In *Proc. of SAFECOMP'98,* Heidelberg, Germany, October, 1998.

Modeling Safety-Critical Systems with Z and Petri Nets

Monika Heiner[1] and Maritta Heisel[2]

[1] Brandenburgische Technische Universität Cottbus, Institut für Informatik, D-03013 Cottbus,
email: mh@informatik.tu-cottbus.de
[2] Otto-von-Guericke-Universität Magdeburg, Fakultät für Informatik, Institut für Verteilte
Systeme, D-39016 Magdeburg, Germany, email: heisel@cs.uni-magdeburg.de

Abstract. We show how to combine the specification notation Z with Petri nets for modeling safety-critical systems. The combination preserves the strengths of the two formalisms, while ameliorating their drawbacks. We illustrate our approach by modeling a part of a production cell and validating that model with respect to safety-related properties.

1 Introduction

Petri nets [Sta90] are a well-established formalism for modeling the behavior of concurrent systems. They have a formal semantics and can be animated by tools. Moreover, there exist sophisticated analysis techniques to demonstrate properties of Petri net models. Animation and validation are particularly important for safety-critical systems, making Petri nets a suitable formalism to use in that area.

A drawback of Petri nets is that they tend to become very large for systems of realistic size. Taking into account not only behavioral but also data-related aspects of the modeled system further increases the size of the Petri net. Data-oriented aspects concern the internal data that the system must maintain to adequately react to environmental or internal conditions. Safety-critical systems (like other computerized systems, too) usually need such an internal data state.

In contrast to Petri nets, the specification notation Z [Spi92b] was designed to specify data and the evolution of data. It does not provide any means to explicitly specify behavior. In Z, we can only specify sets of operations, but we cannot express that we want to occur the operations in a certain order. As compared to other formal specification languages, Z is fairly well-accepted and well equipped with tools, such as type checkers [Spi92a,BGHH98] and theorem provers [KSW96,Saa97].

To adequately specify safety-critical systems, both aspects, behavioral as well as data-oriented ones, must be taken into account. Therefore, we investigate a combination of Z and Petri nets. We use Z to specify the data-oriented aspects of the system, and Petri nets to specify its behavioral aspects. Combining the two languages, we achieve a separation of concerns, which results in better comprehensible, smaller and thus better analyzable system models. Hence, the combination keeps the advantages of both specification formalisms, while ameliorating their drawbacks.

In Section 2, we describe the way in which systems are modeled, using the two formalisms. Section 3 is devoted to a case study that illustrates the approach and shows how combined specifications can be validated. We conclude by comparing our combination of Z and Petri nets with other combinations of data-based and behavioral specification formalisms and by pointing out directions for future research (Section 4).

M. Felici, K. Kanoun, A. Pasquini (Eds.): SAFECOMP'99, LNCS 1698, pp. 361-374, 1999
© Springer-Verlag Berlin Heidelberg 1999

2   Modeling Principles

A goal of our combination of Z and Petri nets is to obtain nets that are much smaller and better analyzable than when using Petri nets alone to model a safety-critical system. When using the combination, data aspects need not be encoded in the nets, but can be specified in Z.

We define the system state and operations that specify how that state can evolve in Z. In Z, it cannot directly be expressed in which order the Z operations should "happen" (indeed, there is not even a notion of executing an operation in Z). To express behavior, we use Petri nets, where Z operations correspond to transitions of the Petri net. Moreover, we assume that Z operations can only be "executed" if their precondition is fulfilled. The precondition of an operation states that there exists an after-state and values for the output variables such that the schema predicate is fulfilled. In this paper, we always give the preconditions explicitly. The following figure illustrates this approach:

The model of a safety-critical system is then made up of both specifications, i.e., the *conjunction* of the constraints imposed by the two specifications must be fulfilled. To obtain a useful system model by combining specifications in different formalisms, we must show that the two specifications do not contradict each other. To ensure compatibility of the two specifications, we have identified several proof obligations. Checking these compatibility conditions may reveal errors in the model and thus contributes to the quality of the specification.

 - The initial marking of the Petri net must be consistent with the initiality conditions of the Z specification.
 - The conditions associated with incoming places of transitions correspond to preconditions of Z operations, the conditions associated with outgoing places of transitions correspond to postconditions established by Z operations. Hence, for chains we have the obligation to show that the postcondition of an operation implies the precondition of its successor in the chain.
 - If the Petri net admits concurrent execution of operations op_1 and op_2 that work on common state components, we must show that
   - the operations do not exclude each other, i.e., $\neg$ (pre op_1 $\wedge$ pre op_2 $\Leftrightarrow$ *false*)
   - for all states where pre op_1 $\wedge$ pre op_2 holds, both orders are possible and lead to the same final state. This allows us to use an interleaving semantics of concurrency for Z operations.

Usually, a transition is enabled if the precondition of its corresponding Z operation holds. But to keep the Petri net sizes small by concentrating on the essential control flow, the precondition of a transition may be weaker than the precondition of its Z operation. To highlight this fact, the letter "Z" appears in the transition symbol (see Figure 2). Z-labeled transitions, if considered only on the Petri net level, exhibit more behavior than allowed by the Z specification. This mechanism may be used to resolve dynamic conflicts in the combined Z - Petri net specification. If two transitions are in a dynamic conflict, whose corresponding Z operations have incompatible preconditions, then only the transition can actually take place whose corresponding Z operation holds, if any. The fact that the Petri net considered in isolation can engage in more behavior than permitted by the Z specification is not a problem when we analyze the Petri net for safety-related properties. There, we show that unsafe system states cannot be entered. Therefore, if the net with the more liberal behavior is safe, than the more restricted behavior is also safe.

To obtain self-contained and analyzable models, we not only consider the control software, but also model parts of the environment, for example sensors (see Section 3).

3   Case Study: Production Cell

To illustrate our approach, we model a part of a production cell [LL95]. The production cell, an existing industrial facility, consists of six physical components: two conveyor belts, a rotable robot equipped with two extendable arms, an elevating rotary table, a press, and a traveling crane (which has been added to make the cell self-contained). The machines are organized in a (closed) pipeline, see Figure 1. Their common goal is to transport and process metal plates. Altogether, 14 sensors and 34 actuators can be used to control the cell.

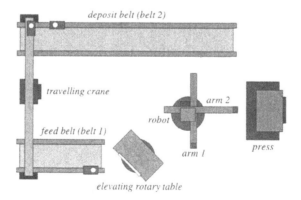

Fig. 1. Production cell

As a first step to develop the control software, we develop a formal and executable system specification. To save space, we restrict ourselves to the first two components, the feed belt and the elevating rotary table, which are quite different technical devices.

While the feed belt may just be switched on and off, the motion of the table is controlled by position engines. In addition, the feed belt has two sensors that indicate whether a plate is at its front or end, respectively.

The original task description considers only the case where at most one plate is on the feed belt at a time. In our model, the maximal number of plates allowed to be present on the feed belt (henceforth called feed belt capacity) is a parameter of the specification. In this way, our model is more general than required by the original task description.

In Section 3.1, we model the two subsystems in Z and specify how their state can change via operations. The order in which the state-changing operations can occur is specified by a Petri net given in Section 3.2. In Section 3.3, the Petri net is analyzed using tools. The coherence of the two specifications is demonstrated in Section 3.4, and some application-dependent safety-related properties of the model are analyzed in Section 3.5.

3.1   Z Part of the Specification

The specification models the two subsystems feed belt and table separately[1]. It exhibits the situations where the two subsystems must communicate or cooperate to achieve a desired state transition. For validation purposes, the whole Z specification was type-checked.[2]

States of the Subsystems   For the feed belt, we need to know whether it is switched on (i.e., whether it moves) or not, and how many plates it carries. We partition the feed belt into three zones: the front, where new plates are dropped, and where a sensor signals the presence of a plate; the end, where the plates are passed on to the elevating rotary table, which is signaled by another sensor; and the zone in between the range of the two sensors.

$$
\begin{array}{l}
\text{— } feed\_belt \text{ —————————————} \\
\hline
at\_front, at\_end : 0 .. 1 \\
in\_between, number\_of\_plates : 0 .. maxplates \\
fb\_mvt : OnOff \\
\hline
number\_of\_plates = \\
\quad at\_front + in\_between + at\_end
\end{array}
$$

$$
\begin{array}{l}
\text{— } Init\_feed\_belt \text{ —————} \\
\hline
feed\_belt' \\
\hline
number\_of\_plates' = 0 \\
fb\_mvt' = off
\end{array}
$$

Here, $maxplates$ is the feed belt capacity, and the type $OnOff$ is defined as an enumeration type $OnOff ::= on \mid off$. In its initial state, the feed belt is switched off, and there are no plates on it. The decoration "'" of variable names means that they describe the state *after* an operation is completed. Plain variables describe the state in which an operation is started.

---

[1] A first version of this specification was based on the partial specification given in [LS96].

[2] Readers not familiar with Z are referred to [Spi92b].

For the elevating rotary table (just called "table" in the following), we need to know its position (modeled by a basic type *Table_Position*), whether it moves or not, and whether there is a plate on it or not. The type *YesNo* is defined as $YesNo ::= yes \mid no$. Whether or not the table is ready to receive a plate is expressed by the derived state component *can_receive*. The two extreme positions of the table are called *load_position* and *unload_position*.

```
┌─ table ──────────────────────────────────
│ t_loaded : YesNo
│ t_position : Table_Position
│ t_mvt : OnOff
│ can_receive : YesNo
├──────────────────────────────────────────
│ can_receive = yes ⇔
│     t_position = load_position ∧
│     t_loaded = no ∧ t_mvt = off
└──────────────────────────────────────────
```

```
┌─ Init_table ─────────────────────
│ table'
├──────────────────────────────────
│ t_loaded' = no
│ t_position' = unload_position
│ t_mvt' = off
└──────────────────────────────────
```

Table control operations We assume a total ordering relation $<$ on the type *Table_Position*, where *load_position* is the smallest and *unload_position* is the largest position. The function *next* increases the position by one unit, the function *prev* decreases it. "$\Delta table$" means that the state of the table may change.

```
┌─ start_load_to_unload ───────────
│ Δtable
├──────────────────────────────────
│ t_loaded = yes
│ t_position = load_position
│ t_mvt = off
│
│ t_loaded' = yes
│ t_position' = load_position
│ t_mvt' = on
└──────────────────────────────────
```

```
┌─ move_load_to_unload ────────────
│ Δtable
├──────────────────────────────────
│ t_loaded = yes
│ t_position < unload_position
│ t_mvt = on
│
│ t_loaded' = yes
│ t_position' = next(t_position)
│ t_mvt' = on
└──────────────────────────────────
```

The operation *start_load_to_unload* starts the motor in the *load_position*, the operation *move_load_to_unload* increases the position of the table by one unit. When the table has reached the *unload_position*, the motor must be switched off, as specified by the operation *stop_at_unload*. Because we do not model how the plate is passed on from the table to the robot, the operation *unload_table* just resets the state component *t_loaded*, i.e., *unload_table* acts as a consumer.

```
┌─ stop_at_unload ──────────────────┐
│ Δtable                            │
│ ──────────────────────────────── │
│ t_loaded = yes                    │
│ t_position = unload_position      │
│ t_mvt = on                        │
│ ──────────────────────────────── │
│ t_loaded' = yes                   │
│ t_position' = unload_position     │
│ t_mvt' = off                      │
└───────────────────────────────────┘
```

```
┌─ unload_table ────────────────────┐
│ Δtable                            │
│ ──────────────────────────────── │
│ t_loaded = yes                    │
│ t_position = unload_position      │
│ t_mvt = off                       │
│ ──────────────────────────────── │
│ t_loaded' = no                    │
│ t_position' = unload_position     │
│ t_mvt' = off                      │
└───────────────────────────────────┘
```

The operations $start\_unload\_to\_load$, $move\_unload\_to\_load$, and $stop\_at\_load$ are defined analogously.

Operations related to the feed belt environment These operations correspond to phenomena that cannot be influenced by the control software of the feed belt but are reported by sensors. Plates are dropped on the feed belt by a producer, which causes the sensor at the front of the feed belt to respond (operation $load\_fb$). When the feed belt is moving, the sensor will eventually report that there is no longer a plate at the front of the feed belt, as specified by the operation $leave\_front$. Furthermore, the sensor situated at the end of the feed belt will eventually report that a plate has reached the point where it can be passed on to the table (operation $detect$).

```
┌─ load_fb ────────────────┐
│ Δfeed_belt               │
│ ──────────────────────── │
│ number_of_plates         │
│     < maxplates          │
│ at_front = 0             │
│ ──────────────────────── │
│ at_front' = 1            │
│ in_between' = in_between │
│ at_end' = at_end         │
│ fb_mvt' = fb_mvt         │
└──────────────────────────┘
```

```
┌─ leave_front ────────────┐
│ Δfeed_belt               │
│ ──────────────────────── │
│ fb_mvt = on              │
│ at_front = 1             │
│ ──────────────────────── │
│ in_between' =            │
│     in_between + 1       │
│ at_front' = 0            │
│ at_end' = at_end         │
│ fb_mvt' = fb_mvt         │
└──────────────────────────┘
```

```
┌─ detect ─────────────────┐
│ Δfeed_belt               │
│ ──────────────────────── │
│ fb_mvt = on              │
│ at_end = 0               │
│ in_between > 0           │
│ ──────────────────────── │
│ at_end' = 1              │
│ in_between' =            │
│     in_between − 1       │
│ at_front' = at_front     │
│ fb_mvt' = on             │
└──────────────────────────┘
```

Feed belt control operations The feed belt controller must decide when to switch on or off the feed belt. To take these decisions in such a way that the safety of the system is guaranteed, it must communicate with the table, i.e., the feed belt control operations import either $\Xi\,table$ (if the state of the table is only queried but not changed) or $\Delta table$.

The operation $switch\_on$ specifies that the feed belt may only be switched on if the table is ready to receive a plate or if there is no plate at the end of the feed belt. The feed belt must be switched off if a plate has arrived at the end of the feed belt but the table is not ready to receive it (operation $switch\_off$). Otherwise, the plate is passed on from the feed belt to the table, as specified by the operation fb_to_table.

Note that the Z specification cannot entirely describe the behavior of the production cell. It only restricts possible behavior via preconditions of operations.

```
┌─ switch_on ──────────────────────────
│ Δfeed_belt
│ Ξtable
├──────────────────────────────────────
│ fb_mvt = off
│ number_of_plates > 0
│ can_receive = yes ∨ at_end = 0
│
│ fb_mvt' = on
│ in_between' = in_between
│ at_front' = at_front
│ at_end' = at_end
└──────────────────────────────────────
```

```
┌─ switch_off ─────────────────────────
│ Δfeed_belt
│ Ξtable
├──────────────────────────────────────
│ fb_mvt = on
│ at_end = 1
│ can_receive = no
│
│ fb_mvt' = off
│ in_between' = in_between
│ at_front' = at_front
│ at_end' = at_end
└──────────────────────────────────────
```

```
┌─ fb_to_table ────────────────────────
│ Δfeed_belt
│ Δtable
├──────────────────────────────────────
│ fb_mvt = on
│ at_end = 1
│ can_receive = yes
│
│ at_end' = 0
│ in_between' = in_between
│ at_front' = at_front
│ fb_mvt' = fb_mvt
│ t_loaded' = yes
│ t_position' = t_position
│ t_mvt' = t_mvt
└──────────────────────────────────────
```

3.2 Petri Net Part of the Specification

Figure 2 shows the Petri net that specifies the control flow, i.e., the order in which the various Z operations can be executed. To enhance the readability of the Petri net, we introduce the following two layout conventions. (1) To avoid edge crossing we use *logical nodes* (the gray ones) to serve as connectors between identically named nodes. (2) Each independent process is drawn separately, and synchronization happens by logical nodes (there is place as well as transition synchronization).

Moreover, to avoid unnecessary restrictions of the concurrency degree, we use test arcs (black dots instead of the arrow head) to model side conditions of transitions (i.e., places that are incoming as well as outgoing for a given transition). Under the interleaving semantics, test arcs can be simulated by two opposite arcs between the transition and its side condition.

Following these rules, the Petri net exhibits a strong separation of controller and environment model into different parts. The controller part generally consists of a finite and static set of communicating processes, one for each physical component. The environment part is composed of small reusable net components: the producer/consumer processes of the work flow, and the devices of the controlled plant (as far as they are necessary on the net level).

Each physical device is basically characterized by its finite set of discrete states (e.g., the sensor *at_front* may recognize a plate or not, the feed belt may be switched on or off), whereby a discrete state may represent an equivalence class of a possibly

Production Cell Environment

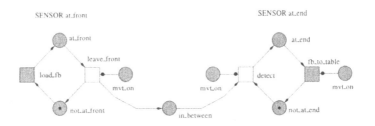

Process Environment

Table Controller

Feed Belt Controller

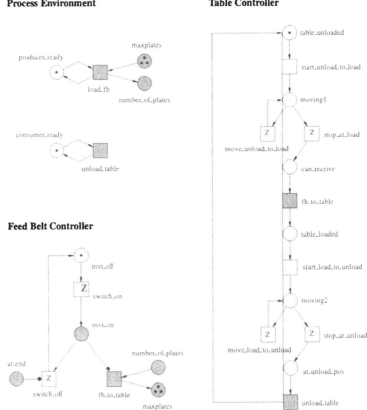

Fig. 2. Petri net for production cell

infinite set of states (e.g. *in_between* summarizes all feed belt states where some plate is located between the two sensors). Obviously, each device must be in one and only one state at any time. In terms of Petri net theory, the states of a device form a place invariant establishing a consistency condition of the system model, see Section 3.3.

To model the assumption of intelligent environment behavior (the producer places a new plate on the belt only if there is room for it), we introduce a place for the state variable *number_of_plates*, and a co-place *maxplates* for its maximal value. In this way, we get a generic system specification - the given feed belt capacity is adapted by the parameter *maxplates*.

Note that there are six Z-labeled transitions, among them all conflicting transitions of the table controller. The transition *fb_to_table*, engaged in a conflict within the feed belt controller, is not a Z-labeled one, because the transition is enabled if and only if the precondition of its Z operation holds. In contrast, the operations *switch_off* and *switch_on* have more detailed preconditions than perceivable in the Petri net structure. Therefore, they are labeled with Z.

For comparison: In [HDS99], a hierarchical Petri net model of the complete production cell has been published, comprising altogether about 200 places and 200 transitions structured into 65 pages. The feed belt–table subsystem needs 46 places and 34 transitions. The Petri net of Figure 2 consists of only 17 places and 13 transitions, which makes a reduction factor of about 2.5.

3.3   Analysis of the Petri Net

Following our approach, the wide variety of available Petri net analysis techniques and tools becomes applicable for computer-aided model analysis. We briefly summarize the results of analyzing the Petri net of Figure 2, using our current Petri net tool box. The following tools have been applied: PED – a hierarchical Petri net EDitor [Tie97] for design, PEDVisor [Men97] for token flow animation, the Integrated Net Analysis tool INA [SR97] for analysis of the consistency conditions, and PEP [BG96] for analysis of the concurrency degree.

After being satisfied with the behavior exhibited by the animation of the Petri net, we perform general analyses. As a general consistency condition for our model, we show that the underlying Petri net is well-formed (which combines boundedness and liveness).

Boundedness. A place invariant x is a set of places, for which the token conservation equation

$$\sum_{p \in P} x(p) \cdot m_0(p) = \sum_{p \in P} x(p) \cdot m(p)$$

holds for all reachable markings m. Our net is covered by the following 8 semi-positive place invariants (where $x(p)$ always equals 1 for the mentioned places, and 0 otherwise):

$inv1 : (at\_front, not\_at\_front)$
$inv2 : (at\_end, not\_at\_end)$
$inv3 : (mvt\_on, mvt\_off)$

$inv4 : (number\_of\_plates, maxplates)$
$inv5 : (at\_front, at\_end, maxplates, in\_between)$
$inv6 : (table\_unloaded, moving1, can\_receive, table\_loaded, moving2, at\_unload\_pos)$
$inv7 : (consumer\_ready)$
$inv8 : (producer\_ready)$

Therefore it is bounded. More concretely: the token sum of the place invariants 1–3, 6–8 equals 1. Therefore, the corresponding places are 1-bounded. The token sum of the place invariants 4 and 5, on the other hand, equals $maxplates$. Therefore, the corresponding places can hold at most $maxplates$ tokens. Hence, we are able to conclude the k-boundedness of the net (with $k = maxplates$). Moreover, by combining the place invariants 4 and 5 we are able to conclude that for all reachable markings holds: $at\_front + in\_between + at\_end = number\_of\_plates$, which reflects an obvious consistency condition of the feed belt model, see Sect. 3.1, invariant of the schema $feed\_belt$.

Liveness. The net structure is extended simple, and the structural property called deadlock-trap property [Sta90] holds. Therefore, we can conclude without construction of the total system space that the pure net is live (which includes deadlock freedom). This is a necessary condition for the liveness of the Z-Petri net.

Concurrency degree. Figure 3 shows the basic concurrent behavior (after the initialization phase) of a production cell with a feed belt capacity of one. It has been derived from the so-called finite prefix of branching processes (produced by PEP), to highlight (and check) the essential behavior of the designed production cell. The derived net demonstrates the behavior of the Petri net shown in Figure 2 under the partial order semantics by showing two concurrent cycles of atomic actions (transitions, Z operations), synchronized by one common operation (fb_to_table). In other words, the action sequence $load\_fb - leave\_front - detect$ to equip the feed belt occurs concurrently with the table's motions from $load\_position$ to $unload\_position$ and back.

The three conflicts (non-deterministic behavior) in the concurrent behavior description are resolved by the Z operations' preconditions, because these exclude each other. Taking those into account, the feed belt is only switched off if the table does not work fast enough. Consequently, the feed belt will still be running while it is empty (because the producer is too slow). Therefore, the net is not reversible: loading the feed belt, and moving the table to the load position while the feed belt is switched off may happen only once at the beginning. This kind of behavior (which may be deemed to be undesirable) hardly becomes obvious by merely inspecting the specification.

If $maxplates = 1$, there only exists concurrency between operations on different subsystems that are independent of each other, i.e., work on disjoint state components. For $maxplates > 1$, however, we can identify the following concurrent operations[3]:

---

[3] Up to now, the theory of (a finite prefix of) branching processes is restricted to 1-bounded Petri nets. Therefore, the identification of the additional concurrent operations was not tool-supported. However, the generalization to bounded Petri nets is an emerging research area in Petri net theory.

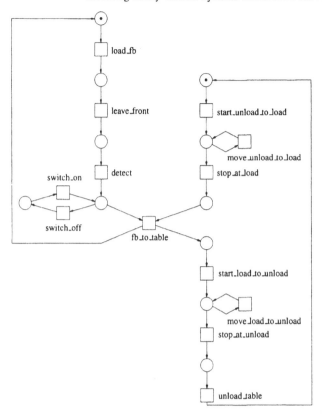

Fig. 3. Concurrent behavior of Petri net of Fig. 2 for *maxplates* = 1

- The operation *load_fb* may happen concurrently with *detect*, *switch_on*, *switch_off*, and *fb_to_table*.
- The operation *leave_front* may happen concurrently with *detect*, and *fb_to_table*.

3.4   Checking Coherence of the Two Specifications

As described in Section 2, we must show the compatibility of the two specifications.

It is easily verified that the initial marking of the Petri net is consistent with the Z specification. For example, there is a token at the place *not_at_front*, which is necessary because the initial condition of the feed belt requires *number_of_plates* = 0.

For the chains in the Petri net, it is also easy to see that the postconditions of all operations in a chain are compatible with the preconditions of their successors. As an example, consider the operations *switch_off* and *switch_on*. The operation *switch_off* establishes the condition *fb_mvt* = *off*, as required by *switch_on*. Because *switch_off* establishes the condition *at_end* = 1, the second precondition of *switch_on*, viz. *number_of_plates* > 0 is also fulfilled. It follows that after a *switch_off* operation, a *switch_on* operation is possible as soon as *can_receive* holds, i.e., as soon as the table is ready.

Finally, we must demonstrate that the order in which concurrent operations are invoked is irrelevant. Considering for example the operations *load_fb* and *detect*, we first identify the set of states where both preconditions hold. For these states, we have $0 < number\_of\_plates < maxplates$, $at\_front = at\_end = 0$, $fb\_mvt = on$, and $in\_between > 0$. Executing the operations *load_fb* and *detect* yields a state where $number\_of\_plates$ is increased by one, $in\_between$ is decreased by one, $at\_front = at\_end = 1$, and $fb\_mvt = on$, independently of the order in which the operations are invoked. For the other concurrent operations, the reasoning proceeds in the same way.

3.5   Application-Dependent Validation of the Model

Lewerentz and Lindner [LL95] enumerate several safety requirements for the production cell control software. The requirements concerning the feed belt and the table are:

1. The blanks have sufficient distance so that they can be distinguished.
2. The table does not move beyond its extreme points.
3. Blanks are not dropped off the feed belt when the table is not ready. The feed belt is stopped before this can happen.

Requirement 1 is reflected in our specification by the precondition of the operation *load_fb*: the state variable *at_front* must be zero, which means that the sensor reports that no plate is present at the front of the feed belt. This condition suffices to fulfill requirement 1. Once the operation *load_fb* is implemented, it must be demonstrated that the implementation indeed faithfully reflects the Z specification.

Requirement 2 is taken care of in the postconditions of the operations *stop_at_load* and *stop_at_unload*. When the table has reached one of the extreme positions, the position engines are switched off, and the operations *move_unload_to_load* or *move_load_to_unload* respectively, are no longer possible. Again, every implemented system being correct with respect to the Z specification fullfills safety requirement 2.

To show that requirement 3 is fulfilled, we must show that if $at\_end = 1 \wedge fb\_mvt = on \wedge can\_receive = no$ then $fb\_mvt = off$ must hold within a certain time bound that is small enough to prevent the plate from being dropped in an unsafe area. If $maxplates = 1$, we can show that $fb\_mvt = off$ holds in the next state after $at\_end = 1 \wedge fb\_mvt = on \wedge can\_receive = no$ holds, because the only operation whose precondition is fulfilled is *switch_off*. If $maxplates > 1$, however, we can only guarantee under the interleaving semantics that $fb\_mvt = off$ holds after at most $2(maxplates - 1)$ operations other than *switch_off* have been executed (these operations are *load_fb* and *leave_front*). An exact proof that the feed belt is switched off fast enough requires a quantitative analysis using time-dependent Petri nets or a partial order semantics. Using transitions whose firing is restricted by time intervals, we would be able to formulate and check the time conditions under which *switch_off* is always faster than *load_fb* and *leave_front*, respectively.

4   Conclusions

Nowadays, it is well recognized that combining data-oriented and behavioral formalisms is an adequate approach to specify embedded systems[4], and in particular safety-critical systems. Z has been combined with a number of other formalisms. We contrast our approach with two such combinations that have been specifically designed for specifying safety-critical embedded systems.

The combination of Z and real-time CSP defined by Heisel and Sühl [HS96] leads to very abstract and concise specifications, but tool support for validating specifications is limited and it is in general impossible to animate such specifications.

The language μSZ developed in the German ESPRESS project [BDG$^+$96] is a combination of the Statemate languages [HLN$^+$90] (namely statecharts and activity charts) and Z. Its advantage is that many engineers are familiar with finite state machines and hence may find μSZ specifications easily accessible.

The combination of Z and Petri nets, however, is superior to both afore-mentioned combinations as far as the means for animation and analysis are concerned. Animation tools provide an executable model of the system that allows customers to get an impression of how the system will behave. Furthermore, a variety of analysis tools (which are available free of charge) provide richer validation facilities than they are available for other formalisms. Checking consistency of the two parts of the specification further enhances confidence in the model.

The reader may see some similarities between our approach and CPN [Jen92] (a quasi-standard of coloured Petri nets), which combines Petri nets with inscriptions written in (a version of) the functional programming language ML. Because our primary objective is formal system specification, however, we prefer to use a pure specification language instead of a programming language in combination with Petri nets.

Our case study has shown that, because of the combination with Z, the Petri net model becomes quite concise and well comprehensible. The reduction of the number of nodes is considerable. Hence, our combination of Z and Petri nets is a promising approach to model safety-critical systems and validate these models.

To make our combined language acceptable to a wider audience, it is necessary to provide methodological support for its application. In the future, we intend to develop methods for

- Setting up combined specifications.
  Here, we need to develop heuristics for the order in which the two parts of a specification are developed, how to separate the software controller from its environment, etc.
- Validating combined specifications.
  A relation to classical safety analysis techniques would be desirable.
- Deriving implementations from combined specifications.

---

[4] This year, an international workshop "Integrated Formal Methods 1999–A Workshop on Combining State-Based and Behavioural Formalisms" on this specific topic takes place.

The combined language, an underlying methodology, and related tool support is likely to lead to a powerful approach for tackling the problem of system and especially software safety.

References

[BDG⁺96] R. Büssow, H. Dörr, R. Geisler, W. Grieskamp, and M. Klar. μSZ – ein Ansatz zur systematischen Verbindung von Z und Statecharts. Technical Report TR 96-32, Technische Universität Berlin, 1996.

[BG96] E. Best and B. Grahlmann. PEP–more than a Petri net tool. In *Proceedings TACAS'96*, LNCS 1055, pages 397–401. Springer-Verlag, 1996.

[BGHH98] R. Büssow, W. Grieskamp, W. Heicking, and S. Herrmann. An open environment for the integration of heterogeneous modelling techniques and tools. In *Current Trends in Applied Formal Methods*. Springer-Verlag, 1998. to appear.

[HDS99] M. Heiner, P. Deussen, and J. Spranger. A case study in developing control software of manufacturing systems with hierarchical Petri nets. *Int. Journal of Advanced Manufacturing Technology*, 15:139–152, 1999.

[HLN⁺90] D. Harel, H. Lachover, A. Naamad, A. Pnueli, M. Politi, R. Sherman, A. Shtull-Trauring, and M. rakhtenbrot. Statemate: A working environment for the development of complex reactive systems. *IEEE Transactions on Software Engineering*, 16 No. 4, April 1990.

[HS96] M. Heisel and C. Sühl. Formal specification of safety-critical software with Z and real-time CSP. In E. Schoitsch, editor, *Proceedings 15th International Conference on Computer Safety, Reliability and Security (SAFECOMP)*, pages 31–45. Springer-Verlag London, 1996.

[Jen92] K. Jensen. *Coloured Petri Nets, Basic Concepts, Analysis Methods and Practical Use, Vol. 1*. Springer-Verlag, 1992.

[KSW96] Kolyang, T. Santen, and B. Wolff. A structure preserving encoding of Z in Isabelle/HOL. In J. von Wright, J. Grundy, and J. Harrison, editors, *Theorem Proving in Higher-Order Logics*, LNCS 1125, pages 283–298. Springer-Verlag, 1996.

[LL95] C. Lewerentz and T. Lindner, editors. *Formal Development of Reactive Systems*. LNCS 891. Springer-Verlag, 1995.

[LS96] N. Lévy and J. Souquières. A "Coming and Going" Approach to Specification Construction: a Scenario. In W. Schäfer, J. Kramer, and A. Wolf, editors, *Proc. 8th Int. Workshop on Software Specification and Design*, pages 115–118. IEEE Computer Society Press, 1996.

[Men97] T. Menzel. Entwurf und Prototypimplementierung eines Petri-Netz-Framework. Technical report, BTU Cottbus, Institut für Informatik, 1997.

[Saa97] M. Saaltink. The Z/EVES system. In J. Bowen, M. Hinchey, and D. Till, editors, *ZUM'97: The Z Formal Specification Notation*, LNCS 1212, pages 72–88. Springer-Verlag, 1997.

[Spi92a] J. M. Spivey. The fuzz manual. Computing Science Consultancy, Oxford, 1992.

[Spi92b] J. M. Spivey. *The Z Notation – A Reference Manual*. Prentice Hall, 2nd edition, 1992.

[SR97] P. H. Starke and S. Roch. INA–Integrated Net Analyser version 1.7. Technical report, Humboldt-Universität Berlin, 1997.

[Sta90] P. H. Starke. *Analyse von Petri-Netz-Modellen*. Teubner, 1990.

[Tie97] R. Tiedemann. PED – Hierarchischer Petri-Netz-Editor. Technical report, BTU Cottbus, Institut für Informatik, 1997.

On Formal Languages for Sequences of Authorization Transformations

Yun Bai and Vijay Varadharajan

School of Computing and Information Technology
University of Western Sydney Nepean, Australia
Email: {ybai, vijay}@cit.nepean.uws.edu.au

Abstract. In a multi-user, information-sharing computer systems, authorization policy is needed to ensure that the information flows in the desired way and to prevent illegal access to the system resource. Usually such policy has a temporal property. That is, it needs to be updated to capture the changing requirements of applications, systems and users. These updates are implemented via transformation of authorization policies. In this paper, we propose two high-level formal languages $\mathcal{L}$ and $\mathcal{L}^d$ to specify the transformation of authorizations in secure computer systems. $\mathcal{L}$ is a simple language that can be used to specify a sequence of authorization transformations. Though it has a simple syntax and semantics, we show that $\mathcal{L}$ is expressive enough to specify some well-known examples of authorization transformations. Language $\mathcal{L}^d$ is an augmentation of $\mathcal{L}$ which includes *default propositions* within the domain description of authorization policies. However, the semantics of $\mathcal{L}^d$ is not just a simple extension of the semantics of $\mathcal{L}$. We show that $\mathcal{L}^d$ is more expressive than $\mathcal{L}$ in that constraints, causal and inherited authorizations, and general default authorizations can be specified.
Key words: Authorization Policies, Policy Transformation, Default logic, Formal language

1 Introduction

In a multi-user, information-sharing computer systems, authorization policy is needed to ensure that the information flows in the desired way and to prevent illegal access to the system resource. Overall, authorization policy provides the ability to limit and control accesses to system, applications and information. In the real world, such policy has a temporal property. That is, it needs to be updated to capture the changing requirements of applications, systems and users. These updates are implemented via transformation of authorization policies. In our previous paper [1], we proposed a model-based approach to specify the transformation of authorizations based on the *principle of minimal change* [3]. Nevertheless, there were some limitations in our previous approach. Firstly, we could not represent a sequence of transformations. Secondly, default authorizations could not be expressed.

In this paper, we propose two high-level formal languages $\mathcal{L}$ and $\mathcal{L}^d$ to specify the transformation of authorization in secure computer systems. In particular,

M. Felici, K. Kanoun, A. Pasquini (Eds.): SAFECOMP'99, LNCS 1698, pp. 375-384, 1999

$\mathcal{L}$ is a simple language that can be used to specify a sequence of authorization transformations. Though it has a simple syntax and semantics, we show that $\mathcal{L}$ is expressive enough to specify some well-known examples of authorization transformations such as separation of duty and Chinese wall security policy. Language $\mathcal{L}^d$ is an augmentation of $\mathcal{L}$ which includes *default propositions* into the domain description. We show that $\mathcal{L}^d$ has more powerful expressiveness than $\mathcal{L}$ in the sense that constraints, causal and inherited authorizations, and general default authorizations can be specified within $\mathcal{L}^d$.

To simplify our presentation, in this paper, we assume the existence of a system security officer administering the authorization transformations. This assumption enables us to concentrate on a single administering agent system and hence avoid the problem of coordination of multiagents.

The paper is organized as follows. Section 2 describes the language $\mathcal{L}$ where both its syntax and semantics are defined. Examples of transformations of authorizations are also illustrated in this section. Section 3 specifies the language $\mathcal{L}^d$, which is an augmentation of $\mathcal{L}$. $\mathcal{L}^d$ is able to represent more complex authorization policies such as constraints, causal and inherited policies as well as default policies. Finally, section 4 presents the conclusion to the paper.

2   Language $\mathcal{L}$

2.1   Syntax of $\mathcal{L}$

Language $\mathcal{L}$ includes the following seven disjoint sorts for *subject, group-subject, access-right, group-access-right, object, group-object* and *transformation* together with predicate symbols *holds*, $\in$, $\subseteq$ and logic connectives $\land$ and $\neg$:

1. *Subject* with finite number of subject constants $S, S_1, S_2, \cdots$, and subject variables $s, s_1, s_2, \cdots$.
2. *Group-subject* with finite number of group subject constants $G, G_1, G_2, \cdots$, and group subject variables $g, g_1, g_2, \cdots$.
3. *Access-right* with finite number of access right constants $A, A_1, A_2, \cdots$, and access right variables $a, a_1, a_2, \cdots$.
4. *Group-access-right* with finite number of group access right constants GA, $GA_1, GA_2, \cdots$, and group access right variables $ga, ga_1, ga_2, \cdots$.
5. *Object* with finite number of object constants $O, O_1, O_2, \cdots$, and object variables $o, o_1, o_2, \cdots$.
6. *Group-object* with finite number of group object constants $GO, GO_1, GO_2, \cdots$, and group object variables $go, go_1, go_2, \cdots$.
7. *Transformation* with finite number of transformations $T, T_1, T_2, \cdots$.

In language $\mathcal{L}$, the fact that a subject S has access right R for object O is represented using a ground atom $holds(S, R, O)$. The fact that a subject S is a member of G is represented by $S \in G$. Similarly, we represent inclusion relationships between subject groups such as $G_1 \subseteq G_2$ or between access right groups such as $GA_1 \subseteq GA_2$.

In general, we define a *fact* F to be an atomic formula of $\mathcal{L}$ or its negation, while a *ground fact* is a fact without variable occurrence. We view $\neg\neg F$ as F. *Fact expressions* of $\mathcal{L}$ are defined as follows: (i) each fact is a fact expression; (ii) if ϕ and ψ are fact expressions, then $\phi \wedge \psi$ is also a fact expression. A *ground fact expression* is a fact expression without variable occurrence. A ground fact expression is called a *ground instance* of a fact expression if this ground fact expression is obtained from the fact expression by replacing each of its variable occurrence with the same sort constant. Now we are ready to formally define the propositions in $\mathcal{L}$.

A *policy proposition* in $\mathcal{L}$ is an expression of the form

$$\phi \textbf{ after } T_1, \cdots, T_m, \tag{1}$$

where ϕ is a ground fact expression and $T_1, \cdots, T_m$ $(m \geq 0)$ are transformations. Intuitively, this proposition means that after performing transformations $T_1, \cdots, T_m$ sequentially, the ground fact expression ϕ holds. If $m = 0$, we will rewrite (1) as

$$\textbf{initially } \phi, \tag{2}$$

which is called *initial policy proposition*.

A *transformation proposition* is an expression of the form

$$T \textbf{ causes } \phi \textbf{ if } \psi, \tag{3}$$

where T is a transformation, ϕ and ψ are ground fact expressions. Intuitively, a transformation proposition expresses the following meaning: at a given state, if the pre-condition ψ is true, then after performing the transformation T at this state, the ground fact expression ϕ will be true in the resulting state.

If the set of ψ is empty, we will rewrite (3) as

$$T \textbf{ causes } \phi, \tag{4}$$

which means that there is no precondition to perform the transformation or the precondition is always true. That is, the transformation can always be performed.

A *policy domain description* D in $\mathcal{L}$ is a finite set of initial policy propositions and transformation propositions.

Example 1. Let us now consider the specification of the Chinese wall access policy [2] using our domain description. The Chinese wall access policy can be viewed as a special kind of dynamic separation of duty. In Chinese wall policy, objects are grouped into *company datasets*, for instance $Company_1$ and $Company_2$. Company datasets whose organizations are in competition are then grouped together into *conflict of interest classes*. A subject can potentially access an object from either company dataset, but if the subject accesses an object in a company dataset 1, it cannot be allowed anymore to access any object in a company dataset that appear in a conflict of interest class with dataset 1. In our language, company datasets can be represented by a *group-object*. For instance, if $Company_1$ and $Company_2$ are in the same conflict of interest class, a subject who has accessed an object of $Company_1$ will not be allowed to access any object in $Company_2$ and vice versa.

Suppose that $Company_1$ and $Company_2$ are in the same conflict of interest class, O_1 is an object of $Company_1$ and O_2 is an object of $Company_2$ and S is a subject. We use $holds(S, Accessable, O_1)$ and $holds(S, Accessable, O_2)$ to represent that S can potentially access both O_1 and O_2. We have the following transformations: $Rqst(S, Access, O_1)$ and $Rqst(S, Access, O_2)$. The domain description D is specified as follows:

> **initially** $O_1 \in Company_1$,
> **initially** $O_2 \in Company_2$,
> **initially** $holds(S, Accessable, O_1)$,
> **initially** $holds(S, Accessable, O_2)$,
>
> $Rqst(S, Access, O_1)$ **causes**
> $holds(S, Access, O_1) \land$
> $\neg holds(S, Accessable, O_2)$
>   **if** $O_1 \in Company_1 \land O_2 \in Company_2 \land holds(S, Accessable, O_1)$,
>
> $Rqst(S, Access, O_2)$ **causes**
> $holds(S, Access, O_2) \land$
> $\neg holds(S, Accessable, O_1)$
>   **if** $O_1 \in Company_1 \land O_2 \in Company_2 \land holds(S, Accessable, O_2)$.

That is, if S accesses O_1, then it will not be able to access O_2 due to the transformation $Rqst(S, Access, O_1)$. Similarly, if S accesses O_2, it will not be able to access O_1.

Note here we only use the simplified specification for constraints and quantifiers for the general statements such as "for any subject S" and "for any object O" to illustrate the examples specified by the language.

2.2   Semantics of $\mathcal{L}$

Now we define the semantics of language $\mathcal{L}$. A *state* is a set of ground facts. Given a ground fact F and a state σ, we say F is *true* in σ iff $F \in \sigma$, and F is *false* in σ iff $\neg F \in \sigma$. A ground fact expression $\phi \equiv F_1 \land \cdots \land F_k$, where each F_i $(1 \le i \le k)$ is a ground fact, is *true* in σ iff each F_i $(1 \le i \le k)$ is in σ. Furthermore, a fact expression with variables is true in σ iff each of its ground instances is true in σ. An *inconsistent state* σ is a state containing a pair of complementary ground facts F and $\neg F$.

A *transition function* ρ maps a set (T, σ) into a state, where T is a transformation and σ is a state. Intuitively, $\rho(T, \sigma)$ denotes the resulting state caused by performing transformation T in σ. A *structure* M is a pair (σ, ρ), where σ is a state, and ρ is a transition function. For any structure M and any set of transformations $T_1, \cdots, T_m$, the notation $M^{T_1, \cdots, T_m}$ denotes the state

$$\rho(T_m, \rho(T_{m-1}, \cdots, \rho(T_1, \sigma) \cdots)),$$

where ρ is the transition function of M, and σ is the state of M.

We denote a policy proposition *is satisfied* in a structure M as $M \models_{\mathcal{L}} \phi$ **after** $T_1, \cdots, T_m$. This is true iff ϕ is true in the state $M^{T_1, \cdots, T_m}$. Given a domain description D, we say that a state σ_0 is the *initial state* of D iff (i) for each initial policy proposition **initially** ϕ of D, ϕ is true in σ_0; (ii) if there is another state σ satisfying condition (i), then $\sigma_0 \subseteq \sigma$ (i.e. σ_0 is the least state satisfying all initial policy propositions of D).

Definition 1. *A structure* (σ_0, ρ) *is a* model *of a domain description D iff σ_0 is a consistent initial state of D, and for any transformation T and state σ, the following conditions hold:*

(i) if D includes a transformation proposition T **causes** ϕ **if** ψ*, and ψ is true in σ, then ϕ is true in $\rho(T, \sigma)$;*
(ii) for each F in D which does not occur in ϕ in proposition T **causes** ϕ **if** ψ*, $F \in \rho(T, \sigma)$ iff $F \in \sigma$;*
(iii) for each F in D which occurs in ϕ in proposition T **causes** ϕ **if** ψ*, and ψ is not true in σ, then $F \in \rho(T, \sigma)$ iff $F \in \sigma$.*

We say that a domain description D is *consistent* if D has a model. A policy proposition ϕ **after** $T_1, \cdots, T_m$ is *entailed* by D, denoted as $D \models_{\mathcal{L}} \phi$ **after** $T_1, \cdots, T_m$, iff it is true in each model of D.

Example 2. Continuation of Example 1. For the Chinese wall policy, the initial state of D is:

$$\sigma_0 = \{O_1 \in Company_1, O_2 \in Company_2, holds(S, Accessible, O_1)$$
$$holds(S, Accessible, O_2)\}.$$

From the above description, it is not difficult to show that

$D \models_{\mathcal{L}} O_1 \in Company_1 \wedge O_2 \in Company_2 \wedge holds(S, Access, O_1) \wedge$
   $\neg holds(S, Accessible, O_2)$
    after $Rqst(S, Access, O_1)$,
$D \models_{\mathcal{L}} O_1 \in Company_1 \wedge O_2 \in Company_2 \wedge holds(S, Access, O_2) \wedge$
   $\neg holds(S, Accessible, O_1)$
    after $Rqst(S, Access, O_2)$,
$D \models_{\mathcal{L}} O_1 \in Company_1 \wedge O_2 \in Company_2 \wedge holds(S, Access, O_1) \wedge$
   $\neg holds(S, Accessible, O_2)$
    after $Rqst(S, Access, O_1), Rqst(S, Access, O_2)$,
$D \models_{\mathcal{L}} O_1 \in Company_1 \wedge O_2 \in Company_2 \wedge holds(S, Access, O_2) \wedge$
   $\neg holds(S, Accessible, O_1)$
    after $Rqst(S, Access, O_2), Rqst(S, Access, O_1)$.

2.3   Properties and Limitations of Language $\mathcal{L}$

Language $\mathcal{L}$ has the following properties:

- *Incomplete information is allowed.* In $\mathcal{L}$, the state of the authorization policies can be specified to be *incomplete* in the sense that some authorizations may not be represented in the state.
- *Denials are expressed explicitly.* As incomplete information is allowed in the state of authorization policies, denials (negations of authorization policies) must be explicitly represented in the state.
- *The entailment relation $\models_\mathcal{L}$ of $\mathcal{L}$ is nonmonotonic with respect to transformation propositions.* The nonmonotonicity of $\models_\mathcal{L}$ with respect to transformation propositions states that adding more transformation propositions into D may result in a policy proposition being no longer entailed in the domain description.
- $\models_\mathcal{L}$ *is also nonmonotonic with respect to policy propositions.* This can be observed from the following example. Suppose a domain description D consists of the following policy and transformation propositions:
  initially $holds(S, Own, File)$,
  $Delete\text{-}own(S, Own, File)$ **causes** $\neg holds(S, Own, File)$ **if** $S \in G$.
  As the pre-condition $S \in G$ does not hold in the initial state, we have $D \models_\mathcal{L} holds(S, Own, File)$ **after** $Delete\text{-}own(S, Own, File)$. However, if $S \in G$ is added into D to form a new domain description D', then we have
  $D' \models_\mathcal{L} \neg holds(S, Own, File)$ **after** $Delete\text{-}own(S, Own, File)$.

But $\mathcal{L}$ has some limitations:

- $\mathcal{L}$ cannot express *inherited* and *causal* authorization policies. For instance, in many situations, a subject can inherit an access right from its group's access right. Unfortunately, this kind of fact cannot be expressed by $\mathcal{L}$.
- $\mathcal{L}$ cannot express default authorization policies. For instance, the *closed world assumption* on the state of authorization policies can be viewed as a general default authorization: any policy that is not explicitly represented in the state will be assumed to be its negation.
- $\mathcal{L}$ cannot express *constraints.* Sometimes we need to specify some restrictions on authorization policies. These restrictions are represented by *constraints* which should be satisfied by any state.

3   Language $\mathcal{L}^d$

3.1   Syntax of $\mathcal{L}^d$

Language $\mathcal{L}^d$ is introduced to overcome the limitations of language $\mathcal{L}$. $\mathcal{L}^d$ has the same sorts and types of propositions as $\mathcal{L}$ but in addition has one more type of proposition called *default proposition* as follows:

$$\phi \text{ implies } \psi \text{ with absence } \gamma, \tag{5}$$

where ϕ, ψ and γ are fact expressions. Note that ϕ, ψ and γ may contain variables. In this case, the default proposition (5) will be treated as a set of default propositions obtained from (5) by replacing ϕ, ψ and γ with their ground instances respectively.

Intuitively, the default proposition says that if ϕ is true in a state σ, and it can not be derived that γ is true in σ, then we will infer that ψ is true in σ.

There is a special form of the default proposition when the set γ is empty in (5). In this case, we rewrite (5) as

$$\phi \text{ provokes } \psi, \tag{6}$$

which is viewed as a *causal* or *inheritance* relation between ϕ and ψ. For example, in many situations, a system should satisfy the following relation:

$$holds(s, Own, o) \text{ provokes } holds(s, Read, o) \land holds(s, Write, o).$$

On the other hand, there is also a special form of (6) when the set ϕ is empty. In this case we rewrite (6) as

$$\text{always } \psi, \tag{7}$$

which represents a *constraint* that should be satisfied by any state in the domain. For instance, we may express a constraint stating that the Root has any right for any object as follows:

always $holds(Root, r, o)$.

We define a transformation-based policy domain description D (or domain description for short) in language $\mathcal{L}^d$ as a finite set of initial policy propositions, transformation propositions and default propositions.

3.2   Semantics of $\mathcal{L}^d$

The semantics of $\mathcal{L}^d$ is not just a trivial extension of the semantics of $\mathcal{L}$ although the syntax of $\mathcal{L}^d$ is a simple augmentation of that of $\mathcal{L}$. The reason is that to define a proper semantics of the default proposition (5), we have to employ a *fix-point semantics* that shares the spirit of fix-point semantics used in *extended logic programs* [4].

Given a domain description D, we first define the initial state of D. First we suppose that a domain description D_p only contains initial policy propositions, default propositions of the special form (6) and transformation propositions.

Definition 2. *A state σ_0 is an initial state of D_p iff σ_0 is the smallest state that satisfies the following conditions:*

(i) for each initial policy proposition **initially** ϕ, ϕ *is true in σ_0;*
(ii) for each default proposition with the form ϕ **provokes** ψ, *if ϕ is true in σ_0, then ψ is also true in σ_0.*

Now we consider a domain description D containing default propositions with the general form (5). To define the initial state of D, we first translate D to domain description D_p described above.

Definition 3. *Let σ_0 be a state. Suppose domain description D_p is obtained from D as follows:*

(i) by deleting each default proposition ϕ **implies** *ψ* **with absence** *γ from D if for some F_i in γ, F_i is true in σ_0;*
(ii) by translating all other default propositions ϕ **implies** *ψ* **with absence** *γ to the form ϕ* **provokes** *ψ.*

Now if this state σ_0 is an initial state of D_p, then we also define it to be an initial state *of D.*

Taking default propositions into account, it turns out that the initial state of a domain description may be not unique, or may not even exist. This is shown by the following example.

Example 3. A domain description D consists of the following propositions:

> **initially** $holds(S, Own, O)$,
> $holds(S, Own, O)$ **implies** $holds(S, Write, O)$
>   **with absence** $\neg holds(S, Write, O)$,
> $holds(S, Own, O)$ **implies** $\neg holds(S, Write, O)$
>   **with absence** $holds(S, Write, O)$,
> $Delete\text{-}own(S, Own, O)$ **causes** $\neg holds(S, Own, O))$.

Clearly, D has two initial states:

> $\sigma_0 = \{holds(S, Own, O), holds(S, Write, O)\}$, and
> $\sigma_0' = \{holds(S, Own, O), \neg holds(S, Write, O)\}$.

Consider another domain description D' consisting of the following propositions:

> **initially** $holds(S, Own, O)$,
> $holds(S, Own, O)$ **implies** $holds(S, Write, O)$
>   **with absence** $holds(S, Write, O)$,
> $Delete\text{-}own(S, Own, O)$ **causes** $\neg holds(S, Own, O))$.

D' has no initial state according to the definition described above.

Similar to that defined in the language $\mathcal{L}$, we define that a *structure* of D to be a pair (σ, ρ), where σ is a state, and ρ is a transition function introduced in section 2. A policy proposition (1) *is satisfied* in a structure M, denoted as $M \models_{\mathcal{L}^d} \phi$ **after** $T_1, \cdots, T_m$, if ϕ is true in state $M^{T_1, \cdots, T_m}$.

To define the model of a domain description, we need to introduce one more definition.

Definition 4. *Let D be a domain description. For any state σ and transformation T, we define a* reduced domain description *(with only default propositions) of D with respect to σ and T, denoted as $D^{\sigma,T}$, consisting of the following propositions:*

(i) *for each ground fact F of σ,* T **implies** F **with absence** $\neg F$ *is a default proposition of $D^{\sigma,T}$;*
(ii) *each default proposition of D is a default proposition of $D^{\sigma,T}$;*
(iii) *if D includes a transformation proposition T* **causes** ϕ **if** ψ, *then ψ* **provokes** ψ *is a default proposition of $D^{\sigma,T}$.*

Definition 5. *Given a domain description D, let (σ_0, ρ) be a structure of D, where σ_0 is an initial state of D, and ρ is a transition function introduced in section 2. (σ_0, ρ) is a* model *of D iff σ_0 is consistent, and for any transformation T and state σ, $\rho(T, \sigma)$ is an initial state of $D^{\sigma,T}$.*

Clearly, a domain description D may have one or more or no models. D is *consistent* if D has a model. A policy proposition ϕ **after** $T_1, \cdots, T_m$ is entailed by D, denoted as $D \models_{\mathcal{L}^d} \phi$ **after** $T_1, \cdots, T_m$ iff it is true in each model of D. A model M of D is *complete* if for any policy proposition ϕ **after** $T_1, \cdots, T_m$, either $D \models_{\mathcal{L}^d} \phi$ **after** $T_1, \cdots, T_m$ or $D \models_{\mathcal{L}^d} \neg \phi$ **after** $T_1, \cdots, T_m$.

Example 4. A credit union divides its customers into two classes G_1 and G_2. The member of G_1 has a credit limit of up to \$5000. The member of G_2 has a credit limit of up to \$10000. The credit union reviews the credits of its customers and upgrade or downgrade their credit limits accordingly. A, B and C are three customers of this credit union. Suppose the information we know is that B belongs to G_2, A has a credit limit of up to \$5000 and C belongs to G_1 and has a credit limit of \$5000. The domain description D for this example is:

initially $holds(A, Credit, \$5000)$,
initially $holds(C, Credit, \$5000)$,
initially $B \in G_2$,
initially $C \in G_1$,
$holds(A, Credit, \$5000)$ **implies** $A \in G_1$
    with absence $A \in G_2$,
$B \in G_2$ **provokes** $holds(B, Credit, \$10000)$.

Suppose x represents a general customer, the *transformation propositions* are:

Upgrade (x) **causes** $x \in G_2$ **if** $x \in G_1$,
Downgrade (x) **causes** $x \in G_1$ **if** $x \in G_2$.

The initial state of D is:

$\sigma_0 = \{holds(A, Credit, \$5000), holds(B, Credit, \$10000),$
$\quad holds(C, Credit, \$5000), A \in G_1, B \in G_2, C \in G_1\}$

Obviously, the following holds:

$D \models_{\mathcal{L}^d} holds(A, Credit, \$10000) \wedge holds(B, Credit, \$10000) \wedge$
    $holds(C, Credit, \$5000) \wedge A \in G_2 \wedge B \in G_2 \wedge C \in G_1$
    after $Upgrade(A),$

$D \models_{\mathcal{L}^d} holds(A, Credit, \$5000) \wedge holds(B, Credit, \$5000) \wedge$
    $holds(C, Credit, \$5000) \wedge A \in G_1 \wedge B \in G_1 \wedge C \in G_1$
    after $Downgrade(B).$

After sequentially executing $Upgrade(A)$ and $Downgrade(B)$, the following will hold:

$D \models_{\mathcal{L}^d} holds(A, Credit, \$10000) \wedge holds(B, Credit, \$5000) \wedge$
    $holds(C, Credit, \$5000) \wedge A \in G_2 \wedge B \in G_1 \wedge C \in G_1$
    after $Upgrade(A), Downgrade(B).$

4   Conclusions

In this paper, we have proposed two high level languages $\mathcal{L}$ and $\mathcal{L}^d$ to specify sequences of authorization transformations. We have shown that the language $\mathcal{L}$ has a simple syntax and semantics, but is expressive enough to represent some well known access policies involving sequences of authorization transformations. Language $\mathcal{L}^d$ is an augmentation of $\mathcal{L}$ which includes *default propositions*. It has more powerful expressiveness than $\mathcal{L}$ in the sense that constraints, causal and inherited authorizations as well as general default authorizations can be specified. We are also at present applying this approach to specification and reasoning about authorizations in object-oriented databases.

References

1. Y. Bai and V. Varadharajan, A logic for state transformations in authorization policies. *the Proceedings of the 10th IEEE Computer Security Foundations Workshop*, pp 173-182, Massachusetts, June, 1997.
2. D.F.C.Brewer and M.J.Nash, The Chinese wall security policy. *Proceedings of IEEE Symposium on Security and Privacy*, pp 215-228, Oakland, May 1989.
3. T.S-C. Chou, M. Winslett, Immortal: a Model-based Belief Revision System, *The 2nd International Conference on Principles of Knowledge Representation and Reasoning*, Morgan Kaufman Publishers Inc. pp 99–110, 1991.
4. M. Gelfond and V. Lifschitz, Classical negation in logic programs and disjunctive databases. *New Generation Computing*, 9:365-385, 1991.

Scheduling Fault-Tolerant Programs on Multiple Processors to Maximize Schedule Reliability

Ireneusz Czarnowski[1], Piotr Jedrzejowicz[1], and Ewa Ratajczak[1]

[1] Chair of Computer Science, Gdynia Maritime Academy,
ul. Morska 83, 81-225 Gdynia, Poland
{irek, pj, ewra}@wsm.gdynia.pl

Abstract. The paper proposes to manage complexity and costs issues of the fault-tolerant programs not at a single program level but rather from the point of view of the whole set of such programs, which are to be run under hard time constraints. A concept of the multiple processor programs is used to model a fault-tolerant program structure. This model, in turn, is used to formulate the fault-tolerant programs scheduling problem under hard time constraints. Since the discussed problem is computationally difficult, three scheduling algorithms, based on three different metaheuristics, have been proposed. To evaluate the proposed algorithms computational experiment has been carried. The proposed global approach has been also compared with scheduling without search for the global optimum. Experiment results prove that the approach could be advantageous by producing more reliable schedules within hard time constraints.

1. Introduction

Recent advances in the following important areas of research have motivated the paper: scheduling in hard real time systems, fault tolerant computing, and software reliability optimization.

In general, scheduling algorithms in hard real-time systems are used to determine a schedule for a set of tasks so that the task's deadlines and resource requirements are satisfied [20]. There exist variety of approaches to scheduling tasks under hard real-time constraints. [19] reviews some of these and proposes heuristic algorithms for distributed scheduling of tasks with deadlines and resource requirements. A review and evaluation of heuristic methods for static task scheduling is offered in [23]. Recent results in the field of scheduling and load balancing in parallel and distributed systems are presented in [24]. It should be noted that several results on scheduling in hard real-time systems to achieve system fault-tolerance in presence of hardware faults have been published in recent years [14], [16], [9].

Somehow in parallel to the above-described efforts, several important techniques for building fault-tolerant (f-t) software out of simplex units have been proposed. Basic models of f-t software are N-version programming (NVP) [2], [25], recovery blocks (RB) [17], [13], [11], [21], and N-version self-checking programming (NSCP) [27], [15]. A hybrid solution integrating NVP and recovery block is known as the consensus recovery block [22]. Yet another approach to software f-t is known as a

M. Felici, K. Kanoun, A. Pasquini (Eds.): SAFECOMP'99, LNCS 1698, pp. 385-395, 1999
© Springer-Verlag Berlin Heidelberg 1999

t/(n-1) variant programming [26]. In all these techniques, the required fault tolerance is achieved by increasing the number of independently developed program variants, which in turn leads to a higher dependability at a cost of additional resources used.

One of the frequently encountered conflicts within complex software-based systems involves high dependability and safety standards required versus system performance and cost. The idea of finding an optimal trade-off between software dependability and a cost of the required resources has motivated research in the field of software reliability optimization. Several optimization models of software with redundancy have been proposed [3], [1], [10]. Self-configuring optimal programming [6] is another attempt to combine some techniques used in RB and NVP in order to exploit a trade-off between software dependability and efficiency.

This paper proposes to manage complexity and costs issues of the fault-tolerant programs not at a single program level but rather from the point of view of the whole set of such programs, which are to be run under hard time constraints. Such an approach contributes by integrating several models, techniques and solutions which, traditionally have been applied in the fields of scheduling in hard real time systems, fault tolerant computing, and software reliability optimization.

In the following parts of the paper a model of the fault-tolerant program structure is introduced. This, in turn, is used to formulate the fault-tolerant programs scheduling problem under hard time constraints. Since the resulting problem is computationally difficult an approach to solving it has been based on using metaheuristics. Three scheduling algorithms solving the discussed problem have been proposed. These include evolution program, tabu search algorithm and social learning algorithm. To compare the algorithms, computational experiment has been carried and its results presented.

2. Problem formulation

A unit of software is fault-tolerant if it can continue delivering the required service after dormant imperfections called software faults have become active by producing errors. When the errors disrupt the expected service one says that software unit has failed for the duration of service disruption. To make simplex software units fault-tolerant, the corresponding solution is to add one, two or more program variants to form a set of $N \geq 2$ units. The redundant units are intended to compensate for, or mask a failed software unit.

The paper focuses on multiprocessor programs. Concept of the multiprocessor program (or task) serves here as a general model of the fault-tolerant program structure. As it was pointed out in [4] and [5], there exist problems where tasks have to be processed on more than one processor at a time. During the execution of these multiprocessor tasks communication among processors working on the same task is implicitly hidden in the "black box" denoting an assignment of this task to a subset of processors during some time interval. To represent multiprocessor problems a $size_j$ parameter denoting processor requirement is used.

It should be noted that the concept of multiprocessor program could be conveniently used to model a majority of the discussed earlier fault-tolerant structures, including NVP and RB schemes. "Size" of the program corresponds to the number of program variants used to construct such a structure. Its execution time covers the worst case requirement for processing, including time needed for internal communication and running of the adjudication algorithm.

Thus, the problem of scheduling a set N of n multiprocessor programs under hard real-time constraints is considered. It is assumed that the following information with respect to each multiprocessor program in N is available:

- ready time - r_j, $j = 1,...,n$;
- ready time - r_j, $j = 1,...,n$;
- deadline - d_j, $j = 1,...,n$;
- maximum size $M = \max\{size_j\}$, $j = 1,...,n$;
- processing time - p_{ji}, $j = 1,...,n$, $i = 1,...,M$;
- reliability R_{ji}, $j = 1,...,n$, $i = 1,...,M$.

The considered problem, denoted as $P|r_j,size_j|R$, is characterized by a set of multiple, identical processors P, and a set of multiple-processor tasks N. Each task has the maximum size M, and the minimum size equal to 1. Tasks are independent and non-preemptable with ready times and deadlines differing per task. Tasks have arbitrary processing times, which may differ per size chosen. Task j of the $size_j = m$ requires m parallel processors for processing. Optimization criterion is schedule reliability $R = \Pi R_{ji}$. Decision variables include assignment of tasks to processors and size of each task. Tasks can not be delayed.

3. Scheduling algorithms

It is easily shown by a polynomial transformation from the result of [7] that the discussed problem of maximizing schedule reliability, ($P|r_j,size_j|R$) is NP-hard. Hence, it is not likely that a polynomial-time algorithm solving it can be found. In view of the above it has been decided to construct three scheduling algorithms based, respectively, on the following metaheuristics: evolution programming (for example, see [18]), social learning [12], and tabu search (for example, see [8]).

3.1. Algorithm EVOLUTION P|r_j,size_j|R

Algorithm *EVOLUTION $P|r_j,size_j|R$* is based on the following assumptions:
- an individual is a vector S of $2*n$ elements, where n is a number of tasks to be scheduled. Tasks are consecutively numbered. Element s_j, $j=1,2,...,n$, represents task number, element s_{j+n} represents its size ($1 \leq s_{j+n} \leq M = \max\{size_j\}$);
- set of potential individuals includes all feasible vectors (i.e. vectors S in which the first n elements contain a combination of task numbers such that all tasks are represented exactly once, and the next n elements contain the respective, allowed, task sizes);
- each individual can be transformed into a solution by applying *EVALUATION $P|r_j,size_j|R$*, which is a specially designed algorithm for list-scheduling multiple-processor tasks;
- each solution produced by the *EVALUATION $P|r_j,size_j|R$* is directly evaluated in terms of its fitness, that is schedule reliability;

– new population is formed   by applying three evolution operators: crossover, random generation of off-springs and transfer of some more "fit" individuals. Some members of the new population undergo further transformation by mean of mutation.

EVOLUTION P|r$_j$,size$_j$|R involves executing steps shown in the following pseudo-code:

Procedure EVOLUTION P|r$_j$,size$_j$|R
Begin
Set population size *PS*;
Generate an initial set of *PS* individuals, half of them with the random size and order, and half with the random size and fixed order, to form initial population I_0;
Set $i := 0$; (iteration counter);
While no stopping criteria is met **do**
    Set i := i + 1
    Calculate, using the *APPROX P|r$_j$,size$_j$|R*, fitness factor for each individual in I_{i-1};
    Form the new population I_i by:
        Selecting randomly some individuals from I_{i-1} (probability of selection depends on fitness of individuals);
        Producing certain number of individuals by applying crossover operator to the previously selected individuals from I_{i-1};
        Generating part of individuals randomly;
        Applying mutation operators to a random number of just created individuals;
EndWhile
End

EVALUATION P|r$_j$,size$_j$|R algorithm used within *EVOLUTION P|r$_j$,size$_j$|R* is carried in three steps:
Step 1. Set loop over tasks ordered as they appear in the first *n* elements of *S*.
Step 2. Within the loop, allocate current task to the multiple processors minimizing beginning time of its processing. Continue with tasks until all have been allocated.
Step 3. If the resulting schedule has task delays, fitness factor of the individual from which the schedule is generated is set to 0. Otherwise, fitness factor is set to $R = \Pi R_{ji}$.

3.2. Algorithm SLA P|r$_j$,size$_j$|R

Algorithm *SLA- P|r$_j$,size$_j$|R* is based on the following assumptions:
– an individual is represented as in *EVOLUTION P|r$_j$,size$_j$|R*;
– set of potential individuals includes all feasible solutions defined as in *EVOLUTION P|r$_j$,size$_j$|R*;
– initial population *J* is generated from the basic individual. Basic individual has all tasks ordered by their non-decreasing ready time as the first criterion and non-decreasing deadlines as the second. All sizes are set to their maximum value;
– part of the initial population is derived from the basic individual by exchanging places of two randomly chosen tasks. Its second part is derived from the basic individual by randomly shuffling order of tasks;

- each solution represented by an individual can be directly evaluated in terms of its fitness, i.e. schedule reliability, using the $EVALUATION$ - $P|r_j,size_j|R$ algorithm;
- fitness of an individual whose tasks cannot be scheduled without delays is set to 0;
- individuals are subject to several stages of learning/improvement and selection leading to a decreasing number of individuals at each subsequent stage.

SLA- $P|r_j,size_j|R$ involves executing steps shown in the following pseudo-code:

Procedure SLA - $P|r_j,size_j|R$
Begin
    $m := 4$;
    Generate the initial population of individuals J ;
    For $i = 1$ **to** m **do**
        For each individual in J **do**
            Apply the learning-improvement procedure L_i ;
        End
        Remove from J all individuals who do not pass the selection criterion SC_i;
    End
End

Procedure L_1
Begin
    For each individual in J **do**
        While individual represents a solution with the delayed tasks **do**
        From among the tasks with sizes greater than 1 choose task numbered s_j, where decreasing size by 1 results in freeing a single processor for the longest period of time;
        $s_{j+n} = s_{j+n} - 1$;
        Evaluate the improved individual using $EVALUATION$-$P|r_j,size_j|R$ algorithm;
        End
    End
End

Procedure L_2
Begin
    For each individual in J **do**
        For $j = 1$ **to** n **do**
            While $s_{j+n} < \max\{size_j\}$ AND individual represents a solution without the delayed tasks **do**
            $s_{j+n} = s_{j+n} + 1$;
            End
        End
    End
End

Procedure L_3
Begin
    For each individual in J **do**
        For $g = 1$ **to** G **do**

Choose randomly an index j, $1 \leq j \leq n$, for which $s_{j+n} > 1$;
Choose randomly indexes k,l, $1 \leq k,l \leq n$, for which $k \neq l$, $s_{k+n} < \max\{size_k\}$
and $s_{l+n} < \max\{size_l\}$;
$s_{j+n} = s_{j+n} - 1$;
$s_{k+n} = s_{k+n} + 1$;
$s_{l+n} = s_{l+n} + 1$;
Evaluate the improved individual using $EVALUATION\text{-}P|r_j,size_j|R$
algorithm;
If fitness of the considered individual $= 0$ **then**
$\quad s_{j+n} = s_{j+n} + 1$;
$\quad s_{k+n} = s_{k+n} - 1$;
$\quad s_{l+n} = s_{l+n} - 1$;
End
 End
 End
End

Procedure L_4
Begin
 For each individual in J **do**
  For $h = 1$ **to** H **do**
   Choose randomly an index j, $1 \leq j \leq n$, for which $s_{j+n} > 1$;
   Choose randomly an index k, $1 \leq k \leq n$, for which $k \neq j$, $s_{k+n} < \max\{size_k\}$;
   $s_{j+n} = s_{j+n} - 1$
   $s_{k+n} = s_{k+n} + 1$
   Evaluate the improved individual using $EVALUATION\text{-}P|r_j,size_j|R$
   If fitness factor of the individual has improved **then**
    accept the change
   else reject it
   End
  End
 End
End

Criterion SC_i for $i = 1,2,3$ requires that all individuals with fitness below an average are rejected. At the final stage criterion SC_4 requires that the best individual only, i.e. the one with the smallest total penalty, be selected. Variables G and H, in L_3 and L_4 represent a positive integer which value should be decided during fine-tuning of the algorithm. In the computational experiment which results are reported in this paper G and H have been set to 200.

3.3. Algorithm TABU-P|r_j,size_j|R

Algorithm $TABU$ $P|r_j,size_j|R$ is based on the following assumptions:
- a solution Q is a list of n objects, each representing a single task. An object has attributes including task number - s_j, $j = 1,...,n$, task size - v_{ji}, $j = 1,...,n$, $i = 1,...,M$, ready and processing times, and deadline;

- tasks are list-scheduled in accordance with their order in Q;
- a move involves moving task s_j from the position sm to the position dm on the list Q changing, at the same time, its size from sv to dv;
- attributes of a move are denoted as $m(s_j, sm, sv, dm, dv, wr)$, where sm, sv, dm, dv are the respective indexes and wr is a move value;
- $Mo(Q)$ denotes a set of possible moves from Q called neighbourhood of Q;
- $Mo'(Q)$ denotes a modified neighbourhood of Q, that is neighbourhood with all tabu-active moves removed;
- TAM denotes list of tabu-active moves;
- SM denotes a short memory of the tabu algorithm, where executed moves are remembered.

$TABU\text{-}P|r_j,size_j|R$ involves executing steps shown in the following pseudo-code:

Procedure $TABU\text{-}P|r_j,size_j|R$
Begin
    $SM = \emptyset$
    $TAM = \emptyset$
    Generate the initial solution: order tasks by their non-decreasing ready times as the first criterion, and non-decreasing deadlines as the second. Choose the smallest allowed size for each task. Calculate total tardiness T;
    If $T > 0$ **then** scheduling problem has no solution;
    else
        max = reliability of the initial solution;
        For $i = 1$ **to** number of iterations **do**
            $best\_value = 0$
            While no move is chosen **do**
                Consider all moves in $Mo'(Q)$, select and remember the best move $m_{best}(s_{j\,best}, sm_{best}, sv_{best}, dm_{best}, dv_{best}, wr_{best})$, where $m_{best} \notin TAM$;
                If the best move can not be found **then** delete from TAM all moves with the least $tabu\_tenure$;
            End While
            If $wr_{best} > best\_value$ **then** $best\_value = wr_{bes}$
            Add the best move to SM;
            Update TAM:
            Add $m1(s_{j\,best}, dm_{best}, 0, sm_{best}, 0, 0)$; $tabu\_tenure = 2 \cdot n$ iterations;
            Add $m2(s_{j\,best}, 0, 0, 0, sv_{best}, 0)$; $tabu\_tenure = (n \cdot (M-1))/2$ iterations;
            Add $m3(s_{j\,best}, 0, 0, sm_{best}, 0, 0)$; $tabu\_tenure = 0.75 \cdot n$ iterations;
            Add $m4(s_{j\,best}, 0, 0, 0, 0, 0)$; $tabu\_tenure = 0.3 \cdot n$ iterations;
            Add $m5(s_{j\,best}, sm_{best}, sw_{best}, dm_{best}, 0, 0)$; $tabu\_tenure = (n \cdot M)/1.75$ iterations;
            Delete moves with $tabu\_tenure = 0$;
            If $best\_value > max$ **then** $max = best\_value$
        End For
End

4. Computational experiment results

To evaluate the proposed algorithms computational experiment has been carried. It has involved 100 randomly generated $P|r_j,size_j|R$ scheduling problems. Within this population the number of available processors varied between 3 and 13, the number of tasks per problem varied between 16 and 28, and the sizes of tasks varied between 3 and 5. Three different algorithms have been used to solve the sample problems: $SLA\text{-}P|r_j,size_j|R$, $EVOLUTION\text{-}P|r_j,size_j|R$, and $TABU\text{-}P|r_j,size_j|R$ - all described in section 3 of the paper. In tab. 1 mean relative errors from the best solution obtained are shown.

Table 1. Mean relative errors from the best solution for the analyzed algorithms.

Number of processors	Relative error (%) SLA vs. MAX	Relative error (%) EVOLUTION vs. MAX	Relative error (%) TABU vs. MAX
3	7,00	2,67	0,33
4	1,75	8,00	6,63
5	0,91	8,91	13,36
6	2,71	3,79	7,14
7	4,00	8,86	11,00
8	0,00	10,53	11,80
9	1,17	12,92	10,75
10	0,00	13,70	6,30
11	0,17	15,50	17,67
12	9,50	27,50	6,50
13	0,00	50,00	38,00
Overall	1,80	10,36	10,22

It is clear from the experiment results that social learning algorithm outperforms the remaining algorithms with respect to the quality of solutions. Moreover, all three algorithms have a comparable time behavior. Obtaining a solution on modern PC has been taking few seconds to few minutes, depending on problems characteristics and size. Since the analyzed class of problems is computationally difficult it has not been possible to compare all approximate solutions with the optimum ones. Such comparison has been possible for a subset of 30 problems from the original population. Optimal solutions have been obtained using branch and bound algorithm. Mean relative errors from the optimum solutions, for the $SLA\text{-}P|r_j,size_j|R$, $EVOLUTION\text{-}P|r_j,size_j|R$, and $TABU\text{-}P|r_j,size_j|R$ are, respectively, 2.14%, 3,00 % and 3.66%.

To support main thesis of the paper stating that exploiting a trade-off between software dependability and efficiency at a global level could be of advantage in comparison to traditional approach, another experiment has been carried. For the previously described sample of the randomly generated FTPS problems a set of solutions without the global optimization has been obtained. In each case the schedule with a maximum schedulable uniform number of program variants for all tasks has been generated. Reliabilities of thus obtained schedules have been calculated and compared with those calculated using SLA algorithm. Fig. 1 shows schedule reliabilities calculated with and without the global optimization.

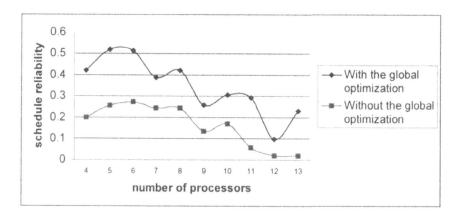

Fig. 1. Comparison of schedule reliabilities obtained with the global optimization (SLA algorithm) and without it, for the sample set of FTPS problems

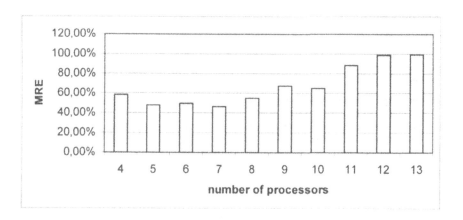

Fig. 2. Mean relative error of solutions obtained without the global optimization as compared with reliabilities of schedules generated by the proposed SLA algorithm.

Fig. 2. shows mean relative error of solutions obtained without the global optimization, as compared to solutions produced by the proposed SLA algorithm. On average, for the analyzed sample, the cost of not searching for a global solution amounts to 67% error margin expressed in terms of the schedule reliability.

5. Conclusion

Main contribution of the paper is a proposal to manage complexity and costs issues of the fault-tolerant programs not at a single program level but rather from the point of view of the whole set of such programs, which are to be run under hard time constraints. It has been suggested to use a concept of the multiple processor program (or task) as a general model of the fault-tolerant program structure. The emerging fault-tolerant programs scheduling problem is, unfortunately NP-hard. To obtain approximate solutions in a reasonable time, three algorithms based on social learning, evolution programming and tabu search have been designed. Computational experiment carried shows that the algorithms can produce satisfactory to good results. Social learning algorithm has proved to generate solutions with the smallest error margin. It has been also shown that searching for a the global optimum can be advantageous by producing more reliable schedules within hard time constraints.

The approach requires further research with respect to both: fault-tolerant software modeling and fault-tolerant programs scheduling algorithms. The latter must be more efficient as far as computational time is concerned. This can be achieved by designing and implementing the parallel versions of the proposed metaheuristics. It is expected, that in the near future, with the advance of software reuse methodologies and mass appearance of COTS, more and more safety critical software systems will be using software redundancy to assure the required dependability. Such solutions may profit from fault-tolerant programs scheduling models and optimization algorithms.

Acknowledgement: This research has been supported by the KBN grant NR 301/T11/97/12

6. References

1. Ashrafi, N., Berman, O.: Optimization Models for Selection of Programs, Considering Cost & Reliability, IEEE Transactions on Reliability 41(2) (1992) 59-65
2. Avizienis, A., Chen, L.: On the implementation of the N-version programming for software fault tolerance during execution, Proc. IEEE COMPSAC 77 (1977) 149-155
3. Belli, F., Jędrzejowicz, P.: An Approach to the Reliability Optimization of Software with Redundancy, IEEE Transactions on Software Engineering, 17(3) (1991) 310-312
4. Błażewicz, J., Drabowski, M., Węglarz, J.: Scheduling Multiprocessor tasks to minimize schedule length, IEEE Transactions on Computers 35 (1986) 389-393.
5. Błażewicz, J., Ecker, K.H., Pesch, E., Schmidt, G., Węglarz, J.: Scheduling Computer and Manufacturing Processes, Springer, Berlin (1996)
6. Bondavalli, A., Giandomenico, F.Di., Xu, J.: Cost-effective and flexible scheme for software fault tolerance, Computer System Science & Engineering, 4 (1993) 234-244
7. Garey, M.R., Johnson, D.S.: Computers and Intractability: A Guide to the Theory of NP-Completeness, W.H.Freeman, New York (1979)
8. Glover, F., Laguna, M.: Tabu Search, Kluver, Boston (1987)
9. Ghosh, S., Melham, R., Mosse, D.: Fault-Tolerance through Scheduling of Aperiodic Tasks in Hard Real-Time Multiprocessor Systems, IEEE Transactions on Parallel and Distributed Systems 8(13) (1997) 272-284
10. Gutjahr, W.: Reliability Optimization of Redundant Software with Correlated Failures, Proc. IX Int. Symposium on Software Reliability Engineering, Paderborn (1998) 293-303
11. Hecht, M., Agron, J., Hochhauser, S.: A distributed fault tolerant architecture for nuclear reactor and safety functions, Proc. Real-Time System Symposium, Santa Monica (1989) 214-221
12. Jedrzejowicz, P.: Social Learning Algorithm, Technical Report nr 7/98, Computer Science Dept. Gdynia Maritime Academy, Gdynia (1998)

13. Kim, K.H.: Distributed execution of recovery blocks: an approach to uniform treatment of hardware and software faults, Proc. 4th International Conference on Distributed Computing Systems, IEEE Computer Society Press (1984) 526-532
14. Krishna, C.M., Shin, K.G.: On Scheduling Tasks with a Quick Recovery from Failure, IEEE Transactions on Computers 35(5) (1986) 448-455
15. Laprie, J.C., Arlat, J., Beounes, C., Kanoun, K.: Definition and Analysis of Hardware-and-Software Fault-Tolerant Architectures, IEEE Computer 23(7) (1990) 39-51
16. Liestman, A.L., Campbell, R.H.: A Fault-tolerant Scheduling Problem, IEEE Transactions on Software Engineering, SE-12(11) (1988) 1089-1095
17. Melliar-Smith, P.M., Randell, B.: Software reliability: the role of programmed exception handling, SIGPLAN Notices 12(3) (1977) 95-100
18. Michalewicz, Z.: Genetic Algorithms + Data Structures = Evolution Programs, Springer, 2nd ed., Berlin (1996)
19. Ramamritham, K., Stankovic, J.A., Zhao, W.: Distributed Scheduling of Tasks with Deadlines and Resource Requirements, IEEE Transactions on Computers 38(8) (1989) 1110-1123
20. Ramamritham, K., Stankovic, J.A., Shiah, P.F.: Efficient Scheduling Algorithms for Real-Time Systems, IEEE Transactions on Parallel and Distributed Systems, 1(2) (1990) 184-194
21. Randell, B., Xu, J.: The Evolution of the Recovery Block Concept, in: M.R.Lyu (ed.): Software Fault-Tolerance, J.Wiley, Chichester (1995) 1-22
22. Scott R.K., J.W.Gault, D.F. Mc Allister: Fault tolerant software reliability modelling, IEEE Transactions on Software Engineering, 13(5) (1987) 582-592
23. Shirazi, B., Wang, M., Pathak, G.: Analysis and Evaluation of Heuristic Methods for Static Task Scheduling, Journal of Parallel and Distributed Computing, 10 (1990) 222-232
24. Shirazi, B., Hurson, A.R., Kavi, K.M.: Scheduling and Load Balancing in Parallel and Distributed Systems, IEEE Computer Society Press, Los Alamitos (1995)
25. Tso, K.S., Avizienis, A.: Community error recovery in N-version software: a design study with experimentation, Digest of 17th FTCS, Pittsburgh (1987) 127-133
26. Xu, J., Randell, B.: Software Fault Tolerance: t/(n-1)-Variant Programming, IEEE Transactions on Reliability, 46(1) (1997) 60-67
27. Yau, S.S., Cheung, R.C.: Design of Self-Checking Software, Proc. Int. Conf. on Reliable Software, IEEE Computer Society Press (1975) 450-457

Formal Design of Distributed Control Systems with Lustre *

Paul Caspi[1], Christine Mazuet[2], Rym Salem[1] and Daniel Weber[2]

[1]VERIMAG*, 2 rue de Vignate, F-38610 Gières
{caspi, salem}@imag.fr
[2]Schneider Electric, Usine M3, F-38050 Grenoble Cedex 9
{christine_mazuet, daniel_weber}@mail.schneider.fr

Abstract. During the last decade, the synchronous approach has proved to meet industrial needs concerning the development of Distributed Control Systems (DCS): as an example, Schneider Electric has adopted the synchronous language Lustre and the associated tool Scade for developing monitoring systems for nuclear power plants. But so far, engineers make use of Lustre-Scade for designing separately single components of a DCS. This paper focuses on the use of Lustre-Scade for designing DCS as a whole. Two valuable consequences of this approach are that (1) the same framework can be used for both programming, simulating, testing and proving properties of a distributed system, and (2) the proposed approach is fully consistent with the usual engineering abstractions concerning smooth signals.

1 Introduction

Control systems are of growing importance as they are involved in many safety critical industrial applications: civil aircraft, ground transportation, nuclear power plant, etc. In this field, a lot of activity has been devoted to ensuring and improving hardware and software reliability. Concerning software development, fault avoidance has always been, beside fault tolerance, an important issue: constrained design process, intensive simulation and testing and even formal methods (e.g. [1], [4]) have proved to be good candidates to answer this problem.

Another feature of control systems is that they are often distributed for quite obvious reasons of performance, fault-tolerance, and sensor/actuator location. Distribution is not without consequences on both the development process and the exploitation of the system: the global behavior of the system is more complex since distribution introduces new operating modes —abnormal modes, when a computing site is down for instance— and questions about the synchronization of the different computing sites. Distributed Control Systems (DCS) are hard to design, debug, test and formally verify. Those difficulties are closely related to a lack of global vision of a system when designing it.

✧ This work has been partially supported by Esprit Project CRISYS (EP 25514).
✦ VERIMAG is a joint laboratory of Université Joseph Fourier (Grenoble 1), CNRS, and INPG.

M. Felici, K. Kanoun, A. Pasquini (Eds.): SAFECOMP'99, LNCS 1698, pp. 396–409, 1999
© Springer-Verlag Berlin Heidelberg 1999

However, the distributed systems which are found in the Control field are quite different from those that are addressed in other fields of Computer Science, like protocols, operating systems, data bases, etc. Most of them are organized as several periodic processes, with nearly the same period, but without common clock, and which communicate by means of shared memory through serial links or field busses (e.g. [7]). This class of DCS is quite clearly an important one in the field and thus deserves special attention. This is why we propose to give it a special name, for instance *"Communicating Periodic Synchronous Processes"* or *CPSP* for short.

During the last decade, the synchronous approach [4] has been largely and successfully applied to the development of such distributed control systems. Based on clean mathematical principles, one of its salient benefit is its ability to support formal design and formal verification methods. As regards the synchronous data flow language Lustre [9] and the associated tool Scade [5], several real world systems have been achieved among which monitoring systems for nuclear power plants designed by Schneider Electric [6] [12], the "fly-by-wire" system of Airbus aircrafts [8] and the interlocking system of the Honk Kong subway designed by CS Transport. So far, engineers make use of Lustre-Scade for designing separately single components of a DCS. As regards designing distributed systems as a whole, they have developed pragmatic solutions based on engineering recipes.

In this paper, we intend to show that this Lustre-Scade approach is not restricted to apply only on single components; it can be extended to globally handle this CPSP class of DCS, thanks to the Lustre sampling, holding and assertions mechanisms. One valuable consequence of this result is that the same framework can be used for both programming, simulating, testing and proving properties of a distributed system, thus limiting the risk of errors due to an unformalized design process.

The paper is organized as follows: section 2 briefly describes the Lustre language, the Scade tool and related works on verification. Based on this background, section 3 shows how to represent the CPSP class of DCS within this framework. Section 4 focuses on a case study. Finally, section 5 concludes with future work.

2   Background

2.1   The Lustre language [9]

2.1.1   Basic concepts

A Lustre program has a cyclic behaviour, and that cycle defines a sequence of times. Any variable or expression denotes a flow, i.e. a possibly infinite sequence of values related to the cyclic behaviour of the program.

Usual operators operate pointwise over flows; for instance $1 + 2$ is the flow $[3, 3, 3, ...]$. Similarly,

c	t	f	t	...
x	x_0	x_1	x_2	...
y	y_0	y_1	y_2	...
if c then x else y	x_0	y_1	x_2	...

A unit delay operator *fby* "followed by" (actually -> *pre* in Lustre) can be represented by the diagram:

x	x_0	x_1	x_2	...
y	y_0	y_1	y_2	...
x fby y	x_0	y_0	y_1	...

2.1.2   Advanced concepts

A program is structured into *nodes*. A node contains a set of equations and can be elsewhere used in expressions; for instance:

```
node integr(x:int) returns (y:int)
let
y = (0 fby y) + x;
tel
...
z = integr (x fby z) + u;
```

It may be that slow and fast processes coexist in a given application. A sampling (or filtering operator) *when* allows fast processes to communicate with slower ones:

c	f	t	f	t	...
x	x_0	x_1	x_2	x_3	...
x when c		x_1		x_3	...

Conversely, a holding mechanism, *current* allows slow processes to communicate with faster ones:

c	f	t	f	t	...
x	x_0	x_1	x_2	x_3	...
y		y_0		y_1	...
current(c, x) y	x_0	y_0	y_0	y_1	...

As we can see in the diagrams above, *when* discards its input x when the input condition c is false. Conversely, *current* fills the holes created by *when* with the input value y it got the last time the condition c was true, if any, and otherwise with an initialising sequence x.

Always "true" boolean expressions can be asserted for several purposes, for instance for expressing non independent input properties; for instance

```
assert (c or (true fby c) )
```

says that c will not stay "false" for more than one time unit. We shall see in the sequel how this feature can be used to express properties of independent clocks sharing the same period.

2.2   The Scade tool

Scade[1] (formerly SAGA [5]) is a software development environment based on Lustre, which provides a graphic editor. Some aspects are similar to SADT: the top-down

---

[1] Scade is commercialised by the Verilog company.

design method, the data-flow network interpretation, and the notion of *activation condition*.

An example of Scade diagram is given on Fig. 1. *CONTROL* is a cyclic program which reads sensors and controls actuators. Its inputs and outputs are sampled according to the boolean condition *clock*: intuitively, if *clock* is *true* then *CONTROL* computes its outputs, else the outputs are maintained to their previous values[2]. Default values are required in case *clock* is *false* at the very first cycle.

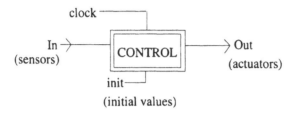

(initial values)

Fig. 1. Example of Scade diagram

The Scade environment includes an automatic C code generator and a simulator. It is also connected to several tools, e.g. Lesar for formal verification of properties (§2.3.1) and Lurette for automatic generation of test cases (§2.3.2).

2.3   Formal verification and automatic testing

As noted in the introduction, control systems often concern critical applications, and thus program verification is a key issue.

2.3.1   Formal verification of properties

Formal verification of properties focuses on safety properties, which states that a given situation should never appear, or that a given statement should always hold. Such properties can be easily expressed with Lustre [3] [10] [11].

Then, the verification principle is based on model checking: the proof is made by an exhaustive exploration of a finite abstraction of the system. However, at that point, an important task is to provide a description of how the environment of the system behaves. Actually, the environment obeys some rules which restrict its possible behaviour. The verification tool would certainly not achieve checking the system without being aware of such an information. Assumptions are therefore necessary: in Lustre, this is done using the assertions mechanisms (§2.1.2).

Properties and assumptions are expressed by means of *synchronous observers* [11]: synchronous observers are programs implementing acceptors of sequences. Then, the program and the observers are gathered in a verification program [10], and the verification tool Lesar decides whether the properties is satisfies; if not, it gives a scenario which leads to violate the property. The main limitation of this approach is the "size explosion" problem. An experimentation is presented in §4.3.

---

[2] Formally, the equivalent Lustre expression is: if *clock* then current(*CONTROL*(*In* when *clock*)) else (*init* fby *Out*)

2.3.2   Automatic generation of test sequences

Program testing is complementary to formal verification: it aims at finding bugs but can not provide any absolute positive results. The automatic generation of test cases follows a black box approach, since the program is not supposed to be fully known. It focuses on two points [14]: (1) generating relevant inputs, with respect to some knowledge about the environment in which the system is intended to run; (2) checking the correctness of the test results, according to the expected behaviour of the system.

The Lustre synchronous observers describing assumptions on the environment (§2.3.1) are used to produce realistic inputs; synchronous observers describing the properties that the system should satisfy (§2.3.1) are used as an oracle, i.e. to check the correctness of the test results. Then, the method consists in randomly generating inputs satisfying the assumptions on the environment [14].

A prototype tool called Lurette has been developed. It takes as input both observers —one describing the assumptions and one describing the properties— written in Lustre-Scade, and two parameters: the number of test sequences and the maximum length of the sequences. An experimentation is presented in §4.4.

3   Application to distributed systems

The above tools quite accurately match the design needs of cyclic programs. Let us see now how we can use them so as to match the needs of our special CPSP case of distributed systems. Let us recall roughly some of the main features of this CPSP class: processes communicate by means of shared memory, they behave periodically and they all have nearly the same period but no common clock. In this chapter, we progressively formalise theses features by means of the Lustre-Scade language. First, we model a shared memory, and based on this, we formalise distributed systems without any hypothesis on clocks. Then, we focus on the relation between clocks: we express the fact that two processes have nearly the same period in order to fit our CPSP class of systems.

3.1   Shared memory

First, we can see that the Lustre sampling primitive, *when*, can be used to model the " reading in a shared memory" operation. It suffices to look at the corresponding diagram of section 2.1.2: let x be the sequence of values held in the memory, and the true values of c, the instants at which a location reads this memory. Then, obviously, "x when c" is the sequence of values read in this location.

Conversely, the "current" operation can be used to model the "writing in the shared memory" operation: looking at the corresponding diagram (§2.1.2), we can use the c sequence to represent the instants at which the memory is written, y will correspond to the written values and a constant sequence x will be used to account for the initial value of the memory. Then, "$current(c,x)y$" will be the current content of the memory. However, this very simple approach is not fully satisfactory because it allows for instantaneous dialogs which do not seem feasible, such as reading and writing at the same time and instantly getting the written value. This is why we insert a delay —by means of the *fby* operator— in the write operation in order to forbid this event:

$$write(v, cw, u) = v \text{ fby (if } cw \text{ then current } u \text{ else } write(v, cw, u))$$

where the delay accounts for short[3] undetermined transmission delays. The behaviour of the shared memory can be represented by the diagram:

cw	t	f	t	f	...
u	u_0		u_1		...
current u	u_0	u_0	u_1	u_1	...
write(v,cw,u)	v	u_0	u_0	u_1	...

3.2   Distributed programs

We are thus able to formalise distributed programs communicating by means of shared memory. Fig. 2 gives the Lustre expression and the corresponding block diagram view for a two location program. An alternative block diagram view is shown at Fig. 3 using the Scade concept of activation condition.

This system corresponds to a possible implementation where each process atomically reads all values issued by other processes. If this is not the case, individual read and write clocks have to be introduced, leading to a more complex, but also tractable program.

However, this formalisation is likely to be inefficient: it will probably not allow properties to be checked, if clocks are considered as free independent boolean sequences. It is here that periodicity is important and has to be taken into account.

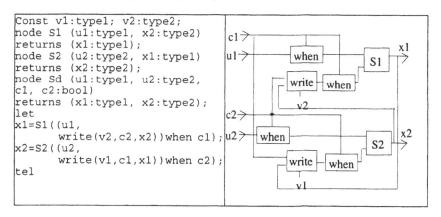

```
Const v1:type1; v2:type2;
node S1 (u1:type1, x2:type2)
returns (x1:type1);
node S2 (u2:type2, x1:type1)
returns (x2:type2);
node Sd (u1:type1, u2:type2,
c1, c2:bool)
returns (x1:type1, x2:type2);
let
x1=S1((u1,
        write(v2,c2,x2))when c1);
x2=S2((u2,
        write(v1,c1,x1))when c2);
tel
```

Fig. 2. A distributed system program

---

[3] Significantly shorter than the periods of read and write clocks. If longer transmission delays are needed, modelling should be more complex.

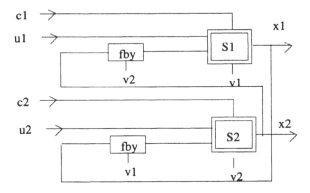

Fig. 3. An alternative equivalent distributed system block diagram

3.3   Formalising periodic clocks

This could be done in some real-time framework, such as timed automata [2] but, for the sake of simplicity, we prefer here to characterize the fact that two independent clocks have approximately the same period by saying that:

Any of the two clocks cannot take the value "t" (true) more than twice between two successive "t" values of the other one.

This can be formalised by saying that the boolean vector stream composed of the two clocks should never contain the subsequence:

$$\begin{bmatrix} t \\ - \end{bmatrix} \bullet \begin{bmatrix} f \\ f \end{bmatrix}^* \bullet \begin{bmatrix} t \\ f \end{bmatrix} \bullet \begin{bmatrix} f \\ f \end{bmatrix}^* \bullet \begin{bmatrix} t \\ - \end{bmatrix}$$

nor the one obtained by exchanging coordinates. (Here, — is a wild card representing any of the two values {t,f}.

Now, such regular expressions yield finite state recognizability and can be associated a finite-state recognizing dynamic system *Same_Period* [4]. Fig. 4 gives an example of clocks satisfying the *Same_Period* property: it may happen that two ticks of clock1 (resp. clock2) are inserted between two ticks of clock2 (resp. clock1). As a matter of fact, data exchanged between the corresponding processes can be lost of duplicated. This protocol does not seem reliable since data can be lost: but we'll see in §3.5 that as far as smooth signals are concerned, this protocol fits engineers practices.

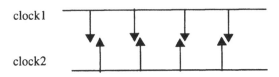

Fig. 4. Periodic clocks

---

[4] This can be automatically generated in Lustre, thanks to the Reglo tool [13].

3.4   Some consequences of periodicity

Intuitively, if read and write clocks have the same period, the read value should not be "too far" from the written one. This can be formalized as the following theorem:

Theorem on Same_Period

$$Same\_Period(cw, cr)$$

implies (write (v,cr,u') = write (v,cw,u)

or   write (v,cr,u') = write (v,cw,v fby u)

or   write (v,cr,u') = write (v,cw, v fby(v fby u))   )

where u' = write(v,cw,u) when cr.

This theorem means that any used internal value must have been produced within a two period time interval. It is automatically proved by the Lustre prover Lesar [9].

3.5   The case of smooth signals

A possible use of this theorem is for smooth (sampled) signals. Given a physical phenomenon and knowing an upper bound on the absolute value of its derivative allows finding a period such that:

$$|u - v\ fby\ u| < \varepsilon$$

This allows us to state the "sampling" property:

$$|\ write\ (v,cr,u')-\ write\ (v,cw,u)\ | < 2\varepsilon$$

This kind of sampling property may help in proving distributed sampled system properties. An example of such property can be found in [3]. We believe this is a kind of abstraction, engineers are used to and which explains why such a CPSP architecture is popular among them.

4   Case study

The method described above is now illustrated on a case study. Through this experimentation, our aim is to study the applicability of the tools based on Lustre — namely Scade, Lesar, Lurette— when applied to distributed systems. First, we apply the proposed formalization: we'll see that the *activation condition* and the *assertion* mechanisms provide a natural way to design distributed systems. Then, we focus on the verification on such a distributed system by applying formal verification and automatic test generation.

4.1   Introduction

The proposed example is that of a single line on which trains can go in opposite directions. The control program has to ensure that no accident happens. We consider the global system composed of three main parts:

- the physical part (Fig. 5): the single line, four tracks, a sensor of train presence on each in_track, switches, sensors for switch presence, actuators controlling switches and traffic lights, and the trains.
- the control part: a Lustre-Scade distributed program which reads the sensors and controls actuators (traffic lights and switches).
- the train drivers who control the train movements. They are supposed to obey traffic lights and not to move the train backward.

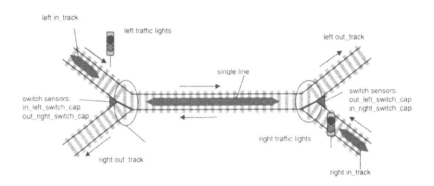

Fig. 5. The single line

4.2   The distributed control system

Given the presence sensors, the control decides the switches position and the state of traffic lights. When trains are present on their in_tracks, a selection of the train to pass must be done with respect to some priority strategy. Such a strategy must ensure that there is no deadlock nor starvation. Of course, if only one train is present it will be selected to pass.

The hardware architecture of the system is composed of three units respectively located on the left in_track, on the right in_track and on the single line. They communicate through networks by means of shared memory. Sensors located on the left track (resp. right track) are connected to the left unit (resp. right unit). The sensor located on the single line is connected to the third unit.

The software architecture follows the hardware one:

- management of the left direction (resp. right direction) is implemented in the left (resp. right) unit,
- the function managing the priorities between the two direction is implemented in the central unit.

The software is developed with Lustre-Scade. The top level diagram is shown at Fig. 6.

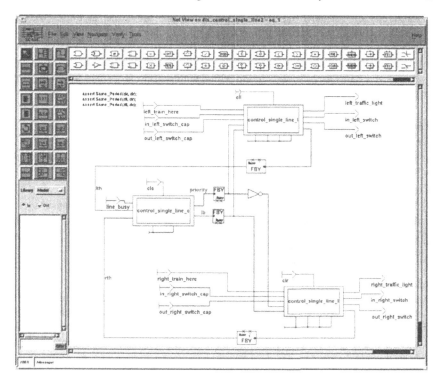

Fig. 6. The distributed control system designed with Scade

The three blocks have their own clock: *cll*, *clc* and *clr*. Data transferred from a block to another one are delayed by means of the *fby* operator: as said in §3.1, the delay accounts for undetermined transmission delay. Relations between clocks are needed to take into account the periodicity of the three units: *assert Same_Period(cll, clr)* states that both clocks cll and clr have almost the same period. *Same_Period* is a Lustre node included in a library.

The proposed formalization provides a simple way to describe CPSP systems. Then, each block can be designed as a single component using the usual engineering practices.

4.3   Formal verification of properties

As said in §2.3.1, formal verification of properties involves defining the properties that the system should satisfy, and the assumptions on the environment behavior.

4.3.1   Properties
The program must verify the following properties:
- Safety: there must be no collision and no derailment. Collision occurs when two trains meet (if going in opposite directions) or reach (if going in the same

direction) one another on the single line or on the same in_track, whereas derailment takes place if the physical path corresponding to the selected direction is not established while a train is moving.

- Fairness: there must be no starvation, i.e it should not be the case that two successive trains go in one direction while another train is waiting in the opposite direction.

4.3.2   Hypothesis

We consider the following hypothesis on the environment:

- The single line is initially not busy. It becomes busy only if a train leaves its in_track.
- Trains removed from their in_tracks will certainly pass on the single line.
- An edge of a switch is set only if it is controlled by the program.
- A switch can't be found in different positions at the same time by two sensors.
- The environment evolves much slower than the control program so that the control program can see all the changes of the inputs. In other words, clocks are fast enough to take samples of each level of each input.

4.3.3   Results

Formal verification with Lesar partly fails because of the state space explosion. The proof ran for 3 days: 1849225 states have been explored without showing the violation of the property but 4515433 states were expecting to be explored. We stopped the proof at this point since this scale of duration is not acceptable in an industrial context.

4.4   Automatic testing

As formal verification is not fully successful, it is interesting to test the distributed control program by means of the automatic testing method (§2.3.2). First, we look at the functional behaviour of the system assuming simplified clocks. Then, we focus on verification of properties.

4.4.1   Simulation of the system behavior

The automatic testing method can be used to simulate a specific behaviour of the system by defining assumptions corresponding to a particular context; thus, the designer can check that the system reacts as expected.

The first step of our experimentation aims at simulating the system behaviour in a restricted context: clocks of the three units are the same deterministic periodic signal as illustrated below:

cll	t	f	f	f	f	t	f	f	f	...
clc	f	f	f	t	f	f	f	f	t	...
clr	f	f	t	f	f	f	f	t	f	...

Hypothesis on the environment are preserved. The results are given on the chronogram of Fig. 7.

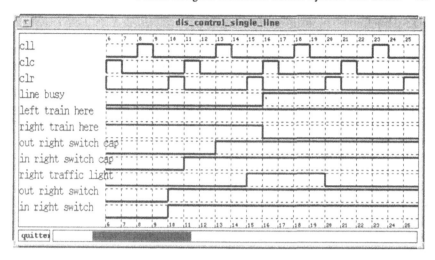

Fig. 7. Results from automatic testing

Let us detail steps from 10 to 20. Values of *cll, clc, ..., in_right_switch_cap*, are automatically generated by Lurette. Values of *right_traffic_light, ..., in_right_switch*, are responses provided by the control program.

1. Step 10: trains are detected on the left in_track and on the right in_track (the corresponding inputs —*left_train_here* and *right_train_here*— are *true*). The single line is empty (*line_busy* is *false*). The control program orders the switch to link the right in_track and the right out_track with the single line (the corresponding outputs —*out_right_switch* and *in_right_switch*—become *true*).
2. Then, the switches slowly move: at step 11, one links the right in_track with the single line (the input *in_right_switch_cap* becomes *true*), and at step 13, the other one links the right out_track with the single line (*out_right_switch_cap* becomes *true*).
3. Since the physical path is now ready, the right unit can allow the train to pass by controlling the right traffic light. This is done at step 15 when the right unit is activated (*clr* becomes *true*): access to the single line is granted (*right_traffic_light* becomes *true*). Then, the train leaves the right in_track (*right_train_here* becomes *false*) and enters the single line (*line_busy* becomes *true*).
4. When the right unit is activated again at step 20, it sets *right_traffic_lights* to *false* thus forbidding access to the single line, since it is busy.

This example shows that the designed system reacts as expected in a given situation. Of course, the properties that the system should satisfied are also examined: they are not violated by the generated test inputs. The next paragraph focuses on intensively testing the distributed program to check whether the properties are satisfied.

4.4.2 Observation of the properties

This experimentation involves the properties defined for formal verification purpose (§4.3.1). Ten test sequences which length is 100 have been generated: this length occurred to be a relevant length to observe trains moving on the single line.

The properties are never violated by the generated test inputs. Of course, this results does not mean that properties are proved. But since formal verification is not tractable, automatic testing is an alternative means to gain a sound confidence in the system safety.

5   Conclusion and future work

In this paper, we show that the considered distributed systems —Communicating Periodic Synchronous Processes— can be thoroughly formalized within the programming language Lustre-Scade thanks to the available sampling and holding mechanisms, and thanks to the assertion mechanism. This result yields valuable consequences:

- the same framework can be used for both programming, simulating, testing and proving properties of a distributed system.
- the Lustre-SCADE available analysis tools, e.g. the Lesar prover and the Lurette test generator, can be directly applied to distributed systems.
- this formalization is fully consistent with the usual engineering abstractions (period, delay) concerning smooth signals.

The next steps of our work are:

- apply the method to a real case study from Schneider Electric;
- try to improve the proof method so as to efficiently cope with these kind of Distributed Control Systems; alternative proof methods are also considered [15].
- go on with further research work on discontinuous signals: the proposed clock formalization works only for smooth signals. When it comes to discontinuous signal (boolean, integers,...) properties, it may be in many cases much better to solve the inverse problem, i.e. instead of distributing a program and then trying to check properties on the distributed program, take a synchronous program with already checked properties and try to safely distribute it while keeping these properties.

Acknowledgement

We wish to thank Christine Bodennec for her constructive comments during the preparation of this paper.

References

1.   J. R. Abrial. *The B-Book*. Cambridge University Press, 1995.
2.   R. Alur and D. L. Dill. A theory of timed automata. *Theoretical Computer Science*, 126:183-235, 1994.

3. S. Bensalem, P. Caspi, C. Parent-Vigouroux and C. Dumas. A methodology for proving control systems with Lustre and PVS. *Proceedings of the 7ᵗʰ Working Conference on Dependable Computing for Critical Applications (DCCA7)*, San Jose, January 1999.

4. A. Benveniste and G. Berry. The synchronous approach to reactive and real-time systems. *Proceedings of the IEEE*, 79(9):1270-1282, September 1991.

5. J.L. Bergerand and E. Pilaud. SAGA: a software development environment for dependability in automatic control. In *Safecomp '88*. Pergamon Press, 1988.

6. A. Billet and C. Esmenjaud. Software qualification: the experience of french manufacturers. *International Conference on Control and Instrumentation in Nuclear Installations*, INEC Cambridge, Great Britain, April 1995.

7. A. Boué and G. Clerc. Nervia: a local network for safety. In *IAEA Specialist Meeting on Communication and data transfer in Nuclear Power Plants (CEA/EDF/FRAMATOME editors)*, Lyon, France, April 1990.

8. D. Brière, D. Ribot, D. Pilaud, and J.L. Camus. Methods and specification tools for Airbus on-board systems. In *Avionics Conference and Exhibition*, London, December, 1994. ERA Technology.

9. N. Halbwachs, P. Caspi, P. Raymond, and D. Pilaud. The synchronous dataflow programming language Lustre. *Proceedings of the IEEE*, 79(9):1305-1320, September 1991.

10. N. Halbwachs, F. Lagnier, and C. Ratel. Programming and verifying real-time systems by means of the synchronous dataflow language Lustre. *IEEE Trans. on Software Engineering*, 18(9):785-793, September 1992.

11. N. Halbwachs, F. Lagnier, and P. Raymond. Synchronous observers and the verification of reactive systems. In M. Nivat, C. Rattray, T. Rus and G. Scollo, editors, *Third Int. Conf. on Algebraic Methodology and Software Technology, AMAST'93*, Twente, June 1993.

12. J.-M. Palaric and A. Boué. Advanced safety I&C system for nuclear power plants. In *ENC'98 World Nuclear Congress*, Nice, France, October 1997.

13. P. Raymond. Recognizing regular expressions by means of data flows networks. In *23rd International Colloquium on Automata, Languages, and Programming (ICALP'96)*, Paderborn, Germany. LNCS 1099, Springer Verlag, July 1996.

14. P. Raymond, X. Nicollin, N. Halbwachs and D. Weber. Automatic testing of reactive systems. In *19th IEEE Real-Time Systems Symposium*, Madrid, Spain, December 1998.

15. M. Säflund and G. Stalmarck. Modelling and verifying systems and software in propositional logic. In *Proceedings of 17th IFAC Safecomp*, pp. 31-36, 1990.

Formal Specification and Development of a Safety-Critical Train Management System

A. Chiappini[1], A. Cimatti[2], C. Porzia[1], G. Rotondo[1], R. Sebastiani[2], P. Traverso[2], and A. Villafiorita[2]

[1] Ansaldo Segnalamento Ferroviario, Via dei Pescatori, 16100 Genova, Italy
[2] IRST, Istituto per la Ricerca Scientifica e Tecnologica, Povo, 38050, Trento, Italy

Abstract. In this paper we describe the on-going specification and development of Ansaldo's Radio Block Center (RBC), a component of the next-generation European Rail Traffic Management System (ERTMS). The RBC will be responsible of managing the movement of trains equipped with radio communication. Its development process is critical: the RBC is a large-scale and complex system, it must provide several novel services at different levels of functionality, it must guarantee interoperability according to European standards, and, last but not least, a high level of safety. We have addressed these issues by devising a development based on formal specifications. ERTMS scenarios have been formalized in order to provide a better understanding of the interoperability requirements. The architecture of the RBC has been formally specified such that the system can be incrementally built as an overlay system (compatible with the existing train detection and interlocking systems) and modularly expanded to control different kinds of trains. The formal specifications of the behaviour of each RBC module have been structured hierarchically: they provide an easy-to-understand documentation for customers and developers; moreover, they can be simulated and validated automatically at the early stage of the development process, thus providing a high level of confidence in their safety in a cost-effective way.

1 Introduction

The next-generation European railway control systems will have to address a set of novel safety, performance, interoperability, and compatibility requirements. One of the goals is to build a safety critical system which improves railway system performances while reducing investment and operating costs. Another goal is to build systems interoperable among different European nations: in practice, a train working for a given railway (e.g. the Italian one) should be able to work in neighboring countries (e.g. in the Austrian, French and German railway's networks). Moreover, the system should be compatible with the existing ones. Finally, it should provide new functionalities incrementally, allowing thus for different levels of increasing sophistication.

The achievement of all these novel and different requirements is a crucial issue for the future of the European railway system. This has led to the set

M. Felici, K. Kanoun, A. Pasquini (Eds.): SAFECOMP'99, LNCS 1698, pp. 410-419, 1999
© Springer-Verlag Berlin Heidelberg 1999

up of a project at the European (rather than national) level, called the European Rail Traffic Management System (ERTMS). In the ERTMS project, the performance requirement has been addressed by conceiving a completely new communication system between trains and signalling systems on the ground, based on GSM mobile radio data transmission and on high-rate balises (EuroBalises). The interoperability requirement has been addressed by designing a European standard communication protocol between the train and the ground system, that has been described by a set of uses cases, called ERTMS scenarios. The system is described in [3] and [2].

The goal of the project described in this paper is the Ansaldo's specification and development of the Radio Block Center (RBC), the ERTMS component responsible for the management of the movement of trains equipped with radio communication. The RBC is a large-scale and complex system: it must interact with several systems beyond trains, e.g. with existing interlocking systems, with the RBC's controlling neighboring parts of the railways line, with a man-machine interface for monitoring and control. It must provide several novel services and guarantee interoperability according to the ERTMS standards, and, last but not least, a high level of safety. It is clear that its specification and development are critical.

We have addressed these issues by devising a development based on formal specifications. One of the main motivations for this choice is the fact that an approach based on formal methods allows for unambiguous specifications which can be validated at the early stage of the development process. Unambiguous specifications are extremely important for the interoperability and compatibility requirements. Their "early validation" is a must in practice for the safety requirements and for the development of a large-scale system. One of the main goals of the project is to devise a development process based on formal techniques which can be cost-effective and really usable by the experts in the signalling field. This has been achieved through some main steps where we have managed to adopt formal notations and formal verification techniques which can be smoothly introduced into the Company's development process. An overview of these main steps is presented in Section 2. The rest of the paper (after a brief description of the application domain in Section 3) describes in detail these steps: the formalization of ERTMS scenarios (Section 4), the formal input/output specification of RBC's software modules (Section 5), the hierarchical formal specification of their behaviour (Section 6) and their early validation (Section 7). In order to keep the paper short and readable, these steps are described through a simple example, which is discussed all through the paper. The whole formal specification and design at the current stage of the project is presented in a detailed project report [1].

2   Overview of the Approach

Cost-effectiveness and real usability of formal methods within the project has been achieved through a specification process based on the following main steps.

First, ERTMS scenarios describing the RBC-train communication have been formalized in order to provide a better understanding of the interoperability requirements. At this stage, it is important to use a language which is easy to understand by signalling experts. Scenarios have been formalized in the "Message Sequence Chart" (MSC) format [6]. MSC's have been designed to represent the dynamic behaviour of protocols. In spite of the fact they are formal and thus provide unambiguous descriptions, their graphical notation is extremely intuitive and easy to read. MSC's have allowed experts in signalling and experts in formal methods to share their respective know-how. As a result, they have allowed us to disambiguate several scenarios and to state clearly the hypotheses under which the scenarios are applicable.

Second, we have designed the high level architecture of the RBC through "Structured Description Language (SDL) block (interconnection) diagrams" [5]. SDL diagrams allow for the definition of software modules and the information exchanged between modules. We have first defined the interconnection diagram between the RBC as a black box and the other systems it interacts with (e.g. the interlocking, the other RBC's, the interface to the operator and the train). We have then decomposed the RBC module into more "elementary" functionalities.

Third, starting from the formalized scenarios (MSC's) and the architectural decomposition in different software modules (SDL block diagrams) we have formally specified the dynamic behaviour of each module. We have used "State Charts" [4] for this purpose. State Charts are a well-known formalism which is used to describe systems components as automata. Automata are a well known technique used in Ansaldo—engineers can easily understand them and use them to describe the system behaviour. The main problem in this task is due to the fact that the system is quite large. A mere one-level and flatten description of the system in terms of state charts would be unpractical and very difficult to maintain. For this reason, state charts have been structured hierarchically: we have developed state charts which describe the behaviour of the system at a high level, abstracting away several details. These state charts are simple (i.e. with a reasonable number of states) and highly non-deterministic: given a state of the system, the system can evolve into more than one next state. In other words, the state chart is not detailed enough to specify the exact conditions under which the system evolves in one of the possibly many behaviours. These automata provide a high level view of the system, are extremely important for the documentation (both for developers and customers), and can be easily validated by railways experts by means of simple inspections.

Then high level state charts are refined in detailed ones. We have specified the detailed behaviour of the system through "SDL processes". SDL processes describe in detail how the system evolves from one state to the next. SDL [5] is a language which has been extensively used in industry. Its notation is not difficult for an engineer which is used to traditional programming and software engineering notations, like data flow diagrams and flowcharts. The signalling expert can still read the detailed specification easily, but a manual validation by inspection is unpractical, since at this level of detail the specification is large.

As a consequence, we have exploited existing tools to automatically simulate the specifications. This is the immediate advantage of having developed formal specifications: they can be simulated far before the code implementation phase. Moreover, we have used "Model Checking" techniques to explore all the possible behaviours of the system exhaustively. The significant added value of Model Checking w.r.t. simulation is that it can guarantee that a safety property is satisfied for all possible behaviours of the system. Indeed, Model Checking has revealed unexpected behaviours of the system as initially specified: specifications errors have been corrected until the specifications have been validated by model checking.

In this project, we have used the ObjectGeode tool [7], which among other languages and features, allows for the use of MSC's, SDL bock diagrams, State Charts, SDL processes, and a simulator and a model checker for SDL processes.

3   Overview of the Application

The main functionality of the RBC is the allocation of Movement Authority (MA) to trains, that is, permission to move for a certain distance. In order to safely allocate MA, the RBC collects information about (but not limited to) the position of trains on the line, emergency situations, and pending orders from human operator(s).

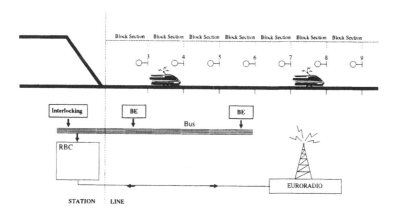

Fig. 1. The ERTMS System.

Figure 1 depicts the situation. The line is logically divided into block sections; the signalling system must guarantee that any block section is occupied at the most by one train. In order to do so, the entrance into a block section is protected by a signal. A train detection system senses the status of occupation of the blocks and sets the signals accordingly. In the station the situation is more complex: an interlocking system is responsible of setting/releasing itineraries, by safely controlling switches and signals. The RBC is connected to all the interlockings installed in the zone it controls. The RBC collects information about the position of trains, the status of occupation of blocks on the line and the itineraries set in the stations, computes MA's based on the information it has collected, and sends them to the trains.

4   Scenarios (via Message Sequence Charts)

The least restrictive way of guaranteeing interoperability is to impose a standardization of the messages and the protocol between RBC and train. The ERTMS project has thus defined a list of correct RBC-train messages, called telegrams, and a set of use cases, called scenarios, that provide examples of the communication protocol. Scenarios are composed of a description in natural language, that explains the rationale of the scenario (e.g. the applicability) and a tabular description of the protocol, that provides examples of how telegrams are exchanged.

Scenarios leave several options open: we must choose among all the options provided by the scenarios the ones that are most suitable, e.g., with the system in which the RBC is going to operate. For instance, the Scenario describing MA allocation to trains does not fix the criteria according to which the RBC decides to allocate MA's: such criteria indeed depend upon the rules governing the signalling system in which the RBC operates (e.g. they are decided on a national basis). This information, however, is essential to provide an executable specification of the RBC.

More to the point, the tabular form used in [2] is kind of ambiguous. The succession of rows does not necessarily correspond to progression of time. Alternatives are difficult to represent.

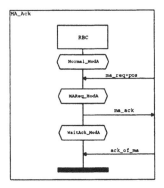

Fig. 2. MSC of MA Allocation with acknowledgement.

The above considerations suggest the need for a more precise notation, with clear syntax and semantics, and easily understandable by experts of the railway system. We adopted the Message Sequence Charts (MSC) notation, as it meets all these requirements. Figure 2 shows an MSC that rationalizes part of the Scenario describing MA allocation to trains. We distinguish an entity, called RBC, that communicates with the environment (framing rectangle). The environment comprehends everything external to the RBC: in our case, trains. The RBC and the environment exchange messages, represented in the MSC by labelled arrows. Time progresses from the top to the bottom. The MSC represents the reception of a request for a MA (ma_req+pos), to which the RBC answers with a MA requiring an acknowledgement (ma_ack). Upon receiving the MA, the train acknowledges the reception (ack_of_ma). The MSC is also marked with "conditions" (e.g. Normal_ModA), that fix the states of the communication between track and train.

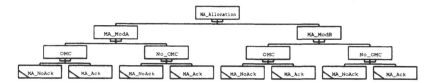

Fig. 3. Abstract MSC of MA Allocation.

In ObjectGeode, MSC's can be combined to form more complex MSC's, using operators like sequence, alternative, and iteration. The composition of MSC's is represented by a tree (called hierarchy), in which the nodes are operators and the leaves are MSC's. Figure 3 shows a hierarchy of MSC's that rationalizes the behaviours of the Scenario describing MA allocation to trains. We individuate two different operating modes, called Mode A and Mode B. In Mode A (leftmost subtree), trains always ask for MA's, whereas in Mode B (rightmost subtree) the RBC allocates MA to trains when it decides to do so. The RBC may request a a change in the operating mode (subtrees marked OMC—Operating Mode Change) and, finally, MA's may require an acknowledgement or not (leaves of the tree). The MSC in Figure 2 is the leaf MA_Ack in the hierarchy in Figure 3.

5   Architectural Description (via SDL Interconnection Diagrams)

MSC's help understand and formally define the way in which the RBC interacts with trains. This is not the whole story, however, as the RBC interacts with several other actors. The second step in the specification of the RBC, thus, is the definition of the environment in which the RBC operates (what we call the "context diagram") and the definition of the constituent blocks of the RBC (architectural decomposition).

Figure 4 shows the context diagram for the RBC. The RBC interacts with actors, that range from devices for the configuration of the RBC at startup

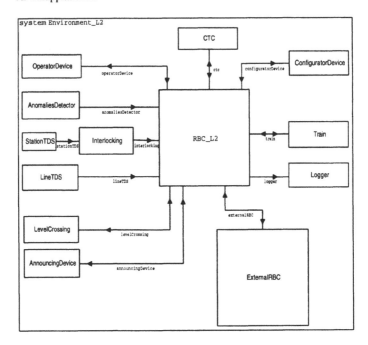

Fig. 4. Context Diagram of the RBC.

(Configurator Device), through devices for collecting the status of the line (Operator, Anomalies Detector, Interlocking, Line TDS, External RBC), to trackside devices directly operated by the RBC (Level Crossing and Announcing Device).

6   Dynamic Behaviour Specification (via State Charts and SDL processes)

We can now start filling the blocks of the interconnection diagram, using the MSC's as a constraint for the I/O behaviour of the RBC. To simplify the process of specification of the blocks, and increase our confidence on the specifications, we start with abstract specifications—using State Charts—that we later refine into SDL code. The abstract specifications hide several details of the behaviour of the RBC (like, for instance, what decisions trigger a transition to a state rather than another): the goal here is providing "high level" specifications that can be validated "by hand".

Figure 5 shows the abstract specification of the communication protocol described in the Scenario describing MA allocation to trains. The left hand side implements the allocation of MA in Mode A. We distinguish three states: Normal_ModA, MAReq_ModA, and WaitAck_ModA. In Normal_ModA the RBC waits for a MA request from the train (ma_req), that causes a transition into MAReq_ModA. From MAReq_ModA the RBC sends a MA to the train and non-deterministically

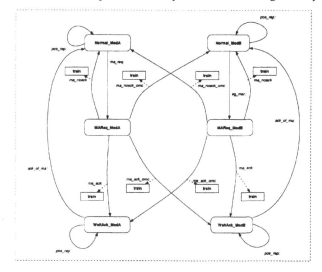

Fig. 5. Abstract State Chart for MA Allocation.

goes into one of the following four states, depending on the MA the RBC decides to send: Normal_ModA (MA that does not require acknowledgement nor operating mode change), WaitAck_ModA (MA that requires acknowledgement but does not require to change operating mode), Normal_ModB (MA that does not require acknowledgement, but that requires an operating mode change), WaitAck_ModB (MA that requires both acknowledgement and to change operating mode). The state chart we just presented does not describe the internal mechanisms and strategies according to which the RBC chooses what MA to send, and, therefore, its next state: our goal, here, is the specification of the generic behaviour of the RBC (e.g., the fact that from MAReq_ModA, the RBC has four possible next states, corresponding to four logically different states of the communication).

State Charts can be automatically translated by ObjectGeode into SDL code. In our case, (a slightly modified version of) the chart of Figure 5 has been automatically translated into SDL code, that has later been refined by hand, adding the details to make its behaviour deterministic. Figure 6 shows the portion starting from MAReq_ModA: the RBC gets information about the occupation of the line (track_path), computes the MA (cma), then decides the next state. Now the transition onto the next state is deterministic and depends upon a call to the function omc (that determines whether to change operating mode) and a parameter cfg_ack (that determines whether to ask for acknowledgements). Depending on which of the four branches is chosen, the RBC sends a different message to the train (one of ma_ack_omc, noma_ack_omc, ma_ack, and ma_noack).

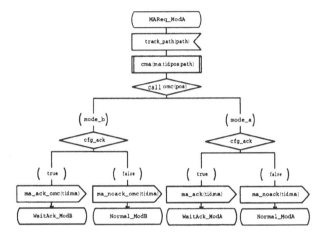

Fig. 6. SDL representation of the State Chart.

7   Early Validation (via Simulation and Model Checking)

The last step is the validation of the specifications. In this step we exploit the executability of the specifications, by running them inside ObjectGeode's simulator and model checker (exhaustive simulator). The goal of this activity is verifying that certain properties hold of the specifications of the RBC. It is important here to observe that, short of a few properties that can be proven with the RBC in isolation (like the absence of deadlocks), in order to verify whether the RBC behaves correctly, we must immerse the RBC into an environment. The environment is composed of, for instance, interlocking and the train detection systems, that provide inputs to the RBC, and trains, that communicate with the RBC and move according to the MA's they receive from the RBC. Thus, by monitoring how trains move, we can check whether the RBC behaves as it should. We can arbitrarily degrade the performances of the environment, by allowing, for instance, telegrams to be lost or corrupted by the radio channel. This allows to test the behaviour of the RBC in a wide range of (critical) situations.

Properties are verified by running simulations (either random or exhaustive) with watches that monitors the behaviour of the system. Such watches can either express properties holding of a state or properties holding along a sequence of states. For instance, we can verify that no block section is occupied by more than one train or that a certain train has reached a certain position.

8   Conclusions

In this paper we have described an on-going project whose aim is the formal specification of a system (the implementation of RBC done by Ansaldo) for the management of trains according to the ERTMS requirements. We have adopted formal methods in order to cope with the safety and interoperability requirements. One of the main issues of the project is the provision of formal specification techniques which can be easily understood and used cost-effectively within the Company's development process. This issue has been addressed by providing formal specifications which are unambiguous and, at the same time, can be easily inspected by the development team; by devising an hierarchical specification of the system which provides an highly structured documentation for customers and developers; by an early validation phase which is performed during the specification and design phase and in which (detailed) formal specifications can be simulated (either interactively or exhaustively) to detect possible expensive specification errors at the early stage of the project.

We have approached the problem of the specification of a quite large and complex system, interacting with several external actors, in a selective and incremental way. At this stage of the project we have formally specified and validated a significant subset of the functionalities. Some of them are (part of) the management of trains inside the area controlled by the RBC, the entry/exit of a train from/to areas controlled/not-controlled by other RBC's, some cases of anomalies handling. These specifications and the methodology used to provide them are now taken as examples and guidelines to complete the specifications and design in the current continuation of the project.

Acknowledgements

The work described in this paper was founded under contract 1607/250000(NA). The authors would like to thank all the people at Ansaldo and IRST involved in the project.

References

1. A. Chiappini, A. Cimatti, F. Giunchiglia, G. Rotondo, R. Sebastiani, P. Traverso, and A. Villafiorita. Formal Specification of the Radio Block Centre (RBC): First Part. RBC I: Ansaldo-IRST Project Report, December 1998.
2. EEIG-ERTMS Users Group, 25 Avenue De Beaulieu 1160 Brussels, Belgium. *Scenarios*.
3. EEIG-ERTMS Users Group, 25 Avenue De Beaulieu 1160 Brussels, Belgium. *System Requirements Specification*.
4. David Harel. Statecharts: A Visual Formalism for Complex Systems. *Science of Computer Programming*, 8(3):231–274, June 1987.
5. ITU-T. *CCITT specification and description language (SDL)*, March 1993. ITU-T Recommendation Z.100.
6. ITU-T. *Message Sequence Chart (MSC)*, October 1996. ITU-T Recommendation Z.120.
7. VERILOG. *ObjectGeode Documentation*. Available at *www.verilogusa.com*.

Formal Validation of the GUARDS
Inter-consistency Mechanism*

Cinzia Bernardeschi[1], Alessandro Fantechi[2], and Stefania Gnesi[3]

[1] Dipartimento di Ingegneria della Informazione, Università di Pisa,
Via Diotisalvi 2, 56126 Pisa, Italy
cinzia@iet.unipi.it
[2] Dipartimento di Sistemi e Informatica, Università di Firenze,
Via S. Marta 3, 50139 Firenze, Italy
fantechi@dsi.unifi.it
[3] Istituto di Elaborazione dell' Informazione, Consiglio Nazionale delle Ricerche,
Via S. Maria 49, 56126 Pisa, Italy
gnesi@iei.pi.cnr.it

Abstract. In this paper we report the experience carried out to specify and validate the Inter-consistency mechanism developed within the European project GUARDS as a component of an architecture for embedded safety-critical systems. The validation approach is based on model checking technique and exploits the verification methodology supported by the JACK environment. The properties that guarantee the desired behaviour of the mechanism are specified as temporal logic formulae; the JACK model checker is then used to verify that the behaviour of the mechanism satisfies such properties also in presence of faults.

1 Introduction

The European project GUARDS (Generic Upgradable Architecture for Real-time Dependable Systems) addresses the development of architectures, methods, techniques, and tools to support the design, the implementation and validation of safety critical systems [12]. Formal approaches were used in GUARDS for the specification and verification of selected critical components, and this was recognised to be one of the main innovative point of the project. In particular, formal validation has addressed four mechanisms of the GUARDS architecture, namely: a) interactive consistency, b) fault diagnosis, c) clock synchronization, and d) multi-level integrity. In this paper we report the formal validation of the interactive consistency mechanism, that focuses on the problem of reliably distributing single source data to multiple processors in presence of faults. The verifications concerning the mechanism were all based on model checking [6]

---

* This work was partly supported by the ESPRIT project GUARDS (Generic Upgradable Architecture for Real-time Dependable Systems) and by Progetto Coordinato CNR "Metodologie e strumenti di analisi, verifica e validazione per sistemi software affidabili"

M. Felici, K. Kanoun, A. Pasquini (Eds.): SAFECOMP'99, LNCS 1698, pp. 420-430, 1999

using the JACK (*Just Another Concurrency Kit*) tool-set [5]. This integrated environment provides a set of specification and verification tools that were used to generate a model of the behaviour of the mechanism and to prove properties formalised as temporal logic formulae. Agreement and validity properties for interactive consistency were proved by expressing them as temporal logic formulae, and by automatically checking the satisfiability of the formula over the model of the system.

The paper is organised as follows: Section 2 describes the Interactive consistency problem, showing how it has been handled inside the GUARDS project. Section 3 describes the validation by model checking of the Inter-consistency mechanism. Section 4 contains some remarks and hints for future work.

2   The GUARDS Project

The GUARDS project has produced a generic architecture for safety critical systems, designed to be instantiated to support different critical applications; it is composed of COTS (Commercial Off The Shelf) components as well as ad hoc defined components, namely the Inter-channel communication network, the Fault Treatment mechanism, the Integrity management mechanism, and the Output data consolidation mechanism. The formal validation policy followed in GUARDS is based on the a priori validation of selected critical components, while COTS components are taken as already validated [1]. A fundamental issue of the Inter-channel communication network and of the Fault Treatment mechanism is the implementation of the *interactive consistency*.

2.1   Interactive Consistency

Interactive consistency focuses on the problem of reaching agreement among multiple processors in presence of faults. The principal difficulty to be overcome in achieving interactive consistency is the possibility of conflicting values sent by faulty processors: such a processor may provide one value to a second processor, but a different value to a third, thereby making difficult for the recipients to agree on a common value. Interactive consistency algorithms overcome this problem by using several rounds of messages exchange during which processor P tells processor Q what value it has received from processor R and so on. This problem is also known as the *Byzantine Generals problem* [11] in the literature. Byzantine agreement is extremely expensive to be implemented and classes of protocols have been proposed to optimise different cost factors (number of messages, number of messages, etc.). Interactive consistency is implemented in GUARDS by the Inter-consistency mechanism, which uses the ZA Byzantine Agreement algorithm described in [9] and briefly reported in Table 1. The algorithm is synchronous and it uses authenticated messages. The assumption of message authentication requires that faulty processors do not make undetectable modifications to messages as they are relayed from one processor to another. The classical *Agreement* and *Validity* properties must be satisfied to reach consistency:

Agreement: if a pair of receivers are non faulty, then they agree on the value ascribed to the transmitter.

Validity: if the receiver P is non faulty, then the value ascribed to the transmitter by P is the value actually sent if the transmitter is non faulty or symmetric faulty; or the distinguished value *error*, if the transmitter is manifest faulty.

In [9] it is shown that the *ZA* algorithm can tolerate a arbitrary, s symmetric, and m manifest faults simultaneously, provided n, the number of processors, satisfies $n > a + s + m + 1, r >= a$ where r is the number of rounds, symmetric faults deliver the same wrong value to every receiver node, while manifest faults produce errors detectable by a receiver.

2.2 GUARDS Implementation of Interactive Consistency

Interactive consistency is implemented in GUARDS by the Inter-consistency mechanism [10], using a non recursive definition of the ZA algorithm, which cannot in this case be generic on the number n of nodes and r of rounds.

In the case of 4 nodes, the implementation of the ZA algorithm for the transmitter node P is given in Table 2. With reference to the table, vp is the private value of node P. In the first phase of the algorithm, the transmitter simply encodes its value, then it sends it to the other nodes. In the next three phases, it waits back the value returned by the receiver nodes. In the last phase, a voting is performed on the three relayed values. Any receiver node, after reception and decoding of a message from the transmitter, relays the message. Node S relays the message in phase 2; node R does it in phase 3 and node Q in phase 4. In the other phases a receiver waits for the message relayed by the other receiver nodes. Then, in the last phase, it votes. The implementation of the ZA algorithm for the receiver node S is given in Table 3.

The GUARDS Inter-consistency mechanism allows a node to behave simultaneously as transmitter and as receiver from every other node, so that each node has at the end a voted knowledge on each value hold by every other node. Therefore, the mechanism is a composition of transmitter and receiver protocols: for example, in the four nodes case, each node includes one trasmitter protocol and three receiver protocols.

3 Formal Verification by Model Checking

Within the GUARDS project, it was considered necessary to submit this high-level implementation to a validation process in order to confirm the satisfaction of the Validity and Agreement properties according to the fault assumptions considered in the project. The generic recursive definition of the algorithm cannot be applied in an embedded system. Moreover, the GUARDS architecture was designed to be exploited by three different pilot applications, namely a nuclear submarine control subsystem, a railway interlocking system, and a space-station payload control system. Of the three cases, the first employs an instance of the

Table 1. The ZA algorithm

ZA(0)

1. The transmitter sends its value to every receiver.
2. Each receiver uses the value received by the transmitter or uses the default *error* value in case of manifest faulty value.

ZA, $r > 0$

1. The transmitter signs and sends its value to every receiver.
2. For each p, let v_p be the value receiver p obtains from the transmitter, or *error* if a manifest faulty value is received. Each receiver p acts as the transmitter in $ZA(r - 1)$ to communicate the value v_p to the other $n - 1$ receivers.

3. For each p and q, let v_q be the value received by the receiver p from receiver q in step 2 of the algorithm $ZA(r - 1)$, or *error* if a manifest faulty value was received. Each receiver p calculates the majority among all non-error values v_q received (at most $n - 1$). If no majority exists, the receiver uses some value.

GUARDS architecture having just two processors, where the interactive consistency mechanism does not apply, the second one employs three processors and the latter four processors. Therefore, only three and four nodes instances of the generic interactive consistency algorithm have been implemented. As a consequence, the formal validation of the interactive consistency algorithm has actually addressed these instances. The adopted approach for the formal validation of these instances was based on model checking.

In a first phase of the project the validation has addressed the three nodes case, producing the specification of the Inter-consistency mechanism (in which each node is composed of one transmitter protocol and two receiver protocols), generating the model and model checking the Validity and Agreement properties [3]. Given the validation effort done for the three nodes case, we could expect that the validation for the four nodes case could exploit the already built model, by performing some kind of incremental extension, that would avoid to generate again the global state space from scratch. Unfortunately, this is not possible due to the structure of the mechanism itself: validation has to be repeated on each instance of the Inter-consistency mechanism generic definition. The validation of the Inter-consistency mechanism to cover the four nodes case has hence required writing a new specification of the nodes of the network. Since every node sends its private value, a greater number of messages is exchanged during any phase of the algorithm and new variables are necessary to record the received messages and their decoded values. Moreover, since the number of nodes also increases, the increment of the number of states of the global model of the mechanism is quite large. This is a typical state explosion problem case. To address this problem, we have decomposed the definition of the four node Inter-consistency mechanism into the four basic protocols (one transmitter and three receivers)

performed by each node. This has been possible since the messages are shown
to be independent between the four protocols.

Table 2. The ZA algorithm of transmitter node P

phase 1:	phase4:
vp:p := p_encode(vp);	p2 := p_decode(msg2);
p_broadcast(vp:p);	msg3 := q_receive();
phase2:	phase5:
msg1 := s_receive();	p3 := p_decode(msg3);
	vp(p) := vote(p1, p2, p3);
phase3:	
p1 := p_decode(msg1);	
msg2 := r_receive();	

3.1   Model Checking

Model checking is an automated verification method for checking finite state
systems against properties specified in temporal logic [6]. The proof of the properties is carried out by means of exhaustive search on the complete behaviour
(model) of the system. The model of the system can be given as a Labelled
Transition System (LTS). LTSs are essentially a variant of classical state machines in which transitions are labelled to describe the actions which cause state
changes. More formally, a system can be specified starting from a finite set of
observable actions *Act* and giving the possible sequences of actions the system
can execute (systems observable behaviour) by means of an LTS. Following the
methodology presented in [2], the LTS expressing the model of the behaviour of
the Inter-consistency mechanism has been built, starting from its description of
section 2.2, using two different languages: the CCS/Meije process algebra and
the graphical language of the ATG tool, based on LTSs and networks of LTSs
[14]. A hierarchical approach in specification is possible: a single mechanism is
obtained by composing the specification of its components. In the modelization
of the Inter-consistency mechanism we have also considered the inclusion of possible faults which may affect the behaviour of the mechanism itself, following the
methodology described in [4]. The branching time temporal logic ACTL logic
[7] has used to express the agreement and validity properties to be checked
on the Inter-consistency mechanism. The tools of JACK [5] support both the
specification and the verification phases of the work. Formulae can be proved by
the model checking algorithm in JACK in polynomial time on the size of the
model and the length of the formula. In [8] JACK was used to specify hardware
components of a buffer system and to verify the correctness of the specification
with respect to some safety requirements. In [13] the formal specification and

verification of some properties of a hydroelectric plant were presented. In [2] JACK has been applied successfully in the verification of a railway interlocking system.

Table 3. The ZA algorithm of receiver node S

phase 1:	phase4:
msg1 := p_receive();	p2 := p_decode(msg2);
	msg3 := q_receive();
phase2:	
p1 := p_decode(msg1);	phase5:
s_broadcast(msg1);	p3 := p_decode(msg3);
	vs(p) := vote(p1, p2, p3);
phase3:	
msg2 := r_receive();	

3.2   Specification of the 4-node Inter-consistency Mechanism

The Inter-consistency mechanism behaviour has been specified as a *network* of four processes: one acting as the transmitter, the other as receivers. The processes communicate values among them on dedicated links and synchronize at the beginning of each phase. Fig. 1 represents the structure of the network, where the links between boxes describe the synchronization between processes through complementary actions. Actions are represented by labelled ports on the box borders. At the bottom of Fig. 1, we can note some "wedges" which represent synchronization between more than two processes (multi-way synchronization).

The specification of the Inter-consistency mechanism has been written along the following criteria:

1. Only 0s and 1s have been considered as correct values. The special value *error* is considered as a separate value.
2. Communication actions between nodes are seen as separate actions on separate links for each possible value transmitted. In this way we have non-parametric actions, that allows a simpler verification process.
3. To maintain coherence with the original interactive consistency algorithm definition, we have specified the variables as distinct processes inside a node, and the reading/writing of the variable are specified as actions performed by the related processes.
4. The injection of the different faults is controlled by ad hoc defined processes, named fault hypothesis processes.

The specification of a node is again a network of processes. The different phases of the algorithm, the variables and the fault hypothesis are processes inside the node. As an example, the specification of the network describing the node S is reported in Fig. 2.

The processes represented in Fig. 2 are described by terms of the CCS/Meije process algebra. For example the process phase1 of node S is expressed by the following term:

```
phase1s = {
RECEIVE = psends_encp_0? : s_m1p_encp_0! : END +
          psends_encp_1? : s_m1p_encp_1! : END +
          psends_omission? : s_m1p_omission! : END
and
END = startphase2! : nil
} in RECEIVE;
```

In the initial state RECEIVE the process may receive a message (of value 0 or 1) from P. A possible fault is the omission of the message. This fault is modeled in the specification by the third choice of the nondeterministic sum. The node upon receiving a message from P (or detecting an omission fault), saves the message into the variable named m1p, by an action which communicates the value to the process modeling the variable . Then it is ready to execute phase 2 of protocol, and signals this by the startphase2! action, on which all the partner nodes have to synchronize. The following faults are modeled in the Inter-consistency mechanism:

1. omission fault. For any P and Q, we use the action ptoq_omiss to inject an omission fault on the communication between the node P and a node Q when P broadcasts a message.
2. transmission fault. The decode operation of a received message may detect an incorrectly encoded message. We can inject the fault "msg incorrectly encoded" for a message received by using the actions: j_inc_enc or j_corr_enc to state whether the message saved into the variable j is incorrectly or correctly encoded. These actions are used when the node decodes the message.
3. a fault which changes the value of the message sent. When the transmitter sends its encoded private value, it actually sends a value different from the correct one (this may lead to inconsistent values received on remote nodes). When a faulty receiver relays a message, it actually modifies the message is relaying. In the case in which a receiver detects "msg correctly encoded", these faults violate the assumption on authentication of messages. In order to model the assumption on authentication of messages, we have to force the detection "msg incorrectly encoded" for the message received in this case.

Arbitrary, symmetric and manifest faulty nodes can be specified by modifying the fault hypotheses processes. The condition of absence of faults is formalised by a fault hypothesis that does not allow faults to occur.

3.3   Generation of the Global Model

The specification of the 4-nodes Inter-consistency mechanism is composed by 64 processes. Tools in JACK have been used to generate the LTS describing the

complete behaviour (model) of the Inter-consistency mechanism starting from its specification. Table 4 reports some figures about the size of the generated model in terms of number of states of the LTSs under the following fault assumptions:
A1 - all nodes are non faulty;
A2 - R is symmetric faulty, S arbitrary faulty;
A3 - S is arbitrary faulty and violates the assumption of authentication.

Table 4. Size of generated models

Fault Assumption	Number of states
A1	3479
A2	109613
A3	122767

3.4   Verification of the 4-nodes Inter-consistency Mechanism

The properties of *Agreement* and *Validity* reported in Section 2 are checked on the global model of the behaviour of the mechanism. In the following, we report the formalisation of the properties as ACTL formulae when nodes are non faulty.
Agreement:
for any execution of the processes, the nodes eventually agree on the value 1 (actions !vp_ofp_eqto_1, !vp_ofq_eqto_1, !vp_ofr_eqto_1, !vp_ofs_eqto_1) or the nodes eventually agree on the value 0 (!vp_ofp_eqto_0, !vp_ofq_eqto_0, !vp_ofr_eqto_0, !vp_ofs_eqto_1 actions) .
Validity:
if in *any* state of the model, it is true that the internal value of the node P is equal to 1 (action !psend_vp_1) or 0 (action !psend_vp_0) , then *for any execution* of the processes, *starting from such a state*, the nodes eventually agree on such a value. The combination of the *Agreement* and *Validity* properties in the case of value 1, is expressed by the following ACTL formula:

```
AG[!psend_vp_1] (A[true{true}U{!vp_ofp_eqto_1}true] &
   A[true{true}U{!vp_ofq_eqto_1}true] &
   A[true{true}U{!vp_ofr_eqto_1} true] &
   A[true{true}U{!vp_ofs_eqto_1}true])
```

A similar formula must be written when P sends the value 0. In the case of faulty nodes, the formulae expressing *Agreement* and *Validity* properties must be modified. As an example, if S is faulty, the formula is independent from S:

```
AG[!psend_vp_1] (A[true{true}U{!vp_ofp_eqto_1}true] &
   A[true{true}U{!vp_ofq_eqto_1}true] &
   A[true{true}U{!vp_ofr_eqto_1}true])
```

Under the assumptions A1 and A2 the formulae have been proved to be satisfied by the model of the system. In the case of A3 the formulae have been proven not to be verified. This asserts that the four nodes Inter-consistency mechanism is able to reach Validity and Agreement even in presence of two faults, provided that the assumption on the authentication of the messages is not violated. In the case of such a violation, even a single fault is not tolerated.

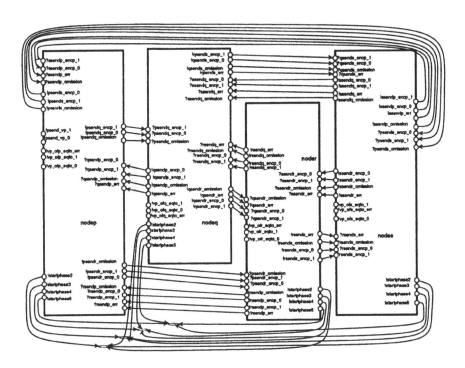

Fig. 1. The network

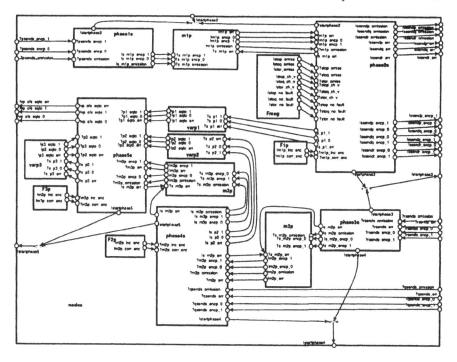

Fig. 2. The node

4   Conclusions

In this paper we have shown the formal validation of a specific mechanism of the GUARDS architecture, by means of model checking. We have shown that the model checking approach is suitable to deal with the considered instances of the Interactive consistency algorithm. Verification based on *theorem proving* has been used instead for the generic algorithm in [9]; this means that the object of our formal validation effort is closer to the actually running code than the generic Interactive Consistency algorithm. The advantage of the model checking approach is that the verification is completely automatic, provided that space explosion problems are solved. This can be in our opinion appealing in the industrial validation of safety critical systems. Moreover, the adopted technique of modelling fault hypothesis by means of specific processes which constrain the occurrence of fault actions allowed us to develop a unified framework to analyze the behaviour of the mechanism under different occurrences of faults. This can be very useful when a careful analysis on the effects of specific faults is desired. The drawback of model checking technique is the capacity of tools in number of states that can be handled. In this respect, a new version of the AMC model checker based on Binary Decision Diagrams (BDDs) is scheduled to join the JACK environment in order to handle larger specifications. In fact, verification tools based on the representation of automata by means of BDD are able o deal with automata with a number of states several orders of magnitude larger than other representations.

References

1. Arlat, J.: Preliminary definition of the GUARDS validation strategy. GUARDS Deliverable D3O1, LAAS -CNRS Report 96378, (1997).
2. Bernardeschi, C., Fantechi, A., Gnesi, S., Larosa, S., Mongardi, G., Romano, D.: A Formal Verification Environment for Railway Signaling System Design. Formal Methods in System Design 12, (1998) 139–161.
3. Bernardeschi, C., Fantechi, A., Gnesi, S., Santone, A.: Automated Verification of fault-tolerant mechanisms. Ercim FMICS98, CWI Press, Amsterdam, (1998).
4. Bernardeschi, C., Fantechi, A., Simoncini, L.: Formal reasoning on fault coverage of fault tolerant techniques: a case study. Proc. EDCC-1, Berlin, Lecture Notes in Computer Science vol. 852, (1994).
5. Bouali, A., Gnesi, S., Larosa, S.: The integration Project for the JACK Environment. Bulletin of the EATCS, 54, (1994) 207–223.
6. Clarke, E.M., Emerson, E.A., Sistla, A.P.: Automatic Verification of Finite-State Concurrent Systems Using Temporal Logic Specification. ACM Transaction on Programming Languages and Systems, 8 (2), (1986) 244–263.
7. De Nicola, R., Vaandrager, F.W.: Actions versus State Based Logics for Transition Systems. Proc. Ecole de Printemps on Semantics of Concurrency, Lecture Notes in Computer Science vol. 469, (1990) 407–419.
8. De Nicola, R., Fantechi, A., Gnesi, S., Ristori, G.: Hardware components within JACK. Proc. CHARME'95, Lecture Notes in Computer Science vol. 987, (1995) 246–260.
9. Gong, L., Lincoln, P., RushbyJ.: Byzantine Agreement with Authentication: Observations and Applications in Tolerating Hybrid and Link Faults. Proc. 5th Conference on Dependable Computing for Critical Applications (DCCA-5), Urbana-Champaign, Il, USA, (1995).
10. Powell, D., Rabéjac, C., Schindler, H.: Inter-Channel Consistency Mechanism. GUARDS Esprit project, D1A3/A0/2008, (1996).
11. Lamport, L., Shostak, R., Pease, M.: The Byzantine Generals Problem. ACM Transactions on Programming Languages and Systems, Vol.4, N. 3, (1982) 382–401.
12. Wellings, A., Beus-Dukic, L., Burns, A., Powell, D.: Genericity and Upgradability in Ultra-Dependable Real-Time Architectures. Work in Progress Proceedings, Real-Time Systems Symp., Washington D.C., IEEE Computer Society Press, (1996) 15–18.
13. Pugliese, R., Tronci, E.: Automatic verification of an Hydroelectric Power Plant. Proc. FME96 Industrial benefit and Advances in Formal methods, Lecture Notes in Computer Science vol. 1051, 1996, pp. 425-444.
14. Roy,V., De Simone, R.: AUTO and Autograph. Proc. Workshop on Computer Aided Verification, Lecture Notes in Computer Science vol. 531, (1990) 65–75.

A Graphical Environment for the Specification and Verification of Reactive Systems

A.K. Bhattacharjee[1], S.D. Dhodapkar[1], Sanjit Seshia[2]*, and
R.K. Shyamasundar[2]

[1] Reactor Control Division, Bhabha Atomic Research Centre, Mumbai 400 025, India
sdd@magnum.barc.ernet.in
[2] School of Technology & Computer Science, Tata Institute of Fundamental
Research, Mumbai 400 005, India
shyam@tcs.tifr.res.in

Abstract. In this paper, we describe the design and implementation of
an environment for the specification, analysis and verification of reactive systems. The environment allows the user to develop specification in
the graphical formalism of Statecharts [1] and a built-in translator tool
translates the specification into ESTEREL [3] program. Through such an
approach, we have been able to integrate the powerful graphical formalism of Statecharts, which is very appealing to engineers, and the power of
formal verification environments for ESTEREL. Since we translate Statecharts, which can be nondeterministic, to ESTEREL programs which
are fully deterministic, the system overcomes the nondeterminism in the
specifications by enforcing priority. The behaviour of ESTEREL programs
generated by the translator follows the Statechart *step* semantics [2]. In
the paper, we describe the main components of the environment, the
principles underlying the translation and illustrate the use of the system
for the specification and verification using an example.

1 Introduction

Significant amount of research has been done in the last decade in the methods for design and development of reactive systems. The class of synchronous
languages and the class of visual formalisms are two approaches that have been
widely accepted and used for the design, analysis and simulation of reactive systems both in academia and industry. The family of synchronous languages are
based on the *perfect synchrony hypothesis* which can be interpreted to mean that
the program reacts rapidly enough to perceive all the external events in order
and produces all the output reactions before reacting to a new input event. Typical examples of embedded control systems can be abstracted in this manner.
Some of the prominent languages of this family that have found wide usage in
the industry include ESTEREL , Lustre, Signal etc. In this work we have selected

---

* Current address: School of Computer Science, Carnegie Mellon University, Pittsburgh,PA 15217, USA, email: Sanjit.Seshia@cs.cmu.edu

M. Felici, K. Kanoun, A. Pasquini (Eds.): SAFECOMP'99, LNCS 1698, pp. 431–444, 1999.
© Springer-Verlag Berlin Heidelberg 1999

ESTEREL due to range of features available which include the availability of rich primitives for concurrency, communication and preemption, a clean and rigorous semantics, a powerful programming environment with the capability of formal verification. The advantages ESTEREL are nicely paraphrased by Gerard Berry, the inventor of ESTEREL , as follows: *What you prove is what you execute.*

Statecharts is a visual formalism which can be seen as a generalization of the conventional finite state automata and supporting features such as hierarchy, orthogonality (concurrency) and broadcast communication between system components. Being a formalism rather than a language, there have been a plethora of semantics corresponding to various plausible implementations. The standard semantics that is normally used (we also use the same) is that of Harel & Naamad [2]. Even though there are powerful programming environments for Statecharts such as STATEMATE [1] including simulators, code generators etc, in general they lack formal verification tools.

Textual and graphical formalisms have their own intrinsic merits and demerits as explained in the following. First, let us consider a reactive system described below, a Statechart representation for which is shown in Fig. 1.:

> The controller required specifies control flow (switching of tasks) among various computing tasks and interrupt service tasks. The computing states (hpt, dt1, dt2 etc.) switch from one to another in a cyclic fashion and are shown as substates of compute_proc. The interrupt service states (rti_isr, wdt_isr, net_isr, nmi_isr) are entered as a result of the occurrence of interrupt events. The history notation has been used to indicate that on return from interrupt states, the system returns to last executing compute state (except when event 100ms occurs, the control returns to computing state hpt). The event wdt_int occurs on system failure and it has to be verified that when wdt_isr is entered, the system will toggle between states wdt_isr and nmi_isr, which is the intended behavior.

Intuitively, one can understand the Statechart in Fig. 1 and its correspondence with the English description above. The above system can be realized in ESTEREL as well. However, writing the program in ESTEREL is somewhat cumbersome than drawing the Statechart shown in Fig. 1. In our experience and opinion, some classes of programs (such as the above) can be modelled/programmed naturally using visual formalisms. Further, visual formalisms are appealing to practicing software designers. Arguing the formal correctness from programs as shown in Fig. 1 however, is quite complex particularly when the number of states are large and hence, the need verification support. In terms of the verification environment, ESTEREL scores over other formalisms.

In this paper, we describe the design and implementation of a programming environment PERTS, that has been designed and implemented in order to leverage the advantages of both visual formalism of Statecharts and simulation &

---

[1] STATEMATE is a registered trademark of I-Logix Inc.

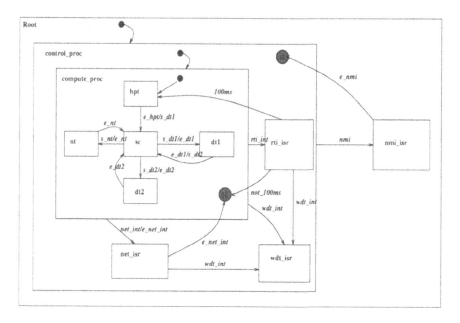

Fig. 1. Example of Switching Interrupts

verification support offered by ESTEREL environment. PERTS environment allows the user to create a model of the software using the user-friendly formalism of Statecharts. The specification is then translated into ESTEREL which then can be subjected to simulation and verification steps. This is possible due to a Statecharts-to-ESTEREL translator tool, STATEST incorporated in PERTS. The translation preserves the correspondence between the Statechart states and the ESTEREL program components for aiding debugging of the programs and verification of the properties at different levels. The primary motivation incorporating the Statecharts-to-Esterel translator tool in PERTS was to open up possibilities of formal verification which seemed easily possible via ESTEREL route, the code generation/optimization capability coming as a bonus. In fact, the implementation of the tool has found to have the important advantage of using Statecharts or ESTEREL for the specifications/modeling of different components of the same system.

In the following, we describe the components of the PERTS environment with a special emphasis on the translation tool i.e., STATEST. The rest of the paper is organized as follows. Section 2 gives an overview of PERTS environment and its main components. In section 3, we describe the translation from Statechart programs to ESTEREL programs as implemented in STATEST. Verification is discussed in section 4 followed by a discussion of related work in section 5.

2   Overview of PERTS

Figure 2 shows the components of the PERTS environment. Presently it consists of a Statechart Editor (SCE) and a translator tool (STATEST) to translate Statecharts into Esterel. The translator forms the link between PERTS and the Esterel environment containing the simulation and verification tools.

The user is required to capture the behaviour of the reactive component using Statecharts notation supported by the SCE. Once the Statecharts specification is ready and is syntactically correct, it can be translated into the ESTEREL using STATEST. The ESTEREL code generated can be used for simulation by using the tool *Xes*. The verification steps can be carried out using tools like *FC2TOOLS* [6], *AUTO/AUTOGRAPH* [7] or Esterel model checker *TEMPEST*[2]. The verification support provides the designer an added level of confidence. The third component SIMSTAT (currently under development) will support simulation of Statecharts based on the same *Step* semantics.

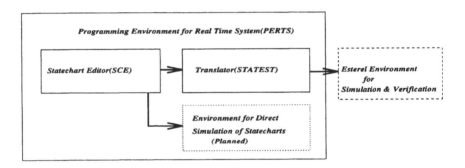

Fig. 2. Components of PERTS

2.1   SCE: Statechart Editor

Figure 3 shows the main window of the Statechart editor SCE along with the expanded *Edit* option menu, that gives the list of the edit functions available to the user. The drawing panel shows a Statechart drawn using the editor. The Statechart Editor SCE provides other useful facilities for storing and retrieving diagrams, loading and browsing previously developed diagrams and for choosing colours for drawing new diagrams. A zoom-in and zoom-out capability to view refinements at various levels is also provided.

Statechart Editor (SCE) allows user to construct Statecharts using the basic building blocks constituting the Statecharts notation. These basic building blocks are *basic states* and *super-states* (OR and AND states) denoted by labeled rectangles, *states with memory* denoted by symbol H, *default transitions* denoted

---

[2] ESTEREL model checker from University of Texas at Austin

by unlabeled arrows with a dot, *transitions* between states denoted by labeled arrows and separate Statecharts showing *refinements* of a given state. When the system is in an OR-state e.g. state S in Fig. 3, it would only be in one of it's immediate sub-states *S1, S2 or S3*. The AND-state e.g. state S2, has sub-states that are related by "and", meaning that when the system is in S2, it would be in all of its immediate sub-states i.e. S21 & S22. AND-state is the mechanism by which concurrent states can be represented. BASIC-states are those at the bottom of the state hierarchy, i.e., those that have no sub-states. The transitions in Statecharts are shown by arrows and they take the system from one set of occupied states to another. The general syntax of an expression labeling a transition in a Statecharts is "e[C]/a", where e is the event that triggers the transition, C is condition that guards the transition from being taken unless it is true when the event e occurs, and a is an action that is carried out if and when the transition is taken. Only the OR-states can have memory and when such states are entered the transition ends on a substate that was last occupied. Figures 1, 3 & 5 show typical Statechart specifications illustrating use of various constructs.

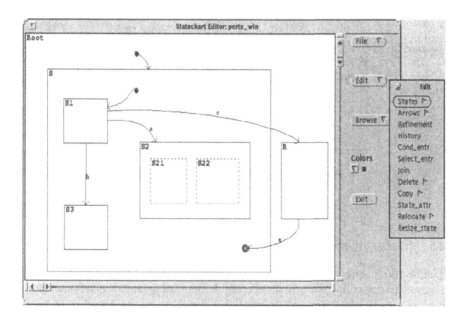

Fig. 3. Main window of Statechart Editor (SCE)

Statechart Editor builds a database, in the background, for use by other tools. In this database a Statechart diagram is represented in the form of a tree and a set of transitions. The Statechart editor is described in details in [5].

3   STATEST: Translator from Statecharts to Esterel

The internal stages of the translator are schematically shown in Fig.4. The first stage is the preprocessing tool **stpp**. The **stpp** module converts syntactical constructs like join points, conditional points etc. into a simpler but equivalent notation. These constructs are designed to provide a crisper notation while drawing Statecharts but can be simplified to simple transitions. This helps in simplifying the implementation of translator which can then expect fewer constructs in the input. It also checks for violation of Statechart syntax and gives warning messages.

The second stage of the translator is the functional form generator **stffg**. The output of **stpp** is fed into the functional form generator **stffg**, which converts the graphical notation into a textual form for further translation. This textual form is described by a context free grammar and hence amenable to rigorous syntax checking and translation. The third stage **stgen** is the ESTEREL code generator. It takes the functional form as input and emits ESTEREL code.

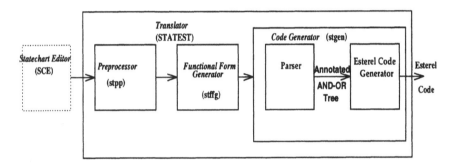

Fig. 4. Schematic Diagram of the Translator

3.1   ESTEREL Code Generator

The ESTEREL code generator is the most complex stage of the translator and its internal structure is shown in the Figure 4. Here we present a brief description but the details along with all translation algorithms can be found in [8,15]. It consists of a parser which parses the input Statechart (in the functional form) and constructs an annotated AND-OR tree by a syntax directed translation scheme. This AND-OR tree is the input to the code constructor.

Translating a "state" in Statechart into ESTEREL means generating a code segment in ESTEREL which will represent the occupied state in Statechart. Such a code segment in ESTEREL , representing an occupied state, has to repeatedly perform ("sustain") the actions expected be carried out in that state, while waiting for events which will cause that code segment to be terminated and other code

segment (a new state) to be entered. Such code segments linked together by Es-
TEREL statements which watch for the events in the system and pass on control
from one code segment to other (as per the specified transitions in Statechart)
constitute the full translation of Statechart program to ESTEREL program. In
ESTEREL code, the transitions are implemented by *await* statements. In principle it is possible to construct a single module in ESTEREL representing the entire
Statechart behaviour. However such a monolithic ESTEREL code is difficult to
understand and also does not permit visualization of occupied/unoccupied states
when simulated using ESTEREL simulator *Xes*. In the code generation strategy
described here, one ESTEREL module is generated for each state in the input
Statechart. This results in the generation of modular ESTEREL code capturing
the behaviour of the Statechart. The only disadvantage of this scheme is that
the code generated contains large number of global signals which are seen on the
simulator panel.

Figure 5 shows a Statechart and its AND-OR tree alongside. Each node of
the AND-OR tree represents the corresponding state in the Statechart and is
annotated with the information like name, type, set of all transitions which enter
and exit this state, history flag indicating whether history exists for this state
etc.

The annotated And-Or tree is the central data structure for the code generation phase. The code generation algorithm traverses the tree in reverse pos-
torder visiting all the children nodes from left-to-right before visiting the parent
node. While visiting each node, the ESTEREL module for each node (State in
Statechart) is emitted and the signals required to interface various modules are
collected. This list is pushed up the tree for the purpose of global signal dec-
larations in each related module. In the following, we explain the structure of
ESTEREL code generated for different types of states in Statechart.

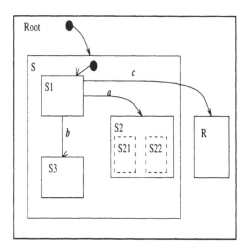
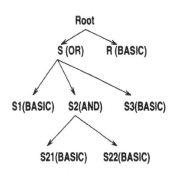

Fig. 5. Statechart and its AND-OR tree

Types of Transitions:

Transitions are important in generating ESTEREL code of each module and are divided into four types as follows:

- Type 1: Transitions between immediate children of same Or-state
- Type 2: Transitions between child to either it's parent or any ancestor
- Type 3: Transitions between ancestor to any of the child state
- Type 4: Transitions between states not governed by the above three rules (inter-level transitions).

In addition to these types of transitions, there is another special type called Loop-type. A transition w.r.t a superstate falls into this type if that transition takes place between two child states (not immediate) of that superstate and the last exited state is one of the immediate children of that superstate. With reference to the state Root in Fig. 5, the transition labeled with event c is of Loop-type.

Restrictions on Transitions

The current implementation of the translator restricts the syntax associated with the transition label $e/[C]/a$ as follows.

- Label e can be a single event or a boolean combination of events
- Guard C can be checking for an internally generated event like IN(S) (which is true only if the current configuration includes state S) or their boolean combinations.
- Action a can only be generation of events .

Priority of Transitions and their Implementation:

Due to nondeterminism permitted in Statecharts multiple transitions can be enabled due to the simultaneous happening of different events. Two transitions are said to be in conflict if there is some common state that would be exited, if any one them were to be taken. The decision as to which transition to take is resolved by priority of transitions. To decide the priority of transitions we use the scope rule [2]. The priority can be determined statically by traversing the AND-OR tree for each transition. We have implemented the priority by introducing a "hide" signal, emitted by a higher priority transition, which is tested while taking all lower priority transitions. Whenever "hide" signal is present all enabled lower priority transitions are blocked. In another type of nondeterminism, two transitions of same priority can be in conflict. Resolution of this type of nondeterminism is explained later.

Structure of ESTEREL Code:

We illustrate the structure of the generated ESTEREL code for each type of states from Statechart. Each state when translated is a module in ESTEREL .

Translation of a Basic state: If A is Basic-state, then the ESTEREL code generated for state A has the form

```
module A :
          emit EnterA;
          do sustain InA watching ExitA;
end module
```

Both "EnterA" and "InA" are global signals. The first statement broadcasts an internal event *EnterA* of entering the state A. The *do sustain InA watching* statement simulates the effect of being in state A by ensuring that while the state A is occupied the *InA* signal is emitted every instant and is available for other states for testing if required. The *do .. watching ExitA* construct ensures that as soon as the signal *ExitA* is emitted, the statement *sustain InA* , terminates in the same instant (strong preemption)

Translation of a Super-state: While translating a superstate of a Statechart, the following has to be implemented.

1. Entry to this superstate
2. Emission of signals to cause entry to substates. The substates may be entered as direct destinations or as a history or as defaults, if the first two are absent.
3. All transitions exiting the substates. Transitions of type 4 are broken into multiple transitions of type 2(child to parent) and type 3(parent to child), happening together in one step.
4. Transitions of loop-type w.r.t this superstate.

Or-State Translation: If S is an OR-state with substates, say, S1, S2,S3 ... Sn, then the structure of the ESTEREL module has the following structure. The || symbol represents parallel execution of three code blocks in ESTEREL syntax.

```
module S :
          Block_1 || Block_2 || Block_3
end module
```

Block_1: This block in the beginning contains statements broadcasting two signals *EnterS* and *InS* signifying entry to superstate S. A local signal ("go" prefixed to the name of the immediate substate to be entered) is then emitted to cause entry to one of the substates. The signal is captured in Block_2.

Block_2: This block of ESTEREL code contains n parallel segments, n being equal to the number of immediate substates, one segment corresponding to each of the substates. This is of this form

```
          Code_for_S1 || Code_for_S2 || .. || Code_for_Sn
```

Each of the segments contain ESTEREL statements for entering the module of each substate as well as code for all transitions exiting that substate.

Block_3: This block of the module handles all inter-level transitions which are of Loop-type w.r.t. this state. This transition is similar to type 1 transition (sibling to sibling) except that the transition originates from deep within one sibling and may terminate deep within another sibling. During a transition this superstate which is the common ancestor of the source and destination state of the transition receives a valued signal from immediate child state exited due to the transition and emits a signal causing entry to the destination state. The emitted signal is simple "go" if the destination is immediate child. Otherwise entry is caused to the ancestor of the destination state, by emitting a valued signal prefixed with "sig_D", the value being the numerical identifier of the destination state. All of the interposing superstates will relay this signal to their substates till the final destination state is reached.

And-state Translation: If S is an And-state with substates S1, S2, ... Sn , the structure of the ESTEREL code has the following form:

```
module S :
        Block_1 || Block_2
end module
```

In And-state the code segment Block_1 is different from the corresponding Block_1 code segment of an Or-state, in that, there is no emission of local *go* signal which causes a substate to be entered as in Or-state. The reason is when an And-state is entered all of its substates are entered at the same instant by definition. There is no Block_3 because there cannot be Loop-type transitions for And-states. The Block_2 code has n parallel segments (n= no of substates) but there is no *await immediate go..* construct as there is no corresponding emission of a go signal in Block_1.

Handling Nondeterminism Some enabled but conflicting transitions cannot be resolved by scope rule [2]. For example, there can be two enabled transitions leaving the same state having the same scope. This type of nondeterminism is permitted in Statechart and is expected to be handled by simulation environment either by randomly taking one transition or allowing the user to decide about which transition to take. Since ESTEREL is a purely deterministic language, the translation scheme has to prioritize the transitions. We resolve this by generating the *await case .. end* construct[3], whereby whichever "case" is positioned first is executed when more than two conflicting events occur. However in case of occurrence of a single event, the corresponding *case* statement will be executed and it will respond to that event only. All possible cases of nondeterminism are reported to the user during the translation process.

The *STEP* signal The translation scheme implements the *step* semantics of STATEMATE [2]. In Statecharts, several *steps* may be executed simultaneously due to the internal generation of events, which enable further transitions before a basic configuration is reached where no more transitions are enabled. This is termed *superstep*. Implementation of such a *superstep* causes semantic problem in ESTEREL as one *superstep* consisting of several steps (transitions) is to be executed in one ESTEREL instant. To overcome this problem, we introduce a

---

[3] Each case statement corresponds to an event triggering the transition

STEP signal and one *step* in Statechart(a transition, including multilevel) is mapped to one ESTEREL instant. The simulation stops for external *STEP* signal to be given, so that next enabled transition can be taken. The *STEP* signal cannot be internally generated in ESTEREL code as it would not create a new instant

In the generated ESTEREL code, when one transition emits an internal signal enabling another transition as in *superstep* semantics, that signal is actually consumed in the same instant, but the execution is broken by *await STEP* statement initiating a new instant. This is operationally equivalent to *step* semantics of Statechart.

3.2   Correspondence between Statechart and ESTEREL Programs

In the structure of the generated ESTEREL code, there is correspondence between *states* in Statechart and *modules* in the ESTEREL code and also a one to one correspondence between an *event* (triggering a transition) in Statechart and a *signal* in ESTEREL . This fact is used to intuitively link the input Statechart with the translated ESTEREL code during process of verification of properties as well as during simulation by ESTEREL tools. The characteristics of the translation is captured below. Consider an arbitrary Statechart program S and its corresponding translated ESTEREL program E. Then, we can establish the following properties from the nature of the translation process:

- For every state in S there is a corresponding code segment in E
- For every transition in S, labeled as *e/C//A* there is a unique corresponding code segment in E that awaits for the event *e*, its guard *C* and emits the signals corresponding to action *A*.
- If the original program is deterministic, then the ESTEREL program generated is causality error free.
- The translation preserves the STATEMATE semantics.

4   Illustration: Verification

We illustrate how the ESTEREL code generated can be used for verification in the ESTEREL environment. Figure 6 shows the specification of a simple lift controller [9]. It is required to verify that the lift cannot move while the door is open. The only relevant events (signals in ESTEREL) are the events *lift_stop* and *door_closed* and the output events are *open_command* and *motor*. To verify the above property, we translate the Statecharts in ESTEREL and obtain the reduced automata by *FC2TOOLS* using the notion of *bisimulation* [14] . The reduced automata is shown in fig 7. The input and output events are prefixed with "?" and "!" respectively. The states are shown by concentric circles and the initial state is the one on top left corner of the figure. If we assume that the door is initially closed(implied by the initial state s0) then the door can remain open only between an emission of *open_command* and the next reception of *door_closed*, and the lift can be moving only between an emission of *motor* and the next reception of *lift_stop*. Since the two states showing the possibility of door remaining open and lift moving are exclusive of each other, the property is true.

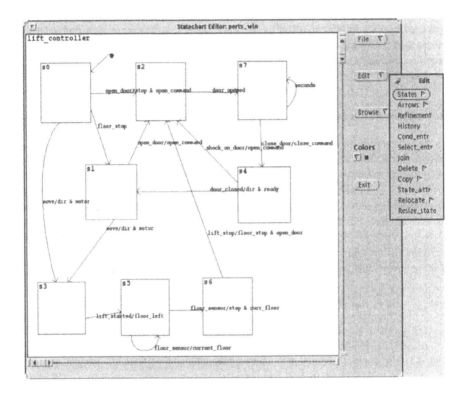

Fig. 6. Specification of a Lift Controller in Statechart

The translator described here has also been applied to the Statechart shown in Figure 1 and the ESTEREL code obtained, tested, simulated and verified. It is also possible to verify temporal properties of the specification using model checking tools like *TEMPEST* on the translated ESTEREL program.

5   Related Work and Conclusion

Recently efforts have been reported in combining Argos and ESTEREL [10]. The translation of Statecharts to Signal has been reported in [11] where the aim has been to use Signal for formal verification purposes. Another effort is translating Statecharts into Promela and has been reported in [12] but it is not clear whether they have taken into account of constructs like *history* of Statecharts. A recent

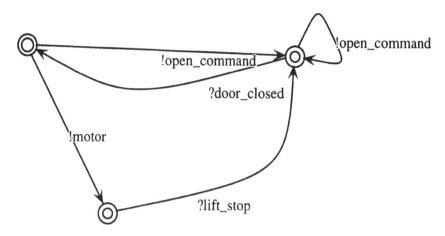

Fig. 7. Reduced Automata obtained using FC2TOOLS

approach based on the work on SyncCharts [13] was aimed at integrating Argos and ESTEREL . However SyncCharts do not allow inter-level transitions and history, which are key features of the version of Statecharts we have considered.

In this paper, we have described an environment for the specification and verification of reactive components. We have been motivated by and concerned with exploiting the advantages of the visual and textual formalisms in the development of reactive systems. The Statecharts follow STATEMATE semantics and our translation of Statechart description into ESTEREL preserves this semantics. In other words the translated ESTEREL programs, when executed would behave exactly like the Statecharts specification from which they were obtained. The prototype system has been tested on a variety of examples and is under use particularly for the design and realization of controllers. We are exploring the use of the system for large scale real-life system developments. It is planned to make this tool available through Internet.

References

1. David Harel: *Statecharts: A Visual Approach to Complex Systems*, Science of Computer Programming, 8:231-274 1987
2. David Harel, Amnon Naamad : *The STATEMATE Semantics of Statecharts*, ACM Transactions on Software Engineering and Methodology, Vol. 5, No. 4, Oct. 1996
3. G. Berry, G. Gonthier: *The ESTEREL synchronous programming languages: Design, semantics, implementation.* Science of Computer Programming, 19(2):87-152, 1992
4. G. Berry : *The Semantics of Pure ESTEREL* . Survey Paper, INRIA, Sophia-Antipolis, France.
5. A. Rai, S.D. Dhodapkar: Statechart Editor (SCE), BARC Technical Report, BARC/1996/E/012, 1996
6. Annie Ressouche et.al. *FC2TOOLS for ESTEREL : Verification by reduction of Synchronous Reactive Programs*, INRIA, Sophia-Antipolis, France.

7. V. Roy, R. de Simone *An Autograph Primer*, INRIA Technical Report, Sophia-Antipolis, France.
8. A.K. Bhattacharjee, S.D. Dhodapkar, S. Seshia and R.K. Shyamasundar: *STAT-EST: A Tool to Translate Statecharts to* ESTEREL . BARC Technical Report BARC/1998/E/014, 1998.
9. N. Halbwachs:*Synchronous Programming of Reactive Systems*, Lecture Notes, 21st AFCET International School of Computer Science, 1991
10. Berry et.al. : *Unpublished note on* ESTEREL *and Argos*, 1995
11. Beauvais. J.R et. al.: *A translation of Statecharts to Signal/DC+.* Tech Rep. IRISA, 1997.
12. E. Mikk et.al.*Implementing Statecharts in Promela/SPIN*, Technical Report, 1997.
13. C. Andre':*A visual Representation of Reactive Behaviours* Tech. Rep. RR 95-52 I3S, Sophia-Antipolis, France, 1995
14. R. Milner:*Communication and Concurrency*, Series in Computer Science, Prentice Hall, 1989.
15. A.K. Bhattacharjee, S.D. Dhodapkar, S. Seshia, R.K. Shyamasundar:*A Translation of Statecharts to Esterel* Accepted for publication in the proceedings of FM'99(Technical Symposium), Toulouse, France, 20-24 Sept., 1999

Dependability Requirements and Security Architectures for the Healthcare/Medical Sector [1]

Gilles Trouessin [2]

CNAMTS [3] / CESSI [4]
14, place St-Etienne – 31000 Toulouse – France
gilles.trouessin@cnamts.fr

Abstract. Firstly the legal and technical aspects of the healthcare area are introduced from a general dependability viewpoint, to clarify the global approach of this article. Then are detailed those main security properties mostly required by any healthcare information system including responsibility. A focus is proposed on different aspects of the confidentiality property. A classification of the generic *TTP* concept is then detailed with legal and technical considerations and three forms and variants of such *TTPs* are distinguished. Anonymisation techniques are described that can be applied for privacy requirements that can be expressed by the healthcare area and reusable by any other sector. After some recommendations on the interoperability of such *TTP* architectures, it is extracted, from all these theoretical concepts and some mentioned applied projects of the healthcare sector, a framework for a global approach towards more secure and more dependable health information systems and exchanges.

1 Introduction

In most of the health/healthcare/medical environments (the healthcare sector), one and usually several of the classical **dependability** constitutive attributes are involved:
- *safety* (if the system is life-critical for the patient) at least, and/or
- *availability* (if the system is in relation with emergency on-line file systems), and/or
- *reliability* (if the system is in charge of electronic healthcare patient records/archives).

These system safety/availability/reliability requirements are derived from legal obligations and/or a medical code of practice enforcing the actors of the healthcare area to pay for various aspects of the dependability technology and especially for one major

---

[1] This article is derived from the theoretical activity held by the author at *AFNOR* and from the applied work handled by *CESSI* within various projects on dependability and security involving *CNAMTS*.

[2] European expert at **CEN/TC251/WGiii** (Working Group III: *"Security/Safety/Quality"*) and french convenor of the AFNOR's *ad hoc* working group on *"Healthcare / Security"*.

[3] The *"Caisse Nationale de l'Assurance Maladie des Travailleurs Salariés (CNAMTS)"* is the french *"National Mandatory Healthcare Insurer for Wage Workers"*.

[4] The *"Centre d'Etudes des Sécurités du Système d'Information (CESSI)"* is the *"Centre for Research and Studies on Information System Security"* of CNAMTS.

M. Felici, K. Kanoun, A. Pasquini (Eds.): SAFECOMP'99, LNCS 1698, pp. 445–458, 1999

concern which is *security* (which is also one of the dependability attributes).[5][6][7]

Organizational, physical and logical security issues in terms of security policies are of great interest in order to obtain trustworthiness and place a justifiable confidence in the healthcare systems that are specified, developed, implemented and used, as is currently the case in many European countries and particularly in France with the deployement of electronic projects based on the *Health-Social Network*, the *Patient Data Card* and the *Health Professional Card*.[8] The security concept, seen as the technologies for removal/provision/forecasting/prevention of intentional faults, is usually defined, as in ITSEC, as the property that combines the *availability*, *integrity* and *confidentiality* properties, merged as the prevention of unauthorized withholding, modification or disclosure of sensible information.

When applied to healthcare information systems handling (store, convey, process) very sensitive data (diagnoses, care acts or pathologies), it is more and more recognized that a forth sub-property is encompassed by the above security property: the system *responsibility accountability* in its *auditability* sense which means the ability to gradually provide *traceability*, *imputability*, *opposability* and *irrefutability* (gradually by means of *audit trail*, *imputation*, *legal evidence* and *scientific proof* facilites), that the system has been correctly specified, faithfully implemented and is actually used in an authorized way with valid controls and active proof constitutions.

In order for both medical staff and the patients to be able to place justifiable trust in those new healthcare systems, a generic security concept and a new kind of security architectures have been developed, respectively the *Trusted Third Party (TTP)* concept and the *Trusted Third Parties (TTPs)* architectures. They are seen as new electronic notaries providing a wide spectrum of specific trusted security services usually accessed *via* a local or a wide public/private area network with the help of some authentication chipcards. This article is in fact a sort of road map, a first step towards a taxonomy, of the *TTP* general concept and its linked terminology, with some focus on the healthcare particularities, such as the auditability property and already build, or currently being implemented, such healthcare-dedicated *TTPs*.

2   Trusted Third Parties (TTPs) *vs.* Trusted Third Party (TTP)

It is important to introduce the *TTP*-terminology exercise by extracting its intrinsic aspects that are currently used and by distinguishing the generic concept of *Trusted Third Party* *versus* its diverse derived forms of *Trusted Third Parties*. The *Trusted Third Party (TTP)* concept is defined here as a generic active entity of the global (healthcare) information system situated in between several natural actors of that system (senders/receivers involved in a data/message or exchange/communication), and on which a justifiable trust, according to its role, can be placed. A *Trusted Third Parties (TTPs)* form is

---

[5] *"Legal"* is used here in its wide acceptation encompassing laws, regulations and juridical aspects.

[6] Or both, as e.g. in french legislation in which the medical staff's *'Code de Déontologie'* is a law.

[7] *"System"* is defined here as the combination of human and technical requirements and interactions.

[8] Respectively: *Réseau Santé Social (RSS)*, *Carte Sesam/Vitale*, *Carte de Professionnel de Santé (CPS)*.

defined as an instantiated trusted role played by an active trustworthy entity of the information system in order to provide trustworthiness services, adapted to the role it is intended to play for the benefit of the system end-users: the main *TTPs* forms concern *certification* services, *confidentiality* facilities, *anonymisation*[9] techniques.

2.1 The *Certification-TTPs*

A first *TTPs* form is the *Certification-TTPs*, mostly known as *Certification Authorities* and recently called *Certification Service Providers*. The role of this first *TTPs* form consists in providing, by means of *Certification* or by *Certifying data*, some trustworthiness on a piece of information usually associated to a end-user declared in- and known from- the information system: identities (or identifiers) and/or cryptographic keys (public keys) are classically certified. For the healthcare sector, in Europe in general (with healthcare professional certification services) and in France in particular (with the French microprocessor: the *Healthcare Professional Card (HPC)* and the *Patient Data Card (PDC)*)[10], many certification projects are currently being deployed in order to provide the healthcare sector (which is strongly growing up with the arrival of electronic communication and exchange networks) with reliable exchange facilites of very sensitive information taking into account, foremost, authenticity and integrity requirements.

The certification needs. Certification needs correspond to a necessity of reliability for the sensitive information used by the information system actors in such a certified way, generally linking a person to a characterizing attribute of that person, but without the need to have to re-build that link, or even to have to check its correctness.

The certification types. Several types of, or requirements for, certificates are used and a wide variety of certificates exists such as identity-, address-, profession- and function-certificates, or just public cryptographic key certificates associated with its owner to be used for authentication, non-repudiation or encryption services. The recognized *de jure* standard dealing with such certificates is ISO/ITU X.509 (v3). However because of flexibility, it is still worth having a standardization of the method and instantiation (as provided by the standard series issued from the PKIX working group) before there is any chance of real interoperability of such certificates.

The certification types. Before any certification activity, many services must be developed in that the end-users of the information system must be known by it and recognized by it in a reliable way (directory services as X.500), new certificates must be calculated with recognized algorithms (certificate generation), certificates must be reliably kept by the system (certificate short-term storage and long-term archiving), correct certificates must be recognized or authenticated as really correct (certificate legal opposability), old certificates must be repudiated (certificate revocation)... *Naming* of

---

[9] *"Anonymisation"* must be understood in its active sense for the *anonymity* property fulfillment: it encompasses actions such as *'anonymizing'* nominative data or *'disanonymizing'* anonymous data.

[10] Respectively: *'Carte de Professionnel de Santé (CPS)'* and *'Carte Sesam/Vitale'*.

certificate owners and certificate *generation, storage/archiving, opposability* and *revocation* are basic services that are to be implemented in the certification context; and most of them are currently elaborated in the French healthcare sector, around the *GIP 'CPS'*, the *GIE 'Sesam/Vitale'* and the *RSS*. [11]

2.2   The *Confidentiality-TTPs*

A second *TTPs* form is the *TTPs for Confidentiality* (too often reduced to its *Escrow-TTPs* variant) usually called *Confidentiality-TTPs*. The role of *TTPs* form consists in giving to the end-users the means, by providing them relevant cryptographic conventions, to place a justifiable trust in the confidentiality protection that they will be able to use in the information system: e.g., asymmetric cryptographic conventions are classically provided in order to protect (by means of asymmetric encryption) symmetric cryptographic conventions which are themselves dedicated to protect (by means of symmetric encryption) the exchanged sensible data or messages.

In the healthcare sector, based on the *IP* technology of the new *RSS* network and on the cryptographic facilites offered by the *CPS*, a *French healthcare confidentiality-TTP* is also in project for a concrete construction. It has the responsibility to providing to each *CPS* owner (*General Practitioner (GP)*), his cryptographic material based on a Diffie-Hellmann key-pair, so called *Key Exchange Key (KEK)*, intended to protect any future session encryption key that will be generated during the lifetime of that *KEK* for that *CPS*, as indicated on the Law dedicated to the *CPS*.

Three different logics must be distinguished for the *Confidentiality-TTPs* form:[12]

- *'distrust'* (cfr. the US *'escrow'* practice as proposed in the *clipper chip* trial);
- *'mistrust'* (cfr. the French *'séquestre'* policy proposed by the Prime Minister services);
- *'entrust'* (cfr. *recovery/recuperation* dual techniques in the French healthcare sector).

Confidentiality by *a posteriori* 'Distrust'. The first *Confidentiality-TTP* logic is well known and could be called *a posteriori 'distrust'* as it mainly had the interest to reveal some crafty practices. It has too strong a drawback to place for many years the concept of *Confidentiality-TTP* in a « *'post-native' 'distrust' logic* ». In fact, the question was: how to relate to end-users interested in using strong encryption and oblige them to adopt a governmental/military imposed encryption package, if not to let them believe, *a posteriori* of the usage of such a package, that the unique decryption means are exclusively in their hand of legitimate users, whereas any security specialist knows that it is perfectly wrong? [13] Defined like this, (apparently) strong encryption is implicit: either restricted in fact to a weak encryption (similar to easy cryptanalysis for the governmental authorities if *a part* of the encryption key, even common to all the users, is escrowed like this), or restricted to some non-encryption (if *the whole* encryption key is escrowed like this)!

---

[11] I.e., *"Groupement d'Intérêt Public 'Cartes de Professionnal de Santé' (GIP 'CPS')"*, *"Groupement d'Intérêt Economique 'Sesam/Vitale' (GIE Sesam/Vitale)"* and *"Réseau Santé Social (RSS)"*.

[12] *'distrust, 'mistrust'* and *'entrust'* in their French senses of *'défiance'*, *'méfiance'* and *'confiance'*.

[13] *'Strong encryption'* is defined as an encryption using high enough key length to prevent from any cryptanalysis (without key knowledge) by brute force attack (successive trails of all the key values).

Such a practice to permit the use of strong confidentiality through *'distrust'*, based on whole or part of the key escrowed by the authorities, is publicly known since the experience (unsuccessful trial) of the US *'clipper'* chip, dedicated to the US electronic commerce sector, or also with other European similar projects. To the discharge of such projects or trials, it must be recalled that, even in any democratic country, the individual liberties in favor of the protection and the assurance of confidentiality stop where the State's obligations of national defense and security begin. A fair compromise between individual and Nation's interests is to be found.

Confidentiality by *a priori* 'Mistrust'. A second logic, well know as well but less problematic, could be called *a priori 'mistrust'* as it has the advantage to be usable and used in very specific contexts, such as the military and national defense sector. However it also had the major drawback to maintain the notion of *Confidentiality-TTP* in a « *culture of preventive 'mistrust'* ». In fact, the question was: how to *a priori* prevent end-users who want to use strong cryptography, if it is not by asking them in advance to escrow their own encryption keys, or, even by enforcing them to adopt *predefined keys*? Like this, a strong encryption (vulnerable to strong cryptanalysis only; with no key knowledge) becomes explicitly equivalent to encryption (for the national authorities) because the decryption key is *a priori* known from these authorities!

Such authorization policies for using strong confidentiality through *'mistrust'*, based on voluntary escrow, or so-called French *'séquestre'*, of the encryption keys or session keys, are publicly well-known, especially in France, considering that the governmental obligation of national defense and security are of major priority when faced with the individual liberties' respect. A fair balance in between the individual interest and the Nation's power is, here again, still to be found.

A posteriori Confidentiality by *a priori* 'Entrust'. The third logic has been much less discussed than the two previous ones, although it is much less problematic since it really allows *a posteriori* confidentiality[14] but could be called *a priori entrust*. It has still not received the legitimate success it should have, inheriting from the drawback of the loss of confidence generated by its two predecessors (cfr. *'escrow'*-like *'distrust'* and *'séquestre'*-like *'mistrust'*) which have oriented the generic term of *Confidentiality-TTP* at the opposite of any « *democratic cryptography perception* ». In fact, the question was: how to assure any end-user wanting to use strong encryption techniques of the necessary and sufficient *a priori* confidence in the system he intends to use, if it is not by guaranteeing to the State's authorities the whole power (*a posteriori* but in perfect legitimacy) of their obligations of national security? Like this, a strong encryption will be able to really subsist under the condition that an accurate and unambiguous legal framework, such as the one provided by the French cryptographic law revised in *July 1996* and its linked decrees, may be proposed and *a priori* adopted by the end-users (cfr. *a priori* 'entrust'), but also imposed and *a posteriori* respected by the State's authorities (cfr. *a posteriori* confidentiality)!

Such techniques for the liberalization of the strong encryption usage through confidence, based on the key encryption **recovery**, are not only theoretically but also practically viable and reliable, in France in particular and in Europe in general, emphasing

---

[14] 'a posteriori *confidentiality*' is sometimes synonymous with *'forward secrecy'*.

on the result that a fair balance is now possible in between the individual liberties' respect (thanks to real strong encryption liberalization) and the governmental obligations of national defense and security (thanks to the French law of *July 1996* and its decrees in law of *Feb. 1998* concerning the agreement of *Confidentiality-TTPs*).

The Confidentiality-relevant Services. Before any form of confidentiality, many services are necessary in that end-users must be known and recognized by a reliable identification (directory services), cryptographic conventions must be calculated with recognized algorithms (key generation), key generation proofs must be kept (reliable storage) and old cryptographic conventions must be really dropped (key revocation). *Naming* of the cryptographic convention owners, *generation, storage/archiving, opposability* and *revocation* of those cryptographic conventions are basic services for the *Confidentiality-TTP* context, in addition to the key encryption recovery services for the State's authorities (*via* legal and regulated procedures) and to the key encryption recuperation services for the end-user (for his own availability and reliability needs). In the healthcare sector these services are currently being implemented around the *GIP* '*CPS*' and over the *RSS* network.

2.3   The *Anonymisation-TTPs*

The third *TTPs* form is the *TTPs for Anonymity*, or *Anonymisation-TTPs*, more faithfully called *Data Matching Agencies*. [15] The role of this form consists in providing, by **Anonymisation** and **Disanonymisation**, trustworthiness in the preservation of individual privacy of the persons concerned by those primarily nominative information contained in such anonymised information systems. Both directly nominative information (identities or addresses) or indirectly nominative information (through a characterization of the corresponding persons, as the French national identification number used by the French social security organisms) are usual information that need to be anonymised. In any case, this new and innovative new form of *TTPs* can be seen:

- either, as a sort of refinement of the previous *TTPs* form (the *Confidentiality TTPs*), like some *Anonymty-TTPs* viewed as a refined case of confidentiality preservation by anonymity protection and by the control of any anonymity removal;
- or, as a really new form of *TTPs*: some *Privacy-TTPs* viewed as the manager of the private relationship[16] loosely associating/disassociating/reassociating nominative information and the corresponding anonymous/anonymised data.

Anonymity-TTPs or *Privacy-TTPs*, in any case this form of *TTPs* can only exist if it is recognized as legal and legitimate and if any anonymisation action, or, more importantly, any disanonymisation request, should only be possible under a restrictive legal framework, taking into account the high sensitivity of the bijective relationship: *nominative-anonymous*. This form of *TTPs* is still unknown and not very used, although it will be essential in some sectorial activities as sensitive as the health/social sector when statistical studies are made on the basis of individual but anonymous data. More

---

[15] '*Data Matching Agency*', in its primary Australian sense.

[16] '*Private*', in the primary English sense of '*Privacy*'.

and more countries are looking to it with great interest, in Europe (United Kingdom, France and Scandinavian countries), in North America (e.g., USA and Canada (Quebec)) and the southern hemisphere (e.g., Australia).

The Disanonymisation Functions. Giving some more details about this new form of *TTPs*, it is first possible to show that *Anonymisation* requirements, addressing the *Anonymity* property, are a quite interesting family of new security needs, as well as: *Identification, Authentication, Authorization, Accreditation* (in the French *Etebac5* sense) or *Certification* (in the ISO/ITU X.509 sense), *Imputation* (of an action to its author), *Non-repudiation* (of an action held by any author in order to address the opposability property), *Integrity/Authenticity* (of data/actions). A first interesting characterization of this new family of security needs concerns the possibilities of anonymity removals (called anonymisation objectives) that must imperatively be fixed before any approach for the development of such anonymisation systems, as it determines the appropriate anonymisation techniques that must be developed and implemented. Three anonymity removal cases can be considered:

- *'never'*: the anonymity removal is in that case *'(absolutely) never'* possible (i.e., *absolute irreversibility* objective), if using one way functions robust enough to *irreversibly* transform nominative identifiers into anonymous ones;
- *'always'*: it is *'(implicitly) always'* possible (*implicit reversibility* objective), if using cryptographic algorithms like encryption/decryption which must be *reversible* to allow to transform nominative identifiers to the corresponding anonymous one (encryption) and conversely (decryption);
- *'sometimes'*: it is *'(explicitly) sometimes'* possible (*explicit inversibility* objective), if using a coherent set of statutory texts (fixing the *inversibility* legal framework), organisational procedures (organizing its kinematic), public authorizations (legal compliant) and auditing means (ensuring its auditability).

Towards a Taxonomy of the Anonymisation Concepts. In addition to these needs and those objectives dedicated to the anonymisation context, two kinds of requirements, to be imposed to any anonymisation system, must now be introduced: the *'chaining'* requirements and the *'robustness'* requirements. The *'chaining'* requirements[17] concern both nominative identifiers (proposed by the French Ministry of Health for the *Identification Permanente du Patient (IPP)*[18]) and anonymous ones (by similarity: *Anonymisations Potentielles des Personnes (APPs)*[19]). As the chaining requirement can be null, partial or total (*3* options) and applied in time and/or in space (*3* contexts), the following (*9 = 3 * 3*) potential chaining cases are defined:

- three cases on the space only axis followed by three cases on the time only axis and by five cases on the dual space-time axes:
  - *(spatial) opacity* (i.e., *nowhere*): this form of no (spatial) chaining is viewed as some identifier *randomization* on the space axis (egal to *perdition* and *unicity*),
  - *(spatial) cooperation* (i.e., *somewhere*): these partial (spatial) chaining forms are understood in the sense of *partial coordination* between anonymity systems,

---

[17] *'Chaining'* means that the same identifier is attributed to the same person in time and/or in space.

[18] *"Identification Permanente du Patient (IPP)"* for *'Permanent Patient-Identifier (PPI)'*.

[19] *"Anonymisations Potentielles des Personnes (APPs)"* for *'Potential Person-Anonymisations (PPAs)'*.

- *(spatial)* **coordination** (i.e., *everywhere*): this total (spatial) chaining form is understood in the sense of the *total cooperation* between anonymity systems;
- *(temporal)* **perdition** (i.e., *never*): this form of no (temporal) chaining is viewed as some identifier *randomization* on the temporal axis (egal to *opacity* and *unicity*),
- *(temporal)* **perenniality** (i.e., *sometimes*): these partial (temporal) chaining forms are understood in the sense of *partial perpetuity* between anonymity systems,
- *(temporal)* **perpetuity** (i.e., *ever*): this total (temporal) chaining form is understood in the sense of the *total perenniality*, between anonymity systems;
- *(space-time)* **unicity** (i.e., *nowhere/never*): this form of no (space-time) chaining corresponds to the complete *opacity* and also to the complete *unicity*,
- *(space-time)* **uniformity** (i.e., *somewhere/ever*): each partial-total (time-space) chaining forms correspond to a combination of *coordination* and *perpetuity*,
- *(space-time)* **university** (i.e., *somewhere/sometimes*): each partial-partial (space-time) chaining forms correspond to a combination of *coordination* and *perenniality*,
- *(space-time)* **ubiquity** (i.e., *everywhere/sometimes*): each total-partial (space-time) chaining forms correspond to a combination of *cooperation* and *perenniality*,
- *(space-time)* **universality** (i.e., *everywhere/ever*): this full (space-time) chaining form corresponds to the combination of *cooperation* and *perpetuity*.

The *'robustness'* requirements, concerning exclusively illicit *'disanonymisation'*, can be divided into two distinct cases: robustness to *'reversion'* and to *'inference'*:

- the *reversion* robustness, or robustness to *'anonymous identifier disanonymisation by means of forbidden anonymous identifier re-building'*, is twofold:
  - either **direct** *reversion* by cryptanalysis, if the used cryptographic techniques are not strong enough: e.g., one way function (irreversibility) with too high collision rates or encryption with a too small encryption key length (reversibility),
  - or **indirect** *reversion* by means of the reconstitution (if wiretapping communication channels) of corresponding tables that make the bijective link between clear (i.e., nominative) identifiers and the corresponding unclear (i.e., anonymous) ones;
- the *inference* robustness, or robustness to *'anonymous data disanonymisation by means of unauthorized nominative information calculation'*, is fourfold:
  - *inference* by **deduction**[20]: it consists in inferring, mainly in first-order logic calculation, unauthorized information on the only basis of publicly available data;
  - *inference* by **abduction**[21]: it consists in inferring, having set various plausible assumptions, unexpected secret information from valid available data;
  - *inference* by **adduction**[22]: it consists in inferring internal inaccessible secret data, by correlation of public information obtained by requesting the information system and private information obtained by external observation;
  - *inference* by **induction**[23]: it consists in inferring, by some recurrence and generalization logic, global information and inference rules issued from the generalization of a set a valid and verified information.

---

[20] A *'deductive'* logic is a proved (sound and consistent) logic based on first order calculation.

[21] An *'abductive'* logic is a logic which allows to infer some plausible but valid extrapolations.

[22] An *'adductive'* logic is a logic which allows to infer some internal and valid correlations.

[23] An *'inductive'* logic is a logic which allows to infer some generalized presomptions.

To finalize the taxonomy of the anonymisation concept, a first characterization of the different families of anonymisation solutions must be introduced: they address above-mentioned anonymisation needs/objectives/requirements and are threefold:

- the *type* of the solutions that are to be developed: organizational procedures, cryptographic algorithms and/or one way functions;
- the *plurality* of the solutions that are to be implemented: simple-/double-/mutli-anonymisation in order to be able to deal with direct or indirect reversions;
- the *interoperability* of the solutions that are to be selected; it is threefold:
  - *transcoding*: (manually) transcoding an anonymisation system (the origin one) of anonymous identifiers into another anonymisation system (the destination one) of anonymous identifiers, for some continuity reasons,
  - *translating*: (mathematically) translating an anonymisation system (the origin one) of anonymous identifiers into another anonymisation system (the destination one) of anonymous identifiers, for some coherence-consistency reasons,
  - *transposing*: (automatically) transforming several anonymisation systems of anonymous identifiers into a unique anonymisation system (the pivot system) of anonymous identifiers, in order to open/authorize or, at the opposite, in order to close/forbid, the natural matching of diversely and variously anonymized data.

The Anonymisation-relevant Services. Before any form of anonymisation, many services are necessary because authorized end-users must be recognized by a reliable identification service (i.e., directory services), cryptographic conventions must be used for generating anonymisation systems (i.e., anonymisation cryptographic key generation), a trusted proof of these generations must be kept (i.e., non-repudiable storage/archiving), correct anonymisation cryptographic conventions must be recognized (i.e., anonymisation-key certification) and anonymisation systems must be interoperable (i.e., anonymisation-key composition/interoperability). *Naming* of anonymisation system end-users, *generation, storage, anthenticity* and *interoperability* of cryptographic conventions used by anonymimsation services are basic services that must be provided in the context of *Anonymisation-TTPs*. In the healthcare sector, all these services are currently being developed (especially within regional, national and, possibly, European projects in which *CESSI/CNAMTS* is already, or will soon be, officially involved).

3 Concepts/Terminology for TTPs Interoperability/Dependability

Several types of interoperability problems must be solved:

- either *horizontal* interoperability: two or more *TTPs* belonging to the same form of *TTPs*, and to the same variant of that form of *TTPs*; e.g.: interoperability between a *Recovery-TTP* and another *Recovery-TTP* (i.e., the same *Confidentiality-TTP* variant),
- or *vertical* interoperability: two or more *TTPs* belonging to the same form of *TTPs*, but belonging to distinct variants of that form of *TTPs*; e.g.: interoperability between an *Escrow-* and a *Recovery-TTP* (i.e., two variants of the *Confidentiality-TTP*),
- or *transversal* interoperability: two or more *TTPs* belonging to different forms and to distinct variants of those different forms of *TTPs*; e.g., interoperability between a *Certification-TTP* and an *Anonymisation-TTP*.

3.1   Prerequisite to any *TTPs* Interoperability

In order to fulfil interoperability requirements, a terminology interpretation phase is necessary at least for the cryptographic conventions that must be handled by the different forms of *TTPs* and by the various variants of *TTP* forms. A given number of notions must be introduced and explained, before using them and showing the needs and solutions they address in connection with the interoperability requirement.

Notion of Cryptographic Convention. Beyond the software or software version problems, not addressed in this article, *TTPs* interoperability concerns first of all cryptographic problems, because it is essential for all the entities of a same area to:
- speak the same *'cryptographic language'*: i.e., notion of *cryptographic convention*,
- use the same *'cryptographic syntax'*: i.e., notion of *cryptographic protocol*,
- adopt the same *'cryptographic semantics'*: i.e., notion of *cryptographic function*.

Like the software/version problems, the notions of cryptographic protocol and cryptographic function are not addressed in this article, whereas the notion of cryptographic convention, which regroups algorithms conventions and their connected parameters, is fundamental for the solution of the interoperability paradigm. I.e., the actors of any information exchange, who want to apply/verify a digital signature, may encrypt/decrypt a message or need to anonymize/disanonymize data, should, before any exchange of such signed/ciphered/anonymized information, have agreed on:
- the signature generation algorithm (and thus the signature verification algorithm), or the message encryption algorithm (and thus the message decryption algorithm), or lastly the data anonymisation algorithm (and thus the disanonymisation algorithm);
- and the connected parameters and cryptographic keys to use for the signature verification, or also for the message decryption, or even for data disanonymisation.

The notion of cryptographic convention regroups the notion of algorithm and the notion of cryptographic parameter/key.

Notion of Public/Private Cryptographic Convention. It is necessary to distinguish:
- the *public cryptographic conventions*, published like a public signature (for signature verification) key, a public encryption key (for asymmetric ciphers) or a restrictedly published secret parameter for a common anonymisation one way function;
- the *private cryptographic conventions*, considered privative to their unique owner, like a private signature key, a decryption key (for asymmetric ciphers), or even a secret parameter exclusively dedicated to a given disanonymisation authority.

Notion of Delivered/Exchanged Cryptographic Convention. To distinguish also:
- the *delivered cryptographic conventions*, distributed or issued, for example by a *TTP*, to any of its clients such as an RSA signature key-pair (public key/private key) or a Diffie-Helmann key-pair (public part/private part) for asymmetric encryption, or even a distributed secret parameter issued by a central anonymisation authority;
- the *exchanged cryptographic conventions*, exchanged between users that have mutual confidence, such as the result of a challenge-response, or public part of an RSA or a Diffie-Helmann key-pair exchanged between *Alice* and *Bob*.

Notion of Common/Shared Cryptographic Convention. To distinguish laslty:

- the *common cryptographic conventions*, commonly adopted by two or more *TTPs* in order to use the same cryptographic algorithms/parameters, for the generation of a signature or a confidentiality key-pair, delivered to their own clients;
- the *shared cryptographic conventions*, shared by two end-users that have to exchange confidential information, in order to be the only two entities able to share the same knowledge about their shared random session key (i.e., encryption key for protecting any message exchanged during one session), or the key exchange key (i.e., encryption key for protecting any session key) shared for a given period of time.

3.2   Inter-TTPs Interoperability *via* the Common Conventions

The *inter-TTPs* interoperability (horizontal/vertical/transversal) is assured by the means of common cryptographic conventions (*TTPs* agreement and mutual recognition):

- in the *horizontal* case: two *Anonymisation-TTPs* (e.g.) may have in common their own anonymisation method (e.g., double-anonymisation by one way functions, with a common secret and a universal chaining of the anonymous identifiers) and the same certification convention, before any exchange of anonymous identifiers;
- in the *vertical* case: e.g. an *Escrow-TTP* and a *Recovery-TTP* may need to have in common their own way of confidentiality protection and their common confidentiality cryptographic convention, before any exchange of secrete information;
- in the *transversal* case: e.g. a *Certification-TTP* and an *Anonymisation-TTP* may have to shared their own way of certification (X.509 v3) and their own common certification cryptographic convention, before any exchange of certificates.

Common Negotiated Conventions: Proposed/Adapted. In order to really have in common *common cryptographic conventions* of any type, they can be negotiated, if:

- firstly, they are proposed by one of the *TTPs* to all the other concerned *TTPs*;
- secondly, they are adapted by each of the concerned *TTPs* in order to respect the same requirements for all the *TTPs*.

Common Non-Negotiated Conventions: Imposed/Adopted. In order to have in obtain *common cryptographic conventions*, it is also possible not to negotiate, if:

- firstly, they are imposed by one of the *TTPs* (let's say the master *TTP* or the older);
- secondly, they are adopted, with no modification, by any of the concerned *TTPs*.

3.3   Inter-Users Interoperability *via* the Shared Conventions

For a real *inter-TTPs* interoperability, the end-users also need to understand one another; this corresponds to the *inter-users* interoperability problem: it can be naturally obtained if the previous *inter-TTPs* interoperability notion is complemented by an efficient management of shared conventions.

Implicitly Shared Conventions: a Coordinated Management. This *inter-users interoperability* can naturally occur by implicit sharing of their shared conventions, under the condition of a *coordinated management*, by the *TTP*, of the convention it delivered to its users, as in the *French-TTP* project:

- in fact, with the establishment at the *TTP* level of common cryptographic conventions for the generation of Diffie-Helmann key-pairs (conventions for the generation of key exchange keys), a first level of sharing between *Alice* (the sender) and *Bob* (the receiver) is reached: their key exchange key knowledge sharing level;
- then, a second level of sharing of shared conventions is also necessary: this is the sharing of the knowledge of the session key which in fact has been generated by the message sender, or the session initiator; using this method the session key can be sent encrypted (by means of a shared algorithm between *Alice* and *Bob*) with the help of the key exchange key which is already implicitly shared.

Explicitly Shared Conventions: an Autonomous Generation. This *inter-users* interoperability could exceptionally occur by means of the explicit sharing of their shared conventions, if an *autonomous management*, disconnected from the *TTP*, of those shared cryptographic conventions takes place:

- in that case *Alice* (sender or exchange initiator) generates herself the conventions that are to be shared and explicitly proposes them to *Bob* (receiver or exchange non-initiator): this can be a session key protected by a key encryption key she had beforehand also explicitly proposed to him;
- but, even in such a case, more complicated than the previous one (cfr. the implicitly shared case), a level of implicitly shared convention is necessary, at least for the sharing protocol of the shared cryptographic conventions, i.e. the "*Alice*-proposal and *Bob*-adoption" protocol,.

3.4   Minimal Facility Kernel for TTPs Interoperability

Around the three forms (and variants) of *TTPs*, more and more complete and complexe security services with associated tools and mechanisms for data storage, computation, transportation are continuously in construction and restruction taking into account emerging security needs (e.g., the anonymity property) and new security technologies (e.g., the *TTP* concept).

A *minimal facility kernel based on security services/tools/mechanisms* is progressively available for security infrastructures intended to provide data/network security facilities. Most services are common to two or more forms of *TTPs* (e.g., certification services issued from a *Certification-TTP* used by a *Confidentiality-TTP* for its own public cryptographic convention certification). However, some security services are still dedicated to their original *TTP*, since this is by excellence the primary trusted place for such services (e.g., name certification services dedicated to a *Certification-TTP*, cryptographic convention recovery services dedicated to a *Confidentiality-TTP*, anonymity removal services dedicted to an *Anonymisation-TTP*).

Many security services/tools/mechanisms are in fact placed at the disposal of the end-users themselves on the basis of the confidence established between them and the

TTPs to which they belong, for the *Certification-TTPs* as well as for the *Confidentiality-TTPs* or for the *Anonymisation-TTPs*. This reinforces the requirement for security architecture interoperability between the different *TTPs* forms and contributes also to the requirement for higher dependability,. All these aspects address the *horizontal*, *vertical* and *transversal* interoperability cases, and thus also the global dependability requirement, of the future global information systems, in perfect independence from the concerned sectorial domains. In fact, under the condition that regulatory frameworks are available which allow such interoperability and dependability fufillment, and if anticipating on any mono-sectorial as well as multi-sectorial interoperability problem, it should be possible to build wide information systems in which ethics and deontology are implicit because they are taken into account at the very beginning of its specification, and where interoperability issues and some of the dependability issues are intrinsic as they are anticipated at the very beginning of its construction.

4 Conclusions

In order to establish or keep some *confidence* between the healthcare sector end-users (above all citizens when seen from the healthcare viewpoint) and the new generation of healthcare information systems (more and more internet-compatible and thus unreliable and also at the opposite of most of the elementary privacy rules), it is necessary to preserve *trust* by the way of the *trusted* aspects of this new growing electronic world, first for healthcare electronic exchanges. This obviously means that these trusted aspects must be *trustworthy*, but trustworthiness is a very difficult challenge to reach when it concerns such sensible information as diagnoses, care activity or pathologies.

Secrecy in its respective **confidentiality** and **privacy** concerns (i.e., **protection** by means of respectively **encryption** or **anonymisation**) is the major concern of the security property as it is much more difficult to establish trust around any security notion than discredit a single security service/tool/mechanism, and in that occasion all the other security services/tools/mechanisms, by the means of some domino effect (cfr the US *'distrust'* practice or the french *'mistrust'* policy *versus* the healthcare *'entrust'* techniques). All the concepts and terminology expressed in this article try to contribute to this global trustworthiness, especially dedicated to health/healthcare/medical systems.

In order to obtain a satisfying dependability level for the future electronic interconnected systems, it is not sufficient to address the security issues, but it is at least a first step towards some interesting results for building dependable systems, recalling that security (dedicated to intentional faults) encompasses data availability-integrity-confidentiality (i.e., three of the constitutives attributes of the dependability basic concept).

Nowadays, as a concrete result concerning the health/healthcare/medical electronic and interconnected systems, having trusted-reliable identification/authentication, trusted-secure authorization, trusted-agreed certification, trusted-strong encryption and trusted-robust anonymisation... services begins to contribute to fulfil some of the other dependability attributes (e.g., system safety/reliability/maintainability and also global system availability/integrity) that are requested by the medical staff and the patients' population in the sense that all the secure services contribute to provide an acceptable level of confidence in the global healthcare information systems.

But it is still worth saying that the most relevant security architectures (based on the security notions, concepts, services, tools and techniques described in this article) are those that are both *flexible* enough to be adaptive to any previous or new legitimate situation and *robust* enough to be adopted by all the end-users and sectorial communities which strongly need for real security facilities, as it is particularly the case for the health/healthcare/medical sector which primary and essential justification is to globally prevent illnesses for all the population and to care each person individually:

* any *secure*, but either *unreliable* or *unsafe*, health/healthcare/medical information system will never be *dependable* enough to obtain some necessary trustworthy properties for being adopted by the citizens or by the professional population;
* conversely, any *reliable* and *safe*, but *non-secure*, health/healthcare/medical information system will never be *dependable* enough to reach the necessary trustworthiness that should be able to be proved in many critical situations (e.g., in front of a judge), by means of (e.g.) the auditability requirement (i.e., responsibility engagement) and the auditability fulfillment (i.e., responsibility demonstration).

Bibliography

1. *"L'anonymisation : autour et alentours"*, AFNOR, G.Trouessin, Sept. 1998.
2. *"La tenue du dossier médical en médecine générale"*, ANDEM, Sept. 1996.
3. *"Chaînage des informations individuelles se rapportant à un même bénéficiaire et reconstitution des séquences de soins"*, CNAMTS, Nov. 1997 (diffusion restreinte).
4. *"Towards a European Framework for Digital Signatre and encryption"*, COM(97) 503, European commission (European parliement, economic social committee and regions committee).
5. *"Les nouveaux tiers de confiance dans les échanges électroniques"*, Ialta, Nov. 1998.
6. *"L'identifiant Permanent du Patient dans les systèmes d'information de santé : orientations et propositions"*, Direction des Hôpitaux, C.Attali, Mai 1997 (diffusion restreinte).
7. *"L'identifiant Permanent du Patient dans les systèmes d'information de santé"*, Direction des Hôpitaux, G.Weil, Dec. 1998 (restricted broadcast).
8. *"Information Technology Security Evaluation Criteria (ITSEC)"*, ISBN 92-826-3004-8, Office for Official Publications of the European Communities, L-2985 Luxembourg, 1991.
9. *"Guide de la Sûreté de Fonctionnement"*, J.C.Laprie (Ed.) 2° ed., 324 P., ISBN2-85428-341-4, Cépaduès Ed., Toulouse, France, 1995.
10. *"Licensing of trusted third parties for the provision of encryption services"*, Minister for Science & Technology, I.Taylor, March 1997.
11. *"Minimum Interoperability Specification for PKI Components (v1)"*, NIST, Jan. 1998.
12. *"Etude formelle de l'interopérabilité de politiques de sécurité"*, F.Cuppens & C.Saurel, ONERA/DTIM, Jul. 1998 (restricted).
13. *"La tierce partie de confiance"*, CESSI/CNAMTS, Déc. 1996 (document de travail).
14. *"Cahier des charges de la TPC Santé/FRANCE"*, GIP 'CPS' - CESSI/CNAMTS, 1998.
15. *"Combining TTP-based key mangement with key escrow"*, Information Security Group, N.Jefferis, C.Mitchell & M.Walker, Apr. 1996.

Three-Pass Hybrid Key Establishment Protocol Based on ESIGN Signature

Sung-Min Lee and Tai-Yun Kim

Dept. of Computer Science & Engineering, Korea University
1, 5-Ga Anam-Dong Seongbuk-Gu Seoul 136-701 Korea
{smlee, tykim} @netlab.korea.ac.kr

Abstract. In this paper we propose 3-pass hybrid key establishment protocol. Different from conventional protocol it doesn't need to share secret key with key distribution center (KDC) in advance since it uses both public key and symmetric key schemes. The proposed key establishment protocol guarantees mutual entity and key authentication via ESIGN signature[7] with only 3-message exchange. As each entity has the same number of messages sent or received, it also guarantees load balance of each entity's processing. Using timestamp, it supports key freshness. It can be efficiently applied to various systems in distributed computing environments since the protocol provides security, efficiency and reliability.

1 Introduction

In today's distributed systems, secure communication is very important. It is also important to use a secure and efficient key establishment in distributed computing environments. For this reason, much effort has been invested into providing security services in a variety of network and operating system environments[6]. There are many protocols based on public key scheme and symmetric key scheme respectively. In some of these protocols, limitations and flaws are discovered[4,10].

Most of conventional key establishment protocols based on symmetric key scheme assume that each entity shares its secret key with a trusted third party in advance. In key establishment protocol based on public key scheme, each entity doesn't need to share secret key with KDC secretly but just publishes its public key. In general, public key encryption is slower than symmetric encryption. Existing protocols do not consider load balance of each entity. So processing complexity is biased mostly on initiator.

In this paper we solve these problems. We propose three-pass hybrid key establishment protocol which uses both symmetric and public key schemes in order to guarantee security and efficiency. The proposed protocol provides explicit key authentication and mutual entity authentication via ESIGN signature which is superior to other signatures in efficiency. The proposed protocol needs only 3 messages for key establishment and distributes load equally among the entities. In addition, it prevents reuse of a session key by using a timestamp.

M. Felici, K. Kanoun, A. Pasquini (Eds.): SAFECOMP'99, LNCS 1698, pp. 459–467, 1999
© Springer-Verlag Berlin Heidelberg 1999

This paper is organized as follows. An overview of our protocol is given in the next section. Section 3 describes the proposed hybrid key establishment protocol in more detail. In section 4, the proposed protocol is analyzed and compared with conventional protocols. Finally section 5 provides the conclusion to this paper.

2 Overview of Our Protocol

As in Kerberos[3], three types of principals are involved in our protocol: clients, servers and key distribution centers(KDCs). The KDC is a trusted third-party which issues tickets and signatures for authentication. The goal of the proposed protocol is authentication and key distribution with minimizing the number of message flows and distributing a balanced load (i.e. the messages sent and messages received) to each entity.

We assume that the distributed computing environment is untrusted; communication links may be susceptible to wiretapping, interception and replay of messages.

2.1 The Number of Messages and Load Balance

The number of message flows affects efficiency of key establishment protocol. We make the proposed protocol exchange only 3-message among entities. And we consider the number of messages sent or received as load. It affects each entity's processing complexity. So the proposed protocol is designed to balance the each entity's load in number of messages. Fig. 1 shows the proposed key establishment protocol and Fig. 2 shows Needham-Schroeder protocol[1]. The proposed protocol needs only 3 messages for key establishment and the number of message sent or received on each entity is equally one. The Needham-Schroeder protocol needs 5 messages and load is biased on initiator A: number of messages sent – 3, number of messages received – 2.

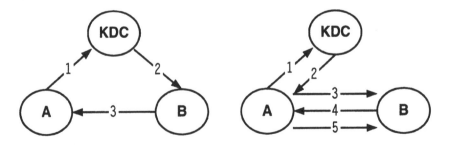

Fig. 1. The Proposed Protocol   **Fig. 2.** Needham-Schroeder Protocol

2.2 Ticket Distribution

In our protocol, different from Kerberos, KDC K issues ticket for B then sends it to B. B receives the ticket then issues ticket for A. Each ticket consists of a pair. Only session key is encrypted with the public key and the other information is encrypted with the symmetric key for efficiency. The ticket for B is:

$P_b(k_{ab})$, Ek_{ab}(id of initiator: A, timestamps, lifetime, signature of sender K, A' public key)

where:
- P_b is a public key of B for encryption and k_{ab} is a session key that will be shared A and B. E is a symmetric encryption algorithm.
- The timestamps are comprised of A's and B's in order to verify freshness of key. The timestamps are used as nonces. The session key cannot be reused since the timestamps are generated by each entity sequentially.
- The lifetime is expiration time of a session key k_{ab}.
- Using the signature of K, B can verify identity of K, A and integrity of information. K's digital signature contains identity of A, session key k_{ab}, A's timestamp T_a, K's timestamp T_k, lifetime of the session key L and B's public key for verification of B's signature. S_a denotes signature of A.

The ticket for A is:

$P_a(k_{ab})$, Ek_{ab}(id of sender: B, timestamps, lifetime, signature of K, signature of B, B's public key)

where B's public key is for verification B's digital signature. A makes sure B's public key as A verifies K's and B's signature. A can authenticate K's and B's identity and integrity of the message. As K's signature contains B's public key, an intruder cannot pretend to be B.

2.3 Authentication using Digital Signature

For authentication, conventional key establishment protocols based on symmetric encryption use a nonce. The proposed hybrid protocol uses digital signature. While a none-based protocol authenticates only each entity, the proposed protocol guarantees both integrity of messages and entity authentication. Using a digital signature scheme, we authenticate mutual entity, integrity of message and session key with only 3 messages. The flaw of a digital signature based authentication is slower than a nonce-based authentication. But using ESIGN signature, we can improve efficiency when each entity authenticates each other and integrity of messages.

3 The Proposed Hybrid Key Establishment Protocol

In this section, the key exchange steps of the proposed protocol and explicit key authentication via ESIGN signature are discussed. The proposed protocol uses a trusted third party KDC. Session key and its lifetime are issued by KDC. A session key is valid for a finite interval called its lifetime. Our protocol uses both public key encryption and symmetric key encryption. We encrypt only small message such as a session key using public key encryption scheme, the others are encrypted using symmetric key scheme. Each entity of our protocol signs its messages using ESIGN in order to prove its identity and integrity of the messages. Fig. 3 shows key exchange steps in our protocol.

The proposed protocol is designed to minimize the number of messages and to optimize the load balance of each entity. It is assumed that the KDC has the public keys of Client A and Server B respectively to verify each entity's digital signature in advance.

3.1 Key Exchange Steps

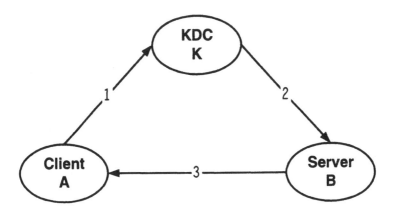

(1) $A \rightarrow K$: $A,B,T_a,S_a(A,B,T_a)$

(2) $K \rightarrow B$: $P_b(k_{ab})$, $E_{k_{ab}}(A,T_a,T_k,L,S_k(A, k_{ab},T_a,T_k,L, P_b),P_a)$

(3) $B \rightarrow A$: $P_a(k_{ab})$, $E_{k_{ab}}(B,T_a,T_k,L,S_k(A, k_{ab},T_a,T_k,L, P_b),T_b,S_b(T_b),P_b)$

Fig. 3. Key Exchange Steps of the Proposed Protocol

The proposed protocol begins with client A initiating authentication by sending message (1) to KDC K containing name of A and B, A's timestamp T_a, together with A's signature of A,B,T_a. It uses timestamp as nonce. K receives the message then authenticates A's identity and integrity of the message via A's signature. K then issues a ticket allowing B to share a session key k_{ab} with A until lifetime specified by K. The protocol splits a ticket into two parts: one is encrypted with session key, another is encrypted with public key. For efficiency only session key is encrypted with public key scheme and the other information such as timestamp, lifetime are encrypted with symmetric key scheme. In message (2), K sends the ticket to B with session key k_{ab}. B first decrypts the ticket to obtain session key using his private key then decrypts another part using the session key k_{ab}. B verifies integrity of the message and authenticity of K and A using K's signature. In message (3), B issues timestamp and signature for the timestamp then constructs ticket for A. The ticket contains identity of sender B, timestamp of A and K, lifetime L, K's signature, timestamp of B, signature of the timestamp and B's public key. Finally A can verify B's and K's identity via ESIGN signature and key freshness by checking T_a matches that sent in message (1). For the complete key establishment, only 3 messages are required in the proposed protocol.

3.2 Explicit Authentication via ESIGN

ESIGN is a digital signature scheme from NTT Japan whose security relies on the difficulty of factoring integers. It is touted as being at least as secure and considerably faster than either RSA[12] or DSA[13], with similar key and signature lengths[14,15]. It is a signature scheme which requires a one-way hash function h: $\{0,1\} \overset{*}{\longmapsto} Z_n$.

In the proposed protocol, each entity creates a public key and corresponding private key for authentication via digital signature. They exchange their public key with Key Distribution Center (KDC) in advance. Fig. 4 shows the process of key generation for ESIGN. Each entity of our protocol generates public and private key pair then publish the public key (n,k).

Select random primes p and q such that $p \geq q$ and p, q are roughly of the same bit length.
Compute $n = p^2q$.
Select a positive integer $k \geq 4$.
Entity A's public key is (n,k); A's private key is (p,q).

Fig. 4. The ESIGN Key Generation Step of Entity A

By using ESIGN signature generation and verification, each entity of the proposed protocol can authenticate each other. In the proposed protocol, 3 pairs of the entities (i.e. A and K, K and B, B and A) need authentication using ESIGN signature. Fig. 5 shows an example of explicit authentication procedure between K and B via ESIGN signature. K generates message m which is concatenated k_{ab}, T_a, T_k, L, P_b. Then it computes $v = h(m)$ and selects a random secret integer x, $0 \leq x < p$ and then computes $\varpi = \lceil ((v-x^k) \mod n)/(pq) \rceil$ and $y = \varpi(kx^{k-1})^{-1} \mod p$. Finally K computes signature: $s = x + ypq \mod n$ then sends it to B. To verify K's signature s on m, B computes $u = s^k \mod n$ and $z = h(m)$ using K's public key (n,k). If $z \leq u \leq z + 2^{\lceil 2/3 \lg n \rceil}$, accept the signature; else reject it. Using ESIGN signature, each entity can authenticate each other and the integrity of message efficiently.

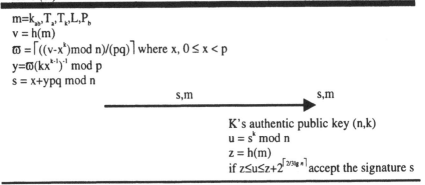

Fig. 5. Explicit Authentication between K and B via ESIGN

Proof the signature verification works.

$s^k \equiv (x + ypq)^k \equiv \Sigma_{i=0}^{k}\binom{k}{i}x^{k-i}(ypq)^i \equiv x^k + kypqx^{k-1}(mod\ n)$. $But \quad kx^{k-1}y \equiv w(mod\ p)$

$and\ ,thus\ ,kx^{k-1}y = w + lp \quad for \quad some \quad l \in Z.Hence\ ,s^k \equiv x^k + pq(w + lp) \equiv x^k + pqw \equiv$

$x^k + pq\left\lceil\dfrac{(h(m) - x^k)\ mod\ n}{pq}\right\rceil \equiv x^k + pq\left(\dfrac{h(m) - x^k + jn + \varepsilon}{pq}\right)(mod\ n),where \quad \varepsilon = (x^k - h(m))$

$mod \quad pq\ .\quad Therefore\ ,s^k \equiv x^k + h(m) - x^k + \varepsilon \quad (mod\ n).\quad Since \quad 0 \leq \varepsilon \leq pq\ ,it \quad follows$

$that \quad h(m) \leq s^k\ mod\ n \leq h(m) + pq \leq h(m) + 2^{\left\lceil\frac{2}{3}lg\ n\right\rceil}, as \quad required$.

4 Analysis

In this section, important properties of key establishment protocol are discussed. Characteristics of the proposed protocol are analyzed and compared with conventional protocols in some factors.

In key establishment protocols, it is important to satisfy following characteristics.

- nature of the authentication: entity authentication and key authentication may be provided.
- reciprocity of authentication: each of entity authentication and key authentication may be unilateral or mutual
- key freshness: a session key if fresh (from the viewpoint of one party) if it can be guaranteed to be new, as opposed to possibly an old session key being reused through actions of an adversary.
- efficiency: considerations include the number of message exchanges (passes) required between parties, bandwidth required by message (total number of bits transmitted), processing complexities by each party.
- third party requirements.

The proposed protocol provides mutual entity authentication and explicit key authentication. It guarantees key freshness since each entity issues timestamp then signs it and KDC issues lifetime of a session key. In the protocol, authenticating parties must have access to synchronized and reliable clocks in order to get timestamps and to verify them. The protocol needs only 3-message exchanges for complete key establishment and spreads an equal load (i.e. messages sent or received) among each of the entities. The protocol uses a trusted third-party KDC. Table 1 compares our protocol with existing protocols. The items compared are encryption scheme, server type, use of timestamp, authentication and use of digital signature.

Table 1. Characteristics of Each Protocol

Properties Protocol	Encryption scheme	Server type	Use of Timestamp	Authentication	Use of Digital signature
Shamir's no-key protocol[14]	Symmetric key	None	No	No	No
Kerberos[3]	Symmetric key	KDC	Yes	Optionally mutual	No
Needham-Schroeder shared key[1]	Symmetric key	KDC	No	Yes	No
Otway-Rees[2]	Symmetric key	KDC	No	Yes	No
Needham-Schroeder PK[14]	Public key	None	No	Mutual	No
Beller-Yacobi[8]	Hybrid	None	No	Mutual	Yes (RSA or Elgamal)
The proposed protocol	Hybrid	KDC	Yes	Mutual	Yes (Esign)

Table 2 shows the number of messages for key establishment in each protocol. The number of messages is one of important factors which affects efficiency of the protocol. The number of messages sent or received also affects each entity's processing complexity. The proposed protocol is only a 3-pass key establishment protocol but it provides all the properties supported by other protocols with only 3 messages. Also, the load balance of messages for each entity has been considered. Load is not biased on some entities since the number of message sent or received is 1. Therefore, the proposed protocol is more efficient than existing protocols.

5 Conclusion

In this paper we proposed 3-pass hybrid key establishment protocol. When designing an authentication protocol certain tradeoffs must be made. It is important to understand the issues in order to choose the best solution[5]. Issues of our protocol are

Table 2. The Number of Messages in Each Protocol

Number of Messages Protocol	Number of total messages	Number of messages sent			Number of messages received		
		A	B	KDC	A	B	KDC
Shamir's no-key protocol	3	2	1	None	1	2	None
Kerberos	4	2	1	1	2	1	1
Needham-Schroeder shared key	5	3	1	1	2	2	1
Otway-Rees	4	1	2	1	1	2	1
Needham-Schroeder PK	3	2	1	None	1	2	None
Beller-Yacobi	4	2	2	None	2	2	None
The proposed protocol	3	1	1	1	1	1	1

the number of messages required, load balance of each entity's computation, authentication of entity and key, and key freshness.

The proposed protocol needs only 3 messages for complete key establishment. It also needs not securely share secret key with KDC in advance since it use both symmetric and public key encryption schemes. Using hybrid mechanism, it guarantees entity and key authentication with 3-pass, and load balance of each entity's computation. The protocol authenticates using ESIGN signature whose efficiency is superior to other digital signatures. And it guarantees key freshness, as it uses timestamp to prevent session key from replaying. It is efficiently applied to various authentication systems in distributed computing environments.

The future work is to verify security and reliability of our protocol by using formal method such as process algebra CSP[16] and its model checker FDR.

References

[1] R.M. Needham and M.D. Schroeder, "Using Encryption for Authentication in Large Networks of Computers," Communications of the ACM, VOL. 21, NO. 12, pp. 993-999, Dec 1978.
[2] D. Otway and O. Rees, "Efficient and Timely Mutual Authentication," Operating Systems Review,VOL. 21, NO. 1, pp. 8-10, 1987.
[3] John T. Kohl, B. Clifford Neuman, and Theodore Y. T'so, "The Evolution of the Kerberos Authentication System. In Distributed Open Systems," IEEE Computer Society Press, pp. 78-94, 1994.
[4] S.M. Bellovin, M. Merritt, "Limitations of the Kerberos Authentication System," ACM SIGCOMM Computer Communication Review, pp. 119-132, October 1990.
[5] B. Clifford Neuman, Stuart G. Stubblebine, "A Note on the Use of Timestamps as Nonces," Operating Systems Review, Vol. 27, No. 2, pp. 10-14, April 1993.
[6] R. Molva, G. Tsudik, E.Van Herreweghen and S. Zatti, "KryptoKnight Authentication and Key Distribution System," Proceedings of European Symposium on Research in Computer Security, Toulouse, France, Nov 1992.

[7] A. Fujioka, T. Okamoto, and S. Miyaguchi, "ESIGN: An Efficient Digital Signature Implemenation for Smart Cards," Advances in Cryptology-EUROCRYPT '91 Proceedings, pp.446-457, Springer-Verlag, 1991.

[8] M.J. BELLER and Y. YACOBI, "Fully-fledged two-way public key authentication and key agreement for low-cost terminals," Electronics Letters, pp. 999-1001, May 1993.

[9] M. Tatebayahi, N. Matsuzaki, and D.B. Newman Jr., "Key Distribution Protocol for Digital Mobile Communication Systems," Advances in Cryptology: Proc. Crypto '89, Lecture Notes in Computer Science 435, pp. 324-333. Springer-Verlag, 1990.

[10] Gavin Lowe, Bill Roscoe, "Using CSP to Detect Errors in the TMN Protocol," IEEE TRANSACTIONS ON SOFTWARE ENGINEERING, VOL. 23, NO. 10, pp. 659-669, OCTOBER 1997.

[11] W. Diffie and M. Hellman, "New Directions in Cryptography," IEEE Transactions on Information Theory, November 1976.

[12] R.L. Rivest, A. Shamir and L. Adleman, "A Method for Obtaining Digital Signatures and Public-Key Cryptosystems," Comm. ACM, Vol. 21, No. 2, pp. 120-126, Feb. 1978.

[13] D. Naccache, D. M'Raihi, D. Raphaeli, and S. Vaudenay, "Can D.S.A. be Improved? Complexity Trade-Offs with the Digital Signature Standard," Advances in Cryptology-EUROCRYPT '93 Proceedings, Springer-Verlag, 1994.

[14] Alfred J. Menezes, Paul C. van Oorschot, Scott A. Vanstone, *HANDBOOK OF APPLIED CRYPTOGRAPHY*, CRC PRESS, 1996.

[15] BRUCE SCHNEIER, *APPLIED CRYPTOGRAPHY*, SECOND EDITION, John Wiley & Sons, Inc., 1996.

[16] C.A.R. Hoare, *Communicating Sequential Processes*, Prentice Hall, 1985.

The Integration of Safety and Security Requirements

David Peter Eames[1] and Jonathan Moffett[2]

[1]ASACS Safety and Standards Unit, RAF, UK
deames@assu.org.uk
[2]Department of Computer Science, University of York, UK
jdm@cs.york.ac.uk

Abstract. This paper investigates safety and security requirements specification methods, and proposed techniques for the integration of contrasting methodologies. The nature of interaction between safety and security requirements, and problems relating to their independent development, are discussed. The requirements specifications of an Air Traffic Control system are used to highlight the problems inherent in the independent approach to requirements development. From investigation of the literature and the case study, we identify several areas that can cause problems when we attempt to harmonize safety and security requirements techniques. The most important of these are: different system models used for safety and security; different documentation structures for the analyses and their results; the interaction of safety and security requirements; isolation of safety and security requirements processes.

1 Background

Computer systems are increasingly used in areas where their failure could have serious consequences. There are many opinions as to the properties such critical systems should possess, and the techniques that should be used to develop them. Two such properties are safety and security. Within their domains, specialised methods have been developed to investigate and generate requirements specifications.

However, systems that are now being built are frequently required to satisfy these properties simultaneously. Due in part to the evolutionary growth of the approaches to safety and security specification techniques, they have largely been developed in isolation. As a result, there is growing interest in the degree to which techniques from one domain complement or conflict with those from the other.

Although there has been some work in the area of integrating techniques, this has concentrated on the techniques themselves, identifying similarities and differences, or presenting ways in which they can be brought together. The aim of this work is to investigate the nature of integration, and its influence on requirements specification.

Section 2 discusses methodologies for risk assessment in the safety and security domains. Section 3 presents a case study of an air traffic control system that is to be modernised in the near future, and has both safety and security requirements. Section 4 discusses the case study in the light of the integration framework presented, and section 5 draws conclusions from the analysis and provides pointers for the future.

M. Felici, K. Kanoun, A. Pasquini (Eds.): SAFECOMP'99, LNCS 1698, pp. 468–480, 1999
© Springer-Verlag Berlin Heidelberg 1999

2   Survey of Safety and Security Risk Analysis Techniques

2.1   Introduction

In this section we present a discussion of accepted methodologies for risk assessment within the safety (2.2) and security (2.3) domains. We then investigate work carried out to integrate security and safety risk analysis (2.4). Section 2.5 identifies the common structure of safety and security analysis. The final part of this section (2.6) is a summary and discussion of these analyses.

2.2   The Safety Risk Analysis Process

The safety risk analysis process has the aim of specifying the safety requirements of the system. There are four distinct stages in this process:

1.   *Functional and Technical Analysis.* The first stage is to gather data on the system; its functional and technical characteristics. The aim is to develop a picture of how the system works. Characteristics to investigate include: the system functions or missions, the system structure, how the system is operated, the environment within which the system functions, and the system boundaries.

2.   *Qualitative Analysis.* The purpose of qualitative analysis is to investigate the failure causes and hazards that could affect the system. Many hazard analysis techniques are available to produce a thorough and consistent investigation. Choosing the most appropriate technique must take into account the overall goals of the analysis, the system being analysed, and the assets available to support the analysis. This analysis develops an understanding of the failure mechanisms of the system and the combinations of failures that could lead to hazardous situations.

3.   *Quantitative Analysis.* Quantitative analysis involves putting numbers to the findings of stage 2. The data used to quantify the identified hazards will always have a degree of uncertainty; it will be probabilistic in nature, taken from sources such as test results, operational records, etc. Quantitative analysis can, however, provide developers with a measure of the relative threat of the hazards, thus allowing attention to be focussed in critical areas, and may be useful in comparing the reliability of alternative features of designs [1].

4.   *Synthesis and Conclusions.* Combining qualitative and quantitative analysis identifies critical components and important functions. It allows developers to identify the measures and requirements of the system which must be put in place if it is to be acceptably safe. It is this work that generates the system requirements specification.

2.3   The Security Risk Analysis Process

The methodology of security risk analysis also comprises a number of basic steps. These differ between authors, but in general include:

1.   Asset Identification. The asset identification phase should identify the resources that require protection. These will include: hardware, software, data, documentation, and computer services and processes. Financial values can be readily applied to some of these assets, but others are more difficult to price.

2.   Vulnerability Analysis. Having listed the assets of a computer system, the next stage is to determine their vulnerabilities. This stage is more difficult than the first, as it requires a degree of imagination to predict what damage might occur to the assets and from what sources [2]. The general aims of computer security are to ensure data secrecy, data integrity and availability. System vulnerabilities are situations that could cause the loss of any of these qualities. A thorough understanding of the threats to the system is required if all the vulnerabilities are to be identified. Methodical and structured approaches are required if threat identification and vulnerability analysis is to be successful.

3.   Likelihood Analysis. The aim of likelihood analysis is to ascertain how often the system will be exposed to each of the vulnerabilities identified. Likelihood relates to the current security safeguards and the environment in which they are applied. Estimating the probability of exposure to a threat can be difficult. Sources of data for this estimation include: operations logs, local crime statistics and user complaints.

4.   Countermeasure Evaluation. All the analysis so far reflects the current situation. If, from this analysis, it is determined that the projected loss will be unacceptable, new or alternative countermeasures will have to be investigated. New controls will have to be identified, and their effectiveness evaluated.

2.4   Integration of Safety and Security

The term "integrate" can mean many things. A thesaurus will provide a number of synonyms, such as: consolidate, combine, synthesise, unify, and harmonise. In the main, the meaning of these is epitomised by the word *unify* (the dictionary meaning of which is 'make or become one'). This meaning has also been adopted by a number of authors who have investigated methods for the integration of safety and security requirements specification techniques. The result of this approach is a single set of requirements describing the safety and security functions of a system.

An alternative meaning is encapsulated by the word *harmonise* (the dictionary meaning being 'cause to agree, reconcile'). Rather than combining techniques to produce a single, unified methodology, here we are considering adjusting or modifying techniques to bring them into alignment with each other. The aim of this would be to produce individual sets of requirements for safety and security that can be compared and analysed for conflicts without having to utilise intermediate techniques.

The Unification Approach. The idea of unifying safety, security and other criteria together under the heading of 'dependability' has been investigated by a number of authors. The notion of dependability has been around for a long time. One definition is "that property of a computing system that allows reliance to be justifiably placed on the service it delivers" [3]. Within this definition, dependability thus includes attributes such as reliability, availability, *safety* and *security*. Work by McDermid [4], and Sanders and Meyer [5] adopt this approach.

Harmonising Approaches. A number of general papers have been written discussing the differences and/or similarities between safety and security properties. Cullyer presents a general paper [6] on the nature of safety and security, in which he recognises the differences between the two, but also states that both groups subscribe to similar development techniques. Rushby [7] also presents an extremely pertinent paper in this context, in which he draws a conclusion (among many) that safety and security techniques could be applicable to each other's domains. Brewer [8] also presents an interesting slant on this theme, by considering the application of security techniques to the development of safety systems and looking at the relationship between safety and security. He concludes that security could benefit from fault tolerant approaches typically found in safety techniques, and that security system developers might benefit from a greater understanding of the hazard analysis methods used by safety engineers. However, he also notes that safety might be improved by the use of fault preventative methods often used in the security domain.

2.5   Canonical Risk Analysis Process

An observation from the early work was that although texts talk about 'safety hazard analysis' and 'security risk analysis', the processes involved in each of the analyses are not actually dissimilar. If sections 2.2 and 2.3 are compared, we can see that they each have the same general stages:

1.   An investigation of the system, its components, its functions, its connections to other systems, its environment, the users, etc. The information gained from this investigation is used to develop a model of the system. Although these investigations go by different names and vary slightly they are essentially **system modeling**.

2.   A **qualitative analysis** of the weaknesses in the system, and dangers to its continued correct operation. In security these are called vulnerabilities and threats, in safety they are called failure mechanisms and hazards, but again, they can be considered to be alike.

3.   A **quantitative analysis** of the weaknesses and dangers. Safety and security domains both attempt to quantify the risks using probabilistic approaches. In security this often results in estimated expected financial losses, while in safety this is expressed as a likelihood of system failure resulting in an accident. Once more, in principle they are similar.

4.   The final stage involves combining the qualitative and quantitative analyses to allow developers to make judgements about the measures that need to be put in place to counter the risks. Examples in safety are redundancy, protective equipment, monitoring devices, etc., while in security examples are access controls, firewalls, etc. In both cases, this last stage involves **defining the requirements** of the system that will ensure that the risks are reduced to acceptable levels.

While accepting that this is a simplification, we believe that that meaningful inferences can be drawn from it. Significantly, this initial observation supports the idea that safety and security *can* be integrated. The next important step is to determine exactly how best the two domains could be brought together.

2.6   Initial Discussion

The amount of published work on integration of safety and security analysis techniques is not large, but it covers a broad spectrum of approaches. These papers generally adopt one of two standpoints, either aiming to unify techniques into a single methodology, or investigating the similarities of techniques from each.

An observation made while reviewing these papers, in light of the earlier investigation of risk analysis, is that safety and security are closely related. As mentioned before, both deal with risks. Also, both safety and security risk analyses result in constraints (which may be regarded as negative requirements) that can conflict with functional and other performance-related system requirements [9]. Both involve protective measures, and both produce requirements that are considered to be of the greatest importance. These similarities indicate that some of the techniques applicable to one field could also be applicable to the other.

However, the conclusion that we draw from the analysis of the papers discussing 'integration' is that, while the definition of safety or security could be extended to include both concepts, in the majority of situations it is inappropriate to attempt to *unify* safety and security risk analysis techniques. Such unification would have the benefit of producing a single set of requirements, and conflict resolution could form an inherent part of the resultant approach, but this has to be weighed against the disadvantages. We believe that consolidation of safety and security could reduce developers' understanding of the system being analysed, and prevent a thorough analysis of either property. Specialised techniques in each domain have evolved with the aim of producing a thorough and complete analysis. Attempts to unify two such techniques would involve compromises in each, which in turn could lead to an *in*complete analysis, with subsequent safety and security risks going unobserved and being incorporated in the final system. An additional danger is that a unified approach might actually hide the requirements conflicts that it aims to resolve. Also, the process of resolving conflicts itself can actually be worthwhile, as it engenders better understanding of the system and its domain. This value could be lost in a unified approach. Finally, trade-offs between qualities could be hidden by a global abstraction, with unnoticed detrimental effects. For example, it is possible to increase reliability while decreasing safety without it being apparent that an increase in risk has occurred [1].

Our analysis leads us to believe that the value in integrating safety and security lies with harmonising techniques from each domain. Such an approach would provide numerous benefits without the disadvantages associated with unification approaches:

- The specialised techniques developed in each domain would not have to be compromised.

- Conflicts could become more apparent than if the techniques were applied in isolation, as comparisons between the two sets of requirements could be simpler.

- The cross-fertilisation of ideas from one domain to the other could promote better understanding of the system and its environment, and might lead to the recognition of risks that could otherwise be overlooked.

- Separation of properties would permit recognition of conflicts and trade-offs, and allow judgement-based decisions to be made, rather than have an 'automated' method make choices, and perhaps screen them from the system developers.

From our initial analysis of integrating safety and security requirements we conclude that safety, security and their associated risk analysis techniques are closely related and have sufficient similarity to make integration a reasonable and achievable goal. Further analysis shows that *unification* of methods has disadvantages that outweigh the benefits they may provide. Finally, *harmonising* safety and security techniques could provide advantages over independently producing requirements in each field, and would not present developers with the drawbacks of the unification approach.

3   The Case Study

3.1   Introduction

This section presents the case study that has been analysed as part of this work. The case study is a military air traffic control system (MATCS) that is due to undergo major modernisation in the near future. The purpose of this work is to replace obsolete hardware and software with current generation equipment. The system safety and security requirements for the programme have been produced via a lengthy analysis process.

In sections 3.2 and 3.3 respectively, we describe the development of the safety and security requirements. These requirements have been developed in isolation from each other, using established approaches from their respective disciplines:

- The safety requirements have been produced within a safety case framework. Preliminary Hazard Identification and systematic hazard analysis has been used to produce high-level safety requirements documented in a safety case.

- The security requirements have been produced via the development of system security policies. Security risk/threat assessment has been carried out using a qualitative approach incorporating evaluation criteria cont-ained in the UK Communications-Electronics Security Group (CESG) guidelines [10, 11].

3.2   Development of MATCS Safety Requirements

A four-part safety case, as defined in UK MoD Defence Standard 00-56/2 [12], has been adopted for the MATCS modernisation project. The main objective of the safety case is to produce arguments and evidence that the system is suitably safe for its int-ended purpose. The work that has been carried out to date has resulted in the prod-uction of the Safety Case Part 1, which contains the user-defined safety targets and high-level safety requirements. This section of the paper describes the process used to produce the safety requirements that are detailed in the Safety Case Part 1.

Safety Requirements Determination. The purpose of the safety analysis was to define the high level safety requirements for the system, which would in turn form the basis for the contractual safety requirements to be met by the implementation contractor. During the process of identifying the safety requirements, the following activities were performed:

Definition of the system boundaries and functions.   The first stage of the safety analysis was to define the system boundaries, functions and interfaces. Much of the system functional model could be developed from the existing system; the replacement is required to provide the same functionality, with minor exceptions. From the required high level functionality, a Safety Context Diagram (SCD) was produced, showing the system and the interfaces with external agencies. From the SCD, more detailed Functional Interface Diagrams (FIDs) were developed, whose purpose was to detail the information that would be passed between the system sub-functions.

Preliminary Hazard Identification (PHI).   Once the system functions had been identified, a PHI could be performed to record hazards or hazardous failures identified by the project team and operational experts. Known hazards from similar systems were also taken into account, and available documentation on the current system was examined to identify potential future hazards. Although a systematic Preliminary Hazard Analysis (PHA) was expected to identify functional failures of the system, the 'brainstorming' aspect of the PHI was carried out to ensure that known hazards in the existing system were taken into account. As well as specific discussions to identify hazards, based on the system functions, ad-hoc questions were raised and potential hazards identified.

Preliminary Hazard Analysis (PHA).   Following the PHI, a PHA was undertaken. The PHA was expected to identify the functional failures that could lead to hazardous states. Once this analysis had been carried out, a process of rationalisation took place to relate the PHA-identified hazards to those from the PHI, removing any duplicates and producing a set of system hazards that could be used to generate the safety requirements. The primary tool used to perform the PHA was Functional Failure Analysis (FFA). The FFA used a systematic approach to determine the impact of failures of each identified function. The basis for discussion involved in the FFA was the SCD and FIDs. Each of the potential outputs shown on a diagram is investigated to determine the consequences of failures of the output, the effect on the function, and the influence on the system as a whole. The ways in which outputs could fail were: data not provided, erroneous data provided, and data output being delayed. For every data output of a sub-function, each failure type was considered in turn to determine whether the subsequent functional failure modes could affect the safety of the system.

Generating the MATCS Safety Requirements.   The final safety requirements presented in the Safety Case Part 1 were derived from a number of sources, including the analysis described above, consideration of the system as a whole (including expert knowledge of the existing system), good engineering practice and guidance provided by the Independent Safety Advisor (ISA). As well as defining requirements to avoid the functional failure modes highlighted by the FFA, the general safety requirements (such as Safety Integrity Levels for software) were defined, as were human factors requirements (for which a separate analysis was carried out). In this way, the Safety Case Part 1 provided the basis from which further, implementation-specific, analysis could be carried out, and against which the implementation contractor could demonstrate the safety of the proposed solution.

3.3   Development of MATCS Security Requirements

While work was being carried out to produce the high-level safety requirements for MATCS, a separate team was developing the security requirements for the project. These requirements were generated and documented via a System Security Policy (SSP). As for the safety requirements, this policy was produced according to government guidelines; in this case, those of the CESG [10]. In accordance with these guidelines, electronic communications and computer systems handling protectively marked information should be accredited, to ensure that their use does not present an unacceptable risk to national security. The basis for this accreditation is the SSP, which represents an agreement between the project manager and the accreditor with respect to system security.

Security Requirements Determination. The SSP describes the scope of the system, the nature of the security requirement and the specific security measures that are to be implemented. The elements of an SSP include:

Definition of the MATCS for Security. This was a concise definition of the system, encompassing security-relevant information, accounting for the role of the system, the data to be handled, the number and security clearance of the users and the system configuration. The system is defined using free text and diagrams. The role and physical distribution of elements and sub-systems is exactly the same as for the generation of the safety requirements. However, the numerous diagrams and text are much less readily understood and intuitive than the SCD.

Security Threat Assessment for MATCS. The threat assessment was carried out following the CESG guidelines. This process is similar to that mandated by the US Department of Defence 'Orange Book' [13] but takes into account the later work of the European ITSEC standard [14]. The first stage was to identify the threat sources, such as hostile intelligence, disaffected users, erroneous system operation, etc. Each of these were then investigated in turn to determine the possible origins of the threat and methods of attack that the system may have to face. From this, the rationale for a security system was formed. In the case of the MATCS, the most significant threat was determined to be authorised users who, for whatever reason, disrupt the system or compromise information. Having considered the threats, it was necessary to carry out an evaluation to determine the level of assurance that was required to protect the system. This evaluation took into account the threats, the system vulnerabilities (numbers of authorised users, modes of operation, clearances and technical characteristics of the system), and marking and/or sensitivity of the information. With the system information at hand, tables in [11] could be referenced to determine the required assurance level. This took a value in the range E0 (low) to E6 (high).

Definition of the MATCS Security Measures. The final stage was to describe the measures necessary to achieve the required level of security, as determined by the threat assessment. This defined what would traditionally be called the system security requirements. The measures were organised by stating the security principles and risks which had been associated with each of the eight ITSEC-identified general security principles (access control, authentication, accounting, audit, object reuse, accuracy, reliability of service and data exchange). Following this, the SSP specified how the risks would be addressed, either by means of assertions, or by measures to be applied (technical or procedural).

4   Case Study Analysis and Discussion

4.1   Introduction

Having described the case, this section documents the analysis carried out in the context of the concepts and ideas presented earlier in the paper. The analysis begins by presenting the authors' views on the concept of integration of safety and security requirements (4.2): the idea that the requirements themselves can be conflicting and/or inconsistent; but also that the requirements are inter-related. This relationship needs to be understood if successful integration is to be achieved. Following this, the safety and security requirements generation processes from the case study are analysed and documented (4.3, 4.4). The final section (4.5) presents a number of recommendations, with respect to the case study, that could allow the safety and security specifications to be better integrated.

4.2   Interaction between Safety and Security

From the initial literature review and investigation of the case study, two kinds of interaction between safety and security requirements have been identified.

The first form of interaction is the obvious case where requirements from each of the two domains are incompatible. As an example, we can consider a computer-controlled door locking system in a modern building. A requirement from the safety domain could be that the system must 'fail safe'. In this case, this would mean that on failure, the doors should be unlocked, thereby allowing personnel to vacate rooms in the event of an emergency. On the other hand, the security developers may identify a requirement for the system to 'fail secure', that is; all the doors should be locked to prevent unauthorised access. Although there are technical solutions to this particular example, it serves to demonstrate how two groups of developers working in isolation can produce incompatible requirements.

The second form of interaction is subtler, and generally not as easily recognised. Here we are considering the interaction that produces what we can call 'primary' and 'derived' requirements. Primary requirements are those that have their foundations in their own domain. For example, primary security requirements have their foundations in the security domain. From investigation of security threats, requirements engineers identify those security measures needed to counter the threats. We might say 'somebody may wish to steal or corrupt this data, so we must control access, limiting it to those personnel that we trust'.

We can think of derived requirements as those that are brought about (their essential rationale) as the result of analysis undertaken *outside* their own domain. An example of this could be *security* requirements identified as the result of *safety* analysis. In this case, these requirements are not specified to protect the system from traditional security threats per se, but rather have been identified as part of the process of reducing the threats to the system's safety performance. We might say 'if this particular data is corrupted in any way, the overall safety of the system could be compromised. Therefore, we must make sure that the equipment cannot fail in a way that causes data corruption, but we must also control access so that people who should not be tampering with it cannot cause a corruption'. In these examples, both primary and derived requirements result in access controls, but there are important differences in the rationales.

These requirements interactions need to be fully understood for two main reasons:

Conflict Resolution. If conflicts are to be properly dealt with, developers need to appreciate how they have arisen. Only then can they be sure that the processes they use to resolve them do not introduce new problems. With the first type of interaction, this should not be a problem. However, the subtle nature of the second form of interaction means that it needs more careful handling; changes to derived requirements could affect not only the parent document, but also the analysis and requirements in the associated opposite domain.

Integration of Requirements. Not until requirements interactions are understood can processes to *integrate* them effectively be developed.

4.3   Safety Case Development

The process used to develop the MATCS safety requirements has followed established and well-documented procedures. A preliminary hazard identification was followed by systematic analysis, all documented via a Safety Case Part 1.

In the Safety Case Part 1, among the General Safety Requirements there is the following conflict resolution policy: "Wherever there is a conflict between the safety requirements and other requirements for the system, the safety requirements shall always have precedence". However, in the System Attribute Safety Requirements, we find a subsection titled 'security requirements' which calls for:

- Access controls to be applied to the operational and system management interfaces.

- Appropriate mechanisms for maintaining secure copies of system configuration and software versions, and for verifying that they have not been altered.

- Sub-contracted systems and commercial-of-the-shelf (COTS) equipment to be free from unapproved or hazardous features including software viruses.

- Security measures or devices implemented in the system not to affect the safety performance of the operational system.

These security requirements and the placement of them in the safety documentation raise two issues:

- First, from where were these specific security requirements derived and why specify these requirements in particular? Traceability within the safety case documentation is incomplete, making it difficult to determine the rationale for specific requirements.

- If a conflict were to occur between one of the derived security requirements and a requirement contained elsewhere in the Safety Case, which would have precedence? This highlights a weakness of a simplistic approach to conflict resolution.

4.4   Security Policy Development

The security policy document states: "In the event of a conflict between security and safety requirements it shall be presumed that safety has precedence until a ruling has been obtained from the System Manager". This differs from the safety document-ation's approach to conflict resolution, in which safety requirements *shall always* have the highest precedence.

4.5   Discussion

From investigation of the literature and the case study, we can identify a number of areas that can cause problems when we attempt to harmonise safety and security requirements techniques. The most important ones are:

- Different system models developed for safety and security.
- Different documentation structures for the analyses and their results.
- The interaction of safety and security requirements.
- Isolation of safety and security requirements processes.

System Models. We have found that security system models and safety system models can differ greatly. The problem with having broadly differing abstract system models is that they lead developers to take different views of the system. However, the physical system for which the case study safety and security requirements were produced was the same for each development team. Production of different models hindered communication as well as being a duplication of effort. Although it may be essential to have different models to reflect the different concerns of safety and security, it must be possible to map between them.

Documentation Structure. Documentation of analyses can differ greatly between safety and security. The problem with these differences is that they can make it difficult to find and compare requirements. We believe that it would be relatively straightforward to harmonise safety and security documentation, with few, if any, problems. Having similar documentation structures would allow easier identification of conflicts and subtle differences in things like the wording of concepts and the levels of detail.

Interaction of Requirements. In section 4.2, we described two ways in which safety and security requirements can interact. The first of these was a simple conflict of requirements, while the second was a more subtle form of interaction due to the way in which security could support safety, and vice versa. We have been unable to identify problems of the first type in the case study. As might be expected of a project that has undergone such extensive work, cursory reading of the documentation has revealed no obvious requirements conflicts. There is, however, a clear example of the second type of interaction as described in section 4.2. The safety requirements contain a number of derived security requirements. There might also be cases where safety could support security, although we could find no examples of this in the case study. In order to identify interaction of safety and security requirements, there needs to be improved traceability in the documentation, particularly where primary and derived requirements are involved. Requirements in safety documentation must be cross-referenced to security analysis, and vice versa, so that the effects of changes can be fully evaluated.

Interaction of Requirements Processes.   The final topic we wish to discuss concerns the interaction of the requirements generation processes themselves. It is now widely accepted that in generating requirements an iterative lifecycle is required, rather than the long-standing 'waterfall' lifecycle. But what about the effects that changes to the safety requirements can have on the security requirements, and vice versa? As well as the processes being iterative within their own domain, we believe that they also need to be 'cross-iterative'. By this we mean that changes in one set of requirements may need to be investigated in *both*. Requirements engineers need to be aware of this interaction if costly errors are to be avoided in system development, and analysis is not to be undermined.

5   Conclusions and Future Work

We can summarise the findings of this paper as follows. If safety and security requirements are defined in isolation from each other, there is the danger that unrecognised, and therefore unresolved, conflicts or inconsistencies between them will arise, as demonstrated in the case study. Some form of integration is therefore required; but it is neither practical nor desirable to unify the two kinds of requirement into a single process. The most appropriate form of integration is the harmonisation of the two processes, enabling any conflicts to be recognised and resolved.

Our suggested approach to harmonisation is, first, to identify appropriate relationships between the stages and documentation of the safety and security requirements processes. We identified in section 2.5 a close correspondence between the processes, which should make this possible. It will then be necessary to introduce, into the over-all systems requirements process, additional steps for the identification and resolution of conflicts and inconsistencies. In this way the aim of integration can be achieved.

In this work we have only begun the task of enabling the integration of safety and security. Further work is required:

- To verify, by examination of other systems, that the concerns which we have raised here are generally applicable.

- To make concrete proposals for the alteration of the general systems requirements process to enable integration of safety and security.

- To verify, on new systems developments, that the proposals are practicable and do indeed provide the benefits that we envisage.

We believe that progress in this work will make a contribution to the production of genuinely dependable systems for the future.

6   References

1.   Leveson, N., G.: Software Safety: Why, What and How. In: ACM Computing Surveys, Vol. 18, No. 2 (1986).
2.   Pfleeger, C., P.: Security in Computing. Prentice Hall Inc (1997).
3.   Avizienis, A., Laprie, J. C. (eds.): Dependable Computing for Critical Applications. Springer-Verlag/Wien (1991).
4.   McDermid, J., A.: On Dependability, its Measurement and its Management. In: High Integrity Systems, Vol. 1, No. 1 (1994).
5.   Sanders, W., E., Meyer, J., F.: A Unified Approach to Specifying Measures of Performance, Dependability and Performability. In Dependable Computing for Critical Systems. Springer-Verlag/Wien (1991).
6.   Cullyer, J.: The Technology of Safety and Security. In: The Computer Bulletin, Vol. 5, No. 5 (1993).
7.   Rushby, J.: Critical Properties; Survey and Taxonomy. In: Reliability Engineering and System Safety, Vol. 43, (1994).
8.   Brewer, D. F. C.: Applying Security Techniques to Achieve Safety. In: Directions in Safety-Critical Systems, Proceedings of the Safety-Critical Systems Symposium, Bristol 1993. Springer-Verlag London Ltd (1993).
9.   Leveson, N., G.: Safeware, System Safety and Computers. Addison-Wesley Publishing Company Inc (1996).
10.   CESG.: CESG INFOSEC Memorandum Number 5 - System Security Policies, Issue 3.0 (July 1994).
11.   CESG.: CESG COMPUSEC Memorandum No 10 - Minimum Computer Security Standards for HMG Information Handled by Information Technology Systems, Issue 2.2, (October 1996).
12.   UK Ministry of Defence: Defence Standard 00-56/Issue 2 (DS 00-56/2), Safety Management Requirements for Defence Systems, dated 13 December 1996 (1996).
13.   Department of Defense Trusted Computer System Evaluation Criteria. US Department of Defense (1985).
14.   Common Criteria for Information Technology Security Evaluation Part 1: Introduction and general model, Common Criteria Implementation Board. CCIB (96/011) (1996).

Author Index

Lecture Notes in Computer Science

For information about Vols. 1–1610
please contact your bookseller or Springer-Verlag